7/2/00

PALATINE ORIGINS

OF SOME

PENNSYLVANIA PIONEERS

PALATINE ORIGINS

OF SOME

PENNSYLVANIA PIONEERS

by

Annette Kunselman Burgert,
F.G.S.P., F.A.S.G.

AKB Publications
Myerstown, Pennsylvania
2000

Library of Congress Catalog Card Number: 00-130444
International Standard Book Number: 1-882442-17-2

Available from:
AKB PUBLICATIONS
691 Weavertown Road
Myerstown, PA 17067-2642

Manufactured in the United States of America
using acid-free paper

CONTENTS

LIST OF ILLUSTRATIONS AND MAPS

*Modern map of the area showing location
of the Palatine villages involved in this study.*

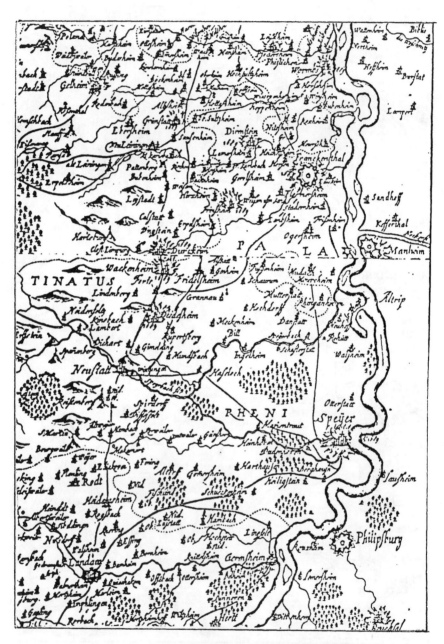

Part of a map by Nikolaus Person in 1689
showing the location of the Palatine villages studied here.

iv

PREFACE AND ACKNOWLEDGMENTS

This author's research in this area started in 1976 with a study of the church books at Niederhochstadt and Oberhochstadt, two Palatine villages combined today into one called Hochstadt. This research resulted in a small publication titled *The Hochstadt Origins of Some of the Early Settlers at Host Church, Berks County, Pennsylvania,* and was originally published in 1977 to commemorate the 250 anniversary of the founding of Host Reformed Church. This small booklet was later revised and published in 1983, as part of a Monograph Series that was to eventually include several more Palatine villages. In 1978, an article was compiled and published in *Der Reggeboge,* a periodical publication of The Pennsylvania German Society, titled *Eighteenth Century Pennsylvania Emigrants from Hassloch and Böhl in the Palatinate.* Soon out of print, this article was revised and incorporated into the Pennsylvania German Monograph Series, with the permission of the editor of the Society.

Several other titles were later added to the Pennsylvania German Monograph Series, including works on the villages of Mutterstadt, Friedelsheim, Gönnheim, Lachen, Speyerdorf, and Freinsheim. Gradually, over the years since their publication, these monographs have gone out of print. Rather than reprint, since much new data has been located and additional immigrants have been identified, it was decided to do a full revision of the previously published materials, and to add to them documentation on other immigrants who have been located in the ensuing years. Also, there were several villages in the vicinity of those previously published from which there was some emigration, and much of that research had not been published in the monograph series. Additionally, there were emigrants from both Hochstadt and Hassloch who were not included in the earlier publications. The Hochstadt monograph, for example, included only those immigrants who were early settlers in the vicinity of Host Church in Berks County, Pennsylvania. There were several other emigrants from Hochstadt who settled elsewhere in Southeastern Pennsylvania. They are included in this new publication. The Hassloch monograph included only research from the Reformed records of Hassloch and Böhl; there were also several more immigrant families from the Hassloch Lutheran records. They, too, are included here.

In addition to the revised materials from the villages in the monograph series, the following villages have been researched and emigrant materials are included in this volume: Dannstadt, Heuchelheim, Kleinniedesheim, Oggersheim, Friesenheim, Maudach, Ruchheim, Weisenheim am Sand, Ober and Niederlustadt, Erpolzheim, Kallstadt, Freisbach, Gommersheim, Klein Schifferstadt, Iggelheim, Böblingen, Duttweiler, Lambsheim,

Kleinfischlingen, Assenheim, Wachenheim, Bad Dürkheim, Ungstein, Grosskarlbach, Schwegenheim, and Leinsweiler.

****

This study would not have been possible without the help of some very special people.

Betty B. Bunting has spent many years researching her Bressler family from Hochstadt. We had a special visit to Hochstadt together, and enjoyed the hospitality of Gerd Pressler, the historian of Hochstadt, and his wife Elie.

William Grenoble transcribed the confirmation lists for several villages in the Duchy of Leiningen and shared his findings on the emigrant families several years ago.

Dr. Arta F. Johnson spent several years transcribing the Hassloch and Böhl church records. Her families came from that area in the nineteenth century. She laboriously transcribed the Hassloch Reformed KB, the Hassloch Lutheran KB, and the Böhl Reformed KB, then compiled a typed transcript of each church book. Several years ago, she presented me with a copy of her work. She has also compiled several lists of Swiss who moved into these Palatine villages, and shared this information, as well as data on several families from Klein Schifferstadt. See the Appendix: Swiss Origins starting on page 417 for Swiss in the area.

C. Frederick Kaufholz, FASG, has worked extensively on the Lachen-Speyerdorf families. He has shared his research on the nineteenth century emigrant families and his 1996 publication titled *The Families of Hamman, Reiff, and Hoos of Lachen-Speyerdorf, Pfalz.*

Alice B. Spayd again has spent many hours entering the manuscript of this book into my computer. Her genealogical knowledge along with her computer skills have been a great help.

Dr. Ken McCrea has been researching some of the emigrants in the church books of Rotterdam, and he located data there on one of the immigrants in this book.

Pastor Frederick S. Weiser has always been interested in this research, and offered many words of advice and encouragement through the years.

Klaus Wust has very generously shared some lists of names of prelist immigrants located on ship's contracts and agreements, making possible the identification of several of these elusive early immigrants.

Thanks, too, to Jeff Godshall for the photograph of the Hans Martin Göhrig house, and to Viola Kohl Mohn for permission to use her sketch of the Isaac Meier house in Myerstown, Pa.

My gratitude, also, to Jane Adams Clarke for her help in obtaining copies of Philadelphia probate records for several families, and for sharing data on her Weidman family.

Many other individuals have shared information on one or more of the families presented here; since this study has spanned more than twenty years, they are far too numerous to list here, but I gratefully acknowledge their contributions.

My husband, Richard A. Burgert, Sr., has, once again, exhibited great patience and understanding for the large amount of time consumed by this research.

Last, but by no means least, I am grateful to the Family History Library in Salt Lake City, Utah, whose microfilming program makes it possible to do this research.

Annette K. Burgert, F.G.S.P., F.A.S.G.

Myerstown, PA, 2000

ABBREVIATIONS AND SHORT CITATIONS

A. or a.	= acres		MD	= Maryland
Adm.	= Administration		mo.	= month(s)
Admr.(s)	= Administrator(s)		nat.	= naturalized
b.	= born		NC	= North Carolina
bp.	= baptized		N.N.	= no name recorded
ca.	= about		PA	= Pennsylvania
Co.	= County		[q.v.]	= which see
Conf.	= confirmed		Rev.	= Reverend, Pastor
d.	= died		Sh.	= shillings
dau.	= daughter		Sp.	= Sponsor (at baptism)
dec'd.	= deceased		trans.	= translation, translator
Est.	= estate		Twp.	= township
Ex, Exr.	= Executor		VA	= Virginia
Exrs.	= Executors		Wit.	= witness(es)
H.	= Herr		y.	= year(s)
KB	= Kirchenbuch (church book)		£	= currency,
m.	= married			British Pound.
mm.	= manumitted			

SHORT CITATIONS

S-H, I:	Ralph Beaver Strassburger and William John Hinke, *Pennsylvania German Pioneers*. 3 vols. (Norristown, 1934). This citation refers to Vol. 1.
Prelist:	The term used to designate the arrival of an immigrant before 1727 when the published passenger lists start.
PfFWKde:	*Pfälzische Familien und Wappenkunde*. (A German genealogical periodical). See list of selected articles on page 413.
Hassloch Beiträge	G. Wenz, Oberlehrer, *Beiträge zur Geschichte der Pflege Hassloch*. (Hassloch/Pfalz, 1985).
Hassloch Gerichtsbuch	"Gerichtsbuch zu Hassloch" photocopy of 509 pages of the original document, records start in 1590. Copy provided by Dr. Arta F. Johnson.

ANNOTATIONS

The Pennsylvania Church records have been studied from existing translations and/or microfilms of the originals in various libraries and archives. The researcher studying a specific family is urged to try to locate and consult the original records where ever possible. There are mistakes in most translations, especially the earliest Lutheran records that were translated in the late nineteenth century, such as Pastor John Caspar Stoever's records and the Augustus Lutheran Church at the Trappe and the New Hanover Lutheran Church, both in Montgomery County. Unfortunately these records have been reprinted without any attempt at correction, thus perpetuating the errors.

Abstracts of wills, administrations, and orphans' court records have been used, and as is the case with the church record translations, the researcher is advised to obtain a copy of the original documents for their family of interest. References to wills are abstracted as follows:
Decedent's name, location, occupation if given, date of will-date of probate. Wife; children (or other heirs). Executors; Witnesses.

The term "prelist" has been used to designate an immigrant who arrived before 1727 when the ship's passenger lists start. If the year of arrival is available from another source, it is also given.

All names, both given and surname, are given as they appear in the various records (both European and American) with no corrections made even when the spelling error is obvious. This is also true of the place name spellings; an index to places is included and places located today in France or Switzerland are so designated. For further information on the indexes, see page 455.

In many German church records, the pastors were inconsistent about recording given names. A woman named Anna Barbara might be given in the next record as Maria Barbara, and then return to Anna Barbara again. She might be baptised as Anna Barbara, but appears in the marriage records as Maria Barbara. A man named Johann Georg also appears in the records as Hans Jörg and other variations. In the Palatine records, the first name, Johann, is frequently abbreviated as Joh. Usually these individuals were known by their second name, i.e. Johann Georg would have been known as Georg. Maria Barbara or Anna Barbara would have been known simply as Barbara. Researchers should keep this in mind when reading the family records presented here, and when searching a name in the index.

Certain German words and phrases have been left untranslated in the text. These words appear in italics, and a Glossary has been added to give an approximate meaning for the words and phrases. See page 415.

INTRODUCTION

Emigration from the Palatinate had its roots in the destruction of the Thirty Years' War. This war can be summed up in three words: plunder, hunger and pestilence. The war began in 1618 and gradually spread over central Europe with certain regions suffering more than others.[1] The part of the Palatinate covered by this volume experienced the horrors of war mainly in 1621 and 1622, and again from 1632 to 1636. Mansfeld appeared in the Rhine region at the end of October in 1621. His 10,000 troops committed rape and plundered the villages; they were guilty of unheard-of atrocities, and when Mansfeld left the area in mid-1622, only ¼ of the population was still living. The material damages were huge, with fields and vineyards destroyed, and many villages for the most part gone up in flames. In Hassloch one farmer's house remained, and has been restored as a Heimat Museum. This house dates from 1599[2] and is the only building in Hassloch that survived the turmoil of the Thirty Years' War. When the building was renovated, two secret chambers were discovered in the upper story; they may have served as a place of concealment for the inhabitants during the time of distress.[3] From 1632 to 1636 this region was once again invaded by the Swedes and French troops. With the troops again plundering the villages, food became very scarce, until by 1636 it had reached the starvation level and many more died. This terrible war lasted another 12 years until 1648 and the Treaty of Westphalia. Before 1618, the start of the war, Hochstift Speyer had 13,000 residents, including the village of Schifferstadt. By 1648, this number was reduced to about 1000 inhabitants. "In 1666 the plague began on the 24th of September and the illness lasted five months; 160 persons, old and young, died." By 1667 the village of Schifferstadt had 292 inhabitants, of which 136 were local residents, and 156 were those who had migrated in from elsewhere. By 1729, the history of Schifferstadt states that "our poor village consisted of only 15 persons".[4]

Many other villages in this region were similarly reduced in population by the Thirty Years' War and other wars that followed. Also contributing to the population loss was the plague, which swept through the area in the 1660s and 1670s. Some villages were totally depopulated and the

---

[1] Sturm, Georg. *Geschichte Meiner Heimatgemeinde Schifferstadt.* 1961

[2] 1599 is the date over the cellar entrance.

[3] undated brochure titled *Heimatmuseum Hassloch.*

[4] Sturm, Georg. *Geschichte Meiner Heimatgemeinde Schifferstadt.* 1961.

rulers of the territories offered certain inducements to attract new settlers, particularly from Switzerland. The late seventeenth century was a time of population movement in central Europe, caused not only by the wars, but also religious oppression.[5] There are references in the Palatine church books to Separatists, Pietists and other religious dissenters. They came into these villages to rebuild following the devastation of the wars, along with Huguenots from France and Mennonites from Switzerland. When Karl Philipp became Elector of the Palatinate in 1716, these Separatists and other religious dissenters encountered difficulties, and this, in turn, triggered a surge in emigration.

There are notations in various church books in the region that provide us with some insight into this repopulation and then subsequent emigration. For example, the pastor at Ungstein recorded in his churchbook that families moved into his village in the waning years of the seventeenth century from elsewhere "to improve their situation because the village and the Pfalz were then empty of people". This pastor also mentions in his record several instances in which the entire village fled to Dürkheim and the safety of the Castle Hartenburg there.

Mutterstadt is located in the Palatinate, southwest of Ludwigshafen am Rhein and northwest of Speyer. The village was uninhabited following the devastation of the Thirty Years' War. The few surviving citizens were staying in Speyer and Frankenthal. To encourage repopulation of the villages, Elector Karl Ludwig offered certain privileges in 1650. The resettlement of Mutterstadt started in 1651, with Huguenot families from Mannheim and Frankenthal. After the war of 1672-1678, Elector Karl Ludwig's son Karl extended the privileges; this, combined with the revocation of the Edict of Nantes, brought new religious refugees into the area. The Mutterstadt church records clearly show the gradual repopulation. There is one baptism recorded in the Reformed record in 1676, one in 1679, and one in 1689. Then three baptisms were recorded in 1695, three more in 1697, then six in 1699. By 1707 and 1708, there were eighteen baptisms recorded in each of these years.

The church records, in the marriages and burials, also show the former villages of residence. The new inhabitants came from the German- and French-speaking areas of Switzerland; there were Walloons and there were other Germans from the regions of Hessen, Nassau, Hanau, and

---

[5] See Durnbaugh, Donald F. *European Origins of the Brethren.* 1958. Pages 30-31 pertain to conditions in the Palatinate. Palatine Elector Karl Ludwig "permitted Mennonites and other outlawed dissenters to settle in his land because of their skill and industry".

Isenburg. Some of the new residents came from other Oberamts in the Kurpfalz, including Heidelberg and Mosbach.[6]

At least four families left Mutterstadt and went to England in 1709, three of them arriving at St. Catharine's 2 June 1709. The Tribbeko and Ruperti lists, Board of Trade Miscellaneous Vol. 2, no. D68, gives the following information about them:[7]

Husbandmen & Vinedressers:
Jeremy Hess age 34, wife, sons age 7 & 5, daughter age 2, Lutheran
Paul Heyn age 39, wife, sons age 8 & 3, daughter age 11, Lutheran

Butchers:
Michel Andrus, age 30, wife, daughter age 2, Reformed

The Hess and Heim families were among those who returned to Germany in 1711, but eventually they carried out their decision to emigrate. Paul Heim arrived in Pennsylvania in 1727 and Jeremias Hess came in 1730. A son of Michael Andreas came to Pennsylvania in 1748.

Ten other families are mentioned in the Mutterstadt records as having left for the new land before 1727. Although they arrived before the start of the ship lists, eight of these families can be documented in the early Pennsylvania records.

The European documentation on the emigrating families of Mutterstadt is unique in one respect. Usually the church books are the only source of information available. In the case of Mutterstadt, however, another source exists. At the Landesarchiv Speyer, there is a Briefprotokolle nr. 154, titled *Mutterstadt Kontraktenprotokolle, 1714-1747.* containing many entries with notations on individuals who had gone to Pennsylvania. This volume and the Mutterstadt Reformed Churchbook provided most of the European documentation on the families from Mutterstadt. However, a few other German church books were consulted for supplementary data on a few of the families. Where other European villages are mentioned in the text, a postal number (*die Postleitzahl*) has been included for location and identification of the village.

---

[6] For further history of Mutterstadt, see Heinrich Eyselein, *Mutterstadt in Vergangenkeit und Gegenwart*, published in Mannheim, 1967.

[7] See Michael Tepper, ed. *Immigrants to the Middle Colonies*, Baltimore: 1978. Pages 84-123 contain "Lists of Germans from the Palatinate Who Came to England in 1709" by John Tribbeko and George Ruperti, excerpted from Vols. XL and XLI (1909, 1910) of *The New York Genealogical and Biographical Record.*

The villages of Hassloch and Böhl are located in the Rheinland-Pfalz just east of Neustadt. Entries for residents of both villages are found in the Hassloch Reformed Church books; a separate church book for the Reformed congregation at Böhl starts in 1730. Also a separate church record exists for the Hassloch Lutheran congregation. The Hassloch Reformed record starts in 1700. The first book contains entries to 1734; the second book is dated 1734-1769; the third book starts in 1769. Dr. Arta F. Johnson has transcribed the eighteenth century records of the Hassloch Reformed KB, the Hassloch Lutheran KB, and the Böhl Reformed KB, and these transcripts were used, along with the microfilmed original records, to compile the families from Hassloch on the following pages. Two other sources exist for Hassloch:

G. Wenz, Oberlehrer, *Beiträge zur Geschichte der Pflege Hassloch*, and the Hassloch Gerichtsbuch, both sources containing lists of names of residents who have received citizenship rights, and the date plus the original village of origin. Many of these settlers were from Switzerland, and Dr. Johnson has also compiled a list of the Swiss settlers in Hassloch giving their earlier Swiss village. See the appendix for further information.

Freinsheim is a small Palatine village located about eight miles west of Frankenthal. It is one of the wine villages, and there are extensive vineyards in every direction. In the middle ages, walls and towers were erected to protect the inhabitants of the village from outside enemies. At Freinsheim, these walls and towers still stand and Freinsheim is often called the "Rothenburg of the Palatinate". The church, as in most Palatine towns, is the largest and most imposing structure.[8]

Freinsheim had both a Lutheran and a Reformed congregation, and a separate church book exists for each denomination. The earliest surviving Reformed book contains records dating from 1698 to 1788. The Pastor Johann Adam Scheffer started keeping the record on 1 May 1704 with a statement of his own ancestry; he mentioned that an earlier record had been burned when the French troops swept through the area in 1688. Earlier, 101 baptisms were recorded in the book before this page by his predecessor. The first entry in the burial records is dated 1705.

The Freinsheim Lutheran record contains 17 baptisms from 1698 to 1708. The regular entries in this book start in 1708 and continue to 1797.

Several of the Freinsheim families emigrated before 1727, when the Pennsylvania ship lists start, and they are designated in the text as prelist. Few of the emigrants appear in archival emigration records, and only one

---

[8] An article describing Freinsheim as it appeared in the late nineteenth century was published in *The Perkiomen Region, Past and Present*, Vol. II, pages 20-21 : "Days Devoted to Research Abroad" by Henry S. Dotterer, Part II: Freinsheim, in the Palatinate.

reference to the emigration appears in the Freinsheim church books; in the 1723 confirmation record of the Böttig and Mülleman children, the Pastor mentions that they are preparing to emigrate to America with their parents and siblings. Otherwise, the records are silent about all others who left.[9]

Friedelsheim and Gönnheim are two small villages located close together about 12 miles west of Ludwigshafen. Although separate records were kept for each village, they are recorded in the same churchbook. The first churchbook contains the baptismal, marriage and death entries for the following years at Friedelsheim:

Baptisms: 1680-1688, 1693-1727, 1798-1802
Marriages: 1655-1657, 1666-1697, 1714-1748
Deaths: 1708-1730

The Gönnheim portion of this record contains these entries:

Baptisms: 1654-1725, 1729-1730
Marriages: 1657-1750
Deaths: 1655-1659, 1681, 1689, 1712-1721

A second book contains later baptismal entries for both villages. It will be noted that the records on the emigrating families from Friedelsheim and Gönnheim may not be complete, due to the gaps in the church records of each village. There are also many faded pages in these church books, as well. The entries in the Gönnheim record from 1699 to 1707 are too faded to read on microfilm. It is possible that they are more legible in the original record. For these reasons, it is suggested that the materials presented here are offered as a guide for further research: a thorough search of the original records there might provide more information on these families.

It has frequently been stated by serious students of the Pennsylvania German immigration that neighbors in the old world remained neighbors in the new world. The emigrants from Friedelsheim and Gönnheim provide a good example of that statement. Several of them settled at Creutz Creek and Conewago, in York County. They continued to sponsor each other's children after arrival in this country.

---

[9] Other helpful sources exist for Freinsheim families:
Heinrich Herzog, "Schweizer Namen im reformierten Kirchenbuch Freinsheim" in *Pfälzisch-Rheinische Familienkunde,* Band 9, Heft 4 (1979), pg. 208-209. Also, Heinrich Herzog, "Freinsheimer im deutsch-reformierten Kirchenbuch Frankenthal 1618-1650" in *Pfälzisch-Rheinische Familienkunde,* Band 11, Heft 1 (1986), pg. 13.

There were other emigrants from Friedelsheim and Gönnheim in the eighteenth and nineteenth centuries.[10] Two Mennonite emigrants from Gönnheim, Johann Jacob Stutzmann and Nicolaus Ellenberger, have been documented in the article by Friederich Krebs, "New Materials on the 18th Century Emigration from the Speyer State Archives." in Don Yoder, ed., *Rhineland Emigrants,* Baltimore (1981). Being Mennonites, they of course do not appear in the church records studied for this compilation.

The emigrants from Friedelsheim and Gönnheim chose two areas of settlement, Creutz Creek and Conewago, that were both involved in boundary disputes with Maryland. At that time, the Pennsylvania-Maryland boundary had not been firmly established, and both colonies claimed the same land. Some of these early settlers became actively involved in the resulting disputes. For example, Martin Schultz and wife Catharine were settled in Hellam township (now York County) prior to 1736 and they suffered violence at the hand of the Marylanders. Authorities in Maryland issued a warrant for arrest dated 21 Oct. 1736. Among the names listed, we find Jacob Lonus (Lanius) and Jacob Welchhutter (Weltzhoffer). Jacob Weltzhoffer was actually arrested by the Maryland authorities. Although their names appear in court records and other legal records of the time, these people were not criminals. They simply settled on land whose ownership was disputed at the time.[11]

Oberhochstadt and Niederhochstadt are two small villages located near Landau in the Rheinland-Pfalz. Today they are combined into one town called Hochstadt.[12] The large emigration from these villages appears to have started in 1732, although there may have been earlier emigrants from the area; one Valentin Pressler was among the Palatine families of

---

[10] The nineteenth century Mennonite emigration from Friedelsheim has been documented in: Fritz Braun, "Auswanderer aus der Mennoniten-gemeinde Friedelsheim im 19. Jahrhundert". *Mitteilungen zur Wanderungsgeschichte der Pfälzer,* 1955, Folge 1 u.2.

[11] For further study of the problems resulting from these disputed land claims, see Abdel Ross Wentz, *The Beginnings of the German Element in York County, Pennsylvania.* Proceedings of the Pennsylvania German Society, Vol. XXIV (1916).

[12] A history of the community of Hochstadt, compiled by Gerd Pressler and others, was published in 1982. It is titled *Über 1200 Jahre Hochstadt.*

New York in 1710.[13] The Hochstadt emigration continued over a period of more than 20 years and was large in proportion to the population of the villages. An interesting fact about this particular migration is the large number of emigrants from this area that can be found mentioned in St. John's (Host) Reformed Church record in Berks County, Pennsylvania. Contrary to other migratory patterns, where large groups came on the same ship but then settled in wide-spread areas in Pennsylvania, these immigrants came a few at a time on several ships, but many seem to have settled, at least temporarily, near Host Church.

The church record at Niederhochstadt starts in 1708, and many of the early Oberhochstadt records are entered in this book. There are gaps in the records: in the death records there are no entries from March 1712 to 1729. Marriages are recorded for the years 1708 to 1716, then skip to 1730. The church record at Oberhochstadt starts with a few baptisms for the period 1727-1729; under the baptism of a child in 1729 is the following notation: "This child was baptized at the new church in Oberhochstadt". The regular record appears to start in 1730.

Lachen and Speyerdorf are two small villages located southeast of Neustadt an der Weinstrasse, and slightly southwest of Hassloch in the Palatinate. Each village has a church, but for the early years, records of both villages were kept in the same parish registers. Emigration from the villages started in 1709, when the family of Ulrich Schmidt went to England and from there to New York.[14] The emigration continued throughout the eighteenth and nineteenth centuries.

In many Palatine villages, including Hassloch, Weisenheim am Sand, Schifferstadt, Lachen and Speyerdorf, there was a large influx of Swiss families following the Thirty Years War. Descendants of several of these Swiss families eventually joined the emigration to Pennsylvania. Included in the Bibliography on page 413-414 of the text, there is a list of articles published in *Pfälzisch-Rheinische Familienkunde* and *Pfälzische Familien und Wappenkunde* that contain much information about the Swiss who came into these villages, and their earlier residence in Switzerland. For a list of many of these Swiss families, see the Appendix: Swiss Origins, starting on page 417 of this volume.

---

[13] See Henry Z Jones, Jr., *The Palatine Families of New York, 1710* for more about Valentin Bresseler. Also by the same author, *More Palatine Families,* (1991), pages 322-323 for additional Pressler discoveries.

[14] See Henry Z. Jones, Jr., *The Palatine Families of New York 1710,* immigrant family #673, pages 889-893, for details of this family.

This volume is part of an ongoing effort to locate and identify the European village of origin of the colonial Pennsylvania German immigrants. The following information is utilized in this search:

1. Data from previously published lists containing European villages of origin.
2. Notations in Pennsylvania church records with reference to villages of birth.
3. Information from several other sources, such as family histories, private knowledge, articles published in Germany, etc.
4. Emigration notations found in some European church records.

Working with this compiled data, additional emigrants can then be established by using the following research steps:

1. Study the names of the other passengers on the ships that were identified by the initial research. Then study the German church record to determine if these other passengers might be from the same village.
2. Verify that the family in question disappears from the German records by the presumed date of emigration (ca. 6 weeks or more prior to the date of the ship's list.)
3. Try to find evidence that the individual first appears in American records soon after the presumed date of emigration.
4. Supporting evidence from Pennsylvania records, showing association with other families from the same village or region; also a coinciding date of birth, a corresponding list of children, or a wife with the same given name as that found in the German record. Step four is often difficult; children died young and their deaths are not always recorded. Sometimes the wife and children died on the voyage, and the immigrant remarried after his arrival.

For some of the immigrants presented here we have emigration records from archival sources. These are designated in the text as:

Emigration record:

Werner Hacker, *Auswanderungen aus Rheinpfalz und Saarland*: this source citation is then followed by the specific emigration record.

There are also emigration notations found in the church records and cited in the text. Additionally, we have available many published lists of emigrants from this region, compiled by Fritz Braun, Friedrich Krebs and translated and published here by Don Yoder and others. They provided welcome clues to the emigrants.

For many of the emigrants the evidence of immigration is circumstantial, and some of the names are offered only as possibilities. In the following pages, each emigrant group is headed with the name of the head of family who appears in the published Pennsylvania ship passenger lists. If the family arrived on one of the ships that included the names of women and children, they are also listed in the heading of the family data. The village of origin is given, along with the current zip code number. This heading is then followed by data from the European church books and any other European records that were consulted for the compilation. American data follows, and was compiled from a variety of sources, all cited in the text.

In all cases, the names are given as they appear in the various records, and there are variations particularly in Pennsylvania records and the ship lists. Place names are also found with variations, and a corrected version is given in square brackets. Each family group contains the village of origin and the German Postal Code number. Since the reunification of Germany, the German postal code number is a 5-digit number. Villages in France also have a 5-digit number preceded by F-. A 4-digit number preceded by CH- indicates villages that are located in Switzerland.

The Pennsylvania material was compiled from a variety of sources, and a bibliography of published sources appears on pages 405-414 in this volume. There can be no guarantee that the individual found in Pennsylvania records is identical with the person of the same name in the German records. The Pennsylvania materials are presented here merely as a guide for further research. Where church records and abstracts of wills, deeds, etc. are mentioned in the text, secondary transcripts of these records were used. Researchers are urged to consult the original records whenever possible on their specific family.

This volume is not intended to be a complete record of the families mentioned. The sole purpose is to provide the information on the emigrating generation from the German church records, with enough substantiating evidence from Pennsylvania records to attempt to prove the connection. In some cases, more information was found on certain families than on others. On a few emigrants, only the emigration record in Europe was located along with a listing in Strassburger and Hinke, *Pennsylvania German Pioneers*. All attempts to locate the individual in Pennsylvania records failed. There are several possible reasons for this:

1. A few of the immigrants died soon after their arrival.

2. A few of the emigrants left Pennsylvania immediately after their arrival and settled in another colony. Additional information is presented on some of these immigrants, from records in Maryland and North Carolina; there is quite likely much more information to be found on many of them.

3. The compiler of this book possibly did not look in the right records, leaving the researcher some work to complete on his own family. Usually, the later the immigrant, the more difficult they are to locate in American records, the reason being the much larger territory that had opened for settlement, and the tendency of the immigrant to move to the more remote areas where land was cheaper. Also many of the later immigrants were single young men. The records from the European sources are sparse, and they are far more difficult to document than a married man with a large family.

xvii

The researcher should also be aware that this volume is not intended to be a complete record of every emigrant from the villages in this region. For example, there were many emigrants from Lambsheim[15] who have been documented in several sources and are readily available for study; there are emigrants from Lambsheim included here, but only those for whom there was new material available that had not been included in the earlier published studies. Another factor that enters into the difficulty of locating every emigrant is the lack of certain records. An example of this is found in the Lustadt records where there are no early marriages, at least not available on microfilm. Another problem in this area is the starting dates for many of the records. The dates for some of the parish records in the region, as given in the microfilm catalog in the Family History Library in Salt Lake City, are misleading. For example, the village of Heuchelheim, near Worms, is listed with a church record dated 1683 to 1763. When you get into the actual record, you find one baptism dated September 1683, then nothing further until the regular record starts in 1703. Also, not every church record in the area was studied, and it is virtually certain that there are many more emigrants from villages in the Vorder Pfalz yet to be located.

Presented here are more than 600 names of individuals who appear in the passenger lists or who arrived prelist, before 1727 when the ship lists were first kept. The actual count of immigrants is much higher, since in most cases only the immigrant head of family is given in the lists. There were 61 of the immigrants who arrived before 1727, most of them with large families.

---

[15] See Don Yoder, ed. and trans., "Emigration Materials from Lambsheim in the Palatinate" in *Pennsylvania Folklife,* Winter 1973-74. This is a translation of Heinrich Rembe's work *Lambsheim,* with Yoder's additional notes on the emigrants. Also available in a reprint of *Pennsylvania Folklife* articles titled *Rhineland Emigrants: Lists of German Settlers in Colonial America* also edited by Dr. Yoder and published in 1981.

THE EMIGRANTS

ACKER, CASPER   Ruchheim=
Prelist   67071 Ludwigshafen am Rhein

EUROPEAN RECORDS

Ruchheim Reformed KB:
Rudolff Acker and wife Maria Johanna had children:
1. Casper, bp. 12 Dec. 1687
2. Rudolff, bp. 14 Feb. 1694
3. Hans Adam, bp. 28 Dec. 1696
4. Franz, bp. 20 Mar. 1699
5. Petrus, bp. 26 Mar. 1705
6. Antonius, bp. 25 Jan. 1708

AMERICAN RECORDS

Philadelphia County Wills and Adms.:
Casper Acre, Adm. G: 6, 1754, estate # 4.

Casper Acker, Chester Co., nat. by Act, 1729/30.

ALTENBERGER, JOHANNES   67454 Hassloch
St. Andrew Galley, 1737   CH-8173 Neerach, ZH
S-H, I: 179, 181, 183

EUROPEAN RECORDS

Hassloch Reformed KB:
Johannes Altenberger, son of Johannes Altenberger of Neerach, Canton
Zurich, Switzerland, m. 27 Apr. 1718 Maria Magdalena, daughter of
Johannes Lindenschmidt.

Hassloch Gerichtsbuch:
Johannes Aldenberger (no origin given) granted citizenship 5 Jan. 1729.

AMERICAN RECORDS

First Reformed KB, Lancaster, PA:
Johannes Altenberger and his wife Anna Magdalena Linninschmidt are listed
as sponsors at a baptism in 1740.

Lancaster County Deed Book D, p. 223, dated 14 Jan. 1755:
150 acres at Muddy Creek; John Altenberger of Brecknock Twp., mortgage
to Michael Bachman.

Lancaster County Deed Book G, p. 400, dated 5 Dec. 1745:   Queen St.,
Lancaster; John Aldebarger and wife Maria Magdalena to Adam Kellin.

ALSTATT, MARTIN   67251 Freinsheim
Mortonhouse, 1729
S-H, I: 24, 26

EUROPEAN RECORDS

Freinsheim Reformed KB:
Johann Martin Altstatt from "Dreyeicher Hayn Isenburgischer Graffschafft"
[today Dreieichenhain = 63303 Dreieich], citizen and master smith here, m.
13 Feb. 1726 Johanna Judith, daughter of Rudolff Walter [q.v.]. They had
one child born in Freinsheim:
> 1. Nicolaus, b. 27 Apr. 1727
>   Sp.: Nicolaus Walter, single son of Rudolff Walter and
>   Jacob Seltzer [q.v.] and his wife Elisabetha.

AMERICAN RECORDS

Martin Altstat, Exeter Twp., Berks Co., nat. 24 Sept. 1760.

Nicholas Alstatt appears on the tax lists for Oley Twp., Berks Co., in the
years 1767 through 1780, taxed with 240 to 250 acres.

New Hanover Lutheran KB, Montgomery Co., Pa.:
Martin Alstadt and wife Judith were sponsors at the baptism of Anna
Margaretha Härdi, daughter of Rudolph and Margareth Barbara Härdi on
13 June 1747.

Rev. John Caspar Stoever's records:
John Albrecht of Oley had a daughter Judith b. 1 June 1734, bp. 9 Aug.
1734. Sp.: John Altstatt and wife Judith [likely John Martin Altstatt].

Rev. John Waldschmidt's records:
Catharina Allstadt, daughter of Martin Allstadt, m. 8 Nov. 1764 Johannes
Soder, son of Nicolaus Soder, deceased.

ANDREAS, HANS ADAM
67112 Mutterstadt
Edinburgh, 1748
S-H, I: 371

EUROPEAN RECORDS

Mutterstadt Reformed KB:
Hans Michel Andres, butcher here, and wife Maria Elisabetha had children:
1. Anna Barbara, bp. 1709 in England
2. **Hans Adam,** bp. 23 May 1717
   notation in KB: "in Pennsylvania 1748"
3. Valentin, bp. 16 Dec. 1725

PfFWKde, Band 6, Heft 5, p. 162:
Joh. Michael Andreas, butcher, son of the late Wentz Andreas, citizen at [68535] Edingen, Oberamts Heidelberg, died 21 Jan. 1758, age 76 y. 5 mo. His wife Maria Elisabeth d. 26 Nov. 1754, age 68 y. 3 mo. 2 days. She was a daughter of Joh. Seelinger, citizen and master shoemaker in [64846] Gross Zimmern (Kr. Dieburg).

Knittle, *Early Eighteenth Century Palatine Emigration:*
Third party: embarked 5 June to 10 June 1709
Andries, Hans Mighel and Vrouw, 1 child
Andries, Peter and Vrouw, 3 children

AMERICAN RECORDS

Philadelphia Adm. Book F, p. 492:
One Adam Andreas of Philadelphia, shopkeeper, left a will dated 5 May 1753; names wife Tabitha and two children, Adam and Ann. Mentions lot of ground and wharf in the Northern Liberties, on the road to Germantown. Adm. granted 31 May 1753 to Tabitha Andreas, widow of Adam.

ANDREAS, RUDOLF
67459 Böhl
Thistle of Glasgow, 1730
S-H, I: 31, 33, 34

EUROPEAN RECORDS

Hassloch Reformed KB:
Rudolf Andreas and wife Anna Catharina of Böhl had children:
Anna Barbara, b. 24 Mar. 1721; bp. 30 Mar. 1721

Johann Martin, b. 18 Aug. 1724; bp. 20 Aug. 1724
Johann Michael, b. 16 Sept. 1728; bp. 19 Sept. 1728

AMERICAN RECORDS

Rudolf Andreas: warrant for 50 acres, Bucks County, PA, 25 May 1738 and another warrant for 60 acres, Bucks County, PA, 21 Mar. 1749.

Emmaus Moravian Family Register:
Barbara Ernhard, nee Andreas, was born in *Boehn* [?67459 Böhl] near Manheim in Germany on 3 Mar. 1722. Her father was Rudolph Andreas and her mother was Anna Catharina Braun, both Reformed. She came with her father to Pennsylvania in the Fall of 1731. She married in 1740 Jacob Ehrnhardt and had eight children. She died 8 Sept. 1777.

Jacob Ehrnhardt of Salisbury Twp., Northampton County, left a will dated 4 Feb. 1760, probated 27 Feb. 1760.

ANTES, FRIEDERICH   67251 Freinsheim
Prelist, ca. 1721

EUROPEAN RECORDS

Freinsheim Reformed KB:
Philip Friederich Antes [in later records he is named as Friederich Antes] and his wife Anna Catharina had children:
1. Joh. Henrich, b. 11 July 1701; bp. 17 July 1701. Conf. 1715.
   Sp.: Joh. Henrich Linter and wife Ursula from
   [67229] Laumersheim.
2. Joh. Jacob, bp. 17 Oct. 1703; conf. 1719.
   Sp.: Johan Jacob D'ore.
3. Joh. Sebastian, bp. 14 Nov. 1706; d. 28 Apr. 1715
   Sp.: Joh. Sebastian Heyner, Lutheran, citizen in
   [67229] Laumersheim, and wife An. Juliana.
4. Conradt, bp. 25 Aug. 1709; d 7 May 1710, age 8 months.
   Sp.: Conradt Leppoldt and wife Dina.
5. Maria Elisabetha, b. 25 Mar. 1711; bp. 29 Mar. 1711
   Sp.: Valentin Neunzehenhöltzer and wife Maria Elisabetha.
6. Johannes, b. 7 Sept. 1716; bp. 13 Sept. 1716; d. 24 June 1718.
   Sp.: Johannes Wigandt, single, from Hessen and Elisabetha,
   single daughter of Rudolff Walter, citizen here.

AMERICAN RECORDS

W. J. Hinke, *Life and Letters of the Rev. John Philip Boehm:*
Philip Frederick Antes and his family came to Pennsylvania in 1721 and settled in Germantown. On 20 Feb. 1723 he moved to New Hanover Twp. His second wife was Elisabeth Catharina Nayman whom he married 9 Apr. 1742. His will was probated 26 Nov. 1746. His son John Henry married Christina Elisabetha Dewees on 2 Feb. 1726. John Henry Antes d. 20 July 1755, age 54 years.

Philadelphia Will Book H: 196, dated 15 Aug. 1746, probated 26 Nov. 1746:
Frederick Antes, New Hanover Twp.
Exrs: wife Elisabeth Catharine and son Henry.
To son Henry, lands in New Hanover, making provisions for wife, and paying daughter Anna Elisabeth £50.
[A complete transcript of the will may be found in *Perkiomen Region, Past and Present,* Vol. 2: 176-177.]

A History of the Beginnings of Moravian Work in America (Bethlehem, 1955) pg. 121-129 gives the father of Henry Antes as a Baron Frederick von Blume. There is no indication in the Freinsheim records of noble lineage for this family. Friederich Antes' name is never preceeded by the title Herr nor any distinguished designation. Nowhere in the church book is he ever referred to as "Baron". This same article states that Henry Antes was baptized in the Lutheran Church at Freinsheim; his baptism is recorded in the Reformed record there.

More detail on the life of Henry Antes may be found in:
Hinke. *Ministers of the German Reformed Congregations in Pennsylvania and Other Colonies in the Eighteenth Century* (1951), pg. 314-318.

McMinn, *Life and Times of Henry Antes* (Moorestown, 1886), Chapter XXII: pg. 284-304.

The Perkiomen Region, Past and Present, Vol. I: 50-51, and Vol. 2: 160-169 and 176-178.

Philadelphia Will Book K: 346: dated 20 July 1754, probated 18 Aug. 1755:
Henry Antes, Frederick Twp., wheelwright.
Wife: Christina. Children: Frederick, Wilhelm, Cathrina, Margaretha, Elisabeth, Henry, John, Mary, Beningna.
Codicil dated 8 July 1755 concerns some land in North Carolina.

Friederich Antes was nat. in Philadelphia Co., 24 Sept. 1742.

APPEL, JOH. HENRICH   67251 Freinsheim
Johnson, 1732
S-H, I: 72, 76, 78

EUROPEAN RECORDS

Freinsheim Reformed KB:
Hans Peter Appel from [67259] Beindersheim m. 27 July 1706 Anna
Catharina, widow of Hans Reichardt Gabel. They had:
  1. **Joh. Henrich**, bp. 5 Jan. 1707
     Sp.: Henrich Grossman, shoemaker, and his wife.
  2. Anna Margaretha, b. 22 July 1708. She m.
     Henrich Müller [q.v.]
     Sp.: Hans Jacob Grossman, Reformed, and
     his wife Margaretha.
  3. Joh. Jacob, b. 12 Apr. 1711
     Sp.: Joh. Jacob Born of [67259] Heuchelheim and
     wife Anna Catharina.

AMERICAN RECORDS

First Reformed KB, Philadelphia:
Died 24 Jan. 1748 - Henry Apel, from Frenzheim, Palatinate, age 38 years.

Philadelphia Wills and Administrations:
Henry Apple, 1747 [?1748] file # 1, Adm. F:129.

Rev. John Waldschmidt's records;
Johannes Appel, son of the deceased Heinrich Appel, m. 8 Aug. 1780 Maria
Elisabeth, daughter of Georg Weber, in Weber's house in the presence of
Mary Weber.

APPEL, PETER   67251 Freinsheim
Mary, 1733
S-H, I: 131, 133, 134
  [other passengers on list: Clara Appel]

EUROPEAN RECORDS

Freinsheim Reformed KB:
Hans Peter Appel from [67259] Beindersheim m. (1) 27 July 1706 Anna
Catharina, widow of Hans Reichardt Gabel.

Hans Peter Appel and wife Catharina had children:
  1. Joh. Henrich [q.v.], bp. 5 Jan. 1707
     Sp.: Henrich Grossman, shoemaker, and his wife.
  2. Anna Margaretha, b. 22 July 1708. She m.
     Henrich Müller [q.v.]
     Sp.: Hans Jacob Grossman, Reformed, and
     his wife Margaretha.
  3. Joh. Jacob, b. 12 Apr. 1711
     Sp.: Joh. Jacob Born of [67259] Heuchelheim and
     wife Anna Catharina.

Peter Appel's wife Anna Catharina was buried 3? Mar. 1731 in Freinsheim.

Peter Appel, widower, m. (2) 21 Oct. 1731 Anna Clara, widow of the late
Peter Nickel from [67256] Weisenheim am Sand.

Emigration records;
Werner Hacker, *Auswanderungen aus Rheinpfalz und Saarland im 18.*
Jahrhundert:
#1 Peter Appel from Freinsheim, 61\9123:107 n. 5, 20 Dec. 1732.

AMERICAN RECORDS

Philadelphia Wills and Administrations:
Peter Appel 1739 file # 3 Adm. D: 116: Letters of Adm. to Henry Miller,
County of Phila., yeoman, kin to Peter Appell, late of said county, yeoman,
dec'd., with a codicil annexed, widow Anna Clara having renounced, 13 Mar.
1739/[40].

Another Peter Apfel (Appel, Apple) arrived in Pa. in 1732.
S-H, I: 102, 104, 106 with Apolonia. He appears to be the Peter Apple who
settled in Maryland, and was naturalized there in 1749. See Tracey & Dern,
Pioneers of Old Monocacy, pg. 199-201 for this other Peter Apple.

Date stone on a building in Freinsheim

BACH, JOHANN NICOLAUS   67251 Freinsheim
Adventure, 1754
S-H, I: 601, 602, 603

EUROPEAN RECORDS

Freinsheim Lutheran KB:
Sebastian Bach, son of Herr Joh. Georg Bach, *Rathsverwanden* here, m. 2
Feb. 1728 Susanna, daughter of Hans Georg Seidemann. Sebastian Bach
was confirmed in 1715 at the age of 14. See immigrants Philip Jacob Bach
and Georg Daniel Bach for more detail on the family of Joh. Georg Bach.
Sebastian Bach and wife Susanna had children:
1. Anna Catharina, b. 7 Nov. 1728
2. **Johann Nicolaus,** b. 3 June 1730, bp. 7 June 1730; conf. 1745.
   Sp.: Johann Nicolaus, son of Michael Sebastian,
   and Sybilla, daughter of Jacob ?Gilgen.
3. Joh. Henrich, b. 15 Nov. 1731
4. Maria Clara, b. 17 Dec. 1733
5. Maria Catharina, b. 6 Jan. 1736
6. Joh. Georg, b. 10 May 1737
7. Johannes Sebastian, b. 18 Feb. 1739
8. Georg Lorentz, b. 4 Aug. 1741
9. a son, b. 10 Apr. 1743

Tower entrance in the protective wall surrounding Freinsheim

Emigration records:
Friedrich Krebs. "Pennsylvania Dutch Pioneers" in *The Pennsylvania Dutchman* (1954); reprint in Boyer, *Ship Passenger Lists, Pennsylvania and Delaware* (Newhall, 1980): from Freinsheim, Johann Niclaus Bach son of Sebastian Bach who died at Freinsheim in 1753 - "who is now, however, in Pennsylvania" (document dated 25 June 1768). Niclaus Bach was a resident of the city of New York as appears from a letter written from there.

BACH, PHILIP JACOB   67251 Freinsheim
BACH, GEORG DANIEL
Mortonhouse, 1729
S-H, I: 24

EUROPEAN RECORDS

Freinsheim Lutheran KB:
Joh. Georg Bach and Anna Maria had several children born before the church book starts; the older children are mentioned in the confirmation records and as sponsors for other children. They had:
1. **Georg Daniel**, conf. 1713, age 14
2. Sebastian, conf. 1715, age 14.
3. Anna Elisabetha, conf. 1715, age 13
4. **Philip Jacob**, conf. 1720
5. Anna Maria, b. 23 Nov. 1708
   Sp.: Anna Maria Bach, grandmother.
6. Maria Margaretha, b. 16 Mar. 1710
   Sp.: Jacob Bach, the child's father's brother from Erbelsheim [67167 Erpolzheim] and his wife Maria Margaretha.
7. Catharina Margaretha, b. 15 Jan. 1713
8. Anna Catharina, b. 10 Apr. 1715
9. Johann Michael, b. 20 Sept. 1718

Anna Maria, wife of Joh. Georg Bach, died 26 Nov. 1722, age 44 years, 1 month and 6 days.

Joh. Georg Bach m. (2) 2 June 1723 Maria Magdalena, widow of the *Schultheis* Jacob Christ of [67167] Erpolzheim.

Emigration record:
Werner Hacker, *Auswanderungen aus Rheinpfalz und Saarland im 18. Jahrhundert,* pg. 213: Bach, Phil. Jakob and Gg. Daniel (no place given) in New Land, record dated 18 Apr. 1739.

AMERICAN RECORDS

Philadelphia Wills, Book F. pg. 62, abstracts:
George Daniel Bach of Philadelphia.
Wife: Elizabeth. Child: Mary Magdalena.
Exrs: Peter Ash and Frank (?Frantz) Shunck.
Witnesses: Michael Gebert, Philips Jacob Bach and George Scholtz.
Dated: 7 Mar. 1737, proved 18 Mar. 1737.

BACHMAN, HENRICH   Duttweiler=
Snow *Lowther,* 1731   67435 Neustadt a. d. Weinstrasse
S-H, I: 54 [appears on A list as Henrick Bowman, on B list as
      Henrich Bruner; step-son of Hans Jacob Brunner q.v.]

EUROPEAN RECORDS

Lachen Reformed KB:
Henrich Bachman, son of Georg Bachman, *Schultheiss* at Duttweiler, m. 23
Apr. 1704 Anna Barbara, daughter of Hans Peter Sautor, *Gemeinsmann*
here.

Duttweiler (Böbingen) Reformed KB:
Henrich Bachman, widower at Duttweiler, m. 27 July 1707 Sophia Louisa,
daughter of the late Jost Bock, gardener at Ohfenbach am Mayn [=63067
Offenbach am Main]. They had children:
    1. Anna, b. 24 Sept. 1708, bp. 30 Sept. 1708
    2. Anna Maria, b. 17 July 1710
    3. **Joh. Henrich,** b. 7 Sept. 1712

Died 21 May 1714, Hans Henrich Bachman, age 31 y. buried 22 May 1714.
His widow Sophia Louisa m. (2) 22 Aug. 1714 Hans Jacob Brunner [q.v.],
and they also emigrated, arriving on the snow *Lowther,* 1731.

AMERICAN RECORDS

Rev. John Casper Stoever's Records:
Heinrich Bachmann and wife were sp. in 1749 for Christina, daughter of
Jacob Moser, Swatara.

Muddy Creek Reformed KB, Lancaster Co., PA:
Heinrich Bachman signed the Reformed Church Doctrine, 19 May 1743.

Henrich Bachman and wife Christina were sp. in 1744 for Henry, son of Ulrich Gilgen.

Swatara Reformed KB, Jonestown, Lebanon Co., PA:
Henry Bachmann and Christina had a daughter:
     Anna Catharine, bp. 13 July 1747
     Sp.: Peter Hetrich and wife Anna Delila.

BAMBERGER, ARNOLD   67251 Freinsheim
BAMBERGER, MARTIN
BAMBERGER, RUDOLFF
Prelist, before 1727

EUROPEAN RECORDS

Freinsheim Reformed KB:
Arnold Bamberger, son of the late Hans Bamberger, m. 11 Jan. 1702 Anna Elisabetha, daughter of the late Philip ?Kremer formerly of Hohlen Lindenfels [?64678 Lindenfels, Odenwald]. Arnold Bamberger was possibly the son of Hans Baumberger from Namikan, Zurich [CH-8606 Nänikon, ZH], son of Felix Baumberger, who married 10 May 1663 at [67256] Weisenheim am Sand, Anna Margaretha, daughter of Johannes Lippert.

Arnold Bamberger, Reformed, and wife Anna Elisabetha, Lutheran, had:
    1. Martin, bp. 6 Jan. 1706, conf. 1719
       Sp.: Martin Schenckel, single son of Conrad
       Schenckel, miller at Gross Carlbach. [67229 Grosskarlbach].
    2. Joh. Nicolaus, bp. 2 Oct. 1709, died 6 Apr. 1710
    3. David, twin, bp. 2 Oct. 1709
       Sp.: *Unterschultheiss* Nicholaus Bassler and H. Davidt Seltzer,
       des Raths and his wife Anna
    4. Anna Elisabetha, bp. 24 Jan. 1712
       Sp.: Jost Wollheit, Reformed, and Anna
       Elisabetha Felsinger, Lutheran.
    5. Joh. Rudolff, bp. 15 Sept. 1715
       Sp.: Rudolff Maurer and wife Veronica
    6. Joh. Peter, bp. 6 Mar. 1718
       Sp.: Joh. Peter Bartscherer, citizen and baker here, and wife.

AMERICAN RECORDS

Abstracts of Philadelphia County Wills:
BAMBERGER, ARNOLD. Northern Liberties, Co. of Philadelphia.
Yeoman. 17 Jan. 1748/9 - 15 Feb. 1748. Book J, pg. 63.
Children: Rudolph and Martin Bamberger and Elisabeth Knerr.
Exr.: Rudolph Bamberger. Wit.: William Shute, John Adam Galer, Christian
Lehman.

St. Michael's and Zion Lutheran KB, Philadelphia:
Rudolph and Catharina Bamberger had children:
      1. Arnold b. Nov. 1744, bp. Mar. 1745
         Sp.: the grandparents Arnold and Elisabetha Bamberger
      2. Agnesa b. 5 Mar. 1749, bp. 14 Apr. 1749
         Sp.: the parents

Catharina Bamberger (an Adultress), wife of Rudolph Bamberger, had an
illegitimate daughter Johanna Catharina b. 25 Aug. 1753, bp. 6 July 1754.
Father given as Meyer De la plain.

Lancaster Will Abstracts: Will Book F-I: 541
Martin Bamberger (d) 27 Mar. 1783, (p) 17 Feb. 1794
Exrs: George Messersmith and George Reitzel; Lancaster (borough).
Wife: Mary Dorothea; child: John; stepchildren: George, Jacob and Peter
Messersmith and Eve, wife of Francis Bug.

A later generation of Bambergers with the given names Arnold and Martin
appear in the 1770s in the Trunity Lutheran KB, Lancaster.

Arnold Bamberger nat. by act 1725, Philadelphia Co.
A Martin Bamberger of Lancaster, Lancaster Co., nat. 24 Sept. 1753.

BARTH, JACOB age 50   67251 Freinsheim
Harle, 1736
S-H, I: 155, 156 [other passengers on list: Anna Catharina Barth, age 38]

EUROPEAN RECORDS

Freinsheim Lutheran KB:
Johann Jacob Barth, son of the late Clemens Barth from Rotha, Hessen-
Darmstadt Ober Ambt Lichtenberg, m. 27 Dec. 1726 Catharina, widow of
the late Georg Daniel Saidemann here. [See also Seidemann]. She was a
daughter of Daniel Sebastian.

Jacob Barth and wife Anna Catharina had:
1. Johannes Peter b. 28 Feb. 1730, bp. 5 Mar. 1730
   Sp.: Johannes Röhmer and his wife Maria Margretha,
   Peter Scheffer and wife from [67167] Erpoltzheim.
2. Susanna Catharina b. 18 Dec. 1732, bp. 21 Dec. 1732
   Sp.: Adam Schaffner and wife Anna Catharina and
   Susanna, widow of Adam Reipold.

Emigration record:
Werner Hacker, *Auswanderungen aus Rheinpfalz und Saarland*, pg. 217:
582: Jacob Barth, Freinsheim "ins Neue Land" dated 9 Mar. 1736.

Half-timbered house in Freinsheim

AMERICAN RECORDS

New Hanover Lutheran KB, Montgomery Co., PA:
Confirmed 29 Apr. 1745: Hans Peter Barth
                        Susanna Catharina Barth

BARTHOLOMAUS, SEBASTIAN   67112 Mutterstadt
Edinburgh, 1748
S-H, I: 371

EUROPEAN RECORDS

Mutterstadt Reformed KB:
Hans Görg Bartholomaus m. 8 Jan. 1708 Anna Barbara Diez. They had children:
    1. Maria Elisabetha bp. 16 July 1710
    2. Maria Catharina bp. 11 Nov. 1713
    3. **Sebastian** bp. 2 Aug. 1716
       "is going to Pennsylvania 1748"
    4. Joh. Peter bp. 13 Sep. 1718
    5. Joh. Georg bp. 13 Sep. 1718
    6. Joh. Michael bp. 22 May 1721, d 22 Oct. 1780
    7. Anna Rosina b. 10 Apr. 1730, bp. 11 Apr. 1730
    8. Joh. Adam b. 21 Sep. 1734 bp. 26 Sept. 1734
       "going to Pennsylvania 1748"

PfFWKde, Band 6, Heft 5, p. 163:
Joh. Georg Bartholome died 21 Dec. 1740, age 57 years and 1 month, son of Joh. Georg Bartholome, citizen at Unterschefflenz [=74850 Schefflenz], Oberamts Mosbach. Married Anna Barbara Dietz; in 33 years of marriage had 6 sons and 5 daughters.

AMERICAN RECORDS

Rev. Jacob Lischy's personal records, York Co., PA:
Sebastian Barthleme and wife Gertraut had a daughter:
       Anna Barbara bp. 6 Aug. 1752
       Sp.: Friedrich Hercher (?Herget) and wife Anna Barbara

BAST, JOH. GEORG age 46   67259 Heuchelheim
Pink *Plaisance,* 1732
S-H, I: 78, 81, 82
  Also on ship: Anna Maree Basst, age 44; child, Johannes Bast.

EUROPEAN RECORDS

Heuchelheim Lutheran KB:
Joh. Georg Bast, linenweaver, and wife Anna Maria had children:
    1. Johannes, b. 28 Jan. 1717, evidently died young

2. Joh. Henrich, b. 14 June 1718
3. Maria Catharina, b. 7 Jan. 1720
4. Johannes, b. 9 July 1721
5. Joh. Georg, b. 29 Sept. 1722, d. 1 Feb. 1723

AMERICAN RECORDS

Moselem Lutheran KB, Berks Co., PA:
Georg Bast, master weaver and widower, m. 20 Trinity 1748 Elisabetha Dorothea Eppler, widow.

Johannes Bast and Magdalena (nee Papst) had:
1. Barbara, b. 11 Apr. 1748, bp. Dom. 4 Trin. 1748
   Sp.: Michael Wolfgang, Barbara Majer
2. Maria Eva, b. 20 Jan. 1751, bp. 25 Feb. 1751
   Sp.: Eva Baur

John Bast was a witness to the will of Philip Grauel [son of Joh. Michael Grauel, q.v.] in Maxatawny Twp., Berks Co. in 1762.

BASTIAN, ADAM see SEBASTIAN, ADAM

BASTIAN, ANDREW see SEBASTIAN, JOH. ANDREAS

BAUERSACHS, HANS NICKEL   Ober Lustadt=
Royal Union, 1750   67363 Lustadt
S-H, I: 432

EUROPEAN RECORDS

Ober Lustadt Reformed KB:
Hans Nickel Bauersachs and wife Maria Elisabetha had children:
1. Maria Elisabetha, b. 9 Apr. 1735, d. before 1750
   Sp.: Herr Philipp Barthol Schmitt and wife
2. Maria Barbara, b. 3 Aug. 1738, d. 9 June 1740
   Sp.: Maria Barbara Hellmann, single
3. Johan Valentin, b. 7 July 1741
   Sp.: Joh. Valentin Bauersachs and Maria Barbara Hellmann
4. Jörg Adam, b. 26 Feb. 1744

AMERICAN RECORDS

Six immigrants are listed together on the passenger list of the *Royal Union,* and all are found in the Lustadt records: Henrich Hauenstein, Casper Schmidt, Philip (X) Prike, Hans (X) Prike, **Hans Nichel Bauersachs**, and Andreas Hertzog.

Old Goshenhoppen Lutheran KB, Family Register, Montgomery Co., PA:
Johann Nicol Bauersax, b. 14 Nov. 1702, bp. 15 Nov. 1702 at Memelsdorf [96117 Memmelsdorf], a tailor, son of Johann Bauersachs, a butcher, and his wife Elisabetha in [96274] Itzgrund. In 1727 he moved to Nider Lustadt [67363 Lustadt], three hours above Speier [67346 Speyer], where he married in 1727 Maria Elisabeth, daughter of Velten Gothe and Eva Elisabeth. They had children:
  1. Joh. Valentin, b. 7 July 1741
  2. Georg Adam, b. 26 Feb. 1744
  3. Elisabeth, died
  4. Maria Barbara, died
Anno 1750 Joh. Nicol Bauersachs with his wife and two children came to America.

Joh. Nicolaus Bauersax appears on the communicants lists, 1751-1756. The 1753 list mentions his wife is Reformed.

Conf. 15 Mar. 1761, Palm Sunday:
Georg Adam Baur Sax, aged 15 y., son of Johan Nicolaus Baur Sax.
Johann Valentin Baur Sax, aged 17 y., son of Johan Nicolaus Baur Sax.

Both sons served in the Revolutionary War, and after their release from service settled in Frederick County, Maryland. References to both families appear in the records of St. David's Lutheran Church near Hanover, Pennsylvania, on the Maryland border. The family of *Georg Adam Bowersox* is later named in the records of St. Mary's Lutheran Church, Silver Run, Maryland, where members of the family are buried. His own gravestone and that of his wife and his son Christian are at Uniontown, Maryland. *Georg Adam Bowersox* took the oath of citizenship to Maryland on June 19, 1779.

BAUMANN, JACOB   67245 Lambsheim
BAUMANN, SUSANNA NEE MÜLLER   67459 Böhl
Adventure, 1727
S-H, I: 14, 15

EUROPEAN RECORDS

Hassloch Reformed KB:
Jacob Bauman, born in Switzerland, citizen and carpenter at Lambsheim, m. 10 Aug. 1717 at Böhl, Susanna, daughter of Christoph Müller from Böhl. (Note: entry very faded; date questionable.)

Other European Data:
Heinrich Rembe, in his book on Lambsheim families, identifies Hans Jacob Baumann, carpenter, citizen of Lambsheim in 1717, as coming from [CH-4437] Waldenburg, Canton Basel, Switzerland.

St. Peter's Reformed Church, Waldenburg, Basel, contains many Baumann family entries. Several of them are designated carpenters by trade, and the name Jacob is common. The following entry is offered as the most probable:
Hans Jacob Baumann the carpenter, and wife Madlen Lüdin had an infant Johannes bp. 2 Apr. 1711. Sponsors were Jacob Berger, Hans Bidermann and Anna Baldnerin. There are no further entries for this Hans Jacob Baumann in the record book.

AMERICAN RECORDS

Emigration materials from the Rembe volume on Lambsheim were translated and edited by Don Yoder in an article published in *Pennsylvania Folklife,* Winter, 1973-74. Jacob Bauman, carpenter, of Germantown, left a will, probated 19 May 1749 (Philadelphia Wills, Vol. G, p. 271). A complete copy of this will and additional detail on the family of Jacob Bauman is found in M. T. Graff, *Early History of Truby-Graff and Affiliated Families* (1941) pp. 105-109.

Philadelphia County Will Abstracts:
Jacob Bowman, Germantown, County of Philadelphia, carpenter. Dated 30 Apr. 1748/49. Probated 19 May 1748. Wife: Margaret. Children: Margaret, Susannah, Elisabeth, Catharine and Sybilla. Exrs: Dirck Keyser and Christopher Meng. Wit.: Christopher Sowers, Christ Lehman and John Dewald End.

BECHTLUF, TOBIAS age 43   67169 Kallstadt, Pfalz
Plaisance, 1732
S-H, I: 79, 81, 83
    with Eliza, age 32; also on ship: Soffia Catarina Picktlen (child).

EUROPEAN RECORDS

Kallstadt Lutheran KB:
Hans Nickel Bechtloff, *Messerschultheissen,* and wife Anna Maria had a son:
Tobias, b. 29 July 1688, bp. 1 Aug. 1688
Sp.: Tobias Lung, and Margretha, wife of Georg Kauck.

Tobias Bechtloff, son of the late Hans Nicolaus Bechtloff, former *Gerichts-schultheissen* at Callstadt, m. 19 Jan. 1717 Anna Christina, daughter of Hans Georg Münch, *Messergerichtsverwander.*
Conf. 1730, age 12: Sophia Catharina Bechtlof.

Tobias Bechtloff m. (2) 3 Nov. 1721 Anna Elisabetha Koch, daughter of Hans Nickel Koch from Ungstein [=67098 Bad Dürkheim].

AMERICAN RECORDS

Rev. John Casper Stoever's Records:
Tobias Bechtel and wife Maria Elisabetha were sponsors in 1735 for Georg, son of Georg Valentin Klapp in Oley.

Bern Reformed KB, Berks Co. & Heidelberg Moravian KB, Berks Co., PA:
Tobias Bechtel and wife Anna Elisabetha were baptismal sponsors for the following children:
Tobias Beckel, b. Mar. 1738, son of Tobias Beckel [q.v.] and Christina [nee Kuster].
Eva Elisabetha Beckel, b. Oct. 1740 (Heidelberg) daughter of Tobias and Christine Beckel, bp. 28 Nov. 1739 (Bern Ref. KB).
Tobias Meyer, b. 21 Sept. 1740 in Bern, son of Johannes Meyer [q.v.] and Maria Margaretha nee Beckel.

Christ Lutheran KB, Stouchsburg, Berks Co., PA:
Buried 16 June 1748, Tobias Bechtel on the Northkill.

Publications of GSP, Vol 5, Abstracts of Wills of Philadelphia Co.:
Tobias Bechtell; dated June 11, 1748; son John Nicklas Bechtell to maintain his mother Anna Elizabeth; mentioned son John George; daughter Anna Margred, to have a cow and heifer, which she had of her god father; daughter Anna Maria; mentioned Ludwig Bush; son John Nicklas Bechtell to pay unto daughter Anna Margred, her share of plantation two years after his decease; the youngest child's share three years after; George Bechtell's share four years after, and Catrina Knop, her share five years after his

decease; witnesses, Fredrick Gerhart, Tobias Bechel and John Zerben; administration to Anna Elizabeth Bechtell, widow of Tobias Bechtell, late of Lancaster County, June 29, 1748.

Rev. John Casper Stoever's Records:
Nicholaus Bechtell (Bern) had:
    John Nicholaus, b. 28 Apr. 1754, bp. 5 May 1754

BECKEL, FRIEDRICH, age 21   67169 Kallstadt, Pfalz
Harle, 1736
S-H, 1: 155, 158 (X) Biegel, 160 (X) Bökel
    with Anna Beckelin, age 23, p. 156

EUROPEAN RECORDS

Erpolzheim Reformed KB:
Conf. 1730, Easter, Johann Friederich Böckel from Kallstadt.

Kallstadt Lutheran KB:
Georg Friedrich Böckel, son of Gotthard Bockel here, m. 15 Apr. 1736
Anna Elisabetha, daughter of Conrad Rohrbach, citizen here.

Georg Friedrich Böckel was b. 19 Mar. 1716 at Dürkheim and was a brother of Tobias Böckel [q.v.] and Maria Magdalena Böckel, wife of Johannes Meyer [q.v.].

AMERICAN RECORDS

Heidelberg Moravian KB, Berks Co., PA:
Friedrich Beckel was a baptism sponsor for Anna Elisabetha Beckel, b. 1736 in Unkstein. She was a daughter of Friedrich's brother Tobias Beckel. Friedrich and Anna Elisabeth Boeckel later sponsored another child of Tobias Böckel's, son Friedrich, b. in Heidelberg (now Berks Co.) 20 Nov. 1743, bp. 29 Nov. 1743.

In 1743, a room was added to Friedrich Boeckel's house, to provide housing for the Anton Wagners, Moravian teachers.

On Apr. 1745 the Heidelberg Moravian congregation was organized. Among the first members were:
        Friedrich and Anna Elisabeth Böckel
        Tobias and Christina Böckel
        Johannes and Margaretha (Böckel) Meyer

On 16 Feb. 1747, the Friedrich Böckels moved to Bethlehem.

Heidelberg Moravian Member Catalog, 1746:
Fredrich Böckel and wife Anna Elisabetha were members of Heidelberg in 1746 along with these children:
1. Peter, b. 6 Jan. 1737
2. Tobias, b. 3 Feb. 1740
3. Caspar, b. 2 Apr. 1742
4. Christina Elisabetha, b. 4 Dec. 1744
5. Maria, b. 28 Dec. 1746

Moravian Cemetery Records, Bethlehem, PA:
Georg Frederick Beckel, 1773-1824, youngest son of Frederick Beckel of Bethlehem; a stocking weaver. Married A.M. Kindig and left two sons: Charles F. and Lewis Beckel.

Frederick Boeckel, 1716-80, born in the Palatinate. He came with his wife to PA in 1736, settling in Berks County, heard Count Zinzendorf preach and was one of the founders of the church at Heidelberg. Later he was employed in the School at Germantown and on the farms at Christiansbrunn and Bethlehem, at which place after the common household ceased he took charge of the farm entirely. Of his first marriage there were one son and five daughters; of his second marriage, one son.

Anna Elizabeth Boeckel, maiden name Rohrbach, 1717-71, born at Carlstadt [67169 Kallstadt] in the Palatinate. In 1736 she m. Fred. Boeckel and the same year emigrated with him to America, settling near Reading. She was converted in 1741. Since 1761 she served as a midwife. She left six children.

Peter Boeckel, oldest son of Frederick Boeckel, born at Heidelberg, PA. He died 10 Oct. 1749, about eleven years old.

Tobias Boeckel, 1740-1815, born in Heidelberg Twp., Berks Co.; a shoemaker; played trumpet and trombone. He m. A. Barbara Heckedorn and had 3 sons and 3 daughters.

BECKEL, GEORG VALENTIN age 32   67161 Gönnheim
Mary, 1732
S-H, I: 94, 95, 96

EUROPEAN RECORDS

Gönnheim Reformed KB:
Georg Velten Böckel from Gönnheim m. 29 Jan. 1723 Anna Maria
Rheinhard. They had children:
1. Maria Margaretha bp. 28 Oct. 1725
   Sp.: Philipp ?Müller and Maria Margaretha (faded entry)
2. Anna Catharina bp. 17 July 1728
   Sp.: Hans Adam Hoff and Anna Catharina
3. Joh. Michael bp. 8 Mar. 1731
   Sp.: Joh. Michael Reinhard and Anna Barbara, daughter of
   Marx Hummel from [67158] (E)llerstadt, both single.

NOTE: The record was checked for the birth ca. 1700 of George Valentin
Böckel, but the entries in the Gönnheim record 1700-1702 are too faded to
read on microfilm. A Philip Böckel and a Joh. Daniel Böckel were both
having children baptized in that time period there.

AMERICAN RECORDS

Conewago Reformed KB, near Littlestown, Adams Co., PA.:
George Valentine Beckel was sp. for a child of Ludwig Klemer [q.v.] and
wife Maria Elisabetha Beckel.

BECKER, JOHANNES   Oberhochstadt=
Em. after Apr. 1749   76879 Hochstadt, Pfalz
In Pa. Feb. 1752   67483 Kleinfischlingen
(There are 4 Johannes Beckers in the ship lists 1749-1751.)

EUROPEAN RECORDS

Oberhochstadt Reformed KB:
Johannes Becker, son of the deceased Joh. Georg Becker from
Kleinfischlingen, m. 17 Feb. 1733 Anna Catharina Meyer, daughter of
Michael Meyer.
They sponsored several children in the Oberhochstadt records, the last one
being a child of Georg Wolff [q.v.] and Maria Apolonia [nee Meyer] in 1749.

Kleinfischlingen Reformed KB:
Johannes Becker and his wife (unnamed) had children:
1. Anna Margretha b. 4 Apr. 1737, bp. 7 Apr. 1737
   Sp.: Hans Jacob Wolff and his wife from Oberhochstadt
2. Ann Abbel b. 30 Oct. 1739, bp. 1 Nov. 1739

(probably Appollonia)
Sp.: Hans Georg Wolff and his wife from Oberhochstadt
3. unnamed child b. 7 Mar. 1742, bp. 7 Mar. 1742
Sp.: Hans David Giessler

AMERICAN RECORDS

Rev. John Caspar Stoever's Records:
Johannes Becker (Atolhoe) had a child:
      Catharina Barbara b. 5 Jan. 1752, bp. 2 Feb. 1752
      Sp.: Jacob Wolf and wife

Rev. Henrich Diefenbach's Travel Diary:
An early Reformed minister, Rev. Henrich Diefenbach, kept a travel diary. His comments recorded in that diary about his relationships to some of these Host Church families is of interest. A brief review of his lineage will clarify the relationships.

Henrich Diefenbach was b. 5 Dec. 1771 near Williamsport, Maryland, a son of Johann Balthasar Diefenbach and Anna Maria Becker. In 1784 the family moved to Staunton, Virginia. Henrich studied to become a Reformed minister; in 1800 he went to North Carolina as a licensed candidate. In 1802 he traveled to Pennsylvania to be examined and ordained by the Synod at the request of several of his North Carolina congregations. Rev. Diefenbach later served congregations in Ohio, where he mysteriously disappeared in 1837.

The 1802 diary contains the following account of his visit to Tulpehocken while he was in Pennsylvania for ordination:

"Friday, the 28th (May 1802) George Ruth rode with me to his brother-in-law George Vonnieda's, who lives near a mill on the Dolpehacken. We found him sick, but had a visit with his wife and son Georg and daughters Barbara and Elisabeth and stayed overnight with them. On Saturday the 29th, Mr. Ruth rode with me to Daniel Wolf's who lives with his sister Eva Kate (die Eva Kät). On the way there we rode past Grandfather Becker's old place, so that we could see it. Mr. Ruth said a daughter of Daniel Meyer was married to one of Peter Leiss' sons and lived on this place. They had built a new barn, but the old house was still standing. Then we came to Host Church, a large stone church with a wooden schoolhouse nearby, and the cemetery is surrounded with a stone wall. Here Grandmother and her four brothers and sisters are buried. Then we came to Henrich Meyer's mill. Mr. Ruth tells me that H. Meyer went to Seyothy (Scioto, in Ohio) and his children of his first wife did not go along. But he was married nineteen years to the second wife, and had children enough with her to go with him. When we came to Daniel Wolf's, Mr. Ruth asked him if he knew me. But he looked at me and said he did not, yet I belonged in Johannes

Becker's family (Freundschaft). When I told him who I was he called in his sister but she didn't know me either. When she learned who I was, she was very much surprised, and asked about all the relatives."

The relationships of the people mentioned in the 1802 diary are:
Children of Michael Meyer of Oberhochstadt:
>   1. Johannes Meyer, conf. 1713, Oberhochstadt [q.v.]
>   A son, Heinrich, inherited the mill property.
>   2. Daniel Meyer [q.v.]
>   A daughter, Barbara, m. Heinrich Leiss, son of Peter.
>   3. Maria Apolonia Meyer m. Georg Wolff [q.v.] and had:
>   A son, Daniel
>   A daughter, Catharina
>   4. Anna Catharina Meyer m. Johannes Becker
>   (Grandparents of Rev. Henry Diefenbach)

In 1935, Dr. W. J. Hinke copied the text of this German-script diary. His transcript is in the Hinke Collection, Philip Schaff Library, Lancaster, Pennsylvania.

BEITELMAN, FELTEN (VELDE)   67126 Assenheim
BEITELMAN, DEITRICH
BEIDELMAN, ELIAS
Thistle of Glasgow, 1730
S-H, I: 31, 33, 34 [Appears on list as Bydleman].

EUROPEAN RECORDS

Assenheim Lutheran KB:
Hans Marti Beutelman had a son:
>   Johann Dieterich, b. 12 June 1706
>   Sp.: Dietert Schweitzer and his wife

Velten Beutelmann m. Anna Clara Biermann and had children:
>   1. Maria Elisabeth, bp. 22 Feb. 1706
>   2. Elias, bp. 25 Sept. 1707
>   Sp.: Elias Brand and his wife
>   Sibilla Christina of [67157] Wachenheim
>   3. Elisabetha, bp. 7 Dec. 1709
>   4. Johann Leonhard, bp. 3 Oct. 1716
>   5. Johann Jacob, bp. 7 Jan. 1720

AMERICAN RECORDS

Berks County Will Abstracts:
Dietrich Beidelman, Alsace, 27 July 1791-23 Mar. 1793. To daughter
Elizabeth, wife of Francis Shalter [q.v. Frantz Schalter], 20 shillings having
provided for her children out of my real estate which I sold to my grandson
Dietrich Shalter. Remainder to wife Susanna who is also executor. Wit:
George Heckman and David Betz.

Susanna Beidleman, widow, Alsace. 30 Aug. 1794-22 Nov. 1794. To
granddaughter Rebecca Rothenberger, wife of Peter, bond of George Kiehn
for £30. To granddaughter Catharine, wife of Abraham Kissinger, £30.
Remainder of estate to be divided equally between 4 grandchildren, viz:
Dieter Shalter, Susanna wife of George Kiehn and 2 named above. Exr:
Dieter Shalter. Wit: Susanna Katzenmeyer and John Spyker.

St. Paul's (Blue) Lutheran KB, Upper Saucon Twp., Lehigh Co., PA:
Communicant members: Elias Beutelmann and wife Anna Maria, 1750.

Joh. Jacob Beutelmann and wife Susanna Cath. had:
    Daniel, b. 3 Nov. 1750, bp. 11 Nov. 1750
    Sp.: Elias Beutelmann and Anna Maria

Rev. J. Wm. Boos Records (Berks Co., PA):
Johann Dieter Beutelman (Alsace), b. June 1709, d. 18 Feb. 1793. (First
burial in a private burial ground at what is now Shalter's Church).

Elias Beutelman, Bucks Co., Quaker, nat. Apr. 1747.
Jacob Beutelman, Bucks Co., Quaker, nat. Sept. 1745.

BENCKER, CHRISTOPHEL   67157 Wachenheim an der Weinstrasse
Mortonhouse, 1728
S-H, I: 17, 19

EUROPEAN RECORDS

Wachenheim Reformed KB:
Christophel Bencker and wife Anna Eva had children:
    1. Maria Saloma, bp. 19 Feb. 1702
       m. Peter Mittelkauff [q.v.]
    2. Juliana, bp. 9 Oct. 1704

3. Catharina, bp. 26 July 1707, d. 17 Nov. 1712
4. Anna Margaretha, bp. 1 Oct. 1710
5. Casimir, bp. 1 May 1715, d. same day
6. Joh. Jacob, bp. 25 Nov. 1717
7. Margaretha Eleonora, bp. 12 May 1722

AMERICAN RECORDS

Christ (Conewago) Lutheran and Reformed KB, Littlestown, Adams Co.:
Martin Kützmüller from Waldorf and wife Julianna, daughter of Christopher Bencker, had a child:
Juliana, b. 22 Mar. 1747
Sp.: Anna Eva Bencker, grandmother

Henry Kassel and wife Anna Margaret nee Bencker had a daughter:
Anna Eva, b. 25 Feb. 1748
Sp.: Anna Eva Bencker, grandmother

John Jacob Bencker and wife Esther had:
1. John Jacob, bp. 25 July 1746
Sp.: Martin Kutzmüller and wife
2. Maria Margaretha, bp. 15 June 1745
Sp.: John Henry Knuss [?Knauff] and wife
3. John, b. 24 Mar. 1749
Sp.: John Jungling and wife.

BENDER, VALENTIN Oberhochstadt =
Dragon, 1749 76879 Hochstadt, Pfalz
S-H, I: 423

EUROPEAN RECORDS

Oberhochstadt Reformed KB:
Valentin Bender and his wife Margretha had children:
1. Joh. Friedrich bp. 2 Aug. 1727
2. Anna Catharina bp. 26 Mar. 1730

AMERICAN RECORDS

Rev. John Caspar Stoever's Records:
Valentine Bender (Atolhoe) had a son:
Georg Valentin b. 2 Feb. 1752, bp. 1 Mar. 1752
Sp.: Valentine Meyer and Elisabeth Stein

Host Church, Tulpehocken, Berks Co., PA:
Catharina, daughter of Valentin Bender, conf. 1753

Christ Lutheran Church, Tulpehocken, Marion Twp., Berks Co., PA:
Adam Bender, son of Valentine Bender m. 13 Apr. 1773 Catharina Behny,
daughter of Peter Behny, Heidelberg, Lancaster Co.

Pennsylvania Archives, 3rd Series, Vol. XVIII, pp. 413, 541, 677, 800:
A Valentin Bender appears on the Berks County tax lists, in Tulpehocken
Twp. in 1780, 1781, 1784, and 1785. His occupation is given as a cooper and
as a carpenter.

BENTZ, JÖRG   67459 Iggelheim
BENTZ, JOHANN LUDWIG
BENTZ, JACOB
Phoenix, 1749
S-H, I: 407

EUROPEAN RECORDS

Schifferstadt-Iggelheim Reformed KB:
Joh. Georg Bentz, shoemaker, son of Johannes Bentz, m. 29 Aug. 1719 Anna
Barbara Büllinger, daughter of the late Jacob Büllinger. They had children:
1. Johannes, b. 3 June 1720, bp. 5 June 1720
2. Joh. Valentin, b. 8 Jan. 1723, d. 3 June 1728
3. Johann Ludwig, b. 29 Dec. 1724, bp. 31 Dec. 1724
4. Johann Jacob, b. 8 Dec. 1727, bp. 14 Dec. 1727
5. Valentin, b. 18 Jan. 1730

Possibly the eldest son Johannes is the emigrant on p. 466, S-H.

Emigration record:
Werner Hacker, *Auswanderungen aus Rheinpfalz und Saarland*:
#1248 Hans Georg Benz, from Iggelheim, 1749.

A later generation of Bentz's appear in the Frederick Reformed KB,
Frederick, MD, where other Schifferstadt immigrants settled; no clear
connection with the above family has been made.

BENZEL, CONRADT   Ruchheim=
BENZEL, HANS GEORG   67071 Ludwigshafen am Rhein
Prelist

EUROPEAN RECORDS

Ruchheim Reformed KB:
Conradt Benzel and wife Maria had children:
1. Hans Georg, bp. *auff Johanni 1695*
   Sp.: Hans Georg Hertel of [67112] Mutterstadt and
   Johannes Cochoy
2. Hans Michel, bp. Mar. 1696 at [67136] Fussgönheim
   Sp.: Michael Borsler and Anna Margaretha

Hans Georg Bentzel, Lutheran, b. here in Ruchheim, weaver, and Anna Barbara, Reformed, b. in Ruchheim, daughter of Rudolff Sager, had children:
1. Maria Elisabeth, bp. 3 July 1719
   Sp.: Jacob Eitzer and Elisabetha
2. Johanna Maria, bp. 29 Aug. 1721
   Sp.: Carl Ludwig Adam and wife Johanna Maria.

AMERICAN RECORDS

Philadelphia Will Abstracts:
Conrad Benzell, weaver, Northern Liberties. Dated 21 Oct. 1738 - probated 1 Sept. 1748. Executor wife Dorothy, son Hans George Benzell, 1 shilling plus what he had received of me. Balance of estate to wife Dorothy.

Philadelphia Will Abstracts:
George Bensell, Germantown, Philadelphia co., dated 8 July 1763, probated 7 Nov. 1763. Shopkeeper "advanced in years". Executors: wife and son Charles. Wife Anna Barbara, est. during her life; at her death to the 4 children (Charles, George, James and Sarah), of my son Charles; daughter Elisabeth; daughter's children (George, Anna Elisabeth, Charles, Mary); daughter Mary; grandson George Bensel.

Lower burial ground, Germantown (Germantown Ave. and Logan St.):

Johann Georg Bensels
b. in Ruchheim in Palatinate 1695
d. 29 Oct. 1763

Anna Barbara, widow of Johann George Bensel
b. in Ruchheim in the Palatinate 29 Sept. 1698
d. 6 Aug. 1775

Germantown Reformed KB, Philadelphia Co., PA:
Charles Bensel and wife Margaret had a son:
>   Charles, b. 28 May 1774, bp. 11 Sept. 1774
>   Sp.: Parents

Signature of George Bensel from the estate records of Christoph Dallmer, 1738, Philadelphia:

George Bensel

BERGHEIMER, CASPAR   67259 Kleinniedesheim
Prelist

EUROPEAN RECORDS

Gross- and Kleinniedesheim Lutheran KB:
Balthaser Birckheimer had children, born in Kleinniedesheim before the church record there starts. (The KB contains baptisms from 1727-1730, then a major gap until 1755 when the record resumes on a regular basis.):
>   1. Johann Casper (to America before 1730, presumed prelist).
>   2. Johann Wilhelm, [q.v.], to America 1732.
>   3. Susanna, to America 1732 with her brother.

AMERICAN RECORDS

Augustus (Trappe) Lutheran KB, Montgomery Co., PA:
Johann Caspar Bergheimer m. 20 Oct. 1730 Elisabetha Catharina Haüser. (This marriage also recorded in Stoever's records, below, with a different translation for the bride's surname.)

Rev. John Casper Stoever's Records:
Casper Bergheimer (Conewago) had children:
>   1. Anna Eva, b. 30 Sept. 1734, bp. 22 May 1735
>   Sp.: Anna Eva Kuntz
>   2. John Ludwig, b. 8 Dec. 1735, bp. 27 Apr. 1736
>   Sp.: John Ludwig Schreiber and wife.
>   3. John Leonhardt, b. 13 Nov. 1737, bp. 23 May 1738
>   Sp.: John Leonhardt Bernitz, Johann Morgenstern and wife.
>   4. Maria Elisabetha, b. 23 May 1741, bp. 25 June 1741
>   Sp.: Maria Elisabetha Morgenstern.

BERGHEIMER, WILHELM age 20   67259 Kleinniedesheim
Samuel, 1732
S-H, I: 59, 61, 63, 65
 with Salome, age 25 and Leonhard Bergh----, age 8, and Veltin Bergh---,
age 6; also on ship Susanna Bergheimer, age 18.

EUROPEAN RECORDS

Gross- and Kleinniedesheim Lutheran KB:
Wilhelm Berckheimer and wife Salome had children:
 1. Leonhard, b. before church records start in 1727
 2. Valentin, b. before church records start in 1727
 3. Magdalena Louisa, b. 22 Aug. 1727, bp. 24 Aug. 1727
   Sp.: Magdalena Louisa, daughter of Peter Hausman at Worms
 4. Joh. Georg, b. 22 Feb. 1729, bp. 23 Feb. 1729
   Sp.: Joh. Georg Dackermann

AMERICAN RECORDS

Old Goshenhoppen Lutheran KB, Upper Salford Twp., Montgomery Co., PA:
Family register, # 14: Johann Leonhardt Berckheimer, age 29 years, b. 3
Mar. 1722, bp. 5 Mar. 1722, son of Joh. Wilhelm Berckheimer of Klein
Niddesheim [67259 Kleinniedesheim] in the Pfalz and of his wife Maria
Salome. He came with his parents to America in the year 1732. Anno 8 Jan.
1744 he married Maria Catharina Kerger, b. 1720, daughter of Philip Kerger,
Lutheran from Kreuznach [55543 Bad Kreuznach] and of his wife Anna
Maria, Lutheran, deceased. She came to America with her parents in the
year 1743. They had children:
 1. Joh. Michael Wilhelm, b. 3 days before Michaelmas, died.
 2. Maria Salome, b. 8 Sept. 1745
 3. Joh. Georg, b. 17 Feb. 1747
 4. Joh. Henrich, b. 3 Apr. 1751
 5. Joh. Jacob, b. 14 Oct. 1753
 6. Joh. Jacob Wilhelm, b. 23 July 1755
 7. Andreas, b. 20 Apr. 1758
 8. Maria Magdalena, b. 15 June 1760

Joh. Valentin Berckheimer and wife Jacobina had:
 1. Johann Wilhelm, b. 21 Apr. 1753

BICKEL, see BECHTLUF, BECKEL, BÖCKEL

BISCHANTZ, JOHANN THOMAS   Ungstein=
Neptune, 1754   67098 Bad Dürkheim
S-H, I: 620, 621, 622

EUROPEAN RECORDS

Bad Dürkheim Lutheran KB:
Abraham Bischantz, son of the late (Hans) Johannes Bischantz, m. 23 Jan. 1703 Magdalene Rossel, daughter of David Andreas Rossel, *Schlossermeister* from [67227] Franckenthal.
(An earlier record indicates that Johan Bisantz was from *"Corsi aus der Schweitz."* [Possibly Corsy, VD = CH-1093 La Conversion])

Sebastian Bischantz, citizen of Bad Dürkheim, son of Abraham Bischantz, *Wingertsmann,* m. 22 Aug. 1730 Maria Magdalena Grüneisen, daughter of Johannes Jacob Grüneisen of Roht [76835 Rhodt unter Rietburg].

Ungstein Lutheran KB:
Sebastian Bisanss, *Metzgermeister,* and wife Maria Magdalena had a son:
    Johann Thomas, bp. 2 Aug. 1731
    Sp.: Herr Johann Jacob Gryneisen, *Gerichtsschreiber*
    und Praeceptor in dem Fleckin Rhod-unter Rippurg
    (today *Rhodt unter Rietburg*); Herr Johann Thomas
    from Mannheim and his wife Maria Magdalena.

AMERICAN RECORDS

St. Michael's and Zion Lutheran KB, Philadelphia:
Johann Thomas Bischantz m. 6 Jan. 1761 Anna Margaretha Münster. Wit.: Marcus Münster and Engelbert Lack.
Thomas Bischantz and wife Margretha had children:
    1. Johannes, b. 8 Dec. 1761, bp. 27 Dec. 1761
        Sp.: Johannes Biegler and Magdalena Schmiedt, single.
    2. Anna Maria, b. 18 Feb. 1766, bp. 9 Mar. 1766
        Sp.: Matthias Sähler and Anna Maria.

BITTING see BÖTTIG

BLEYENSTEIN, HANS JERG   67112 Mutterstadt
York, 1725
    [Signed ship's agreement contract]

EUROPEAN RECORDS

Mutterstadt Reformed KB:
Recorded with the 1724 marriages, but dated 1723 (no month or day given):
Johann Georg Bleyenstein and Anna Maria _____ (faded)

Hans Georg Bleienstein and wife Anna Maria had one child bp. at Mutterstadt:
Anna Katharina, bp. 1 Dec. 1724

AMERICAN RECORDS

No record located for Georg Bleyenstein; the only record found for a similar surname:
Berks County Wills and Administrations, abstracts:
John Jacob Bleistein, Tulpehocken. On 28 Sept. 1775, adm. was granted to Susanna Fulhaver, widow, his sister.

BLUM, FRANTZ   67259 Heuchelheim
Alexander & Anne, 1730
S-H, I: 35, 36

EUROPEAN RECORDS

Heuchelheim Lutheran KB:
Frantz Blum m. 13 Apr. 1723 Elisabeth Müller. Children:
1. Anna Elisabetha, b. 10 Apr. 1726, bp. 14 Apr. 1726
2. Maria Magdalena, b. Sept. 1729, bp. 18 Sept. 1729

AMERICAN RECORDS

Life and Letters of the Rev. John Philip Boehm:
Franz Blum, b. in the Palatinate 1 May 1700, d. 2 Jan. 1777, Nazareth Moravian Graveyard. Frantz Blum was an Elder of the Saucon Creek Congregation in 1740.

Nazareth Moravian KB, Northampton Co., PA:
Franz Blum and wife Catharine had:
1. David, b. 12 May 1743
2. Daniel, b. 27 May 1746
3. Anna Maria, b. 7 July 1750 (Bethlehem Moravian KB)
4. Christina, b. 18 Nov. 1756

BÖCKEL, TOBIAS   Ungstein=
St. Andrew Galley, 1737   67098 Bad Dürkheim
S-H, I: 179, 180, 183
  Signed Dobias Böckell; arrived with Jacob Kuster.

EUROPEAN RECORDS

Kallstadt Lutheran KB:
Gotthart Böckel and wife Maria Sibylla had a son:
      Tobias, b. 15 Feb. 1712, bp. 29 Feb. 1712
      Sp.: *Mstr.* Tobias Lung, and Anna Catharina, wife of
      Mstr. Joh. Matheis Bruch at Leustatt.

Erpolzheim Lutheran KB:
Married 18 Apr. 1734, Tobias Böckel with Kuster's daughter.

Tobias Böckel, inhabitant of Ungstein, and wife Anna Christina, both
Reformed, had children:
      1. Catharina Elisabetha, b. 20 Dec. 1734, bp. 21 Dec. 1734
          Sp.: Joh. Niclaus Schmitt and wife Catharina Elisabetha
      2. Anna Elisabetha, b. 13 Mar. 1736, bp. 18 Mar. 1736
          Sp.: Joh. Friderich Böckel, single and Anna
          Elisabetha, daughter of Georg ____?

AMERICAN RECORDS

Heidelberg Moravian KB, Berks Co., PA:
Tobias Böckel, Sr., widower, m. 24 Aug. 1779 Maria Elisabeth Glatt, widow.

Burials:
Christina Boeckel, nee Kuster, b. 6 Mar. 1714 in Unkstein, Hardenburg
[Ungstein = 67098 Bad Dürkheim]. Her father was Jacob Kuster and her
mother was Elisabeth Diliken of the same place. She was baptized in the
Reformed religion.   On Palm Sunday 1734 she was married to Tobias
Boeckel by Pastor Seiler. In 1737 she came to this land with her husband,
her father and two brothers. The Lord blessed her with 15 children, 7 of
whom died before she died. The 8 living are 5 who are members of our
church here and 3 in North Carolina.   She is also survived by 12
grandchildren. She died 31 Jan. 1775.

Tobias Boeckel was born in the Palatinate 13 Nov. 1711 and came to this
land in 1737. After he was here 3 years [? should read 3 years before
arriving here] he married Christina, a born Kuster. They had 14 children

and he was survived by 7 of them. After his wife died he remarried in the year 1779 to widow Maria Elisabetha Dock, widow of Nicolaus Glat.

Heidelberg Moravian Family Register:
Tobias Beckel, born in November 1711 in Kallstadt near Dürkheim-an-der-Hardt in County Hartenburg. His father was Johann Gotthard Beckel, citizen and member of the local court, and his mother was Sybilla, a born Gossenberger. He was baptized in November at the same place by the pastor there. He was married on Palm Sunday, 1734, to Christinen (now deceased) daughter of Jacob Kuster, citizen of Unkstein, and his wife Elisabeth. Christinen was born 6 May 1714. In their marriage the Lord gave them the following children:

1. Catharina Elisabeth, b. in Unkstein, near Dürkheim-an-der-Hardt, bp. 30 Nov. in the church at that place by Pastor Seiler. Sp.: Hans Nicolaus Schmidt and his wife Catharina Elisabeth. Catharina Elisabeth d. January 1735.
2. Anna Elisabeth, b. in Unkstein in the middle of Lent in 1736, and was baptized 8 days later, by Pastor Seiler of the same place. Sp.: Friedrich Beckel and Anna Elisabeth Borkert. She d. in July 1737 at Helvo sluys on the journey to PA.
3. Tobias, b. March 1738 in Heidelberg in Lancaster Co., bp. by Pastor Götschy of the Reformed Church in Bern Township. Sp.: Tobias Bechtel and his wife Anna Elisabeth. Tobias d. Dec. 1738.
4. Eva Elisabeth, b. middle of Oct. 1740 in Heidelberg, Lancaster Co., bp. by Pastor Götschy in the Reformed church in Bern. Sp.: Tobias Bechtel and wife Anna Elisabeth. She d. in Feb. 1743.
5. Johann Nicolaus, b. 20 Oct. 1741 in Heidelberg; bp. by Caspar Stöver in the Lutheran church on the Northkill in Bern. Sp.: Johann Nicolaus Holler and his wife Anna Maria.
6. Friedrich, b. 9 Nov. 1743 in Heidelberg, bp. 18 Nov. 1743 by Jacob Lischy at home. Sp.: Friedrich and Elisabeth Beckel.
7. Maria, b. 19 Nov. 1745, old style, in Heidelberg; bp. 23 Nov. 1745 at home by Brother Joseph Spangenberg. Sp.: Elisabeth Wagner, Elisabeth Beckel, Anna Margaretha Meyer and Maria Glat.
8. Daniel, b. 8 Jan. 1748, old style, in Heidelberg. Bp. 10 Jan. 1748 after the sermon by Brother Leonhard Schnell. Sp.: Johannes Meyer, Friedrich Gerhard, and Daniel Neubert. Daniel d. 1 Feb. 1748.

9. Phillip Jacob, b. 17 Dec. 1748 in Heidelberg. Bp. 22 Dec. 1748 by Brother Philipp Meurer. Sp.: Phillip Hoen, Jacob Conrad, Johannes Meyer, Friderich Gerhart.
Phillip Jacob d. 9 Feb. 1749.
10. Johannes, b. 26 Mar. 1750, old style, in Heidelberg.
Bp. 28 Mar. 1750 in the house of the parents by Brother Christian Rauch. Sp.: Daniel and Hanna Neibert.
11. Magdalena, b. 23 Apr. 1752 in Heidelberg, bp. 3 May 1752, old style, by Brother Mattheo Reus in the meetinghouse.
Sp.: Margaretha Meyer, Maria Barbara Hön, Anna Maria Schmid, Maria Catharina Conrad, Elisabeth Müller, Barbara Frey and Magdalena Reüs.
12. Johannes Tobias, b. 6 Dec. 1754, bp. 8 Dec. 1754 by Brother Anton Wagner. Sp.: Friedrich Gerhard, Johannes Meyer, Heinrich Leonhardt, Georg Brendel, Jacob Greder.
13. Anton, b. 23 Feb. 1757, bp. 24 Feb. 1757 by Bro. Anton Wagner. Sp.: Friedrich Gerhard, Johannes Meyer, Jacob Müller, Valendin Frey, Georg Brendel, Jacob Greder, Peter Folz, and the father.
14. Elisabeth, b. Good Friday, 13 Apr. 1759, bp. 14 Apr. by Brother Anton Wagner. Sp.: Elisabeth Wagner, Elisabeth Weiser, Elisabeth Müller, Elisabeth Keller and Mrs. Elisabeth Vols.

BOGENREIFF, SIMON   Niederhochstadt=
Davy, 1738   76879 Hochstadt, Pfalz
S-H, I: 234, 235, 236
(appears on list: Simon Bogeriss)

EUROPEAN RECORDS

Niederhochstadt Reformed KB:
Jacob Bogenreif and wife Anna Rosina had a son:
        Johan Simon bp. 6 Mar. 1709
        Sp.: Simon Fischer and Apollonia

Johannes Wittner and wife Anna Catharina had a daughter:
        Catharina bp. 18 Dec. 1712

Joh. Simon Bogenreiff, son of Jacob Bogenreiff, m. 15 Jan. 1732 Catharina Elisabetha Wittner, daughter of Johannes Wittner. They had children:
        1. Jacob bp. 3 Aug. 1732
        Sp.: Jacob Schmidt and Maria Barbara
        2. Georg Henrich bp. 30 Aug. 1733
        Sp.: Georg Heinrich Peter and Christina Lehr, single

3. Catharina bp. 23 Aug. 1735
   Sp.: Catharina Völcker, widow

AMERICAN RECORDS

Christ "Little Tulpehocken" Church Records, Heidelberg Twp., Berks Co.:
Simon Bogenreiff and wife had children:
4. Joh. Valentin b. 17 Oct. 1741, bp. 7 Dec. 1741
   Sp.: Valentin Unruh and wife
5. Jerg Adam b. 17 Apr. 1756, bp. 9 May 1756
   Sp.: Jerg Adam Bartdorff and wife

Christ Tulpehocken Lutheran KB, Stouchsburg, Marion Twp., Berks Co.:
Simon Bogenreif (Northkill) and wife Catharina had a daughter:
6. Margaret Elisabeth b. before 4 May 1747, bp. 6 Jan. 1747
   Sp.: Martin Schell and wife

Host Reformed KB, Tulpehocken, Berks Co., PA:
Simon Bogenreif m. 15 July 1755 Margaret Elisabeth Schell.

Henrich and Adam, sons of Simon Bogenreif, both had children baptized at this church.

Berks County Orphans' Court Records, Vol. 1, p. 224, dated 16 Aug. 1765:
Petition of Simon Bogenreiff on behalf of Peter and Christian Shell, minor children of Martin Shell, deceased. The widow of Martin Shell is now married to Simon Bogenreiff. Martin Shell died leaving 6 children, two of them under 14 years of age.

Berks County Will Abstracts:
Simon Bogereiff of Tulpehocken, dated 28 June 1782, probated 25 Sept. 1782. The will mentions the following heirs: son Henry; the children of Simon Bogereiff; the children of Valentine Bogereiff; Martin Bogereiff; Catharina Mountz; Eva Fengel; son John Adam Bogereiff. Letters of Administration to: Frederick Gerhart and John Fengel. Witnessed by: Frederick Gerhart and David Miller.

Lancaster County Land Warrants, Pennsylvania Archives:
Simon Poncrife, 100 acres, 7 Feb. 1738. Simon Baugenreif, 100 acres 19 Sept. 1752.

Old Reed's Lutheran Church, Tulpehocken Twp., Berks County:
Simon Bogenreif and wife Catharina sponsor a child of Johannes and Maria Elisabeth Schaffer in 1738.

BÖHLER, HANS MARTIN   67161 Gönnheim
Thistle, 1738
S-H, I: 221, 223, 224

EUROPEAN RECORDS

Gönnheim Reformed KB:
Hans Martin Böhler and wife Catharina had children:
  1. Hans Martin bp. 19 June 1712
     Sp.: Martin Sorg and Maria Elisabetha Blaul
  2. Catharina Elisabetha bp. 26 Aug. 1714
     Sp.: Anna Elisabetha Bechdoll from [67245] Lambsheim
     She probably md. ca. 1735 Joh. Jacob Pfarr [q.v.]
  3. Anna Barbara bp. 15 Nov. 1716
  4. Maria Johannata bp. 6 Aug. 1719
  5. Joh. Ludwig bp. 20 Sep. 1722
     Sp.: Joh. Ludwig Weis
  6. Catharina bp. 6 Apr. 1732
     Sp.: Andreas Kiesch from [67136] Fussgönheim and
     Catharina, widow of Conrad Werntz

AMERICAN RECORDS

Rev. Jacob Lischy's records, York Co., PA:
Niclaus Freytag [q.v.] and wife Anna Elisabetha had a son Joh. Martin bp.
31 Aug. 1755. Sp. at his bp. were Joh. Martin Böhler and wife Catharina.

BÖRSTLER, JOH. GEORG   67126 Assenheim
Edinburgh, 1754
S-H, I: 615, 617, 629

EUROPEAN RECORDS

Assenheim Lutheran KB:
Johann Michael Börstler m. 26 Jan. 1734 Anna Catharina, nee Kröll. It is
recorded in the marriage record that the marriage was necessary due to
pregnancy. Joh. Michael Börstler and Anna Catharina had a son:
     Joh. Georg Börstler, bp. 15 Apr. 1734
     Sp.: Johann Georg Schalter and Elisabeth

AMERICAN RECORDS

Berks County Will Abstracts:
A Georg Berstler of Alsace Twp., Berks Co., d. ca. 1791. Ltr. of Admin. granted to Polly, his widow.

Rev. John Wm. Boos' burial records, Schwartzwald, Berks Co., PA:
George Börstler, (Alsace) b. 12 Apr. 1734, d. 8 Aug. 1791

BORTNER, BALTHASAR age 34   Oberhochstadt=
Adventure, 1732   76879 Hochstadt, Pfalz
S-H, I: 84, 85, 86, 87
  Other family members on ship: Merreles (Maria Elisabetha) age 37; Hanna Mela, age 8; Jacob, age 10

EUROPEAN RECORDS

Niederhochstadt Reformed KB:
Balthasar Bortner from Oberhochstadt confirmed 1710.

Oberhochstadt Reformed KB:
Balthasar Bortner and wife Elisabetha had a son:
        Johan Jacob bp. 10 Aug. 1731
        Sp.: Jacob Sauter and Apollonia Meyer, both single

AMERICAN RECORDS

Christ "Little Tulpehocken" Church records, Heidelberg Twp., Berks Co.:
Balthasar Bortner and wife had a daughter:
        Mary Eliesabetha b. 8 Mar. 1738, bp. 30 Apr. 1738
        Sp.: Joh. Wilhelm Leitner and wife

Christ Lutheran Church, Tulpehocken, Marion Twp., Berks Co., PA:
Henry Raun (Kahn), from beyond the Susquehanna, m. 17 Feb. 1748 Maria Barbara Bortner, daughter of Balser Bortner, beyond the Susquehanna.

Host Reformed KB, Tulpehocken, Berks Co., PA:
Jacob Bortner, son of Balthasar Bortner, confirmed 1753.
(Note: the ship's list gives Jacob's age as 10. However, it appears that the age of 1 would be more accurate, in view of the baptismal date and also the confirmation date.)

Philadelphia Administrations F, p. 133, 1747, Philadelphia:
Balthasar Bordner died before Berks county was erected; records on his estate are found in Philadelphia county.

Host Reformed KB, Tulpehocken, Berks Co., PA:
Jacob Bordner and wife Sarah had a daughter:
> Anna Maria b. 9 Dec. 1756, bp. 27 Dec. 1756
> Sp.: Johannes Meyer and Anna Maria

Jacob Portner and wife were sponsors in 1754 for a child of Joh. Bastian Weber.

Berks County Land Warrants, Pennsylvania Archives, Third Series:
Jacob Bortner, 60 acres, 3 Apr. 1792

Jacob Bordner, Tulpohockon, Berks County, nat. Apr. 1761.

BOTT, HERMANUS, age 46   Oggersheim=
Loyal Judith, 1743   67071 Ludwigshafen am Rhein
S-H, I: 335, 337, 338

EUROPEAN RECORDS

Oggersheim Reformed KB:
Hermann Bott, Lutheran, and Anna Kunigunda, Reformed, had a daughter:
> Gertraud, b. 19 Sept. 1721, bp. 23 Sept. 1721

AMERICAN RECORDS

York County, PA, Deed Book 2, pg. 522-525:
12 Mar. 1760: Harmanus Butt of Manchester Twp. to Adam Butt of Yorktown, for the sum of £300 a house and lot # 106 on the main street of York Town. Signed Harmanus Bott.

12 Feb. 1762: Harmanus Bott of Manchester twp., Yeoman, and Katrina his wife to Adam Bott of York Town, Blacksmith. Patent dated 13 Aug. 1750 granted to Hermanus Bott a tract of land in Manchester twp. on the west bank of Codorus Creek, cont. 279 A. Harmanus Bott sells part of this tract to Adam Bott for £25 cont. 5 acres, adj. part of the above recited Patent which Hermanus Bott formerly conveyed to John Guchus, thence by Guches' land to adj. land of Johan Rynard Bott, also part of the above recited tract.

York County, PA, Deed Book 2, pg. 529-531:
20 Feb. 1762: Harmanus Bott of Manchester Twp., Yeoman, and Katrina his wife to John Rynard Bott. Part of the above Patent cont. 279 A. Johan Rynard Bott pays £460 for 218 A, part of the Patented land, to Harmanus Bott, adj. to land sold to John Gucchus.

Additional deeds recorded in Deed Book 1, pg. 63-64 (Hermanus Bott to John Guckes) and Book 1, pg. 128-130 (Hermanus Bott to John Wagoner).

York County Will Abstracts:
Herman Bott. Manchester Twp. dated 9 Oct. 1764, probated 28 July 1772. Wife, no name recorded. Children: Reinhard, Jacob, daughter m. John Cookas? [Guckes, Guches] and Adelia m. John Wagener. Exr: Jacob Bott.

Herman Bott, York Twp., York Co., nat. 25 Sept. 1750.

BÖTTIG [BITTING], HENRICH   67251 Freinsheim
likely on *The Globe,* 1723
    [one Hans Bieting signed the charter agreement for this ship]

EUROPEAN RECORDS

Freinsheim Reformed KB:
Henrich Böttig [surname also given in the records as Bettig, Pettig] is mentioned in the early records as the town janitor. He and his wife Anna Catharina had children:
1. Martin, born before the records start, conf. 1712
2. Anna Sophia [surname Pattich], bp. 22 Nov. 1699
    Sp.: Christopffel Scheffer from Anhalt in Sachsen
    and Anna Sophia Kohlschmidt
3. Johann Ludwig, b. 14 May 1702, bp. 21 May 1702, conf. 1715
    Sp.: Johan Ludwig von Rodebach and Margaretha,
    daughter of Hans Adam Gifft
4. Anna Catharina, bp. 9 Mar. 1704, died 21 Apr. 1706
5. Henrich, bp. 20 Dec. 1705
    Sp.: Henrich Rasp, single, Reformed and Dorothea
    Elisabetha, daughter of the Reformed schoolmaster Quantz
6. Anna Dorothea Elisabetha, bp. 7 Mar. 1708, conf. 1723
    Sp.: Philip Rasp, Reformed, and Dorothea Elisabetha,
    daughter of the schoolmaster Quantz

7. Joh. Peter, bp. 5 Oct. 1710, conf. 1723. It is
   mentioned in the 1723 confirmation lists that these
   two children of Henrich Böttig were confirmed just
   prior to going to Pennsylvania with their parents
   and siblings. Sp.: Peter Besch, citizen here, and his wife
8. Justus, bp. 2 July 1713 [appears in PA records as
   Jost Bitting]. Sp.: Justus Freudenstein and wife Susanna
9. Johanna Juliana, b. __ Apr. 1716, died 20 Sept. 1717
   Sp.: Johannes, son of Herr Clemens Ludwig Böhm,
   schoolmaster and Juliana, daughter of Herr Jacob Leppoldt,
   both 8 years old.
10. Joh. Melchior, bp. not found, d. 15 Nov. 1722, age 4 years.

AMERICAN RECORDS

See an article on Henry Bitting in *The Perkiomen Region, Past and Present*,
Vol. I: 59-60. This article lists the children of the sons Martin, Ludwig,
Henry and Justus Bitting.

New Goshenhoppen Reformed KB, Montgomery Co., PA:
Confirmed 1748-1758: Ludwig Bitting, Henrich Bitting, Anton Bitting, Anna
Maria Bitting, Elisabetha Bitting, Catharina Bitting and her sister.

Conf. 1758: Philip Bitting

Buried 27 Dec. 1775: Ludwig Bitting, b. 1703, age about 73 years.

Philadelphia Will Book Q: 257:
Ludwig Bitting, Lower Milford Twp. 25 Sept. 1771 - 24 Feb. 1776.
Exrs.: brother Jost Bitting, wife Elisabeth and son-in-law Gabriel Kline.
Children: Ludwig, eldest son; Henry; Antony; Philip; Mary wife of Andrew
Graven; Elisabeth wife of Gabriel Kline; Mary Catharina; and Christina wife
of Frantz Lydich.

Oley Moravian Records, Berks Co., PA:
Just Bitting or Bütting was born in Germany "in the Palatinate in the village
of Franzheim" [67251 Freinsheim] in the year 1713, June 24, and
immediately baptized by the Pastor of the place. He was raised in the
Reformed religion. His father was Henrich Bütting, his mother Catharina
nee Schäffer. In 1723 he and his parents emigrated; he was a farmer. In
1743, at the age of 32, he married Agnes nee Dotter. In 1743 he joined the
Moravians. They had 13 children. [See *Der Reggeboge*, Vol. 14, no. 1 (Jan.
1980):3]

Epitaphs, Leidig's Burial Ground, pub. in *The Perkiomen Region, Past and Present,* Vol. 1: 59-60:

Jost Bitting	Agnes Bitting
b. 5 July 1713	b. 14 Feb. 1727
d. 25 Dec. 1801	d. 2 Nov. 1785
age 88 y. 5 mo. 18 days	age 58 y. 6 mo. 8 days

Montgomery County Will Abstracts:
Jost Bitting, New Hanover. Dated 8 Nov. 1793, prob. 26 Jan. 1802.
To son Ludwig, a farm of 30 acres. To son Philip, 21 acres, 125 perches at £4 per acre, and also 6 acres. To son John, 10 acres at £4 per acre; at his death, to be sold and money divided among his children. Rem. to be sold, and divided equally among children. To Henry, Joseph, John, Peter and Philip and daughter Sophia each £10; remainder to be divided among 11 children. To son-in-law George Bechtell, what is left of daughter Catharine's December share. Daughter Rebecca to have full portion, unless she marries again (if she marries, to have interest only.) Exrs: sons Henry and Joseph. Wit: Francis Leidig, Samuel Bartolet, Jacob Shoemaker.

Rev. Boos' Records, Schwartzwald, Berks Co., PA, burials:
Ludwig Buding (Bitting), Cumru;
b. 1731, d. 18 Sept. 1796.

Berks County Will Abstracts:
Ludwig Bitting, Cumru. 16 Sept. 1796 - 17 Oct. 1796.
Provides for wife Susanna and directs her to leave £100 to the children of daughter Catharine, wife of Philip Siesholtz. Christian Bechtel to be their guardian. Mentions having settled unto the children their share of the real estate by deeds. Exrs: wife Susanna and friend Peter Filbert.
Wit.: George Englehart and John Bingaman.

His widow Susanna Bitting also left a will dated 6 Nov. 1801- 28 Jan. 1802. Names son Philip, daughters Catharine, wife of Philip Siesholtz and Esther, wife of William Reyland, and sons John and Daniel. Son Daniel, exr.
Wit.: John Spyker and Paul Maurer.

Ludwig Bitting and Martin Bitting nat. 1734/5.

BRACK, VALENTIN   Oberhochstadt=
[Brock on list; did not sign]   76879 Hochstadt, Pfalz
Queen of Denmark, 1751
S-H, I: 472

EUROPEAN RECORDS

Niederhochstadt Reformed KB:
Hans Jacob Brack, b. in Canton Bern, Switzerland, m. 7 Oct. 1710? Anna
Maria _____ Bergerin, Oberhochstadt.

Valentin Brack, son of the late Jacob Brack, former citizen at
Oberhochstadt, m. 1 May 1742 Anna Margretha, daughter of the late
Henrich ?Lischer, former citizen at Altdorff [=67482 Altdorf, Pfalz].
They had children:
   1. Eva Barbara, b. 27 July 1746, bp. 31 July 1746
       Sp.: Jacob Kern from [76833] Böchingen, single
       and Eva Barbara Unruh, widow.
   2. Valentin b. 13 Sept. 1749, bp. 17 Sept. 1749
       Sp.: Valentin Mayer and Margaretha Bender, both single

Emigration record:
Werner Hacker, *Auswanderungen aus Rheinpfalz und Saarland*:
2096 Valden Brück, wife and 3 children, from Oberhochstadt, mm. 1751.

BRAUN, MELCHIOR   Lachen-Speyerdorf=
Edinburgh, 1748   67435 Neustadt an der Weinstrasse
S-H, I: 372

EUROPEAN RECORDS

Werner Hacker, *Auswanderungen aus Rheinpfalz und Saarland im 18.
Jahrhundert:* #1985 Braun, Melchior, Lachen, deserted. (date of emigration
not given but before 1760).

#1997 Braun, Paul. Citizen of Lachen. Emigrated to Hungary. Record dated
22 Feb. 1770.

No entries for the Braun family were located in the Lachen-Speyerdorf
Reformed KB.

AMERICAN RECORDS

Berks County Will Abstracts:
Melchior Braun, Richmond Twp., dated 28 Sept. 1766, proved 25 Oct. 1766.
To wife Catharina the improvement containing 25 acres as long as she lives;
at her death, godson Melchior Gollinger shall have the property. Remainder

of estate to "my full brother Paul Braun who lives in the village of Lachen in the Electoral Palatinate, and to my full sister Catharina Braun." To the Lutheran church in Richmond #3 for an organ. Step-son Michael Gollinger executor.

BREINIG, JERG Ober Lustadt=
Lydia, 1749 67363 Lustadt
S-H, I: 422

EUROPEAN RECORDS

Ober Lustadt Reformed KB:
Joh. Jacob Breunig, Jr. and wife Magdalena had a son:
Johann Georg, b. 7 Feb. 1732; bp. 10 Feb. 1732
Sp.: Joh. Georg Emlich and Appolonia Reiffel, both single

AMERICAN RECORDS

First Reformed KB, Philadelphia, PA:
One George Breunig with wife Catharina had children:
1. John, bp. 26 Nov. 1760
2. Susanna, b. 3 Feb. 1765, bp. 28 Feb. 1765
3. Conrad, b. 26 Nov. 1767, bp. 12 Dec. 1767
4. Abraham, b. 25 Feb. 1769, bp. 20 Mar. 1769
5. Rebecca, twin, b. 5 July 1772, bp. 20 July 1772
6. Elizabeth, twin, b. 5 July 1772, bp. 20 July 1772
7. Isaac, b. 1 Dec. 1775, bp. 14 Dec. 1775.

Died 21 Feb. 1776, Georg Braunig, age 45 years.

BRENDEL, MARX 67459 Böhl
possibly on *Phoenix,* 1749
S-H, I: 406 [appears on list as Marx Springel; did not sign.]

EUROPEAN RECORDS

Hassloch Reformed KB:
Married 9 Jan. 1709 in [67454] Hassloch: Joh. Balthasar Brendel and Anna Catharina, daughter of Christoph Müller. His father is not named in this record. Joh. Balthasar Brendel was buried 20 Jan. 1756, age 77; Anna Catharina Brendel was buried 7 Apr. 1756, age 70. They had a son:
Johann Marx, b. 18 Feb. 1712, bp. 21 Feb. at Böhl

Married 8 Jan. 1710 in Hassloch: Joh. Philipp Wolf, son of the deceased
Hans Jacob Wolf, *gewesenen Gerichts* at Böhl, with Anna Maria, widow of
the deceased Hans Michael Würth. Anna Maria (Würth) Wolf was buried
at Böhl 12 Apr. 1712. Johann Philipp Wolf married (2) at Böhl 15 Feb.
1713 Anna Elisabetha, daughter of Hans Georg Brunner. Johann Philipp
Wolf was buried 5 Feb. 1736 at Böhl, age 51.

Johann Philipp Wolf and Anna Elisabetha had a daughter:
    Anna Elisabetha, bp. 24 Aug. 1713

Böhl Reformed KB:
Married 25 May 1734 at Böhl: Marx, son of Balthasar Brendel, with Anna
Elisabetha, daughter of Hans Philipp Wolff. They had children:
    1. Johannes, b. 4 Aug. 1735; bp. 4 Aug. 1735
    2. Maria Catharina, b. 9 Oct. 1736; bp. 14 Oct. 1736;
       buried 8 July 1740.
    3. Lorentz, b. 15 May 1738; bp. 16 May 1738
    4. Mattess, b. 24 Oct. 1740; bp. 30 Oct. 1740
    5. Hans Georg, twin, b. 14 May 1743, bp. 16 May 1743,
       buried 3 Dec. 1745.
    6. Johann Nickel, twin, b. 14 May 1743, bp. 16 May 1743
    7. Conrad, b. 29 Sep. 1745; bp. 3 Oct. 1745
    8. Anna Margaretha, b. 8 Aug. 1747, bp. 10 Aug. 1747,
       buried 21 Jan. 1748.
    9. Anna Margaretha, b. 12 Feb. 1749; bp. 16 Feb. 1749

Emigration Data:
Strassburger & Hinke, *Pennsylvania German Pioneers*, Vol. 1, pg. 406:
This immigrant is probably listed in the Pennsylvania passenger lists as Marx
Springel. The immigrant arrived on the ship *Phoenix*, 15 Sept. 1749 with
other passengers from Hassloch and Böhl. He did not sign his name, but
made his mark "B". (Strassburger & Hinke, *Pennsylvania German Pioneers*,
Vol. 2, pg. 453.) Emigration records from Speyer Archives indicate that J.
Marx Brendel from Böhl left for PA 31 March 1749. (Entry # 2052, Werner
Hacker, *Auswanderungen aus Rheinpfalz und Saarland im 18. Jahrhundert.*)

AMERICAN RECORDS

Johann Marx Brendel and wife Anna Elisabetha possibly had children, born
after their arrival in PA:
    10. Samuel, b. ca. 1753, baptism not located
    11. Marx, b. 13 Jan. 1755, bp. 31 Mar. 1755 by Rev. Waldschmidt
    (Recorded in Pa. Archives, Series 6, Vol. 6.)

New Holland Lutheran KB, Lancaster Co., PA:
Married 22 June 1762, Johannes Brendel, son of the late Marcus Brendel of Warwick Twp. and Catharina Marret, daughter of Nicholaus Marret of Warwick.

Pastoral Record of the Rev. John Conrad Bucher 1763-1769, (Hinke trans. 1941). Baptisms in Fredericktown alias Hummelstown:
John Brundle and wife Catharina were sponsors at the baptism of Johannes Ram, son of Melchior Ram and Rebecca, in 1765, and again sponsored a daughter Cathrina, b. 1768, for these same parents.

John Brundle and wife Catharina had children:
> Johan Melchior, b. 16 Feb. 1766, bp. 17 Feb. 1767,
> Sp.: Melchior Ram and Rebecca, his wife.
> Cathrina, b. 4 Aug. 1768, bp. 21 Aug. 1768
> Sp.: Melchior Ram and Rebecca, his wife.

Lorenz Brundle and wife Ferena (Verena) had a son:
> Johannes, b. 27 Mar. 1767, bp. 5 Apr. 1767
> Sp.: John Brundle and Cathrina.

Baptism at Misc. places: (Maytown? or Sharpsbourg?):
Lorenz Brundle and wife Ferena had a daughter:
> Elizabeth, b. 2 Apr. 1768, bp. 26 Apr. 1768
> Sp.: Matheys Eip (Eib?) and Anna Maria, his wife.

History of Franklin Co., PA: p. 594:
Taxables 1786:   Lawrence Brindle
> Samuel Brindle

Manheim Lutheran KB, Lancaster Co., PA:
Lorentz Brendle and Fronica had:
> 1. Joh. Georg, b. 13 Feb. 1772, bp. 10 May 1772
> Sp.: Joh. Georg Gaust and Marg. Brendle

American Revolutionary Soldiers of Franklin County, Pennsylvania:
John Brindle
Served as a private under Capt. John Lamb, 1780--4th Comp., 3rd Batt., Cumb. Co. Militia. He was born 1734, d. 1817. His wife Catherine b. 1743, died 1818. Malachi Brindle d. 1862, aged 96 yrs. Buried in the old Brindle graveyard, St. Thomas Twp. In 1793, John and Malachi Brindle, late of Cumb. Co. Penna., bought from Adam and Sarah Holliday 486 ac. land

which pioneer John Holliday had willed to his son Adam. In Dec. of 1800, John Brindle transferred all his interest in 2 tracts of land, called "Wrangle"

and "The Addition to Wrangle" to John and Saml. Holliday. The Witnesses were Elliott T. Lane and John Riddle. In 1789, David Casner and wife, Catherine sold to John Brindle, a tract in Peters Twp., called "Ipswich" joining James Campbell and others. Burials of the above family are in the "Old Brindle Graveyard," St. Thomas Twp., a cement wall enclosing the graves. **(Penna. Arch. 5th Ser. Vol. 6, p. 219, 225.)**

Lawrence Brindle (Brendle)

Appears as a pvt., 1780-81-82, with Capt. Wm. Strain, Cumb. Co. Militia. He is shown as a taxable in Lurgan Twp., 1778 to 1782, with land, horses and cattle and in Southampton Twp., in 1786, with both state and county taxes. The tax list of 1796 is signed by Geo. Johnston, Daniel Nevins and Lawrence Brindle. He removed to Westmoreland Co., Penna. where he died in 1809, one dau. having mar. _____Harshman. **(Penna. Arch. 5th Ser. Vol. 6, p. 142, 397, 416, 429.)**

Samuel Brindle (Brendle)

Of Southampton Twp., served under Capt. Wm. Strain, 1780-82, undated rolls, also with Capt. Benj. Blythe, Cumb. Co. Militia. Samuel Brendle is shown as a taxable 1778 to 1782 in Lurgan Twp., with land, horses and cattle. His will, dated and prob. 1804, in which he requested his youngest son Wm. to be sent to school "if a school can be had." He names six children: Peter; George; Catherine Brindle; Uley Brindle; Wm.; John; son John's son Samuel and dau. Elizabeth. **(Penna. Arch. 5th Ser. Vol. 6, p. 142, 152, 398, 430.)**

Land records, Pennsylvania Archive, Harrisburg, Original Warrants, Lancaster County. Film # 3.73: Warrant no. 533:

Whereas Marks Brendel of the County of Lancaster has requested we grant him 50 acres, adjoining Christian Frederick and John Rish (or Bish?) in Warwick Twp., Lancaster County for which he agrees to pay to our use at the rate of £15, 10 shillings for 100 acres and the yearly quitrent of one halfpenny sterling per acre. Dated 21 Feb. 1750.
[On reverse of document: returned 23 Sept. 1767.]

Film # 5.8, part 2: returns 13 May 1767-2 Oct. 1767:

23 Sept. 1767, Warrant dated 21 Feb. 1750 granted to John Marks Brendel, there was surveyed unto Christian Hershaw a tract called "Hershaw's Purchase" in Warwick Twp., Lancaster County adjoining Abraham Reyst, Ulrich Gingrich, Christopher Frederick, John Reyst [Reist], containing 16 ¼ acres plus allowances (for roads).

Another document: John Marks Brendle to Christian Hershaw: Brendle's right by virtue of a deed dated 16 Mar.? 1750 from Brendle to Jn° Whisand. J. Whisand sold this right on 21 Jan. 1755 to P. Hershaw.

Lancaster County Deed Abstracts:
Deed Book P, page 10. Dated 23 Jan. 1769. Paxton Twp. [note: in 1769, this was Lancaster County; in 1785, Dauphin County was cut off from Lancaster and Paxton Twp. is in Dauphin Co. after that date.]
Jacob Lentz of Paxton Twp. sold to Melcher Raam and John Brindle of said County and Province for £400 "all that certain plantation and tract of land in Paxton Twp., Lancaster Co., adjoining Albright Segelly, John Shoemaker, Philip Fischer, Joseph Sherrer and the Swahatara Creek, containing 260 acres.

Marks Brendle appears on Lancaster County tax lists in Warwick Twp. in 1756 and 1759. Marcus Brendel died intestate in Lancaster County, ca. 1760-1762.

Lawrence Brundle, Derry Twp., Lancaster Co., nat. Sept. 1765

John Brundle, Derry Twp., Lancaster Co., nat. Sept./Oct. 1765.

BRESSLER, GEORG   Niederhochstadt=
Lydia, 1749   76879 Hochstadt, Pfalz
S-H, I: 421
EUROPEAN RECORDS

Niederhochstadt Reformed KB:
Georg Pressler and wife (not named) had a son:
>   Joh. Georg bp. 10 Aug. 1728
>   Sp.: Georg Stettler of Roth, and Elisabetha, single
>   (He was probably a brother of Jerg Simon Bressler, also an
>   immigrant on this same ship.)

Died 1 Jan. 1744, Georg Pressler age 50 years.

AMERICAN RECORDS

Host Reformed KB, Berks Co., PA:
George Bresler m. 27 Jan. 1754 Anna Eva Bollinger. They had children:
>   1. Anna Margaretha b. 30 May 1756, bp. 27 June 1756
>   (Rev. John Caspar Stoever's records)

2. Nicolay b, 3 Feb. 1759, bp. 4 Mar. 1759 at Host Church
   Sp.: Nicolay Bressler
   He d. 12 May 1826 and is buried at Long's Church,
   Halifax Twp., Dauphin County.

Berks County Land Warrants, Pa. Archives, Third Series:
George Bressler, 100 acres, 27 June 1753 (others later).

George Presler, Tulpehoccon Twp., Berks Co., nat. Fall 1765.

BRESSLER, GEORG ADAM   Ober Lustadt=
Polly, 1765   67363 Lustadt
S-H, I: 704

EUROPEAN RECORDS

Ober Lustadt Reformed KB:
Heinrich Bressler and wife Anna Barbara had a son:
     Jörg Adam, b. 5 June 1750, bp. 7 June 1750
     Sp.: Jörg Adam Lehr and Anna Maria Haaf, both single

AMERICAN RECORDS

Fourteen passengers on the ship *Polly* in 1765, listed in close proximity to
one another on the list (S-H, I: 704), all appear in the Oberlustadt records:
Andreas Heintz, Christian Wunder, Conrad Hauenstein, Georg Jacob
Hauenstein, Christoph Strigel, Johann Leon[d] Devil (Deubel), Andres
Ehresmann, Peter Zeiler, **Georg Aadam Bresler**, Johan Michael Dühmer,
Jacob Wunder, Jacob Faut, Georg Simon Haushalter, Geo. Adam Teis.

BRESSLER, JERG SIMON   Niederhochstadt=
Lydia, 1749   76879 Hochstadt, Pfalz
S-H, I: 421

EUROPEAN RECORDS

Niederhochstadt Reformed KB:
Hans Georg Pressler from the Closter (Heimbach) was confirmed 1709.

Hans Jeorg Pressler and wife Eva Magdalena had a son:
     Joh. Georg Simon bp. 29 June 1722
     Sp.: Georg Simon Stutz and Anna Catharina Bauer, both single

AMERICAN RECORDS

Host Reformed KB, Berks Co., PA:
Georg Simon Pressler and wife were sponsors in 1750 for Catharina Barbara, daughter of Ludwig Kornman [q.v.].

Georg Simon Bressler and wife Anna Barbara had children:
1. Georg, bp. 8 Apr. 1751 at Blue Mountain Church, Berks Co.
   Sp. Peter Laucks [q.v.] and wife.
   Georg Bressler m. Maria Catharina Gamber, daughter of Joh.
   Wilbert Gamber and Maria Elisabetha Gamber [q.v.].
2. Georg Peter, conf. at Host, Whit Sunday 1765
   He m. Eva Barbara Ulrich, daughter of Georg
   Jacob Ulrich [q.v.] and Maria Elisabetha Wolff.
3. Johannes, b. 1753, d. 1835
   Tombstone at Summer Hill (St. Paul's Union) Church
   He m. Anna Maria Ulrich, daughter of Georg Jacob
   Ulrich [q.v.] and Maria Elisabetha Wolff.
4. Johann Nicholas, b. 8 June 1758, bp. 11 June 1758
   at Host Church. He m. Catharina Elisabetha Boyer.
5. Michael, b. 15 Aug. 1764, Tulpehocken Twp.
   He m. Barbara Heltzel. Both are buried at Friedens Church,
   Hegins, Pa.

After the Revolutionary War, Simon Bressler settled on the Deep Creek in Pine Grove Twp., Berks County (now Wayne Twp., Schuylkill County). He d. 12 Nov. 1802, age 81 years, 7 months, 10 days, and is buried at Hetzel's Church, Wayne Twp., Schuylkill Co., PA.

Pennsylvania Genealogical Magazine, Vol. XXVII, No. 1 (1971), "Palatines and Servants," pp. 54-57, concerning the indentures of immigrants imported on the ship *King of Prussia,* 1764: dated 8 Oct. 1764:
   "Cash of Simon Bresler at Tulpohocken Dr to Nicholas Bresler and wife's passage - 29.15 pounds. Ditto to Philip Jacob Bresler - 14.18.6 pounds."

The amounts paid for their passage indicates that Philip Jacob Bresler was single, and Nicholas Bresler and his wife were a childless couple. They were probably kinsmen of Georg Simon Bressler.

Simon Pressler, Tulpehoccon Twp., Berks County, nat. Fall 1765, without taking an oath.

BRESSLER, JOHANNES   Niederhochstadt=
ca. 1749,   76879 Hochstadt, Pfalz
[not in ship lists]

EUROPEAN RECORDS

Niederhochstadt Reformed KB:
Valentin Pressler and wife Anna Catharina had a son:
        Johannes, bp. 22 Aug. 1716, conf. 1731

Johannes Bressler, son of the deceased Valentin Bressler, m. 29 July 1738
Eva Maria Öhli, daughter of Nicolai Öhli, citizen here. Children:
        1. Johann Georg, b. 4 Sept. 1738, bp. 5 Sept. 1738
            Sp.: Joh. Georg Bressler from here and Anna Elisabetha
        2. Stephan, b. 17 Apr. 1740, bp. 21 Apr. 1740
            Sp.: Stephan Franck, schoolteacher at Metzheim
            [possibly 67271 Mertesheim] and his wife Eva Catharina
        3. Elisabetha, b. 4 Apr. 1743; her baptism is not recorded at
            Niederhochstadt. Her date of birth from the family Bible.
        4. Johannes, b. 30 Oct. 1744, bp. 1 Nov. 1744
            Sp.: Ulrich Guth and Anna Barbara
        5. Barbara, b. 13 Jan. 1748, bp. 14 Jan. 1748
            Sp.: Hieronimus Kornmann and wife Barbara

Buried 16 Feb. 1736, Valentin Pressler, age 67 years.

Buried 8 Sept. 1743, Catharina Pressler, age 66 years.

AMERICAN RECORDS

For the American descendants of this immigrant, see an article by Elizabeth
B. Bunting, "The Bresslers/Presslers of Niederhochstadt" published in
Mennonite Family History, Vol. XI, No. 1 (Jan. 1992).

BRESSLER, NICLAS   Niederhochstadt=
Lydia, 1749   76879 Hochstadt, Pfalz
S-H, I: 421

EUROPEAN RECORDS

Niederhochstadt Reformed KB:
Georg Simon Pressler and wife Eva Magdalena had a son:
        Joh. Nickel bp. 17 Nov. (1724?)

He was probably a brother of Jerg Simon and Georg Bressler, both also on this ship. The father of Jerg Simon is given as Hans Georg Pressler, but the mother mentioned in both baptismal records is Eva Magdalena.

AMERICAN RECORDS

Host Reformed KB, Berks County, PA:
Nicolay Bressler was a sponsor in 1759 for the son of Georg Bressler and Anna Eva.

A Nicholas Bressler is listed as a taxpayer at Penns Creek in 1776. Family tradition indicates that this Niclas Bressler was murdered in the Indian incursions, and left a large family in Union and Snyder counties. (The Penns Creek Massacre occurred in 1778.)

The name Pressler is still found in Hochstadt.
The vineyards surrounding these Palatine villages
are an important part of the economy.
Pressler-Weine is made in Hochstadt today.

BRESSLER, PHILIP JACOB   Niederhochstadt=
King of Prussia, 1764   76879 Hochstadt, Pfalz
S-H, I: 694
   (also Nicholas Bressler, not on ship's list)

EUROPEAN RECORDS

Niederhochstadt Reformed KB:
Joh. David Bressler and wife Margaretha had a son:
      Philip Jacob b. 19 Nov. 1744
      The mother of the child died shortly after the birth.

AMERICAN RECORDS

Berks County Abstracts of Wills and Administrations:
Jacob Bressler of Tulpehocken, 8 Oct. 1770. Adm. to Maria Sarah Bressler,
the widow.

Berks County Orphans' Court Records, dated 1773:
Maria Sarah Bressler, widow and administratrix of the estate of Philip Jacob
Bressler, late of Tulpehocken, deceased, asks for guardian for three year old
daughter Maria Elisabeth. Nicolaus Kintzer of Tulpehocken was appointed.

Pennsylvania Genealogical Magazine, Vol. XXVII, No. 1 (1971), "Palatines
and Servants," pp. 54-57, Redemption of immigrants imported on the *King
of Prussia,* 1764:
   "Cash of Simon Bresler at Tulpohocken Dr to Nicholas Bresler and wife's
passage 29.15 pounds. Ditto to Philip Jacob Bresler 14.18.6 Pounds." Dated
8 Oct. 1764.

Philip Jacob Bresler appears on the ship's list, but Nicholas Bresler does
not.

Berks County Will Abstracts:
A Nicholas Bressler of Pine Grove Twp., Berks County: will probated 12
Dec. 1794. His children were:
      1. Barbara m. Benjamin Battdorf
      2. Elizabeth m. William Becker
      3. Michael only son

BRICK (PRIKE), PHILIP
BRICK (PRIKE), HANS
Royal Union, 1750
S-H, I: 432

Ober Lustadt=
67363 Lustadt

EUROPEAN RECORDS

Ober Lustadt Reformed KB:
Friedrich Brick and wife Margaretha had sons:
1. Philip, b. 6 Apr. 1721
   Sp.: Philip Häger, single
2. Johannes, b. 26 Sept. 1724, bp. 1 Oct. 1724
   Sp.: Johannes Emmenet and Catharina Groh, single

AMERICAN RECORDS

Six immigrants are listed together on the passenger list of the *Royal Union,* and all are found in the Lustadt records: Henrich Hauenstein, Casper Schmidt, **Philip (X) Prike, Hans (X) Prike**, Hans Michel Bauersachs, and Andreas Hertzog.

BRICKERT, JACOB
BRICKERT, CHRISTOPH
Britannia, 1764
S-H, I: 693 [surname appears as Brückert on list]

Lachen-Speyerdorf=
67435 Neustadt an der Weinstrasse

EUROPEAN RECORD

Lachen-Speyerdorf Reformed KB:
Jacob Brickert, son of the late Friederich Brickert, m. 28 Mar. 1742 Anna Maria nee Zöller. It is mentioned in the marriage record that she was formerly married to Henrich Kugeler, who deserted her 7 years ago, and then went to Pennsylvania. This previous marriage was not found in the Lachen KB; a search of nearby records revealed the earlier marriage was recorded in the Hassloch Lutheran KB, dated 14 May 1733: at Böhl, Henrich Küchler, single married Anna Maria Zöller from Lachen.

Jacob Brickert and Anna Maria had children:
1. Joh. Christoph b. 2 May 1742, bp. 6 May 1742; conf. 1755, age 13
   Sp.: Christoph Schmitt, single son of Jacob & Christina Schmitt

2. Georg Michael b. 11 Nov. 1743, bp. 17 Nov. 1743; conf. 1757.
   Sp.: Georg Michael Clamm [q.v. Klamm], son of Stephan Clamm
   of Duttweiler [=67435 Neustadt a. d. Weinstrasse] and Anna
   Margretha, daughter of the late Georg Theobald.
3. Joh. Adam b. 21 July 1745, bp. 25 July 1745
   Sp.: Joh. Adam Bartel, son of Ernst Bartel of Speyerdorf,
   Eva Elisabetha, daughter of Hans Wolfgang Grabler, linenweaver
4. Maria Catharina b. 25 Feb. 1747, bp. 28 Feb. 1747
   Sp.: Maria Catharina, daughter of the late Blasii Rosen
5. Maria Barbara b. 5 Jan. 1749, bp. 7 Jan. 1749
   Sp.: Maria Barbara, daughter of Jacob Haag of Neustatt
6. Joh. Jacob b. 22 July 1751, bp. 25 July 1751
   Sp.: Joh. Jacob Fauth of Neustatt & Amalia Louisa ?_____
7. Anna Maria b. 30 May 1753, bp. 2 June 1753
   Sp.: Anna Maria, daughter of Görg Müller of Neustatt [67435
   Neustadt a. d. Weinstrasse].
8. Johan Görg b. 22 Jan. 1755, bp. 23 Jan. 1755
   Sp.: Johan Gorg Zöller and wife Anna Maria
9. Wilhelm Daniel b. 29 June 1756, bp. 1 July 1756
   Sp.: Wilhelm Daniel ?Schauser & wife Maria Catharina
10. Maria Helena b. 22 Apr. 1761, bp. 26 Apr. 1761
    Sp.: Maria Helena, daughter of Josua Gross

Emigration record:
Friedrich Krebs, "Palatine Emigrants from the District of Neustadt, 1750" in
the *The Pennsylvania Dutchman,* (May, 1953):
Peter Franck and Jacob Brickert, inhabitants of Lachen, are permitted along
with their wives and children, and upon payment of the "Tenth Penny"___
which amounts to 27 florins for the former, and 5 florins 30 kreuzer for the
latter, to go to Pennsylvania.

[note that although permission to emigrate was granted in 1750, five more
children were born in Lachen after that year. One Jacob Bricker appears on
the ship Sandwich in 1750 but emigration records indicate another Jacob
Bricker emigrated from Kleeburg that year; a comparison of the signatures
of these two men indicates that they are not the same signature.]

AMERICAN RECORDS

Old Goshenhoppen Reformed KB, Montgomery Co., PA:
Conf. 17 Apr. 1771: Wilhelm Daniel Bruckert, aged 16 years.

Christoph, son of Jacob Bruckert, of Old Goshenhoppen, m. 22 Aug. 1769 Magdalena, daughter of Georg Kuchler, of Old Goshenhoppen. They had children:

> 1. Johann Wilhelm b. 22 Jan. 1773
>   Sp.: Wilhelm Brickert and Margaretha Somni
> 2. Johannes b. 3 Sept. 1774
>   Sp.: Valentin Kugler and Elisabetha Kebler
> 3. Georg b. 28 Feb. 1776
>   Sp.: Georg Kessler and Catharina Martin

BRICKERT, MATHIAS   Lachen-Speyerdorf=
Brotherhood, 1750   67435 Neustadt an der Weinstrasse
S-H, I: 447

EUROPEAN RECORDS

Lachen-Speyerdorf Reformed KB:
Conf. 1743: Matthias Brickert, son of the late Friederich Brickert of Lachen, age 15 years.

Friedrich Brickert, master baker, died in Lachen 26 Nov. 1731. [no age given in burial record.]

Emigration record:
Friedrich Krebs, "Palatine Emigrants from the District of Neustadt, 1750" in *The Pennsylvania Dutchman,* (May, 1953):
   Mathias Brickert of Lachen is permitted to go to Pennsylvania gratis.

AMERICAN RECORDS

New Goshenhoppen Reformed KB, Montgomery Co., PA:
Undated marriages, between 1747-1758; #119 Mathys Brickerdt and Maria Elisabetha (no other names recorded).

Matthys Bruckerdt and wife Maria Elisa had children:
> 1. J. Jacob bp. 7 Dec. 1757
>   Sp.: J. Nicol Jung and wife
> 2. J. Henrich bp. 24 June 1759
>   Sp.: J. Nicolaus Jung and wife Anna Gertraudt

Matthys Brickerdt and wife Maria Gertraudt had a son:
> 3. Andreas bp. 22 Feb. 1761
>   Sp.: Andreas Jung and Elisa Barb. Wannemacher

Dauphin County Wills:
Mathias Brickert, Derry Twp., dated 13 Jan. 1803, proved 3 Mar. 1803.
All lands to son Jacob. Mentions two grandsons, Mathias Plasser and
Christian Plasser. Wife, Cattrout.
Exrs: sons Jacob and Christley Brickert
Wit.: Fredrich Wagner, Henry Shaffner, Amos Atkinson

Mathias Brukert, Weisenburg Twp., Northampton Co., naturalized by
affirmation in 1765.

BRUNNER, HANS JACOB   Duttweiler=
Snow *Lowther*, 1731   67435 Neustadt a. d. Weinstrasse
S-H, I: 54, 55, 56
  with Sophia Brunner, Jeremiah (Georg?), Jeremiah (Georg?) Michael,
Wolf Henrich, Appollonia, Margert, Margreeden Brooner.

EUROPEAN RECORDS

Duttweiler (Böbingen) Reformed KB:
Hans Jacob Brunner, single, m. 22 Aug. 1714 Louisa Sophia, widow of
Henrich Bachman [q.v.].

Hans Jacob Brunner and wife Louisa Sophia had children:
    1. Hans Adam, b. 24 Mar. 1715
    2. Johannes, b. 2 Feb. 1716
    3. Hans Jörg, b. 6 June 1718
        [Jeremiah on passenger list]
    4. Jörg Michel, b. 5 Mar. 1720
        [Jeremiah Michael on passenger list]
    5. [Faded entries in KB] probably
        Wolf Henrich, ca. 1722-3
    6. Maria Appollonia, b. 28 Sept. 1725
    7. Jacob, b. __ Nov. 1728
    8. Anna Margretha, b. 13 Mar. 1731

AMERICAN RECORDS

Rev. John Casper Stoever's Records:
George Michael Bronner m. 21 June 1748 Barbara Templemann, Lebanon.

Wolf Heinrich Bronner, m. 10 Oct. 1748 Anna Catharina Enssminger, Cocalico.

Jacob Bronner m. 1 May 1772 Anna Stoppelbein, Hanover and Lebanon.

Muddy Creek Lutheran KB, Lancaster Co., PA:
Sophia Lowisa, wife of Jacob Brunner was sp. in 1732 for Sophia Lowisa, daughter of Jacob Kissinger. She was also a sp. in 1736 for Sophia Lowisa, daughter of Michael AmWeg.

Georg Michael Bronner was a sp. in 1743 for a daughter of Michael Kissinger.

Appolonia Bronner was a sp. in 1742 for a child of Nicolaus Zöllner, Muddy Creek.

Georg Michael Bronner and his wife, and Wolff Heinrich Brunner and his wife Anna Catarina were sp. in 1749 for Anna Catarina, daughter of Philipp Schäffer, Cocalico.

Muddy Creek Reformed KB, Lancaster Co., PA:
Hans Jacob Brunner, elder, and Görg Brunner signed the Reformed Church Doctrine, 19 May 1743.

Georg Michael Brunner and Maria Appolonia Brunner were sp. in 1743 for a child of Jacob Birckenhauser.

George Michael Brunner and wife Barbara had:
>   John George, b. 20 May 1754, bp. 2 June 1754
>   Sp.: Martin Burkhalter; Eva Amweeg

Conf. 1746: Anna Margaret Brunner
>   Barbara Brunner
Conf. 1767: Geo. Michael Brunner, 19 years

Rev. John Waldschmidt's Records, Penna. Archives, Sixth Series, Vol. 6:
Gorg Michael Brunner and wife had:
>   1. Margretha, bp. 4 Nov. 1749
>   2. Anna Catharina, bp. 12 Apr. 1752?
>   3. Johannes, bp. 17 May 1752?
>   4. Anna Maria, bp. 17 Apr. 1764

Wolf Heinrich Brunner and wife had:
>   1. Margaretha, b. & bp. in 1749, no other date given

BRUNNER, JOHANNES   67105 Schifferstadt
BRUNNER, JOSEPH
Allen, 1729
S-H, I: 27

EUROPEAN RECORDS

Schifferstadt Reformed KB:
Joseph Brunner m. 23 Nov. 1700 Catharina Elisabetha Thomas, daughter of
Christian Thomas. They had children:
1. Anna Barbara, b. 21 Sept. 1701; conf. 1715;
   She m. 20 Apr. 1723 Christian Götzendanner [q.v.]
2. Johann Jacob, b. 25 Feb. 1703; conf. 1716
3. Gabriel, b. 14 Feb. 1706; conf. 1719
4. Johannes, b. 3 Oct. 1708; conf. 1722
5. Johann Valentin, b. 3 Dec. 1711
6. Johann Henrich, b. 25 Feb. 1715; conf. 1727
7. Maria Catharina, b. 9 Sept. 1718; conf. 1729
8. Elias, b. 15 Feb. 1723

Emigration record:
Werner Hacker, *Auswanderungen aus dem Früheren Hochstift Speyer nach
Südosteuropa und Übersee im XVIII Jahrhundert*, Heimatstelle Pfalz, 1969:
Brunner, Josef, Klein-Schifferstadt, ref., with wife and 3 children (Joh. 18,
Heinr Elias 6, MCath 19). Paid emigration tax 26 Apr. 1729. Arrived on the
ship *Allen* together with Christian Götz(endanner) [q.v.]   and Johann
Waydmann.

AMERICAN RECORDS

Frederick Reformed Church, Frederick, MD:
Johannes Brunner and wife Anna Maria had a daughter:
      Elisabetha, b. 22 May 1748
      Sp.: Catharina Götzendanner [q.v.]

Elias Brunner and wife Albertina had children:
1. Stephan, b. 7 May 1749
2. Johann Peter, b. 31 Mar. 1753
3. Johannes, b. 21 Oct. 1759
4. Johannes, b. 21 June 1761

Henry Brunner and wife Magdalena had:
1. Anna Maria, b. 18 Jan. 1753
2. Anna Margaretha, b. 16 Mar. 1761
3. Jacob, b. 16 Mar. 1764

BRUNNER, JOHANN JACOB   67105 Schifferstadt
Mortonhouse, 1728
S-H, I: 19

EUROPEAN RECORDS

Schifferstadt Reformed KB:
Joseph Brunner m. 23 Nov. 1700 Catharina Elisabetha Thomas, daughter of
Christian Thomas. (See above for their complete family). They had a son:
>   Johann Jacob, b. 25 Feb. 1703, conf. 1716.
>   Sp.: Johann Jacob Siegel from Mussbach and wife Cathrina

Johann Jacob Brunner, son of Joseph Brunner, m. Nov. 1725 Maria Barbara
Sturm, daughter of Christian and Anna Barbara (nee Gah) Sturm. They
had a son:
>   Johann Peter, b. 30 Aug. 1726
>   Sp.: Johann Peter Keck and Helena Sturm.

AMERICAN RECORDS

Reformed Church records, Frederick, MD:
Jacob Brunner and wife Maria Barbara appear in these records as early as
1746.

Peter Brunner and wife Anna Maria had children:
>   1. Johannes, b. 11 Aug. 1751
>   2. Charlotta, b. 27 Mar. 1754
>   3. Susanna, b. 8 Oct. 1758

Monocacy Lutheran KB, Frederick, MD:
Johann Jacob Brunner and wife Maria Barbara were sp. in 1746 for a child
of Thomas Schley.

BURLÄMMER, DIETER   67112 Mutterstadt
Prelist

EUROPEAN RECORDS

Mutterstadt Kontraktenprotokolle:
Record dated 1717: Johann Michael Hoffacker, grinder and citizen here,
sold property in the name of his brother-in-law Diter Burrlämmer, as he had

moved to Pennsylvania. The property was sold at public auction to the honorable Claudine Magin and Anna Maria his wife. The transaction was recorded 5 June 1737. In another transaction dated 1718, further property was sold; recorded 7 June 1737.

PfFWKde, Band 6, Heft 5, p. 165:
Anna Barbara Burlämmer, nee Kissel, died in Mutterstadt 20 Sept. 1733. Her husband has gone from here with the Separatists.

BUSS, JOH. JACOB   67259 Kleinniedesheim
Pennsylvania Merchant, 1732
S-H, I: 66, 67, 69, 70
    with Anna Puss and Cathrina Puss

EUROPEAN RECORDS

Gross- and Kleinniedesheim Lutheran KB:
Joh. Jacob Buss, apprentice weaver, born in Ramroth [Ramrath = 41569 Rommerskirchen] in the Dukedom Darmstadt, m. 21 Sept. 1728 Maria Catharina Ritter. They had a daughter:
    1. Anna Catharina, b. 6 Apr. 1730, bp. 7 Apr. 1730
       Sp.: The late Adam Heilman's widow Anna Catharina.

AMERICAN RECORDS

Great Swamp Reformed KB, Lower Milford Twp., Lehigh Co., PA:
Jacob Buss and wife Catharina had:
       Christina, bp. 4 Nov. 1750
       Sp.: Melchior Wecher, Christina Wecher.

BÜTTNER, CASPAR   67125 Dannstadt
Thistle of Glasgow, 1730
S-H, I: 31, 32, 34

EUROPEAN RECORDS

Dannstadt Reformed KB:
Johann Caspar Büttner, Lutheran from Maudach [= 67067 Ludwigshafen], m. 14 June 1729 Maria Elisabetha Münch, daughter of Jean Noe Münch, citizen at Dannstadt.
Caspar Büttner and wife Maria Elisabetha nee Münch had a son:
    Joh. Henrich, b. 11 Apr. 1730, bp. 12 Apr. 1730
    Sp.: Joh. Henrich Schmid and Anna Maria

The book *Die Einwohner von Maudach*, by Hans Jung and Irmgard König, indicates that Caspar is probably a son of Christoph Büttner of Maudach who m. 14 May 1699 at Mundenheim [= 67061 Ludwigshafen] Maria Margaretha Hertler(?).

The church at Dannstadt

CHRIST, CHRISTIAN   67459 Iggelheim
Phoenix, 1749
S-H, I: 406 [surname Creeste on list; did not sign.]

EUROPEAN RECORDS

Schifferstadt-Iggelheim Reformed KB:
Christian Christ m. 17 June 1698 Margaretha Huber. They had children:
    1. Anna Margaretha, b. 22 Mar. 1699
    2. Joh. Adam, b. 29 Aug. 1700
    3. Maria Christina, b. 9 July 1702
    4. Anna Elisabetha, b. 5 Oct. 1704
    5. Anna Katharina, b. 19 June 1707
    6. Joh. Peter, b. 20 Oct. 1709
    7. Joh. Henrich, b. 6 Mar. 1712
    8. **Christian**, b. 9 Sept. 1714
    9. Maria Philippina, b. 21 May 1717; the father is mentioned as
deceased in this last baptismal record.

Christian Christ and wife Maria Catharina, nee Bergdalt, had the following
children baptized at Iggelheim:
    1. Anna Margaretha, b. 13 May 1741
    2. Daniel, b. 30 Jan. 1744
    3. Anna Elisabetha, b. 28 Oct. 1746
    4. Joh. Marx, b. 26 Mar. 1749
        Sp.: Marx Brendel from Böhl, a fellow passenger

Emigration record:
Werner Hacker, *Auswanderungen aus Rheinpfalz und Saarland*:
#2367 Christian Christ, Iggelheim, 1749

AMERICAN RECORDS

Emmaus Moravian KB, Northampton Co., PA:
Christian Christ and Maria Catharina had children:
    Margaretha, b. 26 Sept. 1750
    Georg, b. 12 Feb. 1753
    Catharina, b. 21 May 1758
    Christian, b. 12 Oct. 1760

Allemengel Moravian KB, Berks Co., PA:
Christian Christ b. 9 Sept. 1714 in Igelheim, Pfalz, son of Christian Christ
and Margaretha Huber, m. 1741 Maria Catharina Bergdoll; came to America
in 1749.

Lititz Moravian Burials, Lancaster Co., PA:
Daniel Christ, b. 1744, d. 1815, son of Christian Christ.

CLAUER see KLAUER

COBLENTZ, NICLAUS age 45   67159 Friedelsheim
St. Andrew, 1743
S-H, I; 349, 350, 351

EUROPEAN RECORDS

Friedelsheim Reformed KB:
David Cobelentz m. 14 Jan. 1693 Magdalena ?Turck. They had a son:
    Johann Niclaus, bp. 14 Jan. 1697
    Sp.: Niclaus Klingler and Maria Margaretha _____, both single

David Coblentz died 26 Dec. 1734, age 70 years.

Niclas Coblentz, son of David Coblentz of Friedelsheim, m. 10 June 1727 at
[67161] Gönnheim (name of wife not recorded in KB).

Nickel Coblentz and Anna Catharina had children:
    1. Joh. Jacob, bp. 25 Apr. 1728, d. 16 May 1732
        Sp.: Jacob Orth and Anna Maria
    2. Joh. Adam, bp. 11 July 1729
        Sp.: Joh. Adam Metzger from Gönnheim and wife Anna Eva
    3. Joh. Philip, bp. 19 Nov. 1730
        Sp.: Joh. Philip Orth from Gönnheim
        and Elisabetha, daughter of the late Gabriel Schultheis
    4. Joh. Peter, bp. 11 Mar. 1733
        Sp.: Joh. Peter Coblentz from [67256] Weisenheim-am-Sand
        and wife Agnes
    5. Joh. Herman, bp. 1 May 1735
        Sp.: Joh. Herman Messing and Maria Magdalena
    6. Maria Margaretha, bp. 29 Sep. 1737
        Sp.: Joh. Adam Zimmermann of Gönnheim and
        Maria Margaretha
    7. Anna Maria, b. 1 July 1740, bp. 3 July 1740
        Sp.: Anna Catharina, daughter of Joh. Herman Messing
    8. Johanna Dorothea, bp. 19 Apr. 1742
        Sp.: Johanna Dorothea, daughter of Adam Zimmermann

AMERICAN RECORDS

Conewago Reformed KB, near Littlestown, Adams Co., PA.:
John Schreyer from Friedelsheim and wife Maria Margaret, daughter of
Gerhard Rener from Hundsbach, Zweibrucken, had a child Catharina, b. 17
Oct. 1746. Sp.: Joh. Nicholas Coblenz and wife.

Nicholas Koblentz and wife had:
Maria Margaret b. 1747 bp. 10 Apr. 1748
Sp.: John Schreier and wife Maria Margaret

Peter Koblentz was a sp. in 1753.

Frederick Reformed KB, Frederick, MD.:
Peter Coblenz m. 6 May 1759 Susanna Keller. Peter Coblentz and Susanna
had children:
1. A son, b. 11 July 1760, bp. 2 Oct. 1760
   Sp.: Herman Coblentz and Elisbetha
2. Johan Adam, b. 19 May 1762, bp. 17 Oct. 1762
3. Elisabetha, b. 17 Jan. 1764, bp. 13 Apr. 1764
   Sp.: Henrich Scheffer and wife

Peter Kobelenz m. 5 Nov. 1764 Elisabetha Steffan.

Middletown Reformed Cemetery, MD.:
Herman Cobelance, b. 1735, d. 31 July 1806
Youleamia Cobelance, b. 1742, d. 12 Jan. 1806

Peter Coblentz, b. 28 Feb. 1732, d. 9 June 1808
wife Elizabeth b. 14 Feb. 1745, d. 11 Dec. 1824

CRON, JOHANN MARTIN   Ungstein=
St. Andrew Galley, 1737   67098 Bad Dürkheim
S-H, I: 179, 181, 183

EUROPEAN RECORDS

Ungstein Lutheran KB:
Died 23 Dec. 1700 in Ungstein, Johann Jacob Cron, a linenweaver from
Mittelfischach [= 74423 Obersontheim] in the Grafschaft Öhringen, age 41.

Johann Jacob Cron m. 1689 Anna Margaretha, daughter of Peter Göfft of Ungstein. Their son:
Hans Martin, b. ca. 1695, conf. 1709, age 14.

Johann Martin Cron m. 27 Apr. 1723 in [67229] Grosskarlbach Maria Margaretha Kroop, daughter of Hans Henrich Kroop, innkeeper at the Gasthaus Zur Cronen in Grosskarlbach. They had children:
1. Catharina Elisabetha, b. 11 Mar. 1724, conf. 1737
   [it is mentioned in her confirmation record that she is "going with her parents to the New Land."]
2. Johann Georg, b. ca. 1726 in [67229] Grosskarlbach,
   d. 4 Aug. 1729 in Ungstein
3. Andreas, b. 4 Dec. 1728
4. Johann Valentin, b. 18 Nov. 1731, d. 17 Feb. 1733
5. Maria Margaretha, b. 13 Apr. 1734
6. Jacob Lorentz, b. 22 Mar. 1737

AMERICAN RECORDS

Berks County Will Abstracts:
Martin Cron, Alsace. 27 Feb. 1765, adm. to Margaret Haas, widow of the intestate.

Berks County Administration Bond, Estate of Martin Cron:
Margaret Haas, formerly Margaret Cron, widow of Martin Cron late of Alsace Twp., now in Berks County (formerly in Philadelphia County) weaver, deceased, Laurence Cron of the said twp., eldest son of the said deceased, and Henry Vanderslice of Exeter Twp., in the county aforesaid, Yeoman.....
their bond in the sum of £ 600; they will make or cause to be made an inventory of the estate by 27 Mar. 1766. Signed in German script; Margred Hasin; Laurence (his + mark) Cron; H. Vanderslice. Wit.: Jacob Hoffmann, Ludwig Heller.

CUSHWA, ISAIAH   67112 Mutterstadt
Johnson Galley, 1732
S-H, I: 71, 75, 77 appears on list as Isau Cushwa

EUROPEAN RECORDS

Mutterstadt Reformed KB:
Isaac Coschwa m. 15 Sept. 1705 Elisabetha Catharina Hofmann. They had children, surname spelled Cochoy, Coschois, Coschoi, Gousay, Gouschoy:

1. Balthasar, bp. 29 May 1706 d. young
2. Balthasar, bp. 22 June 1707
3. Anna Clara, bp. 26 Aug. 1708
4. Johannes, bp. 24 Nov. 1709
5. Hans Jacob, bp. 15 Sept. 1711
6. **Esaias**, bp. 19 June 1714
7. Louisa, bp. 1 May 1717

PfFWKde, Band 6, Heft 5, p. 165:
Elisabetha Catharina Couchoy, nee Hoffmann, died 21 Apr. 1729, age 54 years; daughter of Jacob Hoffmann, citizen at Weydenthal (= 67475 Weidenthal). She m. Isaac Couchoy. The surname appears in the Mutterstadt records with many variant spellings: Cussai, Cusay (1655), Kussai (1660), Coussuay (1662), Coschway (1702), Cosway (1705), Cuswar, Cuschway, Cochois, Gussai, Goussay, Gouschoy, etc.

Mutterstadt Kontraktenprotokolle:
Recorded 19 Dec. 1738: Joh. Adam Fried and Catharina his wife had bought property of Isaac Cuswa, "as he had moved to Pennsylvania."

AMERICAN RECORDS

Swatara Reformed KB, Lebanon Co., PA:
Isaiah *Guschweyd* and his wife Anna Christina were sponsors at the baptism in 1740 for Anna Christina, daughter of Johannes Heyl.

St. Paul's (Klopps) Reformed KB, Bethel Twp., Lebanon Co., PA:
Isaiah Cuschwa and wife Anna Christina had:
>   Anna Catharina, bp. 8 Feb. 1756
>   Sp.: Tobias Bickel and wife.

John Guschwa and wife Catharina Elisabetha had:
>   John David, b. 10 Aug. 1777, bp. 24 Aug. 1777
>   Sp.: Philip Gebhard and Anna Christina.

Isaiah Guschwa and wife Margaret had:
>   David, b. 1 Mar. 1796, bp. 27 Mar. 1796

Berks County, PA, Will Abstracts:
Isaiah Cushwa, Bethel Twp., dated 7 Feb. 1788, probated 12 June 1788. Mentions eldest son John, youngest son Isaiah; four daughters: Catharine wife of Conrad Wolf; Margaret, wife of John Hahn, son of Adam Hahn; Esther, wife of John Hain, miller; Anna, wife of Conrad Sherman. Son Isaiah executor.

DAUBENSPECK, JACOB 67251 Freinsheim
Harle, 1736
S-H, I: 155, 158, 160

EUROPEAN RECORDS

Freinsheim Reformed KB:
Joh. Georg Daubenspeck m. 7 July 1705 Anna Dorothea Wylly. They had a son:

      Johann Jacob, b. 27 July 1715; conf. 1731
      Sp.: Jacob Fischer and wife Sophia

Dorothea Daubenspeck d. 30 Oct. 1726, age 56 years.
George Taubenspeck d. 3 Jan. 1743, age 73 years.

AMERICAN RECORDS

Egypt Reformed KB, Lehigh Co., PA:
Jacob Daubenspeck and wife Juliana had a daughter:

      Anna Magdalena, b. 16 Feb. 1753
      Sp.: Conrad Bloss and wife Anna Magdalena

Tohickon Reformed KB, Bucks Co., PA:
Confirmed Easter 1757 in Heidelberg Twp., Maria Barbara Daubenspeck.

The Reformed KB at Heidelberg, Lehigh Co., has been destroyed or lost, so the family of Jacob Daubenspeck must be reconstructed from other sources.

It appears from the existing records that Jacob Daubenspeck had three sons:
    1. Georg who was a sponsor at a baptism in 1763, in Heidelberg Lutheran Church.
    2. Jacob who appears on the Heidelberg tax list in 1762.
    3. Philip who served in Capt. Adam Stahler's company, Sept. 1781.

Jacob and George Daubenspeck also served in the Revolutionary War. Later branches of the family resided in West Penn Twp., Schuylkill Co. and Luzerne Co., and Butler and Armstrong Co., in Western Pennsylvania. In some areas, the surname became Doverspike.

Jacob Taubenspeck, Heidelberg Twp., Northampton Co., nat. 1765.

DE FRENE, PETER   Ruchheim=
prelist   67071 Ludwigshafen am Rhein

EUROPEAN RECORDS

Ruchheim Reformed KB:
Hans Adam von Esch and wife Anna had a daughter:
    Catharina, bp. 25 Mar. 1692

Peter DeFrene, son of Jacob DeFrene, m. 10 Feb. 1711 Maria Catharina, daughter of Joh. Adam Esch [q.v.] and Anna.

Peter DeFrene, *Huffschmidt* (farrier), and wife Catharina had one child born at Ruchheim:
    1. Maria Margaretha, b. 6 Dec. 1711, died.
    (no further entries)

AMERICAN RECORDS

Philadelphia Will Abstracts, F. pg. 120:
Peter DeFroen, will translated 22 Jan. 1747/8.
Wife: Catharine
Children mentioned but not named; youngest son to have *smith's* tools. Legacy to youngest daughter.
Wit: Christian Brauer, Jacob Back or Brack, Peter Esh [q.v.], Johannes Madlung.
Adm. to Catherine DeFroen, Philadelphia 23 Jan. 1747/8.

Catharina DeFrain on Vincent Twp., tax list, 1753.

Peter DeFrain, b. 1733, d. 23 Mar. 1782, buried Vincent Reformed Cemetery. He resided in Coventry Twp., Chester Co., Pa. His wife was Eva, and they had sons Peter and John.

DEICKERT, JOH. MICHAEL   67459 Böhl
Ship data not located, 1749

EUROPEAN RECORDS

Böhl Reformed KB:
Died 26 Nov. 1742 Anna Helena Deickert, the Lutheran schoolmaster's wife, age 42 y. 6 mo.

Hassloch Lutheran KB:
Johann Michael Daiekert, *Ev. Schuldiener and Ludi Magister* at Böhl, m. 30 May 1743 Anna Christina Schumann, widow. [She was nee Hauck and m. (1) Philipp Schumann on 23 Oct. 1736. He d. 1742] Children:
  1. Anna Catharina [Daicker], bp. 18 May 1744
  2. Johann Peter [Daikert], b. 13 Jan. 1747

Conf. 1748 in Böhl, Anna Margaretha Dieckert

Emigration record:
Werner Hacker, *Auswanderungen aus Rheinpfalz und Saarland*:
#2412, 2464, 2976, 2986: J. Michael Dackert, Böhl, Emigrated to PA, 22 May 1749; additional records for the names: Deickert, Dricker, and Druckert also appear in this source.

DEISERT, GEORG PETER   Niederhochstadt =
King of Prussia, 1764   76879 Hochstadt
S-H, I: 694

EUROPEAN RECORDS

Niederhochstadt Reformed KB:
Hans Peter Deisserth (name also given in various records as Deysser, Teissert, Deysserd, Deissert) and wife Anna Margretha had children:
  1. Johannes Georgius, bp. 27 Feb. 1718
  2. Joh. Daniel, bp. 5 Aug. 1723
  3. Maria Margretha, bp. 19 Mar. 172? (recorded in 1723 with above baptism)
  4. Jeorg Henrich, bp. 25 Mar. 1728
  5. **Georg Peter**, b. 5 Sept. 1732, bp. 8 Sept. 1732; conf. 1745.
     Sp.: Joh. Georg Ladermann and Maria Catharina Gamber, both single.

Died 23 June 1735, Anna Margretha, wife of Peter Deissert, age 42 years.

Peter Deysserd, widower, m. (2) 9 Feb. 1736 Anna Maria Meyer, widow from Oberlustadt [= 67363 Lustadt].

Died 23 Jan. 1758, Johann Peter Deissert, aged 72 years, 7 months.

AMERICAN RECORDS

Christ (Conewago) Reformed KB, Littlestown, Adams Co., PA:
Georg Peter Deisert and wife Wilhelmina, nee Hünd, had children:
1. Maria Catharina, b. 5 Nov. 1770, bp. 16 Nov. 1770
    Sp.: Stephan Bart and Catharina.
2. Elisabeth, b. 26 Oct. 1773, bp. 31 Oct. 1773
    Sp.: Henry Herchelroth and Maria Catharina.
3. Johann Georg, (twin) b. 18 Mar. 1778, bp. 25 Mar. 1778
    Sp.: Georg Weickert and Anna Margaretha.
4. Johannes, (twin) b. 18 Mar. 1778, bp. 25 Mar. 1778
    Sp.: Joh. Unruh and Maria Julia.
5. Juliana Margaret, b. 8 Feb. 1781, bp. 4 Mar. 1781
    Sp.: Conrad Ditter and Juliana Margaret.

Georg Peter Deisert became a *Fraktur* artist in PA. Identified examples of his work appear in Frederick Weiser's book titled *The Gift is Small The Love is Great*, York, PA (1994).

View of the main street in Hochstadt.

DELATER, DAVID age 31   67105 Schifferstadt
St. Andrew, 1741   67480 Edenkoben
S-H, I: 304, 305, 306

EUROPEAN RECORDS

Schifferstadt Reformed KB:
A David Delatre from Flanders d. 14 Jan. 1726, age 70 yr. He was married
3 times and had 9 children.

David Delatre, son of David of Schifferstadt, m. 27 Sept. 1718 Anna
Elisabetha Geringer, daughter of the late Jacob Geringer of Edigkoben
[Edenkoben].

Edenkoben Reformed KB:
David Delater and wife Anna Elisabetha had the following children:
1. Christina, bp. 21 Feb. 1728
2. Joh. Henrich, bp. 1 Apr. 1731
3. Maria Catharina, bp. 30 Mar. 1738

AMERICAN RECORDS
Frederick, MD, Lutheran KB:
David Dellarter (and wife, not named) had:
    Maria Catrina, b. 6 Jan. 1744, bp. 1 Apr. 1744
    Sp.: Johannes Brunner and wife Maria Catrina

Joh. David Delatre and wife Anna Barbara were sp. in 1758 for a child of
Christoph Wölfflin.

Frederick Reformed KB, Frederick, MD.:
David DeLatere and wife Barbara had:
    Johannes, b. 6 Aug. 1749, bp. 1 Nov. 1749
    Sp.: Johannes Brunner

Married 18 Mar. 1759, Gabriel Leidig and Catharina Delater.
Married 26 Sept. 1764, Andreas Adam and Catharina Delater.
Married 21 Feb. 1790, Jacob Delater and Catharina Mähn.

Jacob Delater and wife Elisabetha had:
    Anna Barbara, b. 28 Dec. 1752, bp. 1753
    Sp.: Anna Barbara Brunner.

David Delater naturalized at Annapolis, Apr. 1749.

DETEMER, HANS MICHAEL   Friesenheim=
Mortonhouse, 1728   67063 Ludwigshafen am Rhein
S-H, I: 18, 19

EUROPEAN RECORDS

Oggersheim Reformed KB:
Johann (Hans) Michael Dedemer, *Gerichtsschöffe und Wirt,* Lutheran, and
wife Maria Barbara, Reformed, had children:
    1. Anna Barbara, bp. not found, m. 13 May 1727 Friederich Scholl
      at Friesenheim.
    2. Anna Maria, b. 19 May 1711, bp. 24 May 1711.
      She d. 21 May 1716.
    3. Johannes Hartmann, b. 22 Feb. 1716; bp. 29 Feb. 1716
      at Friesenheim.

AMERICAN RECORDS

Tohickon Reformed Church, Bucks Co., PA:
Jacob Dettemer (at Saucon) and wife Elisabeth had a child:
    Anna Margaret, bp. 18 Feb. 1750
    Sp.: Martin Lahr and Margaret Scholl

Hartman Ditmer (Dettemer, Dettmer) and wife Anna Catharina had
children:
    1. Anna Catharina, bp. 29 Sept. 1754
        Sp.: Henry Hertzel and Margaret
    2. Catharina Magdalena, bp. 18 Apr ? bp. 18 Nov. 1759
        Sp.: Adam Schmitt and Sophia Catharina Jost
    3. A son, bp. 15 Aug. 1762
        Sp.: _____ Jost
    4. John Michael, bp. 27 Mar. 1764
        Sp.: John Wolf Lizel (Lutheran Pastor at Tohicon)

Blue (Saucon) Lutheran KB, Northampton Co., PA:
Jacob Dethmer and wife Maria Elisabeth had children: (see also above)
    2. Joh. Georg, b. 26 Sept. 1755, bp. 14 Dec. 1755
        Sp.: Joh. Georg Weber and Susanna Weber
    3. Catharina, b. 5 Feb. 1758
        Sp.: Peter Zehrsch and Catharina Koch

DEUBEL, JOH. LEONHARD Ober Lustadt =
(Joh. Leon d Devil) 67363 Lustadt
Polly, 1765
S-H, I: 704

EUROPEAN RECORDS

Ober Lustadt Reformed KB:
Jörg Deubel and wife Margaretha had a son:
Leonhard, b. 3 May 1740, bp. 8 May 1740

AMERICAN RECORDS

Fourteen passengers on the ship *Polly* in 1765, listed in close proximity to one another on the list (S-H, I: 704), all appear in the Oberlustadt records: Andreas Heintz, Christian Wunder, Conrad Hauenstein, Georg Jacob Hauenstein, Christoph Strigel, **Johann Leon[d] Devil (Deubel)**, Andres Ehresmann, Peter Zeiler, Georg Aadam Bresler, Johan Michael Dühmer, Jacob Wunder, Jacob Faut, Georg Simon Haushalter, Geo. Adam Teis.

DIEMER see DÜHMER

DITLO, (DITLEAU), ABRAHAM Friesenheim =
Prelist 67063 Ludwigshafen am Rhein

EUROPEAN RECORDS

Oggersheim Reformed KB:
Abraham Ditleau, son of Abraham Ditleau, m. 26 Nov. 1715 Margaretha, daughter of the late Hans Jacob Ohlinger, *Hufschmied und Gerichtsschöffe* of Edichheim [67069 Edigheim]. They had children baptized at Friesenheim:
1. Johannes, bp. 5(?) Oct. 1716, d. 1716
2. Heinrich, b. 9 Sept. 1717, bp. 11 Sept. 1717, d. 1717
3. Anna Margaretha, b. 20 Sug. 1718, bp. 28 Aug. 1718
4. Philip Heinrich, b. 8 Mar. 1721, bp. 9 Mar. 1721
5. Anna Maria, b. 21 Jan. 1723, bp. 24 Jan. 1723

AMERICAN RECORDS

Abraham Ditlo appears as an early member at Great Swamp Church (now Lehigh Co.).
A Henry Titlow b. 1719, d. 1793 is buried at Brownback's Church, Chester Co., PA.

Old Goshenhoppen Lutheran Family Register, Montgomery Co., PA:
Anna Margaretha, b. ca. 1719, daughter of Abraham Ditloh and Anna
Margareth, dec'd, Reformed, m. in 1736 to Georg Weigele, b. 1714 son of
Johann Michael Weigele and wife Anna Maria, dec'd., both Mennonites.

Philadelphia Adm. G., pg. 129:
Estate of Abraham Titlo, Philadelphia, 1758, Est. #81.

DRACH, JOHANN RUDOLFF   67125 Dannstadt
Thistle of Glasgow, 1730
S-H, I: 31, 32, 33 [Draugh on list]

EUROPEAN RECORDS

Dannstadt Reformed KB:
Johann Rudolf Drach and wife Maria Elisabetha had:
> Elisabetha, bp. 14 Aug. 1728;
> Sp.: Elisabetha Oberbeck

Emigration record:
Werner Hacker, *Auswanderungen aus Rheinpfalz und Saarland*:
#2934 Elisabeth Drach married Andr. Overbeck [q.v.], Dannstadt
#2935 Drach siblings from Dannstadt emigrated 40 years ago to America,
> record dated 27 May 1788.
#2936 Rudolf Drach from [67126] Assenheim, in the New Land, 1749.

AMERICAN RECORDS

Tohickon Lutheran KB, Bucks Co., PA:
Rudolph and Maria Elisabetha Drach had:
> Anna Maria, b. 8 Apr. 1750

Tinicum Lutheran KB, Bucks Co., PA:
> Susanna, bp. Sept. 1761

Tohickon Reformed KB, Bucks Co., PA:
Peter Drach m. 21 Nov. 1758 Catharina Schaeffer. They had children:
> 1. Anna Margaret, b. 31 Aug. 1759
> 2. Catharine, b. 15 Feb. 1761
> 3. Jacob, bp. 4 Nov. 1764
> 4. Maria Elisabeth, b. 25 Sept. 1774, (Tohickon Lutheran KB)

Henry Drach and Anna Maria had:
>Joh. Rudolph, b. 16 Oct. 1759
>Susanna, 30 Apr. 1769

Adam Drach and Eva had:
>John Rudolph, b. 19 Aug. 1770, bp. 9 Oct. 1770
>Sp.: John Rudolph Drach and Maria Elis.

DREYBELBISS see TREIBELBISS

DÜHMER, (DIEMER) JOH. MICHAEL
Polly, 1765
S-H, I: 704

Niederlustadt=
67363 Lustadt
76351 Linkenheim

EUROPEAN RECORDS

Linkenheim Lutheran KB:
Jacob Heinrich Dehmer, a weaver here, and wife Maria Agnes, had a son:
>Joh. Michael Dehmer, b. 12 Nov. 1731
>Sp.: Michael Leonhard Pflüger, servant of the *Anwald*;
>Maria Margaretha, widow from Liedolsheim [= 76706 Dettenheim];
>Anna Maria (n.n.) from Elffingerhoff by [75433] Maulbronn, single;
>Rosina (n.n.) from Liedolsheim, single.

[No other records at Linkenheim; the parents did not marry there]

Ober Lustadt Reformed KB:
Joh. Michael Diemer and wife Eva Catharina had children:
>1. Anna Margaretha, b. 27 July 1758, bp. 1 Aug. 1758
>   Sp.: Johannes Hausser and Anna Margaretha
>2. Jörg Adam, b. 10 Sept. 1760, bp. 14 Sept. 1760
>   Sp.: Jörg Adam Schmitt and Barbara Stettler, both single
>3. A. Elisabetha, b. 6 Feb. 1763, bp. 7 Feb. 1763
>   (Niederlustadt)
>   Sp.; Anna Elisabetha Schmidt, single
>4. Joh. Daniel, b. 12 Nov.1764, bp. 14 Nov. 1764
>   (Niederlustadt)
>   Sp.: Joh. Daniel Haaff von N. Lust. and Maria Magdalena.

*A unique half-timbered structure in Lustadt with
decorated corner timbers, one bearing the date 1746.*

AMERICAN RECORDS

Fourteen passengers on the ship *Polly* in 1765, listed in close proximity to
one another on the list (S-H, I: 704), all appear in the Oberlustadt records:
Andreas Heintz, Christian Wunder, Conrad Hauenstein, Georg Jacob
Hauenstein, Christoph Strigel, Johann Leon[d] Devil (Deubel), Andres
Ehresmann, Peter Zeiler, Georg Aadam Bresler, **Johan Michael Dühmer**,
Jacob Wunder, Jacob Faut, Georg Simon Haushalter, Geo. Adam Teis.

Augustus Lutheran KB, Trappe, Montgomery Co., PA:
Tombstone inscription in cemetery:
        Here rests Johann Michael Diemer, born in Linkenheim in
Deutschland 12 Oct. 1731; died 13 Aug. 1794, age 62 yrs., 10 months, 1 day.

Confirmed 21 June 1778 at Trappe:
        George Diemer, son of Michael Diemer.

Muhlenberg's Journals, Vol. 3, pg. 270:
Michael Diemer and his wife Catharina were sp. in Oct. 1779 for a daughter
of Heinrich Rohrman.

Montgomery County Will Abstracts:
Michael Diemer, Limerick Twp., Montgomery Co., dated 6 Oct. 1793, probated 2 Oct. 1794. Vol. 1: 411:
To wife Catharine, income of ¼ part of estate. At her death equally divided among three children: George, Daniel and Eve. To son George, farm containing 100 acres. He to pay £ 25 more than ¼ of estate to exrs. To son Daniel, farm of 30 acres in Limerick. To daughter Eve, to be paid by son George, what will amount to £ 25 less than ¼ part. Personalty to be sold, money divided among children. Exrs: Isaiah Davis, James Stall. Wit: Adna Evans, Mordecai Evans.

DUPPEL, MORITZ, age 24   67454 Hassloch
St. Andrew, 1741
S-H, I: 304, 305, 306
  [Appears on A list as Maurice Edzebell, age 24; on B list as Johan Maurice Double; on C list as Johan Morritz Dubel. Did not sign his name.]

EUROPEAN RECORDS

Hassloch Reformed KB:
Confirmed 1734 at Hassloch, Moritz Duppel, age 18.

Joh. Moritz Duppel, son of the late Ludwich Duppel, m. 21 May 1738 Anna Barbara, daughter of the late Ulrich Werle.

AMERICAN RECORDS

Swatara Reformed KB, Lebanon Co., PA:
Moritz Dubel and wife Anna Barbara sp. in 1749 a child of Bernhard Rauch.

Millbach Reformed KB, Lebanon Co., PA:
Mauritius [Moritz] Duppel and wife Anna Maria had:
  1. Sophia Elisabeth, b. 5 June 1773, bp. 13 June 1773
     Sp.: Anna Maria Lang
  2. Catharina Margaret, b. 8 Oct. 1774, bp. 16 Oct. 1774
     Sp.: Jacob Mohr and Catharine
  3. John, b. 14 Jan. 1776, bp. 14 Feb. 1776
     Sp.: John Saltzgeber and Catharine.

DÜNNDORFF, ANNA BARBARA   67229 Grosskarlbach
ship unknown, 1738

EUROPEAN RECORDS

Grosskarlbach Lutheran KB:
Joh. Jacob Dünndorff, Miller in the Haumühl, and wife Anna Catharina had
a daughter:
    Anna Catharina Margretha, bp. 17 May 1708
    Sp.: Dominicus Nicolaus Hosbach, Ref. schoolmaster, and
    wife Margaretha; Anna Catharina, wife of Hans Georg Christmann.

Joh. Jacob Dünndorff and wife Anna Maria had a daughter:
    Anna Barbara, bp. 24 July 1710

EUROPEAN RECORDS

Frederick Lutheran KB, Burials, Frederick, MD:
Buried 16 Sept. 1774, Anna Barbara, wife of Jacob Haehn, b. 24 June 1710.
Her father was Joh. Jacob Dundorff and mother Anna Catharina, in
Groscarbach [Grosskarlbach] in the Palatinate, bp. on the 6th Sunday after
Trinity. In the year 1738, May 3, en route to America, in Rotterdam, she
married her surviving widower and had 6 daughters and 1 son with him of
whom one daughter died before the mother. From the five daughters who
lived she has 52 grandchildren and 1 great grandchild. Died of Gühlfluss
[jaundice?] Sept. 14 at 11 P.M. 64 years, 2 months, 3 weeks.

DÜTTENHÖFFER, JOHAN PAUL   67454 Hassloch
Thistle of Glasgow, 1730
S-H, I: 32, 33, 34

EUROPEAN RECORDS

Hassloch Reformed KB:
Married 29 June 1701 in Hassloch: Johann Georg Diedenhöffer, joiner, with
Maria, daughter of the deceased Abraham Munier, carpenter of Tramelan
[CH-2720 Tramelan, BE], Canton Bern. Hans Georg Didenhöffer was buried
26 May 1739, age 60 y., 4 mo., 10 days. Maria, wife of Georg Diettenhöffer,
was buried 6 May 1733, age 57 years. They had a son:
    Paulus, bp. 3 Oct. 1706.

The marriage of the emigrant is not recorded in the Hassloch records, but his wife is given in a later entry as Anna Maria. Paul Diedenhöffer, master joiner, and wife Anna Maria had a son:

    Joh. Christoph, bp. 3 Aug. 1729
    Sp.: Joh. Christoph Hügel, apprentice tailor from Meckenheim
    and Anna Maria ?Habü, also from [67149] Meckenheim.

Hassloch Gerichtsbuch:
Georg Düttenhöffer from Mannheim granted citizenship 28 Jan. 1706. [68159-68169 Mannheim].

AMERICAN RECORDS

Lancaster Deed Book G, p. 205, dated 20 Mar. 1748 mentions a tract of land containing 120 acres in Warwick Twp., patented in 1739 to Paul Tettenhaver; he and wife Anna Maria sold to Christian Sanseny in 1747.

Lancaster County Orphans' Court records, dated 7 Mar. 1749/50:
Anna Maria Dettenhelfer widow of Paul Dettenhelfer, deceased, and Jacob Lanius and Herman Miller are appointed guardians over Christopher, Michael, George, Sophia, Elisabeth, Juliana, and Catharine, orphan children of Paul Dettenhelfer.

Paul Dittenhaver purchased an improvement about 3 miles west of York in 1746. George Dittenhoefer also appears in York county records, and two of his children were baptized at Blimyer's Church. The records of the First Reformed Church at York name the wife of George Dietenhöffer as Margaretha nee Wilhelm.

Frederick Reformed KB, Frederick, MD:
Michael Düttenhofer m. 3 Jan. 1764 Rachel Wilkens.

York County Deed Book 1, pg. 176-180:
24 July 1756: Several deeds are recorded, disposing of land of the late Paul Tittenhaver; Warrant dated 26 Apr. 1746 for 251 acres on Little Codorus Creek County of Lancaster, now York County. Said Paul Tittenhaver died intestate leaving a widow Anna Maria, and children: Christopher, his eldest son; Sophia married to Jacob Heible; Elisabeth married to Michael Valentine; Michael; George; Juliana; and Catharine. Three deeds dispose of part of this warranted land. On page 212-213 of Deed Book 1, another deed pertaining to this land was sold, and the other heirs sign a release to Christopher Deetinhefer, oldest son and heir of Paul Deetinhefer, dec'd.

EHLY (ELI), CHRISTIAN age 49   Niederhochstadt=
EHLY (ELI), HANS DAVID age 20   76879 Hochstadt, Pfalz
Loyal Judith, 1732
S-H, I: 88, 89, 91

EUROPEAN RECORDS

Niederhochstadt Reformed KB:
Christian Öhli, son of Hans Lorentz Öhli m. 26 Nov. 1709 Anna Maria
Unruhe, daughter of Hans David Unruhe. They had children:
1. Joh. David, bp. 14 Jan. 1711
   Sp.: Hans David Weber from Zaiskam [67378 Zeiskam] and
   Anna Catharina Degen from Niederhochstadt
2. Nickolaus, bp. 19 Mar. 1713
   Sp.: Nicklaus Becker and Anna Margretha
3. Simon, bp. 1 Oct. 1714
   Sp.: Simon Schirmann and Maria Catharina
4. Philip Jacob, bp. 1 Dec. 1720
   Sp.: Philip Jacob Hirth and Anna Barbara
5. Georg Christophel, b. 26 Dec. 1731
   Sp.: Georg Unruh and Anna Barbara

AMERICAN RECORDS

Berks County Will Abstracts:
David Ely, Richmond Twp., dated 23 Feb. 1761, probated 24 Mar. 1761.
Names wife Elizabeth and children: son John (under 21), Samuel, Jacob,
Elizabeth, David, Daniel, Abraham, and James. (All of the children were
minors when the will was written.)

David Ely, nat. as a "Quaker," Richmond Twp., Berks Co., 10 Apr. 1754.

EHLY (ELIE), NICHOL age 27   Niederhochstadt=
Winter Galley, 1738   76879 Hochstadt, Pfalz
S-H, I: 198, 200, 202

EUROPEAN RECORDS

Niederhochstadt Reformed KB:
Christian Öhli, son of Hans Lorentz Öhli m. 26 Nov. 1709 Anna Maria
Unruhe, daughter of Hans David Unruhe. They had a son: (See Christian
Ehly for other children.)

Nickolaus bp. 19 Mar. 1713
Sp.: Nicklaus Becker and Anna Margretha

Oberhochstadt Reformed KB:
Nicolaus Öhli, son of Christian Öhly m. 9 Oct. 1734 Anna Barbara Licht,
daughter of the cowherd.

AMERICAN RECORDS

Rev. John Caspar Stoever's Records:
Nicolaus Eli, Tulpehocken, and wife had children:
1. Maria Catarina b. 14 Aug. 1745; bp. 1 Sep. 1745
   Sp.: John Meyer and wife
2. Christian b. 2 Mar. 1748; bp. 6 Mar. 1748
   Sp.: Christian Meyer and wife

Host Church, Tulpehocken, Berks Co. PA:
3. Barbara Eli, daughter of Nicol Eli, conf. Christmas 1753

Nicol Eli and wife had a son:
4. Joh. Jacob b. 14 July 1754
   Sp.: Joh. Jacob Portner and wife

Married 2 Oct. 1759 Valentin Gress and Barbara Eli, daughter of Nicol Eli.

Berks County Land Warrants:
Nicholas Ely, 50 acres, 28 Sept. 1752

EHRESMAN, ANDREAS   Ober Lustadt=
Polly, 1765   67363 Lustadt
S-H, I: 704

EUROPEAN RECORDS

Ober Lustadt Reformed KB:
Andreas Erisman (Erismann) and wife Anna Maria had children:
1. Maria Eva, b. 8 Feb. 1747, bp. 12 Feb. 1747
   Sp.: Jacob Rübel and Maria Eva Roch, both single
2. Jörg, b. 4 Jan. 1754, bp. 6 Jan. 1754
   Sp.: Jörg Spick and Catharina

AMERICAN RECORDS

Fourteen passengers on the ship *Polly* in 1765, listed in close proximity to
one another on the list (S-H, I: 704), all appear in the Oberlustadt records:
Andreas Heintz, Christian Wunder, Conrad Hauenstein, Georg Jacob
Hauenstein, Christoph Strigel, Johann Leon[d] Devil (Deubel), **Andres
Ehresmann**, Peter Zeiler, Georg Aadam Bresler, Johan Michael Dühmer,
Jacob Wunder, Jacob Faut, Georg Simon Haushalter, Geo. Adam Teis.

First Reformed KB, Lancaster Co., PA:
One Andrew Ehresman m. 15 May 1805 Maria Baer of Manor.

EHRHARD, PHILIP REINHART   67459 Böhl-Iggelheim
Prelist
  (in PA 1723)

EUROPEAN RECORDS

Iggelheim - Schifferstadt Reformed KB:
Hans Michael Erhard and wife Maria Catharina had a son:
        Philip Reinhardt, bp. 1 Apr.1696
        Sp.: H. Philipps Reichardt and wife Agnes.

Philipp Reinhard Ehrhardt, son of Hans Michel Ehrhardt, m. 19 May 1716
at Igelheim Anna Barbara Blum, daughter of the late Hans Jacob Blum from
Böhl. They had children:
    1. Johann Peter, b. 16 Jan. 1718
        Sp.: Peter Geibel and Maria Elisabetha Catharina Erhard
    2. Johann Jacob, b. 22 Apr. 1719, bp. 23 Apr. 1719
        Sp.: Jacob Lysi, single and Maria Christina Erhardt, single
    3. Philipp Jacob, b. 1 Aug. 1721, bp. 3 Aug. 1721
        Sp.: Philipp Jacob (torn) and Anna Margareta
        nee Schuh (torn)

AMERICAN RECORDS

Perkiomen Region Past and Present Vol I, no. 7, March 1895:
Brief Notices of Colonial Families: Philip Reinhart Erhard.
        "Under date of February 20, 1723. Philip Reinhart Erhard
purchased of Henry Van Bebber two hundred and six acres of land, part of
five hundred acres bought November 4, 1718, by Henry Van Bebber, which
was part of the Great Tract (22,377 acres) granted to the Frankfort

Company. On March 25, 1738, Erhard sold one hundred and three acres of this land to Michael Bachman; and March 20, 1739, he sold to Simon Smith, of New Hanover Township, the remaining one hundred and three acres, which adjoined lands of Henry Antes, Philip Brant, Michael Fedley and Michael Bachman. At the last mentioned date Erhard lived in Lancaster County.

The tract sold to Michael Bachman was afterwards the Falkner Swamp church parsonage farm, upon which General John F. Hartranft was born."

Philadelphia County Will Abstracts:
Phillip Ehrhard, dated 25 Feb. 1739/40; prob. 11 Mar. 1739.
Children: Jacob, Phillip, David, Hannah and Elizabeth.
Exrs. (or Curators): Martin Orner and John Stein.
Wit.: Wilhelmus Kuepper and Martin Orner.

EICHELIN, JOH. ADAM 67256 Weisenheim am Sand
Pennsylvania Merchant, 1731
S-H, I: 43, 46 [other passengers on ship: Barbara Egling]

EUROPEAN RECORDS

Freinsheim Luth. KB, Weisenheim am Sand Luth. Records:
Hans Adam Eichelein, son of the late Hans Georg Eichelein, former *Gemeinsmann* at Sultzbach an d. Kocher, [Sulzbach am Kocher = 74429 Sulzbach-Laufen], Graffschaff Limburg, m. 24 June 1726 Maria Barbara daughter of the late Jacob Wollschläger, former *Gemeinsmann* at Weisheim ahm Sand [Weisenheim am Sand]. Married here in our church at Freinsheim. They had a child:
1. Johann Geörg, b. 12 Oct. 1727, bp. 14 Oct. 1727
Sp.: Johann Geörg, son of Michael Ohleschläger

Lambsheim Reformed KB:
Johann Jacob Wollschläger and wife Margaretha of Weisenheim am Sand had a daughter Maria Barbara, bp. 1 Apr. 1703.

AMERICAN RECORDS

Old Goshenhoppen Lutheran KB, Montgomery Co., PA:
Anna Maria, daughter of Adam Euchlen, was a sponsor in 1755.
A Leonhard Eichlen appears in record in 1768.

Christoph Fehr, Luth., son of Hannes Fehr and Anna from Wuertemberg in Amt Maulbrunn m. 1 Nov. 1757 Maria Barb. Euchlin, Luth., single daughter of Joh. Adam Euchlin.

New Goshenhoppen Lutheran KB, Montgomery Co., PA:
Joh. Adam Eucheling and wife had:
> Leonhard, bp. 24 Nov. 1732
> Sp.: Leonhard Schmid and Anna Maria Herbig, both single

St. Paul's (Red Hill) Lutheran KB, Montgomery Co., PA:
Married 3 Jan. 1764 Melcher Eukling and Anna Catharina Specht.

Conf. 1753:
Anna Maria Eichly, almost 15, daughter of Eichly, slow, mediocre in knowledge, good habits.

Adam Eichely nat. Apr. 1741, Phila. Co.

ERB, JOHAN JACOB   Lachen-Speyerdorf=
Recovery, 1754   67435 Neustadt an der Weinstrasse
S-H, I: 660
  [name on list: Jacob Earp]

EUROPEAN RECORDS

Lachen-Speyerdorf Reformed KB:
Johann Jacob Erb, son of Joh. Georg Erb, citizen at Musbach [=67435 Neustadt a. d. Weinstrasse], m. 26 Sept. 1753 Anna Margaretha, daughter of Hennerich Sauter [q.v.].

Emigration Record:
Werner Hacker, *Auswanderungen aus Rheinpfalz und Saarland im 18. Jahrhundert:* #3297 Erb, J. Jacob, Lachen, married A. Marg. Sauter, permitted to go to Pennsylvania with his father-in-law Henr. Sauter. Record dated 30 May 1754.

Names and date 1746 on a corner timber
with floral decoration on a building in Lustadt.

ERISMAN (EHRESMAN), GEORG JACOB   Ober Lustadt=
Brothers, 1752   67363 Lustadt
S-H, I: 481
EUROPEAN RECORDS

Ober Lustadt Reformed KB:
Jacob Erisman and wife Barbara had children:
      Maria Ursula, bp. 15 Mar. 1722
      Sp.: Joh. Adam Muffel and Maria Ursula
      Barbara, bp. 25 Apr. 1723
      Sp.: Peter Roch and Barbara
      Georg Jacob, b. 20 Apr. 1727, bp. 27 Apr. 1727
      Sp.: Georg Hauenstein and Maria Barbara

AMERICAN RECORDS

York County Abstracts of Wills:
Jacob Ehresman, Manchester Twp., dated 2 Nov. 1793.
Exrs.: Peter and Andrew Shultz. (There is no will, letters of administration
were granted to the parties named.)

ESCH, ADAM   Ruchheim=
ESCH, SAMUEL   67071 Ludwigshafen am Rhein
ESCH, PETER
Prelist

EUROPEAN RECORDS

Ruchheim Reformed KB:
Hans Adam von Esch and wife Anna had:
1. Catharina, bp. 25 Mar. 1692
2. Samuel, bp. __ Feb. 1696
3. Maria, bp. __ May 1700
4. Petrus, bp. 25 May 1707
5. Anna Barbara, bp. 20 Apr. 1710

Samuel von Esch and Anna Margaretha had:
    Anna Margaretha, bp. 20 June 1720

AMERICAN RECORDS

Futhey and Cope, *History of Chester County, PA:*
Adam Esch appears on Coventry tax list 1753.

Peter Esch appears on East Vincent tax list 1753.

Samuel Esch signed the Call to Rev. Jacob Lischy, as an elder of Brownback's Reformed Church, dated 10 Apr. 1743 in Coventry Twp., Chester Co., PA.

One Adam Esch d. 21 June 1778, Falkner Swamp, Montgomery Co., PA.

Philadelphia County Will Abstracts:
Peter Esh witnessed the will of his brother-in-law Peter DeFrene [q.v.] in 1747.

Peter Ash was named executor for the will of Georg Daniel Bach [q.v.] in 1737.

Peter Ash, Chester Co., nat. 1743.

FAUT (FAUTH), JACOB   Ober Lustadt=
Polly, 1765   67363 Lustadt
S-H, I: 704

EUROPEAN RECORDS

Ober Lustadt Reformed KB:
Bernhard Fäth and wife Catharina (nee Haf) had a son:
    Joh. Jacob, b. 7 Sept. 1738, bp. 14 Sept. 1738
    Sp.: Joh. Unruh and Margaretha

Fritz Braun and Friedrich Krebs. "Pennsylvania Dutch Pioneers from South
Palatine Parishes", *The Pennsylvania Dutchman,* 8 (Spring, 1957):
Hacker #3481:
Johann Jacob Fauth, born at Oberlustadt 7 Sept. 1738, son of Bernhard
Fauth [church register: Fäth] and wife Katherine Haf "went away to America
about 8 years ago (Document dated 18 Mar. 1783); married Louisa Theiss,
born at Oberlustadt 24 Dec. 1741, daughter of Johann Adam Theiss and wife
Magdalena Schmitt, "who married Jacob Fauth from here and likewise went
to PA." (Document dated 3 Dec. 1765).
Brother-in-law of Georg Jacob Heintz [q.v.].

Emigration record:
Werner Hacker, *Auswanderungen aus Rheinpfalz und Saarland*:
#3481 J.Jacob Fauth, Oberlustadt, to America, 1765.

FEHL, GEORG VALENTIN   Oberhochstadt=
Anderson, 1751   76879 Hochstadt, Pfalz
S-H, I: 451

EUROPEAN RECORDS

Oberhochstadt Reformed KB:
Confirmed Easter 1744, Georg Valentin Vehl [also appears as Vöhl].
Martin Vehl and wife Sara had:
    1. Georg Valentin, b. 14 June 1731, bp. 17 June 1731
        Sp.: Georg Valentin Schmidt and
        Catharina Margaretha Hubing(in), both single
    2. Johann Wilhelm, b. 31 Mar. 1734, bp. 4 Apr. 1734
    3. Margaretha, b. 10 June 1740, bp. 12 June 1740
        Sp.: Michel Gamber and Margaretha.

AMERICAN RECORDS

Rev. Waldschmidt's Records, Lancaster Co., PA:
Valentin Fehl, son of Görg Fehl, m. 30 June 1776 Elisabeth, daughter of the late Adam Bahmer.

Salome Fehl, daughter of the late Johannes Fehl m. 28 Sept. 1784 Nicolaus Kammer, son of Peter Kammer.

Valentin Fehl and wife Elisabeth had:
1. Johan Philip, b. 18 July 1777, bp. 3 Aug. 1777
   Sp.: Michael Bohmer
2. Anna Margaretha, b. 7 Mar. 1780, bp. 29 Apr. 1780
   Sp.: Anna Margaretha Bohmer
3. Johann Adam, b. 1 July 1781, bp. 27 Sept. 1781
   Sp.: Adam Bohmer and Margretha, daughter of Michael Roth.

Lancaster County Will Abstracts:
Dec. 5, 1815-Dec. 29, 1815. George Fehl. Wife, Elizabeth Fehl. Children: Jacob, George, Catharine, John, Mary wife of Melchoir Brenneman and Elizabeth. Grandchild: Elizabeth Brenneman.

FEHL, HEINRICH, age 27   Oberhochstadt=
Winter Galley, 1738   76879 Hochstadt, Pfalz
S-H, I: 199, 201, 203

EUROPEAN RECORDS

Oberhochstadt Reformed KB:
Henrich Fehl from the Hanauischen Dorf Wallroth [= 36381 Schlüchtern] m. 22 Feb. 1735 Eva Barbara, daughter of Henrich Gützler. They had:
1. Nicolaus, b. 24 Dec. 1735, bp. 25 Dec. 1735
   "ist nur 14 tag alt worden"
   Sp.: Nicolaus Dennhart and Eva Barbara Fehl, both single
2. Johann Nicolaus, b. 7 Apr. 1737, bp. 11 Apr. 1737
   Sp.: Joh. Nicolaus Dennhart from Oberhochstadt and
   Eva Barbara Fehl from *"Wallroth aus dem Hanauischen",*
   both single.

FINCK, CONRAD   67157 Wachenheim an der Weinstrasse
St. Mark, 1741
S-H, I: 297, 298, 300

EUROPEAN RECORDS

Wachenheim Reformed KB:
Joh. Conrad Finck, son of the late Johannes Finck of Breitenbach in Hesse, [several Breitenbachs in Germany; possibly = 36381 Schlüchtern] m. 11 Jan. 1729 Anna Margaretha, daughter of Johannes Ille. They had children:
1. Anna Martha, bp. 27 Dec. 1730
2. Anna Martha, bp. 12 May 1731
3. Anna Elisabetha, bp. 2 May 1734
4. Johannes, bp. 10 May 1737

AMERICAN RECORDS

A Conrad Fink, weaver, appears on the Hereford Twp., Berks Co., tax lists in 1779, 1780, 1781, taxed with 26 A.

A Conrad Fink appears on the Windsor Twp., Berks Co., tax lists in 1780 and 1781, taxed with 225 A.

Berks County Abstracts of Wills & Administrations:
One Conrad Fink, deceased, of Richmond Twp.; on 3 Nov. 1806, administration on his estate was granted to Catharine, the widow, and George and Peter Fink, sons.

FISCHER, JACOB   67251 Freinsheim
Prelist, before 1723
    [with wife Sophia Elisabetha & family]

EUROPEAN RECORDS

Freinsheim Reformed KB:
Johann Jacob Fischer and wife Sophia Elisabetha had children:
1. Joh. Jacob, bp. 9 Aug. 1699
   Sp.: Wendel Albertus and wife & Anton Fischer
2. Joh. Philip, bp. 22 Aug. 1700
   Sp.: Johan Philip Günther and wife Sophia Elisabeth

3. Anna Maria, bp. 26 Nov. 1702
   Sp.: Gabriel _____ and wife Anna
4. Joh. Herman, bp. 7 Jan. 1705
   Sp.: Joh. Herman Basler and H. Leopold's
   oldest daughter, both single
5. Joh. Henrich, bp. 3 July 1707
   Sp.: Joh. Henrich Rasp and Elisabetha Byrin, both single
6. Maria Magdalena, bp. 12 Oct. 1710
   Sp.: Hermann Bassler and Maria Magdalena, his wife
7. Johanna Margaretha, bp. 28 Aug. 1712
   Sp.: Herr J. Theobald Beyer, saddler at [67227] Franckenthal,
   and Johanna Margaretha, his wife.

AMERICAN RECORDS

Jacob Fischer signed a 1723 petition for a road in Limerick Twp. through Falkners Swamp to Oley. Jacob Fischer and wife Sophia sponsor a child of Wendel Wiand [q.v.] at New Goshenhoppen Reformed Church in Montgomery Co. Herman Fischer was an Elder in the New Goshenhoppen Reformed congregation on 18 Mar. 1740.

The Journals and Papers of David Shultze, Vol. I: 75-79:
Jacob Fisher died 8 Mar. 1748, leaving a will which was contested by some of the heirs. A full transcript of the will, along with David Shultze's comments and advice in the matter, are included in the published Shultz papers.

Jacob Fisher, Upper Hanover Twp. will dated 18 Apr. 1747 names heirs as follows: John Jacob Fisher, eldest son of his son Herman; Sophia Totter, a daughter of Michael Totter and Anne Mary his wife "who is my daughter"; Sophia Wyant eldest daughter of Wendell Wyant and his wife Anne Margareth "my daughter". After legacies are paid the remainder of the estate to Wendell Wyant, "my well beloved son-in-law".
Exrs: Andrew Gräber, Casper Holtzhausen and Michael Rheder.
Witnessed by David Schultze, Jöhannes Hoffman, Michael Moll.
The court set the will aside, and an administration was granted to the son Herman Fisher. Inventory and appraisement was made on Dec. 11, 1752.

Philadelphia Will Book L: 526:
Herman Fischer, Upper Hanover Twp. dated 18 July 1760, prob. 30 Sept. 1760. Names wife Margaret. Children: Jacob, John, George, Herman, Wendell, Anna Mary, Catharina, Barbara, Margaret, Sophia and Christina. Exrs: Margareth and Jacob Fisher, John Mock. Wit.: Wendal Wiand, David Shultze, Christopher Zeigler.

Additional data on the family was published in:
The Perkiomen Region, Past and Present, Vol. I: pg. 6-7 & 22-26: This article contains a complete transcript of Herman Fischer's will and an appraisal of his real estate from the estate inventory.

FISCHER, JOHANN GEORG   Lachen-Speyerdorf=
permit to emigrate 1749   67435 Neustadt an der Weinstrasse
    [There are two immigrants named Hans Jerg Fischer in 1749: one on the ship *Albany* (S-H, I: 395) and one on the ship *Leslie* (S-H, I: 420). One of them likely emigrated from Wuerttemberg according to the Gerber list of emigrants.]

EUROPEAN RECORDS

Lachen-Speyerdorf Reformed KB:
Johann Görg Fischer, son of Balthasar Fischer, parish farmer here, m. 28 Aug. 1726 Maria Ursula, daughter of the late Conrad ?Gentzer (or ?Bentzer). They had children:
    1. Anna Margretha, b. 8 June 1732
    2. Joh. Peter, b. 24 Oct. 1734
    3. Apollonia, b. 13 June 1737
    4. Philipp Jacob, b. 19 Jan. 1740
    5. (Joha)n Peter, b. 6 Apr. 1746

Emigration record:
Werner Hacker, *Auswanderungen aus Rheinpfalz und Saarland im 18. Jahrhundert:* #3667 Fischer, J. Georg, Lachen/Neustadt, with 5 children, manumitted to Pennsylvania. Record dated 18 Mar. 1749.

AMERICAN RECORDS

One Georg Fisher nat. 1765, Whitemarsh, Philadelphia Co., PA.
Another Georg Fisher nat. 1765, Cumberland in Jersey.

FISCHER, PHILIP JACOB   Lachen-Speyerdorf=
permit to emigrate 1765   67435 Neustadt an der Weinstrasse
[not located in PA ship's lists]

EUROPEAN RECORDS

Lachen-Speyerdorf Reformed KB:
Philip Jacob Fischer, son of the master tailor Peter Fischer here, m. 7 June 1757 Maria Martha, daughter of the master linenweaver Peter Franck. They had children:
> 1. Anna Catharina, b. 27 June 1758, bp. 29 June 1758
>   Sp.: Anna Catharina, daughter of Peter Franck
> 2. Anna Helena, b. 7 Dec. 1759, bp. 9 Dec. 1759
>   Sp.: Anna Helena, daughter of Jacob Fischer, tailor
> 3. Philipp Lorentz, b. 23 Nov. 1760, bp. 25 Nov. 1760
>   Sp.: Philip Lorentz Deobald and wife Margretha
> 4. Maria Apollonia, b. 24 Nov. 1762, bp. 28 Nov. 1762
>   Sp.: Maria Apollonia, wife of Elias Hoffsas
> 5. Johan Peter, b. 3 Feb. 1765, bp. 7 Feb. 1765
>   Sp.: Joh. Peter Deobald the younger and wife
>   Catharina Elisabetha.

Emigration record:
Werner Hacker, *Auswanderungen aus Rheinpfalz und Saarland im 18. Jahrhundert:* #3670 Fischer, Jacob, together with his father-in-law Ptr. Franck, Lachen, to America.

FORNEY, JOH. ADAM   67157 Wachenheim an der Weinstrasse
(FORNICK)
Prelist, 1721

EUROPEAN RECORDS

Wachenheim Reformed KB:
New communicants 1705: Hans Adam Fornick

Joh. Adam Fornick and Elisabeth Louise had children:
> 1. Marx, bp. 20 Nov. 1713
>   Sp.: Marx Oberle and wife
> 2. Niclas, bp. 7 July 1715
>   Sp.: Nickel Fornick at Dürckheim=[67098 Bad Dürkheim] and wife.

Joh. Adam Fornick and Louysa had:
> 3. Louysa Charlotta, bp. 26 Apr. 1718

Hans Adam Farnie and Elisabetha had:
>   4. Maria Eva, bp. 8 Jan. 1721
>   Sp.: Maria Eva, daughter of Matthaus Häseler

AMERICAN RECORDS

York Co. Will Abstracts:
Feb. 3, 1783-Mar. 25, 1783. Philip Forney. Executors: Adam Forney and Andrew Shriner. Heidelburg Township. Wife: Elizabeth Forney. Children: Adam, Samuel, David, Peter, Jacob, Mary m. Ludwick Shriver, Louise m. Leonhard Lease, Elizabeth m. Daniel Saunnot, Hannah, Susanna, and Salome.

York Co. Will Abstracts:
Apr. 30, 1800 - Feb. 20, 1804. Marks Forney. Executor: Adam Forney. Manheim Township. Children: Christian, Marks, Adam, Eve m. Christian Werts, Catharine m. Nicholas Kiefbraler, and Daniel.

FRANCK, PETER   Lachen-Speyerdorf=
permit to emigrate 1750 & 1765   67435 Neustadt an der Weinstrasse
  [not located in PA ship's lists]

EUROPEAN RECORDS

Lachen-Speyerdorf Reformed KB:
Peter Franck, son of the late Martin Franck of [76726] Germersheim, m. 16 May 1731 Anna Barbara, daughter of the late Peter Zimmerli. They had children:
>   1. Joh. Peter, b. 14 Sept. 1732, conf. 1746
>   2. Maria Martha, b. 16 Nov. 1734; m. 7 June 1757
>   Philip Jacob Fischer [q.v.]
>   3. Johannes, b. 5 Feb. 1737, conf. 1751. He
>   Married 23 Nov. 1761 Anna Maria, daughter
>   of Henrich Kreuter
>   4. Joh. Georg, b. 20 Aug. 1739, conf. 1755
>   5. Catharina, b. 9 Apr. 1742
>   6. Maria Magdalena, b. 11 Oct. 1744
>   7. Joh. Wilhelm, b. 12 Mar. 1747
>   8. Philip Lorentz, b. 3 May 1749

Emigration record:
Werner Hacker, *Auswanderungen aus Rheinpfalz und Saarland im 18. Jahrhundert:* # 3795 Franck, Peter, Lachen, with wife & children, permission to go to PA, record dated 1 Apr. 1750. [As will be noted above, he continued to appear in the Lachen records, and did not emigrate in 1750]. #3808 Franck, Peter, Lachen/Neustadt, with son Johann to Am. [1765]. See also son-in-law Jacob Fischer.

AMERICAN RECORDS

Colonial Maryland Naturalizations:
Peter Frank and Philip Lawrence Frank were nat. in Maryland, 25 Sept. 1772.

Pennsylvania Naturalizations:
Another Peter Franck nat. without oath in Upper Saucon, Northampton Co., PA, Fall 1765.

FRANZ, FRANZ BALTHASAR	67126 Assenheim
Adventure, 1727
S-H, I: 14, 15

EUROPEAN RECORDS

Assenheim Lutheran KB:
Hans Ulrich Frantz and wife Anna Elisabeth had twin sons:
Georg Christoffel, b. 30 Jan. 1698; conf. 1712
Frantz Balthasar, b. 30 Jan. 1698; conf. 1712
Sp.: Joh. Christoffel Gross (?) and Christina Margaretha, Frantz Balthasar Werning and Anna Rosina

Dannstadt Reformed KB:
Frantz Balthaser Frantz of Assenheim m. 2 Jan. 1727 Anna Barbara Fechtern of Assenheim.

AMERICAN RECORDS

Trinity Lutheran KB, New Holland, Lancaster Co., PA:
Frantz Balthazer Frantz had:
George Adam, b. 13 Dec. 1730
Sp.: Joh. Adam Leitner and wife

Lancaster Co. Orphan's Court records:
Dated 5 Mar. 1755 and 10 June 1755. Balser Frances, dec'd. Tract of land containing 236 A in Cocalico Twp. Heirs named in OC records: widow, Anna Barbara; eldest son John, son George, daughters Anna Maria (elsewhere Margaret) m. to Michael Frantz, Catharina m. to Conrad Charles, Elisabeth m. to Michael Kitch, sons Abraham and Christophel.

For additional detail on this family and the disposal of F. Balthaser Frantz's property, see Lancaster County Deeds, Book H, p. 97; Book D, p. 400; and Book H, p. 134.

FREIDEL, PETER FREDERICH   67454 Hassloch
St. Andrew, 1734   Niederhochstadt=
S-H, I: 137, 141, 142   76879 Hochstadt, Pfalz
The ship's list A gives the names of the following family members: Peter Freytle (Freidel on B list); Anna Veronica Frytle, Maria Ingle Frytle, and Philip Frytle.

EUROPEAN RECORDS

Hassloch Reformed KB:
Peter Friedrich Freudel and wife Anna Veronica had children:
1. Anna Catharina, b. 26 Dec. 1724; bp. 31 Dec.; d. 10 May 1729
2. Maria Engel, b. 8 May 1727; bp. 12 May 1727
3. Joh. Philip, b. 31 Dec. 1729; bp. 6 Jan. 1730

Niederhochstadt Reformed KB:
Peter Friderich Freydel from Hassloch and his wife Anna Veronica had a son:
4. Georg Theobald, b. 21 May 1732; bp. 25 May 1732

FREYTAG, NICHOLAS   67161 Gönnheim
Thistle, 1738
S-H, I: 222, 223, 225

EUROPEAN RECORDS

Gönnheim Reformed KB:
Nicholaus Freytag m. 7 May 1720 Maria Catharina, widow of the late Nicolaus Klingler.

Nicholaus Freytag and wife Maria Catharina had a son:
1. Nicolaus, bp. 14 July 1720
   Sp.: Nicolaus Coblentz and Anna Margaretha Klingler

In 1733 there is a very faded marriage entry:
Nicolaus Freytag and _____.

Niclas Freytag and wife Anna Elisabetha had children:
2. Catharina Elisabetha, bp. 3 Nov. 1734
   Sp.: Johan Jacob Pfarr and Catharina Elisabetha, daughter of Hans Martin Böhler (q.v.).
3. Johann Martin, bp. 5 May 1737
   Sp.: Joh. Martin Böhler and wife Anna Catharina.

AMERICAN RECORDS

Rev. Jacob Lischy's records, York Co., PA:
Niclaus Freytag and Anna Elisabetha had children:
4. Catharina Elisabeth, bp. 26 May 1745
   Sp.: Joh. Adam Krämer and Anna Catharina Welshöfer
5. Joh. Martin, bp. 31 Aug. 1755
   Sp.: Joh. Martin Böhler and Catharina.

FROSCHAUER, HANS GEORG   67157 Wachenheim an der Weinstrasse
Mary, 1732
S-H, I: 93, 94, 95

EUROPEAN RECORDS

Wachenheim Reformed KB:
Hans Conrad Froschauer and wife Sybilla had a son:
   Hans Georg, bp. 3 Apr. 1701
   Sp.: Georg Seitz of Roth [=67827 Becherbach] and Anna Barbara

Hans Conrad Froschauer, cartwright here, d. 15 Mar. 1702.

Hans Görg Froschauer and Anna Catharina had children:
1. Joh. Georg, bp. 6 June 1728
   Sp.: Hans Görg Gutermann and Maria Catharina
2. Maria Elisabetha, bp. 29 Sept. 1730
   Sp.: Hans Jacob Stempel [q.v.] and Maria Elisabetha

AMERICAN RECORDS

Conewago Reformed KB, Adams Co., PA:
John George Froschauer and wife Catharina daughter of Adam Graf from Lichtenberg near [76829] Landau had:

Andrew, b. 30 Sept. 1746, bp. 6 May 1747
Sp.: Andrew Schreiber and wife

John George Froschauer and wife had a son (name not given):

_____, b. 29 Jan. 1748
Sp.: Martin Kützmueller and wife

George Froschauer and Magdalena had a daughter:

Catharine, b. 28 July 1763
Sp.: Jacob Froschauer and Catharine Krebs.

FRUHMANN [FREEMAN], BARBARA   67259 Heuchelheim
FRUHMANN [FREEMAN], JACOB
FRUHMANN [FREEMAN], CATRINA
FRUHMANN [FREEMAN], MARGARET
St. Andrew, 1734
S-H, I: 139 [listed with their mother, Catrina Romfiel [Rumpfelt, q.v.]

EUROPEAN RECORDS

Heuchelheim Lutheran KB:
Johan Jacob Fruhmann m. 26 Aug. 1710 Anna Catharina Foltz. They had children:

1. Abraham, b. 21 May 1711
2. Anna **Barbara**, b. 20 Feb. 1715
3. Anna **Catharina**, b. 22 Mar. 1717
4. Johan **Jacob**, b. 28 June 1719
5. Anna Maria Elis., b. 14 Dec. 1721, d. 1724
6. Susanna **Margaretha**, b. 16 May 1724

Jacob Fruhmann d. 2 Feb. 1724, age 35 yr.

His widow Anna Catharina Fruhmann m. (2) 8 May 1725 Joh. Jacob Rumfeld [q.v.], shoemaker. They had a child:

1. Catharina Margaretha Rumfeld, b. 20 Nov. 1727
Sp.: Catharina Margaretha, daughter of
Johannes Bauniger? of Hessheim? [67258 Hessheim].

AMERICAN RECORDS

St. Paul's (Blue) Lutheran KB, Lehigh Co., PA:
Henrich Rumfeld and wife Barbara had six children here. Two of them were
sp. by Johan Jacob Rumfield and Barbara. Henrich Rumfeld was a son of
Joh. Jacob Rumfeld. There is no mention of the Fruhmann children in this
record.

FULMAN, JOHAN JACOB   67259 Heuchelheim
Harle, 1736
S-H, I: 155, 158, 160
   Passengers on ship: Jacob Vellmann, age 55, and Barbara Vollmanin, Age
41. He signed Follman and Fellman on Lists B and C.

EUROPEAN RECORDS

Heuchelheim Lutheran KB:
Johan Jacob Fulman m. 30 Jan. 1703 at Heuchelheim, Anna Barbara
(maiden name not given in marriage record, but see Pennsylvania records.)
They had children:
   1. Johannes, b. 14 Dec. 1703; conf. 1716;
      d. 11 Nov. 1720, age 17 yrs.
   2. Sybilla Elisabetha, b. 6 Feb. 1708;
      conf. 1718; m. 8 July 1724 Johann Michael Grauel [q.v.]
   3. Apollonia, b. 7 Oct. 1706, d. 14 Oct. 1706
   4. Joh. Wendel, b. 3 Feb. 1708; conf. 1720 [q.v.]
   5. Andreas, b. 26 Dec. 1709, d. 16 Sept. 1710
   6. Joh. Jacob, b. 7 July 1711, d. 9 Sept. 1712
   7. Anna Gertraut, b. 8 Oct. 1713, d. 9 Sept. 1712
   8. Joh. Jacob, b. 9 Oct. 1715, d. 3 June 1717
   9. Anna Maria, b. 28 Mar. 1718, d. 16 May 1721
   10. Joh. Georg, b. 7 July 1719, d. young
   11. Joh. Dieterich, b. 21 Aug. 1720, d. 9 May 1721
   12. Magdalena, b. 27 Apr. 1722, d. 10 Nov. 1724
   13. Philip, b. 10 June 1724, [to America with parents]
   14. Joh. Georg, b. 18 Apr. 1726, d. 4 Jan. 1730
   15. Henrich, b. 9 Feb. 1728, d. 11 Jan. 1730

Nicolaus Fulman died at Heuchelheim 19 June 1724, age 74 yrs.

Joh. Georg Seÿfried died 25 Nov. 1712, age 52 yrs.

Sybilla Seyfrid, died 16 May 1726, age 64 yrs.

AMERICAN RECORDS

Old Goshenhoppen Lutheran Family Register, Montgomery Co., PA, 1751:
Johann Jacob Fillmann, age 70 yrs., b. 22 Dec. 1681. Father: Nicolaus Fillmann from Heichelheim near Worms; Mother: Anna Barbara, both Lutheran. In 1703 he m. Anna Barbara, b. 1683, daughter of Georg Seigfried and wife, Margaretha, both Lutheran, also from Heichelheim. In 1736 he came to America. (This record then names their 15 children with some slight discrepancies in names and dates.)

Johann Jacob Filmann d. 14 Feb. 1753. His obituary, recorded in the Old Goshenhoppen Lutheran burial records, mentions that he was married almost 50 yrs., had 15 children, 19 grandchildren, and 5 great-grandchildren. There are still living 2 sons, 1 daughter, 14 grandchildren, and 5 great-grandchildren. He was buried in the cemetery at the New Stone Church in Old Goshenhoppen, 16 Feb. 1753.

Philip Filmann, son of Jacob, is also listed in this family register: Philip Filmann, age 23 yrs., b. 9 June 1724, son of the above. In 1736 he came with his parents to America. In 1748 he was married to Catharina, b. 1727, daughter of Johann Juncker and Hanna Regina. They had children: (from family register and church records)

1. Johannes, b. 9 Dec. 1748
2. Jacob, b. 25 Aug. 1750
3. Philippus, b. 5 July 1752 (Old Goshenhoppen Lutheran)
4. John Leonard, b. 18 July 1755 (Indianfield Lutheran, surname Philmon)
5. Catharina, b. 8 July 1756 (Old Goshenhoppen Lutheran)
6. Conrad, b. 10 Apr. 1759 (Old Goshenhoppen Lutheran)
7. Maria Magdalena, b. 19 Dec. 1761 (Old Goshenhoppen Luth.)
8. Friedrich or Friedrica, b. 24 Oct. 1764 (Old Goshenhoppen Lutheran)

(The surname is occasionally spelled Philman in these records.)

Philip Filman was buried 31 Aug. 1765. He was a church elder.

FULLMAN, JOH. WENDEL   67259 Heuchelheim
_____, 1752 (Ship data not located)

EUROPEAN RECORDS

Heuchelheim Lutheran KB:
Joh. Jacob Fulman m. 30 Jan. 1703 Anna Barbara. They had 15 children baptized at Heuchelheim, many of them died in childhood [See 1736 immigrant Joh. Jacob Fulman for list.] One of the surviving children was:
Joh. Wendel, b. 3 Feb. 1708; conf. 1720. He remained in Heuchelheim when the rest of the family emigrated to Pennsylvania in 1736. Joh. Wendel Fullman and wife Anna Elisabetha had children:
1. Johannes, b. 28 June 1734, bp. 29 June 1734
   Sp.: Johannes Heÿn, son of Johannes Heÿn of Hessheim;
   d. 15 Sept. 1734
2. Eva Catharina, b. 30 July 1735
3. Joh. Jacob, b. 18 Sept. 1737
4. Anna Maria, twin, b. 3 Sept. 1740
5. Catharina Margaretha, twin, b. 3 Sept. 1740
(No further record at Heuchelheim)

AMERICAN RECORDS

Old Goshenhoppen Lutheran Family Register, Montgomery Co., PA:
Joh. Wendel Filmann, b. 3 Feb. 1708; m. 1733 Elis. Heim, b. 1707, daughter of Joh. Heim [?Heÿn] and Catharina. She came with her husband in 1752 to America.

Old Goshenhoppen Lutheran communicants register:
17 June 1753, Anna Barbara Filman, widow of the late Jacob Filman.
Jacob Filman, single son of Vendel Filmann, grandson of the above.

FÜSSER, JOHANN NICKOLAUS   67454 Hassloch
Thistle of Glasgow, 1730
S-H, I: 31, 32, 35

EUROPEAN RECORDS

Hassloch Reformed KB:
Christoph Füsser and his wife Anna Margaretha (married before the KB begins) had at least ten children, many of whom died in infancy. Two sons were immigrants:
1. **Johann Nickolaus** m. 1722 Juliana Sophia Hautz (see below)
2. Clara Elisabetha m. 15 Apr. 1722 Joh. Daniel Hering
3. Anna Margretha, bp. 31 May 1700
4. Johann Wendel, bp. 16 May 1701 [q.v.] m. 1728

5. Johann Fridrich, bp. ? Feb. 1703
6. Maria Catharina, bp. 23 Sept. 1705
7. Maria Sara, bp. 24 June 1708, died 1710
8. Catharina Elisabetha, bp. 16 Feb. 1710,
   daughter of the late Christoff Fieser,
   m. 23 Nov. 1734 Balthaser Becker, son of Jacob Becker
9. Maria Magdalena, b. 18 Sept. 1711, bp. 23 Sept. 1711
10. Maria Elisabetha, b. 7 June 1713, daughter of the late
    Christoph Fieser, m. 4 Apr. 1736 Christoph Pister, widower
11. Christina Margretha, b.23 Feb. 1715, bp. 27 Feb.; d. 1715
12. Christoph, b. 27 Jan. 1716, bp. 2 Feb. 1716, d. 23 Jan. 1724
13. twin, Johann Georg, b. 10 Aug. 1718, bp. 13 Aug. 1718
14. twin, Georg Ludwig, b. 10 Aug. 1718, bp. 13 Aug. 1718;
    Both died 1718
15. Georg Ludwig, b. 16 June 1720, bp. 19 June 1720;
    Died 24 July 1720.
16. Johann Georg, b. 12 June 1722, bp. 17 June 1722;
    Died 5 July 1722.

Christoph Füsser d. 19 Oct. 1733, age 60 years. His widow Anna Margaretha nee Gummer from Böhl was buried 16 May 1753, age 76 years, leaving 57 grandchildren.

Married 7 Apr. 1722, in Hassloch, **Joh. Nickolaus Füsser,** son of Christoph Füsser, with Juliana Sophia, daughter of Wendel Hautz, *Gemeinsmann* and master potter here. She was a sister of Johan Philip and Philip Lorentz Hautz, both emigrants from Hassloch. Their children:
1. Maria Catharina, b. 26 Dec. 1722; bp. 27 Dec. 1722
2. Philip Jacob, b. 3 Mar. 1724; bp. 6 Mar. 1724
3. Anna Catharina, bp. 26 Dec. 1725
4. Johan Jacob, b. 16 Apr. 1728; bp. 18 Apr. 1728
5. Philip Peter, b. 5 Apr. 1730; bp. 10 Apr. 1730
   Sp. at this last bp. was Johann Peter Ohler from [67149]
   Meckenheim, a fellow passenger on the *Thistle* in 1730.

Clara Elisabetha Füsser, daughter of Christoph, m. 15 Apr. 1722 Joh. Daniel Hering, son of Johannes Hering, *Gemeinsmann* here.

AMERICAN RECORDS

Muddy Creek Reformed KB, Lancaster Co., PA:
The surname appears as Fieser and Fisser in Pennsylvania. Joh. Niclaus Fisser signed the Muddy Creek Church Doctrine in Lancaster county in 1743.

Joh. Nicl. Fisser and Anna Sophia sponsor children of both Adam and Peter Wisenant in 1743. The Wisenant family was also from Hassloch [q.v. Visenant]. Other members of the family appear in the Muddy Creek records, and in the death record for that church: d. 25 Nov. 1791, Peter Fiesser, age 61 y. 7 mo. 17 days.

The Protestant Church at Hassloch.
The tower of the church is quite old;
the newer addition is dated 1752.

Fritz Braun in *Auswanderer aus der Umgebung von Ludwigshafen a. Rh. auf dem Schiff "Thistle of Glasgow" 1730* names the following additional children:

      6. Maria Margaret, b. 10 May 1735;
          m. 16 Apr. 1754 Philip Lorentz Grünewald [q.v.]
      7. Susanna m. Andreas Rhum [more likely Andreas Riehm of Muddy Creek].
      8. possibly Peter
      9. possibly George
     10. possibly Christina, sp. at bp. in 1751, Muddy Creek.

FÜSSER, JOHAN WENDEL   67454 Hassloch
Pennsylvania Merchant, 1732
S-H, I: 66-70
   Passengers on ship: Wendel Fiseir and Susanna Fiseir

EUROPEAN RECORDS

Hassloch Reformed KB:
Joh. Wendel Füsser was b. 16 May 1701, son of Christoph and Anna Margaretha Füsser. He was conf. in 1715, age 14. [See his brother, Johann Nickolaus Füsser, above, for additional family data].

Married 7 Apr. 1728, Joh. Wendel Füsser, son of Christoph Füsser, with Maria Susanna, daughter of the deceased Emanuel Müller, the old schoolmaster. [No children of this marriage listed in KB].

Died 17 May 1727, Herr Emanuel Müller, former schoolmaster here, age 65 years. His widow Maria Elisabetha was buried 10 Apr. 1748, age 70 years.

AMERICAN RECORDS

Muddy Creek Reformed Church records, Lancaster Co., PA:
Wendel Fisser was one of the signers of the Muddy Creek Church Doctrine, dated 19 May 1743. Wendel Feezer had 100 acres of land surveyed in Lancaster County on 12 Oct. 1737.

York County tax lists:
Wendel Feeser was taxed in Codorus Twp., York Co., in 1762.
[He and wife Susanna appear in area church records as sponsors in 1751 and 1756.]

GABEL, PETER 67251 Freinsheim
Johnson, 1732
S-H, I: 72, 76, 78

EUROPEAN RECORDS

Freinsheim Reformed KB:
Reichard Gabel and wife Anna Catharina had a son:
    Joh. Peter, bp. 30 Jan. 1704, conf. 1719.
    Sp.: Peter Abresch, citizen at Freinsheim and wife Susanna.

AMERICAN RECORDS

New Goshenhoppen Reformed KB, Montgomery Co., PA:
A Peter Gabel and wife are sponsors in 1766 and 1770.
Johan Fischer m. 8 Oct. 1759 Catharina Gabel.

One Peter Gabel, Newhanover, Philadelphia Co., nat. 1763.
One Peter Gabel, Philadelphia, nat. 1765.

GAMBER, JOHANNES Oberhochstadt=
Royal Union, 1750 76879 Hochstadt, Pfalz
S-H, I: 433

EUROPEAN RECORDS

Oberhochstadt Reformed KB:
Johannes Gamber, conf. 1739

One Johannes Gampfer was bp. 14 Nov. 1722, son of Rudolph Gampfer and Anna Maria nee Unruh.

Rudolph Gamber m. (1) 27 Sept. 1712 at Niederhochstadt Anna Maria Unruh.

GAMBER (GAMBERT), WILBERT Niederhochstadt &
GAMBER, JOHANNES Oberhochstadt=
Dragon, 1749 76879 Hochstadt, Pfalz
S-H, I: 423

EUROPEAN RECORDS

Niederhochstadt Reformed KB:
Nickolaus Gamber and wife Maria Catharina had a son:
    Joh. Williberth, bp. 9 May 1717
    Sp.: Joh. Wiltperth Gamber and Anna Barbara Deutsch, both single.

Oberhochstadt Reformed KB:
Nicolaus Gamber d. 8 Feb. 1731 (no age given).
Maria Catharina Gamber d. 16 Nov. 1734, age 49 years.

Johann Gamper conf. 1731
Joh. Philibert Gamber conf. 1732

Joh. Williberth Gamber m. 18 Feb. 1741 Maria Elisabetha Seger from
Postorff [= F-57930 Fénétrange] in Lotharingen. They had children:
    1. Rudolff, b. 24 Sept. 1742; bp. 27 Sept. 1742
       Sp.: Rudolff Gamber Sr. and Anna Barbara
    2. Joh. Wilhelm, b. 9 Nov. 1744; bp. 11 Nov. 1744
       Sp.: Joh. Wilhelm Schmidt, schoolmaster, and Maria Barbara
       d. 3 Jan. 1745, age 1 month, 3 weeks, 4 days
    3. Maria Barbara, b. 30 Oct. 1745; bp. 1 Nov. 1745
       Sp.: Joh. Wilhelm Schmidt, schoolmaster, and Maria Barbara
    4. Joh. Fredrich, b. 7 Dec. 1747; bp. 10 Dec. 1747
       Sp.: Friederich Gamber and Apollonia Kolb from
       [76877] Offenbach

Diedendorf [= F-67260 Sarre-Union] Reformed KB, Bas Rhin, France:
Johann Jacob Sager, *Schürmer*, of Postorf and wife Magdalena nee Betsche
had a daughter:
    Maria Elisabetha, b. 23 May 1723

AMERICAN RECORDS

Host Reformed KB, Tulpehocken, Berks Co., PA:
Joh. Wilberth Gamber and wife had children:
    5. Maria Catharina, bp. 23 Dec. 1749
       Sp.: Unruh and husband
    6. Joh. Valentine, b. 28 Apr. 1754 bp. 30 July 1754
       on the other side of the Blue Mountain
       Sp.: Valentin Unruh and Maria Catharina
    7. Johannes, b. 12 Apr. 1757 bp. 22 May 1757
       Sp.: Johannes Trautman and wife

Berks County Land Warrants, Pennsylvania Archives, Third Series:
Wilput Gamber, 277.1 acres, 3 Nov. 1774; Wulpert Gamber, 270 acres, 11
Nov. 1784; Wulpert Gamber, 50 acres, 11 Nov. 1784.

Berks County Tax Lists, Pennsylvania Archives, Third Series, Vol. XVIII:
Residing in Pinegrove twp. 1779-1785: Wilbert, Johannes, and Valentine
Gambert.

Emigration record:
Werner Hacker, *Auswanderungen aus Rheinpfalz und Saarland*:
#4152 & #4153: Johann Gampert and Wilhelm Gampert, Oberlustadt
(possibly an error in transcribing or recording and Oberhochstadt intended.)
Each is listed with three children, and both are manumitted to go to
Pennsylvania in 1749.

GEISEY, see GŸSI, GIESSI

GENSEMER, GEORG DANIEL age 45   Niederhochstadt=
GENSEMER, JOHANNES age 17   76879 Hochstadt, Pfalz
Friendship, 1738
S-H, I: 226, 228, 230

EUROPEAN RECORDS

Niederhochstadt Reformed KB:
Georg Daniel Gentzheimer and wife Christina had children:
    1. Johannes, bp. 15 June 1720
      Sp.: Johannes Degen and Anna Maria Fischer
    2. Catharina, bp. 19 Oct. 1722
      Sp.: Hans Peter Völcker and Maria Catharina Hermann
    3. Jörg Jacob, bp. 25 May? 1725 (very faded entry)
    4. Margretha, bp. 15 Sept. 1728

AMERICAN RECORDS

Christ "Little Tulpehocken" Church, Tulpehocken, Berks Co., PA:
George Daniel Gensemer and wife had a daughter:
    5. Maria Apollonia, b. 21 Mar. 1740; bp. 30 Mar. 1740
      Sp.: Jacob Vollmar and wife

Rev. John Caspar Stoever's Records:
Geo. Daniel Gaensemer and wife of Tulpehocken had children:
      6. Johannes, b. 27 July 1744; bp. 19 Aug. 1744
        Sp.: Johannes Knoll and wife
      7. Catharina Barbara, b. 18 Dec. 1746
        Sp.: John Heinrich Deck and Anna Barbara Teuber

Host Reformed KB, Tulpehocken, Berks Co., PA:
Georg D. Gensemer and wife had a daughter:
      8. Susanna, bp. Dec. 1749
        Sp.: Libo and husband

Anna Apollonia Gensheimer, daughter of Geo. Daniel Gensheimer, confirmed 1753.

Christ Lutheran Church, Tulpehocken, Marion Twp., Berks Co., PA:
Fiedler Numan, son of Walter Numan in Heidelberg Twp., m. 30 May 1748 Anna Margaret, daughter of Georg Daniel Gensomer.

Died Dec. 1772 Maria Catharina Gensemer, widow, aged about 63 years. Buried at Frederick Weiser's; b. in Miflingen in the Palatinate; m. 1738 Daniel Gensemer. Had 5 children, 2 sons and 3 daughters.

Lancaster County Land Warrants, Pennsylvania Archives, Third Series:
Daniel Gansomyer, 100 acres, 14 Dec. 1749. Geo. Dan'l Kinsemer, 50 acres, 17 Oct. 1752.

Berks County Tax Lists, 1767, Pennsylvania Archives, Third Series, Vol. XVIII, p. 75:
A Catharina Gissemenen appears, taxed with 50 acres in Tulpehocken.

GERTON, FELIX
Dragon, 1749
S-H, I: 423

Oberhochstadt=
76879 Hochstadt, Pfalz

EUROPEAN RECORDS

Oberhochstadt Reformed KB:
Confirmed 1739 at Oberhochstadt, Felix Gerton.

AMERICAN RECORDS

Germantown Reformed KB, Philadelphia Co., PA:
Felix Gerdun (also Gertun in another record) and wife Eva had children:
1. Abraham, bp. 30 Sept. 1753
    Sp.: Abraham (surname unknown) and Margaret
2. George Felix, bp. 16 Nov. 1755
    Sp.: George Felix Beck and wife.

GIESSE, GIESY, see GYSI

GLUCK, JOHANN CONRAD   67125 Dannstadt
Lydia, 1749
S-H, I: 421

EUROPEAN RECORDS

Dannstadt Reformed KB:
Hans Marc Gluck and Anna Maria had:
    Hans Conrad, b. 27 May 1708

Johann Conrad Glück, son of H. Johann Marx Glück, *Gerichtsman* of Dannstadt m. 6 July 1734 Suzanne Jardin, daughter of the deceased Jacque Jardin, University Hoff. Johann Conrad Glück and wife Susanna nee Jardin had:
1. Maria Catharina, bp. 15 Apr. 1736
2. Johan Marc, bp. 31 Oct. 1738
3. Ludwig Henrich, bp. 23 Mar. 1741
4. Maria Barbara, bp. 21 Jan. 1744
5. Johannes, bp. 22 Apr. 1746

Died 13 Mar. 1754 - Johan Marx Glück, *Gerichtsmann,* son of the late Hyeronimus Glück, former mayor here. Age 75 y. 30 mo. He m. (1) Anna Maria Wessa. They were m. 18 years and had 4 sons, 3 daughters, 20 grandchildren. He m. (2) Louisa Reuter; married for 28 years; no children to second marriage.

Emigration record:
Werner Hacker, *Auswanderungen aus Rheinpfalz und Saarland*:
#4661 J. Conrad Gluck from Dannstadt; emigration record dated 1749, destination not given.

AMERICAN RECORDS

Anita L. Eyster, "Notices by German and Swiss Settlers --- in the *Pennsylvanische Staatsbote*" [newspaper]. Published in *Pennsylvania German Folklore Society*, Vol. III, 1938.
Issue dated 4 Aug. 1775, Simon Keppler expects in three weeks time to make another trip to Germany. He has already gone six times, will visit many places. He advertises that he has letters for several people or wishes to find others, including Joh. Conrad Gluck from *Darm*stadt.

The Berks County home of Hans Martin Gerich.
Photo by Jeff Godshall.

GÖHRIG, JOH. MARTIN   67112 Mutterstadt
Prelist

EUROPEAN RECORDS

Mutterstadt Reformed KB:
Joh. Martin Gerich, cooper from [67229] Gerolsheim m. 28 Oct. 1721 Anna Catharina Schad.

Mutterstadt Kontraktenprotokolle:
Record dated 1720, recorded 2 June 1737: Johann Martin Göhrig, citizen here, who "had moved to Pennsylvania with his family," property sold at public auction to Christoph Emmerich.

AMERICAN RECORDS

Rev. John Casper Stoever's Records:
Martin Gaehrich in Oly had children:
1. Johann Jacob, b. 31 Jan. 1731, bp. 22 Feb. 1731
   Sp.: Johann Jacob Dieburger
2. Susanna, b. 9 Nov. 1733, bp. 17 Nov. 1733
   Sp.: Christoph Bechtel and wife Susanna

Sower's newspaper, dated 16 Mar. 1750: Hansz Martin Gerig, Exeter County (sic: Exeter Twp., Berks Co.) in the Schwartzwald, 3 miles from Justice Buun [=Boone], offers a plantation for rent.

Berks County Wills Abstracts:
Hansz Martle Gerick of Exeter Twp. 1 Mar. 1757 - 30 May 1757.
Mentions son George Mertel Gerick; son-in-law Henry Hersten; wife Catharina. Lands in Exeter Twp., and houses and lots in Reading.

Hans Martin Gerich nat. by Act. of 1730/31.

GÖTZENDANNER, CHRISTIAN   67105 Schifferstadt
Allen, 1729
S-H, I: 27   (Kitsintander, Kitsenlander)

EUROPEAN RECORDS

Schifferstadt Reformed KB:
Christian Götzendanner, son of Jacob Götzendanner, a Swiss, m. 20 Apr. 1723 Anna Barbara, daughter of Joseph Brunner. They had children:
1. Susanna Margareta, b. 12 July 1724
2. Gabriel, b. 15 Jan. 1727

Emigration record:
Werner Hacker, *Auswanderungen aus dem Früheren Hochstift Speyer nach Südosteuropa und Übersee im XVIII Jahrhundert,* Heimatstelle Pfalz, 1969: Götz[endanner], Christian. Schifferstadt, Reformed, with wife and son and daughter. Paid emigration tax to go to Pa. on 26 Apr. 1729, together with Joseph Brunner [q.v.].

AMERICAN RECORDS

Frederick Reformed Church, Frederick, MD:
Gabriel Götzendanner and Christian Götzendanner both appear here as early as 1749. Christian's wife is given in these early records as Anna Barbara, and they sponsor children of other Schifferstadt families.

Jacob Giezendanner m. 3 Apr. 1757 Catharina Kast.
Balthasar Giezendanner m. 11 May 1758 Anna Steiner
Georg Thomas Schley m. 16 May 1758 Maria Giezendanner.

Naturalized in Maryland:
Gabiel Getsedanner nat. 14 Apr. 1761.
Christian Getson Tanner nat. 19 Oct. 1743.

GRENOBLE, JACOB   67167 Erpolzheim
Snow *Charlotta*, 1743
S-H, I: 339, 340

EUROPEAN RECORDS

Inhabitants List of Married and Unmarried Men for the Graffschafft Leiningen-Hartenburg, 1706:
    Moeritz Grenobel, age 45   Erpolzheim

Erpolzheim Lutheran KB:
Moritz Kronobus [Cronoby, Grenoble] and wife [Anna] Elisabeth had children:
1. Anna Margretha, bp. 22/12 Feb. 1699
2. Anna Barbara, bp. 24 Feb. 1701
3. A son **[Jacob]**, b. 4 May 1702, bp. 7 May 1702;
   Conf. 1716, age 14, [67169] Kallstadt Lutheran KB.
   Sp.: Jacob Bach, son of Philip Bach and Anna Catharina,
   dau. of Henrich Cronoby (Grenoble) from Dürkheim [= 67098 Bad Dürkheim].
4. Anna Catharina, bp. 7 Feb. 1706
5. Joh. Valentin, bp. 23 Jan. 1708
6. Margaretha, b. 11 Jan. 1712, bp. 17 Jan. 1712

Joh. Jacob Grenoble and his wife Agnesa had children:
(he was Lutheran, she was Reformed)
1. Anna Barbara, b. 16 Feb. 1741, bp. 19 Feb. 1741; d. 1742.

2. Lorentz, b. 10 Jan. 1743, bp. 13 Jan. 1743
Sp.: Lorentz Haintz of [67169] Kallstadt, and
Juliane Stützgen of [67229] Grosskarlbach.

AMERICAN RECORDS

Christ Lutheran KB, Stouchsburg, Berks Co., PA:
Jac. Gränobel was a communicant at Christ Church in 1743 (at Christmas), 1744, 1745, and 1746.

Berks County Will Abstracts:
Jacob Cronople, Greenwich, 21 Dec. 1762 - 12 May 1777. To stepson Conrad Beaber my estate where I now live for £50, as follows: to his sister Lisa Margreth £10 and to my daughter Mary £10 and a cow; to son Lawrence £15; to son Henry £15. Also provides fo wife Odilia. Exr: Conrad Beaver. Wit: Jacob Leiby, Christian Henry, and George Haws.

GRAUEL, JOHAN MICHAEL 67259 Heuchelheim
Harle, 1736
S-H, I: 154, 156, 158, 160
Michel Kraul, age 53, (he signed Graul) and Sibila Elisabeth Kraul, age 30

EUROPEAN RECORDS

Heuchelheim Lutheran KB:
Johann Michael Grauel, master carpenter, m. 8 (July?) 1724 Sybilla Elisabetha Fulmann. They had children at Heuchelheim:
1. Johan Georg, b. 21 Nov. 1725
2. Johan Nicolaus, b. 25 Mar. 1727
3. Joh. Henrich, b. 14 May 1729; bp. 18 May 1729
4. Jacob, b. 2 Jan. 1731
5. Joh. Philip, b. 18 Aug. 1732
6. Johannes, b. 2 Oct. 1733; bp. 9 Oct. 1733

AMERICAN RECORDS

Old Goshenhoppen Lutheran Family Register:
Michael Graul m. Sybilla Filmann, b. 1705, daughter of Joh. Jacob Filmann [q.v.] and Anna Barbara.

Reading Lutheran KB, Berks Co., PA, Burials:
Sibilla Kraul, wife of Michael (elsehwere in records mentioned as widow of Michael), d. 4 Apr. 1776, age 71 years, 1 month, 3 weeks, 5 days.

Berks County Will Abstracts:
Philip Grauel of Maxatawny, will dated 29 Mar. 1762, probated 14 Apr. 1762, names wife Eva Catharina and mother Sibilla Grauel. Mentions children, but not by name. Exrs: wife Eva Catharina and friend, Sebastian Levan. Wit: Nicholas Schroyer, John Bast, Jost Vollert.

Berks County Abstracts of Wills and Adm.:
Adm. on the estate of John George Graul of Berks Co., was granted 29 Dec. 1753 to Elisabeth Graul, the widow. Orphans Court records dated 16 May 1754 mention 4 young children (not named), and a tract of land in Maidencreek Twp., 100 A.

Mertz's Lutheran Church, Rockland Twp., Berks Co., PA:
Georg Graul and wife Elisabetha nee Lerch had a daughter:
Sibylla, b. 11 Mar. 1751, bp. 12 May 1751
Sp.: Sibylla Graul

Heinrich Graul and wife Anna Margretha, nee Bader, had a son baptized on the same date:
Johann Debald, b. 8 Apr. 1751, bp. 12 May 1751

Reading Lutheran KB, Berks Co., PA:
Jacob Kraull, b. in the Palatinate 14 Jan. 1730, d. in Reading 19 July 1811, age 81 yr., 6 mo., 5 da. He m. (1) May 1759 Anna, daughter of Balthasar Schmidt and Dorothea, from Gibelstadt, Anspach [97232 Giebelstadt]. They had three sons and one daughter, one son survived. His first wife d. 21 Jan. 1770, and he m. (2) Catharina, daughter of Henry Christ. They had several children baptized at Reading and one child, Susanna, b. 31 Jan. 1774, was sponsored by Sybilla, widow of the late Michael Grauel.

Heinrich Grauel and wife Margaret moved to Frederick Co., MD, where he d. in 1784 and later descendants moved to Darke Co., OH. The surname appears in records as Croull, Crowel, etc.

GROH, JOH. SIMON   Ober Lustadt=
Lydia, 1749   67363 Lustadt
S-H, I: 423
                        EUROPEAN RECORDS

Ober Lustadt Reformed KB:
Peter Croh and wife Magdalena had a son:
Joh. Simon, b. 28 Oct. 1730, bp. 29 Oct. 1730
Sp.: Joh. Simon Hoffmann and Margaretha _____, both single

AMERICAN RECORDS

Blue Mountain Reformed KB, Upper Tulpehocken Twp., Berks Co.:
Simon Groh and wife (not named) had a daughter:
Maria Margaret, bp. 28 Apr. 1771

Simon Groh naturalized Fall, 1765 - Tulpehocken, Berks Co.

GROSCOST, PHILIP   67112 Mutterstadt
Thistle of Glasgow, 1730
S-H, I: 30, 31, 33

EUROPEAN RECORDS

Mutterstadt Reformed KB:
Hans Philip Grosskost and wife Anna Margaretha had children:
   1. Wilhelm, bp. 10 May 1715
      Sp.: Wilhelm Heim (q.v.) and Anna Margaretha Reisiger,
      both single.
   2. Christoph, bp. 14 Feb. 1717; married 22 Feb. 1735 by the
      Lutheran pastor: Christoph Groscost, Lutheran, son of Joh. Philip
      Groscost "now in Pennsylvania," and Johanna Steiger, daughter of
      Joh. Theobald Steiger.
   3. Anna Elisabetha, bp. 19 Mar. 1719
   4. Philip Daniel, bp. 8 Nov. 1721

PfFWKde, Band 6, Heft 6, p. 195:
Hans Philipp Grosskost m. Anna Margaretha Heim. The family emigrated
in 1730 to America, arriving on the ship *Thistle of Glasgow.* They had four
children born between 1715 and 1721 in Mutterstadt.

Additional Data:
See also Fritz Braun, "Auswanderer aus der Umgebung von Ludwigshafen
a. Rh. auf dem Schiff *Thistle of Glasgow* 1730," publication #8, *Schriften zur
Wanderungsgeschichte der Pfälzer.*

AMERICAN RECORDS

They possibly settled in York County, where a Daniel Grosscast appears on
later tax lists along with a John Grosscast.

GROW (GROH), PETER Ober Lustadt=
Lydia, 1749 67363 Lustadt
S-H, I: 423

EUROPEAN RECORDS

Ober Lustadt Reformed KB:
Peter Groh and wife Maria Magdalena had a son:
    Peter, b. 14 Apr.1733, bp. 19 Apr. 1733
    Sp.: Peter Roch and Anna Barbara

AMERICAN RECORDS

Peter Kroh naturalized Fall, 1765, in Weisenburg.

GRUMBACH, CONRAD Oberhochstadt=
Dragon, 1749 76879 Hochstadt, Pfalz
S-H, I: 423

EUROPEAN RECORDS

Oberhochstadt Reformed KB:
Conrad Grumbach and wife Anna Catharina had children:
    1. Eva Catharina, b. 27 Oct. 1737, possibly died young.
    2. Eva Catharina, b. 17 June 1739
    3. Johann Adam, b. 20 Jan. 1742
    4. Anna Maria, b. 8 July 1744
    5. Georg Heinrich, b. 8 Dec. 1745

The records of Oberhochstadt and Niederhochstadt were searched for a marriage record and only the following was found:
Married 22 Jan. 1732, Joh. Krummbach, son of Johann Krummbach of Duttweiler, and Maria Catharina Dörr, daughter of the deceased Daniel Dörr. [Note by compiler: this is possibly the marriage record of Conrad Grumbach, above; if his full given name was Joh. Conrad Grumbach, the pastor might have just recorded the Joh. part of the name.]

Emigration record:
Werner Hacker, *Auswanderungen aus Rheinpfalz und Saarland*:
#4991 Grumbach, Konrad, Oberlustadt, manumitted, with two children to Pennsylvania, 12 Mar. 1749.

The Grombach surname appeared in the Niederhochstadt records prior to the 30 Years' War. The church records here start in 1708, and any research before that date must depend on other sources. There exist three village account books (much like our tax lists) dated 1619, 1626, and 1628. They are located in the Landesarchiv in Speyer. The name appears in these lists as Grombach, Grombächer, and Crombächer.

> a Georg Grombach, Dorfmeister, appears on the 1619 and 1626 lists.
>
> a Hanns Grombach appears in 1619 and 1626.
>
> a Heinrich Grombächer appears in 1619.
>
> a Hans Crombächer appears in 1628.

The Oberlustadt records start in 1720, and a thorough search of the records there failed to reveal the surname in the records there, nor any mention of Conrad Grumbach, specifically. The surname Dörr appears briefly in the Oberlustadt record in 1723. It is possible that Conrad and Catharina lived there briefly before emigrating to America in 1749, in light of the emigration record in Werner Hacker's book; or this could be an error, and Oberhochstadt was intended; the two villages are within walking distance of each other.

AMERICAN RECORDS

Egypt Reformed KB, Lehigh Co., PA:
Confirmed 1753: Eva Catharina, daughter of Conrad Grumbach.

Rev. Abraham Blumer's Pastoral Records (Reformed, Lehigh Co., PA):
Died 25 Jan. 1781: Conrad Grumbach, aged 71 years less 17 days.

Northampton County Will Abstracts:
Conrad Crumbach, Easton, will dated 20 Jan. 1781; probated 8 Feb. 1781. Names wife Catharina and the following children: Christina, Eve, George Henry, Conrad and Margaret. Exrs: son George Henry Crumbach and George Groff. Wit.: Peter Rhoads, Lorentz Hauck, Mathias Riegel.

Zion Reformed KB, Allentown, Lehigh Co., PA:
Baptized 13 Apr. 1775 after instruction: Esther Sewitz, wife of George Henry Crumbach.

George Henry Grumbach and wife Esther had children:
> 1. Anna Catharina, b. 27 Dec. 1774, bp. 8 Jan. 1775
>   Sp.: John Epler; Catharine Knaus.
> 2. Eva Catharina, b. 22 July 1776, bp. 25 Aug. 1776
>   Sp.: Leonard Grumbach; Catharina Deschler.

Conrad Grumbach and his wife Catharine were sponsors in 1776 for David Fuchs, b. 12 Sept. 1776, son of John Nicholas Fuchs and wife Margaret.

Andrew Rieb and wife Eva Catharina had children:
1. John Adam, b. 13 July 1769, bp. 23 July 1769
   Sp.: George Henry Grumbach; Maria Marg. Grumbach; Jacob Hauk.
2. Eva Catharine, b. 26 Dec. 1771, bp. 7 Jan. 1772
   Sp.: Jacob Hauck in place of his brother Peter Hauck; and Christine Grumbach.
3. Maria Catharina, b. 1776
   Sp.: Conrad Grumbach and wife Catharina.

Land Warrants, Northampton Co., from Pennsylvania Archives:

Conrad Grumbach	30.141 acres	6 Feb. 1772
	46.109 acres	6 Feb. 1772

GRÜNEWALD, PHILIP LORENTZ   67459 Böhl
Phoenix, 1749
S-H, I: 407
Name on list: Hann Filb Grünewalt

EUROPEAN RECORDS

Hassloch Reformed KB:
Mathaes Grünewald, son of the deceased Johannes Grünewald, m. 8 Nov. 1724 at Böhl, Maria Catharina (faded and incomplete entry: her maiden name not given). They had children:
1. **Philip Lorentz,** b. 10 June 1725; bp. 12 June 1725 at Böhl
2. Johann Conradt, b. 19 Sept. 1727, bp. 21 Sept. 1727
3. Johann Michel, b. 20 Apr. 1730, bp. 23 Apr.; d. 2 Apr. 1733.
Böhl Reformed KB:
4. Johann Jacob, b. 10 July 1734, bp. 11 July 1734
5. Catharina Barbara, b. & bp. 27 Jan. 1737; d. 16 Feb. 1738
6. Maria Magdalena, b. 12 June 1739, bp. 14 June 1739.

AMERICAN RECORDS

Rev. John Waldschmidt's pastoral records, Pa. Archives, Series 6, Vol. 6:
Philip Lorentz Grünewald m. 16 Apr. 1754 Maria Margaret, daughter of Johan Nickel Füsser [q.v.].

Egle, *History of Lebanon County, Pennsylvania,* **p. 240:**
Philip Lorenz Greenawalt, b. 10 June 1725 in Hassloch in Boehl, Germany, died 28 Feb. 1802; m. Maria Margaret Foeser, b. 10 May 1735, d. 10 May 1806 at Lebanon, and with her husband there buried. They had issue:
1. John Philip, b. 17 June 1756, m. Catharine Shaffner
2. Christian, b. 14 Dec. 1758, m. Elizabeth Kelker
3. John, b. 14 Oct. 1760
4. Elizabeth, b. 1 Mar. 1763, m. Henry Kelker
5. Margaret, b. 17 July 1765, m. Philip Stoehr
6. Matthias, b. 17 Oct. 1767
7. Jacob, b. 14 Feb. 1770
8. Catharine, b. 20 July 1772, m. John Zinn
9. Michael, b. 21 Jan. 1775
10. Leonard, b. 21 Jan. 1775, m. Catharine Pool
11. Maria Magdalena

[Additional data on descendants is given in this history. See also page 272 for the military service record of Col. Philip Greenawalt].

GUCKER, JOHAN BARTHEL   67256 Weisenheim am Sand
Pennsylvania Merchant, 1731   67435 Neustadt a. der Haardt
S-H, I: 43, 45, 46
(A list: Bartel Kooker, Katrina Kooker
  Laurence and Christian Kooker (under 16) [see Laufer]

EUROPEAN RECORDS

Weisenheim am Sand Reformed KB:
Joh. Barthel Guckert, son of Joh. Guckert from Neustadt a. der Haardt m. 16 Jan. 1731 Catharina, widow of the late Heinrich Leufers. Catharina was nee Schmidt, the daughter of Wilhelm Schmidt. She m. (1) 14 Apr. 1716 Joh. Heinrich Eberle and (2) 7 Sept. 1718 Heinrich Laufer. Two children of her second marriage appear on the list as:
        Laurence and Christian Kooker [surname actually Laufer, q.v.].

AMERICAN RECORDS

New Goshenhoppen Reformed Ch. Record, Montgomery Co., PA:
Bartholomeus Gucker and wife Catharina had children:
        1. Susanna, bp. 24 Nov. 1732
           Sp.: Christopher Schmit [q.v.] and wife
           She married Jacob Riedi

2. Eva Lisabeth, bp. 9 May 1736
   She married Andreas Ohl
3. Elisa Barbara
   She married _____ Ohl

New Goshenhoppen Reformed KB, Burials, Montgomery Co., PA:
Buried: 3 June 1772 Catharina Gucker, b. 1696, aged about 76 years.

Members of New Goshenhoppen Reformed Church (1736-1739)
   Joh. Bartholomeus Kuker

Conf. 1748-1758:
   Elisa Barbara Gucker
   Eva Gucker
   Susanna Gucker

St. Paul's Lutheran KB, Red Hill, Montgomery Co., PA:
Barthold Gucker and Catharina sp. a child of Daniel Müller in 1745.
Elisabetha Barbara Gucker sp. a child of Peter Busz in 1749.

GŸSI (GIESSE), JACOB   67454 Hassloch
Snow *Lowther*, 1731   CH-4434 Hölstein, BL
S-H, I: 54, 55, 56
Name on the lists: Keesey, Giss(e), Kerzey.
Passengers on ship: Jacob, John Wendel, Anna Barbara, David Vincent,
Conrad, Ulrich, and Catharina.

EUROPEAN RECORDS

Hassloch Reformed KB:
Married 11 Nov. 1705 at Hassloch: David Güller, son of Conrad Güller, with
Anna Barbara, daughter of the deceased Ludwig Michel. They had two sons,
neither of whom lived to adulthood. David Güller died after the baptism of
the second child, 3 Feb. 1709.
Married 11 June 1710, Jacob Gysi from Switzerland with Anna Barbara,
widow of David Güller. Children born at Hassloch:
   1. Joh. Wendel, b. 23 July 1711, bp. 16 July 1711
   2. Anna Catharina, b. 29 Jan. 1716, bp. 1 Feb. 1716
   3. Joh. David, b. 6 Aug. 1718, bp. 7 Aug. 1718
   4. Joh. Conrad, b. 17 Mar. 1723, bp. 21 Mar. 1723
   5. Joh. Ulrich, b. 17 Oct. 1725, bp. 21 Oct. 1725

Since there were evidently three different emigrants named Jacob Gysi (Giese, etc.) and to further complicate matters, each had a wife named Barbara at the time of emigration, data on the two men from Hassloch is presented here. The third Jacob Gysi emigrated directly from Switzerland, and data on that family may be found in Faust and Brumbaugh, *Lists of Swiss Emigrants to the American Colonies in the Eighteenth Century.*

Title page of the Hassloch Reformed Church record, dated 1769.

Jacob Gysi was a son of the deceased Hans Gyssi and the deceased Anna Bleyer "aus der Gruende bei Höllstein" (Amt Waldenburg, Basel-Land, Switzerland). Jacob had lived for 8 years in Hassloch in the Kurpfaltz and there married Anna Barbara Christian. He applied to Basel for manumission on 13 Jan. 1717 and at that time he had three children. (Staatsarchiv Basel, D 6, 172.)

[Note that only two children were found in the Hassloch baptismal record before 1717. There is a burial record for an unnamed 8 year old daughter who died 22 May 1721.]

Hassloch Gerichtsbuch:
20 Jan. 1721: Jacob Gysse *aus dem Baselerisch Schweitzerisch Gebieth* [from the Canton Basel-Land, Switzerland] was granted citizenship.

AMERICAN RECORDS

New Holland Lutheran Church, Lancaster County:
One Joh. Jacob Guisie and wife (not name) had children:
1. Elisabeth, b. 17 Mar. 1734
2. Philip Jacob, b. 7 Mar. 1736

Lancaster County Orphans' Court record, dated 7 Dec. 1757:
Guardians are appointed for the following children of Jacob Geesy, deceased: eldest son Philip, son John, son Henry, and daughter Maria Elisabeth wife of Ulrich Seiler.

GYSI (GIESSI), JACOB 67454 Hassloch
Princess Augusta, 1736 67459 Iggelheim
S-H, I: 162, 164, 166
Name on list: Jacob (X) Kese, Kissy age 28

EUROPEAN RECORDS

Hassloch Reformed KB:
Heinrich Giessi, a swineherder in Hassloch m. 11 Nov. 1704 Maria Magdalena daughter of the deceased Heinrich Burckhard. They had:
1. Anna Barbara, bp. 22 Nov. 1705
2. **Joh. Jacob,** bp. 3 July 1707; conf. 1721
3. Anna Helena, bp. 13 Apr. 1710; d. 17 Sept. 1718
4. Susanna, b. 1 Jan. 1713, bp. 8 Jan. 1713
5. Anna Catharina, b. 9 Feb. 1716; bp. 12 Feb. 1716
6. Joh. Conradt (emigrant in 1741, q.v.), b. 27 Mar. 1718
7. Johannes, bp. 19 May 1723; d. 1725

Hassloch Gerichtsbuch:
20 Jan. 1721: Henrich Gyssi *von Hollstein Berner Gebiets* [actually CH-4434 Hölstein, Canton Basel] was granted citizenship.

Schifferstadt-Iggelheim Reformed KB:
Married (1) 10 Feb. 1728 at Iggelheim, Hans Jacob Gyssi, son of Henrich Gyssi of Hassloch and Anna Maria Erhard daughter of Hans Peter Erhard.

Died 10 Apr. 1728 at Iggelheim, Anna Maria Giesi, nee Erhard, daughter of Peter Erhard and Maria Magdalena nee _____(faded), age 25 years, 2 months, 10 days. Wife of Joh. Jacob Giesi of Hassloch.

Hassloch Reformed KB:
Married (2) in Hassloch 29 June 1728, Jacob Gysi, widower, and Anna Barbara, daughter of the deceased Jacob Biber, shoemaker here. They had a daughter:
> Elisabetha, bp. 29 Oct. 1730
> [This child died in Hassloch 12 Mar. 1732. It will be noted that the first Jacob Gysi emigrated in 1731.]

Anna Barbara Biber was bp. 20 Aug. 1702, daughter of Jacob Biber and Maria Catharina. Jacob Biber, shoemaker, died 30 Apr. 1715.

AMERICAN RECORDS

See the 1731 immigrant Jacob Gyssi (Giesse, Geisey etc.) for possible American data.

GYSI, CONRADT age 23   67454 Hassloch
St. Andrew, 1741
S-H, I: 304, 305
  Name on list: Kiesie, Gissy

EUROPEAN RECORDS

Hassloch Reformed KB:
Henrich Gysi and wife Maria Magdalena had a son: (See emigrant Jacob Gysi, 1736, for their marriage and other children)
> Johann Conradt, b. 27 Mar. 1718; bp. 30 Mar. 1718; conf. 1732.

Joh. Conrad Giesi, son of Henrich Giesi, m. 15 Apr. 1738 Anna Barbara, daughter of the deceased Ulrich Werle. They had children:
> 1. Catharina Barbara, b. 3 June 1739; bp. 7 June 1739
> 2. Maria Elisabetha, b. 16 May 1740; bp 22 May 1740

Dannstadt Reformed KB:
Conf. Pfingsten, 1732: Anna Barbara, daughter of the deceased Ulrich Werle from Hassloch, age 18 years. From the Roman Catholic to the Reformed Religion.

AMERICAN RECORDS

Lancaster and York County Church Records:
A Conrad Geisi (Güsse, Giese, Giesy) with a wife Maria Agatha appears in Reformed Church records in Lancaster and York. In one record, his wife is given as Maria Agnes nee Baer. The earliest record for this family is found in the First Reformed Church records, Lancaster. Conrad Geise and wife Mary Agatha had a son John Conrad b. 12 July 1750. Sponsors at the baptism were Ulrich Seyler and wife Maria Elisabeth (nee Giesi?). Later entries for this family are found in First Reformed Church records, York, and Blimyer's Church records, York county. The evidence found does not determine whether these York entries are for Johann Conrad the 1741 emigrant or for Joh. Conrad b. 1723, son of the 1731 emigrant.

Lancaster County Deed Books:
Conflicting information on Conrad Geisi's wife Maria Agatha appears in two Lancaster county deeds. The first of these deeds, recorded in Deed Book GG:2, pp. 170-172, dated 17 Sept. 1771, states that Maria Agatha Geesy, wife of Conrad Geesy of York county, is the full sister of Elizabeth Wolf of Lancaster county. Elizabeth Wolf was the widow of Samuel Wolf, and her maiden name was Bär. She was a daughter of Joh. Ulrich Bär, 1732 immigrant who arrived on the ship *Dragon.*

The second deed, Book GG:2, pp. 313-316, dated 17 Dec. 1787, contains the conflicting statement that Agatha Geesy was the only child of Elisabetha and Samuel Wolf. This second deed is in error. Maria Agatha Bär was b. 28 Feb. 1720, daughter of Joh. Ulrich Bär. [For full detail on the Bär family, see Burgert, Annette K., *Eighteenth Century Emigrants from German Speaking Lands,* Vol. I: The Northern Kraichgau. Pennsylvania German Society, Vol. XVI (1983).]

Rev. Jacob Lischy's records, York Co., PA:
Conrad Kissy and wife Sussanna had a daughter:
    Maria Magdalena, bp. 24 May 1752
        Sp.: Ludwig Schreiner and Maria Magdalena.

HAAS, GEORG LUDWIG   67454 Hassloch
Thistle of Glasgow, 1730
S-H, I: 31, 32, 33

EUROPEAN RECORDS

Hassloch Lutheran KB:
Abraham Haas and his wife Anna had children:
1. Barbara, bp. 6 Sep. 1700; not conf.
2. **Georg Ludwig**, bp. 31 July 1703; conf. 1716
3. Anna Maria, bp. 16 Oct. 1703; conf. 1716
4. Anna Catharina, bp. 6 Apr. 1706; bur. 11 Aug. 1707
5. Anna Engel, bp. 26 Apr. 1710; not conf.

Anna Maria Haas m. 27 Aug. 1720 Johann Philipp Reyer.

Abraham Haas was buried 12 July 1731, age 70 years 7 months. His wife
Anna was buried 29 Nov. 1724, age 56 years.

Georg Ludwig Haass m. 23 Jan. 1725 Anna Margaretha Stahler. "They went
to the Island of Pennsylvania in the year 1730." (Pastor's note).
They had children:
1. Maria Barbara, b. __ Feb. 1726, bp. 28 Feb. 1726
   Sp.: Maria Barbara Stahler
2. Johann Balthasar, b. 1 Sep. 1727, bp. 3 Sep. 1727
   Sp.: Johann Balthaser Haass

Hassloch Reformed KB:
Johannes Stahler and his wife Anna Margaretha had a daughter:
      Anna Margaretha, bp. 18 Apr. 1703

Johannes Stahler was bur. 30 Mar. 1737 age 64 years. Anna Margaretha
died sometime after the birth of a child 26 Apr. 1707 and before Johannes
married again about 1712.

Hassloch Gerichtsbuch:
Abraham Haas from "*Prokau by Loschitz*" granted citizenship 26 Nov. 1700.
Peter Staller (no origin given) granted citizenship 6 Nov. 1676.
Johannes Staller "from here" granted citizenship 26 Nov. 1700.

AMERICAN RECORDS

Philadelphia Adm. Book D: 161: 1741, est. # 46:
Letters of Administration to Margaret Haas, widow of Lodowick Haas, twp. of Heidelberg, co. of Philadelphia, dec'd. 26 May 1741.

Philadelphia Adm. # 46, 1741, probate packet:
Ludowich Hass; Bond taken out by Margaredt Haas of Heidelberg twp., Lancaster co., widow; Michael Rith of Tulpehocken in said county, Yeoman; and Michael Meyser of Heidelberg twp.; dated 6 May 1741. She signed with her mark (H).
The inventory of the estate totaled £231.15.4; the plantation was valued at £90. Also mentioned in the inventory: the goods belonging to the smith shop of the deceased. Signed by George Graff and Anderes Saltzgeber.
The account was filed by Nicholas Swingle and Marg^t, his wife, formerly Haas, late widow of Lodowich Haas. The account indicates that money was paid to Conrad Weiser to pay the Proprietors for conveying of the plantation. Balance of est. to be divided between widow and 4 daughters. Account dated 5 May 1753. Margaret Swingle signed with her mark; he signed Nicolaus Schwingel.

Lancaster Deed Book G: 258:
Widow Margaret Haas patented 149 A on Tulpehocken Creek in 1741.

Margaret, the widow of Ludwig Haws of Tulpehocken m. (2) Nicholas Schwingle. The children of her first marriage were:
1. Anna Barbara, m. 6 Feb. 1753 John Georg Zöller,
   son of Henry Zöller, Sr., of Tulpehocken at
   Millbach Reformed Church.
2. Anna Margaret, m. 19 May 1752 Christian Schrack
   from Providence twp., Philadelphia co., at Christ
   Lutheran Church, Stouchsburg
3. Anna Catharina m. 9 Dec. 1760 John Adam Meusser,
   youngest son of Michael Meusser at Millbach Reformed Church
4. Fredrica Elisabeth m. 10 Mar. 1771 John Adam Steumle at
   Christ Lutheran Church, Stouchsburg

Johann Georg Zeller, b. ca. 1725; d. in Tulpehocken Township before 21 Apr. 1792; m. at Millbach Reformed Church 6 Feb. 1753, Anna Maria Barbara Haas, daughter of Ludwig *Hast of Muehlbach*; b. ca. 1731; d. 30 July 1815, aged 84. The entry of her death at Christ Tulpehocken states she had 14 children, 65 grandchildren and 111 greatgrandchildren. Trinity Reformed Church records show the baptisms of seven of the children:
1. Anna Maria, bp. 26 June 1754. Sp.: Henry Zeller
2. Andrew, bp. __ Sept. 1755
   Sp.: Andrew Saltzgeber and Anna Maria (the child's aunt)

3. Elizabeth, bp. __ June 1757
4. Margaret Elizabeth, bp. 15 June 1758.
    Sp.: Margaret Elizabeth Haas
5. Susanna, bp. 15 June 1767.
    Sp.: Leonard Schwartz and wife Elizabeth (the child's aunt)
6. John, bp. 14 Feb. 1768 at Christ Lutheran. Sp.: John Pontius
7. Jacob, bp. 25 Jan. 1770
8. Peter, bp. 25 Dec. 1771

Georg Zeller's will, written 26 Jan. 1791, and accepted for probate 21 Apr. 1792 provided for his wife Maria Barbara, and that she was to have the use of his plantation in Tulpehocken until his son Henry came of age. His son John was to have the plantation of 135 acres for £860, of which £200 was to be his portion. His son Adam was to have four tracts of land, 26 acres in all, with George's mill in Tulpehocken for £600, of which £200 was to be his portion. The son Henry was to have a plantation in Tulpehocken of 139 acres for £970, of which £200 was to be his portion. Andrew, the eldest son, having already received £200, was to have only £5. Jacob, the youngest son, was to have £200 when he came of age. Each of the daughters was also to receive £200: Elizabeth, wife of John Rigel, Margaret Elizabeth wife of John Kaderman, Catharina, wife of John Pottdorf (Battorf), Susanna, wife of Jacob Schneider, Maria Barbara Zeller, and the heirs of deceased daughter Maria. Exrs: sons Andrew and John. Wit: Henry Mayer and Frederick Miller.

HAAS, HYERONIMUS   67251 Freinsheim
Prelist
                        EUROPEAN RECORDS

Freinsheim Lutheran KB:
Hyeronimus Haas, citizen here, and wife Christina had one child bp. at Freinsheim:
1. Johann Hennrich bp. 15 July 1714
    Sp.: Johann Eberhardt Hass and Anna Margaretha ?Männgin, born in ?Wisick in Darmstattischen bey Giessen.

Although no marriage record for this couple appears in the Freinsheim records, it appears from a Pennsylvania record that the wife Christina might be Anna Christina, widow of Alexander Kraus [see immigrant Nicolaus Krauss].

                        AMERICAN RECORDS

Trappe Lutheran KB, Montgomery Co.:
Buried 22 Dec. 1752 - Haas, wife of Hieronymus Haas.
Buried 30 Jan. 1751 - Johan Heinrich Haass.

Conf. 1754 - Catharina Kraus, daughter of Nicolaus Kraus, granddaughter of Hieronymus Haas, age 18 years; reads fairly well.

Conf. 1758 - Jacob Lorentz Krohn, step-son of Hieronymus Haas, age 21.

Philadelphia Wills & Administrations index:
Johann Henry Haas   1750? (1751?) file 236   Will I: 366
Heronimus Hause   1761   file 53   Will M: 86

Hieronimus Hans, Philadelphia Co., nat. Sept. 1740
Henrich Hans, Philadelphia Co., nat. Sept. 1740

HAMERICH, HANS GEORG   67454 Hassloch
Snow *Lowther,* 1731   67251 Freinsheim
S-H, I: 54-57
Passengers on ship: Hans Jerg, Amaryllis Eliza, Paul, Margaretta, and Clara

EUROPEAN RECORDS

Hassloch Reformed KB:
Married 20 Feb. 1719 at Hassloch: Joh. Georg Hammerich, linen weaver, son of the deceased Hieronimus Hammerich from Freinsheim, with Maria Elisabetha, daughter of the deceased Jacob Biber, shoemaker here. Their children:
>   1. Johann Paul, b. 8 June 1720; bp. 9 June 1720
>   2. Johannes, b. 9 Apr. 1722; bp. 9 Apr. 1722; bur. 19 Apr. 1722
>   3. Anna Margretha, b. 19 Mar. 1723; bp. 19 Mar. 1723
>   4. Johann Peter, b. 13 Mar. 1724; bp. 15 Mar. 1724
>   5. Johann Henrich, b. 10 Jan. 1725; bp. 14 Jan. 1725
>   6. Maria Cretha, b. 4 Apr. 1726; bp. 7 Apr. 1726; bur. 15 Apr. 1726
>   7. Anna Margaretha, b. 15 Mar. 1727; bp. 16 Mar. 1727
>   8. Philip Lorentz, b. 2 Feb. 1730; d. soon after bp.

Jacob Biber, shoemaker, d. 30 Apr. 1715, no age given. His wife was Maria Catharina, named in the baptisms of their children 1701 and 1702; her death was not located in the KB.

Hassloch Gerichtsbuch:
Jacob Biber of Hassloch granted citizenship 19 Jan. 1703.
Hanss Georg Hammerich from Wiegmanshaussen granted citizenship 20 Jan.
1721. [Possibly Wichmannshausen = 36205 Sontra].

AMERICAN RECORDS

New Holland Lutheran KB, Lancaster Co., PA:
Joh. Georg Hammerich had a son Johan Jacob b. 26 Aug. 1733; sp. at the
baptism were Jacob Guisie and wife.

First Reformed Church, Lancaster, PA:
George Hamrick and wife had a daughter Maria Elisabeth bp. 1 May 1737.

Oley Hills Reformed KB, Berks Co., PA:
Paul Hammerich had a daughter bp. in 1756.

HAMMAN, PETER   Lachen-Speyerdorf=
HAMMAN, PHILIP   67435 Neustadt a.d. Weinstrasse
not in S-H

EUROPEAN RECORDS

Lachen-Speyerdorf Reformed KB:
Joh. Jacob Hammann and wife Anna Margretha had children:
　　　　1. Johann **Peter**, b. 15 Apr. 1733, bp. 19 Apr.; conf. 1748
　　　　2. Anna Elisabetha, b. 14 Sept. 1735
　　　　3. **Philip** Lorentz, b. 22 Oct. 1737
　　　　4. Georg Michael, b. 1741, died
　　　　5. Georg Michael, b. 25 Mar. 1742, bp. 27 Mar. 1742
　　　　6. Johann Paul, b. 7 Aug. 1745, bp. 8 Aug. 1745
　　　　7. Anna Catharina, b. 18 Mar. 1748, bp. 22 Mar. 1748

AMERICAN RECORDS

Maryland Black Books:
Philip and Peter Hammen signed a petition in Western MD in 1766.

Philip Haman nat. MD, 11 Sept. 1765

HAMMAN see also SAUERHEBER
Maria Catharina nee Theobald, married (1) Peter Hamman, m.(2) Jacob
Sauerheber; Hamman children came to PA with their mother.

HAMMAN, THOMAS Lachen-Speyerdorf=
Thistle of Glasgow, 1730 67435 Neustadt a. d. Weinstrasse
S-H, I: 31, 33, 34

EUROPEAN RECORDS

Lachen-Speyerdorf Reformed KB:
Georg Christoph Hamman, son of the late Georg Hamman, m. 9 Feb. 1689
Anna Catharina, daughter of the late Hans Jacob Schmitt. They had a son:
  Hans Thomas, bp. 22 Nov. 1700, conf. 1714

Thomas Hammann, son of Georg Christoph Hammann, m. 12 Oct. 1725
Susanna, daughter of Benedict Raderli of Mussbach [= 67435 Neustadt],
now living in Eysersthal. They had:
  1. Joh. Görg, b. 28 Apr. 1727, bp. 1 May 1727
    Sp.: Görg Hoos and Anna Elisabetha

Georg Christoph Hamman died 3 Dec. 1727, age 66 years, 7 months

AMERICAN RECORDS

New Goshenhoppen Reformed KB, Montgomery Co., PA:
Thomas Hamman and wife Susan had children:
  2. Anna Maria, bp. 4 June 1732
    Sp.: Anna Maria, wife of Christian Lehman [q.v.]
  3. Susan, bp. 9 May 1736
    Sp.: Christian Leeman and daughter Anna Mary

Tohickon Reformed KB, Bucks Co., PA:
Thomas Haman and Susanna were sp. in 1754 for a child of John Leil.

George Haman and wife Maria Magdalena had:
    1. Maria Catharina, b. 20 June 1756, bp. 11 July 1756
      Sp.: John Haman, Catharina Gilger.
    2. Anna Barbara, b. 26 June 1758, bp. 13 Aug. 1758
      Sp.: Valentin Rohr and wife.

Philadelphia Wills and Administrations:
Thomas Hamon, 1755   Adm. G: 40.

HAMMEL, JACOB   Lachen-Speyerdorf=
Leslie, 1749   67345 Neustadt a. d. Weinstrasse
S-H, I: 419

EUROPEAN RECORDS

Lachen Reformed KB:
Hans Wilhelm Hamel, son of Hans Hammel, *Anwalt* at Speyerdorf, m. 25
Jan. 1682 Maria Catharina, daughter of Hans Lenhard Meck. Son:
        Johannes, bp. 7 Sept. 1684

Died 29 Oct. 1690 - Hans Wilhelm Hammel, elder here.

Died 16 Nov. 1690 - the deceased Hans Wilhelm Hammel's widow, named
Maria Catharina.

Johannes Hammel, single, son of the late Willhelm Hammel former
Gemeinsmann here, m. 13 Mar. 1715 Anna Catharina, widow of the late
Martin Pranck, former linenweaver at [76726] Germersheim. Children:
        1. Anna Maria, bp. 7 May 1716, died 1717
        2. Anna Christina, b. 4 June 1718; conf. 1732
        3. Johann Henrich, bp. 24 Aug. 1720; conf. 1734
        4. Anna Maria Barbara, bp. 17 Jan. 1723
        5. Johann Jacob, b. 16 May 1727; conf. 1741
            Sp.: Jacob Lehemann

Died 25 July 1730, Johannes Hammel, *Gemeinsmann* here, age 46 years.

HAUENSTEIN, CONRAD   Ober Lustadt=
HAUENSTEIN, GEORG JACOB   67363 Lustadt
Polly, 1765
S-H, I: 704

EUROPEAN RECORDS

Ober Lustadt Reformed KB:
Conrad Hauenstein and wife Barbara had children:
        1. **Georg Jacob**, b. 23 Jan. 1746, bp. 25 Jan. 1746
            Sp.: Georg Jacob (into center of book) and
            Maria Ursula Hauenstein

2. Maria Elisabetha, b. 4 May 1749, bp. 7 May 1749
   Sp.: Sebastian Herder and Maria Elisabetha
3. Jörg Nicolaus, b. 20 Aug. 1755, bp. 24 Aug. 1755
   Sp.: Jorg Nicolaus Ott and Maria Apollonia Ott,
   both single

AMERICAN RECORDS

Fourteen passengers on the ship *Polly* in 1765, listed in close proximity to one another on the list (S-H, I: 704), all appear in the Oberlustadt records: Andreas Heintz, Christian Wunder, **Conrad Hauenstein, Georg Jacob Hauenstein**, Christoph Strigel, Johann Leon[d] Devil (Deubel), Andres Ehresmann, Peter Zeiler, Georg Aadam Bresler, Johan Michael Dühmer, Jacob Wunder, Jacob Faut, Georg Simon Haushalter, Geo. Adam Teis.

HAUENSTEIN, HENRICH   Ober Lustadt=
Royal Union, 1750   67363 Lustadt
S-H, I: 432

EUROPEAN RECORDS

Ober Lustadt Reformed KB:
Johannes Hauenstein and wife Anna Appolonia had the following son:
   Joh. Heinrich, bp. 29 Mar. 1722
   Sp.: Joh. Heinrich Theiss, single

AMERICAN RECORDS

Six immigrants are listed together on the passenger list of the *Royal Union,* and all are found in the Lustadt records: Henrich Hauenstein, Casper Schmidt, Philip (X) Prike, Hans (X) Prike, Hans Michel Bauersachs, and Andreas Hertzog.

Lancaster County, PA, Deed Abstracts, H282b, L33:
Henry Houenstein is mentioned as a adj. landowner in several deeds in Rapho Twp., Lancaster Co. in 1765. The deeds pertain to land of Tobias Kuster, and name the children of Tobias Kuster: John, Anna, Henry, and Abraham.

Lancaster County Will Abstracts:
One George Hauenstein is named exr. of the will of George Blattenberger, Rapho Twp., dated 9 Oct. 1791. George Hauenstein is also named as a son-in-law in this will, married to Blattenberger's daughter Rosina.

Pennsylvania Census, 1790: Manheim, Lancaster Co., PA:
George Howenstone, 1 male over 16, 3 Males under 16, 4 females.

HAUERWAS, HEINRICH   67454 Hassloch
Snow *Lowther,* 1731
S-H, I: 55, 56, 57
Names on list: Henrich, Margaretta, Margaretta Jr., Philippena, and Anna
Barbara (Havervass, Howervass)

EUROPEAN RECORDS

Hassloch Reformed KB:
Married 17 Aug. 1712: Joh. Henrich Hauerwas, son of the deceased Philip
Hauerwas of [35039] Marpurg in Hessen, with Ursula Elisabeth, daughter
of the deceased Melchior Glässer. Their children:
    1. Anna Margaretha, b. 2 Sept. 1714, bp. 5 Sept. 1714
    2. Anna Maria, b. 21 July 1718; bp. 24 July 1718, d. 2 Aug. 1718
    3. Philippina Margaretha, b. 18 Sept. 1721; bp. 21 Sept. 1721
    4. Maria Catharina, b. 6 May 1724; bp. 10 May 1724

Hassloch Lutheran KB:
Buried 22 Nov. 1716: Anna Barbara Glässler, age 67 years. [This may be the
widow of Melchior "Glässer"; the name is consistently Glässler in the
Lutheran KB.]

Buried 20 July 1724: Ursula Elisabetha Haurwass, age 40 years, 10 months.

Hassloch Reformed KB:
Henrich Hauerwas, widower, m. (2) 28 Oct. 1724 Maria Margaretha,
daughter of the deceased Joh. Heinrich Scholl. One child of this marriage
recorded at Hassloch:
    Anna Barbara, bp. 12 Sept. 1725

Johann Heinrich Scholl, master joiner, d. 9 Dec. 1716, age 68 y. His widow,
Maria Sara Scholl, was buried 21 Aug. 1732, age 73 y.

Hassloch Gerichtsbuch:
Henrich Hauerwas from [35039] Marburg, *hochfürstl. Hessen Casselisch.
Jurisdiction,* was granted citizenship 20 Jan. 1721.

Henrich Scholl from [67157] Wachenheim was granted citizenship 27 Feb. 1708.

AMERICAN RECORDS

New Holland Lutheran Church, Lancaster County, PA:
In 1735, Anna Margaretha Auerwassin sp. a child of Carl Burckhardt.

Henrich Aurwasser signed the Muddy Creek Reformed Church Doctrine in 1743. In 1748, Henrich and wife Anna Gretha were sp. at a baptism there.

Muddy Creek Moravian records, Lancaster Co., PA;
Anna Barbara, daughter of Henrich Auwasser, m. in Dec. 1741 Heinrich Brendel.

Berks County Abstracts of Wills:
Henry Auerwasser of Brecknock Twp., Berks County, left a will dated 24 Nov. 1763, probated 5 May 1764. He names his wife Margaret and the following heirs: Henry Brendle, Philipina Merkin. Conrath Hart and his wife were disinherited "because of their bad and good-for-nothing words." Young Henry Brendle was named executor.

HAUSAMEN, JOHANN VALENTIN   67259 Heuchelheim
Prelist

EUROPEAN RECORDS

Heuchelheim Lutheran KB:
Joh. Valentin Hausamen m. 13 Aug. 1709 Susanna Strupp, born in Epstein [Eppstein, Pfalz = 67227 Frankenthal]. They had chidlren:
1. Anna Catharina, b. 14 June 1710
   Sp.: Joh. Jacob Fruhman and Anna Catharina [She em. 1734 with her second husband Jacob Rumfeld, q.v.]
2. Anna, b. 3 Oct. 1711
3. Joh. Andreas, b. 15 Jan. 1714
4. Johannes, b. 19 Aug. 1715
5. Joh. Georg, b. 23 Aug. 1716

There are indications in the record that the Hausamen family was originally from Switzerland.

AMERICAN RECORDS

Valentin Hausamen was residing in Skippack in 1730. He signed a letter that year. (See History of Goshenhoppen Charge).

Trappe Lutheran Church, Montgomery Co., PA:
Conf. 1753 - Susanna Hausamin, daughter of Jurg Hausamin, deceased, and step-daughter of Melchior Herter, age 15.

HAUSHALTER, CHRISTIAN   Ober Lustadt=
Britannia, 1764   67363 Lustadt
S-H, I: 693

EUROPEAN RECORDS

Ober Lustadt Reformed KB:
Jörg Simon Haushalter and wife Anna Maria had a son:
  Christian, b. 3 Dec. 1743, bp. 8 Dec. 1743
  Sp.: Christian Hellman, single and his
  mother Anna Barbara

AMERICAN RECORDS

Seven passengers from Oberlustadt are listed together on the passenger list of the ship *Britannia* in 1764: Johann Bernhart Ott, Johann Andreas Schmitt, **Christian Haushalter,** Georg Heinrich Schmitt; further on the list are Johann Martin Ott, Carl Garaus (see Jahraus), Vallentin Stettler.

HAUSHALTER, GEORG SIMON   Ober Lustadt=
Polly, 1765   67363 Lustadt
S-H, I: 704

EUROPEAN RECORDS

Ober Lustadt Reformed KB:
Jörg Simon Haushalter and Anna Maria had children:
  1. Jörg Simon, b. 20 Mar. 1741
   (probably the 1765 imm.)
   Sp.: Jacob Lehr and Maria Eva
  2. Christian, b. 3 Dec. 1743, bp. 8 Dec. 1743 [q.v.]
   Sp.: Christian Hellmann, single and his
   mother A. Barbara

3. Eva Maria, b. 5 Sept. 1746, d. 29 Sept. 1746
4. Maria Eva, b. 27 Oct. 1749
5. Anna Margaretha, b. 1 mar. 1753, bp. 4 Mar. 1753
6. Stillborn child, b. 14 May 1756, d. 14 May 1756
7. Joh. Jörg, b. 28 Sept. 1757, bp. 29 Sept. 1757

Fritz Braun and Friedrich Krebs. "Pennsylvania Dutch Pioneers from South Palatine Parishes", *The Pennsylvania Dutchman,* **8 (Spring, 1957):**
Haushalter, Georg Simon - arrived in Philadelphia on the ship *Polly,* 24 Aug. 1765, with the brothers Christian and Johann Jakob Wunder as well as Johann Jacob Fauth. Since he wrote his name immediately after Fauth in the ship's list and the name Haushalter appears in Ober- and Niederlustadt in the period involved, we may assume that the emigrant is connected with the Haushalter family listed in the Church Register of Oberlustadt. The only point of uncertainty is whether the father Jörg Simon Haushalter emigrated with the family or whether the son Jörg Simon Haushalter emigrated alone.

AMERICAN RECORDS

Fourteen passengers on the ship *Polly* in 1765, listed in close proximity to one another on the list (S-H, I: 704), all appear in the Oberlustadt records: Andreas Heintz, Christian Wunder, Conrad Hauenstein, Georg Jacob Hauenstein, Christoph Strigel, Johann Leon[d] Devil (Deubel), Andres Ehresmann, Peter Zeiler, Georg Aadam Bresler, Johan Michael Dühmer, Jacob Wunder, Jacob Faut, **Georg Simon Haushalter**, Geo. Adam Teis.

HAUSMAN, JOHANN PHILIPP   67256 Weisenheim am Sand
Lydia, 1749
S-H, I: 422

EUROPEAN RECORDS

Weisenheim am Sand:
Johannes Haussman and wife Anna Elisabetha had:
1. Joh. Dietrich, bp. 1717
2. Joh. Peter, bp. 1718
3. Johannes, bp. 2 Feb. 1723
   Sp.: Johannes Sahler, single
4. **Joh. Philipp**, bp. 1 Aug. 1725
   Sp.: Joh. Philipp Waldman from Hessen

5. Anna Margaretha, bp. 6 Aug. 1732
   Sp.: Joh. Wilhelm Lentz and Anna Margaretha
   (daughter of Christoph Sahler).

AMERICAN RECORDS

York County Abstracts of Wills:
Philip Houseman, York Twp. 20 Mar. 1758 - 26 Apr. 1758
Mentions minor children (not named).
Exrs: Christian Zangrey and Anthony Kirkhart.

York Orphans Court Book A p. 142, dated 27 May 1760
Heirs of Christian Zangree, dec'd:
Widow (named in one record as Anna Margareta, in another record as Anna Maria).
Ch.: Christian Zangree, Jr., Mary Housman, widow, Elisabeth wife of George Myer, Susannah wife of Joseph Burkert.

Rev. Jacob Lischy's records, York Co., PA:
Philip Hausman and wife Maria had:
      1. Heinrich, bp. 31 Aug. 1755
        Sp.: Heinrich Amend

HAUTZ, JOHANN PHILIP   67454 Hassloch
Thistle of Glasgow, 1730
S-H, I: 31, 33, 34

EUROPEAN RECORDS

Hassloch Reformed KB:
Johann Wendel Hautz and his wife Anna Catharina had children, the first two born before the church record starts:
      1. Juliana Sophia m. 7 Apr. 1721 Joh. Nickolaus Füsser [q.v.]
      2. Anna Catharina m. 2 Feb. 1723 Herr Johann Wilhelm
        Leichthammer, Organist.
      3. Johann Jacob, bp. 22 Jan. 1702, died 1702.
      4. Johann Jacob, bp. 9 Feb. 1703
      5. Catharina Margretha, bp. 9 Apr. 1704;
        she m. 20 Feb. 1726 Moses Völckle.
      6. Johann Ulrich, bp. 1 Sept. 1706
      7. Johann Philipp, bp. 28 Oct. 1708

8. Johann Henrich Christoph, bp. 15 Feb. 1711;
  he m. 3 Feb. 1734 Maria Clara Elisabetha Müller.
9. Philipp Lorentz [q.v.], b. 10 Sept. 1713, bp. 11 Sept. 1713

Anna Catharina, wife of Joh. Wendel Hautz, d. 16 Mar. 1716.
Johann Wendel Hautz, master potter, m. (2) 26 Apr. 1719 Anna Catharina, widow of Joh. Henrich Knorr, former shoemaker at B---feld, Oberamt Otzberg. [No children to this marriage. Wendel Hautz died 5 Feb. 1723 in Hassloch, age 54 years.]

AMERICAN RECORDS

Johann Philip Hautz m. Anna Margaret Royer (Rheyer, Reyer), b. 1 June 1713, daughter of Sebastian Rheyer from Böhl [q.v.] They lived in Bethel Twp., then in Lancaster County, now in Lebanon County, PA.

Swatara Reformed KB, Jonestown, Lebanon Co., PA:
Philip Hautz and wife Anna Margaret had:
  Philip Lorentz, bp. 16 Dec. 1740
    Sp.: Philip Lorentz [probably Hautz] and wife Eva.
  John Christopher, b. 20 Jan. 1753
    Sp.: Christopher Reier and wife Catharina

Joh. Philip Hautz d. 4 Dec. 1766, leaving a will recorded in
Lancaster Will Book Y-2, p. 289:
Wife: Margaretha. Dated 2 Dec. 1766.
To son Henry, the old plantation on Swatara Creek; to son George the plantation on the other side of Swatara Creek. Son Wendel to have £5 aforehand, before his brothers and sisters. Sons Philip Lawrence and Stophel have a tract between them at Rough Mountain, son Philip Lawrence to have 150 A. and youngest son Stophel to have 100 A. thereof. My two youngest daughters shall have £10 before their brothers and sisters. Whereas I have four children under age, son Philip Lawrence Hautz and son-in-law John Weber are appointed guardians. Wit.: John Casper Stover, Jr., Philip Wolff.

Will of Anna Margaritha Hautz, dated 1 Dec. 1788, probated 24 Apr. 1789. Bethel twp., Dauphin co., widow of 22 years of the deceased Philip Hautz. Names children: son Henry, son Wendel, daughters Magdalene and Elisabeth, son Philip Lawrence, daughter Juliana, son Christopher, daughters Eva and Anna Mary. To the heirs of my deceased son George, namely Catharine, Philip Jacob and Henry, to have income from their father's plantation. Executor: Samuel Royer of Bethel Twp., Berks Co., PA. Wit.: Heinrich Battorf, Fredrick Siebert.

HAUTZ, PHILIP LORENTZ age 23   67454 Hassloch
Friendship, 1738
S-H, I: 226, 228, 230

EUROPEAN RECORDS

Hassloch Reformed KB:
Philip Lorentz Hautz was b. 10 Sept. 1713, the son of Johann Wendel and Anna Catharina Hautz.
[For additional family data, see his brother Johann Philip Hautz.]

AMERICAN RECORDS

Christ Lutheran Church, Stouchsburg, Berks Co., PA:
Philip Lorentz Hautz m. Eva Walborn. Baptisms of the following children were found:
  1. Maria, b. 23 Jan. 1744; bp. 27 Mar. 1744 Christ Lutheran Church
  2. Anna Catharina, b. 6 Aug. 1745; bp. 3 Mar. 1746, Christ Lutheran Church
  3. Anna Maria, bp. 3 days before Pentecost (?1751), Swatara Reformed Church, Lebanon Co.
  4. Balser, b. 3 July 1757; bp 17 Aug. 1757, Christ Lutheran Church

Lancaster County Will Abstracts:
Philip Lorentz Hautz of Bethel Twp. left a will dated 17 May 1787, filed at Lancaster. The will mentions his wife and the following children: Wendel, Baltzer, Christian, Catharina wife of Leonard Gunckel, and son-in-law Samuel Royer.

Additional family records appear in St. Paul's (Klopp's) Church records, Bethel Twp., Lebanon County, PA.

HAUTZ, SUSANNA   67454 Hassloch
HAUTZ, EVA ELISABETH
Ship unknown, exact date of emigration unknown but before 1745.

EUROPEAN RECORDS

Hassloch Reformed KB:
Christoph Hautz, son of the dec'd Jacob Hautz, former *Gerichtsverwandten,* m. 22 Feb. 1713 at Hassloch, Anna Margaretha, daughter of Hans Adam

Neu. They had nine children baptized at Hassloch. Two of the daughters appear in Pennsylvania records. It is possible that the entire family emigrated; therefore the children are all listed here; the father listed as a master potter in some records:

1. Joh. Barthol, b. 26 Oct. 1713
2. Juliana Sophia, b. 27 Aug. 1715; conf. 1729, age 14.
3. Joh. Jacob, b. 18 Dec. 1716; conf. 1731, age 14
4. Susanna, b. 9 Nov. 1718, bp. 11 Nov. 1718
5. Joh. Andreas, b. 25 Mar. 1723; d. 4 June 1729
6. Eva Elisabetha, b. 25 Mar. 1723; conf. 1737, age 14
7. Joh. Friedrich, bp. 2 Feb. 1726; conf. 1741, age 15
8. Johannes, b. 13 Jan. 1728; conf. 1741, age 13
9. Joh. Nicolaus, b. 26 May 1732

Died 12 Sept. 1739, Joh. Christoff Hautz, age 54 years, 5 months.

Hans Adam Neu, father of Anna Margaretha Hautz, d. 7 Mar. 1726, age "from 70 to 80 years."

Hassloch Gerichtsbuch:
Hans Adam New from Geysselberg [67715 Geiselberg] Oberamt Lautern, granted citizenship 1 Dec. 1712.

AMERICAN RECORDS

Heidelberg Moravian Church, Berks Co., PA:
Died 20 Apr. 1777, Eva Elisabeth Keller, widow, nee Haus. She was born in Hassloch 29 Mar. 1723. She came to this country single and was married to the widower Johannes Keller on 13 Oct. 1745. He d. 14 Jan. 1767.

Muddy Creek Lutheran KB, Lancaster Co., PA:
Susanna Hauts m. 16 June 1745 Johan Philip Hertz. Three of their children were bp. at Muddy Creek:

1. Susanna Catharina, bp. 25 May 1746
2. Philip Petrus, bp. 9 Aug. 1749
3. Hans Bernhart, bp. 12 June 1751

HAUTZ, PHILIP PETER   67454 Hassloch
Minerva, 1768
S-H, I: 721

EUROPEAN RECORDS

Hassloch Reformed KB:
Joh Ulrich Hautz, tailor, son of Joh. Barthel Hautz, master tailor, m. 15 May 1721 Hedwig Sophia Susanna, daughter of the late Johann von der ?Vohl or ?Nahl, former citizen at [67346] Speyer. They had children:
1. Sophia Christina, b. 26 Mar. 1722, bp. 29 Mar. 1722
2. **Philip Peter**, b. 6 Mar. 1724, bp. 12 Mar. 1724, mother listed as Sophia Magdalena.
3. Johann Marx, bp. 26 Aug. 1725; conf. 1739; d. 1749.
4. Joh. Jacob, posthumus, b. 27 June 1727; conf. 1742, age 14.

The father Ulrich Hautz d. 28 Apr. 1727, age 28 years. The widow of Ulrich Hautz married (2) 12 Jan. 1729 Johann Georg Löchner [q.v.], tailor, son of the late Joh. Georg Löchner, master tailor in [67149] Meckenheim.

AMERICAN RECORDS

Rev. Anthony Hautz, b. 4 Aug. 1758, in Germany is identified by Dr. Hinke in *Ministers of the German Reformed Congregations in Pennsylvania and Other Colonies* as a son of the Philip Peter Hautz who arrived on the ship Minerva in 1768. Rev. Anthony Hautz studied theology at Lancaster and served as pastor at Muddy Creek and Cocalico in 1787.

Philip Peter Hautz evidently resided elsehwere prior to his emigration to Pennsylvania. His marriage and the birth of the son Anthony are not recorded in the Hassloch Church records.

St. John's Union KB, Fredericksburg, Lebanon Co., PA:
Philip Peter Hautz and wife Catharine were sp. in 1782 for a child of George Philip Eisenhauer.

HEGELY (HÄGELE), TOBIAS
Johnson, 1732
S-H, I: 71, 75, 77

Ober Lustadt=
67363 Lustadt

EUROPEAN RECORDS

Ober Lustadt Reformed KB:
Tobias Hägely and Anna Appolonia had children:
1. Joh. Adam, b. 2 June 1726, bp. 7 June 1726
   Sp.: Joh. Adam Deubel and Maria Ursula
2. Anna Maria, ? Mar. 1729
   Sp.: Nicolaus Wenner and Anna Maria

AMERICAN RECORDS

Trinity Lutheran KB, New Holland, Lancaster Co.:
Tobias Högele had:
1. Joh. Mattheis, b. 30 Aug. 1733, bp. 16 Sept. 1733
   Sp.: Mattheis Wendrich
2. Maria Margaretha, b. 3 Feb. 1735, bp. 17 Feb. 1735
   Sp.: Philip Eckert and wife Maria Margaretha

HEILMAN, ANDREAS, age 29
Harle, 1736   67259 Kleinniedesheim
S-H, I: 155, 158, 160
   with Maria Elisabeth, age 28

EUROPEAN RECORDS

Gross- and Kleinniedesheim Lutheran KB:
Joh. Valentin Heylman and wife Anna Catharina had children:
1. Anna Margaretha, b. 1700
   Sp.: Anna Margaretha, wife of Nicolas Vesper of Heuchelheim
2. Catharina Christine, b. 170?
   Sp.: Hans Jacob Tackerman and Catharina Christina
3. **Andreas, b. 30 June 1707, bp. 3 July 1707**
   Sp.: Andreas Heÿlmann of Kleinniddesheim
4. Joh. Valentin, b. 3 Apr. 1710, bp. 6 Apr. 1710
   Sp.: Joh. Valentin, son of Ludwig Schreiber of Heuchelheim
5. Anna Barbara, b. 12 Sept. 1714, bp. 14 Sept. 1714
   Sp.: Anna Barbara, wife of Hans Jacob Fillman of Heuchelheim

Joh. Valentine Heÿlman died in 1715.

Andreas Heÿlmann, son of the late Valentin Heÿlmann m. 21 Feb. 1730
Maria Elisabetha, [b. 23 June 1709], daughter of the late Johannes Müller
of Heuchelheim. They had:
1. Joh. Wendel, b. 10 Dec. 1730
2. Maria Catharina, b. 30 Nov. 1732
3. Georg Bernhard, b. __ ___ 1734 (entry not complete)

Emigration record:
Werner Hacker, *Auswanderungen aus Rheinpfalz und Saarland*:
#5453 Heilmann, Andreas, Grossniddesheim/Freimersheim, wishes to go to PA, 11 Apr. 1736.
#5454 Heilman, Valentin, Grossniddesheim, manumitted, to go to PA, 11 Apr. 1736.

HEILMAN, ANTON   67259 Kleinniedesheim
ca. 1721
prelist

EUROPEAN RECORDS

Gross- and Kleinniedesheim Lutheran KB:
Anthon Heilman and wife [Maria Salome] had sons:
    Johannes, b. 16 Oct. 1710, bp. 21 Oct. 1710
    Heinrich, dates unknown

AMERICAN RECORDS

Muhlenberg's Journals: Vol III, p. 180-181: Aug. 3, 1778.
Johannes Heilman, son of Anthon Heilman, b. 16 Oct. 1710 in Kleinniedesheim, and bp. on 21 same month. He came to this country with his parents when he was young, married Anna Maria Croesman in 1736, had 10 children, 8 still living and all married. Johannes Heilman was buried 3 Aug. 1778 in Skippach near the Mennonite meeting house. The deceased formerly lived in this neighborhood and was an Elder of the Providence Congregation. Several years ago he bought a place a few miles from Barren Hill Church and he was also an Elder of that congregation. He had a very large family, but he still had to undergo the experience of being plundered by the English during those war times and robbed of his personal property. His parents had helped to establish the burial place near the Mennonite meeting house, and therefore had burial rights there.

Augustus (Trappe) Lutheran KB, Montgomery Co., PA:
Johannes and Anna Maria Heilmann had children:
    1. Antonius, b. 25 Sept. 1737, bp. 11 Oct. 1737; conf. 1752
       Sp.: Antonius Heilmann and wife Marri Salmen
    2. Anna Katarina, b. 7 Aug. 1739, bp. 31 Aug. 1739
       Sp.: Johannes Crössman and wife Anna Katarina
    3. Marri Salmm, b. 23 Feb. 1741, bp. 15 Mar. 1741
       Sp.: Andon Heilman and wife Marri Salmm

4. Johannes, b. 27 Sept. 1742, bp. 6 Jan. 1743
    Sp.: Frithrig Mahrsteller and Anna Barbara
5. Lisa Margreda, b. 24 Jan. 1744, bp. 4 Feb. 1744
    Sp.: Andon Heilmann and wife Marri Salm
6. Johannes, b. 12 Nov. 1747, bp. 2 Dec. 1747
    Sp.: Nicolaus Moritz and wife Catharina
7. Anna Maria, b. 8 Apr. 1750, bp. 28 May 1750
    Sp.: Heinrich Heilman's wife Anna Maria
8. Johann Jacob, b. 27 Nov. 1751, bp.28 Jan. 1752
    Sp.: Johann Jürg Croesmann of Indianfield
9. Johann Heinrich, b. 20 Jan. 1754, bp. 19 Feb. 1754

Heinrich Heilman and wife Anna Maria had:
1. Anthonius, b. 8 Nov. 1742, bp. 19 Dec. 1742
    Sp.: Anthoni Heilman
2. Heinrich, b. 24 Mar. 1745, bp. 14 Apr. 1745
    Sp.: Anthonius Heilmann
3. Anna Maria, b. 15 Aug. 1747, bp. 27 Sept. 1747
    Sp.: Johannes Heilmann's wife Anna Maria
4. Johann Henrich, b. 20 June 1752, bp. 21 June 1752
    Sp.: Anthon Heilmann
5. Sarah, twin, b. 4 May 1754, bp. 28 May 1754
6. Anna, twin, b. 4 May 1754, bp. 28 May 1754
7. Margretha, b. 1 Mar. 1756

Johan Michel Heilman and Anna Maria had:
1. Elisabetha, b. 3 Dec. 1742, bp. 21 Apr. 1743
    Sp.: Johan Wendel Ernst and wife Anna Katarina
2. Maria Margretha, b. 9 Aug. 1746, bp. 2 Sept. 1746
    Sp.: Melchior Heiter
3. Margretha, b. 11 Oct. 1747, bp. 1 Dec. 1747
    Sp.: Johan Wendel Ernst and wife Margretha
4. Catharina, b. 24 Dec. 1749, bp. 1 Mar. 1750
    Sp.: Parents

Conf. 1749 - Elisabeth Heilman nee DuFrenin, age 19 y.
Jurg Adam Heilman m. __ Feb. 1745 Elisabeth Dufrene, beyond the Schuylkill.
Jurg Adam Heilmann and Elisabeth had:
1. Johannes, b. 2 July 1745, bp. 15 Aug. 1745
    Sp.: Wendel Ernst
2. Michael, b. 11 June 1748, bp. 1 Oct. 1748
    Sp.: Michael Heilmann and wife

3. Catharina, b. 25 Sept. 1750, bp. 1 Feb. 1751
    Sp.: Parents

Buried 26 Sept. 1745, Maria Salome Heilman, wife of Anthon, age 73 y.

Buried 16 July 1759, Anthon Heilman, church warden of this congregation, age 88 years.

Anthon Heilman, son of Johannes Heilman, m. 27 Nov. 1760 Sarah Thomas.

Philadelphia Co. Will Abstracts:
Hallman, Anthony. Skippack, Co. of Philadelphia, Yeoman. January 25, 1755. August 3, 1759. L.300.
Children: John, Dorothy Heizer, Christian Seffebber, Catherine Kresseman, Mary Salome Perkymer, Barbara Jacobs, Anna Maria Ketchy and Henry. Son-in-law: John Heizer. Grandchildren: Leonard, Valentine and George Perkymer. Exec: Henry Hallman. Witnesses: Deter Welchor, Charles Cornelius Rabotcaw.

Montgomery County Will Abstracts:
Hallman, Henry. Perkiomen and Skippack. January 31, 1800. October 10, 1803. 2.346.
To son Henry and son Anthony and daughter Catharine, wife of Jacob Creasamer, daughter Christiana, wife of Jacob Snyder, daughter Mary, wife of Matthias Ritter, 5 pounds each. To son Abraham, 100 pounds. To son Daniel, 95 pounds. Remainder of estate to be divided among 6 sons and 4 daughters: Jacob, Benjamin, John, Isaac, Daniel, Sarah, wife of Christian Mattis, Margaret, wife of Jacob Iset, Elizabeth, wife of Jacob Frontfield, Susanna, wife of John Groves. Execs: Sons Jacob and John. Wit: Henry Hunsicker, John Tyson.

HEIM, PAUL   67112 Mutterstadt
HEIM, HANS
James Goodwill, 1727
S-H, I: 10
Passengers: Paul and Hans Heim, 2 men, 6 in family

EUROPEAN RECORDS

Mutterstadt Reformed KB:
Hans Paulus Heim from Schweigenheim by Weissenburg m. 30 June 1706 Anna, daughter of Henrich Volcker from [67227] Epstein. (There is a 76889

Schweigen located in the southern Rheinland Pfalz, on the border near Wissembourg, Alsace.) They had children:
>   1. Anna Maria, b. 29 Dec. 1709 bp. 1713 in Ireland
>   2. Johannes, bp. 10 July 1712

Knittle, *Early Eighteenth Century Palatine Emigration:*
Appendix, p. 281
Returned to Holland in 1711: Heym, Paul and 2 persons

AMERICAN RECORDS

Rev. John Caspar Stoever's personal records:
Johannes Heim (Coventry) had a son:
>   Joh. Caspar, b. 9 Sept. 1740 bp. 19 Sept. 1740
>   Sp.: Caspar Kuehner

HEIM, WILHELM   67112 Mutterstadt
Thistle of Glasgow, 1730
S-H, I: 30, 31, 33

EUROPEAN RECORDS

Mutterstadt Reformed KB:
In 1715, Wilhelm Heim sponsored a child of Philip Groscost, a fellow passenger on the *Thistle of Glasgow.*

Mutterstadt Kontraktenprotokolle:
In 1729, Johannes Altmann and wife Maria Elisabeth bought property of Wilhelm Heim and Judith his wife, "as they had moved from here to Pennsylvania." Transaction recorded 1 June 1737.

Additional Data:
See also Fritz Braun, "Auswanderer aus der Umgebung von Ludwigshafen a. Rh. auf dem Schiff *Thistle of Glasgow* 1730," publication #8, *Schriften zur Wanderungsgeschichte der Pfälzer.*

AMERICAN RECORDS

Rev. John Caspar Stoever's records:
Wilhelm Heim of Coventry had children:
>   1. Joh. Christian, b. 1 Oct. 1731 bp. 24 Oct. 1731
>   Sp.: John Christian Schunck

2. Joh. Casper, b. 17 May 1734, bp. 22 May 1734
   Sp.: John Casper Schunck
3. Frantz Hugo, b. 17 Sept. 1738 bp. 10 Jan. 1739
   Sp.: Frantz Schunck and wife Elizabeth

HEINTZ, ANDREAS   Ober Lustadt=
Polly, 1765   67363 Lustadt
S-H, I: 704

EUROPEAN RECORDS

Ober Lustadt Reformed KB:
Jörg Adam Heintz and Maria Eva had a son:
       Andreas, b. 5 Oct. 1747, bp. 8 Oct. 1747
       Sp.: Andreas Kirchner and Agnesia

AMERICAN RECORDS

Fourteen passengers on the ship *Polly* in 1765, listed in close proximity to one another on the list (S-H, I: 704), all appear in the Oberlustadt records: **Andreas Heintz**, Christian Wunder, Conrad Hauenstein, Georg Jacob Hauenstein, Christoph Strigel, Johann Leon[d] Devil (Deubel), Andres Ehresmann, Peter Zeiler, Georg Aadam Bresler, Johan Michael Dühmer, Jacob Wunder, Jacob Faut, Georg Simon Haushalter, Geo. Adam Teis.

First Reformed KB, York, PA:
Andreas Heintz m. 18 Mar. 1783 Elisabet Rothrauf.

HEINTZ, GEORG JACOB   76835 Rhodt unter Rietburg
before 1765   Ober Lustadt=
                                                          67363 Lustadt

EUROPEAN RECORDS

Ober Lustadt Reformed KB:
Johann Adam Theiss of Oberlustadt and wife Maria Magdalena had children:
       1. Anna Maria, b. 22 Aug. 1729, bp. 27 Aug. 1729

    2. Anna Elisabetha, b. 11 Dec. 1731
    3. Maria Eva, b. 16 Apr. 1734, bp. 18 Apr. 1734
    4. **Maria Catharina**, b. 20 Feb. 1736, bp. 23 Feb. 1736
       She m. **Georg Jacob Heintz** of Roth; to Am.
    5. Joh. Georg, b. 17 June 1738, bp. 19 June 1738
    6. Lowisa, b. 21 Dec. 1741, bp. 24 Dec. 1741
       She m. Joh. Jacob Fauth [q.v.]; Em. 1765.

Braun and Krebs, "Pennsylvania Dutch Pioneers from South Palatine Parishes" in *The Pennsylvania Dutchman,* 8 (Spring, 1957):
Georg Jakob Heintz from Rhodt unter Rietburg, m. Maria Catharina Theiss, born at Oberlustadt, 20 Feb. 1736, daughter of Johann Adam Theiss of Oberlustadt and Magdalena Schmitt, "who married Georg Jakob Heintz from Roth and went with him to Pennsylvania..." (Document of December 3, 1765). [Brother-in-law of Johann Jakob Fauth, q.v.]

HEIPEL (HEYBEL), PAUL   67112 Mutterstadt
Prelist

EUROPEAN RECORDS

Mutterstadt Reformed KB:
Joh. Paul Heypel m. (1) 16 Nov. 1706 Anna Catharina, widow of the late Ulrich Neüman. Hans Paul Heybel and wife Anna Katharina had a son:
    Johannes, bp. 25 Nov. 1708

Paul Heybel, widower, m. (2) 2 May 1726 Agnes, daughter of the deceased Johann Rudolff of [55283] Nierstein.

Paul Heypel and wife Anna sponsors for Paul Ullrich, bp. 7 Jan. 1714, son fo Georg and Anna Maria Ullrich. This Paul Ullrich was a later emigrant from Mutterstadt, arriving in 1748 (q.v.).

No other children for Paul Heipel listed in the Reformed KB.

Mutterstadt Kontraktenprotokolle:
Several entries in this volume refer to disposition of land owned by Paul Heipel. All of them contain the notation "as he has moved to *Pensilvania* with his family." The land was sold at public auction. The entries are dated 1726 and 1728; the date of the recorded transactions was 1737.

Emigration record:
Werner Hacker, *Auswanderungen aus Rheinpfalz und Saarland*:
5575, Paul Heipel, from Mutterstadt, with his family to PA, sold property
1726. Record dated 29 May 1737.

HELLER, RUDOLFF   67454 Hassloch
HELLER, JACOB
prelist

EUROPEAN RECORDS

Hassloch Reformed KB:
Conf. Easter 1710, Rudolph Haller from Rhÿnach, Bern. [There is a CH-
5734 Reinach, AG, and CH-4153 Reinach, BL.]

Rudolff Heller and Anna Catharina had children:
1. Johann Jacob, b. 1 Apr. 1712, bp. 3 Apr. 1712
2. Anna Engel, b. 19 June 1714, bp. 24 June 1714
3. Joh. Conrad, b. 30 Dec. 1716, bp. 3 Jan. 1717; d. 30 Jan. 1717
4. Maria Magdalena, b. 4 July 1718, bp. 10 July 1718
[none of these chlidren were confirmed there.]

One Hans Jacob Heller, *Gemeinsmann*, and Anna Maria had one child:
Anna Helena, b. 13 Feb. 1716 in Böhl, bp. 16 Feb. 1716.

AMERICAN RECORDS

Heller's Reformed Church (also called Hill Church and Schaeffer's Church), Lancaster Co., PA:
Rudolff Heller, died 1734, took up a tract of land in Upper Leacock Twp.,
Lancaster Co., which was warranted to Jacob Heller in 1735. Jacob Heller
was an adjacent landowner to this tract in 1735; other adj. landowners to
Jacob Heller's land were Johannes Lein [John Line] and Michael Weidler.
The first church for this oldest Reformed congregation in Lancaster County
was built along the property line of Rudolff Heller [by 1735, belonging to
his son Jacob Heller] and Conrad Tempelman's tract (all Warrants dated
1735.) This congregation dates from 1727-1730; Conrad Tempelmann was
schoolmaster and reader for this congregation. Unfortunately, no early
church register for this congregation is known to survive; in fact, no records
exist before 1824.

Trinity Lutheran KB, New Holland, Lancaster Co., PA:
Jacob Heller and wife had a son:
> Johann Martin, b. 28 Sept. 1744

HELLMAN, PETER   Ober Lustadt=
Brothers, 1752   67363 Lustadt
S-H, I: 481

EUROPEAN RECORDS

Ober Lustadt Reformed KB:
Peter Hellmann and wf. Gertrud had a son:
> Joh. Peter, b. 17 Apr. 1739, bp. 19 Apr.1739
> Sp.: Joh. Peter Speck and Anna Maria
> Haaf, both single.

AMERICAN RECORDS

York County Land Records:
One Sebastian Hellman was taxed in Codorus Twp., York Co., PA in 1762.
He received a Warrant for 100 A on 3 July 1773; also 70 A on 28 Sept.
1774. Both tracts were patented to Peter Hellman in 1801.

HELLMAN, SEBASTIAN (BASTIAN)   Ober Lustadt=
Brothers, 1752   67363 Lustadt
S-H, I: 481

EUROPEAN RECORDS

Ober Lustadt Reformed KB:
Jacob Hellman and wife Anna Barbara had a son:
> Jörg Bastian, b. 8 Jan. 1725, bp. 14 Jan. 1725
> Sp.: Hans Jörg Schmitt and Cath.

Jörg Sebastian Hellman and wife Christina had a son:
> Theobald, b. 29 Apr. 1752, bp. 30 Apr. 1752

AMERICAN RECORDS

Rev. Jacob Lischy's records, York Co., PA:
One Sebastian Hellman and wife Margretha were sponsors for a child of
Lorentz Stambach in Mar. 1752; if this date is correct, it appears that this
is *not* the immigrant on the ship *Brothers*, 1752. He and wife Margretha had
four children bapt. in Lischy's records from 1752-1765, and they served as
sponsors in 1767 for a child of Christian Wonner [?Wunder, q.v.] and wife
Catharina.

HERCHELROTH, LORENTZ	67169 Kallstadt, Pfalz
Prelist	67167 Erpolzheim

EUROPEAN RECORDS

Kallstadt Reformed KB:
Hans Heinrich Herchelroth m. (1) 10 May 1664 Anna Catharina Leopold.
They had children:
    1. Hans Nickel, bp. 12 May 1667 at Dürkheim
    2. **Johannes Laurentius**, bp. 25 Apr. 1669 at Kallstadt

Hans Henrich Herchelroth m. (2) 6 Sept. 1681 Anna Elisabetha Keller.
Children of second marriage:
    3. Johann Henrich, bp. 10 Sept. 1682
    4. Sophia Elisabetha, bp. 31 May 1684
    5. Johannes Joachim, bp. 31 May 1684
    6. Johannes Joachimus, bp. 5 May 1686
    7. Jost Martin, bp. 3 Aug. 1687
    8. Maria Elisabetha, bp. 6 Nov. 1689

Erpolzheim Reformed KB:
Confirmed Pentecost, 1683, Lorentz Herchelroth, age 14, son of Henrich
Herchelroth of Callstatt.

AMERICAN RECORDS

Philadelphia Will Abstracts: Will Book G, p. 163:
Lorence Herkelbrod, Lampeter, Lancaster Co., cooper, dated 30 Aug. 1740 -
probated 17 Feb. 1744. Children: Henry, Valentine, John.
Exr: Henry Herkelbrod. Wit: Daniel Herman and Emanuel Carpenter.

Rev. John Casper Stoever's Records:
Valentin Herchelrodt m. 29 Dec. 1747 Elisabetha Meusser, Lebanon.

Valentin Herckelroth (Herckelroad, etc.) lived along the Tulpehocken Creek in what is today Myerstown. Myerstown as early as 1738 appeared on Scull's map as Herclerodes. The Herchelroth/Meier House, Myerstown, Pennsylvania.   Sketch by Viola Kohl Mohn.

Christ Lutheran Tulpehocken KB, Stouchsburg, Berks Co., PA:
Velte Herchelroth, widower, m. 31 May 1748 Barbara Unruh, widow of the late George Unruh [q.v.].

St. John's Reformed KB, Host, Berks Co.:
Conf. 1754, Henrich Herchelroth, Valentin's son.
Conf. 1754, Barbara Herchelroth, Valten's daughter.

Married 10 June 1754, Isaac Meyer and Catharina Herchelroth.

Trinity Tulpehocken Reformed KB, Jackson Twp., Lebanon Co., PA:
Jonas Fortune and wife had a son:
John Henry, bp. 10 June 1754
Sp.: John Henry Herchelroth and Catharine Meyer,
wife of Isaac Meyer of Conestoga.

Isaac Meyer and Catharine had:
1. Elizabeth, bp. 4 July 1755
   Sp.: Valentine Herchelroth and wife Barbara
2. Anna Maria, b. 5 Jan. 1759, bp. 25 Mar. 1759
   Sp.: Christian Ohrendorff
3. Catharine, b. 18 Nov. 1767, bp. 18 Nov. 1767
   Sp.: The mother

Burials, Trinity Tulpehocken Cemetery:
Isaac Meyers, b. 4 Jan. 1730, d. 15 July 1770
(Founder of Myerstown)

Valentine Hergelrat, Lancaster County, nat. by act, 1739.

HERGET, GEORG FRIEDRICH   67112 Mutterstadt
Edinburgh, 1750
S-H, I: 372

EUROPEAN RECORDS

Mutterstadt Reformed KB:
Joh. Peter Herget m. 25 May 1708 Maria Appolonia Funck. They had:
   1. **Georg Friedrich,** bp. 18 Apr. 1709
      Sp.: Georg Friedrich Krick, single, and Elisabetha Steinkonig
   2. Anna Maria, bp. 12 Feb. 1711
   3. Blasius, bp. 17 May 1717; died 16 Apr. 1796
   4. Joh. Peter [q.v.], bp 21 Nov. 1719

Georg Friederich Herget, son of Joh. Peter Herget, m. 10 Apr. 1736 Anna
Barbara Gärtner, daughter of the late Herr Conrad Gärtner, Reformed
schoolmaster here.   A notation by their marriage record: "moved to
Pennsylvania 1748." They had one child baptized at Mutterstadt:
      Georg Friederich b. 12 Mar. 1738 bp. 16 Mar. 1738
      Sp.: Friederich Krick and Anna Katharina nee Renner. Note under
this child's bp. record: "to Pennsylvania 1748."

PfFWKde, Band 6, Heft 5, p. 168:
Herr Joh. Conrad Gärtner died 10 Sept. 1732, age 54 y. 5 mo. less 5 days.
He had been the Reformed schoolmaster at Mutterstadt for over 26 years.
He was a son of Georg Gärtner, schoolmaster at Eppfenbach [= 74925
Epfenbach by Sinsheim]. He married Maria Elisabetha Scheiner, daughter
of Joh. Scheiner, citizen at [69198] Schriesheim. She died 13 Jan. 1733, age
55 y. 6 mo. 18 days. They had 6 sons and 2 daughters.

AMERICAN RECORDS

Rev. Jacob Lischy's personal records, York Co., PA:
One Freidrich Hercher (?Herget) and wife Anna Barbara were sponsors in
1752 for a child of Sebastian Barthleme (q.v.).

HERGET, PETER   67112 Mutterstadt
Two Brothers, 1750
S-H, I: 438 [Hergedt on list]

EUROPEAN RECORDS

Mutterstadt Reformed KB:
Joh. Peter Herget m. 25 May 1708 Maria Appolonia Funck. They had:
1. Georg Friedrich [q.v.], bp. 18 Apr. 1709
   Sp.: Georg Friedrich Krick, single, and Elisabetha Steinkönig
2. Anna Maria, bp. 12 Feb. 1711
3. Blasius, bp. 17 May 1717; died 16 Apr. 1796
4. **Joh. Peter,** bp. 21 Nov. 1719

Oggersheim Reformed KB:
Johann Peter Herget, son of Peter Herget of Mutterstadt, m. 26 Apr. 1746 Catharina, widow of the late Isaac Derein. They had children:
1. Susanna Elisabetha, bp. __ July 1747
2. Anna Catharina, b. 3 Apr. 1749 bp. 11 Apr. 1749

PfFWKde, Band 6, Heft 3, p. 77:
Isaac Derein, b. 21 Jan. 1714 at Oggersheim [=67071 Ludwigshafen], d. 10 June 1745. He m. (2) at Oggersheim 7 June 1738 Maria Catharina Marquart, daughter of the late Gabriel Marquart, citizen at [68161-69] Mannheim. She had previously married in 1735 Joseph (Johannes) Braun. She married (3) the emigrant Joh. Peter Herget. The four Derein children of her second marriage died young.

Joh. Peter Herget emigrated to Pennsylvania in 1750 with wife and children and his step-son Christian Braun. The Braun family was originally from Neckarelz [=74821 Mosbach].

Additional Data:
Fritz Braun, "18th Century Palatine Emigrants from the Ludwigshafen Area," *The Pennsylvania Dutchman* (1954): Johann Peter Herget, citizen of Oggersheim, received in 1750 permission to emigrate to Pennsylvania with his wife and children. This was granted upon payment of 60 florins tax plus 30 florins for his step-son Christoph Braun.

AMERICAN RECORDS

Frederick, MD, Reformed KB:
Died 16 Aug. 1789, Catharina Herget, wife of Peter Herget, age 70 y., 6 mo.

Christoph (Stoffel) Braun m. 9 Sept. 1761 Magdalena Mann [Mehn, daughter of George Mehn].

Frederick County Will Book GM2: 383:
Will of Peter Hargate, Sr. (evidently Peter Herget).
Christopher Brown was named as an heir.

1798 Land Assessment Book for Frederick Co., MD:
Stoffel Braun was assessed on a tract of land called "Okus Hime" (evidently a phonetic rendition of Oggersheim, the home in Germany.)

HERTZOG, ANDREAS   Ober Lustadt=
Royal Union, 1750   67363 Lustadt
S-H, I: 432

EUROPEAN RECORDS

Ober Lustadt Reformed KB:
Peter Herzog and wife Catharina had children:
1. Maria Catharina, bp. 2 Nov. 1721
   Sp.: Georg Schmitt and Catharina
2. Hans Georg, b. 3 Aug. 1724, bp. 7 Aug. 1724
   Sp.: Hans Georg Presler and Anna Barbara Weggler, single
3. Joh. Andreas, b. 27 Oct. 1730, bp. 29 Oct. 1730
   Sp.: Joh. Andreas Sch(mitt?) and Margaretha
4. Georg Nicolaus, b. 29 Oct. 1736, bp. 1 Nov. 1736
   Sp.: Georg Nicolaus Weppler and Anna Maria Weppler,
   both single.

Emigration record:
Werner Hacker, *Auswanderungen aus Rheinpfalz und Saarland*:
#6050, Andreas Hertzog from Niederlustadt to PA.

AMERICAN RECORDS

Six immigrants are listed together on the passenger list of the *Royal Union,* and all are found in the Lustadt records: Henrich Hauenstein, Casper Schmidt, Philip (X) Prike, Hans (X) Prike, Hans Michel Bauersachs, and **Andreas Hertzog**.

First Reformed Church, Philadelphia, PA:
Andrew Hertzog appears on a subscription list for salary of a minister in 1756.
Andrew Herzog from the Palatinate and wife Barbara had children:
1. Rebecca, b. 30 Apr. 1759, bp. 27 Oct. 1759; Sp.: parents
2. Andrew, bp. 14 Jan. 1761; Sp.: parents
   Sp.: Andrew Seiss and Cleophea Ludwig
3. Sarah, bp. 1763, 10 mo. old; d. 1763; Sp.: parents

4. Joseph, bp. 23 Feb. 1764; Sp.: parents
5. Andrew, b. 14 Mar. 1766, bp. 14 Apr. 1766; Sp.: parents
6. Jacob, b. 11 July 1768, bp. 16 Sept. 1768; Sp.: parents
7. Esther, b. 1 Dec. 1770, bp. 6 Jan. 1771; Sp.: parents
8. Maria, b. 26 Feb. 1773, bp. 8 Mar. 1773; Sp.: parents.

HESS, JEREMIAS   67112 Mutterstadt
Thistle of Glasgow, 1730
S-H, I: 30, 32, 33

EUROPEAN RECORDS

Mutterstadt Reformed KB:
Jeremias Hess and his wife Anna had been among the earlier emigration to England and Ireland in 1709. The pastor of Mutterstadt recorded in the church book that they sponsored Anna Maria Heim, daughter of Paul Heim [q.v.], baptized in Ireland. Two of the Hess children died in Ireland. The Hess and Heim families were among those returned to Holland in 1711.

Jeremias Hess and his wife Anna had children:
1. A son, b. ca. 1703
2. Hans Conrad, b. 3 May 1705 Mutterstadt; d. in Ireland
3. Elisabeth, b. 21 Oct. 1708 Mutterstadt; d. in Ireland
4. Christian, b. 14 July 1713 Mutterstadt; d. in Mutterstadt
5. Hans Conrad, bp. 19 Aug. 1714
6. Balthasar, bp. 8 Dec. 1717

Knittle, *Early Eighteenth Century Palatine Emigration:*
Appendix D, p. 281: Returned to Holland 1711: Jeremias Hess and 3 persons: Paul Heym and 2 persons.

Additional Data:
See also Fritz Braun, "Auswanderer aus der Umgebung von Ludwigshafen a. Rh. auf dem Schiff 'Thistle of Glasgow' 1730," publication #8, *Schriften zur Wanderungsgeschichte der Pfälzer.*

AMERICAN RECORDS

Jeremias Hess first appears in the records at Falckner Swamp, Montgomery County, when he sponsored a child of Johan Georg Schweinhart in 1730.

Jeremias Hess took up a warrant for a tract of land containing 100 acres on 9 Sept. 1734.

Philadelphia Will Book G, p. 101:
Jeremias Hess.
Dated 18 Apr. 1739, probated 11 Apr. 1743; mentions his children, 3 sons and 1 daughter: "Son Peter Hess, and my daughter Eve living in Maryland, they both received already their portion of Heritage;" balance of estate to two youngest sons, Conrad Hess and Baltzer Hess. The sons are to provide for his wife as long as she lived. No executor was named; on 11 Apr. 1743, Anna Hess, widow, renounced administration to her son Conrad Hess, Philadelphia County.

New Goshenhoppen Reformed KB, Montgomery Co., PA:
Peter Hess and wife had a son:
  Johann Henrich, bp. 12 Aug. 1733
  Sp.: Heinrich Rether [Roeder, q.v.] and wife

Williams Township congregation, Northampton Co., PA:
Balthasar Hess and wife Anna Maria had a son:
  Wilhelm, b. 18 June 1741 bp. 2 July 1741
  Sp.: Georg Wilhelm Ruhl and Gertraud

Balthaser Hess and wife Catharina sponsored a Volprecht child in 1752.

Peter Hess and wife Anna Margaretha had a child:
  Michael, b. 12 July 1741 bp. 21 July 1741
  Sp.: Michael Raupp and Anna Maria

HEYER, JOHAN FRIDERICH age 23   67161 Gönnheim
HEYER, VALLENDIN age 18
Lydia, 1743
S-H, I: 341, 342, 343
 (Surname spelled Hayer on A list. A Philip Hayer, age 31,
 also appears on the list. He is possible also a member of this family.
 There are many faded entries in the Gönnheim record.)

EUROPEAN RECORDS

Gönnheim Reformed KB:
Joh. Philip Heyer of Rummershausen, Hesse-Cassel (possible Rummelhausen = 63694 Limeshain) m. 6 Jan. 1711 Anna Elisabetha Bergtold. Their children:

1. Appolonia, bp. 8 Nov. 1711 at Friedelsheim
   Sp.: Joh. Georg Sorg and Anna Barbara
2. Joh., bp. 28 May 1713 at Gönnheim
   (Was his full name Joh. Philip?)
3. Anna Barbara, bp. 21 Aug. 1718; she m. Christian Kramer,
   [see Hans Adam Kramer family].
4. **Joh. Friderich,** bp. 1 Apr. 1720
   Sp.: Johannes Spannknebel and Anna Margaretha
5. Anna Elisabetha, bp. 24 Jan. 1723
6. **Joh. Valentin,** b. ca. 1724
   (All entries from June 1723 to Mar. 1725 faded.)

AMERICAN RECORDS

Pennsylvania Archives, Second Series, Vol. IX: 140:
Lititz Moravian Marriages, Lancaster Co.:
Frederick Hayer m. 1746 (no other date given) Margaret Schmoker.

Rev. Jacob Lischy's records, York Co., PA:
Friedrich Hayer and wife Catharina were sp. in 1747 for a child of Christian Krämer.

Valentin Heyer and Anna Catharina (her maiden name given in the First Reformed KB, York, is Weltzhoffer) had children:

1. Johann Jacob, bp. 3 Feb. 1751 (Lischy's record)
   Sp.: Jacob Welshoffer [q.v.] and Anna Catharina
2. Maria Elisabeth, bp. 26 Nov. 1752 (Lischy's record)
   Sp.: Johannes Comfort and Maria Elisabetha Welshoffer
3. Johannes, bp. 9 Mar. 1755 (Lischy's record)
   Sp.: Johannes Schultz and Eva Welshöfer
4. Joh. Georg, bp. 10 Jan. 1757 (Creutz Creek KB)
   Sp.: John George Spangeler and wife
5. Anna Maria, b. 7 Mar. 1760 bp. 4 June 1760 (Creutz Creek KB)
   Sp.: Anna Maria Schultz
6. Eva, b. 26 Feb. 1763, bp. 20 Mar. 1763 (First Ref. KB, York)
   Sp.: Killian Schmahl and wife

York County Deeds, Vol. 2, pp. 449-451:
Katrina Welshofer, widow of Jacob Welshofer, late of Hallam Twp., yeoman, deceased, Valentine Heyer, Taylor, and Anna Katrina his wife, John

Comfort, yeoman, and Maria Elizabeth his wife, all of Hallam Twp., and Kyllyan Small of York Town, joyner, and Eva his wife of the one part and Jacob Welshofer of Hallam Twp., eldest son and heir at law of Jacob Welshofer, deceased. A warrant was granted to the father for 200 A of land in the Manor of Springetsbury, dated 30 Oct. 1736. The above heirs sell 173 A to Jacob for £150. (Land adjoins Martin Shultz, q.v.)

HILL, JOHANN JACOB   67259 Heuchelheim
Prelist

EUROPEAN RECORDS

Heuchelheim Lutheran KB:
Jacob Hill m. 8 Jan. 1709 Anna Elisabetha Müller. They had children:
1. Joh. Jacob, b. 13 Nov. 1719, d. young
2. Johannes, b. 12 Jan. 1711, d. 25 Nov. 1712
3. Joh. Deobald, b. 9 Nov. 1713
4. Joh. Jacob, b. 17 Jan. 1716
5. Joh. Peter, b. 8 July 1718, d. 1 Feb. 1719
6. Joh. Philip, b. 1 Nov. 1719
[Entire family drops out of Heuchelheim record.]

AMERICAN RECORDS

A Johan Jacob Hill with wife Elisabeth lived in Windsor Twp., now Berks Co. before 1740.

Philadelphia County Administration Book D, page 93: #23:
Letters of Adm. to Ann Elizabeth Hill, county of Philadelphia, widow, adm. of **Jacob Hill**, dec'd., 9 Aug. 1739.

[The following records probably are for the Joh. Jacob Hill, born 1716:]
Moselem Lutheran KB, Berks Co., PA:
Joh. Jacob Hill and wife Maria Apollonia (nee Merkle) had:
1. Magdalena, b. 29 Jan. 1749
    Sp.: Joh. Daniel Hill, Helena Merklin
2. Johann, b. 20 June 1751
3. Joh. Jacob, b. 3 June 1756
4. Johann Friderick, b. 21 Oct. 1758

Peter Hill and wife Anna had:
    Joh. Georg, bp. 7 July 1754

Philip Hill and wife Christina had:
1. Andreas, b. 16 Jan. 1766 at Zion Union, Perry Twp.
2. Maria Magdalena, b. 21 Mar. 1768 at St. Paul's, Windsor

Johannes Hill and wife Hanna (nee Kuhn) had:
1. Hanna Marta, b. 30 May 1746
   Sp.: Gottfried Kramer and Hanna Hill
2. Anna Catharina, b. 15 Oct. 1747
   Sp.: Joh. Daniel Hill and Anna Maria Rausch
3. Eva Rosina, twin, b. 22 Mar. 1750
4. Hanna Martha, twin, b. 22 Mar. 1750
5. Johann Jacob, b. 11 July 1752
6. Maria Christina, b. 22 Apr. 1755

Moselem Lutheran KB, Berks Co., PA:
Gotfrid Kramer, single son of Sebold Kramer, m. Jubilate 1747 Hanna Martha Hill, single daughter of Jacob Hill.

Johann Daniel Hill, single son of Jacob Hill, m. 28 Nov. 1749 Anna Catharina Sibert, single daughter of Mathaus Sibert.

Georg Merklin, son of Christian Merklin, m. 18 De.c 1750 Christina Hill, daughter of Jacob Hill.

Jacob Hill, Philadelphia Co., naturalized by Act, 1735.

HILLEBRAND, JOH. MICHAEL   67246 Dirmstein
St. Andrew, 1738
S-H, I: 237, 238, 239

EUROPEAN RECORDS

Heuchelheim Lutheran KB:
Joh. Michael Hillebrand of Dirmstein was conf. in 1713, age 13 yrs.

AMERICAN RECORDS

Moselem Lutheran KB, Berks Co., PA:
Johannes Georg Nicolaus Hildebrand, son of Michael Hildebrand, m. 26 July 1757 Maria Hill, single daughter of Johann Jacob Hill. [q.v.]

Philadelphia Wills and Administrations:
Michael Helleprant 1739, Estate #22, Adm. D, p. 75:
Letters of Adm. to Henry Reiser, County of Lancaster, yeoman, adm. of
Michael Helleprant, dec'd, during minority of Nicholas Helleprant, an infant
son of said deceased, 14 Apr. 1739.

HOCK, ANNA APPOLLONIA   67112 Mutterstadt
_____, 1748
EUROPEAN RECORDS

Mutterstadt Reformed KB:
Johann Georg Hock and Anna Margaretha had a child baptized:
      Anna Appollonia, bp. 7 Sept. 1719
   [There is a note in the church record under the child's name, "in
   Pennsylvania, 1748."]

HOFF, JOHAN ADAM   67159 Friedelsheim
Joyce, 1730
S-H, I: 37, 38, 39
   appears on A list: John Hoaf, age 27

EUROPEAN RECORDS

Friedelsheim Reformed KB:
Johann Adam Hoff m. 21 Jan. 1727 Catharina, daughter of Christian Müller.
They had one child:
      Elisabetha Barbara, bp. 12 Dec. 1728
      Sp.: Hennrich Müller and Elisabetha Barbara Clemmer

AMERICAN RECORDS

York Moravian Records, York, PA:
Adam Hoff on the Codorus, born at Friedelsheim near Dürckheim an der
Hard in the Electoral Palatinate. He d. 20 Nov. 1785, age 81. He became
a Moravian at Lancaster 11/22 Feb. 1752. He m. in 1735 Juliana Seib of
Ebingen, 9 hours from Heidelberg in the Electoral Palatinate. She was born
18 Feb. 1720. [See Burgert, *Eighteenth Century Emigrants, Vol. I: The
Northern Kraichgau* (1983), p. 339 for this Seib family from 75031 Eppingen.]

Adam Hoff and Juliana had children:

    1. Ludwig, b. 13 Sep. 1737, d. Jun 1761
      (First Reformed KB, Lancaster: b. 9 Sep. 1736)
    2. Franz, b. 4 Feb. 1739
    3. Joh. Adam, b. 29 July 1740
      (First Reformed KB, Lancaster: bp. 29 Jun 1739)
    4. Joh. Peter, b. 29 Oct. 1742
    5. Johannes, b. 2 Feb. 1744, died
    6. Christina, b. 8 Nov. 1745
      (Rev. Lischy's record: bp. 11 Dec. 1747)
    7. Joh. Jacob, b. 26 Dec. 1747
      (Rev. Lischy's record: bp. 11 Dec. 1747)
    8. Daniel, b. 5 Feb. 1750
    9. Andreas, b. 23 Nov. 1751
   10. Gottfried, b. 25 Nov. 1753
   11. A son, b. 23 Nov. 1755 stillborn twin
   12. A daughter, b. 23 Nov. 1755 stillborn twin
   13. Philipp, b. 5 Feb. 1757, d. 1 Jan. 1771
   14. Joh. Henrich, b. 6 Aug.1760
   15. Juliana, b. 30 Mar. 1762, d. 13 May 1765

York County Wills:

Adam Hoff, Codorus Twp., dated 5 May 1776, probated 24 Dec. 1785. Executors: Juleana and Francis Hoff. Son Francis named in will, but names and number of other children not given.

Adam Hoff, Codorus Twp., York Co., nat. 18 Sep. 1762, without oath.

HOFF, JOHANNES   67112 Mutterstadt
Prelist

EUROPEAN RECORDS

Mutterstadt Reformed KB:

Johannes Hof and wife Susanna had children:

    1. Susanna, bp. 9 Mary 1705
    2. Anna Barbara, bp. 29 Sept. 1707
    3. Anna Clara, bp. 26 Dec. 1712
    4. Anna Sophia, bp. 8 May 1718
    5. Anna Eva, bp. 1 June 1720

Mutterstadt Kontraktenprotokolle:
Entry dated 1728: some land of Johannes Hoff was sold at public auction "as he has moved to Pennsylvania".: Adjoining landowners were Daniel Möck and Lambert. The transaction was recorded 28 May 1737.

Another entry, dated 7 Nov. 1730: Johannes Berg and Anna Catharina his wife bought property of Johannes Hoff, citizen and wagonmaker, and Susanna his wife, "as they have moved to the new land."

An entry, record dated 1728, recorded 28 May 1737: Joh. Georg Wentz and Dorothea his wife bought property of Johannes Hoff, and again the record mentions that he had moved to Pennsylvania.

AMERICAN RECORDS

Muddy Creek Reformed KB, Lancaster Co., PA:
One John Hof and wife Anna Barbara had a daughter:
      Maria Apollonia, bp. 13 June 1743
      Sp.: John Adam Renner and Maria Apollonia Brunner

HOFFMAN, DANIEL   Ober Lustadt=
Neptune, 1754   67363 Lustadt
S-H, I: 621

EUROPEAN RECORDS

Ober Lustadt Reformed KB:
Joh. Jacob Hoffman and wife Susanna Christina had a son:
      Daniel, b. 17 Feb. 1727, bp. 18 Feb. 1727
      Sp.: Daniel Kamp and Catharina

Emigration record:
Werner Hacker, *Auswanderungen aus Rheinpfalz und Saarland*:
#6298 Daniel Hoffmann, Oberlustadt, emigrated to the New Land

Fritz Braun and Friedrich Krebs. "Pennsylvania Dutch Pioneers from South Palatine Parishes", *The Pennsylvania Dutchman*, 8 (Spring, 1957):
Daniel Hoffmann born at Oberlustadt, 17 Feb. 1727, son of Johann Jacob Hoffmann and wife Susanna Christina Brückner, "who went to the New Land" (Document of August 30, 1758).

AMERICAN RECORDS

St. Michael's and Zion KB, Philadelphia: Burial records:
7 June 1790 Daniel Hoffman, b. 17 Feb. 1727 in Oberlustat in the Pfalz, son of Joh. Jacob Hoffman and Susanna Christina. He m. 28 July 1761 Margretha Baumänn and had 12 children. Died age 64 y., 3 months, 3 weeks.

HOLLER, JOHANN NICOLAUS   Ungstein=
St. Andrew Galley, 1737   67098 Bad Dürkheim
S-H, I: 179, 181, 183

EUROPEAN RECORDS

Ungstein Lutheran KB:
Andreas Holler, b. ca. 1656 Engwiller [Engwiller = F-67350 Pfaffenhoffen], Alsace, son of Georg Holler and Ottilia, d. 11 Oct. 1704 at Ungstein. He m. ca. 1684 at Engwiller Maria Müller. They moved to Ungstein in 1693, and had a son:
Johann Nicolaus, b. ca. 1700, conf. 1715, age 15.

Johann Nicolaus Holler, son of Andreas Holler, m. 7 Apr. 1722 at Ungstein Anna Maria Koch, daughter of Hanns Nicol Koch. They had children:
1. Johann Nicolaus, b. 8 Dec. 1722, d. 27 Feb. 1724
2. Anna Maria, b. 17 Mar. 1725, conf. 1737, age 13
   [It is mentioned in her confirmation record that she is "going with her parents to the New Land."]
3. Johann Philipp, b. 2 June 1728, d. 29 Dec. 1732
4. Johann Nicolaus, b. 30 Aug. 1731
5. Maria Elisabetha, b. 15 Aug. 1734
6. Stillborn son, 14 Apr. 1737

AMERICAN RECORDS

Heidelberg Moravian KB, Berks Co., PA:
Philipp Stör [Stöhr] from Langensulzbach [Langensoultzbach = F-67360 Woerth] in Lower Alsace, m. in May 1742 by Caspar Stöver, Miss Anna Maria Holler, daughter of Johan Nicolaus Holler, citizen of Unkstein and his wife Anna Maria; married at Warwick. 6 children are listed, surname Stor, in the Moravian family register. [For Stöhr data, see Annette K. Burgert, *Eighteenth Century Emigrants from the Northern Alsace*, p. 490-92].

Muddy Creek Reformed KB, Lancaster Co., PA:
Nicholas Hoeller and wife had a son:
>John, bp. 29 July 1751
>Sp.: Nicholas Koerber and wife

HOLTZINGER, JACOB   67454 Hassloch
Snow *Lowther,* 1731
S-H, I: 55, 56, 57
[other family members on ship: Barbara Holtsinger, Jacob Holtsinger,
Barbara Holtsinger, Jr.]

EUROPEAN RECORDS

Hassloch Lutheran KB:
Johann Jacob Holtzinger m. 19 Apr. 1718 at Hassloch Maria Barbara [no
surname given]. Children:
>1. Bernhard, b. 21 Feb. 1720, bp. 25 Feb. 1720
>2. Anna Barbara, b. 13 Dec. 1724, bp. 17 Dec. 1724
>3. Johannes, b. 7 Feb. 1730, bp.12 Feb. 1730

AMERICAN RECORDS

Trinity Lutheran KB, New Holland, Lancaster Co., PA:
Bernhard Holtzinger was a bp. sponsor in 1739. Jacob Holtzinger and wife
Maria Veronica were sponsors in 1744 and 1752.

Muddy Creek Lutheran KB, Lancaster Co., PA:
Jacob Holtzinger [wife not named] had children:
>1. Anna Maria, b. 15 Mar. 1743, bp. 25 Mar. 1743
>   Sp.: Leonhardt Breitenstein and wife Anna Maria
>2. Johannes, b. 12 Feb. 1745, bp. 10 Mar. 1745
>   Sp.: Johannes Ulrich and wife Margaretha
>3. Cunradt, b. 30 Aug. 1748, bp. 25 Sept. 1748
>   Sp.: Cunradt Wirnss and wife

Seltenreich Reformed KB, Lancaster Co., PA:
Joh. Peter Becker, widower and elder, m. 1 Jan. 1767 Veronica Holdsinger,
widow of Jacob Holdsinger of Cocalico.

Hocker, *German Settlers of Pennsylvania:* 161:
Philadelphische Zeitung 4 Nov. 1757:
Bernhard Holtzinger of York sells Almanancs.

Christ Lutheran KB, Lischy's Records & First Reformed KB, all York Co.:
Bernhard Holtzinger and wife Elisabetha had:
1. Joh. Georg, bp. 17 Aug. 1746 [Lischy's record]
2. Martin, b. 5 Jan. 1749, bp. 20 May 1749, d. 1749
3. Catharina, bp. 24 May 1750
4. Joh. Jacob b. 10 Sept. 1753
5. Elizabeth, b. 30 Oct. 1756, d. 1 May 1759
6. John, b. 20 Feb. 1759
7. Anna Maria, b. 2 Apr. 1761
8. Bernhard, b. 22 Feb. 1766 [York Reformed KB]

Several deeds recorded in Deed Books A and B, York co. list Bernhard Holtzinger's occupation as blacksmith. He purchased 262 acres on 16 Mar. 1759, and also owned lots # 28, 51 and 76 in York Town.

Bernhard Holsinger nat. 25 Sept. 1750, York, York Co., PA.

HOLTZINGER, JERG   67454 Hassloch
Phoenix, 1751
S-H, I: 470

EUROPEAN RECORDS

Hassloch Lutheran KB:
Petter Holtzinger m. 24 June 1710 Anna Elisabetha Herter. They had:
Joh. Georg, b. 1 Apr. 1715, bp. 3 Apr. 1715
Conf. 1729 - Johann Georg Holtzinger

Johann Georg Holtzinger m. 17 Apr. 1742 Catharina Margaretha Wallenfelss from D_Ickenheim [Delkenheim = 65205 Wiesbaden] in the Herrschafft Ebstein.

AMERICAN RECORDS

Rev. John Waldschmidt's records: (Lancaster Co.)
Johann Gorg Holtzinger, widower, m. 21 Oct. 1783 Magdalena, widow of Abraham Kessler. Five years ago Mrs. Kessler was married by Rev. Boos to Friedrich Luckart, but the latter went away about three years ago without any cause.

HOOS, PHILIP age 25   Lachen-Speyerdorf=
Snow *Fox,* 1738   67435 Neustadt an der Weinstrasse
S-H, I: 231, 232, 233

EUROPEAN RECORDS

Lachen-Speyerdorf Reformed KB:
Johannes Hoos, son of Herr Niclaus Hoos, *ChurPfaltz Schultheissen* at
Lachen, m. (1) 2 Oct. 1709 Catharina, daughter of Niclaus Freytag.

Johannes Hoos and wife Catharina had a son:
> 1. Hans Philipp, b. 2 Apr. 1712, bp. 3 Apr. 1712, conf. 1727.
> Sp.: Hans Philipp Scherrer. The mother died at the
> birth of this child.

Joh. Philip Hoos, son of Johannes Hoos, m. 11 Nov. 1733 Anna Margretha,
daughter of Peter Müller, shoemaker in [67454] Hassloch. They had one
child, bp. in the Hassloch Reformed Church:
> 1. Johann Henrich, b. 20 Jan. 1734

AMERICAN RECORDS

Strayer's (Salem) Lutheran KB, York Co., PA:
One Philip Hoss m. 17 June 1768 Anna Salome, daughter of Johann Martin
Schumacher. They had a son:
> 1. Johan Dieter, b. 29 Jan. 1770, bp. 25 Mar. 1770
> Sp.: Johan Dieter Ruppert and wife Margreth.

Philip Hoss of Manchester Twp., York Co., nat. Apr. 1762.

HORLACHER, MICHAEL   67256 Weisenheim am Sand
Pennsylvania Merchant, 1731
S-H, I: 43, 44, 46, 47
> Frenech Horloger and Maria Horloger under 16 on list.

EUROPEAN RECORDS

Freinsheim Lutheran KB, Weisenheim am Sand Lutheran entries:
Johann Michael Horlacher m. 8 Feb. 1724 Maria Fronica, daughter of
Wilhelm Schmidt.

Joh. Michel Horlacher, master tailor, and wife Maria Fronica had:
1. Johann Jacob, b. 3 Nov. 1724, bp. 7 Nov. 1724
   at Weisenheim am Sand, he d. 21 May 1728.
   Sp.: Joh. Jacob, son of Paul Droutz? of [67229]
   Gerolsheim and Barbara Ohleschläger of Weisenheim
2. Johann Peter, b. 23 Sept. 1728
   Sp.: Joh. Peter Appel and his wife

AMERICAN RECORDS

St. Paul's Lutheran "Six-Cornered" Church, Upper Hanover Twp., Montgomery Co., PA:
Johann Michael Horlacher and wife Maria Veronica sp. children of Peter Wetzstein in 1736 and 1739.

Michael Horlacher and Maria Veronica had:
    Susanna, b. 4 May 1741, bp. 24 May 1741
    Sp.: Susanna Gucker
    Johann Peter, b. 25 Oct. 1742, bp. 7 Nov. 1742
    Sp.: Joh. Peter Klingenschmidt

St. Paul's (Blue) Lutheran KB, Upper Saucon, Lehigh Co., PA:
Daniel Horlacher married in 1758 [no other date given] Maria Margaretha Brunner, daughter of Henrich Brunner from Upper Saucon.

Tombstone inscriptions:

Daniel Horlacher	Margaretha Horlacher
b. 4 Aug. 1735	nee Brunner
d. 24 Sept. 1804	b. 4 Jan. 1741
Revolutionary War	d. 2 Apr. 1806
	14 children

Michael Horlactior (?Horlacher), Lower Milford Twp., Bucks Co., nat. 1761.

HORTER, GEORG ADAM   Ober Lustadt=
    ca. 1756   67363 Lustadt

EUROPEAN RECORDS

Emigration record:
Werner Hacker, *Auswanderungen aus Rheinpfalz und Saarland*:
#6506 Gg. Adam Horter, Oberlustadt, to Pennsylvania, 1756.

Fritz Braun and Friedrich Krebs. "Pennsylvania Dutch Pioneers from South Palatine Parishes", *The Pennsylvania Dutchman*, 8 (Spring, 1957):
Georg Adam Horter, born at Oberlustadt, 27 May 1738, son of Jacob Horter and wife (Maria) Agnes Sohland, "already gone to Pennsylvania 12 years ago" (Document of April 20, 1768). The emigration must therefore have taken place around 1756.

Ober Lustadt Reformed KB:
Jacob Horter and wife Maria Agnesia had a son:
>   Georg Adam, b. 27 May 1738, bp. 1 June 1738
>   Sp.: Georg Horter and Anna Barbara

HORTER, GEORG JACOB   Ober Lustadt=
Ship data not located, before 1758   67363 Lustadt

EUROPEAN RECORDS

Ober Lustadt Reformed KB:
Joh. Georg Horter and wife Anna Barbara had:
>   1. Anna Christina, b. 2 Feb. 1724, bp. 6 Feb. 1724
>   2. Anna Barbara, b. 17 Sept. 1726, bp. 22 Sept. 1726
>   Sp.: Theobald Nutz and Anna Barbara
>   3. Anna Maria b. 21 July 1729, bp. 24 July 1729
>   Sp.: Anna Maria Spuler, single
>   4. **Georg Jacob,** b. 9 July 1733, bp. 12 July 1733
>   Sp.: Jacob Horter and Agnesia
>   5. Joh. Valendin, b. 12 July 1739, bp. 14 July 1739
>   Sp.: Joh. Valendin Tischer and Margaretha
>   6. Joh. Valentin [q.v.], b. 16 Sept. 1740, bp. 18 Sept. 1740
>   Sp.: Joh. Hauenstein and Anna Appolonia

AMERICAN RECORDS

Germantown Reformed KB, Philadelphia:
George Jacob Horder and wife Magdalena had children:
>   1. Catharina, b. 9 May 1758, bp. 21 May 1758; conf. 1774
>   Sp.: Georg Nicholas Unruh [q.v.] and Catharina Franck
>   2. Maria Magdalena, b. 30 Jan. 1767, bp. 1 Mar. 1767
>   Sp.: Valentin Horder [q.v.] and Maria Magdalena
>   Reiss, single
>   3. George, b. 14 Sept. 1769, bp. 5 Dec. 1769

Died 1 Dec. 1796 Jacob Horter's wife Magdalena, age 61 y. 9 mo.

HORTER, JOH. VALTIN   Ober Lustadt=
Britannia, 1764   67363 Lustadt
S-H, I: 693

EUROPEAN RECORDS

Ober Lustadt Reformed KB:
Georg Horter and Barbara had 6 children, including the following [see
Georg Jacob Horter, above, for a complete record]:
>   Anna Maria, b. 21 July 1729; m. Johann Jacob Wunder [q.v.]
>   Georg Jacob, b. 9 July 1733 [q.v.]
> * **Johann Valentin**, b. 16 Sept. 1740, bp. 18 Sept. 1740
>   Sp.: Johannes Hauenstein and Anna Appolonia

Fritz Braun and Friedrich Krebs. "Pennsylvania Dutch Pioneers from South
Palatine Parishes", *The Pennsylvania Dutchman,* 8 (Spring, 1957):
Anna Barbara Horter, married before 1733 to Georg Horter, citizen and
town councilor at Oberlustadt; died before 1764. "Whereas Barbara Horter,
widow and relict of Georg Horter, deceased citizen at Oberlustadt, went
from here about one year ago to the so-called New England with her son
Velten Horter, also a son of hers named Georg Jacob Horter had gone there
several years previously, so then both brothers and sisters and in-laws of hers
still residing here, namely Jacob Wunder and his wife Anna Maria, and
Jacob Sager, sent a manuscript letter asking here therein, since one of them
had the desire to go to the above-mentioned New Land, if he should sell or
convert into money the inheritance still coming to her here and bring it to
her.   Now since Jakob Wunder and his wife Anna Maria have likewise
resolved to go to their respective mother and brothers and sisters and
therefore have petitioned for permission, to convert into cash the properties
of their inlaws still coming to them and take them to them," hence a
complete inventory of the properties of Georg Jakob and Velten Horter was
drawn up and the results of the sale given to the brother-in-law, Jacob
Wunder, who emigrated in 1765 (Document of April 19, 1765).

AMERICAN RECORDS

Germantown Reformed Church, Philadelphia Co., PA.:
Married 2 Apr. 1767 Valentine Horter and Mary Magdalena Reuss. They
had children:
>   1. Anna Margaret, b. 7 Jan. 1768, bp. 16 June 1768
>   2. Maria Magdalena, b. 14 July 1769, bp. 27 Aug. 1769
>   3. Catharina, b. 4 Sept. 1771, bp. 18 Sept. 1771
>   4. Catharine, b. 14 Aug. 1772, bp. 27 Dec. 1772

5. Susanna, b. 27 Sept. 1774, bp. 25 Dec. 1774
6. Joh. Valentin, b. 1 Sept. 1776, bp. 8 Sept. 1776
7. Georg, b. 30 May 1784, bp. 23 Apr. 1786

Died 3 Dec. 1772 Maria Barbara Horter, age 68 years, 13 days.

*A typical half-timbered house
located in the village of Hochstadt.*

JÄGER, ANDREAS   Lachen-Speyerdorf=
Britannia, 1764   67435 Neustadt an der Weinstrasse
S-H, I: 693

EUROPEAN RECORDS

Lachen-Speyerdorf Reformed KB:
Andreas Jäger, son of the late Jacob Jäger, conf. 1745, age 13 years, 6 months. He married 11 Feb. 1755 Anna Barbara, daughter of the late Philip Schuster.

Johann Philip Schuster, son of the late Stephan Schuster, m. 16 Jan. 1727 Anna Helena, daughter of Jacob Weyhenacht of Gimmeldingen [=67435 Neustadt a.d. Weinstrasse]. Their daughter, Anna Barbara, b. 15 Feb. 1733. Philip Schuster died 30 Sept. 1738, age 37 years less one month.

Andreas Jäger and Anna Barbara had children:
1. Johanna Maria, b. 24 Nov. 1755, bp. 27 Nov. 1755
   Sp.: Johanna Maria, wife of Joh. Adam Schmit
2. Anna Maria, b. 10 Jan. 1757, bp. 13 Jan. 1757
   Sp.: Anna Maria, wife of Joh. Adam Schmit
3. Maria Christina, b. 27 Oct. 1758, bp. 30 Oct. 1758
   Sp.: Maria Christina, wife of Henrich Möck
4. Anna Barbara, b. 24 Feb. 1761, bp. 27 Feb. 1761
   Sp.: Joh. Nickel Gleich and wife Anna Barbara
5. Joh. Christophel, b. 11 Mar. 1763, bp. 13 Mar. 1763
   Sp.: Joh. Christopher, son of the schoolmaster
   Roos and Anna Margaretha.

AMERICAN RECORDS

Wentz' Reformed KB, Montgomery Co., PA:
Andreas Jaeger and wife Anna Barbara had children:
6. Johannes, b. 26 Jan. 1766, bp. 30 Mar. 1766
   Sp.: Johan Eitel and wife Agnes
7. Elisabetha, b. 26 Feb. 1768, bp. 23 May 1768
   Sp.: Abraham Lefeber and wife Elisabeth

St. David's Reformed KB, Killinger, Dauphin Co., PA:
Conf. 1780: Joh. Christophel Jaeger, age 17.

Buried 27 July 1779: Mrs. Anna Barbara Jäger nee Schuster, was born 15 Feb. 1733 in Lachen, Ober-Amt Neustadt in der Pfaltz.

JÄGER, JOHANN NICOLAUS   Lachen-Speyerdorf=
permit to emigrate 1749   67435 Neustadt an der Weinstrasse
[not located in PA ship's lists]

EUROPEAN RECORDS

Lachen-Speyerdorf Reformed KB:
Johann Nicolaus Jäger, son of the late Jacob Jäger, Reformed, m. 21 Feb.
1746 Anna, daughter of the late Johannes Hilger, formerly
Gerichtsverwandten in Duttweiler [= 67435 Neustadt a.d. Weinstrasse],
Catholic. It is mentioned in the record that there is an illegitimate two year
old child.

Emigration record:
Werner Hacker, *Auswanderungen aus Rheinpfalz und Saarland im 18.
Jahrhundert:* # 6782 Jäger, Nikolaus, Lachen/Ger; manumitted to leave for
PA. Record dated 18 Mar. 1749.

AMERICAN RECORDS

New Goshenhoppen Reformed KB, Montgomery Co., PA:
Undated marriages, between 1747-1757: One Nicolaus Jeger m. Anna
Hillikas.

Berks Co. Orphan's Court: one Nicholas Hunter of Oley died before 10
Mar. 1772, leaving minor children. No firm evidence has been located to
connect to the Lachen emigrant.

JÄGER, PETER   Niederlustadt=
St. Andrew, 1734   67363 Lustadt
S-H, I: 137, 141, 142

EUROPEAN RECORDS

Niederhochstadt Reformed KB:
Heinrich Jäger and Anna Barbara had a son:
        Joh. Peter, bp. 20 Oct. 1709 at Niederlustadt.

JARAUS (GARAUS), CARL Ober Lustadt=
Britannia, 1764 67363 Lustadt
S-H, I: 693

EUROPEAN RECORDS

Ober Lustadt Reformed KB:
Carl Jaraus and Dorothea had a child:
    Carl, b. 31 Dec. 1741, bp. 1 Jan. 1742
    Sp.: Carl Becker and Appolonia Roland, both single

AMERICAN RECORDS

Seven passengers from Oberlustadt are listed together on the passenger list of the ship *Britannia* in 1764: Johann Bernhart Ott, Johann Andreas Schmitt, Christian Haushalter, Georg Heinrich Schmitt; further on the list are Johann Martin Ott, **Carl Garaus (Jahraus)**, Vallentin Stettler.

JORDAN, ADAM Niederhochstadt=
Janet, 1751 76879 Hochstadt, Pfalz
S-H, I: 474

EUROPEAN RECORDS

Niederhochstadt Reformed KB:
Philip Adam Jordan m. 17 Jan. 1741 Barbara Wagner. Barbara Wagner was bp. 30 Mar. 1717 at Niederhochstadt, a daughter of Caspar Wagner [q.v.] and wife Anna Maria nee Laux. They had children:
    1. Anna Maria, b. 1 Aug. 1741, bp. 6 Aug. 1741
      Sp.: Joh. Andreas Menges and Anna Maria Laux, both single
    2. Catharina, b. 15 Jan. 1744, bp. 19 Jan. 1744
      Sp.: Valentin Butz and Catharina
    3. Maria Catharina, b. 7 May 1746, bp. 8 May 1746
      Sp.: Conrad Bungel and Maria Catharina Schwartz, both single
    4. Philip Jacob, b. 27 Apr. 1749, bp. 1 May 1749
      Sp.; Jacob Ott and Maria Catharina

*The vineyards near Hochstadt continue to be
a major economic factor in this area.*

AMERICAN RECORDS

Host Reformed KB, Tulpehocken, Berks Co., PA:
Philip Adam Jordan and his wife Eva Barbara sponsor a child of J. Leonard
Groff in 1754

Berks County Probate Records:
Estate of Adam Jordan of Tulpehocken. Administration was granted 28
Mar. 1761 to Eva Barbara Jordan, the widow.

Berks County Orphans' Court Records, Vol. 1, p. 140, dated 13 Nov. 1762:
Adam Jordan died intestate, leaving a widow Eva Barbara and 4 children;
two of the children are under 14 years of age: Philip Jacob, age 13 years, and
Maria Elisabetha, age 9 years. John George Laucks of Tulpehocken was
appointed guardian.

Berks County Orphans' Court Records, Vol. 1, p. 160, dated 6 Mar. 1763:
Distribution of the estate of Adam Jordan. Shares to: son Philip Jacob, age
13; daughter Catharina married to Peter Lebo; daughter Maria Catharina,
age 16; daughter Elisabetha, age 9. Maria Catharina Jordan, daughter of the
deceased Adam Jordan, chooses Valentine Moyer of Tulpehocken as
guardian.

KAUFFMAN, AUGUSTUS   67454 Hassloch
St. Andrew, 1741
S-H, I: 305, 306 [on A List, p. 304, as Hans Kaufman, age 25.]

EUROPEAN RECORDS

Hassloch Reformed KB:
Johan Andreas Kauffman, son of the late Melchior Kauffman, former
Huffschmid here, m. 14 Aug. 1700 Anna Elisabetha, daughter of the late
Caspar Weinlandt, former *Gemeinsmann* at [69488] Birkenau by Weinheim.
Joh. Andreas Kauffman and wife Elisabetha had children:
  1. Anna Catharina, bp. 31 Apr. 1701
  2. Maria Christina, bp. 25 Feb. 1703
  3. Johannes, bp. 4 May 1704
  4. Susanna, bp. 12 Sept. 1706
  5. Susanna, bp. 29 July 1708
  6. Catharina Elisabetha, bp. 4 Jan. 1711
  7. **Augustus**, b. 1 Oct. 1717; bp. 3 Oct. 1717;
     conf. Easter 1732, age 15.

Andreas Kauffman was buried 18 July 1747, age 85 years.

Hassloch Lutheran KB:
Elisabetha Kauffmann was buried 28 Oct. 1736, age 60 y. less 10 days.

Ottersheim Reformed KB:
Augustus Kauffmann, born in Hassloch, single, m. 17 Sept. 1739 Anna
Catharina Hatzenböhler from [76879] Ottersheim [no parentage given].
Notation in KB by marriage record: *sind d. 1 May 1741 in Americam verreist.*
[No baptisms recorded in this KB 1740-1742].

AMERICAN RECORDS

Muddy Creek Reformed KB, Lancaster Co., PA:
Justus Kaufman signed the Muddy Creek Reformed Church Doctrine in
1743.
Justus Kaufman and wife Catharina had a son bp. in the church records:
        Christophel, bp. 12 Aug. 1743
          Sp.: Christopher Steinel and Anna Catharine
Augustus Kaufman and Catharina had a daughter bp. in the church records:
        Catharina Margaretha, bp. 7 Sep. 1746
          Sp.: Cath. Margaret Schuessler

KAUFFMANN, JURG age 20   67454 Hassloch
Friendship, 1738
S-H, I: 225, 228, 230

EUROPEAN RECORDS

Hassloch Reformed KB:
Joh. Conradt Kauffman, son of Herr Philip Kauffman, *Licenter und Gauerben Hubschultheiss* here, m. 10 Nov. 1706 Anna Barbara, daughter of the late Lorentz Feldman. They had children:
1. Johann Conradt, bp. 11 Sept. 1707
2. Anna Barbara, bp. 27 Sept. 1708
3. Maria Magdalena, bp. 16 Feb. 1710
4. Anna Catharina, b. 29 Jan. 1712, bp. 31 Jan. 1712
   She m. 1730 Henrich Guth.
5. **Johann Georg,** b. 29 Dec. 1713, bp. 31 Dec. 1713
   Conf. Easter, 1728, age 14.
6. Christina Philippina, b. 4 Apr. 1716, bp. 8 Apr. 1716.
   She m. 1737 Hans Adam Ritter.
7. Maria Christina, b. 1 Dec. 1718, bp. 4 Dec. 1718
8. Maria Elisabetha, b. 25 May 1721, bp. 28 May 1721
9. Maria Elisabetha, b. 12 July 1722, bp. 15 July 1722.

KAYSER, LORENTZ   67167 Erpolzheim
St. Andrew Galley, 1737
S-H, I: 179, 180, 183

EUROPEAN RECORDS

Inhabitants List of Married and Unmarried Men for the Graffschafft Leiningen-Hartenburg, 1706:
     Hans Adam Keyser, age 26   Erpolzheim

Erpolzheim Reformed KB:
Conf. 1722: Agnes Margaretha Kaÿser, daughter of Hans Adam Kaÿser
Conf. 1727: Johann Lorentz Kaÿser, son of Hans Adam Kaÿser of
            Erpolzheim.
Conf. 1730: Johann Peter Kaÿsser from Erpolzheim
Conf. 1733: Johann Conrad Kaÿser

AMERICAN RECORDS

Frederick Lutheran KB (Monocacy), Frederick Co., MD:
Lorentz Käÿser had a son:
>   Johann Adam, b. __ Feb. 1750, bp. 29 July 1750;
>   Sp.: He himself and wife.

Lincoln County, NC, Deed Book 3: 275-276:
Adam and George Kiser divide 300 acres which was granted to their father, Lawrence Kiser on 10 Apr. 1761.

KEIBER, WENDEL	Lachen-Speyerdorf=
KEIBER, CARL LUDWIG	67435 Neustadt an der Weinstrasse
Prelist, before 1727	67112 Mutterstadt

EUROPEAN RECORDS

Lachen-Speyerdorf Reformed KB:
Carl Ludwig Keiber, son of Wendel Keiber, master wagonmaker at Lachen, was conf. 1711.

Mutterstadt Reformed KB:
Carl Ludwig Keiber from Lachen m. 17 June 1719 Maria Catharina Koch. They had a son:
>   Joh. Michael b. 8 Aug. 1721
>   Sp.: Joh. Michael Hofacker and wife Maria Rachel

Mutterstadt Kontraktenprotokolle:
Johann Adam Rebarlie bought property from Daniel Koch's widow here and her son-in-law Carl Keyper who has moved to Pennsylvania. Record dated 17 Apr. 1738. In another entry dated 1739. concerning this sale, Daniel Koch's widow Elisabeth and her daughter Catharina "who is in Pennsylvania" are mentioned.

AMERICAN RECORDS

History of Goshenhoppen Charge, Vol. I, p. 59:
Carl Ludwig Keipper was a member of the Skippack congregation in 1730. Wendel Keupper was one of the elders of this congregation in 1730. Both signed the letter of complaint to the Classis of Amsterdam about the ordination of Pastor Boehm.

Great Swamp Reformed KB, Lehigh Co., PA:
Michel Keiber and wife Magdalena had a daughter:
    Maria Elisa bp. 8 Sept. 1749
    Sp.: Daniel Heller and Maria Elisabetha Keiber

St. Paul's (Blue) Lutheran KB, Upper Saucon Twp., Lehigh Co., PA:
Michael Keuper and wife Magdalena Catharina had a daughter:
    Magdalena b. 24 Oct. 1751 bp. 8 Dec. 1751
    Sp.: Daniel Heller and Elisabeth

Carl Ludwig Keiper and wife Catharina had a son:
    Jacob b. 16 Aug. 1760 bp. 14 Sept. 1760
    Sp.: Christoff Heller and Elisabeth

KELLER, HANS JACOB   67112 Mutterstadt
Prelist

EUROPEAN RECORDS

Mutterstadt Reformed KB:
Hans Jacob Keller from Canton Bern, Switzerland, m. 3 Apr. 1714 Anna
Barbara ?Riedt from Unterscheflentz [= 74850 Schefflenz], Oberamts
Mospach. Their children:
    1. Anna Margaretha, bp. 7 July 1716
    2. Johannes, bp. 3 Sept. 1721
    3. Joh. Jacob, bp. 26 Sept. 1723

AMERICAN RECORDS

Jacob Keller was residing in Skippack in 1730 and signed the letter from
that congregation to the Classis of Amsterdam protesting the ordination of
Pastor Boehm.

Jacob Keller and wife were sponsors for a child of Wilhelm Schmitt in 1731
at New Goshenhoppen.

Great Swamp Reformed KB, Lehigh Co., PA:
A later Jacob Keller had a daughter:
    Anna Barbara, bp. 5 Feb. 1765
    Sp.: Simon Walter and wife

KERCHNER (KIRCHNER), ANDREAS

Ober Lustadt=

Dragon, 1749

67363 Lustadt

S-H, I: 423

EUROPEAN RECORDS

Ober Lustadt Reformed KB:
Andreas Kirchner and wife Agnesia had a son:
  Daniel, b. 11 July 1748, bp. 15 July 1748

KERN, JOH. THOMAS age 36

67361 Freisbach

Samuel, 1737

S-H, I: 169, 170, 172

EUROPEAN RECORDS

Freisbach Lutheran KB:
Joh. Thomas Kern m. 17 Feb. 1733 Maria Margretha, daughter of Michael
Jopp from [76879] Ottersheim. They had children:
  1. Anna Elisabetha, b. 20 Nov. 1733, bp. 22 Nov. 1733
     notation in KB: "In Pensyl."
  2. Joh. Christoph, b. 25 Jan. 1736, bp. 28 Jan. 1736
     notation in KB: "In Pensyl."

AMERICAN RECORDS

Christ "Little Tulpehocken" Lutheran Church:
Thomas Kern had a son:
  Simon, b. 24 Feb. 1742, bp. 18 Apr. 1742
  Sp.: Simon Bogenreif and wife

Berks Co. Abstracts of Wills and Administrations:
Thomas Kern of Tulpehocken, will dated 3 Apr. 1761, probated 30 May
1761. Son-in-law Johann George Rieth to have the place on paying £300.
Names wife Maria Kreth Kern. Names children: Stophel, Simon, Johann,
Nickel, and Eva Kretha. Son Stophel is the eldest son. Letters of
Administration to Maria Margaretha Kern, the widow.

Margaret Kern, widow, Tulpehocken; Administration on her estate granted
25 Mar. 1776 to Christopher Kern, eldest son.

First Reformed Church, Lancaster, PA:
Thomas Kern and wife Maria Margaretha Jop had a child:
    John Michael, bp. 12 May 1739

Berks Co. Orphans Court Records:
Dated 16 Jan. 1771 - Petition of Nicholas Kern, one of the children of
Thomas Kern, deceased. States that his father died sometime past seized of
a tract of land in Tulpehocken of 170 acres. That the said Thomas Kern
made a will (proved since his death) devising said land to Johannes George
Rith, upon condition that he pay £300 to the children of said Thomas Kern.
The said Johannes Georg Rith refuses to accept the land at the price - it
then vests in the children of said deceased, to be as an intestate estate.
Prays for an inquest to divide or value and divide among the children of
Thomas Kern, deceased to wit: Christopher, Simon, Nicholas, Anna
Elizabeth wife of Johannes George Reed, and Eva Margaret wife of Philip
Waggoner.

KIRCHER (KERCHER), CATHARINA   Lachen-Speyerdorf=
Emigrated 1764   67435 Neustadt an der Weinstrasse
    with uncle Andreas Jäger, q.v.

EUROPEAN RECORDS

Lachen-Speyerdorf Reformed KB:
Johann Philip Schuster, son of the late Stephan Schuster of Speyerdorf, m.
16 Jan. 1727 Anna Helena, daughter of Jacob Weyhenacht of Gimmeldingen
[= 67435 Neustadt a.d. Weinstrasse]. They had children:
    1. Johannes, b. 24 Apr. 1729, bp. 1 May 1729
    2. Anna Maria, b. 28 May 1731, bp. 3 June 1731
        Sp.: Anna Maria, daughter of Andreas Jäger, shepherd here
    3. Anna Barbara, b. 15 Feb. 1733. She m. 1755 Andreas Jäger [q.v.]
        Sp.: Anna Barbara, wife of Philips Rheinhard Clos, shepherd
    4. Catharina Elisabetha, b. 12 Jan. 1736
    5. Anna Elisabetha, b. 23 Dec. 1737

Johannes Kircher, son of the late Johannes Kircher of Musspach [Mussbach
= 67435 Neustadt a.d. Weinstrasse], m. 31 Oct. 1752 Anna Maria, daughter
of Philip Schuster. They were likely the parents of Catharina Kircher, but
her baptismal record has not been located in the Lachen KB.

Emigration record:
Fredrich Krebs, "Pennsylvania Dutch Pioneers" in *The Pennsylvania Dutchman,* 1954-56:
From Lachen (Kreis Neustadt) Andreas Jaeger went from Lachen to America in the year 1764 and took his niece Catharina Kircher (or Kercher) with him. The latter married in America Johannes Brunner of Passyunck near Philadelphia. Andreas Jaeger lived in Upper Paxtang, Lancaster County.

KIRSCHNER, JOH. GEORG   67112 Mutterstadt
Edinburgh, 1748
S-H, I: 371

EUROPEAN RECORDS

Mutterstadt Reformed KB:
Joh. Henrich Kirschner from Muttgers, Schwartzenfelser Amt, Hessen [Mottgers = 36391 Sinntal] m. 24 Sept. 1715 Apollonia, daughter of Hans Ritter from Maulich, Graffschaft Ahnspach (Maulach = 74564 Crailsheim). They had a son:
> Joh. Georg, bp. 18 Sept. 1718
> Sp.: Joh. Georg Weinacht and Anna Margaretha Weber, both single

Joh. Henrich Kirschner died 6 Dec. 1733, age 63 y., son of the late Tobias Kirschner, smith and inhabitant at ?Motgens in Schwartzenfels Ambt, Hessen [Mottgers = 36391 Sinntal].

AMERICAN RECORDS

St. Paul's (Blue) Church, Upper Saucon Twp., Lehigh Co., PA:
Died 19 Mar. 1750: Maria Kerschner, daughter of George Kerschner, age 6 mo. 19 days. Buried 21 Mar. 1750.

Jürg Kerschner and wife Anna Margaretha were sponsors in 1757 for a child of Johannes Heuger, and for a child of Jürg Walter.

A George Kershner, Saucon Twp., Northampton County, was naturalized 10 or 11 Apr. 1761.

182   *Palatine Origins of*

KISSLE (KISSEL), HANS JEORG   67459 Iggelheim
KISSLE (KISSEL), JOH. JACOB (sick)
Allen, 1729
S-H, I: 27, 29, 30

EUROPEAN RECORDS

Schifferstadt Reformed KB:
Joh. Georg Kissel m. (1) 11 Feb. 1706 Anna Maria, daughter of Hans Mäny
of Wintzingen [Winzingen = 73072 Donzdorf]. They had children:
1. Anna Barbara, b. 17 Apr. 1707; conf. 1720
2. Joh. Jacob, b. 2 Dec. 1708; conf. 1724
Joh. Georg Kissel, widower, m. (2) 30 Mar. 1712 Christina Elisabetha Stein.
They had children:
3. Maria Benedicta, b. 22 Feb. 1714, d. 1720
4. Joh. Niclaus, b. 24 Sept. 1716
5. Joh. Friedrich, b. 27 Aug. 1719, d. 1720
6. Joh. Georg Friedrich, b. 13 June 1721
7. Maria Benedicta, b. 24 Feb. 1725

AMERICAN RECORDS

Warwick Moravian Burials, Lancaster Co., PA:
1762 John George Kiesel, b. 1680 in Igelheim, Palatinate.

Joh. Niclaus Kiesel, d. 3 Nov. 1791; b. 24 Sept. 1716 in *Ingels*heim (sic),
Palatinate, son of John George and Christine Margaret (Stein) Kiesel.
Married Barbara Boehler and had 12 children. The following are listed in
the **Lititz Moravian KB:** (from John Humphrey's *Pennsylvania Births,
Lancaster County* volume):
1. Anna, b. 31 Jan. 1748
2. Johann Georg, b. 16 July 1750
3. Johann Georg, b. 30 Oct. 1751
4. Christina, b. 17 July 1754
5. Benigna, b. 9 Feb. 1757
6. Johannes, b. 12 June 1759
7. Johan Friedrich, b. 15 July 1762

George Frederick Kiesel, d. 6 Oct. 1798; b. 13 June 1721 in the Palatinate.
Came to Warwick 1729. Married Veronica Leuthold. They had children:
1. Anna Maria, b. 2 Jan. 1757
2. Veronica, b. 12 Nov. 1758
3. Christina, b. 10 Dec. 1760
4. Georg Friedrich, b. 6 July 1763

5. Nathaniel, b. 5 Sept. 1765
6. Anna, b. 21 Aug. 1767
7. Johannes, b. 4 Sept. 1769
8. Abraham Friedrich, b. 6 Jan. 1772
9. Anna Maria, b. 14 Sept. 1774

Died 3 Dec. 1773, age 89 years, Christina Margaretha Kiesel, nee Stein. Born on Christmas day, 1684 in Boeht [67459 Böhl] near Speier. Married John George Kiesel in 1712; had 7 children, survived by sons Nicholas and Frederick.

First Reformed Church, Lancaster, PA:
George Frederick Kissel, son of George Kissel of Warwick twp., m. 9 Nov. 1742 Anna Maria Werntz, daughter of Conrad Werntz of Earltown, Lancaster co.

York Moravian KB, York, PA:
Barbara Kiesel m. (1) Vincent Stauffer, and had children:
1. Christina, b. 7 Apr. 1734
2. Anna Margaretha, b. 16 May 1735
3. Anna Barbara, twin, b. 6 Sept. 1739
4. Heinrich, twin, b. 6 Sept. 1739
5. Vincent, b. 12 Mar. 1741
6. Frederich, b. 11 Oct. 1743
7. Joh. Georg, b. 15 May 1746
8. Daniel, b. 9 Oct. 1748.

Barbara (Kiesel) Stauffer m. (2) Christopher Haller

KLAMM (CLAMM), GEORG MICHEL Lachen-Speyerdorf=
KLAMM (CLAMM), JACOB 67435 Neustadt an der Weinstrasse
Hero, 1764
S-H, I: 699
EUROPEAN RECORDS

Lachen-Speyerdorf Reformed KB:
Georg Michael Clamm, son of Stephan Clamm, *Gerichtsverwandten* at Duttweiler [= 67435 Neustadt a.d. Weinstrasse], m. 29 Jan. 1744 Anna Margretha, daughter of the late Georg Theobald, inhabitant here. They had:
1. Johannes, b. 8 Jan. 1745, bp. 13 Jan. 1745
Sp.: Johannes, son of Peter Otterstätter

2. Johann Jacob, b. 3 July 1747, bp. 9 July 1747 conf. 1761
   Sp.: Jacob Möck and wife Anna Margretha
3. Maria Elisabetha, b. 15 Oct. 1749, bp. 18 Oct. 1749, conf. 1763
4. Johannes, b. 1 Sept. 1751, bp. 5 Sept. 1751, conf. 1764
   Sp.: Johannes, son of Peter Ottenstätter and wife Apollonia
5. Maria Catharina, b. 10 July 1753, bp. 12 July 1753
   Sp.: Maria Catharina, daughter of Philip Scherer
6. Christina Margretha, b. 20 Dec. 1754, bp. 26 Dec. 1754
7. Johan Peter, b. 11 Aug. 1756, bp. 15 Aug. 1756
8. Anna Margretha, b. 27 Sept. 1758, bp. 7 Oct. 1758
9. Anna Barbara, b. 31 May 1760, bp. 5 June 1760
10. Johan Nickel, b. 4 Mar. 1763, bp. 6 Mar. 1763

Emigration record:
Werner Hacker, *Auswanderungen aus Rheinpfalz und Saarland im 18. Jahrhundert:* #7746 Clamm, Gg. Michael, citizen of Lachen/Neustadt, wishes to emigrate (no destination given). Record dated 15 May 1764.

KLAPP (CLAP) JOST   67273 Weisenheim am Berg
KLAPP, JOHANN LUDWIG
KLAPP, JÖRG VALENTIN
James Goodwill, 1727
S-H, I: 10, 12

EUROPEAN RECORDS

Erpozheim Lutheran KB:
Conf. 1717, Anna Catharina Klapp from Weisenheim am Berg.

Conf. 1722, Anna Margaretha Klapp, daughter of Johann Jost Klapp from Weisenheim.

Dackenheim Lutheran KB:
Conf. 5 June 1726, Johann Ludwig Klapp from Weisenheim am Berg.

AMERICAN RECORDS

Rev. John Caspar Stoever's Records:
Georg Valentin Klapp in Oley had children:
   1. Joh. Philipp, b. 20 Feb. 1731, bp. 22 Feb. 1731
      Sp.: Joh. Jost Klapp

2. Maria Veronica, b. 14 Jan. 1733, bp. 19 Jan. 1733
   Sp.: Philipp Carl Jäger and wife Maria Veronica
3. Georg, b. 18 Jan. 1735, bp. 30 May 1735
   Sp.: Tobias Bechtel and wife Maria Elisabetha

Heidelberg Moravian KB, Heidelberg Twp., Berks Co., Family Register:
Heinrich Schuchardt, born in Eckartshausen [= 63654 Büdingen, Hesse], district of Marienborn, County Ysenburg, in the year 1695. He m. (1) Miss Catharina Baus and they had one daughter, Anna Maria. His first wife, Catharina, died in 1728. He m. (2) Anna Catharina Klapp, daughter of Jost Klapp of Iste, Hesse. They were married in Oley. Anna Catharina Klapp was born in 1707. They had children:
1. Johann Jost, b. 7 Feb. 1731, bp. by Caspar Stöver
2. Johannes, b. __ Aug. 1733, bp. by Johannes Müller
3. Anna Maria, b. 9 Mar. 1735, bp. by Philip Boehm
4. Maria Catharina, b. 9 May 1736, bp. by Philip Boehm
5. Maria Christina, b. 1737, bp. by Philip Boehm
6. Johann Heinrich, b. 8 Sept. 1741, bp. by Philip Boehm
7. Carl, b. 1743, bp. in Bern by Jacob Lischy
8. Tobias, b. 8 Feb. 1747, bp. Same day
9. Anna Elisabeth, b. 4 Dec. 1749, bp. 11 Dec. 1749

[For additional data on Heinrich Schuchardt, see Annette K. Burgert, *Eighteenth Century Emigrants from Langenselbold in Hesse to America,* 1998].

Heidelberg Moravian Member Catalog, 1746:
#9. Heinrich Schuchart, b. in Ekertshausen, Marienborn, son of Johannes and Christina Schuchart. He m. (1) July 1728 by Pastor Böhm in Wittpentown, Catharina; she died 1730. He m. (2) Catharina from Weistheim [Weisenheim] am Berg in the Graffschafft Leiningen. Her father was Jost Klopp in Olÿ, her mother Anna Maria. They were m. __ Oct. 1730 by George Bone [Boone], J.P. The catalog then names the children, as above, with a few date discrepancies.

KLAUER, GEORG   67251 Freinsheim
The Globe, 1723
   Signed the charter agreement as Jürich Clauer,
   arrived with others from Freinsheim.

EUROPEAN RECORDS

Freinsheim Reformed KB:
Georg Klauer m. 29 Jan. 1704 Anna Margaretha, daughter of Christopfel
Mülleman. They had children:
>   1. Susanna, bp. 21 Jan. 1705, conf. 1722
>   Sp.: Peter Abresch and Susanna
>   2. Joh. Niclaus, bp. 14 Apr. 1706
>   Sp.: Niclaus Seltzer, single son of Jacob Seltzer, here
>   and Fronick Klauer, single sister of Georg Klauer
>   3. Joh. Jacob, bp. 27 Nov. 1707
>   Sp.: Mstr. Hans Jacob Grossman, cooper and citizen here
>   4. Anna Margaretha, bp. 10 Nov. 1709
>   Sp.: Jacob Grossman and Anna Margaretha
>   5. Joh. Philip, bp. 6 Sept. 1711
>   Sp.: Philip Beyer and wife
>   6. Barbara, bp. ?16 July 1713 (mother named Susanna in this
>   one record; possibly an error).
>   Sp.: Balthasar Seiler and Anna Barbara his wife
>   7. Charlotta Eleonora, bp. 2 Jan. 1718
>   Sp.: Valentin Stadeler and Charlotta Eleonora, his wife
>   8. Johannes, bp. 21 Feb. 1720
>   Sp.: Johannes Klauer and Anna Margaretha, his wife.

The 1708 marriage record of this last sponsor, Johannes Klauer, names his
father as the late Gregory Klauer of Rockeweil, Canton Bern, Switzerland
[possibly CH-4914 Roggwil, BE]. The immigrant Georg Klauer is named in
an early record as *Herr von Juncken's Hoffman* here.

AMERICAN RECORDS

Rev. John Caspar Stoever's records:
Joh. Georg Klauer and wife Anna Margaretha sp. a child of Christoph
Amborn in 1735, in Coventry.

Trappe Lutheran KB, Montgomery Co., PA:
Christoph Amborn m. 21 May 1734 Susanna Klauer(in).

Johannes Klauer and wife Anna Maria had:
>   1. Johann Jacob, b. 2 Aug. 1748, bp. 31 July 1749
>   Sp.: Johannes du Frene

St. Matthew's Lutheran KB, Hanover, York Co., PA:
Philip Klauer had children:
>   1. Maria Barbara, b. 5 Sept. 1743, bp. Dec.1743
>   2. Susan Catharina, b. 5 Feb. 1745, bp. 23 Jan. 1746

Rev. Jacob Lischy's records, York Co., PA:
A Johannes Clauer with wife Margretha had a child bp. 1751.

Philadelphia Will Abstracts:
George Cloward, Chester Co., PA. Yeoman. 1 Feb. 1747/8- 21 Mar. 1747.
Will Book H: 523. Exr.: Wife Margaret. Children: Lyte, Jacob, John,
Susanna, and Barbara. Wit: Samuel Brockdin, Emanuel Bailey.

KLEMMER, HENRICH   67159 Friedelsheim
KLEMMER, JOHANNES
Alexander and Anne, 1730
S-H, I: 35, 36, 37
   (Johannes on A list: he signed the B list and C list as Johan Andreas
   Klemmer.)
                        EUROPEAN RECORDS

Friedelsheim Reformed KB:
Jacob Klemmer and wife Anna Catharina had a son:
        Joh. Hennrich, bp. 13 June 1688
        Sp.: Johannes Wingert and wife Anna

Hans Jacob Klemmer died 3 Oct. 1728, age 78 years

Hennrich Klemmer and Catharina his wife were sp. in 1728 for a child of
Johannes Klemmer.

Additional European Data:
"Eighteenth Century Emigrants to America from Palatine Parishes," by
Friedrich Krebs. *Pennsylvania Genealogical Magazine,* Vol. XXVI, No. 1
(1969). The material below in quotation is taken from this article.

        Alsheim - Gronau [= 67127 Rödersheim-Gronau]

"On 24 Jan. 1742, was married Johann Ludwig Klemmer, legitimate son of
Johann Henrick Klemmers, formerly an inhabitant of Gronau, but now a
citizen of Philadelphia in the so-called New World, to Anna Elisabetha
Böckels, legitimate daughter of Joh. Adam Böckels, formerly an inhabitant
of Friedelsheim. (Reformed Church book, [67149] Meckenheim.)"

[Note by AKB: Maria Elisabetha Böckel, bp. 26 June 1718, daughter of
Hans Adam Böckel, who married 28 Nov. 1714 Salome, daughter of the late
Hennrich Sinn of Friedelsheim.]

"Johann Henrick Klemmer landed in Philadelphia as "Henerich Clemer" in the year 1730 on the Ship *Alexander and Anne.* The oath of abjuration followed on 5 September 1730. (Hinke-Strassburger, *Pennsylvania German Pioneers,* I, Lists 12 A-B.) The birth entry of Johann Ludwig Klemmer, who is probably the "Ludewig Klemmer" who emigrated to Philadelphia in 1751 (ship *Neptune,* 1751, Hinke-Strassburger, I, List 172-C), was not to be found in the records of the Reformed Church of Alsheim."

[Note by AKB: Ludwig Klemmer of Friedelsheim had already returned to Pennsylvania by 1747, and had a child baptized at Conewago that year.]

"According to an entry in the church records of the Reformed Congregation of Alsheim, the Johann Henrich Klemmer who emigrated to America in 1730 had married Catharina, widow of Michael Davernier, on 16 Sept. 1710. The son of Jacob Klemmer and Anna Catharina, he was baptized 13 June 1688, in the Reformed Church in Friedelsheim. This Jacob Klemmer had emigrated to the Palatinate from the district of Zurich as "Hannss Jacob Klemmer"; in Friedelsheim on 17 Sep. 1678 he married a daughter of Hans Jacob Pfaffmann, a citizen of Friedelsheim. As may often be observed, this American immigrant family is of Swiss extraction."

AMERICAN RECORDS

Conewago (Christ Church), near Littlestown, Adams Co., PA:
Ludwig Klemer from Friedelsheim, Pfalz, and wife Maria Elisabetha had a son:
>
>   George Valentine, b. 10 Feb. 1747, bp. 6 May 1747
>   Sp.: George Valentine Beckel

Other later Klemmers appear in this church record.

York County Will Abstracts:
Valentine Climmer, dated 7 Oct. 1785, probated 31 Oct. 1785. Executors: Elizabeth Climer and Adam Winteroth. Wife: Margaret. Children: John, George, Elemer (!), Susanna.

A branch of this Klemmer family of Conewago appears to have gone to Virginia. One George Klemmer left a will in Rockbridge county, VA., in 1828. His wife was Modlena and he had 8 children. A George Klemmer with wife Magdalena had children baptized at Conewago in 1775, 1780, and 1782.

KNOLL, JOHANNES age 29   Niederhochstadt=
Elizabeth, 1733   76879 Hochstadt, Pfalz
S-H, I: 113, 114, 115, and Appendix, 765
Other family members on ship: Anna Maria, age 26; Elisabetha age 3 3/4;
Margaretha, age 1 1/2.

EUROPEAN RECORDS

Niederhochstadt Reformed KB:
Johann Knoll and wife Johanna Maria had a daughter:
     Anna Margretha, bp. 3 Apr. 1732
     Sp.: Georg Valentin Schmidt and Catharina Margretha

AMERICAN RECORDS

Christ "Little Tulpehocken" Church, Tulpehocken, Berks Co., PA:
Johannes Knoll had a daughter:
     Maria Catarina, b. 21 July 1741 bp. 4 Sept. 1742
     Sp.: Georg Daniel Gensemer [q.v.]

Christ "Little Tulpehocken" Church, Berks Co., PA.

190   *Palatine Origins of*

Christ Tulpehocken KB, Stouchsburg, Berks Co., PA:
Married 20 Jan. 1748, John Knoll, widower, and Gertrude Faust.

Died 12 Apr. 1748, John Knoll.

Philadelphia Administration Book F, p. 148: John Knoll, 1748

Lancaster County Orphans' Court Docket, dated 6 Dec. 1748:
Mary Margaret Knull, a minor orphan child of John Knull, chooses Peter
Lowker to be her guardian. John Jacob Knull chuses (sic) Valentin
Herclerod as his guardian. John Valentin Knull chuses (sic) Valentine
Unrough to be his guardian. (These three children would be over 14 y. of
age.)

John Troutman is appointed guardian over Anna Catharina Knull. (She
would be under 14 years of age.)

Host Reformed KB, Tulpehocken, Berks Co., PA:
Confirmed Easter 1755: Jacob Knoll, son of Johannes Knoll, and Valentin
Knoll, son of Johannes Knoll.

Reed's Cemetery, Tulpehocken, Berks County:
Buried: Elisabeth Knoll, b. 19 June 1729; d. 11 Aug. 1797, wife of Leonard
Rieth; m. 48 years, 9 months; had 9 children.

KOCH, CONRAD   67256 Weisenheim am Sand
Pennsylvania Marchant, 1731
S-H, I: 43, 45, 46
   Children on list under 16: Johannes and Julian Koog

EUROPEAN RECORDS

Weisenheim am Sand Reformed KB:
Conrad Koch m. 23 Apr. 1715 Anna Barbara, widow of Johannes Lippert.
They had children:
   1. Johannes, b. 25 June 1719
   2. Anna Juliana, b. 21 Mar. 1723

Conrad Koch from Nassau Erfurth in Hessen m. 15 Feb. 1682 Ursula, widow
of Johannes Wirth, nee Zentner from Langen Kandel [= 76870 Kandel,
Pfalz]. She m. (1) 14 Jan. 1679 Johannes Wirth from Hundsweil in
Switzerland [CH-9064 Hundwil, AR].

Lambsheim Reformed KB:
Johannes Lippert from Weisenheim am Sand and wife Anna Barbara had:
1. Elisabeth, b. 30 Jan. 1701
2. Maria Barbara
   m. 24 May 1729 Johannes Mehn, son of Friederich Mehn
3. Joh. Jacob, b. 1708 [q.v.- em. 1736].
   m. 13 July 1734 Anna Maria Schwab, daughter of
   Johannes Schwab from Canton Bern, Switzerland.

KOCH, PHILIP JACOB   67112 Mutterstadt
Edinburgh, 1748
S-H, I: 372

EUROPEAN RECORDS

Mutterstadt Reformed KB:
Philip Daniel Koch and wife Maria Elisabetha had a son:
      Philip Jacob, bp. 6 Mar. 1709
      notation in KB: "To Pennsylvania 1748"

Philip Jacob Koch m. 23 Jan. 1731 Anna Barbara Brandt, daughter of Johan
Ludwig Brandt of Igelheim (=67459 Böhl-Iggelheim). They had children:
      1. Maria Katharina, b. 27 Sept. 1731 bp. 30 Sept. 1731
      2. Clara Elisabetha, b. 11 Mar. 1733 bp. 15 Mar. 1733
      3. Maria Elisabetha, b. ?5 Mar. 1736 bp. 3 Apr. 1736

The marriage of Philip Daniel Koch is not recorded in the Mutterstadt
Reformed KB, nor the baptism of his daughter Catharina who married Carl
Ludwig Keiper and also emigrated to Pennsylvania.

AMERICAN RECORDS

Tohickon Reformed KB, Bucks Co., PA:
Philip Jacob Koch and wife Anna Barbara had a son:
      Carl Ludwig, bp. 27 May 1750
      Sp.: Carl Ludwig Keiper [q.v.] and wife

Lower Saucon Reformed Church, Northampton Co., PA:
Philip Jacob Koch d. 10 June 1792, bur. 12 June 1792; age 83 y. 4 mo.

KOHL, CONRAD   67256 Weisenheim am Sand
Lydia, 1749
S-H, I: 421

EUROPEAN RECORDS

Lambsheim Reformed KB:
Johannes Kohl and Elisabetha had:
    1. Anna Catharina, bp. 15 Mar. 1699
    2. Georg Conrad, bp. 18 Sept. 1701
    3. Henrich, bp. 9 Aug. 1703

Weisenheim am Sand Reformed KB:
Conrad Kohl, son of the late Johannes Kohl, m. 1732 Maria Christina, daughter of Michael Schick. They had children:
    1. Catharina Elisabetha, b. 2 May 1734
    2. Johan Caspar, b. 7 Mar. 1736
    3. Elisabetha, b. 14 Sept. 1738
    4. Anna Amelia, b. 4 Sept. 1740
    5. Johan Michael, b. 13 Jan. 1743

KORNMANN, LUDWIG age 24   Niederhochstadt=
Samuel, 1737   76879 Hochstadt, Pfalz
S-H, I: 169, 170, 172

EUROPEAN RECORDS

Niederhochstadt Reformed KB:
Anna Sybilla Unruhe was bp. 12 Nov. 1713, the daughter of Hans Philips Unruhe and wife Anna Barbara. Sponsors at her baptism were Velten Chard and Anna Sybilla Laux.

Ludwig Kornmann, son of Nicolai Kornmann m. 17 Jan. 1736 Sybilla Unruh, daughter of Hans Philip Unruh. They had a son:
    Johann Adam, bp. 6 Oct. 1736
    Sp.: Joh. Adam Öhli and Anna Maria Bressler, both single

AMERICAN RECORDS

Rev. John Caspar Stoever's Records:
John Ludwig Kornmann and wife sponsor a child of Valentin Meyer at Atolhoe in 1746.

Host Reformed KB, Tulpehocken, Berks Co., PA:
Ludwig Kornmann and wife had children:
    1. Johannes, bp. 30 Nov. 1748
       Sp.: J. Mayer [q.v.]
    2. Catharina Barbara, bp. 21 Feb. 1750
       Sp.: Georg Simon Pressler and wife [q.v.]

Loodwick Cornman of Lancaster County nat. 4 Oct. 1749.

KRÄMER, HANS ADAM   67161 Gönnheim
Pennsylvania Merchant, 1731   55270 Essenheim
S-H, I: 43, 44, 45, 46
   (He arrived with wife Elisabetha and sons-in-law Jacob Lanius and Martin
   Schultz. There are other Krämers on this ship list: a Henrich Krämer
   listed with the men, another Elisabeth Kreemer listed with the women and
   the following children: Eve, Christian, Adam, Maria, and Christina
   Kreemer.)

EUROPEAN RECORDS

Essenheim Reformed KB:
Johannes Kramer and Elisabeth had a son:
       Hans Adam, bp. 14 Sept. 1679
       Sp.: Hans Adam Wagner

Johan Adam Krämer, son of the late Johannes Krämer, inhabitant here, m.
19 Nov. 1708 Maria Eliesabeth, dau. of Wentz Wolff. They had children:
    1. Catharina, b. 19 Apr. 1710, bp. 21 Apr. 1710
       Sp.: Eliesabeth Catarina, daughter of the late Johannes Vetter
       [She m. Martin Schultz [q.v.]
    2. Anna Juliana, b. 2 Dec. 1711, bp. 6 Dec. 1711
       Sp.: Anna Juliana, wife of Kilian Iber
       [She m. Jacob Lanius [q.v.]
    3. Maria Elisabetta, bp. 3 June 1714
       Sp.: Maria Elisabetta, wife of Hans Adam Bloth
    4. Eva, bp. 29 Mar. 1717
       Sp.: Eva, wife of Hans Adam Wagner
    5. Christianus, bp. 6 Jan. 1721
       Sp.: Christianus Schmahl, inhabitant here.

Died Jan. 1711 - Wentz Wolff, the younger, age 42 y. and 10 mo.

Gönnheim Reformed KB:
Hans Adam Krähmer and wife Maria Elisabetha had a daughter:
Christina Appolonia, bp. 18 Dec. 1729
Sp.: Christina Appolonia, daughter of Philip Heyer

Anna Catharina, daughter of Hans Adam Krämer of Gönnheim, m. 3 Sep. 1728 at Friedelsheim Hans Martin Schultheis [q.v., Schultz].

Juliana daughter of Joh. Adam Krähmer, m. 13 June 1730 at Gönnheim Joh. Jacob Lanius from [67149] Meckenhiem. [See Lanius].

AMERICAN RECORDS

York Moravian KB, York Co., PA:
Information recorded in the York Moravian KB provided the clue that the Krämer family may have come to Gönnheim from [55270] Essenheim, near Mainz. Juliana Krämer Lanius is listed in that record as b. 2 Jan. 1712 at Eysenheim. Other York co. families, Fischel and Schmahl, also came from Essenheim.

Rev. Jacob Lischy's records, York Co., PA:
Joh. Adam Krämer and Anna Catharina Welshöfer sponsored a child of Niclaus Freytag in 1745.

Christian Krämer and wife Anna Barbara [nee Heyer, q.v.] had children:
1. Anna Catharina, bp. 24 Aug. 1747
   Sp.: Friedrich Hayer and Catharina
2. Maria Elisabetha, bp. 19 Jan. 1752
   Sp.: Maria Elisabetha Lanius
3. Eva, bp. 14 July 1754
   Sp.: Eva Bahn

Adam Krämer and wife Susanna had children:
1. Joh. Heinrich, bp. 7 June 1752
   Sp.: Heinrich Bahn and Eva
2. Maria Elisabetha, bp. __ Oct. 1764
   Sp.; Maria Elisabetha Schultz

Joh. Adam Krämer and wife Catharina had a child:
Catharina, bp. 6 Aug. 1758
Sp.: Niclaus Schram and Catharina

Joh. Adam Krämer and wife Anna Elisabeth had a child:
>   Maria Elisabetha, bp. 24 Jan. 1762
>   Sp.: Phil. Jacob Zinn and Maria Elisabetha

York County Will Abstracts:
Adam Cramer of York, dated 2 June 1798, probated 8 Feb. 1800. Executors:
Martin Gartner and Adam Bahn. Wife: Ann Elizabeth Cremmer. Children:
Elizabeth, Adam, Jacob, Catharina, Eve, Abraham, Peter.

KRAUSS, NICKEL   67251 Freinsheim
Prelist, with Hyeronimus Haas [q.v.]

EUROPEAN RECORDS

Freinsheim Reformed KB:
Alexander Kraus of Lamersheim [67229 Laumersheim] m. 22 Oct. 1698
Anna Christina (no name recorded). They had children:
>   1. Anna Barbara, bp. 10 Jan. 1700
>   Sp.: Hans Velten, son of Meister Velten Schaffner
>   and Anna Barbara, daughter of Hans Bartel ?Krifft
>   2. Valentin, b. 26 Nov. 1701, bp. 30 Nov. 1701
>   Sp.: Velten Schaffner and wife Maria Catharina
>   3. Niclas, bp. 13 Apr. 1705
>   Sp.: Niclaus Koch from [67245] Lambsheim, Lutheran and
>   his wife, Reformed
>   4. Catharina, bp. 28 Jan. 1709
>   Sp.: Jost Willi and wife Catharina

AMERICAN RECORDS

Trappe Lutheran KB, Montgomery Co., PA:
Conf. 1754, Christian Krause, son of Nicolaus Krause, age 20 years, cannot
read fluently.
Conf. 1754, Catharina Kraus(in), daughter of Nicolaus, granddaughter of
Hieronymus Haas, age 18 years. Reads fairly well.

Nicolaus Krauss and Eva Catharina had:
>   Anna Maria, b. 6 Apr. 1747, bp. 29 May 1748
>   Sp.: Anna Maria Schmidin and Jurg Krauss

New Hanover Lutheran KB, Montgomery Co., PA:
Jürg Oxlein m. 2 Jan. 1759 Maria Catharina Kraus.

KREBS, JOH. CHRISTIAN   67361 Freisbach
Peggy, 1753
S-H, I: 546, 548

EUROPEAN RECORDS

Freisbach Lutheran KB:
Joh. Christian Krebs and wife Anna Barbara had children:
  1. Christine Barbara, b. 29 Jan. 1748, bp. 31 Jan. 1748
     There is a notation in the KB: "in America".
  2. Maria Barbara, b. 11 Aug. 1750, bp. 12 Aug. 1750
     again, the notation "in America".
  3. Anna Maria, b. 4 Jan. 1753, bp. 6 Jan. 1753
     notation in the KB: "in Pensyl."
     Sp.: Anna Maria, wife of Nicklaus Krebs of [67377]
     Gommersheim.

The village of Freisbach.

KREDER, MORITZ   67251 Freinsheim
Mortonhouse, 1729
S-H, I: 24
  [name on list: Moret Creetor]

EUROPEAN RECORDS

Freinsheim Reformed KB:
Anton Kreder and wife (Anna Margareth) had a son:
     Joh. Moritz, bp. 28 May 1703
     Sp.: Joh. Moritz Hiski and wife Catharina

AMERICAN RECORDS

Chambers, *Early Germans of New Jersey,* pg. 636:
one Moritz Creter appears on an early list (ca 1754) of N.J. residents.

KREITER, HENRICH
St. Andrew Galley, 1737
S-H, I: 179, 181, 183

Lachen-Speyerdorf=
67435 Neustadt a.d. Weinstrasse

EUROPEAN RECORDS

Lachen Reformed KB:
Henrich Kreiter, apprentice cartwright, son of the late Henrich Kreiter, *Gemeinsmann* at [68119] Mannheim, m. 13 Sept. 1730 Anna Barbara, daughter of Görg Hammann, *Gemeinsmann* here.

AMERICAN RECORDS

St. Joseph's Lutheran and Reformed KB, Pike Twp., Berks Co., PA:
One Heinrich Kreiter with wife Elisabeth had a daughter:
Anna Eva, b. 8 Oct. 1765

KÜCHLER, HENRICH age 33   67454 Hassloch
St. Andrew, 1741
S-H, I: 303 [appears on A list as Hendrick Kugley, not on B or C lists.]

EUROPEAN RECORDS

Hassloch Lutheran KB:
Joh. Georg Küchler, single, from Heydenheim [?89518 Heidenheim a. d. Brenz], m. 23 June 1705 at Böhl, Anna Catharina Stutter, single.
Joh. Georg Küchler and Anna Catharina had:
1. Joh. Jacob, bp. 9 May 1706, Böhl
   Sp.: Johann Jacob Blum
2. Maria Judith, b. 24 Feb. 1708, bp. 26 Feb. 1708
   Sp.: Maria Judith Haffner
3. Johannes, bp. 30 July 1709, Böhl
   Sp.: Johannes Stubler
4. **Henrich,** bp. 23 Nov. 1710, Böhl
   Sp.: Henrich Stuter; Anna Elisabetha Bomlin
5. Anna Margretha, b. 17 Feb. 1712, bp. 21 Feb. 1712
   Sp.: Anna Margretha Christ
6. Hans Adam (surname Kiechler)
   b. 27 Sept. 1714, bp. 30 Sept. 1714
   Sp.: Hans Adam Hasslinger

7. Philipp Rheinhard, b. 22 Mar. 1717, bp. 26 Mar. 1717
   Sp.: Philipp Rheinhard Bommel
8. Johann Petter, b. 18 Aug. 1720, bp. 19 Aug. 1720
   Sp.: Johann Petter Blum
9. Lorentz, b. 9 Oct. 1726, bp. 13 Oct. 1726
   Sp.: Lorentz Metzger

Henrich Küchler, single, m. 14 May 1733 at Böhl Anna Maria nee ?Zöller from Lachen [= 67435 Neustadt a. d. Weinstrasse].

See immigrant Jacob Bricker from Lachen who married Henrich Kugeler's deserted wife.

KUDER, [KUTRER] ENGELHARDT   67454 Hassloch
Ann, 1749
S-H, I: 416

EUROPEAN RECORDS

Hassloch Lutheran KB:
Johann Caspar Kuder from Neckargartach [=74078 Heilbronn] m. 13 Sept. 1718 at Hassloch Anna Catharina Holtzinger. Their son:
        Engelhard Ludwig, b. 13 June 1719, bp. 18 June 1719

Conf. 1733: Engelhard Kutterer

Lutheran Church Record in Rotterdam, Holland (record located by Kenneth McCrea):
Married 31 May 1749:
Engelhart Kutter, J.M. van Neustad in de Paltz [Neustadt, Pfalz]
Anna Catharina Lucas, J.D. uit Z Graaffsclap Leidingen [Graffschafft Leiningen].   Comment recorded in KB: to Nieuw Engeland.

AMERICAN RECORDS

Christ Lutheran KB, York, PA:
Engelhard Kuder and Catharina had:
        1. Juliana, b. 29 July 1758, bp. 6 Aug. 1758
           Sp.: John Adam Bott and wife Juliana

York Reformed KB, York, PA:
Engelhard Kuder and wife sp. a child of Bernhard Holtzinger [q.v.] in 1766.

KÜHLWEIN, DOROTHEA   67256 Weisenheim am Sand
prelist, 1719   67245 Lambsheim

EUROPEAN RECORDS

Weisenheim am Sand Reformed KB:
Theobald Kühlwein m. 29 Sept. 1663 Dorothea Weber, daughter of Johannes Weber of Weisenheim am Sand.

Lambsheim Reformed KB:
Theobald Kühlwein and wife Dorothea had children:
1. Sara, b. ca. 1665, m. Johannes Fischer
2. Sebastian m. Margareta Weissbecker
3. Veronica m. Abraham Zimmerman on 24 Apr. 1719 sold property and left for Pennsylvania
4. Albert
5. Catharina m. Matthäus Baumann; emigrated to PA ca. 1714
6. Anna Maria m. Joh. Valentin Stahl
7. Maria Elisabeth m. Joh. Adam Pfarr
8. Philipp, emigrated 1709

Lambsheim from Merian's Topographia Germaniae, 1672

Theobald Kühlwein's widow Dorothea sold her property in Lambsheim in 1719, with the intention of going to Pennsylvania. Her daughter Veronica married Abraham Zimmerman and also emigrated to Pennsylvania; Her daughter Catharina married Matthäus Baumann, who is mentioned in the Lambsheim records as a Pietist. They also emigrated to Pennsylvania about 1714, and founded a sect called "Baumannites" or "New-Born" in the Oley Valley. The first of this group to come to America was the son Philipp

Kühlwein who arrived in 1709. He married a daughter of Jean LeDee and settled in Oley. For further detail on all of these families and other emigrants from Lambsheim, see:

"Emigration Materials from Lambsheim in the Palatinate" by Heinrich Rembe, edited by Don Yoder, published in *Rhineland Emigrants. Lists of German Settlers in Colonial America.* Baltimore, 1981.

KUNTZ, LORENTZ   Lachen-Speyerdorf=
Johnson, 1732   67435 Neustadt an der Weinstrasse
S-H, I: 72, 76, 77
   [passengers on ship: Lorentz Kuntz; women above 14: Maria Konce; girls under 14: Gertrudt Konce, Margt. Konce & Maria Konce.]

EUROPEAN RECORDS

Lachen-Speyerdorf Reformed KB:
Lorentz Cuntz, son of Michel Kuntz, was confirmed 1713.

Lorentz Kuntz and wife Maria Eva had children:
   1. Hans Georg, b. 11 Sept. 1723   twin
   2. Maria Helena, b. 11 Sept. 1723 twin
      Sp.: Hans Görg Hoos and wife Maria Helena
   3. Maria Gertraud, b. 2 Oct. 1724
      Sp.: Gertraud, wife of Michel Blumm
   4. Hans Melchior, b. 7 July 1726, died June 1731
   5. Johannes, b. 29 Oct. 1727
      Sp.: Johannes Möchtersheimer
   6. Anna Margretha, b. 20 Jan. 1730
      Sp.: Anna Margretha, daughter of David Trüb
   7. Anna Maria, b. 9 Mar. 1732
      Sp.: Anna Maria, daughter of Peter Lippert

AMERICAN RECORDS

First Reformed KB, Philadelphia:
Henry Wynheimer from Manheim [68159-69 Mannheim], Palatinate, m. 26 July 1748 Anna Maria Kuntz, daughter of Lorentz Kuntz of our congregation. They had:
   1. Anna Maria, b. 5 Dec. 1749

Philadelphia Wills and Administrations:
Lawrence Kuntz, 1781   Adm. I: 35

LANG, JOHANNES, age 46   Niederhochstadt=
LANG, JOH. VALENTIN, age 16   76879 Hochstadt, Pfalz
Samuel, 1737
S-H, I: 169, 170, 172

EUROPEAN RECORDS

Niederhochstadt Reformed KB:
Johannes Lang and wife Maria Magdalena had children:
1. **Joh. Valentin,** bp. 6 May 1721
   Sp.: Joh. Valentin Bressler and Anna Maria
2. Anna Maria, bp. 16 May 1730
   Sp.: Georg Valentin Degen and Anna Maria Wolff
3. Henrich Frederich, b. 4 July 1732, bp. 6 July 1732
   Sp.: Henrich Friderich Martin and wife
   Elisabetha from Appenhoffen [= 76831 Billigheim].

Died 15 Mar. 1735, Maria Magdalena Lang, age 35 years.

AMERICAN RECORDS

Manuscript Collection, PA State Museum, # 63.19.26:
Document dated 13 May 1737, issued by the Reformed Pastor Joh. Georg Kessler, pastor at Niederhochstadt, lists the above family data from the Niederhochstadt records. Johannes Lang's occupation given as master weaver and the document was issued by the pastor since the family was leaving for America.

Christ "Little Tulpehocken" Lutheran KB, Berks Co., PA:
One Johannes Lang had children:
1. Johannes, b. 21 Aug. 1737, bp. 5 Feb. 1737
   [sic; read 1738]
   Sp.: Johannes Schoff and wife Susanna
2. Anna Margaretha, b. 21 Feb. 1740, bp. 30 Mar. 1740
   Sp.: Ludwig Wagner and his wife
3. Jacob, b. 12 Jan. 1742, bp. 24 Jan. 1742
   Sp.: Jacob Schopff and his wife
4. Joh. Georg Thomas, b. 1 July 1746, bp. 6 Sept. 1746
   Sp.: Joh. Thomas Kern and wife Margaretha

LANIUS, JACOB   67149 Meckenheim
Pennsylvania Merchant, 1731   67161 Gönnheim
S-H, I: 43, 45, 46
(Julian Laamsen on list of women over 16)

EUROPEAN RECORDS

Gönnheim Reformed KB:
Johann Jacob Lanius from Meckenheim m. 13 June 1730 at Gönnheim
Juliana, daughter of Joh. Adam Krähmer.

AMERICAN RECORDS

York Moravian Records:
Jacob Lanius, b. 12 May 1708 in Meckenheim on the Hart. Came to
America in 1731. He lived first at Kreutz Creek, and on 25 Aug. 1762
moved to Yorktown. Reformed religion. He died in Yorktown 1 Mar. 1778.
He married 13 June 1730 Juliana nee Kramer. She was born in Eysenheim
(55270 Essenheim) 2 Jan. 1712. She died at Yorktown 26 Feb. 1769. They
had children:
    1. A daughter, b. 3 June 1731, died
    2. Jacob, b. 14 Aug. 1732
    3. Elisabeth, b. 29 June 1734, m. Weidner
    4. Catharina, b. 12 June 1736, m. Römer
    5. Heinrich, b. 21 Aug. 1738, m. Anna Margaretha Fischel
    6. Juliana, b. 12 Dec. 1740, m. Michael Fischel
    7. Eva, b. 1 May 1742
    8. Maria Magdalena, b. 23 Oct. 1745, m. Ephr. Culver
       (She is listed as Anna Maria in Lischy's record.)
    9. Wilhelm, b. 23 Sep. 1748, m. Elisabeth Heckedorn
    10. Johannes, b. 24 Mar. 1751
    11. Joh. Adam, b. 14 Apr. 1754, d. 20 Apr. 1754

York County Will Abstracts:
Jacob Lanius, Yorktown. Dated 20 June 1775, probated 28 Apr. 1778.
Executors: Jacob, Henry, and William Lanius. Names chidlren: Jacob,
Henry, William, John, Mary wife of Christopher Weider, Catharina wife of
Frederick Rohmer, Juliana wife of Michael Fishel, and Magdalena wife of
Ephraim Colver.

Jacob Lannius, Hellam, York Co., Moravian Sacrament taken 21 Mar. 1761
for naturalization.

LAUFER, CHRISTIAN 67256 Weisenheim am Sand
Pennsylvania Merchant, 1731
S-H, I: 44
Passengers on list: Christian and Laurence Kooker

EUROPEAN RECORDS

Weisenheim am Sand Reformed KB:
Joseph Läufer from Switzerland m. 18 Feb. 1680 Elisabetha, daughter of Ludwig Fischer from Hessen. They had a son:
> Joh. Heinrich, bp. 25 Mar. 1683
> > Sp.: Oswald Weih and wife Maria

The Reformed Church in Weisenheim am Sand

Joh. Heinrich Leuffer, son of Joseph Leuffer, m. (1) 11 July 1708 Feronica, daughter of Melchior Caspar, deceased citizen at [67273] Dackenheim. They had four children, and Fronica, wife of Heinrich Läufer, died 11 Oct. 1717, aged 30 years.

Heinrich Läufer, widower, m. (2) 7 Sept. 1718 Anna Catharina, widow of Joh. Heinrich Eberle of Gross-Carlbach [67229 Grosskarlbach]. She was the daughter of Wilhelm Schmidt. They had children:
    1. Johann Laurent [q.v.], b. 1 June 1719
    2. Maria Ursula, b. 5 Oct. 1721
    3. Johan Christian, b. 17 May 1723
    4. Joh. Jacob, b. 31 Mar. 1726
    5. Johannes, b. 25 July 1728

Heinrich Läufer died and Anna Catharina, his widow, married (3) 16 Jan. 1731 Barthel Guckert [q.v.] from [67435] Neustadt an der Haardt. They emigrated in 1731, bringing with them the 2 surviving sons of her previous marriage.

AMERICAN RECORDS

Stone Reformed KB, Kreidersville, Northampton Co., PA:
List of contributors to the building fund, dated 16 Mar. 1771
Christian Lauffer	£3-0-0
1. his son Bardollomey	£1-0-0
2. his son Petter	£0-10-0
3. his daughter Susanna	£0-10-0

Bartholomew Lafer and wife Anna Maria (nee Drumm, daughter of Philip Drumm) had a son:
    Adam, b. 14 Dec. 1774, bp. 12 Feb. 1775
    Sp.: Adam Lafer and Margaret Trumm (Drumm).

Tohickon Reformed KB, Bucks Co., PA:
Christian Lauffer (also Laffer) and wife Susanna had children:
    4. John Adam, b. 10 Feb. 1758, bp. 29 Mar. 1758
    Sp.: Adam Driesbach and wife
    5. Henry, b. 14 Aug. 1759, bp. 16 Sept. 1759
    Sp.: Henry Beck and wife.

Christian Lauffer and wife sp. in 1758, Susanna, dau. of Nicholas Schneider. Christian Lafer and wife sp. in 1760, Susanna, dau. of Adam Marsh.

Christian Lauffer and wife Susanna Catharina also appear in the Emanuel Reformed KB, Moore Twp., Northampton Co., PA, as baptismal sponsors.

Christian Lauffer and wife Susanna had other children, and the following have been established from Westmoreland County sources:

     6. Magdalena, b. ca 1762, d. 13 Dec. 1737, m. John Bash (from her obit. in *The Pennsylvania Argus,* newspaper in western PA.)

     7. Anna Maria, b. 10 May 1763, d. 11 Apr. 1737, m. Philip Wentzell (from her obit. in *The Pennsylvania Argus.*)

     8. Catharine, b. ca 1765, m. Frederick Reiss

     9. Elisabeth, b. ca 1768, d. 10 Feb. 1853, m. Jacob Christman

     10. John, b. 8 Mar. 1769, d. 18 Feb. 1851, m. Susanna Kemmerer

     11. Christian, Jr. b. ca 1770, d. 2 Oct. 1823

Christian Laffer and family moved to Westmoreland County, PA, and he died there in 1796. On 2 June 1796, letters of adm. on his estate were granted to Bartel Laffer. The son, Bartel Lauffer was a County Commissioner for Westmoreland County in 1796; he also kept a tavern in which temporary courts were held for about three years. In 1797, he appears on a tax list for Brady Twp., Butler Co., PA. In 1810, he was living in Sugarcreek Twp., Armstrong Co., PA, where his wife died in 1814. Bartel Laffer then moved to Tuscarawas Co., OH, where he m. (2) 30 Nov. 1815 Catharina Mosser. Bartholomew Laffer died in Sandyville, OH, 1 Jan. 1822, aged 72 years.

Christian Lauffer, Lehi Twp., Northampton Co., nat. Fall, 1765.

LAUFER, LAURENT [Lorentz]   67256 Weisenheim am Sand
Pennsylvania Merchant, 1731
S-H, I: 44
Passengers on list: Christian and Laurence Kooker

EUROPEAN RECORDS

Weisenheim am Sand Reformed KB:
Joseph Läufer from Switzerland m. 18 Feb. 1680 Elisabetha, daughter of Ludwig Fischer from Hessen. They had a son:
     Joh. Heinrich, bp. 25 Mar. 1683
     Sp.: Oswald Weih and wife Maria

Joh. Heinrich Leuffer, son of Joseph Leuffer, m. (1) 11 July 1708 Feronica, daughter of Melchior Caspar, deceased citizen at [67273] Dackenheim. They had four children, and Fronica, wife of Heinrich Läufer, died 11 Oct. 1717, aged 30 years.

Heinrich Läufer, widower, m. (2) 7 Sept. 1718 Anna Catharina, widow of Joh. Heinrich Eberle of Gross-Carlbach [67229 Grosskarlbach]. She was the daughter of Wilhelm Schmidt. They had children:
1. **Johann Laurent,** b. 1 June 1719
2. Maria Ursula, b. 5 Oct. 1721
3. Johan Christian [q.v.], b. 17 May 1723
4. Joh. Jacob, b. 31 Mar. 1726
5. Johannes, b. 25 July 1728

Heinrich Läufer died and Anna Catharina, his widow, married (3) 16 Jan. 1731 Barthel Guckert [q.v.] from [67435] Neustadt an der Haardt. They emigrated in 1731, bringing with them the 2 surviving sons of her previous marriage.

AMERICAN RECORDS

St. Paul's Church, Red Hill, Montgomery Co., PA:
Lorentz Lauffer and wife Elisabeth Margareth had children:
1. Maria Catharina, b. 21 Nov. 1744
   Sp.: Christian Lauffer and Catharina

Philadelphia Probate Records, Administration # 44, 1757:
Laurence Lawfer, deceased; adm. bond taken out by Michael Long, George Sheafer and John Allbright of Berks in the amount of £200, 12 Jan. 1757. Note: Michael Long married Margaret Lawfer, widow of the deceased, who is unable to travel, being big with child. Documents in the probate packet include accounting of Michael Long, and also the inventory of Lorentz Laffer, late in Oley Hills, Berks County, Turner.

Berks County Orphans Court petition:
The petition of Philip Laufer, eldest son and heir at law of Laurence Laufer, late of Rockland Twp., Berks Co., Yeoman, deceased; that your petitioner's said father died about 30 years since intestate leaving a widow Rachael and issue six children, to wit: Philip Laufer, the petitioner, Eve the wife of John Nicholas Bader, Elizabeth the wife of Conrad Rauenzan, Margaret the wife of Casper Werfel, Barbara the wife of Jacob Boover, and Catharine who is since deceased leaving three children by her husband Conrad Rauenzan: to wit Conrad, George Adam and Magdalena Rauenzan. Laurence Laufer died owning a certain tract of land in Rockland Twp. adj. lands of Gotlob Weida, Ester Kucher and others containing 75 acres. Petitioner prays for an inquest to make partition to divide the premises to and among the children or appraise the same. Dated 21 Mar. 1796. It was determined the property could not be divided and it was valued at £445. The eldest son, Philip Laufer, accepted the property at valuation, and gave bonds to the other heirs.

Lawrence Lawfer, Philadelphia County, nat. 24 Sept. 1741.

LAUX (LAUCKS), PETER age 32   Niederhochstadt=
Friendship, 1738   76879 Hochstadt, Pfalz
S-H, I: 226, 228, 230

EUROPEAN RECORDS

Niederhochstadt Reformed KB:
Johan Peter Laux and wife Anna Catharina had children:
>   1. Georg Theobald, b. 6 Oct. 1730, bp. 8 Oct. 1730
>   Sp.: Georg Theobald Becker and Anna Margaretha
>   2. Catharina, b. 29 Jan. 1733, bp. 1 Feb. 1733
>   Sp.: Valentin Becker and Catharina Heusel, both single
>   3. Catharina, b. 17 Feb. 1735, bp. 20 Feb. 1735
>   Sp.: Georg Valentin Degen and Catharina Heusel, both single
>   4. Johan Jacob, b. 16 Aug. 1737, bp. 18 Aug. 1737
>   Sp.: Johan Jacob Wolff and Agatha

AMERICAN RECORDS

Rev. John Caspar Stoever's Records:
Peter Laucks m. 28 June 1743 Anna Barbara Kuerschner, Tulpehocken.

Lancaster County Land Warrant, Pennsylvania Archives, Third Series:
Peter Laux, 150 acres, 3 Nov. 1738

Host Reformed KB, Tulpehocken, Berks Co., PA:
Confirmed 1755, Joh. Georg Laux, son of Peter Laux.

Georg Deobold Lauchs (Laux) and Maria Apollonia had:
>   1. Maria Elisabeth, b. 21 Apr. 1765, bp. 22 Apr. 1765
>   Sp.: Elisabeth Becker and Christoffel Kayser
>   2. Anna Catharina, b. 28 Mar. 1769, bp. 2 Apr. 1769
>   Sp.: Benjamin Zerbe and wife

George Laux (Lauchs) and wife Anna Catharina had:
>   1. Johann Caspar, bp. 7 Aug. 1768
>   Sp.: Caspar Runkel and wife Eva
>   2. Eva Catharina, b. 25 Oct. 1770, bp. 4 Nov. 1770
>   Sp.: Eva Kayser

3. Maria Gretha, b. 15 Feb. 1773, bp. 28 Feb. 1773
   Sp.: Valentin Mayer and wife
4. Maria Margareth, b. 15 Nov. 1774, bp. 4 Dec. 1774
   Sp.: Adam Kalbach and wife
5. Peter, b. 1 July 1776, bp. 7 July 1776
   Sp.: Jacob Knoll and wife

Peter Laux of Tulpyhoccon, Lancaster County, nat. 25 Sept. 1751.

LAŸE, MARTIN   67454 Hassloch
St. Mark, 1741
S-H, I: 297, 298, 300

EUROPEAN RECORDS

Hassloch Reformed KB:
Recorded in the Hassloch marriage record: Martin Laÿe, son of Johannes
Laÿe of Muspach [Mussbach = 67435 Neustadt a.d. Weinstrasse] and Anna
Margaretha, daughter of the late Martin Fechter formerly of Assernheim
[Assenheim = 67126 Hochdorf-Assenheim], m. 6 Jan.1730. The emigration
of Martin Laÿe in 1741 is verified by the card file at the Heimatstelle Pfalz,
Kaiserslautern.

LE BEAU, (LEBO), JOHANNES   Friesenheim=
Prelist   67071 Ludwigshafen am Rhein

EUROPEAN RECORDS

Oggersheim Reformed KB:
Jean LeBeau, son of Abraham LeBeau, deceased *Gemeinsmann* at [68766]
Hockenheim, m. 4 July 1708 in Friesenheim, Anna, daughter of Pierre
Croiiet, *Gemeinsmann* in Friesenheim. They had children:
1. Anna Margaretha, b. 20 May 1717
2. Maria Magdalena, b. 3 may 1723

AMERICAN RECORDS

Berks County Abstracts of Wills and Adm.:
John Lebo of Alsace Twp., Berks Co., PA left a will, probated 4 June 1759. Mentions his sons; Peter, Abraham, and daughter Margaret. "The above three children being from a former wife". Provides for wife Anna Mary and mentions 8 children by last wife; Paul, Jacob, Leonard, Isaac, Henry, Modleen Sharer, Mary Werner, and Elisabeth Marks.

LEHMAN, CHRISTIAN   Lachen-Speyerdorf=
Thistle of Glasgow, 1730   67435 Neustadt an der Weinstrasse
S-H, I: 31, 32, 33

EUROPEAN RECORDS

Lachen-Speyerdorf Reformed KB:
The earliest mention of the suname in the Lachen records is 1664, Benedict Lehman is mentioned as formerly a citizen of Leützingen, Bern Switzerland. [possibly today: CH-3706 Leissigen, BE].

Conf. 1710: Christian Lehemann, son of Jacob Lehemann of Lachen.

Christian Lehemann and wife Anna Maria had children:
1. Johannes, b. 17 Aug. 1720
   Sp.: Johannes Stumpff, single, master linenweaver
   at Speyerdorf
2. Anna Maria, b. and bp. 8 Mar. 1722
   Sp.: Anna Maria, wife of Johannes Dambach of
   Musspach [= 67435 Neustadt a.d. Weinstrasse].
3. Susanna, bp. 6 Aug. 1724
   Sp.: Susanna, wife of Christian Zoog, Musspach
4. Johannes, b. 19 Apr. 1727, bp. 23 Apr. 1727; d. 10 Apr. 1729
   Sp.: Johannes Otterstätter
5. Johan Adam, b. 16 Nov. 1729, bp. 20 Nov.; d. 16 Dec. 1729
   Sp.: Johann Adam Sauter

AMERICAN RECORDS

New Goshenhoppen Reformed KB, Montgomery Co., PA:
Anna Maria, wife of Christian Lehman, sp. a child of Thomas Hamman [q.v.] in 1732. Christian Leeman and daughter Anna Maria sp. a child of Thomas Hamman in 1736.

Confirmed at New Goshenhoppen, 1748-1759:
    Christian Lehmann's three sons.
    Christian Lehmann's daughter.

Christian Leeman was an elder in the Skippack congregation in 1734.

Philadelphia Wills & Administrations:
One Christian Leaman, 1749   Philadelphia Wills J: 100
Salford, County of Philadelphia. Husbandman. 11 Oct. 1748/9-29 Apr. 1749.
Wife: Ann Margaret. Children: John, Susannah, Anne, George, Hans Adam,
Dority, Jacob and Ludwig. Exrs: Daniel Hester, Jacob Husse. Wit.: Jacob
Arnt, Philip Gable, William Nash.

Christian Leaman, Philadelphia Co., nat. 10 and 11 Apr. 1741
Another Christian Lehman, with John Lehman, Germantown, Philadelphia
nat. Apr. 1743

LEHMAN, JOHANNES   Lachen-Speyerdorf=
Adventure, 1727   67435 Neustadt an der Weinstrasse
S-H, I: 14, 15
[signed Johannes Lemahn]

EUROPEAN RECORDS

Lachen-Speyerdorf Reformed KB:
Hans Jacob Lehman and wife Anna Barbara had a son:
    Johannes, bp. 13 June 1700, conf. 1718
    Sp.: Johannes Otterstätter

Johannes Lehemann, son of the late Jacob Lehemann, m. 10 Nov. 1723
Adriana, daughter of the late Jacob Brunner of Duttweiler [= 67435
Neustadt a.d. Weinstrasse]. They had:
    1. Loysa Eleonora, b. 5 Jan. 1726, bp. 10 Jan. 1726
    Sp.: Loysa, wife of Friederich Metzger, oil miller at Speyerdorf

AMERICAN RECORDS

One Johannes Leman signed the letter dated 10 May 1730 sent by the
Skippack congregation to Amsterdam.

Rev. John Caspar Stoever's records:
Johannes Lehman (Conewago) had:
>Johannes, b. 22 Apr. 1734, bp. 22 May 1735
>Sp.: Johan Theobald Jung

Conewago Reformed KB, near Littlestown, Adams Co., PA:
John Lehman and wife were sp. in 1747.

Johan Leman and wife Anna Maria had:
>John Georg, b. 21 Feb. 1751, bp. 7 May 1751
>Sp.: Georg Spanzeiler and wife Louise

Georg Lehman and wife Maria Salome had:
>Anna Margaret, b. 18 Jan. 1752, bp. 25 Jan. 1752
>Sp.: Anna Margaret Spengel, single

St. Matthew's Lutheran KB, Hanover, York Co., PA:
Georg Spanseyler m. 12 Feb. 1744 Louisa Lehman. They had a son:
>Georg, b. 12 May 1751, bp. 12 June 1751 (Conewago KB)
>Sp.: John Leman and Anna Maria

York County Deeds, Vol. 3: 566-567:
Dated 3 May 1762- John Leman of Berks Co. bought 123 acres (now in York Co.) from Thomas Kenworthy.

Adams Co. Wills, Book B: 182-
Christian Lehman, Menallen Twp. Wife: Hannah. Children: John, Christian, Mary, Rachel.

Philadelphia Adm. G: 61:
John Leaman, 1756

Another Johannes Lehman arrived on the ship York in 1725.

One Johannes Lehmann was naturalized in Philadelphia Co., Apr. 1748.

LEHMAN, LUDWIG   Lachen-Speyerdorf=
Johnson, 1732   67435 Neustadt an der Weinstrasse
S-H, I: 72, 76, 77
[passengers on ship: Lodawick Leeman, Eva Leeman & Maria Leighman]

EUROPEAN RECORDS

Lachen-Speyerdorf Reformed KB:
Hans Jacob Lehman and wife Barbara had:
> Joh. Ludwig, bp. 13 Nov. 1703
> Sp.: Joh. Ludwig Lehman, son of Benedict Lehman

Conf. 1718: Johannes Lehemann and Joh. Ludwig Lehemann, brothers, sons of Jacob Lehman.

Died 20 May 1726, Barbara, widow of the late Jacob Lehemann here, age 54½ years.

Johann Ludwig Lehemann and wife Maria ___ (into center of book) had children:
> 1. Anna Maria, b. & bp. 1 Oct. 1724   twin
> 2. Anna Barbara, b. & bp. 1 Oct. 1724 twin
>   Sp.: Anna Maria, wife of Christian Lehemann and
>   Anna Barbara, the grandmother, widow of the late
>   Jacob Lehemann.

Joh. Ludwig Lehman and wife Anna Eva had children:
> 3. a son, b. and d. 22 May 1727
> 4. Anna Maria, b. 20 July 1728, bp. 25 July 1728
>   Sp.: Anna Maria, wife of Johannes Wiedemann
>   of Gimmeldingen [= 67435 Neustadt a.d. Weinstrasse].
> 5. Johannes b. ca 1730, died 14 Dec. 1731

AMERICAN RECORDS

Hocker, *Genealogical Data, German Settlers of PA:*
Sower's newspaper, dated 16 Jan. 1755: Matheus Schaeuffele, Old Goshen-hoppen (Montgomery Co.) took over the plantation of his father-in-law, Ludwig Lehmann, and gave his brother-in-law, Jacob Keller, a bond for £100. He has now returned the plantation to Lehmann, and issues warning against payments on the bond.

Philadelphia Staatsbote, dated 10 May 1774: Conrad Schwartz, a saddler from Lancaster, has removed to a house opposite Ludwig Lehmann's house on the south side of King Street.

Old Goshenhoppen Lutheran KB, Montgomery Co., PA:
Married at Ludwig Lehmann's place 20 Oct. 1752: Mattheus Scheiffele, Lutheran and single, from the district of Ulm, son of Johann Caspar and Anna Maria Scheiffele still living in Germany, and Margaretha, Reformed,

single daughter of Ludwig Lehmann and wife Eva, both Reformed. She is living with her parents in Fredrich twp.

Philadelphia Wills and Administrations:
Ludwig Lehman, 1772 Philadelphia Wills P: 339; Adm. H: 103.

Ludwick Lehman, Philadelphia Co., nat. 18 Nov. 1769 in Berks co.

LERU, JONAS   Hembshof, Oggersheim=
Prelist   67071 Ludwigshafen am Rhein

EUROPEAN RECORDS

Oggersheim Reformed KB:
Jonas LeRoux, residing on the Hembshof, and Catharina had children:
1. Maria, bp. 31 Dec. 1702
2. Elisabetha, bp. 15 Oct. 1705
3. Ester, b. 13 Apr. 1707, bp. 17 Apr. 1707
4. Catharina, b. 13 May 1708, bp. 17 May 1708
5. Johann Georg, b. 2 Aug. 1709, bp. 4 Aug. 1709
6. Jonas, b. 4 Dec. 1710, bp. 7 Dec. 1710
7. Margaretha, b. 2 Apr. 1712, bp. 10 Apr. 1712
8. Abraham, bp. __ Feb. 1716
9. Peter, bp. 27 Jan. 1717, bp. 31 Jan.1717
10. Johanna Catharina, b. 26 Aug. 1718, bp. 4 Sept. 1718
11. Possibly Isaac (faded), bp. __ Dec. 1719

AMERICAN RECORDS

Trinity Lutheran KB, New Holland, Lancaster Co., PA:
Jonas Läru, Jr., sp. a child of Ignatius Leitners in 1733. Abraham LeRu had a daughter Anna Maria, b. 1 Dec. 1738. Peter Lehru had a daughter Ester Margreth, b. 8 Oct. 1745.

Lower Bermudian KB, Adams Co., PA:
Isaac and Abraham Lero are mentioned in 1745. Isaac Leruh m. 22 July 1759 Agnes Merchene.

Lancaster Co., PA land records:
1725 Jonas LaRou - a request for 100 acres by Daniel Fiere.

PA Archives, Third Series, Vol XIX, p. 729:
1734 Jonas LeRue, warrant for 350 acres.

PA Archives, Third Series, Vol XXIV, p. 457, 458:
1737 Jonas LeRue warrant for 50 acres.

The family Bible of Johann Georg LeRuh, b. 1709, is in the custody of The Genealogical Society of Pennsylvania. In it, Georg recorded on the inside of the back cover: I, Johan Jörg LeRu, b. 4 August 1709, "auff dem Heimbhoff". Another notation in the Bible is: "Anno 1739 August 13 Jonas Larow Sein Biebell". Also recorded in this Bible: "in 1760? (or 1763?) 1 Jan. my father Jonas Leru died."

The son Jonas settled in the area that is today Myerstown, Pa.

LINDENSCHMIDT, DANIEL   67454 Hassloch
Edinburgh, 1748
S-H, I: 372
EUROPEAN RECORDS

Hassloch Reformed KB:
Johannes Lindenschmidt and wife Maria Elisabetha (married before the church record begins) had at least six children, three of whom were immigrants: Maria Magdalena married Johannes Altenberger [q.v.], Johann Daniel, and Johann Ludwig [q.v.].

Maria Elisabetha, wife of Johannes Lindenschmidt, was buried 5 Aug. 1742, age 69 years. Johannes Lindenschmidt was buried 11 Dec. 1747, age 76 years.

Mathes Muschel and his wife Anna Magdalena (married before the church record begins) had a daughter:
Anna Barbara, conf. 1710, age 15

Mathess Muschel was buried 17 Apr. 1742, age 76 years. His widow, Anna Magdalena, nee Leibrock, was buried 1 Jan. 1760, age 88 years, leaving 47 grandchildren and 25 great grandchildren.

Joh. Daniel Lindenschmidt, son of Johannes Lindenschmidt m. (1) 5 Sept. 1719 Anna Barbara Muschel, daughter of Mathes Muschel. Their children:
1. Anna Magdalena, b. 29 Oct. 1720; bp. 3 Nov. 1720
2. Joh. Friederich, b. 24 Dec. 1723; bp. 27 Dec. 1723
3. Anna Margaretha, b. 20 Sept. 1727; bp. 23 Sept. 1727
4. Joh. Valentin, b. 27 June 1731; d. 25 Jan. 1733

D. 25 Jan. 1746, Anna Barbara wife of Daniel Lindenschmidt, age 50 years.

Daniel Lindenschmidt, widower, m. (2) 31 Aug. 1746 Catharina Huber, daughter of the deceased Hans Michael Huber.

Hassloch Gerichtsbuch:
Mathes Muschel from "Webenheimb königl. Schwedischer Jurisdiction" granted citizen ship 1 Dec. 1712.

AMERICAN RECORDS

Trinity Lutheran KB and First Reformed KB, Lancaster, PA:
Johann Daniel Lindenschmidt, Reformed, and his wife Catharina, Lutheran had the following children baptized:
  1. Margaretha, b. 23 Dec. 1749
  2. John George, b. 20 Aug. 1753
  3. Joh. Jacob, b. 16 Apr. 1750
  4. Catharina, b. 29 Aug. 1757

LINDENSCHMIDT, LUDWIG   67454 Hassloch
Edinburgh, 1748
S-H, I: 372

EUROPEAN RECORDS

Hassloch Reformed KB:
Johan Ludwich Lindenschmidt, son of Johannes Lindenschmidt, m. 2 Sept. 1732 Maria Elisabetha, daughter of Jacob Boll. Joh. Ludwig was b. 4 July 1705; confirmed 1721. His wife was b. 24 Dec. 1711, daughter of Jacob Boll and Maria Elisabetha. Ludwig Lindenschmidt and Maria Elisabetha had children:
  1. Johannata Magdalena, b. 26 Sept. 1733; bp. 28 Sept. 1733
  2. Barbara, b. 23 June 1736
  3. Johann Jost, b. 6 Sept. 1738
  4. Johann Jacob, b. 1 May 1741
  5. Anna Sara, b. 23 July 1743
  6. Anna Maria, b. 20 Mar. 1746

Hassloch Gerichtsbuch:
Jacob Boll from Biel was granted citizenship 27 Nov. 1710.

AMERICAN RECORDS

Tochickon Union Church, Bedminster Twp., Bucks County:
Ludwig Lindenschmidt and wife Mary Elisabeth (Eliza) had children:
  7. Maria Magdalena, bp. 19 Nov. 1749
     Sp.: George Henry Seibel [q.v.] and Mary Magdalena.
  8. Mary Elisabeth bp. 26 July 1752 at Saucon
     Sp.: Balthasar Erbach and Mary Elisabeth
  9. Eva Eliza bp. 12 Oct. 1754; Eva confirmed 1770.
     Sp.: Balthasar Erbach and Mary Eliza.

John Jost Lindenschmidt was confirmed at Tohickon on Easter 1758.

LIPPERT, JOH. JACOB   67256 Weisenheim am Sand
Harle, 1736
S-H, I: 156
  with Anna Maria
EUROPEAN RECORDS

Lambsheim Reformed KB:
Johannes Lippert from Weisenheim am Sand and wife Anna Barbara had:
  1. Elisabeth, b. 30 Jan. 1701
  2. Maria Barbara
     m. 24 May 1729 Johannes Mehn, son of Friederich Mehn
  3. **Joh. Jacob**, b. 1708
     m. 13 July 1734 Anna Maria Schwab, daughter of
     Johannes Schwab from Canton Bern, Switzerland.

Weisenheim am Sand Reformed KB:
Johann Jacob Lippert, son of the late Johannes Lippert m. 13 July 1734
Anna Maria Schwab daughter of the late Johann Schwab *"aus dem Berner
Gebiet in der Schweiz"*.

AMERICAN RECORDS

Rev. Boos' records, Schwartzwald burials, Berks Co., PA:
Jacob Lippert (Ruscombmanor), b. 1710, d. 26 Dec. 1783.

Berks County Abstracts of Wills and Adm.:
Jacob Lippert, Ruscombmanor. 11 Aug. 1781 - 29 Dec. 1783.
Wife: Anna Mary. Son John; to grandson Philip Miller £20 in gold or silver
when 21 years old. To daughter Anna Barbara £30 and to daughter Sarah

£15 after wife's decease. At that time, exrs. to sell plantation containing 244 acres and divide proceeds between sons Adam, Michael, Emanuel and daughters Anna Barbara and Sarah. Son Adam and friend Elias Wagner, exrs. Wit.: Peter Fisher and William Reeser.

LOCHBAUM, JACOB age 34   67365 Schwegenheim
LOCHBAUM, CHRISTINA (wife) age 33
LOCHBAUM, (LUGETBOM), ANNA age 10
Hope, 1733
S-H, I: 116, 119, 121

EUROPEAN RECORDS

Schwegenheim Reformed KB:
Jacob Lochbauhm, son of Nicolaus, Reformed, m. 9 July 1720 Maria Christina Rohrbach, Catholic, b. in Bellheim [76756].
Jacob Lochbaum and wife Christina had a daughter:
        Anna Maria Catharina Elisabetha, b. 2 May (1731? - page torn)
        Sp.: Jacob Sch ___?___ and A. Maria Catharina

LÖCHNER, HANS GEORG age 33   67454 Hassloch
St. Andrew, 1741
S-H, I: 304, 305
    [appears on B list as Hans Geo. (X) Legener, on C List as Hans George (X) Lägner; did not sign.]

EUROPEAN RECORDS

Hassloch Reformed KB:
Johann Georg Löchner, tailor, son of the late Joh. Georg Löchner, master tailor in [67149] Meckenheim, m. 12 Jan. 1729 Hedwig Sophia Susanna, widow of the late Ulrich Hautz. They had children:
        1. Anna Margretha, b. 27 Dec. 1729, died.
        2. Anna Margretha, b. 3 Feb. 1731.

The wife of Johann Georg Löchner died in 1735, and he m. (2) 26 Oct. 1735 Maria Magdalena, daughter of the late Huprecht Freÿtag from Gönnheim.

Gönnheim Reformed KB:
Joh. Georg Löchner and wife Maria Magdalena had a daughter:
Maria Magdalena, bp. 25 Nov. 1736
Sp.: Joh. Wilhelm Krebs and Maria Magdalena.

AMERICAN RECORDS

Rev. John Casper Stoever's Records:
George Lechner and wife (n.n.) were sp. in 1751 for Anna Margaretha,
daughter of Stephen Cunradt, Swatara. George Lechner also sp. in 1752
George Philipp Cunradt, son of Stephen Cunradt, Swatara.

Trinity Tulpehocken Reformed KB, Jackson Twp., Lebanon Co., PA:
Georg Lochner and wife Maria Elizabeth were sp. at a bp. in 1778 for a
child of John Aurand. Margaret Lechner, single, was sp. in 1779 for a child
of Georg von Nied. Margaret Lechner was a sp. in 1788 for a child of Frantz
Zeller.

LÖFFEL (LÖFFLER), BALTHASAR   Oggersheim=
Two Brothers, 1750   67071 Ludwigshafen am Rhein
S-H, I: 438

EUROPEAN RECORDS

Oggersheim Reformed KB:
Hans Philipp Löffel, son of the late Dieter Löffel m. 25 Jan. 1707 Anna
Rosina, daughter of the deceased Tobias Schiffel (?) of Edi(gheim?)
[Edigheim = 67069 Ludwigshafen]. They had the following son:
Balthasar, b. 3 Jan. 1721, bp. 6 Jan. 1721

Balthasar Löffel m. 11 Feb. 1749 (page half torn away, name of wife missing
entirely).

AMERICAN RECORDS

Berks County Abstracts of Wills:
Balzer Leffel of Amity Twp., Berks Co., left a will dated 23 Jan. 1796;
probated 3 Aug. 1796. He mentioned his wife (who is not named) and the
following children: John, Jacob, deceased, Mary wife of John Schrader, Eve
wife of Benjamin Boone, Elisabeth wife of Philip Marquart, Sevilla wife of
John Pott, Susanna wife of Henry Remely.

A Sevilla Leffel of Amity Twp., Berks Co., left a will dated 16 June 1804; probated 28 July 1804 which names the same children.

Rev. Joh. Wilhelm Boos' Burial Records:
Sibilla Löffel b. 1 Mar. 1728, d. 21 July 1804.
Balthasar Löffel (Amity), b. 2 Feb. 1721, d. 13 July 1796.

LÖSCHERT [LESCHER], NICHOLAUS   67245 Lambsheim
Globe, 1723
  [signed the ship's contract]

EUROPEAN RECORDS

Lambsheim Reformed KB:
Nicholaus Löschert, Reformed, son of Jacob Löschert, and wife Maria Johanna appear in the Lambsheim records 1696-1718. Children:
    1. Petronella, bp. 15 Dec. 1697
    2. Catharina, ca. 1700
    3. Hans Jacob, b. 31 Dec. 1702
    4. Joh. Jacob, b. 28 June 1704

According to the *"Kaufprotokoll der Gemeinde Lambsheim"* Nicholaus Löschert and wife Maria Johanna sold property on 20 Mar. 1723 and 13 Apr. 1723.

AMERICAN RECORDS

Oley Valley Heritage, p. 177, Appendix 7: Known heads of households and single freemen residing in the Oley Valley 1701-1741.
    Johannes (John) Lesher 1735 Oley
    Nicolaus Lesher, Sr.   1729 Oley
    Nicolaus Lesher, Jr.   1735 Oley
    (Not a son to the one above).

Nicolaus Lesher was a landowner in Oley Twp., Phila. Co. in 1750.

Philadelphia Administrations, F 310:
Nicholas Lesher, 1749, Est. No. 87

Nicholas Leisher, Jr. of Phila. Co. nat. by Act, 1735.

MAURER, RUDOLPH   67251 Freinsheim
MAURER, JACOB
MAURER, FRIEDRICH
MAURER, ANDREAS
Prelist, after 1717

EUROPEAN RECORDS

Freinsheim Reformed KB:
Joh. Rudolff Maurer, tile or brick maker, and wife Fronica had children:
    1. Jacob Maurer, conf. 1717
    2. Friederich Maurer, conf. 1717
    3. Joh. Rudolph, bp. 25 Mar. 1704
       Sp.: Joh. Rudolph Maurer, two of this name, with their wives:
       the one from [67245] Lambsheim and the other from [67273]
       Weisenheim am Berg. [Heinrich Rembe, *Lambsheim:* pg. 172: the
       Rudolf Maurer who lived in Lambsheim came from Jais (?Jeus),
       Canton Bern [possibly CH-2565 Jens, BE].
    4. Anna Maria, bp. 11 Dec. 1707
       Sp.: Joseph Wylly, master baker, and wife Anna Maria
    5. Maria Sophia, bp. 26 May 1709, d. 11 Feb. 1710
       Sp.: Andreas Seltzer and wife Sophia
    6. Andreas, bp. 11 Mar. 1711, same sp. as above
    7. Johannes, b. ca 1713, bp. not located, d. 16 July 1717, age 4.

AMERICAN RECORDS

New Goshenhoppen Reformed KB, Montgomery Co., PA:
Frederich Maurer and wife had children:
    1. Anna Maria, bp. __ Aug. 1731
       Sp.: Anna Maria Segler
    2. Jacob, bp. __ Aug. 1731
       Sp.: Jacob Maurer
    3. Joh. Fridrich, bp. 21 Jan. 1733
       Sp.: Fridrich Hilligas & wife

Jacob Maurer and wife Sophia Lisabeth had:
    1. Andreas, bp. 30 July 1732
       Sp.: Andreas Maurer
    2. Elisabetha Barbara, bp. 19 June 1737
       Sp.: Fridrich Hilligas & wife
    3. Anna Maria, bp. 30 Aug. 1741
       Sp.: Anna Maria Segler

Andreas Maurer and wife Anna Maria had:
  1. Joh. Andreas, bp. 11 Apr. 1737
     Sp.: Andreas Sechler & Anna Maria
  2. Margreda, bp. 4 Sept. 1742
     Sp.: Anna Margreda Lauer
  3. Margreda, bp. 5 May 1744

Rudolph Maurer and wife were sp. at a baptism in 1747.

Undated marriages, # 54 (between 1748-1758):
Andreas Mauerer m. Maria Barbara Steinman.

Confirmed 1748-1758:
Sophia Maurer	Mathys Maurer
Veronica Maurer	Peter Maurer
Barbara Maurer	Rudolf Maurer
Jacob Maurer	John Maurer
Andreas Maurer	Maria Eva Maurer
Jacob Maurer	John Maurer

Confirmed 1759:
  Elisabeth Mauerer
  Anna Maria Mauerer
  Catharina Mauerer

Journals and Papers of David Shultze:
Died 4 July 1768, wife of Friederich Mowrer, age about 60 years.

MAURER, JOH. HENRICH   67157 Wachenheim an der Weinstrasse
St. Mark, 1741
S-H, I: 297, 298, 300

EUROPEAN RECORDS

Wachenheim Reformed KB:
Henrich Maurer, apprentice carpenter m. 21 June 1729 Anna Maria widow
of the late Michel _____(ink blot), from the Anspach region.
They had:
  Margaret Felicitas, bp. 26 Feb. 1730
  Sp.: Felix N.----, swiss, and Anna Margaretha

MAURER, PETER   67157 Wachenheim an der Weinstrasse
ship unknown

EUROPEAN RECORDS

Wachenheim Reformed KB:
Peter Maurer, son of dec'd Görg Henrich Maurer of [67229] Laumersheim,
m. 17 Jan. 1731 Anna Margaretha, widow of the late Joh. Hermann. They
had:
>   1. Joh. Adam, bp. 8 Dec. 1731
>   Sp.: Johannes Haberman, Mayor of Laumersheim and
>   Maria Margaretha, wife of Joh. Adam Hermann

AMERICAN RECORDS

Conewago Reformed KB, Adams Co., PA:
In 1749 Peter Maurer and wife Anna Margaret sp. a child of Philip
Grünewald's at Conewago.

MECK, JOHANN NICOLAUS   Lachen-Speyerdorf=
Brotherhood, 1750   67435 Neustadt an der Weinstrasse
S-H, I: 447

EUROPEAN RECORDS

Lachen-Speyerdorf Reformed KB:
Johannes Möck, son of Caspar Möck m. 21 June 1724 Anna Christina,
daughter of Henrich Reiff. Anna Christina Reiff was bp. 28 Oct. 1699,
daughter of Henrich Reiff and wife Elisabeth nee Beer.

Johannes Meck and Anna Christina had a son:
>   Johann Nicolaus, b. 12 Dec. 1732, bp. 14 Dec. 1732, conf. 1746
>   Sp.: Johann Nicolaus Jung, master baker here

AMERICAN RECORDS

I. Daniel Rupp, *A Collection of Thirty Thousand Names:* pg. 243, footnote:
Johann Nicolaus Meck died at Harrisburg Apr. 16, 1803, age 71 years 4
months and 4 days. He was an ancestor of Rupp's wife.

Dauphin County Deed Book E-I: 248:
dated 19 Apr. 1791, recorded 1 June 1792: Nicholas Meck, Lampeter Twp.,
Lancaster Co. and wife Catharina to Jacob Meck of Upper Paxton Twp.

(their son) 305 3/4 acres in Upper Paxton Twp. patented 1790 to Nicholas Meck.

Dauphin County Will Abstracts:
Nicholas Meck, Borough of Harrisburg, dated 20 Dec. 1802, proven 22 Apr. 1803. Wife: Catharine. Children: Philip, John, Jacob, Henry, and Mary wife of Henry Amend. Grandchildren: George, John, Jacob and Catharine, children of son Philip.
Wit.: Samuel Hill, Wm. McKinzey and J. Downey.

Mennonite Family History, **Vol. XVIII, No. 4, Oct. 1999:**
Article on the Ament (Am Endt) family: Johannes Ament (Am Endt) arrived on the ship *Lydia,* 1743. He was born in 1725, son of Hans Georg Am Endt of [67273] Weisenheim am Berg, and Anna Maria nee Gemlich. Johannes Ament married Maria Appolonia Paulus from [55270] Essenheim. John Amen's estate papers (1788, Dauphin County Adm.) mentions "Philip Meck who intermarried with Catharine, one of the daughters of John Amen, deceased."

MELLINGER, DAVID   Ruchheim=
Snow *Louisa,* 1752   67071 Ludwigshafen am Rhein
S-H, I: 506

EUROPEAN RECORDS

Ruchheim Reformed KB:
Johannes Mellinger and wife Maria Eva had a son:
David, bp. 3 Jan. 1717

AMERICAN RECORDS

Lancaster County Will Abstracts:
George Mumma of Hempfield Twp. 9 Apr. 1785 - 29 July 1786.
Wife: Barbara; children: Elizabeth wife of John Carle, Magdalena wife of Jacob Strickler, Juliana wife of **David Mellinger**, Maria Barbara, George, Henry, David and Jacob. Exrs: John Hertzler and John Shirk.

His widow Barbara Mumma also left a will dated 24 Oct. 1788, naming children: Christian, Henry, Jacob, Magdalena wife of Abraham Hiestand, Juliana wife of David Mellinger, Mary wife of Jacob Hertzler, Barbara, George, and David. Exr: David Brubacher.

Anna Newcomet of Manor Twp., will dated 4 Apr. 1807 - 28 May 1813.
Named her daughter Anna wife of **David Mellinger**, and he is also named as
one of the exrs.

York County Will Abstracts:
David Mellinger, Hellam Twp. 4 Oct.1814 - 26 Apr. 1815.
Children: Frances wife of Martin Slenker, Barbara wife of Christian Lehman,
John, Elizabeth, David, Joseph, Christian, and Abraham.
Exrs: John Mellinger and Joseph Kaufman.

MELLINGER, JOHANNES   Ruchheim=
MELLINGER, BENEDICT   67071 Ludwigshafen am Rhein
St. Andrew, 1749
S-H, I: 396, 397

EUROPEAN RECORDS

Ruchheim Reformed KB:
Johannes Mellinger and wife Maria Eva had a son:
        Benedictus, bp. 25 Jan. 1715
        Sp.: Peter DeFrene and wife

AMERICAN RECORDS

Lancaster County Will Abstracts:
Benedict Mellinger, Manor Twp., 17 Sept. 1794 - 9 May 1795.
Children: David, Christian, John, and Feronica wife of Jacob Ebersole.
Exrs: David and John Mellinger.

MERCKEL, NICOLAUS   67259 Kleinniedesheim
Brothers, 1751
S-H, I: 464

EUROPEAN RECORDS

Gross- and Kleinniedesheim Lutheran KB:
Johann Nicolaus Merckel and wife Anna Catharina had children:
        1. Joh. Niclaus, b. 22 Apr. 1728, bp. 29 Apr. 1728
           Sp.: His father, Herr Johann Niclaus Merckel,
           Schultheiss here.

2. Anna Maria, b. 15 Jan. 1730, bp. 18 Jan. 1730
Sp.: The grandmother on the father's side, Anna Maria

AMERICAN RECORDS

Moselem Lutheran KB, Berks Co., PA:
Georg Michel Dürr, son of Michael Dürr in Rotenburg an der Tauber [91541 Rothenburg ob der Tauber], m. 14 Dec. 1756 Magdalena Merklin, daughter of Nicholaus Merkel.

Joh. Georg Springer, smith, son of Peter Springer from Donegal, m. 14 Dec. 1756 Catharine Merkel, single daughter of Nicholaus Merkel.

Nicolaus Merkle, single son of Nicolaus Merkle, m. 2 May 1758 Maria Margretha Frey, single daughter of Andreas Frey, a master wheelwright.

Wolfgang Mehring, a master weaver from Anspach, m. 16 Oct. 1758 Anna Merkel, single daughter of Nicholaus Merkel.

MERCKLIN, CHRISTIAN   Schillersdorf=
Prelist, ca. 1720   F-67340 Ingwiller
                                 Oppau= 67069 Ludwigshafen
                                          67245 Lambsheim

EUROPEAN RECORDS

Schillersdorf Lutheran KB:
Hans Georg Märcklin, citizen and cartwright, m. 16 June 1672 Esther, daughter of Diebold Haus, citizen and cook at Oberbrunn [Oberbronn = F-67110 Niederbronn les Bains]. They had:
1. Dieboldt, bp. 11 June 1673
2. probably Christian (gap in bp. record 1674-76)
3. Margretha, bp. 29 Dec. 1681
4. Niclaus, bp. 7 Sept. 1684
5. Hans Georg, bp. 12 June 1787

Frankenthal (includes Oppau) Lutheran KB:
Christian Mercklin, apprentice cartwright, son of Hans Georg Mercklin, master cartwright at Schüllersdorf near Buschweiler [Buswiller= 67350 Pfaffenhoffen] in Unter Elsass m. 6 Jan. 1707 in the church at Lambsheim Anna Catharina, dau. of Johannes Benner [surname given as Bender in

Lambsheim records], citizen and smith at Lambsheim, also *vorsteher* of the Ev. Lutheran congregation there.

Heinrich Rembe, *Lambsheim*:
Christian Merkel, Reformed, cartwright, m. 1711 Catharina Bender. He is mentioned in the Lambsheim records in 1704 when his property was valued at 100 florins. On 19 Apr. 1719, he sold his house to Dietrich Roth and emigrated to Pennsylvania.

Christian Merkel and wife Catharina had:
>Maria Catharina, bp. 21 Jan. 1715
>Sp.: Catharina Ursula Schmidt
>(This daughter married in PA the early Lutheran pastor Johann Caspar Stoever.)

AMERICAN RECORDS

Moselem Lutheran KB, Richmond Twp., Berks Co., PA:
Joh. Frederich Kramer, son of Sebold Kramer, m. 10 Dec. 1745 Anna Maria Merklin, daughter of Christian Merklin.

Peter Merkel, son of Christian Merkel, m. 16 Nov. 1750 Catharina, daughter of Egidius Grimm.

Peter Biel, son of Peter Biel, m. 3 Dec. 1750 Magdalena Merkel, daughter of Christian Merkel.

Georg Merklin, son of Christian Merklin, m. 18 Dec. 1750 Christina Hill, daughter of Jacob Hill [q.v.].

Caspar Merklin, son of Christian Merklin, m. 1 Apr. 1755 Elisabetha, daughter of Egydius Grimm.

Berks County Abstracts of Wills:
Christian Merckel, Philadelphia County, 25 Apr. 1749 - 22 May 1766. [Note: will was made before Berks County was formed; Christian Merckel lived in Richmond Twp., which became Berks County by the date of probate.]
To sons Peter and George all estate, real and personal, they paying legacies to my two other sons Christian and Caspar, £100 each. To each of my daughters Catharine Stover, Frankiena Rugh, Mary Hill, Anna Maria Cramer, and Anna Lena Merckel £40 each. Sons Peter and George exrs. Wit.: Andreas Frey and Peter Reiff.

MERTZ, JOHANN GEORG   67256 Weisenheim am Sand
Pennsylvania Merchant, 1732
S-H, I: 66, 68, 69, 70
  Other passengers on ship: Anna Margaretha with Dorothy and Elisabeth

EUROPEAN RECORDS

Lambsheim Reformed KB:
Peter Mertz and wife Anna Dorothea had a son:
> 1. Hans George, bp. 27 Aug. 1702
>   Sp.: Hans Georg Fischer from [67098 Bad Dürkheim]
>   Türkheim and Julianne

Weisenheim am Sand Reformed KB:
Joh. Georg Mertz, son of Peter Mertz, m. 25 May 1723 Anna Margaretha, daughter of Albertus Roth. They had children:
> 1. Maria Catharina, bp. 6 Aug. 1724
> 2. Susanna, bp. 19 Jan. 1727
>   Sp.: Susanna Roth, single
> 3. Anna Elisabeth, bp. 21 Oct. 1731

AMERICAN RECORDS

Jordon Lutheran KB, Lehigh Co., PA:
Georg Mertz and Margaretha had a son:
> Name omitted, bp. 15 June 1740

MEYER, DANIEL   Oberhochstadt=
Queen of Denmark, 1751   76879 Hochstadt, Pfalz
S-H, I: 472, 473

EUROPEAN RECORDS

Oberhochstadt Reformed KB:
Daniel Meyer was probably the son of Michael Meyer, the local judge and church elder. Michael Meyer died at Oberhochstadt on 27 Feb. 1733, aged 61 years. Daniel was also probably a brother of Johannes Meyer [q.v.], who emigrated to Pennsylvania in 1739 with his son Egidius and other children. [The Hochstadt records do not start early enough to verify these relationships.]

Daniel Meyer m. Anna Catharina __. She died 9 Dec. 1750, aged 43 years, 6 months, 3 weeks. Daniel and Anna Catharina had children, baptized at Oberhochstadt:

1. Catharina, d. 6 Oct. 1731, age 5 years. Her bp. is not recorded in the records, since the regular bp. start in 1730, with a few scattered earlier ones entered in the beginning of the book.
2. Anna Margretha, bp. 28 Nov. 1726
   Sp.: Jacob Wolff and Anna Margretha
3. Johan Valentin, bp. 27 May 1731
   Sp.: Joh. Valentin Bender Jr. and Christina his wife
4. Maria Apollonia, bp. 2 Feb. 1734
   Sp.: Bernhard Mayer from [67480] Edenkoben and Maria Apollonia Meyer, both single.
5. Johan Philip, bp. 23 June 1736
   Sp.: Joh. Philip Kupper from Duttweiler [= 67435 Neustadt a. d. Weinstrasse] and Anna Maria
6. Johan Michael, bp. 17 Mar. 1738
   Sp.: Joh. Michael Rühling from [76879] Essingen and Catharina
7. Nickel, bp. 17 Oct. 1741
   Sp.: Nickel Gamber and Anna Margaretha
8. Maria Barbara, b. 7 May 1744, bp. 10 May 1744
   Sp.: Bernhard Meyer and Maria Barbara from [67480] Edenkoben
9. Johan Georg, b. 3 June 1746, d. 9 Feb. 1750
   Sp.: Joh. Georg Wolff and Maria Apollonia [nee Meyer].
10. Maria Elisabetha, b. 20 Jan. 1750
    Sp.: Maria Elisabetha Wolff, single.

AMERICAN RECORDS

Host Church Records, Tulpehocken, Berks county:
Valentin Mayer m. 5 Nov. 1758 Margaret Barbara Werler
Maria Barbara Meyer m. ca. 1764 Heinrich Leiss
Johan Philip Meyer m. Maria Catharina Unruh

Tombstone Inscriptions, Charles Evans Cemetery, Reading, Berks Co., PA:

Maria Apolonia Rhein, nee Meyer(in)	David Rhein
b. 2 Feb. 1734	b. 7 Jan. 1733
d. 4 Nov. 1809	He married Maria Apollonia Meyer
age 75 years, 9 months.	on the 19 June 1759
	d. 7 Aug. 1801

[Photographs of both tombstones provided by a descendant, Clarke H. P. Schneider of Chicago, IL].

Berks County Probate Records:
Daniel Meyer of Tulpehocken: on 28 March 1761, Letters of Administration were granted to Valentine Meyer, eldest son.

A Valentin Mayer, Tulpehockon, Berks County, nat. 10/11 Apr. 1761.
Philip Meyer, Tulpehockon, Berks County, nat. 10-12 Apr. 1762.

MEYER, JOHANNES   67098 Bad Dürkheim
St. Andrew Galley, 1737   67169 Kallstadt, Pfalz
S-H, I: 179, 181, 183
    with Dobias Böckell [q.v.] and Jacob Kuster

EUROPEAN RECORDS

Kallstadt Lutheran KB:
Gotthart Böckel and wife Maria Sibylla had:
    Maria Margaretha, b. 25 Dec. 1714

AMERICAN RECORDS

Heidelberg Moravian KB, Berks Co, PA:
Johannes Meyer was born in Dürkheim-on-the-Hardt in Rhine Palatinate in the jurisdiction of Hardenburg on June 19, 1715 (new style). His father was Johann Philipp Meyer, citizen of Dürkheim, and his mother was Maria Catharina ____. He was baptized at the same place on July 2, 1715 by Herr Gerber, superintendent and pastor in Dürkheim. His sponsors were Johann Sa____, citizen of Dürkheim and member of local court of justice, and his wife Eva. He was married in Dürkheim-on-the-Hardt on May 4, 1737 by Pastor Georg Demler, to Maria Margaretha Beckel, daughter of Johann Gotthard Beckel, citizen of Callstadt. She was born on Christmas 1714. In this marriage the Lord gave them the following children:
    1. Anna Catharina, b. 30 Nov. 1738, old style in Bern in Lancaster County. Bp. by Pastor Schmidt. Sp.: Conrad Kirschner and his wife Catharina Heck (Beck at Moselem)
    2. Tobias, b. 21 Sept. 1740, in Bern Lancaster County, bp. by Caspar Stöver. Sp.: Tobias Bechtel and wife Elisabeth [q.v.]
    3. Johannes, b. 24 Aug. 1742, in Bern, Lancaster County, bp. by Caspar Stöver. Sp.: Johannes Meth. Johannes died.
    4. Christina, b. 19 June 1745, old style, in Heidelberg, Lancaster Co. Bp. 30 June 1745. Sp.: Tobias and Christina Beckel [q.v.]

5. Anna Maria, b. in Heidelberg, Lancaster Co., 17 Oct. 1747, old style. Bp. 8 Nov. 1747. Sp.: Anna Maria Stör, Maria Catharina Conrad, and Christina Beckel.
6. Johann Phillip, b. 1 Nov. 1749, bp. 25 Nov. 1749
   Sp.: Philip Höhn, Friderich Gerhard, Tobias Böckel, Daniel Neibert, and Henrich Antes.
7. Johann Friedrich, b. 19 Nov. 1753, bp. 25 Nov. 1753
   Sp.: Friedrich Gerhard, Christoph Weiser, Tobias Böckel, Heinrich Stöhr, and Johannes Möller.

Johann Tobias Meyer, b. 2 Oct. 1740 in Bern township. In the year 1765 he m. Anna Maria Knaus in Emmaus. They had 7 children of whom 2 died before he died. He d. 9 Oct. 1791, from a "hitzigen fieber", age 51 years and 7 days (in parenthesis - died Sept. 29, between 10 and 11 o'clock, 1791).

Maria Margaretha Meyer, a born Boeckel, b. 25 Dec. 1714 in Kalstadt-an-der-Hart. Married Johannes Meyer 4 May 1737. She was blessed with 4 sons and 3 daughters, of whom 2 have already died. She d. 13 Dec. 1791, age 77 years less 12 days.

Johannes Meyer, born in Dürckheim-an-der-Hardt in the Palatinate in the jurisdiction of Hardenburg, on 29 June 1715. His father was Johan Philip Meyer, and his mother Maria Catharina Meyer. On 4 May 1737 he m. Maria Margaretha Boeckel. After they were married they came to America and had 7 children, 2 sons died and 2 sons and 3 daughters survived. He d. 17 Feb. 1792, age 76 years, 7 months and 17 days.

MEYER, JOHANNES age 40
MEYER, EGIDI age 16   Oberhochstadt=
Friendship, 1739   76879 Hochstadt, Pfalz
S-H, I: 264, 268, 271

EUROPEAN RECORDS

Niederhochstadt Reformed KB:
Joh. Meyer from Oberhochstadt confirmed 1713.

Johannes Meyer, son of Michael Meyer of Oberhochstadt, m. 1721 Catharina Stallmann. They had a son:
   1. Joh. Geidi, bp. 22 Apr. 1722
      Agidius Meyer confirmed at Oberhochstadt 1737

Oberhochstadt Reformed KB:

Johannes Meyer and wife Maria Catharina had children:

2. Valentin, (probably), conf. 1739
3. Eva Barbara, bp. 16 Sept. 1730
   Sp.: Emanuel Gamber and Eva Barbara Gutzler
4. Johann Georg, bp. 17 May 1733
   Sp.: Georg Meyer and Catharina Weyler, single
5. Margretha, b. 22 Aug. 1735, bp. 25 Aug. 1735
   Sp. Philip Adam Peter and Margretha
6. Heinrich, b. 24 Jan. 1738
   Sp.: Henrich Kolb and Eva Catharina from __ (unreadable)

AMERICAN RECORDS

Host Reformed Church in Berks Co., PA was named Host because many of the early members were from Hochstadt.

Rev. John Caspar Stoever's Records:
Johannes Meyer's first wife died; he m. (2) 8 Jan. 1746 Anna Maria Essel at Tulpehocken.

Egudius Meyer (Atolohoe) had a child:
    Maria Eva, b. 23 Nov. 1746, bp. 21 Dec. 1746
    Sp.: Bernhardt Motz and Eva Maria [q.v.]

Valentin Meyer (Atolohoe) had a child:
    John Ludwig, b. 27 Sept. 1746, bp. 28 Sept. 1746
    Sp.: John Ludwig Kornmann and wife [q.v.]

Host Reformed KB, Tulpehocken, Berks County, PA:
Heinrich Meyer confirmed 1753.

Berks County Wills:
Johannes Mayer of Tulpehocken, dated 28 Dec. 1765, probated 12 Aug. 1766, named his wife Anna Maria and the following heirs: Gideon, eldest son (apparently Egidius); Georg; Anna Barbara Wolff; Eva Catharine Stettler; children of daughter Catharina Deissinger; children of deceased son Valentin Mayer; Henry. Sons George and Henry were named executors. The will was witnessed by Valentine Unruh [q.v.] and Johann Christ Seiler. George Wolff [q.v.] was named as guardian of the estate for the funds to be distributed to the children of Catharine Deissinger, and Frederick Wolff guardian of the children of Valentine Meyer. [A complete transcript of this long will appeared in Schuyler Brossman's newspaper column, "Our Keystone Families," *Lebanon Daily News,* Column #425, 21 Nov. 1974. Deeds pertaining to this estate were published in his column #437, 13 Feb. 1975.]

Johannes Mayer, along with Simon Shirman [q.v.] and Johannes Haberling, of Lancaster County, nat. 10-11 Apr. 1746.

MEYSS (MAYSS), GEORG   Lachen-Speyerdorf=
permit to emigrate 1749   67435 Neustadt an der Weinstrasse
[not located in ship's lists]

EUROPEAN RECORDS

Lachen-Speyerdorf Reformed KB:
The earliest Meyss recorded in the Lachen KB was Henrich Meyss from [76889] Klingenmünster. His widow Catharina was buried in Lachen 30 July

1702. Their son, Stephan Meyss m. 30 May 1665 Anna Margreth, daughter of Johann Matthes Schuster. Anna Margretha, wife of Stephan Meys, died 23 Jan. 1718, age 73. Stephan Meyss and Anna Margretha had a son:
Johann Michel, bp. 10 Nov. 1667

Johann (Hans) Michel Meess m. 5 May 1694 Anna Maria Bauer, daughter of the late Nicolaus Bauer. They had children:
1. Joh. Georg, bp. 3 July 1695, died young
   Sp.: Hans Georg Hamman
2. Hans Peter, bp. 24 Mar. 1697
   Sp.: Peter Zimmerli, son of Jacob Zimmerli of Speyerdorf
3. Hans Jacob, bp. 1 June 1698
   Sp.: Jacob Hertzog, carpenter
4. Maria Elisabetha, bp. 1 May 1701
   Sp.: Maria Elisabetha, daughter of Stephen Meess
5. Joh. Agidius, bp. 17 Feb. 1704, died 1727
   Sp.: Johan Agidius Meess
6. Christophel, bp. 13 May 1706, d. 2 Dec. 1706
   Sp.: Christoph Bauer
7. Johan Georg, b. 27 Nov. 1707, d. 21 Mar. 1709
   Sp.: Johan Georg Fischer of [78739] Hardt
8. Anna Margretha, b. 17 Feb. 1710, bp. 23 Feb. 1710
   Sp.: Anna Margretha, wife of Andreas Fischer
9. **Hans Görg**, bp. 20 Aug. 1713, conf. 1727
   Sp.: Görg Hamman of Lachen

Joh. Görg Meyss, son of Michel Meyss, m. 27 Oct. 1734 Anna Maria, daughter of Valentin Dieppel of [67459] Böhl. She was b. 9 June 1713 in Böhl, daughter of Valentin Dippel and his wife Maria Magdalena nee Michel. Johann Görg Meyss and Anna Maria had children:
1. Johannes, b. 18 Dec. 1735, bp. 22 Dec. 1735, conf. 1748
2. Johann Philip Reinhard, b. 10 Oct. 1737, diec 1743
3. Johann Henrich, b. 31 Oct. 1739
4. Johann Nicolaus, b. 24 Nov. 1741
5. Joh. Georg, b. 3 Apr. 1744, bp. 6 Apr. 1744
6. Philipp Carl, b. 5 Oct. 1746, bp. 9 Oct. 1746

Emigration record:
Werner Hacker, *Auswanderungen aus Rheinpfalz und Saarland im 18. Jahrhundert:* #9778 Mass, Georg. Lachen, manumitted, to PA. Record dated 18 Mar. 1749.

AMERICAN RECORDS

Lancaster County Will Abstracts:
Georg Meas, Heidelberg Twp., dated 14 Nov. 1767, proved 16 Dec. 1767,
Wife: Anna. Children: John, Nicholas, Jacob, Georg, Michael, Margaretta,
Catharine and Anna.
Exrs: Georg Swengel and Anna Meas.

Lancaster Co. Miscellaneous Book, dated 1768-1772:
7 Mar. 1769: George Swengel, Anna Maria Meas and Nicholas Meas, exrs.
of the last will and testament of George Meas, deceased. Produced an
account, balance £197, 18 shillings. Jacob Meas, George Meas and Margaret
Meas, minors over 14 years, choose Michael Tice of Lebanon Twp. as their
guardian. Michael Meas, Katharine Meas and Mary Meas, minor children
under 14, court appoints Michael Tice as guardian.

Heidelberg Reformed KB, Schaefferstown, Lebanon Co., PA:
John Nicholas Maes and Susanna had:
      1. a son, b. 5 Aug. 1769, no sp. recorded
      2. Benjamin, b. 31 Jan. 1784
         Sp.: Henry Hergelroth and Christina

George Maes and Elisabeth had:
      1. Elisabeth, b. 12 Feb. 1783
         Sp.: Georg Holstein and Elisabeth
      2. Georg, b. 12 July 1788
         Sp.: Franz Seibert and wife

Jacob Mase and Catharina had:
      1. John Jacob, bp. 6 Dec. 1784
         Sp.: George Maes and Elisabeth

MICHEL, JACOB   67454 Hassloch
Snow *Lowther*, 1731
S-H, I: 55, 56, 57
  with Margaret on list

EUROPEAN RECORDS

Hassloch Reformed KB:
Peter Michael and wife Anna Helena (married before the church record
begins) had children:
      1. probably Susanna, conf. Easter 1710, age 14

2. Johann Christian, conf. Easter 1712, age 14
3. Johann Conradt, bp. 7 Dec. 1701; d. 6 Apr. 1710, age 18
4. Johann Ulrich, bp. 6 Jan. 1704; conf. 1718 [q.v.]
5. Anna Catharina, bp. 21 May 1706; conf. 1720
6. Johan Jacob, bp. 20 June 1708; conf. 1722, age 13 y. 9 mo.

Anna Helena, wife of Peter Michel, died 6 ?Aug. (?July) 1728, age 61 years.
Peter Michel was buried 13 Jan. 1757, age 84 years.

Married 26 Apr. 1730 in Hassloch: Jacob Michel, son of Peter Michel, with
Anna Margaretha, daughter of the deceased Peter Scherer.
(Anna Margaretha Scherer was conf. 1717, age 14.)

Hassloch Lutheran KB:
Married 12 Sept. 1702, Petter Scherer, widower and Anna Maria Guck,
widow. They had a daughter:
     Anna Margaretha, bp. 2 May 1703

Peter Scherer was buried 13 Oct. 1728, age 61 years. The death of Anna
Maria was not found (Luth. or Ref.).

Hassloch Gerichtsbuch:
Peter and Johannes Scherer from Arnisheim were granted citizenship on 27
Nov. 1710.

AMERICAN RECORDS

Oley Reformed Church, Berks County, PA:
A Jacob Michael and wife Margretha appear as sponsors.

Berks County Will Abstracts:
Jacob Michael, Ruscombmanor, 11 Dec. 1776 - 26 Apr. 1777.
Eldest son George Philip, £22; to daughter Susanna £5; Exrs to sell land
(200A) and all moveables and divide the proceeds among all children,
namely: George Philip, Peter Michael, Magdalena, Elizabeth wife of Adam
Koehly, Susanna Koehn, Margaret Kaelchner, and Christina Windbigler.
Son-in-law Frederick Koehn, Exr. Wit: Elizabeth Reeser, Wm. Reeser.

MICHEL, JOH. ULRICH   67454 Hassloch
Snow *Lowther,* 1731
S-H, I: 55, 56, 57
     Names on List: Ulrich, Maria Margaretta, Catharina, and Philip Lawrence.

EUROPEAN RECORDS

Hassloch Reformed KB:
Peter Michel and his wife Anna Helena had a son:
>   Johann Ulrich, bp. 6 Jan. 1704

Joh. Ulrich Michel, son of Peter Michel, m. 6 June 1725 Anna Margaretha, daughter of the deceased Hans Georg Riemer (or Riener), formerly a citizen and master baker of [76889] Klingenmünster in Oberamt Germersheim. Their children, born at Hassloch:
>   1. (no name recorded), bp. 5 May 1726
>   2. Catharina, b. 20 Oct. 1727; bp. 22 Oct. 1727
>   3. Philip Lorentz, b. 4 June 1730; bp. 8 June 1730

Anna Helena Michel d. 6 July 1728, age 61 years.
[For more family data on Peter Michel, see his son Jacob Michel, above.]

AMERICAN RECORDS

Christ "Little Tulpehocken" KB, Berks Co:
Ulrich Michael had a daughter:
>   Margaretha, b. 8 Jan. 1741, bp. 2 Aug. 1741
>   Sp.: Eliesabetha Hassin

Rev. Boos' records, Schwartzwald burials:

Ulrich Michel (Heidelberg)	Widow of Ulrich Michel
b. 30 Sept. 1702 (sic!)	b. 25 July 1704
d. 2 Oct. 1784	d. 15 May 1787

Christian Michel (Heidelberg)
b. 17 Sept. 1732
d. 7 May 1787

Muddy Creek Reformed KB, Lancaster County:
Ulrich Michael and his wife sponsor a child in 1743.

It is interesting to note that a total of 27 people who arrived on the Snow *Lowther* in 1731 are identified in the Hassloch records, and all of the same surnames then appear, at least for a short time, in the Muddy Creek records in Lancaster County, PA.

PA Land Warrants: #17 dated 2 May 1753:
Ulrich Michel: Survey Book C-135-53, Patent P-1-154 to Christian Michel.

Lancaster County Will Abstracts:
Will of Christian Michael, Heidelberg. 3 May 1787 - 4 June 1787.
Wife Maria Margaret to hold the plantation for 10 years to bring up and educate younger children, then to be sold and divided into 13 equal shares to children: Christian, Susanna wife of Andrew Swalm, John, Margaret wife of Henry Shrack, Peter, Frederick, William, Appolonia, Elisabeth, Christian (by 2nd wife), Christina, Philip, Catharine. Neighbor Michael Miller and son John, Exrs. Wit: John Miller and Casper Stein.

MITTELKAUFF, PETER   67157 Wachenheim an der Weinstrasse
Mortonhouse, 1728
S-H, I: 17, 19

EUROPEAN RECORDS

Wachenheim Reformed KB:
Philip Daniel Mittelkauff and wife Maria Eva had a son:
>Johann Peter, bp. 15 Apr. 1703

Joh. Peter Mittelkauff, son of Philip Daniel Mittelkauff, m. 7 Jan. 1727 Maria Saloma, daughter of Christophel Benckert [q.v.]. They had:
>Maria Margaretha, bp. 10 Oct. 1727
>Sp.: Maria Margaretha, wife of Casimir Benedict

AMERICAN RECORDS

Rev. John Casper Stoever's Records:
Peter Mittelkauff had children:
>Catharina, b. 6 Feb. 1735, bp. 22 May 1735
>Sp.: Johan Theobaldt Jung and wife Catharina
>Leonhardt, b. 23 Jan. 1739, bp. 19 Apr. 1739
>Sp.: Johan Leonhardt Bernitz

Conewago Reformed KB:
John Henry Knauff from Maren [? 67297 Marnheim, Pfalz], Palatinate, and wife Maria Margaret, daughter of Peter Middelkauff, had:
>1. Susanna, b. 1 Oct. 1746, bp. 6 May 1747
> Sp.: Peter Middelkauff and wife
>2. A son, b. 29 Jan. 1748, bp. 16 May 1748
>3. Peter, b. 1749, bp. 1750

Jacob Mittelkaff and wife Magdalena Schmidt had:
        Jacob, b. 14 Aug. 1791, bp. 20 Nov. 1791
        Sp.: Andrew Cuntz and Catherine

Lancaster County Will Abstracts:
Juliana Thomas, wife of Philip Thomas, Lancaster Borough. 23 Dec. 1815 -
30 Dec, 1815.
Children: Juliana wife of Jacob Middlekauff, George, and Mary wife of ___
Walker. Exr: Jacob Middlekauff.

Peter Middlecave nat. in Maryland, October term, 1743.

MOHLER, LUDWIG   67454 Hassloch
Thistle of Glasgow, 1730
S-H, I: 32, 33, 34

EUROPEAN RECORDS

Hassloch Reformed KB:
Mathes Mohler from Switzerland and his wife Margretha (Cretha) had
children:
        1. Maria Elisabetha, bp. 6 June 1700
        2. Anna Elisabetha, bp. __ Nov. 1701
        3. Johann Georg, bp. 12 Aug. 1703
            Sp.: Johannes Mohler, also from Switzerland
        4. **Johann Ludwig,** bp. 22 Nov. 1705
        5. Johann Henrich, b. 29 Sept. 1711, bp. 4 Oct. 1711

AMERICAN RECORDS

The Brethren Encyclopedia, p. 868:
"Ludwig Mohler (1696[?]-1754) from Switzerland arrived in Pennsylvania on
Aug. 29, 1730 on the *Thistle* with his wife and three sons. He settled in
Lancaster Co., PA, near Ephrata. Some of the family became Brethren in
the White Oak and Cocalico congregations." Later Generations settled in
VA and OH. This article cites several published Mohler histories.

Cocalico Twp. Tax Lists:
Henry Mohler is listed on the 1751 Cocalico tax list.
Jacob Mohler owned 200 A of land in Cocalico in 1756.
John Mohler owned 200 A of land in Cocalico in 1756.

Tombstone inscription, Mohler's Church (pictured in Journal of the Historical Society of the Cocalico Valley, Vol. XI, 1986, p. 35:
    Henrich Mohler died 20 Apr. 1774, age 46 years, 3 months.

MOLL, MICHAEL   67256 Weisenheim am Sand
Pennsylvania Merchant, 1731
S-H, I: 43, 45, 46
    with Rosina

EUROPEAN RECORDS

Weisenheim am Sand Reformed KB:
Hans Georg Moll, single, from Hessen, m. 19 Nov. 1687 Esther Margaretha, daughter of Adam Schmidt. They had children:
    1. Hans **Michel**, bp. 15 June 1698
        Sp.: Hans Michel Strauss and Maria Margretha
    2. Maria Ursula, bp. 8 May 1701
    3. Joh. Peter [q.v.]

Hans **Michael Moll** and wife **Rosina** had a son:
    1. Hiob, bp. 30 July 1730
        Sp.: Hiob Held, single

AMERICAN RECORDS

New Goshenhoppen Reformed KB, Montgomery Co., PA:
Michael Moll was an early member at New Goshenhoppen Reformed Church.

Michael Moll and wife Rosina had children:
    1. Joh. Christophel, bp. 1 Aug. 1736
        Sp.: Christophel Moll and Anna Catharina
    2. Lisabeth Margreth, bp. 24 Sept. 1740
        Sp. Melchior Süssholz and Lisabeth
    3. Joh. Benedick, b. 13 Nov. 1741, bp. 2 Mar. 1742
        Sp.: Benedick Strohm and Catharina (this baptism recorded at St. Paul's Lutheran KB, Red Hill, Montgomery County.)
    4. Michael, bp. 4 Sept. 1742
        Sp.: Michel Reitenbach

Burials:
1770, Feb. 14 - Michael Moll was buried. Born 1700, aged 70 years.
1779, Aug. 5 - A daughter of the late Michael Moll was buried, born 1739, about March; aged about 40 years.

Michael Moll, son of Michael Moll of Upper Hanover, m. 26 May 1767 Margaretha Schmeck, daughter of the late Johannes Schmeck of Elsass Twp.

Philadelphia County Wills, Will # 361, 1770:
Michael Moll of Upper Hanover, Yeoman. 4 Sept. 1769 - 2 Apr. 1770.
Wife Rosina given certain items: a cow, rows of apple trees, use of land. "Plantation to be sold to one of my children that will give best price as shall agree between them". Eldest son Henry to receive £5 before hand.
Exrs: Eldest son Henry and son in law Daniel Nyer. Wit.: Adam Shneider and Philip Wischan. Codicil dated 12 Jan. 1770 increased items given to wife Rosina.

Inventory and Adm. accounts included in the probate packet; some of the names mentioned in the accounts are: Johan George Moll, Michael Moll, Benedict Moll, Elizabeth Moll.

Citation dated 12 June 1802: Henry Moll surviving executor of estate of Michael Moll states that personal estate went to his mother....no part to his hands except enough to pay debts. Remaining property or nearly so having been converted by her into money and lost during the Revolution on account of depreciation of money. Nothing remained at her death. Real estate was released to Christopher Moll as per release dated 25 May 1771.

Other Molls arrived on this same ship and appear to be related, but due to gaps in the Weisenheim church records, they cannot be documented. They are:
> Christophel Moll
> Women over 16: Margarite Moll and
> > Anlyas [possibly Anna Elisabetha] Moll.
> Children under 16: Conraed Moll, Margarite Moll.

MOLL, JOH. PETER   67256 Weisenheim am Sand
Mortonhouse, 1729
S-H, I: 26, 27

EUROPEAN RECORDS

Weisenheim am Sand Reformed KB:
Hans Georg Moll, single, from Hessen, m. 19 Nov. 1687 Esther Margaretha, daughter of Adam Schmidt. They had children:
1. Hans Michel [q.v.], bp. 15 June 1698
   Sp.: Hans Michel Strauss and Maria Margretha
2. Maria Ursula, bp. 8 May 1701
3. **Joh. Peter,** bp. 25 Mar. 1709
   Sp.: Peter Morra and Susanna

MOTZ, BERNHARD age 46   Niederhochstadt=
Friendship, 1738   76879 Hochstadt, Pfalz
S-H, I: 226, 228, 230

EUROPEAN RECORDS

Niederhochstadt Reformed KB:
Hans Bernhard Motz and wife Maria Elisabetha had children:
1. Eva Elisabetha bp. 6 Oct. 1719
   Sp.: Hans Peter Laux [q.v.] and Eva Magdalena Degin
2. Margaretha bp. 14 June 1724
   Sp.: Jacob Schieffer and Margretha
3. Anna Maria bp. 10 Sept. 1727
   Sp.: Nickel Reintzel [q.v.] and Anna Maria
4. Maria Catharina bp. 27 July 1732
   Sp.: Wolfgang Müller [q.v.] and Margretha

AMERICAN RECORDS

Christ "Little Tulpehocken" Lutheran KB, Tulpehocken, Berks County:
Bernhard Motz and wife were sponsors for a child of Jacob Wilhelm [q.v.] in 1742.

Rev. John Caspar Stoever's Records:
Bernhardt Motz and his wife Eva Maria sponsor a daughter of Egidius Meyer [q.v.] in 1746.

John George Flohr m. 16 Dec. 1753 Maria Catarina Motz, Atolhoe.

MÜHLSCHLÄGEL, ANDREAS   Lachen-Speyerdorf=
Patience, 1750   67435 Neustadt an der Weinstrasse
S-H, I: 427

EUROPEAN RECORDS

Lachen-Speyerdorf Reformed KB:
The schoolmaster Hans Jacob Mühlschlägel and wife Anna Margretha had:
Hans Henrich bp. 20 Apr. 1684

Died 26 Apr. 1706: our schoolmaster Hans Jacob Mühlschlägel

Hans Henrich Mühlschlägel, son of the late Hans Jacob Mühlschlägel (both schoolmasters here) m. 7 Sept. 1707 Maria Apolonia, daughter of Peter Hamman. They had a son:
    Joh. Andreas, b. 15 Apr. 1730, bp. 23 Apr. 1730
    Sp. H. Johann Andreas Riedinger, citizen and innkeeper
    at Statt Neuburg in Mannheim [?68167 Nürburgstr., Mannheim].

Died 2 Jan. 1735: Herr Johann Henrich Mühlschlägel, schoolmaster. Age 50 years, 8 months

Emigration record:
Werner Hacker, *Auswanderungen aus Rheinpfalz und Saarland im 18. Jahrhundert:* # 10593 Mühlschlegel, Andreas, Reformed Schoolmaster, [67475] Weidental, permitted to go to PA, but must pay 10% tax on property. Record dated 26 May 1750.

AMERICAN RECORDS

New Goshenhoppen Reformed KB, Montgomery Co., PA:
Undated marriages, between 1747-1758:
    Andreas Muehlschlagel and Anna Maria Emet.

MÜLLEMAN, PETER   67251 Freinsheim
Prelist, 1723

EUROPEAN RECORDS

Freinsheim Reformed KB:
Conf. 1701: Hans Peter Mülleman
Joh. Peter Mülleman, son of Christoffel Mülleman, m. 25 Mar. 1704
Agnesia, daughter of Christoffel Voltz from the Graffschaft Rödelsheim.

Joh. Peter Mülleman and Agnesia had children:
1. Johann Caspar, bp. 7 Aug. 1707, conf. 1723. There
   is a notation in the conf. record that he and his
   brother were confirmed in preparation of their
   departure for PA with their parents and siblings.
   Sp.: Joh. Caspar Ehmel, Reformed, from Asselheim [= 67269
   Grünstadt] and wife Dorothea, Lutheran
2. Joh. Georg, bp. 26 May 1709, conf. 1723 prior to
   departure for PA. Sp.: Georg Klauer [q.v.] and his wife
3. Anna Maria, bp. 11 Jan. 1711, d. 29 Mar. 1713
   Sp.: Philip Beyer, Lutheran, and Anna Maria
4. Susanna, bp. 5 July 1713
   Sp.: Frantz Poppel and Susanna, his wife
5. Anna Catharina, bp. 5 May 1715, d. 4 Sept. 1717
   Sp.: Andreas Neu from Leystatt [Leistadt=67098 Bad Dürkheim]
   and Anna Catharina, daughter of Daniel Sebastian
6. Eleonora, bp. __ Dec. 1716, d. 18 Sept. 1717
   Sp.: Simon Schantz and Eleonora, his wife
7. Susanna, bp. 26 June 1718, d. 16 Oct. 1719
   Sp.: Henrich Hammel and Susanna Becker, both single
8. Anna Catharina, bp. 15 Dec. 1720
   Sp.: Peter Appel and Anna Catharina, his wife

AMERICAN RECORDS

Chester County administrations:
Peter Milleman, Chester County, Adm. granted 7 Aug. 1738 to Abraham
Dilbeck; Gasper Milleman, eldest son, renouncing.

MÜLLER, JOHANN HENRICH   67251 Freinsheim
Johnson, 1732
S-H, I: 72, 76, 78
[other passengers on list: Marg^t Miller, pg. 73]

EUROPEAN RECORDS

Freinsheim Reformed KB:
Johann Henrich Müller, son of Georg Müller, *Hoffman* on the Margreth
Hoff in the Leiningen Jurisdiction, m. 2 Oct. 1731 in the Lutheran Church
here, Anna Margaretha, daughter of Peter Appel. [See Appel immigrants
for more detail on Appel family.]

AMERICAN RECORDS

Henrich Miller arrived on the same ship as his brother-in-law Henrich Appel and several others from Freinsheim.

First Reformed KB, Philadelphia, PA:
Buried 14 Feb. 1748: Anna Margaretha Müller, wife of Henry Müller, Lutheran. She was born 1712, d. on the 12th, sister of Henry Apel from Frenzheim [Freinsheim]. Her age 36 years.

Philadelphia Wills and Administrations:
Peter Appel 1739 file # 3 Adm. D: 116: Letters of Adm. to Henry Miller, county of Phila., yeoman, kin to Peter Appell, late of said county, yeoman, dec'd., with a codicil annexed, widow Anna Clara having renounced, 13 Mar. 1739/[40].

MÜLLER, JOH. JACOB   67259 Heuchelheim
Alexander & Anne, 1730
S-H, I: 35, 36

EUROPEAN RECORDS

Heuchelheim Lutheran KB:
Johan Caspar Müller and wife Magdalena had a son:
    Johan Jacob, b. 10 Jan. 1706; conf. in 1720.

Caspar Müller d. 10 Feb. 1714, age 54 years. Anna Magdalena, widow of the late Joh. Caspar Müller, d. 19 Dec. 1742, age 74 years, 3 months.

AMERICAN RECORDS

Augustus Evangelical Lutheran Church, Trappe, Montgomery Co., PA:
Buried 26 Nov. 1755 Johan Jacob Müller from Heuchelheim, b. 10 Jan. 1706, d. 24 Nov. 1755. (He married his cousin Anna Christina Müller, b. 2 Nov. 1734, daughter of Joh. Nicolaus Müller [q.v.]).

MÜLLER, JOH. NICOLAUS   67259 Heuchelheim
Imm. between 1746 and 1755
(3 in S-H during that time period)

EUROPEAN RECORDS

Heuchelheim Lutheran KB:
Maria Appollonia, wife of Joh. Nicol Müller, d. 30 Dec. 1730, age 30 years, 10 months, 15 days.

Joh. Nicolaus Müller, widower, m. 14 Jan. 1732 Eva Maria Kraft, daughter of Velten Kraft of Grosnittesheim [67259 Grossniedesheim]. They had:
1. Anna Margaretha, b. 30 Dec. 1732
2. Anna Christina, b. 2 Nov. 1734
3. Joh. Nicolaus, b. 8 June 1737
4. Joh. Adam, b. 17 Sept. 1739, d. 17 Dec. 1739
5. Joh. Philip, b. 31 Jan. 1741
6. Joh. Valentin, b. 4 Nov. 1743
7. Juliana, b. 12 July 1746

AMERICAN RECORDS

Muhlenberg's Journals:
On the 7 Jan. 1777 buried at Trappe Anna Christina Preiss (or Preisse), a widow. She was the daughter of Johan Nicolaus Mueller, deceased, and his still surviving wife Eva Maria. She was b. in Heuchelheim 2 Nov. 1734. Came to America with her parents, brothers and sisters. She m. (1) her cousin, Jacob Müller, and they had 2 sons. She m. (2) Johannes Preisser, they were m. 15 years and had 7 sons.

Augustus Lutheran KB, Trappe, Montgomery Co., PA:
Jacob Müller and wife Christina had:
        Johann Jacob, b. 23 May 1755

Conf. 1755, Joh. Philip Müller, age 13;
Conf. 1756, Joh. Nicolaus Müller, age 18;
Conf. 1758, Joh. Valentin Müller, age 14.

Falckner Swamp Reformed KB, Montgomery Co., PA:
John Preiser and wife (NN) had:
        John Nicholas, b. 27 June 1761

John Preusser and Christina had:
        Frederick, b. 9 Nov. 1768

MÜLLER, JOHAN PHILIP age 38   67259 Heuchelheim
Pink *Plaisance*, 1732
S-H, I: 78, 81, 82
  with Christina Muller, age 35 and
  children: Christopher Muler, Hans Urig Muler, Filip Muler

EUROPEAN RECORDS

Heuchelheim Lutheran KB:
Joh. Philip Müller m. 3 Dec. 1718 Catharina Christina Schweiber. They had:
  1. Johan Christoph, b. 16 Sept. 1718, bp. 14 Feb. 1719.
     Conf. 1731, age 12
  2. Anna Elisabetha, b. 12 Mar. 1721
  3. Johan Georg, b. 7 Feb. 1722
  4. Johan Philip, b. 10 Mar. 1724
  5. Anna Margaretha, b. 20 Nov. 1729

AMERICAN RECORDS

The Müller name is common; the following is offered only as one possibility:

St. Paul's Lutheran KB, Red Hill, Montgomery Co., PA:
One Joh. Philip Müller with wife Anna Barbara had a daughter:
  Eva Elisabeth, b. 23 Aug. 1753

MÜLLER, JOHANNES age 36   67259 Heuchelheim
Pink *Plaisance*, 1732
S-H, I: 78, 81, 82
  with Anna Mare Muller, age 26

EUROPEAN RECORDS

Heuchelheim Lutheran KB:
Johannes Müller m. 6 Jan. 1726 Anna Maria Lachmund. They had:
  1. Anna Maria, b. 21 Sept. 1726
  2. Catharina Elisabetha, b. 12 Apr. 1729

MÜLLER, WOLFGANG age 41   Niederhochstadt=
Elizabeth, 1733   76879 Hochstadt, Pfalz
S-H, I: 113, 114, 115; Appendix 765, 766,767
  Other passengers on ship: Margret Miller age 53; Jacob Miller age 17

EUROPEAN RECORDS

Niederhochstadt Reformed KB:
Wolfgang Müller and wife Margretha had a son:
        Jacobus, bp. 5 Sept. 1716
        Sp.: Jacob Reintzel and Dorothea Dieterin, both single.

Wolfgang Müller and wife Margretha sponsored a child of Bernhard Motz
[q.v.] in 1732.

The Reformed Church in Hochstadt
with a half timbered house in the foreground.

AMERICAN RECORDS

Lancaster County Land Warrant, Pennsylvania Archives, Third Series:
Wolfgang Miller, 200 acres, 31 Oct. 1735. Wolfgang Miller, 50 acres, 30
Aug. 1753.

Lancaster County Orphans' Court Records:
Tulpehocken, 5 Mar. 1747/48, the account of Elisabeth Miller, widow of
Jacob Miller, now intermarried with Peter Zerben. Balance to be distributed
to the widow, Johannes eldest son, and daughters Christina, Margaret, and
Susanna. Wolfang (sic) Miller was appointed guardian over Johannes
Miller. Abraham Cauke (Lauck?), guardian over Christina; Jacob Emerick
guardian over Margaret; Jacob Kantner guardian over Susanna.

Berks County Abstracts of Wills:
Wolfgang Miller of Tulpehocken, dated 29 Nov. 1752; filed 29 Jan. 1753.
One share of estate to grandchildren: Johannes, Christina, and Elisabeth
Miller. One share of estate to wife Eva Madline. One share of estate to
step-sons: Mathias and Johannes Wagner. "£15 current money of
Pennsylvania shall be paid to my grandchild Johannes Miller, abovenamed,
with a new suit of clothes when he goes the first time to the Lord's Table."
Step Son Mathias Wagner [q.v.] and friend and neighbor Johannes
Troutman, exrs. Witnessed by Hans Presler, George Presler, and Bernhard
Mots. Also witnessed and translated by Conrad Weiser.

From this will, it would appear that Margretha, the first wife, died and
Wolfgang Miller married (2) Eva Magdalena Wagner, a widow.

MÜNCH, JOHANNES (HANS MINNIGH)   67125 Dannstadt
Thistle of Glasgow, 1730
S-H, I: 31-33

EUROPEAN RECORDS

Dannstadt Reformed KB:
Johannes Münch m. 6 June 1724 Anna Catharina Gluck. No children listed
in record. The first Münch in this record is Hans Leonhard Münch who
sponsors a child in 1705. In 1708, a Hans Mönch and wife Maria Johanneta
had a daughter Maria Catharina baptized. The Glück family appears in the
record from 1675.

For additional identification of this immigrant, see:
Braun, Dr. Fritz, *18th Century Palatine Emigrants from the Ludwigshafen Area* in the *Pennsylvania Dutchman* Vol. V, no. 13, Mar. 1, 1954, pg. 13.

AMERICAN RECORDS

Exact identification would require extensive research. There were several colonial Minnich-Münch families and the name John appears frequently. A John Minnich died in Albany Twp., Berks Co., PA and letters of administration were granted on his estate 11 Feb. 1755. However, he is listed in the probate records as a newcomer from Holland.

Caspar Büttner [q.v.], a fellow passenger on ship, was married to Maria Elisabetha, nee Münch.

MÜNCH, JOH. PETER   67361 Freisbach
MÜNCH, JOH. SIMON
Samuel, 1737
S-H, I: 169, 171, 172

EUROPEAN RECORDS

Gommersheim Lutheran KB:
Joh. Peter Münch m. 19 Sept. 1724 Christina, daughter of the late Leonhard Oster, citizen at Freÿschbach [Freisbach].

The Palatine village of Freisbach

Joh. Peter Münch and Christina had children:
1. Elisabetha, b. 1726 in Freisbach.
2. Philip Simon, b. 25 Aug. 1728, bp. 29 Aug. 1728
   Notation in KB: "in Pensylvania".
   Sp.: Joh. Simon Münch of [67377] Gommersheim
3. Johann Georg, b. 27 Sept. 1731, bp. 30 Sept. 1731
   Notation in KB: "In Pensylv."
4. Jacob Peter, b. 28 June 1733, bp. 29 June 1733
   Notation in KB: "In Pensyl."

AMERICAN RECORDS

Berks County Abstracts of Wills and Adm.:
Peter Minnich, beyond the Blue Mt. Adm. granted 15 May 1766 to Eva
Minnich, the widow.

Christ "Little Tulpehocken" Lutheran KB, Berks Co., and Stoever's Records:
Peter Muench of Tulpehocken had children:
1. Joh. Michael, b. 2 Jan 1738, bp. 24 Jan. 1738
2. Joh. Conrad, b. 28 Nov. 1740, bp. 21 Jan. 1741

Rev. John Casper Stoever's Records:
George Muench m. 5 Jan. 1752 Catar. Margaretha Guthman, Northkill.

George Muench (Bern) had children:
1. Simon, b. 20 Mar. 1753, bp. 6 May 1753
   Sp.: Simon Muench and wife
2. Catarina Margaretha, b. 5 June 1754, bp. 25 Aug. 1754
   Sp.: Peter Muench and wife Christina
3. Anna Margaretha, b. 24 May 1756, bp. 7 June 1756

Hocker, *German Settlers of Pennsylvania:*
Sower's Newspaper, dated 1 Nov. 1749:
Simon Muench, Bern Twp., on the Northkill (Berks County).

MUSCULUS, JOH. PETER age 30   67361 Freisbach
Peggy, 1753
S-H, I: 546, 548

EUROPEAN RECORDS

Gommersheim Lutheran KB:
Johann Peter Musculus, master weaver, from Unteröwisheim [= 76703 Kraichtal] in Würtenberg, m. 18 Apr. 1747 Anna Ursula, daughter of Johannes Klopp. They had children, in Freisbach:
1. Anna Barbara, b. 16 July 1749, bp. 19 July 1749
   There is a notation in the KB "in America".
2. Joh. Peter, b. 29 Mar. 1751, bp. 31 Mar. 1751
   Again, the notation in the KB "in America".

AMERICAN RECORDS

Trinity Lutheran Church, Lancaster, PA:
Anna Elisabetha, beloved little daughter of Peter Muscatnus and his wife Ursula, died 20 Mar. 1769 and was buried the 21st in the morning. Age 13 years, 6 months, 6 days.

Adam and Catharina Musculus had children:
1. Peter, b. 28 July 1780, bp. 18 Mar. 1781
   Sp.: Peter Musculus and wife Ursula
2. Catharina, b. 2 June 1782, bp. 13 June 1782
   Sp.: Parents
3. Catharina, b. 1 June 1784, bp. 7 June 1784

Adam Musculus - first Communion 20 May 1770.

Ursula Muscatnuss was a sponsor in 1775 for a child of Peter and Barbara Ebel.

Communicants list 31 Mar. 1782:
Adam Musculus and wife, Catharina, confirmed by Mr. Graf.

Lancaster County Intestate Records:
Adam Musketnuss died intestate in 1821. Records are in Vol A-1: 43.

A John Musgetness died intestate in 1792.

NEUNZEHNHÖLTZER, JACOB   67251 Freinsheim
Johnson, 1732
S-H, I: 72, 76, 78
   [other passengers on ship: women: Seville,
   girls: Maria Susanna and Margt. surname spelled Nythelzer]

EUROPEAN RECORDS

Freinsheim Reformed KB:
Velten Neizehöltzer and wife (Elisabetha) had a son:
      Johan Jacob b. 19 Feb. 1701, bp. 23 Feb. 1701; conf. 1714,
      (surname spelled Neunzehenhöltzer in conf. record. The name also
      appears in this KB as 19höltzer!)

Died 13 Mar. 1725: Val. Neunzenhöltzer, citizen here.

AMERICAN RECORDS

Falckner Swamp Reformed KB, Montgomery Co., PA:
Jacob Neuzehenholtzer and wife appear as sponsors at several baptisms.

Died 21 Mar. 1774: Sibilla Neunzehnhöltzer.

Conf. 1750: Michael Neunzehenholtzer, son of Jacob Neunzehenholtzer.

Conf. 1751: Elisabetha Neunzehenholtzer, age 14, daughter of Jacob
Neunzehenholtzer.

Philadelphia Wills, Book L: 467:
Jacob Neiteholtzer, dated 5 May 1760; prob. 16 June 1760.
Exrs: wife Sibilla and son John Michael.
To eldest son John Michael, horse and plantation; wife Sibilla has the right
to remain in the house. Mentions two youngest children. To son John
Michael, the book of sermons; son Jacob to have the Bible; youngest son
Jacob to be bound to a trade 1 Nov. 1760. If wife dies before youngest
daughter comes of age, she is to be free and not bound out.
Witnessed: Jacob Bernhardt and Godfrey Langebein.

Rev. John Waldschmidt's records, PA Archives, Sixth Series, Vol. 6:
Martin Meyer, son of the late Georg Meyer, m. 26 Feb. 1765 Catharina,
daughter of the late Jacob Neunzehnholsser; in Stophel Friedrich's house.

Berks County Abstracts of Wills:
John Neunzehnholtzer, Robeson Twp. dated 13 Aug. 1796; prob. 3 Sept. 1796. Wife: Anna Maria. Children: Jacob, Susanna, Catharina and Elizabeth. Exrs: wife Anna Maria & friend George Weidner. Wit.: John Bear and Philip Heil

Jacob Neunzehelzer. Robeson. 28 July 1815-7 Oct. 1815. Wife Magdalena. Names children: Peter and Jacob (there are others not mentioned by name). Exrs: wife Magdalina and friend John Ziemer.

NUMRICH, JOHANNES 67454 Hassloch
Snow *Charlotta,* 1743
S-H, I: 340

EUROPEAN RECORDS

Hassloch Lutheran KB:
Johannes Numrich m. 1 Aug. 1719 Anna Margretha Schmid. They had:
  1. Conrad, b. 20 Feb. 1720, conf. 1734
  2. Johannes Antoni, b. 26 Sept. 1721, conf. 1735
  3. Maria Magdalena, b. 16 Dec. 1723
  4. Magdalena, b. 13 Nov. 1725
  5. Anna Catharina, b. 23 Feb. 1731
  6. Joh. Jacob, bp. 25 Feb. 1732
  7. Anna Maria, bp. 12 Dec. 1733
  8. Conrad, bp. 21 Oct. 1735
  9. Anna Maria, bp. 10 Jan. 1740

Anna Margaretha Nummerich d. 24 Sept. 1742, age 46 years.

NUSS, JOHANN JACOB age 20 67259 Heuchelheim
Harle, 1736
S-H, I: 156, 159, 161

EUROPEAN RECORDS

Heuchelheim Lutheran KB:
Peter Nuss and his wife Anna Margaretha had a son:
        Johan Jacob, b. 25 June 1716, bp. 29 June 1716
        Sp.: Jacob Nuss and Sybilla Elisabeth, his wife.

AMERICAN RECORDS

Old Goshenhoppen Lutheran KB, Montgomery Co., PA:
Joh. Jacob Nuss d. 20 Sept. 1757, age 41 years, 3 months, 24 days.

Old Goshenhoppen Family Register:
Johann Jacob Nuss, age 37 years, b. 25 June 1716 in Heuchelheim near Worms in the Palatinate, son of Peter and Anna Margaretha Nuss. In 1736 he came to America without his parents. In 1738, he m. Anna Maria Reiher, b. 5 Dec. 1712, daughter of Michael Reiher and wife Anna Maria, deceased. They had children:
  1. Anna Maria, b. 2 Jan. 1740
  2. Maria Elisabetha, b. 27 Nov. 1741
  3. Johan Conrad, b. 17 Mar. 1744
  4. Anna Margaretha, b. 25 Oct. 1746
  5. Anna Catharina, b. 14 Jan. 1750
  6. Johann Jacob, b. 1 Mar. 1753

OBERBECK, ANDREAS   67125 Dannstadt
Johnson, 1732
S-H, I: 71-77
　　[Passengers on ship: Andreas Overbeck (over 16), Elisabeth (women over 14), Johannes and Philips (boys under 16), and Matelina (girls under 14).]

EUROPEAN RECORDS

Dannstadt Reformed KB:
Andreas Oberbeck m. 30 Jan. 1714 Elisabeth Drach. [He is possibly the Andreas Oberbeck who was bp. 24 Aug. 1684 at [67256] Weisenheim am Sand, son of Andrianus and Maria; Sp.: Andreas Scherer and Maria Magdalena]. They had children baptized at Dannstadt:
  1. Hans Georg, bp. 20 Feb. 1715; conf. Easter, 1729.
  2. Anna Catharina, bp. 1 Feb. 1717
  3. Maria Magdalena, bp. __ ___ 1720
     (this entry very faded ink- notation under child's name:
     to PA 1732 with father).
  4. Philip Jacob, bp. 24 Oct 1724
     (notation under this child: Anno 1732 in PA)

AMERICAN RECORDS

Several entries concerning this family are to be found in the Tohickon Union Church records, Bedminster Twp., Bucks Co., PA (records published in Pennsylvania German Society Publications, Vol, XXXI). The earliest baptismal entry for this surname is:

Philip Jacob Oberbeck and Maria Sarah had:
> John George, b. 15 Dec. 1757, bp. 27 Dec. 1757
> Sp.: Joh. George Oberbeck and wife

Additional records on Philip Jacob Oberbeck may be found in the Springfield Reformed Church records, Bucks Co., PA.

Hocker, *German Settlers of Pennsylvania:*
In Christopher Sower's Germantown Newspaper, dated 5 Mar. 1757: Georg Oberbeck of Bucks Co., four miles from Durham Furnace, advertises that a servant, Johannes Schmitt, ran away.

Bucks County Will Abstracts:
Elizabeth Oberbeck, Bedminster Twp. 22 Apr. 1772 - 11 Feb. 1775. Daughters Anna Maria and Maria Magdalena. Four children (not all named). Exr: Jacob Beidleman. Wit.: Jacob Yearling, John Lear.

Andreas Oberbeck was naturalized 10 Apr. 1746. He resided in Nockamixon Twp., Bucks Co., PA, where he d. 10 Apr. 1765.

OECHSLEN, GEORG CHRISTOFF   67459 Böhl
Adventure, 1727
S-H, I: 14, 15 (appears on A List as EXELL)

EUROPEAN RECORDS

Hassloch Lutheran KB:
Georg Christoph Exelin from Sandhaussen [69207 Sandhausen, Baden], m. 27 July 1723 Maria Margretha Müller from Böhl. They had a son:
> Henrich, b. 25 Feb. 1727, bp. 2 Mar. 1727 at Böhl

AMERICAN RECORDS

Augustus (Trappe) Lutheran KB, Montgomery Co., PA:
Jürg Oxlein m. 2 Jan. 1759 Maria Catharina Kraus at New Hanover.

Frederick S. Weiser, Monocacy Lutheran KB, Frederick, MD:
Appendix II: 107
Henrich Oechslein m. 19 June 1785 Catharina Beckert in the church at
Short Hill.

Hocker, *German Settlers of Pennsylvania:*
Apr. 1, 1756 - Sower's Newspaper:
Plantation for sale in Heidelberg Twp., Berks Co. on Cacoosing Creek, and
also an adjoining place where Christopher Oechslen lives.

Christopher Exline, Philadelphia Co., nat. Sept. 1743.

OFFENBACHER, JACOB   67361 Freisbach
Samuel, 1737
S-H, I: 169, 170, 172

EUROPEAN RECORDS

Gommersheim Lutheran KB:
Joh. Jacob Ofenbacher, *Gemeinsmann* at Freyspach, and wife Anna Rosina
had children:
    1. Joh. Leonhard, b. 26 Nov. 1706, bp. 30 Nov. 1706
    2. Joh. Michael, b. 10 Apr. 1711, bp. 12 Apr. 1711
        Sp.: Joh. Michael Heintz and Maria Catharina, his wife
    3. Joh. Jacob, b. 6 Jan. 1713, bp. 8 Jan. 1713
        Sp.: Joh. Jacob Dietz, son of George Dietz, citizen
        at Rath_____? [possibly 67744 Rathskirchen] and Margaretha
        Ursula, daughter of _____?

OHLER, JOHANN WILHELM   67159 Friedelsheim
St. Andrew Galley, 1737
S-H, I: 179, 181, 183

EUROPEAN RECORDS

Friedelsheim Reformed KB:
A very faded entry in the 1734 marriage records:
Joh. Wilhelm Ohler and ____, daughter of Peter ____

Joh. Wilhelm Ohler and wife Ursula had a child:
> Marx Simon, b. 26 Dec. 1734
> Sp.: Marx Fritz and Elisabetha

Joh. Wilhelm Ohler, master smith at Friedelsheim, and Ursula his wife were sponsors for a child of Hans Michel Braun in 1735.

AMERICAN RECORDS

Wentz, *The Beginnings of the German Element in York County, Pennsylvania,* page 116, says the William Oler who arrived in 1737 settled in York County. The same source states that William Oler and Peter Oler took out land grants in York County. (Peter Ohler arrived on the *Thistle of Glasgow,* 1730, from [67149] Meckenheim.)

Pennsylvania Archives, Third Series, Vol. XXIV, page 496, Lancaster Co. land warrants:
> William Ouler 50A, 1 May 1744; Peter Ouler 100A, 3 Mar. 1747.

Rev. John Casper Stoever's Records:
Peter Ohler had a child baptized by Pastor Stoever in 1734, and is listed in that record as residing in Conewago.

ORTH, GEORG DANIEL   67251 Freinsheim
Brotherhood, 1750
S-H, I: 448

EUROPEAN RECORDS

Freinsheim Reformed KB:
Georg Orth and wife Judith had a son:
> Georg Daniel, b. 17 Dec. 1725, bp. 21 Dec. 1725
> Sp.: Georg Daniel Weilbrenner single, and Gertraudt,
> daughter of Jacob Reck.

Georg Daniel Orth, son of the late Johann Georg Orth, m. 8 Aug. 1748 Sophia Elisabetha, daughter of Joh. Daniel Ergenbrod of Schwartzenau, Graffschaft Wittgenstein [= 57319 Bad Berleberg].

Buried 7 Feb. 1732, Juditha, wife of Georg Orth.

Emigration record:
Werner Hacker, *Auswanderungen aus Rheinpfalz und Saarland im 18. Jahrhundert,* pg. 585:
11197, Orth, Joh. Dianich?, Freinsheim, he and his brother are permitted to move to Pennsylvania. Dated 9 Dec. 1749.

Jost Wigandt also received permission to emigrate on the same date, and arrived on the same ship.

AMERICAN RECORDS

Lancaster County Will Abstracts:
Daniel Orth, Donegal Twp. 26 Sept. 1795 - 22 Oct. 1795.
Children: Barbara wife of -- Foglesong; Catharine wife of -- Blazer; Rosina; and Elizabeth wife of -- Kollinger. Grandchild, Matalina Kollinger. Exr: Ulerich Engle.

OTT, ANDREAS   Niederlustadt=
Brothers, 1752   67363 Lustadt
S-H, I: 481

EUROPEAN RECORDS

Ober Lustadt Reformed KB:
Joh. Georg Ott and wife Catharina had a son:
    Joh. Andreas, b. __ Sept. 1728
    Sp.: Joh. Andreas Theiss and Magdalena

Fritz Braun and Friedrich Krebs. "Pennsylvania Dutch Pioneers from South Palatine Parishes", *The Pennsylvania Dutchman,* 8 (Spring, 1957):
Johann Andreas Ott, born at Niederlustadt, 20 Sept. 1728, son of Johann Georg Ott and wife Catharina Groh; "already gone to the New Land ten years ago". Emigration document dated 20 June 1760.

AMERICAN RECORDS

Montgomery County Will Abstracts:
Andrew Ott is named as a son in law and also executor in the will of William Hendricks, Abington, 22 Nov. 1796.

OTT, JOH. BERNHART Ober Lustadt=
Britannia, 1764 67363 Lustadt
S-H, I: 693

EUROPEAN RECORDS

Ober Lustadt Reformed KB:
Bernhard Ott and wife Maria Magdalena had children:
1. Child, bp. __ Jan. 1746
2. Joh. Jacob, b. 28 July 1747, bp. 30 July 1747
3. Jörg Heinrich, b. 9 Jan. 1752, bp. 11 Jan. 1752

or:
Casper Ott and wife Anna Catharina of Niederlustadt had a son:
1. Joh. Bernhard, b. 8 Oct. 1740, bp. 9 Oct. 1740
   Sp.: Georg Schmidt and Anna Catharina.

AMERICAN RECORDS

Seven passengers from Oberlustadt are listed together on the passenger list of the ship *Britannia* in 1764: **Johann Bernhart Ott,** Johann Andreas Schmitt, Christian Haushalter, Georg Heinrich Schmitt; further on the list are Johann Martin Ott, Carl Garaus (see Jahraus), Vallentin Stettler.

OTT, JOH. MARTIN Ober Lustadt=
Brittania, 1764 67363 Lustadt
S-H, I: 693

EUROPEAN RECORDS

Ober Lustadt Reformed KB:
Martin Ott and Catharina Schmitt of Niederlustadt had an illegitimate daughter:
   Maria Eva, b. 4 May 1764, bp. 6 May 1764

AMERICAN RECORDS

Seven passengers from Oberlustadt are listed together on the passenger list of the ship *Britannia* in 1764: Johann Bernhart Ott, Johann Andreas Schmitt, Christian Haushalter, Georg Heinrich Schmitt; further on the list are **Johann Martin Ott,** Carl Garaus (see Jahraus), Vallentin Stettler.

PETER, GEORGE PHILIP   67157 Wachenheim an der Weinstrasse
Two Brothers, 1750
S-H, I: 438

EUROPEAN RECORDS

Wachenheim Reformed KB:
Görg Philip Peter, son of Görg Bernhard Peter, m. 11 July 1730 Maria
Barbara, daughter of the late David Wölter of [67159] Friedelsheim. They
had children:
  1. Maria Eva, bp. 15 May 1731
  2. Joh. Christian, bp. 12 Feb. 1734
  3. Joh. Michael, bp. ? Feb. 1737
  4. Joh. Ludwig, bp. 26 June 1740
  5. Joh. Leonhard, bp. 30 Aug. 1743
  6. Joh. Jacob, bp. 30 Aug. 1743

Emigration record:
Werner Hacker, *Auswanderungen aus Rheinpfalz und Saarland*:
#11318 The deceased Gg. Philipp Peter's widow from Wachenheim, and 6
children; to America in 1752.

AMERICAN RECORDS

Trinity Lutheran KB, Lancaster:
Conrad Schindler, widower from [72639] Neuffen, Wuertemberg, m. 2 July
1753 Maria Barbara Peter, widow from Wachenheim.

PFARR, JOHAN JACOB   67161 Gönnheim
Thistle, 1738
S-H, I: 221, 223, 224

EUROPEAN RECORDS

Gönnheim Reformed KB:
Joh. Jacob Parr, widower from [67227] Franckenthal, m. 14 Jan. 1690 Anna
Maria, widow of *Herr Schultheis* ?Affenstein.

Joh. Jacob Pfarr m. 19 Nov. 1710 Anna Maria Becker.

Herr Joh. Jacob Pfarr, *Schultheis* of Gönnheim, m. 20 Feb. 1715 Maria
Catharina Heltzhausser of [67346] Speyer.

A faded marriage entry in 1735 appears to be the marriage record for Joh. Jacob Pfarr, son of Jacob. Name of wife is not legible.

Joh. Jacob Parr and wife Catharina Elisabetha (nee Böhler) had children:
1. Catharina Elisabetha, bp. 16 Oct. 1735
    Sp.: Catharina Elisabetha, daughter of the late
    Melchior Schneider
2. Anna Barbara, bp. 14 July 1737
    Sp.: Anna Barbara, daughter of Joh. Martin Böhler

Hans Martin Böhler and Joh. Jacob Pfarr appear together on the ship list.

AMERICAN RECORDS

Conewago Reformed KB, Adams Co., PA:
Jacob Parr and wife Catharina Elisabetha had children:
3. A son, b. 14 June 1747, bp. __ Apr. 1748
    Sp.: Jacob Rorbach and wife
4. Louise, b. 20 Oct. 1749, bp. __ _ 1750
    Sp.: George Spanseiler and wife
5. John Adam, bp. 10 May 1751
    Sp.: Peter Mittelkauff [q.v.] and Salome

PFLAUM, JOHANNES   Lachen-Speyerdorf=
Boston, 1764   67435 Neustadt an der Weinstrasse
S-H, I: 1764

EUROPEAN RECORDS

Lachen-Speyerdorf Reformed KB:
Michel Plaum and Anna Ursula had a son:
    Johannes, bp. 13 Sept. 1705, conf. 1720

Johannes Blaum (elsewhere in KB: Plaum, Pflaum), son of Michel Blaum, m. 2 May 1739 Anna Barbara, daughter of Georg Christoph Hamman. They had children:
1. Anna Margretha, b. 7 July 1739, bp. 12 July, conf. 1755
2. Joh. Jacob, b. 16 Nov. 1741, bp. 19 Nov. 1741, conf. 1755
    Sp.: Jacob, son of Nicolaus Hamann
3. Maria Catharina, b. 5 Feb. 1744, bp. 9 Feb. 1744, conf. 1759
    Sp.: Anna Catharina, daughter of the late Georg Christoph Hammann

4. Anna Maria, b. 10 June 1748, bp. 13 June 1748
   Sp.: Anna Maria, daughter of Philip Scherer here
5. Johan Conrad, b. 3 Apr. 1751, bp. 5 Apr. 1751, conf. 1763
   Sp.: Joh. Conrad, son of Johannes Deobald and his mother
   Maria Catharina.

PRESSLER see BRESSLER

QUAST, JOHANNES   67256 Weisenheim am Sand
Crawford, 1772
S-H, I: 742

EUROPEAN RECORDS

Weisenheim am Sand Reformed KB:
Heinrich Quast and wife Anna Martha had a son:
   Johannes, bp. 28 Jan. 1751
   Sp.: Johannes Quast from [68159-68169] Mannheim and wife

Heinrich Quast d. 26 Apr. 1764.

Emigration record:
Werner Hacker, *Auswanderungen aus Rheinpfalz und Saarland*:
#11608 Johann Quast, master butcher, Weisenheim am Sand, residing in
Philadelphia in 1778.

Weisenheim am Sand

RADERLI, BENEDICT Mussbach =
Prelist, before 1727 67435 Neustadt an der Weinstrasse

EUROPEAN RECORDS

Lachen-Speyerdorf Reformed KB:
Thomas Hamann, son of Georg Christoph Hammann, m. 12 Oct. 1725 Susanna, daughter of Benedict Raderli of Musbach [Mussbach = 67435 Neustadt a. d. Weinstrasse], now living in Eysersthal.

AMERICAN RECORDS

New Goshenhoppen Reformed KB, Montgomery Co., PA:
List of heads of families belonging to the congregation of New Goshenhoppen, Reformed members (ca. 1736-1739):
    # 39 Benedict Raderly

Married at New Goshenhoppen 21 Dec. 1735, Daniel Schwartz and Eva Marg. Raderli.

RAHN, GEORG 67454 Hassloch
RAHN, CONRATH
St. Andrew Galley, 1737
S-H, I: 179, 181, 183

EUROPEAN RECORDS

Hassloch Lutheran KB:
Johann Georg Rahn from ?Rheinroth, Amt ?Schotten, Darmstadt jurisdiction m. 15 Jan. 1716 Anna Elisabetha Birckel from Mertzheim [?=67271 Mertesheim]. They had:
    1. Margaretha Elisabetha, b. 29 July 1716
    2. Conrad, b. 10 Dec. 1718, conf. 1731
    3. Jacob, bp. 14 Dec. 1721
    4. Johann Xtophel [Christophel], b. 25 Aug. 1724
    5. Caspar, b. 2 Apr. 1731

AMERICAN RECORDS

St. Michael's and Zion KB, Philadelphia:
Christopher Rahn (Providence) m. 2 Aug. 1753 Cathrina Setzler(in).

Caspar Rahn m. 28 Sept. 1756 Barbara Beutlen(in).

Augustus (Trappe) Lutheran KB, Montgomery Co., PA:
Conf. 13 Apr. 1746 - Johann Caspar Rahn, age 16 years, step son of
Balthaser Sähler [q.v.- Seyler].

Caspar Rahn and Barbara had:
      1. Johannes, b. 29 Mar. 1758
      2. Elisabetha, b. 11 Mar. 1760
      3. Georg, b. 28 Apr. 1761
      4. Samuel, b. 26 Aug. 1763
      5. Jacob, b. 6 Mar. 1765

RAHN, JOH. JACOB   67454 Hassloch
Lydia, 1749
S-H, I: 421 [with Johannes Vogt, q.v.]

EUROPEAN RECORDS

Hassloch Lutheran KB:
Jacob Rahn and wife Anna Maria had children:
      1. Anna Margretha, b. 3 Apr. 1713
      2. Catharina, b. 22 Mar. 1715
      3. Hans Nickel, b. 21 July 1716
      4. **Johann Jacob**, b. 23 July 1720, conf. 1733.
      5. Johann Henrich, bp. 22 Oct. 1722
      6. Johann Christophel, b. 11 Mar. 1727

RAUSCH, JACOB   67125 Dannstadt
Johnson Galley, 1732
S-H, I: 71, 72
   [Passengers: Jacob Rouse, Clara Rouse]

EUROPEAN RECORDS

Dannstadt Reformed KB:
Hieronymus Rausch m. __ __ 1707 Anna Catharina, widow of Henrich
Bickel. Children:
      1. **Hans Jacob,** bp. 18 Sept. 1710
        Sp.: Hans Jacob Becker and Anna

2. Joh. Lorentz, bp. 8 Jan. 1713
3. Maria Salome, b. 26 Dec. 1715
4. Adam, b. 25 ?Apr (faded) 1720
5. Joh. Marx, b. 6 Mar. 1724

Joh. Jacob Rausch, Lutheran, son of Hieronymus Rausch, m. 4 Nov. 1731 Anna Clara Renner, daughter of the deceased Velten Renner.

AMERICAN RECORDS

Philadelphia County Administrations, #132 of 1738:
John Jacob Raush. Codicil to will: Wife Anna Clara to have 1/3 part of real and personal estate. Brother in law John Jacob Krause...debts to be paid with corn... wife to have one years bread supply. Wit.: John Philip Brand, Michael Fidele. Papers taken out by Anna Clara Rausch, widow of John Jacob Raush, late of Philadelphia County, Limerick Twp.; Michael Fedle of Philadelphia, Yeoman, and Philip Brand. 17 Feb. 1738.

RAUSCH, GEORG 67259 Heuchelheim
Prelist

EUROPEAN RECORDS

Heuchelheim Lutheran KB:
Joh. Georg Raush m. 8 Jan. 1709 Magdalena Hill. They had:
1. Joh. Daniel, b. 21 Oct. 1709
2. Joh. Philip, b. 9 Apr. 1711
3. Johannes, b. 5 Sept. 1712
4. Jacob, b. 26 Apr. 1717, d. 1717
5. Anna Barbara, b. 24 Mar. 1717
6. Johannes, b. 24 June 1719

AMERICAN RECORDS

Rev. John Casper Stoever's Records:
Daniel Rausch m. 18 Mar. 1730 Elisabetha Optograef, Providence.

Dunkel's Reformed KB, Berks Co., PA:
A Daniel Rausch had a child baptized at Dunkel's Church in 1749; a Johannes Rausch had a child baptized in 1746, also at Dunkel's Church; sp. of this child was a Magdalena Rausch.

Moselem Lutheran KB, Berks Co., PA:
Johannes Rausch and Catharina (nee Hok ?Hoch) had:
>   Jacob, bp. 15 Apr. 1750, age 6 weeks
>   Sp.: Andreas Seidel and Regina

Joh. Leonhard Kepplinger, Jr., single son of John Leonhard Kepplinger, Sr.,
m. 28 Nov. 1749 Anna Maria Rausch, single daughter of Georg Rausch.

REICHARD, ULRICH   67365 Schwegenheim
Davy, 1738
S-H, I: 234, 235, 236

EUROPEAN RECORDS

Schwegenheim Reformed KB:
Ulrich Reichardt, son of Valentin Reichardt, Reformed, m. 17 Nov. 1722
Anna Maria Meckel, daughter of the late Abraham Meckel, Lutheran. They
had children:
>   1. Anna Maria, b. 28 Mar. 1733
>   Sp.: Joh. Jacob Kübler and Anna Maria
>   2. Johannes, b. 30 Oct. 1737
>   Sp.: Joh. Anthel? and Anna Maria

AMERICAN RECORDS

Lancaster Moravian Burials:
Susanna Reichard b. 1724, daughter of Ulrich and Anna Maria Reichard, of
Schwechenheim [67365 Schwegenheim] near Speyer; m. 1741 Joh. Peter
Ganter. They had nine children. She died 1806.

Lancaster Moravian Records:
Ulrich Reichard, b. 1695 in Schwechenheim near Speyer, died 13 Mar. 1766,
m. Anna Maria Merkel, daughter of Abraham and Margaret Merkel, b. 1701,
d. 30 Oct. 1768. They had children:
>   1. Susanna, b. Sept. 1724, d. 19 Feb. 1806
>   m. 2 Apr. 1741 John Peter Ganter
>   2. Dorothea, m. 19 Aug. 1745 Nicolaus Kontz
>   3. Christoph, b. Feb. 1731, d. 16 Oct. 1783
>   m. 24 Feb. 1756 Susanna Zimmerman
>   4. John Adam, b. 22 Nov. 1738, d. 9 May 1813
>   m. (1) Catharine Zimmerman
>   m. (2) Susanna Rudesil
>   5. Maria Catharina, b. 25 Nov. 1743, d. 8 Sept. 1748

REIMER, BALTHASAR age 40   67112 Mutterstadt
Brothers, 1754
S-H, I: 609, 611, 613

EUROPEAN RECORDS

Mutterstadt Reformed KB:
Hans Bernhard Reimer m. 30 Apr. 1709 Anna Catharina Sager from Ruchheim [= 67071 Ludwigshafen]. They had a son:
  Balthasar, b. 30 May 1715

Balthasar Reimer, son of Bernhard Reimer, m. 11 Feb. 1738 Maria Magdalena Kob, nee Renner, a widow from Fusgonnheim [= 67136 Fussgönheim]. No children listed in Mutterstadt Reformed KB.

Krebs, "Pennsylvania Dutch Pioneers," *The Pennsylvania Dutchman,* 1954, 1955, 1956: Balthasar Reymer of Mutterstadt is permitted to go to the New Land with wife and children, but must pay the tithe on his property that he is taking out of the country." (Protocols of the Oberamt of Neustadt, 1753.)

REIMER, FREDERICK   67112 Mutterstadt
Thistle of Glasgow, 1730
S-H, I: 31, 32, 33

EUROPEAN RECORDS

Mutterstadt Reformed KB:
Dionysius Friderich Reimer m. 1 Oct. 1715 Maria Elisabetha Weynach. They had children:
  1. Elisabetha, bp. 24 Dec. 1716
  2. Maria Salome, bp. 15 Apr. 1719
  3. Susanna Elisabetha, bp. 16 July 1721
  4. Anna Barbara, bp. 2 Jan. 1724
  5. Johanna Maria, bp. 30 May 1726
  6. Joh. Peter, bp. 30 Nov. 1728

Braun, "Auswanderer aus der Umgebung von Ludwigshafen a. Rh. auf dem Schiff *Thistle of Glasgow* 1730," publication #8, *Schriften zur Wanderungsgeschichte der Pfälzer,* 1959, mentions the emigration of Freiderich Reimer.

2

AMERICAN RECORDS

Philadelphia County Will Abstracts:
Frederick Reimer, Frederick, co. of Philadelphia. 9 may 1755- 11 Feb. 1758. Wife: Elizabeth. Children: Elizabeth, Salome, Susanna, Barbara, Anna Maria, Cathrine, John Petter, Johannes and Ludwig. Exrs: wife Elizabeth and son John Peter Reimer. Wit.: Henry Antes, John Philip Leydich.

Wm. J. Hinke, *Life and Letters of the Rev. John Philip Boehm:* "Frederick Reymer arrived in Philadelphia in the ship *Thistle,* 29 Aug. 1730, and settled in Frederick twp. His will was probated 11 Feb. 1758, and names his wife Elizabeth and son John Peter Reimer. One of his daughters, Elizabeth Reimer, married Francis Shunk of Providence twp. She was the grandmother of Governor Francis R. Shunk."

Falckner Swamp Reformed KB, New Hanover Twp., Montgomery Co., PA:
Joh. Peter Reimer m. 28 Nov. 1752 Rachel Zieber.

Elizabeth Schunk, widow of Francis Schunk, nee Reimer, d. 18 Mar. 1802. Age 85 y. 30 mo. Buried at Trappe.

Frederick Reimer and wife Elisabetha appear as sponsors in 1747, 1748, and 1756.
Anna Maria Reimer, single daughter of Frederick Reimer, was a sponsor in 1747.
Frederick Reimmer signed a petition in 1730/31 for laying out Frederick twp.

Frederick Reymer was nat. by Act of 1735.

REIMER, VALENTIN   67112 Mutterstadt
Edinburgh, 1748
S-H, I: 371

EUROPEAN RECORDS

Mutterstadt Reformed KB:
Hans Jacob Reimer m. 5 Feb. 1704 Anna Maria Lindmayer. They had a son:

        Valentin, bp. 29 Apr. 1714
        Sp.: Hans Valentin Reinig from [69412] Eberbach
          a. Neckar and wife Anna Margaretha nee
          Bleyenstein.

Joh. Valentin Reimmer, son of Jacob Reimmer, m. 17 Sept. 1737 Maria Catharina Gartner, daughter of Isaac Gartner. Notation in marriage record: "to Pennsylvania 1748".

AMERICAN RECORDS

St. Paul's (Blue) Lutheran KB, Upper Saucon Twp., Lehigh Co., PA:
Valentin Reimer and wife Anna Margaretha had a daughter:
>Elisabeth b. 29 Nov. 1753, bp. 17 Apr. 1754
>Sp.: Elisabeth Transue

Lower Saucon Reformed KB, Northampton Co., PA:
Valentin Reimer d. 13 Feb. 1794; bur. 15 Feb. 1794; age 80 y.9 mo. 18 d.

Northampton County Will Abstracts:
Valentin Reimer, Williams twp., dated 30 Mar. 1793, probated 31 Mar. 1794. Names his wife Margareth, and children: Isaac; Daniel; Jacob; Henry; Margareth, wife of John Reil; Elisabetha, wife of Peter Unangst; Catharina, wife of Peter Lantz; Sarah, wife of Jacob Miller; Anna Barbara; Anna Eva; Susanna, deceased, had m. ___ Holland and had children.

REINTZEL, CONRAD   Niederhochstadt =
Ship data not located,   76879 Hochstadt, Pfalz
Emigration record dated 1762; there were no ships arriving that year in Philadelphia. One ship arrived in 1756, no arrivals in 1757-1760. One ship arrived in 1761, then nothing until October of 1763.

EUROPEAN RECORDS

Niederhochstadt Reformed KB:
Conrad Reintzel was confirmed in 1735; his birth record was not located but there are several faded and unreadable entries in the KB in the 1720s. There were, however, several Reintzel families in Niederhochstadt. [See next immigrant].

Emigration record:
Werner Hacker, *Auswanderungen aus Rheinpfalz und Saarland*:
#11774 Conrad Reintzel from Niederhochstadt, to America, 1762

AMERICAN RECORDS

Berks County Abstracts of Wills and Adm.:
Conrad Reintzel. On 22 Sept. 1792, letters of adm. were granted to Eva Reintzel, the widow.

REINTZEL, VALENTIN age 17   Niederhochstadt=
Friendship, 1738   76879 Hochstadt, Pfalz
S-H, I: 226, 228, 230

EUROPEAN RECORDS

Niederhochstadt Reformed KB:
Hans Niclas Reintzel and wife Susanna had a son:
    Joh. Valendin, bp. 19 Mar. 1722
      Sp.: Veltin __ (unreadable) and Anna
        Catharina Reintzel, both single.

AMERICAN RECORDS

Host Church, Tulpehocken, Berks Co., PA:
Valentin Reintzel and wife Sarah had children:
    1. Maria Margreth, bp. 7 Apr. 1749
      Sp.: (Maria Margretha) Richel
    2. (Jacob), b. 26 Oct. 1753; bp. 16 Nov. 1753
      Sp.: Jacob Habler and Barbara

PA, Sixth Series, Vol. 6, Rev. Waldschmidt's records:
John Mauntz, son of the late Jacob Mauntz, m. 26 Aug. 1765 in Host
Church, Maria Elisabeth, daughter of Valentin Reintzel.

Valentine Reintzell, Tulpehoccon, Berks County, nat. 10 to 23 Apr. 1764.

REMELY, AMBROSE   67256 Weisenheim am Sand
Lydia, 1749
S-H, I: 421

EUROPEAN RECORDS

Weisenheim am Sand Reformed KB:
Ambrosius Remelli, son of the late Nicolaus Remelli of Gross Carlbach
[67229 Grosskarlbach], m. 10 Jan. 1719 Anna Catharina, daughter of Joh.
Michael Schick. They had children:
    1. Anna Maria, bp. 5 Nov. 1721
      Sp.: Joh. Michael Schick and Anna Maria
    2. Joh. Philipp, bp. 11 Nov. 1725
      Sp.: Joh. Philipp Neckarauer, single

3. Maria Magdalena, bp. 12 Dec. 1728
   Sp.: Johannes Sar and wife Maria Magdalena
4. Joh. Michael, bp. 21 Mar. 1731
   Sp.: Joh. Michael Schick and wife
5. Johannes, bp. 23 Aug. 1733
   Johannes Saar from Gronau [67127 Rödersheim-Gronau]
   and wife Maria Magdalena
6. Joh. Georg, bp. 15 May 1735
   Sp.: Joh. Georg Schick, single
7. Peter, bp. 27 Apr. 1738
   Sp.: Peter Coblentzer and wife Agnesia.

AMERICAN RECORDS

Rev. Abraham Blumer's Records:
d. 27 Aug. 1776, Barbara Remaley, widow of Ambrosius, age 73 y.

Rev. Daniel Schumaker's Baptismal Register:
Michaell Remelÿ and Anna Maria had a daughter baptized in Heidelberg
[today Lehigh Co.]:
   Catharina, b. 29 Jan. 1764, bp. 6 May 1764
   Sp.: Wilhelm Wodringh and Elisabeth, wife of Johannes Rebbert

Northampton County Will Abstracts:
George Remely of Whitehall Twp. 30 Sept. 1800 - 29 Oct. 1800.
Wife: Elizabeth. Children: Ambrosius, Johannes, Elisabeth, Barbara, Jacob,
Maria, Heinrich, Magdalena, George and Peter. Exrs: son Ambrosius and
Peter Roth. Wit.: Fredk. Marting, A. Troxell, J. Strein.

Additional Remely records may be found in Schlosser's Reformed KB,
Unionville, North Whitehall Twp., Lehigh Co., PA.

REMELY, NICHOLAS   67229 Grosskarlbach
Pennsylvania Merchant, 1731   67251 Freinsheim
S-H, I: 43, 45
   appears on A List as Nicholas Reymel,
   on B List as Johann Nicklaus Rei[mel]

EUROPEAN RECORDS

Nicholaus Remely was evidently a son of the late Nicolaus Remelli of Gross
Carlbach [67229 Grosskarlbach]. He names his brother Ambrose Remely
[q.v.] in his Pennsylvania will.

Emigration record:
Werner Hacker, *Auswanderungen aus Rheinpfalz und Saarland*:
#11956 Niklas Remle, from Freinsheim, to PA, 1731.

AMERICAN RECORDS

Philadelphia Will Abstracts:
Nicholas Remely, filed 23 Jan. 1738. Book F, pg. 90:
Mentions brother Ambrose. Exrs.: Jacob Klemmer and Abraham Soler
[Sahler, q.v.]. Wit.: Dilman Kolb, Hannes Huber and Johannes Blyler.

RENN, BERNHARD   67454 Hassloch
Thistle of Glasgow, 1730
S-H, I: 32, 33, 34

EUROPEAN RECORDS

Hassloch Lutheran KB:
Bernhard Renn was a sponsor in 1724 for a child of Valentin Renn [q.v.]

Bernhard Renn (?) m. 31 Aug. 1728 Maria Christina Bommel. They had:
       Philippina, b. 13 July 1729, bp. 17 July 1729
       Sp.: Philippina Renner

AMERICAN RECORDS

New Hanover Lutheran KB, Montgomery Co., PA:
Confirmed 1747 - Philipina Renn, daughter of Bernhard Renn.
Confirmed 1747 - Johann Michael Renn, son of Bernhard Renn.
Confirmed 1750 - Bernhard Renn, age 15.
Confirmed 1752 - Catharina Renn, age 15.

Augustus (Trappe) Lutheran KB, Montgomery Co., PA:
Bernhard Renn, widower, m. 19 Jan. 1749 the widow Sibilla Riegel (?) [the
surname appears in the New Hanover KB as Rüdel.]
Bernhard Renn died 19 Apr. 1749.

The widow, Sybilla Renn m. 20 Nov. 1749 at New Hanover Veit Jürger.

Johan Michael Renn, son of Bernhard Renn, m. 18 Apr. 1754 Salome Kraus,
daughter of Michael Kraus.

Rev. H. M. Muhlenberg's Journals, I: 148:
May 1747, confirmed a deacon's son, 16 years old (Saddler's brother-in-law from Jersey). A footnote in the volume says:
Johan Michael Renn, son of <u>Leon</u>hard Renn but church record says son of <u>Bern</u>hard Renn.

Old Goshenhoppen Lutheran KB, Montgomery Co., PA:
Jacob Schmidt, 22 years old, son of Wilhelm and Margreth (Schmidt) deceased, m. 19 Mar. 1734 Philippina Renn, daughter of Bernt Renn.

Monocacy Lutheran KB, Frederick, MD:
Bernhard Renn (Jr.) and wife Catharina had a daughter:
Maria Elisabeth, b. 15 Aug. 1763, bp. 16 Oct. 1763
Sp.: Johannes Koupferschmidt and Maria Elisabeth

Bernhart Renn, Philadelphia Co., nat. Apr. 1743.

RENN, VALENTIN   67454 Hassloch
[Ship arrival not located -
possibly Valentin Renn was sick on arrival, and does not appear in the lists; his oldest son is likely the following:]
REYN [REIN], BERNARD age 17
St. Andrew, 1741
S-H, I: 304, 305, 306
EUROPEAN RECORDS

Hassloch Lutheran KB:
Hanss Valentin Renn, single, m. 19 Oct. 1723 Philippina Margretha Schmidt. They had:
1. Georg Bernhard, b. 29 July 1724, bp. 2 Aug. 1724
   Sp.: Bernhard Renn
2. Anna Margretha, b. 29 Nov. 1726, bp. 1 Dec. 1726
   Sp.: Anna Margretha Schmid.
   She died 29 Apr. 1728
3. Christina Margretha, b. 12 Feb. 1729, bp. 13 Feb. 1729
   Sp.: Christina Margretha Schmid
4. Anna Catharina, bp. 20 Oct. 1731
   Sp.: Anna Catharina Eisenmeyer.
   She died 1 June 1738, age 7 years

    5. Elisabetha, bp. 2 June 1735
        Sp.: Elisabetha Schmidt, single.
        She died 14 Feb. 1737, age 1 year 9 months 7 days
    6. Johann Friederich, bp. 22 June or July 1738
        Sp.: Friederich Wohlfahrt and wife

Hassloch Beiträge:
1727, Velte Renn from Königshoffen in *Grabfeldherrlich. ?Bibraischer Jurisdiction* [97631 Königshofen i. Grabfeld]

AMERICAN RECORDS

New Hanover Lutheran KB, Montgomery Co., PA:
Jürg Bernhard Renn m. 3 June 1746 Anna Maria Kallbach.

Conf. 1746 - Christina Margaretha Renn, daughter of Valentin Renn.

Berks Co., PA Wills and Administrations:
Bernhard Renn, Windsor Twp., 18 Aug. 1763. Administration granted to John Kiehl and his wife Anna Maria, who was widow of said intestate.

Fred. Renn, Moyamens Twp., Philadelphia Co. nat. Fall 1765.

RENNER, GÖRG BLEES   67112 Mutterstadt
[Görg Blees Rener, signed]
York, 1725
   [Agreement contract with ship's capt.]

EUROPEAN RECORDS

Mutterstadt Reformed KB:
Görg Blasius Renner m. 13 Feb. 1720 Anna Elisabetha Bleyenstein. No children bp. there.

RENNER, JACOB   67112 Mutterstadt
RENNER, JACOB
RENNER, JOHANN GEORG
Edinburgh, 1754
S-H, I: 615, 617, 620

EUROPEAN RECORDS

Mutterstadt Reformed KB:
Hans Jacob Renner and wife Rosina Barbara had a son:
    Hans Jacob, bp. __ Dec. 1702

Oggersheim Reformed KB:
Johann Jacob Renner, son of Hans Jacob Renner of Mutterstadt, m. 12 Feb. 1726 Helena Barbara, daughter of Johann Peter Sachs.

Mutterstadt Reformed KB:
Johann Jacob Renner and wife Helena Barbara nee Sachs had children:
    1. Anna Barbara, bp. 17 Feb. 1727
    2. Anna Maria, bp. 21 Nov. 1728
    3. Maria Katharina, b. 7 July 1731 bp. 20 July 1731
    4. Joh. Jacob, b. 22 Mar. 1735, bp. 27 Mar. 1735
    5. Joh. Georg, b. 16 Nov. 1737, bp. 20 Nov. 1737

Krebs, "More 18th Century Emigrants from the Palatinate," *The Pennsylvania Dutchman,* 1954: "Johann Jacob Renner, of Mutterstadt, permitted in 1754 to emigrate to the New Land with wife and children, but had to pay the tithe on property which he took out of the country."

Emigration record:
Werner Hacker, *Auswanderungen aus Rheinpfalz und Saarland*:
#11970, J. Jacob Renner, Mutterstadt, with wife and children, 1754.

AMERICAN RECORDS

Philadelphia Wills, Book O, p. 28:
Jacob Renner, Worcester Twp., Philadelphia Co., yeoman. Dated 22 Feb. 1766, probated 30 Sept. 1766. Executors: Jacob Wentz and Melchior Wagener. Wife Anna Margaret; sons Jacob, George, and youngest son Adam.

Zion's Lutheran Church, East Pikeland Twp., Chester Co., PA:
Adam Renner, b. 1 Feb. 1740, d. 2 Dec. 1808, from "Fartsch Velly" (Valley Forge?), son of Jacob Renner.

Jacob Renner, Worchester Twp., Philadelphia Co., nat. 11 Apr. 1763.
Jacob Renner, Worchester Twp., Philadelphia Co., nat. Fall, 1765, without taking an oath.

RENNER, WERINA BECKER   67125 Dannstadt
WIFE OF CONRAD RENNER
Arrived between 1737 and 1739

EUROPEAN RECORDS

Dannstadt Reformed KB:
Hans Conrad Renner, son of Hans Martin Renner of [67136] Fussgönheim
m. 28 May 1736 Werina Becker, daughter of Johannes Becker of Dannstadt.
Conrad Renner and Verina nee Becker had a daughter:
    Maria Salome, b. 27 Apr. 1737
    [Note under child's name in record: *ist in PA.*]

Emigration record:
Werner Hacker, *Auswanderungen aus Rheinpfalz und Saarland*:
#8015 Veronica Klopp, nee Becker, from Dannstadt.

AMERICAN RECORDS

Hans Conrad Renner may have died before leaving Europe, or on the
voyage to America. He does not appear in the passenger lists. It is quite
possible that he was one of the many victims of the epidemic of 1738.

**Rev. John Caspar Stoever's Records, also Christ "Little Tulpehocken" KB,
Berks Co.:**
Johannes Heyl m. 2 Aug. 1739 Werina Rönner [27 Aug. in Christ "Little
Tulpehocken" KB]

Swatara Reformed KB, near Jonestown, Lebanon Co., PA:
John Heyl and wife Maria (Werina) had:
    1. Anna Christine, bp. 16 June 1740
       Sp.: Isaiah Guschweyd and wife Anna Christina
    2. Anna Maria, bp. 10 Aug. 1742
       Sp.: Ludwig Born and wife Anna Maria

Lancaster Co. Orphan's Court Docket, dated 7 Mar. 1748/9:
Peter Klopp is appointed guardian of Johannia Renner, daughter of Conrad
Renner, dec'd. In the next item in the same docket, Peter Klopp is also
appointed guardian over Christina, Anny Mary, Margaret Catharine and
Margaret Heil, daughters of John Heil, dec'd.

Hain's Church Burials, Berks Co., PA:
Peter Klopp, b. 22 May 1719, d. 22 May 1794.
Werrina Klopp nee Becker, b. 24 June 1713, d. 22 Nov. 1792.

RENNER, HANS VELTIN   67125 Dannstadt
Johnson, 1732
S-H, I: 71, 75, 77
  [Passengers on ship: Veltin Renner, Margaretha and Catharina]

EUROPEAN RECORDS

Dannstadt Reformed KB:
Hans Dieter Renner and Magdalena of Dannstadt had a son:
      Hans Veltin, bp. 10 Dec. 1703

Joh. Velten Renner, son of the late Dietrich Renner of Dannstadt, m. 12 Apr. 1730 Anna Margaretha Wessa, daughter of Joh. Jacob Wessa of Schauernheim [= 67125 Dannstadt-Schauernheim]. They had:
      1. Maria Catharina, bp. 6 Feb. 1731

Dietrich Renner died in Dannstadt 29 Apr. 1729, age 70 years.

Emigration record:
Werner Hacker, *Auswanderungen aus Rheinpfalz und Saarland*:
#11967 Hans Valentin Renner, Dannstadt to America, 1732.

AMERICAN RECORDS

Tohickon Union Church Records, Bedminster Twp., Bucks Co., PA:
Valentin Renner and wife Magdalena had a child:
      1. Joh. Peter, b. 16 May 1744
          Sp.: Peter Hans and Anna Lucia

Valentin Renner and wife Catharina had a child:
      2. Maria Elisabeth, b. 30 Mar. 1757
          Sp.: Rudolph Drach [q.v.] and wife

Bucks County Will Book 4, pg. 143:
Vallentin Renner, Bedminster Twp., Bucks Co. 15 Apr. 1775 - 5 Nov. 1781. Weaver. Wife: Magtalena. Children: sons John, Jacob, Peter, Henry, Adam, and Michael; daughters Clara, Catharine, Magtalena and Elizabeth. All children to have equal shares, and son John to have 20 shillings extra. Three daughters Catharina, Elisabeth and Magtalena have received £7 which is to be deducted from their shares. Exrs: friend Jacob Ott and wife Magtalena. Wit.: Henry Ott and Michael Ott.

REYER, CHRISTOFFEL   67459 Böhl
Phoenix, 1749
S-H, I: 406

EUROPEAN RECORDS

Hassloch Reformed KB:
Samuel Rheyer, *Gemeinsmann,* son of the deceased Hans Georg Rheyer of
Böhl, m. at [67454] Hassloch 22 Sept. 1716 Anna Magdalena, daughter of
the deceased Johannes Kauffman (faded entry). Samuel Reyher died at Böhl
5 Apr. 1736, age 47 years, 1 day. (This last entry from Böhl Reformed KB.)
Samuel and Anna Magdalena had children:
1. Georg **Christoph**, b. 13 Feb. 1718; bp. 20 Feb. 1718 at Böhl
2. Maria Catharina, b. 12 Oct. 1719, bp. 15 Oct. 1719 at Böhl
3. Anna Margretha, b. 26 Jan. 1722, bp. 1 Feb. 1722 at Böhl
4. Maria Margretha, b. 6 Aug. 1724, bp. 10 Aug. 1724 at Böhl
5. Johann Marx, b. 13 Jan. 1727, bp. 19 Jan. 1727 at Böhl
   d. 29 Sept. 1734, age 7 y. 9 mo. (Böhl Reformed KB)
6. Anna Maria, b. 28 Dec. 1728, bp. 1 Jan. 1729 at Böhl
7. Philippina Margretha, b. 17 July 1731, bp. 22 July 1731 at Böhl
   d. 2 Mar. 1736, age 4 y. 8 mo. 17 d. (Surname Ruher)
8. **Böhl Ref. KB:** Johannes, b. 31 May 1734, bp. 3 June 1734

Georg Christoff Reyher, son of the deceased Samuel Reyher of Böhl, m. 26
Apr. 1741 Anna Barbara Degin, daughter of Henrich Degen. They had the
following children bp. at Hassloch:
1. Anna Margaretha bp. 6 Mar. 1743
2. Joh. Georg bp. 10 Apr. 1746
3. Johannes bp. 3 Mar. 1748
4. Joh. Jacob bp. 3 Mar. 1748

Böhl Reformed KB:
Buried 5 Apr. 1736 Samuel Reÿher, age 47 years and 1 day.

Johannes König, son of Johann Philipp König, m. 4 Sept. 1736 Maria (sic)
Magdalena, widow of Samuel Reyher.

Georg Christoph Reyher (son of the late Samuel Reyher, citizen at Bohl) m.
26 Apr. 1740 Anna Barbara, daughter of Henrich Degen citizen at Hassloch.

Anna Margaretha, daughter of the late Samuel Reyher, m. 14 Aug. 1742
Johannes Gross, widower.

Maria Margaretha, daughter of the late Samuel Reyher, m. 25 Nov. 1744
Johann Arnold Christ, son of the late Marx Christ.

Johannes Reyer, son of the late Samuel Reyher, m. 18 Oct. 1757 Anna Margaretha, daughter of the late Christoph Mattern.

Johannes Brendtel, son of Johannes Brendtel, m. 25 apr. 1758 Anna Maria, daughter of the late Samuel Reyer.

AMERICAN RECORDS

Christoph Reyer appears on tax lists for Bethel Twp., Berks County.

St. Paul's (Klopp's) Reformed KB, Bethel Twp., Lebanon Co., PA:
Samuel Reyer and wife Maria Elisabeth had:
      Christopher, b. 25 Oct. 1770, bp. 16 Dec. 1770
      Sp.: Christoph Reyer and Catharine

Berks County Abstracts of Wills:
Christopher Royer of Bethel Twp. left a will, probated 18 Apr. 1796 at Reading. He names his wife Anna Catharina, and children: Margaret, George, Sebastian, Christian, Christopher, and youngest son Amich. Eldest son George and friend Samuel Royer were named as executors.

RHEYER, SEBASTIAN 67459 Böhl
Prelist; emigrated about 1726

EUROPEAN RECORDS

Hassloch Reformed KB:
Married at Böhl 15 Feb. 1707, Sebastian Rheyer, son of the deceased Hans Georg Rheyer, *des Gerichts,* with Agnes, daughter of the late Johann Wendel Flockerth, miller at [67105] Schifferstadt.

Sebastian Rheyer and his wife Agnes nee Flockirth of Böhl had children:
1. Johann Emich, bp. 18 Dec. 1707
2. Johann George, bp. 24 Aug. 1710
3. Maria Magdalena, b. 1 June 1713, bp. 5 June 1713
4. Anna Margaretha, b. 1 June 1713, bp. 5 June 1713
5. Johann Martin, b. 10 Mar. 1716; buried 30 Nov. 1716
6. Samuel, b. 4 Oct. 1718, bp. 9 Oct. 1718
7. Johann Heinrich, b. 15 Oct. 1721, bp. 26 Oct. 1721
8. Maria Catharina, b. 20 Sept. 1725, bp. 23 Sept. 1725

AMERICAN RECORDS

Sebastian Royer took out a land warrant for 100 acres in Lancaster County, 3 Jan. 1733. Other warrants for the family: George Reyer, 100 acres 18 May 1743; Amos (?Emich) Reyer, 215 acres 18 May 1743; Henry Royer, 200 acres 31 July 1746.

Lancaster Will Book Y-2, p. 518, Abstract:
Sebastian Royer, twp. omitted. 13 Aug. 1758 - 21 Feb. 1759.
Wife: Agness. Children: John (there were others, names and numbers not given). Exr.: John Emich Royer.

Lancaster County Will Abstracts:
Emick Royer, Cocalico Twp. 27 Mar. 1769 - 29 Apr. 1769.
Wife: Catharine Royer. Children: Philip, Christian, Peter, John, Daniel, Elizabeth and Catharine. Exrs: John Landis and Henry Mohler.

Johan Emich Reyer had children bp. at the Muddy Creek Church, Lancaster County. Samuel Reyer appears as a sponsor in the Seltenreich Church records in 1746. There are probate records for Heinrich Reyer recorded at Lancaster in 1767. Anna Margaretha Reyer m. Johann Philip Hautz, another emigrant from Hassloch [q.v.]. Maria Catharina Reyer m. Jacob Conrad, a member of the Heidelberg Moravian congregation in Berks County. Additional records on their children are found in that record.

RIEG, DANIEL   Niederhochstadt=
[listed in S-H index as Ring]   76879 Hochstadt, Pfalz
Britannia, 1764
S-H, I: 692 [actually signed Rieg]

EUROPEAN RECORDS

Niederhochstadt Reformed KB:
Johannes Rieg, son of the deceased Jacob Rieg of Oberlustadt [= 67363 Lustadt], m. 28 Jan. 1738 Anna Catharina Freitag, daughter of the deceased Johann Freitag. They had children:
    1. Eva Barbara, b. 14 Sept. 1738, bp. 16 Sept. 1738
       Sp.: Joh. Erhard Siegrist of Oberlustatt
       and Eva Barbara Wagner
    2. Eva Barbara, b. 16 Dec. 1739, bp. 20 Dec. 1739
       Sp.: Joh. Heinrich Sygerist of Lustatt
       and Eva Barbara Wagner, both single

3. Anna Maria, b. 13 Nov. 1742, bp. 15 Nov. 1742
   Sp.: Georg Jacob Reintzel and Anna
   Maria Knoll of Bornheim(?) [76879 Bornheim, Pfalz]
4. **Daniel,** b. 24 Feb. 1746
   Sp.: Daniel (faded) and Barbara Laux, both single
5. Catharina Margaretha, b. 19 Nov. 1748, bp. 24 Nov. 1748
   Sp.: Geo. Theobaldt Ely and Catharina Butz, both single
6. Maria Eva, b. 18 June 1755, bp. 22 June 1755
   Sp.; Jacob Rieg of Oberlustadt and Maria Eva

Johannes Rieg died 26 May 1761, age 48 years, 1 month, 15 days.

Anna Catharina Rieg d. 19 Jan. 1775, age 56 years, 2 months, 8 days.

Half-timbered house in Hochstadt

AMERICAN RECORDS

Reading Lutheran Marriage Record, Berks Co., PA:
Daniel Rühig, son of Johannes Rühig dec'd from Niederhoff (should be Niederhost) near Landau, Upper Palatinate, m. 17 Dec. 1769 Anna Maria Günther, daughter of Philip Günther, Blue Mtn.

RIHM, JOHANNES   Lachen-Speyerdorf=
RIHM, JOHANN JÜLCH   67435 Neustadt an der Weinstrasse
(did not sign: Johann Julius (X) Reehm)
Edinburg, 1748
S-H, I: 372

EUROPEAN RECORDS

Lachen-Speyerdorf Reformed KB:
Joh. Agidius Riem, son of Herr Johannes Riem, court recorder, m. 9 Jan. 1697 Christina, daughter of the late Jacob Zimmerli. They had a son:
Johannes, bp. 30 Nov. 1701, conf. 1715

Johannes Rihm, son of the late Gilg Rihm, m. 27 Sept. 1724 Maria Elisabetha, daughter of Michel Meyss. They had children:
1. Johann Jülch, b. 1 Sept. 1725, bp. 5 Sept. 1725
2. Johann Adam, b. 5 Jan. 1727, d. 1727
3. Johannes, b. 7 Mar. 1728, d. 1729
4. Johann Georg, b. 28 Nov. 1729, conf. 1744
    He may be the immigrant Johann Georg Rihm on the
    Ann Galley, 1752.
5. Anna Margretha, b. 3 Feb. 1731
6. Catharina Elisabetha, b. 2 Aug. 1732, conf. 1747
7. Johannes, bp. 18 Aug. 1734, d. 1736
8. Gertraud, b. 30 Jan. 1736, d. 1736
9. Johannes, b. 6 Feb. 1737
10. Cunrad, b. 6 Aug. 1739, d. 1739
11. Anna Maria, b. 26 Aug. 1740

AMERICAN RECORDS

One John Ream appears on the Reading, Berks Co., tax list in 1754.

Trinity Lutheran KB, Reading, Berks Co., PA:
One Elisabetha Riem sp. a child of Lorentz Vies in 1754.
Jürg Riem and wife Apollonia sp. a daughter of Balthasar Rickart in 1754.

A Georg Riem and wife Anna Maria had a son:
      Joh. Christian, b. 25 Oct. 1760, bp. 24 Dec. 1760
      Sp.: Christian Maurer and Catharina Elisabetha

George Rehm, Alsace Twp., Berks Co., nat. Apr. 1761.

RIHM, NICLAS   67112 Mutterstadt
York, 1725   Lachen-Speyerdorf=
                    67435 Neustadt an der Weinstrasse
[signed ship contract agreement]

EUROPEAN RECORDS

Lachen-Speyerdorf Reformed KB:
Herr Johannes Riem, schoolmaster and court recorder, son of Hans Riem of Wintzingen [?Winzingen = 73072 Donzdorf], m. 12 Aug. 1674 Barbara Catharina, daughter of the late Valentin Dietrich, former citizen and tanner at [35585] Wetzlar. They had a son:
      Johan Nicolaus, bp. 18 Aug. 1686
      Sp.: Niccel Rohtt

Mutterstadt Reformed KB:
Johannes Bock and wife Anna Margaretha had a daughter:
      Anna Barbara, bp. 23 Oct. 1698

Johannes [Nicholas?] Christian Riem from Lachen m. 27 Apr. 1717 Anna Barbara Bock.

Nickolaus Riem and wife Anna Barbara had children:
      1. Balthasar, bp. 5 Mar. 1719
      2. Johannes, bp. 14 Mar. 1721
          Sp.: Johannes Renner and Maria Susanna Bock

AMERICAN RECORDS

Niecklas Riem signed a petition in September, 1727 requesting a road from the Lutheran meeting house at Tulpehocken to the Quakers meeting house near George Boone's mill in Oley.

ROCH, PETER   Niederlustadt=
Rowand, 1753   67363 Lustadt
S-H, I: 569, 570, 572

EUROPEAN RECORDS

Ober Lustadt Reformed KB:
Peter Roch and wife Anna Barbara had a son:
    Johann Peter, b. 24 Aug. 1724, bp. 29 Aug. 1724
    Sp.: Peter Groh and Anna Barbara

Fritz Braun and Friedrich Krebs. "Pennsylvania Dutch Pioneers from South
Palatine Parishes", *The Pennsylvania Dutchman,* 8 (Spring, 1957):
  Johann Peter Roch, born at Niederlustadt, 24 Aug. 1724, son of Peter
Roch, citizen and farrier at Niederlustadt, and wife Maria (Anna) Barbara
Stadler; married Margaretha Lutz.

Emigration record:
Werner Hacker, *Auswanderungen aus Rheinpfalz und Saarland:*
#12159 Peter Roch, Niederlustadt, m. Margaretha Lutz, Offenbach; to
America 1753.

RÖDER, CATHARINA, widow of Johann Adam Röder 67112 Mutterstadt
Prelist; ca. 1724/1725

EUROPEAN RECORDS

Mutterstadt Reformed KB:
Hans Adam Röder and wife Anna Katharina had children:
    1. Hans Adam, bp.2 July 1706
       Sp.: Adam Röder and wife Anna Maria
       from Maudach [= 67067 Ludwigshafen am Rhein]
    2. Hans Michael, bp. 22 Apr. 1714
    3. Louisa, bp. 18 Oct. 1716
    4. Maria Katharina, bp. 24 Mar. 1720

Johann Adam Röder d. 23 Mar. 1721, age 52 years.

Emigration record:
Werner Hacker, *Auswanderungen aus Rheinpfalz und Saarland:*
#11905 The deceased Adam Röder's widow from Mutterstadt to PA.

Mutterstadt Kontraktenprotokolle:
Record dated 1724: Hans Adam Röder's widow, who is moving to Pennsylvania, sold property to Johannes Krieg and wife Margaretha. Recorded 3 June 1737.

Dated 1726: Adam Fritz, citizen here, bought land from Adam Röder's widow, who moved to Pennsylvania. Recorded 31 May 1737.

Dated 21 July 1726: Sebastian Reimer and Anna Barbara bought property from Röder's widow, who moved to Pennsylvania. Recorded 14 Apr. 1738.

AMERICAN RECORDS

Emmaus Moravian KB, Lehigh County, PA:
Catharina Roeder died 19 April 1751, age 80 years.

Catharina Weiser, nee Roeder, died 12 Mar. 1786, age 66 years less 13 days. She was born in Mutterstadt in the Palatinate 24 Mar. 1720, and in 1724 came to this country with her mother. In 1737 she married Johann Heinrich Knaus, and had four sons of whom Johann Michael Knaus is still living. Her first husband died in 1761, and in 1762 she married Christoph Weiser. He died in 1768 and she lived as a widow for 18 years.

New Goshenhoppen Reformed KB, Montgomery County, PA:
New communicants, 10 Oct. 1736:
   Anna Marg. Raehder, daughter of the late Adam Reder

Michael Reder (Roeder) and wife Susanna had children:
   1. Anna Margreth, bp. 27 Mar. 1737
      Sp.: Georg Welcker and Anna Margreth
   2. Lisabeth, bp. 24 Sept. 1740
      Sp.: Lisabeth Zimmerman
   3. Johannes, bp. 15 Mar. 1747
      Sp.: Johannes Mack and wife

   Michael Roeder m. ca. 1751 Catharina Erb
   Michael Roeder m. 26 Feb. 1760 Barbara Meyer

Falckner Swamp Reformed KB, Montgomery County, PA:
Adam Rader (Röder) is mentioned as a deacon 10 Nov. 1740.

Adam Reder of Philadelphia County nat. Sept. 1740.
Michael Reider of Philadelphia County nat. 24 Sept. 1741.

RÖDER, HENRICH   67112 Mutterstadt
Prelist, ca. 1725

EUROPEAN RECORDS

Mutterstadt Reformed KB:
Johann Henrich Röder m. 4 Apr. 1725 Anna Trummer from Canton Bern, Switzerland.

It is possible that Henrich Röder is a son of Hans Adam Röder and his wife Anna Katharina, born before that couple resided in Mutterstadt. Members of the family resided in Maudach [= 67067 Ludwigshafen], and the records there were studied, but Henrich's baptism was not recorded there.

AMERICAN RECORDS

New Goshenhoppen Reformed KB, Montgomery Co., PA:
Heinrich Rether and wife had a son:
> Joh. Adam, bp. Aug. 1731
> Sp.: Michael Rether and Susanna Zimmerman

Heinrich Reder and wife Anna had a daughter:
> Anna Margaretha, bp. 19 June 1737
> Sp.: Hans Jörg Welcker and Anna Margareth

Henrich Rötter signed a petition in 1734 for a road through Goshenhoppen.

Pennsylvania Dutchman, issue dated 28 July 1949:
About 1740, Henrich Roeder settled near Germansville in Heidelberg Twp., Lehigh County, and had the first grist mill there.

Northampton County Wills and Administrations:
Henry Reeder (Roeder), Heidelberg Twp., yeoman: adm. 20 Feb. 1753 to Ann Reeder, widow, and Nicholas Traxall and Michael Troxall of Egypt. Grist mill and improvements mentioned. Children are not named.

A later Henrich Röder appears in the records of **St. Paul's (Blue) Lutheran Church, Upper Saucon Twp., Lehigh Co.:**
John Heinrich Röhder and wife Anna Maria were sponsors in 1759 for a child of Joh. Franz Fries.

Johann Henrich Röder (Röhder) and wife Anna Maria had children:
> 1. Johann Jürg, b. 10 Aug. 1757
> 2. Juliana, b. 23 June 1760

ROST, MATHIAS   Niederhochstadt=
Anderson, 1751   76879 Hochstadt, Pfalz
S-H, I: 450
   Other passengers on ship: George Valentin Fehl from Niederhochstadt

EUROPEAN RECORDS

Niederhochstadt Reformed KB:
Matthoy Rost and wife Margretha had a son:
        Matthaus, bp. 24 Apr. 1725
        Sp.; Matthoy Koch and Sybilla Catharina

Mathias Rost confirmed 1739.

Mathias Rost m. 27 June 1750 Catharina Elisabetha Koch.

AMERICAN RECORDS

Lancaster County Land Warrants, Pennsylvania Archives, Third Series:
Matthias Raust, 50 acres, 18 Oct. 1751.

Lancaster County Tax Lists:
Mathias Rost, Lancaster Twp., 1771 and 1772, 5 acres.

Host Church, Tulpehocken, Berks County, PA:
Although the name Mathias Rost does not appear in the Host KB, a
Henrich Rost had a daughter Maria Catharina, bp. 20 Dec. 1767. Also, a
Jacob Rost appears in the Christ "Little Tulpehocken" Church records as
early as 1741. Jacob Rost came on the ship *Friendship* in 1738 with
Reintzel, Laux, Motz, and Gensemer, all from Hochstadt.

Mathias Rost, Lancaster Twp., Lancaster County, nat. Fall 1765.

ROTHERMEL, LEONHARD   67459 Böhl
Adventure, 1727
S-H, I: 15 [Rodennill on list]

EUROPEAN RECORDS
Hassloch Lutheran KB:
Confirmed 1703: Joh. Leonhard Rothermel of Böhl.

Hans Leonhard Rothermel m. 30 Oct. 1709 at Böhl Margretha
Zimmermann. They had:
1. [possibly] Christian, bp. not located, conf. 1724
2. [possibly] Anna Margretha, bp. not located, conf. 1725
3. Joh. Peter, twin, b. 3 Feb. 1715
4. Lorentz, twin, b. 3 Feb. 1715
5. Johann Paul, b. 30 Dec. 1718
6. Johannes, b. 9 Feb. 1722

AMERICAN RECORDS

Zion's Lutheran KB, Lower Macungie Twp., Lehigh Co., PA:
Peter Federolf and wife Margaretha [nee Rothermel] had:
Maria Magdalena, bp. 3 Aug. 1755
Sp.: Christian Rothermel and wife

Christian Rothermel and wife Magdalena had:
1. Maria Barbara, bp. 3 Aug. 1755
Sp.: Daniel Schmäyer and Barbara Federolf, both single
2. Johan Peter, bp. 29 May 1757
Sp.: Johan Peter Federolff and wife Margaretha

Conf. 1754: Peter Federolff and Anna Barbara Federolff, son and daughter
of Peter Federolff.
Conf. 1756: Jacob Federolff.

Moselem Lutheran KB, Richmond Twp., Berks Co.:
Peter Rothermel and wife Sybilla (nee Hoch) had:
Daniel, b. 1 Mar. 1741, bp. 12 June 1744
Sp.: Benedict A. Keplinger and Maria Salome Winter

Lorentz Rothermel and wife Maria had:
1. Peter, bp. 12 June 1744
Sp.: Susanna Schantz and Johannes Rothermel
2. Johannes, b. 20 Mar. 1744, bp. 12 June 1744
Sp.: Susanna Schantz

Christian Rothermel and Magdalena had:
1. Maria Magdalena, b. 22 Aug. 1765 bp. 9 Dec. 1765
Sp.: Friedrich Hill and Maria

Martin Rothermel and wife Anna had:
Daniel, b. 3 July 1775

Berks County land warrants, Pennsylvania Archives, Third Series:

Christian Rothermel	150 A, 14 Mar. 1742
	50 A, 5 Sept. 1748
	25 A, 20 June 1753
	25 A, 20 June 1753
Peter Rothermel	100 A, 26 Oct. 1737
	100 A, 30 Aug. 1738
	250 A, 17 Oct. 1738
	100 A, 15 Apr. 1743
Lorentz Rothermel	150 A, 15 Aug. 1738
	100 A, 26 Oct. 1744
	25 A, 24 Oct. 1750
	25 A, 15 Nov. 1751

Hocker, *German Settlers of Pennsylvania:* 24: Sauer's Newspaper dated 16 Dec. 1750: Johannes Rothermel, Weidenthal, Upper Oley (Berks co.).

Johannes Rothermel was taxed in Richmond Twp. from 1754 to 1785. In 1784, his family consisted of 6 persons.

New Goshenhoppen Reformed KB, Montgomery Co., PA:
Undated marriage # 55, ca. 1757:
Married Paulus Rothaermel and Maria Cretha Mauer.

Tax lists show Paul Rothermel resided in Maidencreek Twp., Berks Co. In 1784, there were 10 persons in the family.

Berks County Administration Abstracts:
Lawrence Rodarmel, Windsor Twp; Adm. granted 6 Dec. 1758 to Ursula Rodermel, the widow, and Peter and John Rodermel, brothers.

Christian Rothermel of Oley Twp. Letters of Adm. granted 16 Mar. 1769 to Magdalena Rothermel, widow and relict

Berks County Orphans Court records, dated 8 Feb. 1762:
Petition of Peter Rodarmel states that Lawrence Rodamel died in 1758 intestate, leaving a widow Ursula and four [minor?] children: Maria, above 14 years; Leonard, Catharine, and Elizabeth, all under 14. Letters of Adm. to widow. She has recently married Frederick ?Hauer. The court appoints guardians for the children: Sebastian Zimmerman and Peter Merckel.

Dated 12 Aug. 1774: petition of Leonard Rothermel, only son of Lawrence Rothermel, late of Windsor Twp. He states that his father died intestate about 15 years ago, leaving a widow (Ursula, since married to Frederick

?Haas) and five children: Peter, the oldest son, since deceased; Leonard, the petitioner; Mary, wife of John Romich; Catharine, wife of Henry Bock; Elizabeth, wife of Jonas Petery. Intestate had a tract of land in Windsor Twp. containing 300 acres.

Dated 29 Jan. 1770: petition of Magdalena Rothermel, Admrx. of Christian Rothermel of Oley, deceased, Yeoman. That Christian died intestate about a year since, leaving a widow (the petitioner), and seven children: Martin, aged 20; Peter, aged 10; Catharina, aged 19; Sibilla, aged 17; Maria, aged 15; Margaret, aged 11; Magdalena, aged 4. Personal estate is not sufficient to pay debts - that he was seized of a tract of land in Richmond Twp. of 275 acres, also 4 tracts in Oley containing together 210 acres and one tract of Warrant Land of 50 acres, Prays for order to sell the five last mentioned tracts; granted.

On petition of Magdalena Rothermel, Court appointed Casper Merckel, blacksmith, of Richmond and Frederick Hill, same Twp., Yeoman, guardians of Peter, Margaret, and Magdalena, minor children of Christian Rothermel, deceased. Maria Rothermel chooses her uncle Paul Rothermel of Maidencreek for her guardian.

Nat. 24/25 Sept. 1744, without oath:
>Christian Rodarmale, Philadelphia Co.
>Paul Rodermale, Philadelphia Co.

Nat. Apr. 1743: Peter Rothermel.

ROTHERMEL, PETER   67459 Böhl
Prelist
EUROPEAN RECORDS

Hassloch Lutheran KB:
Hanss Peter Rothermel from Rimbach [8 Rimbachs in *Das Postleitzahlenbuch*] m. (1) 17 ___ 1707 Anna Margretha Brunner. They had children baptized in Böhl:
1. Maria Magdalena, bp. 2 July 1709, d. 1720
2. Catharina, b. 4 Apr. 1712, Conf. 1725
3. Joh. Georg, b. 15 Apr. 1715, d. 1716
4. Joh. Daniel, b. 3 May 1717

Hassloch Reformed KB:
Died 8 Mar. 1718, Anna Margretha, wife of Peter Rothermel of Böhl, age 29 years.

Hassloch Lutheran KB:
Petter Rothermel, widower at Böhl, m. (2) 5 July 1718 Anna Elisabetha
Weber. Children:
     5. Joh. Georg, b. 1 Sept. 1719
     6. Christoph, b. 18 Dec. 1721
     7. Anna Margretha, b. 27 Feb. 1724

AMERICAN RECORDS

Rev. John Casper Stoever's Records:
Unpublished baptisms:
Peter Roth-Ermel in the Falckner's Schwaum had a son:
     8. Leonhardt, b. 15 Sept. 1729, bp. 1 Feb. 1730;
        Conf. at New Hanover, 1745.
        Sp.: Leonhardt Aches

Peter Rothermel and wife Anna Elizabeth sp. a child of Leonhardt Ochs in
1734 in [New] Hanover.

New Hanover Lutheran KB, Montgomery Co., PA:
Conf. 1743: Hans Jürg Rothermel
           Johann Daniel Rothermel
           Christoph Rothermel
Conf. 1745: Leonhardt Rothermel

Philadelphia Adm. Book E: 2:
Will of Peter Rodernell of New Hanover, yeoman. Wife to keep plantation
and house until youngest children are of age. To eldest son, John Daniel,
his due on account of my first wife, his mother, deceased. Eldest daughter
Anna Katherine by first wife. Signed 17 Dec. 1737.
Wit: John Philip Brand and Michael Fedele.
Proved 17 May 1743. Adm. to Elizabeth RodErmell, the widow, testator not
having named an executor.

Augustus (Trappe) Lutheran KB, Montgomery Co., PA:
Leonhard Rothermel m. 31 Mar. 1752 Mary Joakims, daughter of Jonas
Joakims.

New Hanover Lutheran KB, Montgomery Co., PA:
Daniel Rothermel and wife Anna Barbara had:
     1. N.N., bp. 15 Apr. 1745
     2. Maria Elisabeth, bp. 13 June 1747
     3. Maria Barbara, b. 1 Apr. 1751; conf. 1767
     4. Eva Rosina, b. 30 Jan.1 754

5. Christina, b. 5 Aug. 1758; conf. 1773
6. Joh. Christophel, twin, b. 9 May 1762
7. Joh. Peter, twin, b. 9 May 1762

Died 19 Oct. 1764 - wife of Daniel Rothermel, age 41 y.
Died 23 Oct. 1764 - Johann Daniel Rothermel, age 48 y.

Christophel Rothermel and wife Juliana had:
1. Catharina, b. 24 Nov. 1745
2. Johann Friederich, b. 1 July 1747
3. Leonhard, b. 24 Oct. 1750, d. 24 Nov. 1751
4. Felicitas, b. 1 Sept. 1752

Rev. Jacob Lischy's records, York Co., PA:
Christoff Rothermel and wife Juliana had:
5. Johannes, bp. 4 May 1755

Nat. Apr. 1743 without oath: Peter Rodermill, Philadelphia County.
Nat. 24 Sept. 1762: Christr. Rodermill, Codorus, York Co.

RUMPFELT, JACOB   67259 Heuchelheim
RUMPFELT, HENRICH (listed with men)
RUMPFELT, CATHARINA
RUMPFELT, CATHARINA MARGARETHA
St. Andrew, 1734
S-H, I: 137, 139, 141, 142

EUROPEAN RECORDS

Heuchelheim Lutheran KB:
Joh. Jacob Rumfeld, shoemaker, m. 8 May 1725 Anna Catharina Fruhmann.
They had a child:
1. Catharina Margaretha, b. 20 Nov. 1727
    Sp.: Catharina Margaretha, daughter of
    Johannes Bauniger? of Hessheim? [67258 Hessheim].

Other passengers on ship who were children of Anna Catharina Fruhmann
[q.v.] by her first marriage:
    Barbara Freeman, Jacob Freeman, Catrina Freeman, Margaret Freeman

Johan Jacob Fruhmann m. 26 Aug. 1710 Anna Catharina Foltz. They had children:
1. Abraham, b. 21 May 1711
2. Anna **Barbara**, b. 20 Feb. 1715
3. Anna **Catharina**, b. 22 Mar. 1717
4. Johan **Jacob**, b. 28 June 1719
5. Anna Maria Elis., b. 14 Dec. 1721, d. 1724
6. Susanna **Margaretha**, b. 16 May 1724

Jacob Fruhmann d. 2 Feb. 1724, age 35 yr.

AMERICAN RECORDS

St. Paul's (Blue) Lutheran KB, Lehigh Co., PA:
Henrich Rumfeld and wife Barbara had:
1. Joh. Jacob, b. 12 Apr. 1750, bp. 22 Apr. 1750
   Sp.: Johan Jacob Rumfield and Barbara
2. Andreas, b. 15 Aug. 1752, d. Nov. (1752)
   Sp.: Andreas Weltz and Anna Maria
3. Johann Georg, b. 31 July 1756, bp. 1 Aug. 1756
   Sp.: Caspar Brunner and Appolonia
4. Hanna, b. 30 June 1758, bp.1 5 July 1758
   Sp.: Casper Brenner and Appelona
5. Philip Jacob, b. 30 May 1760, bp. 11 June 1760
   Sp.: Jacob Rumfeld
6. Susanna, b. 27 Mar. 1763
   Sp.: Apollonia Brenner

Northampton County Will Abstracts:
Appelonia Brunner (Brenner). filed 13 June 1773.
"To Henry Rumfield, everything: do make my last will and it is hereby made sure that Henry Rumfield shall have all that I leave behind; further, I did send some writing to Lewis Klotz with Michael Smith, which I now repent that I did so; I say hereby that Lewis Klotz shall give the same writing which I sent him by Michael Smith to Henry Rumfield and this is my last will and testament."
Wit.: John Newcomer and Philip Soeller.

Andreas Weltz, Upper Saucon. Yeoman. 15 Aug. 1765 - 24 Oct. 1765.
Brothers: John George, George; sister Appolonia, wife of Casper Brener, deceased. Exr.: Henry Rumfelt.
Wit.: Philip Soller, Conrad Reigle.

RUPP, JOHANNES   67105 Schifferstadt
RUPP, JACOB
Phoenix, 1749
S-H, I: 407

EUROPEAN RECORDS

Schifferstadt Reformed KB:
Johannes Rupp, master miller in Schifferstadt, and wife Anna Maria had:
1. Johann Jacob, bp. 4 Feb. 1731
2. Johannes, bp. 22 Nov. 1733
3. Catharina Christina, bp. 22 July 1735
   Sp.: Joh. Georg Rupp from [67346] Speyer and
   wife Catharina Christina
4. Philipp Henrich, bp. 28 Dec. 1737
   Sp.: Joh. Henrich Thomas and Maria Catharina

AMERICAN RECORDS

Muddy Creek Lutheran KB, Lancaster Co., PA:
Johannes Rupp m. 20 May 1750 [Muddy Creek] Margaretha Frey.

Johannes Rupp of Muddy Creek had children:
1. Maria Catarina, b. 26 Feb. 1751, bp. 24 Mar. 1751
   Sp.: Georg Stiegeler and wife
2. Dorothea, b. Jan. 1753, bp. 4 Feb. 1753
   Sp. not given

Muddy Creek Reformed KB, Lancaster Co., PA:
Jacob Rupp and wife Juliana had children:
1. John Jacob, b. 5 May 1773, bp. 30 May
   Sp.: Valentine Wolff and Male (Molly)
2. John, b. 14 Jan. 1776, bp. 31 Jan.
   Sp.: John Bechtel and wife Anna Maria

Jacob Rub (Rupp) was installed as a deacon on 11 June 1775.

One John Rupe of Cocalico Twp., Lancaster Co., nat. Apr. 1761.

SACHS, DANIEL   Oggersheim=
_____, 1751   67071 Ludwigshafen am Rhein

EUROPEAN RECORDS

Oggersheim Reformed KB:
Johann Peter Sachs and Maria Catharina had a son:
    Daniel, b. 15 Sept. 1721, bp. 19 Sept. 1721

Daniel Sachs, son of Joh. Peter m. 6 June 1740 Maria Barbara Köhler, Lutheran, daughter of the dec'd Joh. Leonhard Köhler. They had children:
    1. Johannes, b. 15 Apr. 1742, bp. 17 Apr. 1742
    2. Maria Christina, b. 6 Jan. 1746, bp. 8 Jan. 1746

Emigration record:
Werner Hacker, *Auswanderungen aus Rheinpfalz und Saarland*:
#12419 J. Daniel Sachs, Oggersheim, with wife and children to PA, 1751.

AMERICAN RECORDS

Pennsylvania Dutchman, 1954, 18th Century Palatine Emigrants from the Ludwigshafen Area:
Daniel Sachs, of Oggersheim, received permission in 1751 to emigrate to PA with wife and children upon payment of a Tithe of 16 florins.

SAHLER see SEYLER

SAHLER, ABRAHAM   67256 Weisenheim am Sand
Pennsylvania Merchant, 1731
S-H, I: 43, 45, 46

EUROPEAN RECORDS

Weisenheim am Sand Reformed KB:
Georg Saler and wife Elisabeth had a son:
        Johann Abraham, bp. 5 July 1705
            Sp.: Joh. Abraham Jung from [67246] Dirmstein, single

Lambsheim Reformed KB:
Georg Sahler, smith in Weisenheim am Sand, and Elisabeth had:
    1. Daniel, bp. 7 May 1697
        Sp.: Daniel Neckerauer, *Schultheiss'* son

2. Christoph, bp. 19 June 1699
    Sp.: Christophus Storck, *Schultheiss* at Ackenheim.

AMERICAN RECORDS

New Goshenhoppen Reformed KB, Montgomery Co., PA:
Abraham Saler and Wilhelm Schmit [q.v.] sponsored 2 sons of Jacob Schmit [q.v.] and wife in 1731.

Philadelphia Will Abstracts:
Abraham Soler was named Exr. of Nicholas Remely's [q.v.] will in 1738.

Augustus (Trappe) Lutheran KB, Montgomery Co., PA:
Abraham Sähler and wife Elisabeth had:
    Rahel, b. 20 Jan. 1746

SAHLER, CONRAD, age 13   67256 Weisenheim am Sand
Lydia, 1743
S-H, I: 341
    with Johannes Roth

EUROPEAN RECORDS

Lambsheim Reformed KB:
Georg Sahler, smith in Weisenheim am Sand, and wife Elisabeth had a son:
    Daniel, b. 2 May 1697

Weisenheim am Sand Reformed KB:
Daniel Sahler and wife Susanna had a son:
    1. **Conrad**, bp. 20 Nov. 1729
        Sp.: Conrad Jung

AMERICAN RECORDS

Lincoln Co., NC, Deed Book 16: pg. 306-308:
Dated 6 Sept. 1789: John Member and wife Hannah Margaret and George Hide and wife Magdalena all of Berks Co., PA, sell their 2/3 interest in 200 acres on Doctor's Creek. Conrad Sailor, deceased, purchased 11 Jan. 1757 from Frederick Hambright, 200 acres. Conrad Sailor died leaving three daughters: Hannah Margaret Member, Magdalena Hide, and Susannah Cloves. On 26 Dec. 1789, John Cloves and wife Susannah of Washington Co., MD, sell their 1/3 interest in this tract.

SANGER, JOHANNES   Ober Lustadt=
St. Andrew, 1734   67363 Lustadt
S-H, I: 137, 141, 142
  other passengers on ship: Catrina Singer and Catrina Singer.
  Surname given as Singer on A List; he signed Senger.

EUROPEAN RECORDS

Ober Lustadt Reformed KB:
Johannes Sanger and wife Anna Catharina had a daughter:
      Anna Catharina, b. 27 Nov. 1732, bp. 30 Nov. 1732
      Sp.: Anna Catharina Haaf, single

AMERICAN RECORDS

Rev. John Casper Stoever's Records:
John Saenger, Perkiomen, had a son:
      John Christian, b. 20 Oct. 1734, bp. 1 Dec. 1734
      Sp.: John Christian Schmidt

Wentz's Reformed KB, Worcester Twp., Montgomery Co., PA:
Christian Saengger and wife Appollonia had:
      Maria Margareta, b. 9 June 1772

Boehm's Reformed KB, Whitpain Twp., Montgomery Co., PA:
Christian Sänger and wife Appollonia had:
      Johann Jacob, b. 3 Jan. 1774.

SAUERHEBER, JACOB   67454 Hassloch
Hero, 1764
S-H, I: 697

EUROPEAN RECORDS

Hassloch Reformed KB:
Henrich Sauerheber, son of Michael Sauerheber of Muspach [Mussbach =
67435 Neustadt a. d. Weinstrasse], m. 26 Nov. 1726 Anna Maria, daughter
of Johan Andreas Gemming.

Henrich Sauerhöffer and Anna Maria had a son:
      Johan **Jacob**, bp. 26 Dec. 1737

AMERICAN RECORDS

In an article titled "Pennsylvania Dutch Pioneers" published in the
Pennsylvania Dutchman in 1956, listed under emigrants from Lachen (Kreis
Neustadt) is the following:
"Maria Catharina Theobald of Lachen, daughter of Johannes Theobald of
Lachen, widow of Peter Hammann, went to Pennsylvania with her second
husband Jacob Sauerheber from Hassloch and the children of her first
marriage (in 1764). Johann Jacob Sauerheber was a resident of Maiden
Creek Twp., Berks County."

SAUERHEBER, MARIA CATHARINA THEOBALD Lachen-Speyerdorf=
(widow **Hamman**)   67435 Neustadt an der Weinstrasse
with husband Jacob Sauerheber
Hero, 1764
S-H, I: 697

EUROPEAN RECORDS

Lachen-Speyerdorf Reformed KB:
Peter Hamman b. 9 Dec. 1714, son of Heinrich Hamman, m. (2) 29 Oct.
1749 Maria Catharina, daughter of Johannes Deobald. They had children:
1. Anna Catharina Hamman, b. 21 Apr. 1752, bp. 23 Apr. 1752;
   conf. 1764; Sp.: Johannes Deobald
2. Joh. Peter, b. 8 June 1753, bp. 11 June 1753
   Sp.: Peter Freytag and Anna Elisabeth
3. Anna Helena, b. 16 Aug. 1755, bp. 18 Aug. 1755
   Sp.: Anna Helena, wife of Lorentz Freytag
4. Johannes, b. 23 June 1758, bp. 25 June 1758
   Sp.: Johannes Hamman and wife Anna Elisabetha
5. Joh. Jacob, b. 17 July 1759, bp. 22 July 1759
   Sp.: Joh. Jacob Öhl and Anna Margretha
6. Joh. Heinrich, b. 19 Nov. 1760, bp. 23 Nov. 1760
   Sp.: Joh. Henrich Hamman and Anna Margretha

Peter Hamman d. 8 Feb. 1761, age 46 years 2 months.

Married 12 Oct. 1762: Philip(!) Jacob, son of Henerich Sauerhobel(!) from
[67454] Hassloch, and Anna(!) Catharina, widow of the late Peter Hamman.
[This was actually Johan Jacob Sauerheber, bp. 26 Dec. 1737 in Hassloch,
son of Henrich Sauerheber and Anna Maria nee Gemming. See above.]

Johan Jacob Sauerheber and Maria Catharina had:
    Anna Maria, b. 24 June 1760, bp. 26 June 1760
    Sp.: Anna Maria, wife of Joh. Christoph Sauerheber
    of [67459] Iggelheim.

Emigration record:
Friedrich Krebs, "Pennsylvania Dutch Pioneers", in *The Pennsylvania Dutchman,* 1954-1956: from Lachen (Kreis Neustadt):
Maria Catharina Theobald of Lachen, daughter of Johannes Theobald, widow of Peter Hamman, went to Pennsylvania in 1764 with her second husband Jacob Sauerheber from Hassloch and the children of her first marriage. Jacob Sauerheber was a resident of Maiden Creek Twp., Berks Co., PA.

AMERICAN RECORDS

1790 census: Jacob Sowerheifer, Abington Twp., Montgomery Co. 3 males over 16; 1 female.

First Reformed KB, Philadelphia:
Married 13 Aug. 1809, Jacob Sauerhever and Maria Barbara Richtel.

SAUTER, HEINRICH   Lachen-Speyerdorf=
Recovery, 1754   67435 Neustadt an der Weinstrasse
S-H, I: 660 [name on list: Sowder]

EUROPEAN RECORDS

Lachen-Speyerdorf Reformed KB:
Heinrich Sauter, son of the late Henrich Sauter of Speyerdorf, m. 19 Nov. 1710 Anna Margretha, daughter of the late Jacob Roth of Lachen. They had children:
    1. Johannes, b. 18 June 1716, bp. 20 June 1716, conf. 1731
       Sp.: Johannes Möchterheimer, der alte
    2. Johann Georg, bp. 8 Sept. 1718, conf. 1733
       Sp.: Joh. Görg Volmar of Neustatt and Cathar. Elisab.,
       daughter of Peter Blattmann of [67435] Neustatt
    3. Anna Maria, b. 3 Mar. 1721, d. 1721.
       Sp.: Anna Maria, daughter of the late Nickel Freytag
    4. Philips Friederich Heinrich, b. 21 Nov. 1722; d. 1736.
    5. Anna Margretha, b. 27 June 1726, bp. 30 June 1726; conf. 1741.
       Sp.: Anna Margretha, daughter of Michel Plaum

6. Johann Henrich, b. 11 Feb. 1730, d. 1730
7. Johann Henrich, b. 29 June 1731, bp. 1 July 1731
   Sp.: Johann Henrich, son of Georg Baur here

Anna Margretha, daughter of Hennerich Sauter, had an illegitimate child:
Anna Margretha b. 19 ?July 1752, bp. 24 ?July 1752
Sp.: Johannes Lutz and wife Catharina

Anna Margretha, daughter of Henrich Sauter, m. Joh. Jacob Erb [q.v.] in 1753.

Emigration record:
Werner Hacker, *Auswanderungen aus Rheinpfalz und Saarland im 18. Jahrhundert:* # 12574 Sauter, Heinrich, widower from Lachen, with daughter (A. Marg. married to Jak. Erb) and single son Heinrich Sauter, along with Martin Schellert of Speyerdorf and his wife and son- to PA. Record dated 15 May 1754.

SAUTER, JOHANNES   Lachen-Speyerdorf=
Dragon, 1749   67435 Neustadt an der Weinstrasse
S-H, I: 423

EUROPEAN RECORDS

Lachen-Speyerdorf Reformed KB:
Johannes Sauter, son of Henrich Sauter [q.v.], m. 7 Feb. 1741 Anna Margretha, daughter of Henrich Fischer of Speyerdorf. They had children:
1. Christina Margretha, b. 27 Sept. 1742, bp. 30 Sept. 1742
   Sp.: Johannes Scherer of Speyerdorf and wife Maria Christina and daughter Anna Margretha
2. Joh. Jacob, b. 14 Jan. 1744, bp. 19 Jan. 1744
   Sp.: Joh. Jacob Öhl, son of Hans Caspar Öhl
3. Maria Barbara, b. 23 June 1746, bp. 26 June 1746
   Sp.: Maria Barbara, daughter of the late Philipp Staud, Speyerdorf
4. Maria Eva, b. 4 Feb. 1749, bp. 7 Feb. 1749
   Sp.: Maria Eva, ?wife of Ludwig Sauter of Speyerdorf

Emigration record:
Werner Hacker, *Auswanderungen aus Rheinpfalz und Saarland im 18. Jahrhundert:* # 12573 Sauter, Johann, Lachen/Neustadt. Manumitted to PA. Record dated 18 Mar. 1749

SAUTER, PETER age 48   Lachen-Speyerdorf=
SAUTER, PHILIP age 17   67435 Neustadt an der Weinstrasse
Loyal Judith, 1732
S-H, I: 88, 90, 92

EUROPEAN RECORDS

Lachen-Speyerdorf Reformed KB:
Hans Peter Sautor and wife Anna Catharina had a son:
>Johan Peter, bp. 11 Apr. 1688, conf. 1703
>Sp.: Peter Hamman

Peter Sauter, weaver, son of Hans Peter Sauter, also linenweaver here, m. 20 Apr. 1712 Anna Margretha, daughter of Hans Michel Schuster. They had children:
>1. Anna Margretha, b. 23 Jan. 1713, d. 1715
>Sp.: Anna Margretha, wife of Hans Conradt Theobald,
>*des Gerichts*
>2. **Philipps**, b. 27 Feb. 1715, bp. 3 Mar. 1715
>Sp.: Philips Hoos
>3. Carl Ludwig, b. 7 Sept. 1717
>Sp.: Carl Ludwig Keiper [q.v.], son of Wendel Keiper, cartwright
>4. Anna Margretha, b. 4 May 1720
>Sp.: Anna Margretha wife of Philip Hoos
>5. Anna Catharina, b. 8 July 1722
>Sp.: Anna Catharina, widow of Niclaus Hoos
>6. Maria Catharina, b. 7 Jan. 1725
>Sp.: Maria Catharina, daughter of Ludwig Leheman
>7. Johann Wilhelm, b. 4 July 1727
>Sp.: Johann Wilhelm Sebach, master baker at [67435] Neustatt
>8. Anna Margretha, b. 18 Dec. 1729
>Sp.: Anna Margretha, wife of Johannes Otterstätter,
>*des Gerichts*

SCHAFFNER, JOHANN HENRICH   67251 Freinsheim
does not appear in lists; emigration record dated 14 Dec. 1749
indicates Henrich Schaffner wishes to emigrate with his brother-in-law Jost Wigandt [q.v.]

EUROPEAN RECORDS

Freinsheim Lutheran KB:
Johann Adam Schaffner m. 2 Nov. 1718 Anna Catharina, daughter of
Sebastian Messinger from Feidenheim [elsehwere Feudenheim = 68259
Mannheim]. They had children:
  1. Joh. Sebastian, b. 2 Sept. 1719, d. young
     Sp.: Joh. Sebastian, son of Georg Bach
  2. Maria Elisabetha, b. 8 Mar. 1721, bp. 16 Mar. 1721
  3. probably Barbara who m. Jost Wygand b. ca 1723
     (gaps in record)
  4. Anna Catharina, b. 15 Aug. 1725
  5. Veit Ludwig, b. 16 Nov. 1727
  6. **Johann Henrich**, b. 27 Apr. 1730, bp. 30 Apr. 1730; conf. 1742
  7. Andreas, b. 1 Nov. 1733
  8. Joh. Peter, b. 11 Mar. 1737

Emigration record:
Werner Hacker, *Auswanderungen aus Rheinpfalz und Saarland*:
#12812 Henrich Schaffner, citizen of Freinsheim, wishes to go to PA with
brother in law Josef Wigandt, dated 14 Dec. 1749.

Jost Wigandt arrived on the ship *Brotherhood*, 1750 with Georg Daniel Orth
[q.v.], also from Freinsheim. Johann Henrich Schaffner may have died on
the voyage, since he does not appear on the list.

SCHALTER, FRANTZ BALTZER   67126 Assenheim
Edinburgh, 1754
S-H, I: 615, 617, 620

EUROPEAN RECORDS

Assenheim Lutheran KB:
Johann Georg Schalter and wife Elisabeth ahd children:
     1. Johannes, b. 16 Sept. 1720
        Sp.: Johannes Börstler, son of Michael Börstler
        of Schauernheim [67125 Dannstadt-Schauernheim]
     2. Frederica Augusta, b. 1728, died young
     3. **Franz Balthasar**, b. 18 Apr. 1735, bp. 24 Apr. 1735
        Sp.: Franz Balthasar Storck and Maria Catharina
     4. Elias, b. 26 Feb. 1739
        Sp.: Elias Storck and Anna Catharina

AMERICAN RECORDS

Berks County Abstracts of Wills and Adms:
Dietrich Beidelman [q.v.] of Alsace Twp. left a will probated 23 Mar. 1793:
He names his daughter Elizabeth, wife of Francis Shalter, and also mentions
his grandson Dietrich Shalter.

Frantz Shalter, will probated Nov. 1813, Maidencreek Twp.
Wife: Elisabeth, sons Michael and Jacob, son-in-law Samuel Bernhart, son-
in-law Abraham Kissinger, Peter Rothenberger, and son-in-law Daniel
Kershner. This will was never signed and settlement was by verdict of jury.

Dietrich Shalter, Berks Co. Adm granted 3 Oct. 1795 to Francis Shalter, the
father.

Philadelphia Will Book M, pg. 208:
Will of Balthasar Shalter of Frederick Twp., Philadelphia Co., PA; dated 24
Nov. 1759; probated 27 Oct. 1761; names as executor, Francis Balthazar
Shalter, son of my brother; other heirs named are: Eva Margreth Kurz,
daughter of my sister, and cousin Ludwig Engelhard.

SCHELLHAMMER, PHILIP JACOB   67256 Weisenheim am Sand
The Globe, 1723
[signed the ship's contract]

EUROPEAN RECORDS

Weisenheim am Sand Reformed KB:
Died 1719, Elisabeth, wife of Philip Jacob Schölhammer, age 28 yr. 7 mo.

Gönnheim Reformed KB:
Philip Jacob Schelhammer, widower, from Weisenheim am Sandt, m. at
[67161] Gönnheim 23 Jan. 1720 Anna Margaretha, daughter of Hans Adam
Lutz.

Weisenheim am Sand Reformed KB:
Philip Jacob Schellhamer and wife had:
      1. Anna Maria, bp. 19 Apr. 1722
        Sp.: Anna Maria Lutz from Gönnheim

AMERICAN RECORDS

New Goshenhoppen Reformed KB, Montgomery Co., PA:
Philip Jacob Schellhammer and wife Anna Margreth had:
> Christophorus, bp. 4 June 1732
> > Sp.: Christophorus Schmitt [q.v.]
> Maria Susanna, bp. 24 July 1737
> > Sp.: Maria Lang and Susanna Schmidt

Philadelphia Adm. F: 172: (1748)
Administration No. 112 or 1748 - Philip Jacob Shellhaber. Bond taken out by Margaret Shellhamer, her son George Shellhamer and Jacob Peters of Berks, Housekipers (sic) for £200 on 9 May 1748.

Appraisement and inventory attached - both in German and translation.

Accounting in pieces...but could read "widow and children to her and remaining in right of children." It looks like it might be 5 ¼ for each child - £ 29.11.03, for a total of £ 57.0.0 (could possibly be pieced together)

Berks County Will Abstracts:
Donat, Jacob, Albany. Nov. 13, 1811-Jan 24, 1814. To son-in-law Abraham Merkel £30 for nursing my deceased wife. The money son William yet owes me to be divided among children. To daughter Elizabeth £91.13.4, £60 which is wages for working over her age 21, daughter Rachel £76.13.4. £60 which is wages for working over her age 21, daughter Susanna £111.13.14 £30 which is wages for working over her age 21, son Jacob £73 £30 which is wages for working over his age 21, daughter Maria £60 £20 is wages. To son Peter's children £30, daughter Catharine £10. Son-in-law Philip Jacob Schellhammer shall keep in his hands the money which comes to his wife until children are 21. Sons Martin and William have received their portions. Mentions daughter Elizabeth Schellhammer and grandson Joseph Donat, Jacob's oldest son. Exrs: Friends George Fusselman and John Smith. Wits: John Brobst and John Brobst, Jr. Translation.

SCHERER, ANNA MARGARETHA   67112 Mutterstadt
SCHERER, VALENTIN
Edinburgh, 1748
S-H, I: 371

EUROPEAN RECORDS

Mutterstadt Reformed KB:
Hans Adam Scherer and wife Anna Kunigunda had children:
1. **Anna Margaretha,** bp. 14 Apr. 1709
   Sp.: Hans Georg Muller from [74889] Sinsheim and
   Anna Margaretha Bock.
   Notation under child's name: "Moved to Pennsylvania 1748"
2. Hans Bernhard, bp. 5 Nov. 1710
3. Hans **Valentin,** bp. 1 Sept. 1715
   Sp.: Hans Valentin Biebinger, single,
   and Maria Elisabetha Flockert of [67105] Schifferstadt
4. Christina, bp. 15 July 1717

AMERICAN RECORDS

Williams Township Congregation, Northampton County, PA:
Valentin Scherer had children:
1. Johan Adam, b. 10 Oct. 1757, bp. 16 Oct. 1757
2. Anna Barbara, b. 21 May 1759, bp. 3 June 1759;
   She m. 1781 Johannes Transue

Northampton County Will Abstracts:
Valentine Shaerer, Williams Twp., dated 23 Apr. 1793, probated 10 Oct. 1797. Wife: Barbara. Children: Adam; Philip; and Barbara, wife of John Transue. Step-son John Vogt.

There were other Valentin Scherers in early Pennsylvania records. One appears in the Trappe Lutheran KB in 1745, and had a daughter confirmed there in 1776. He was nat. in 1761, residing in New Providence.

One Valentine Sherer of Witpain Twp., Philadelphia Co., was nat. 11 April 1763.

SCHERRER, JOH. AUGUSTUS   Lachen-Speyerdorf=
Thistle of Glasgow, 1730   67435 Neustadt an der Weinstrasse
S-H, I: 31, 33, 34

EUROPEAN RECORDS

Lachen-Speyerdorf Reformed KB:
Frantz Scherrer, son of Johannes Scherrer, m. 13 Aug. 1710 Anna Regina, widow of Stephan Schuster of Speyerdorf. They had children:
1. Augustus, b. 22 Aug. 1711, bp. 26 Agu. 1711; conf. 1726

Sp.: Herr Augustus Kieffner, *Rathsverwandter* at [67435] Neustatt
2. Johannes, b. 12 Mar. 1714, bp. 15 Mar. 1714; conf. 1730
Sp.: Johannes Michel.

AMERICAN RECORDS

Augustus Scherrer was a witness to the will of Christian Schreyer, probated at Lancaster 18 Jan. 1744. Christian Schreyer [q.v.] was a prelist emigrant from [67159] Friedelsheim. The testator and witnesses lived in the Conewago settlement, today York and Adams Counties.

York County Deeds, Vol. 2: 537-538:
Dated 7 Apr. 1762: Görg Miller of Germany Twp. sold a 50 acre tract in Germany Twp. to Görg Onstot. One of the adjacent landowners was Augustus Sherr. A witness to the transaction was Augustus Sherrer.

York County Deeds, Vol. 3: 589-590:
Dated 21 Jan. 1752: deed concerns a 200 acre tract adjoining lands of Augustinus Sharrer, John Shaun and Peter Little in Germany Twp.

SCHERRER, JOHANNES   Lachen-Speyerdorf=
Thistle of Glasgow, 1730   67435 Neustadt an der Weinstrasse
S-H, I: 31, 33

EUROPEAN RECORDS

Lachen-Speyerdorf Reformed KB:
Johannes Scherr(er), son of the late Hans Phili Scherr(er), m. 12 Jan. 1698 Anna Margretha, daughter of the late Hans ?Sochen of Speyerdorf. They had children:
   1. Franciscus, bp. 24 Mar. 1690 [see Augustus Scherrer]
      Sp.: Frantz Gerling of Speyerdorf
   2. Hans Ulrich [q.v.], bp. 1 Jan. 1694
      Sp.: Hans Ulrich Isler, citizen and stone-mason
      at Neüstatt [= 67435 Neustadt an der Weinstrasse]
   3. Maria Christina, bp. 18 Sept. 1695
      Sp.: Maria Christina, daughter of the late Hans Jacob Zimmerli
   4. **Johannes,** bp. 24 Feb. 1697
      Sp.: Johannes Majer, baker and citizen at Neüstatt
   5. Catharina Elisabetha, bp. 15 Mar. 1699
      Sp.: Catharina Elisabetha, daughter of the late Henrich Krieger, formerly smith here.

6. Anna Margretha bp. 20 Feb. 1701
   Sp.: Anna Margretha, wife of Hans Jacob Mühlschlagel, schoolmaster here
7. Anna Catharina, bp. 11 Mar. 1703
   Sp.: Anna Catharina, daughter of Benedict Affolder
8. Christophel, bp. 1 June 1704
   Sp.: Christoph Bauer
9. Georg Christophel, bp. 12 Dec. 1707, d. 1714
   Sp.: Christoph Bauer
10. Anna Margreth, b. 16 May 1709, bp. 22 May 1709
    Sp.: Anna Margreth, wife of Hans Philip Klein, miller at Speyerdorf
11. Anna Maria, b. 24 ?Nov. 1711, bp. 29 ?Nov 1711
    Sp.: Anna Maria, daughter of Hans Jacob Rothgeb, Neustatt

Johannes Scherrer, son of the late Johannes Scherrer, m. 14 Nov. 1726 Anna Barbara, daughter of Görg Schmid, the elder. They had one child bp. in Lachen:

1. Joh. Jacob, b. 9 Nov. 1727, bp. 13 Nov. 1727
   Sp.: Joh. Jacob Walckner and sister Anna Maria Walckner

AMERICAN RECORDS

William J. Hinke, *History of the Goshenhoppen Reformed Charge,* Pennsylvania German Society Vol. XXVII, 1916 (1920), pg. 73:
1730 immigrant Johannes Scherer became a member of the Reformed Church in Philadelphia.

Philadelphia Wills & Administrations:
John Scherrer, 1748 Adm. F: 165

SCHERRER, ULRICH   Lachen-Speyerdorf=
Thistle of Glasgow, 1730   67435 Neustadt an der Weinstrasse
S-H, I: 31, 32, 34

EUROPEAN RECORDS

Lachen-Speyerdorf Reformed KB:
See family record of Johannes Scherrer. The second son of Johannes Scherrer and Anna Margretha was Hans Ulrich, bp. 1 Jan. 1694. Confirmed 1709.

Ulrich Scherrer, son of Johannes Scherrer of Speyerdorf, m. 20 Jan. 1717
Margaretha Apolonia, daughter of the late Peter Walckner, at Speyerdorf.
They had children: (wife named Maria Apolonia in bp. records)
1. Maria Elisabetha, b. 6 Nov. 1717, bp. 11 Nov. 1717; died 1718.
   Sp.: Maria Elisabetha, daughter of Hans Görg Voltz of
   Speyerdorf.
2. Joh. Friedrich, bp. 16 Apr. 1719
   Sp.: Joh. Friedrich Schaad of Neustatt [67435 Neustadt]
3. Johannes, b. 30 Nov. 1721, died 1725
   Sp.: Johannes Scherrer, single, the father's brother, and
   Maria Elisabetha, daughter of Görg Voltz of Speyerdorf
4. Wilhelm Otto, b. 17 Jan. 1726, died 1729.

AMERICAN RECORDS

Hocker, *German Settlers of Pennsylvania:*
Sower's newspaper, dated 16 Apr. 1747: Ulrich Scherer, on the Schuylkill,
at Poplar Neck; wife, Maria Aebel (Apolonia).

Sower's newspaper, dated 1 Mar. 1751: Ulrich Scherer, on Saucon Creek.

First Reformed KB, Philadelphia:
Ulrich Scherer on subscription list for salary of minister, 1756.

Another Ulrich Scherer with wife Dorothea appear in the Moselem
Lutheran KB, Berks Co., in 1744.

Ulrich Sherer, Philadelphia Co., nat. 24 Sept. 1741.

SCHILLING, JOHANN MARTIN   67125 Dannstadt
Johnson, 1732
S-H, I: 71, 75, 77
   with Julian on p. 73

EUROPEAN RECORDS

Dannstadt Reformed KB:
Benedict Schilling m. 1700 Barbara Hoffman, daughter of the late Johann
Jacob Hoffman from [67475] Weidenthal. Barbara d. 14 Dec. 1732, age 60
yrs. 9 mo. 11 days. They had 11 children; the following are mentioned in the
Dannstadt record:
1. Maria Martha, m. 16 Oct. 1725 Daniel Juy (Schuy) [q.v.]
2. Johann Valentin, m. 10 Feb. 1733 Anna Eva Hausser

3. Johannes, bp. 31 July 1708
4. **Hans Martin** , b. 22 July 1711
5. Anna Margaretha, b. 1713
6. Anna Catharina, bp. 12 Oct. 1717; conf. Easter 1730

SCHIRMAN, SIMON age 49   Niederhochstadt=
Elizabeth, 1733   76879 Hochstadt, Pfalz
S-H, I: 113, 114, 115; Appendix 765, 766, 767
  Other passengers on ship: Catharina Sherman, age 40; Maria Elisabetha, age 22; Maria, age 19; Georg, age 17; Catharina, age 13; Philip, age 6 ½; Daniel (dead), age 3.
EUROPEAN RECORDS

Niederhochstadt Reformed KB:
Simon Schurmann, son of the deceased Ulrich Schurmann, m. 14 May 1709 Catharina, daughter of the deceased Jacob Heberling. (NOTE: The surname is spelled Schirman and Schermann in the bp. records.)
They had children:
  1. Maria Elisabetha, bp. 14 May 1711
    Sp.: Maria Elisabetha Presslerin
  2. Anna Maria, bp. 4 Nov. 1714
    Sp.: Caspar Wagener and Anna Maria
  3. Georg, bp. 4 July 1716
    Sp.: Georg Peter and Anna Maria
  4. Catharina Elisabetha, bp. 17 Jan. 1720
    Sp.: David Pressler and Elisabetha
  5. Eva Catharina, bp. 30 Jan. 1722
    Sp.: Carl Henrich Bruckner and Eva Catharina
  6. Joh. Carolus, bp. 16 Apr. 1725
    Sp.: Joh. Carl Bruckner and Maria Catharina
  7. Philip Adam, bp. 27 Nov. 1726
    Sp.: Philip Adam Peter and Margaretha
  8. Joh. Daniel, bp. 15 June 1730
    Sp.: Daniel Eli and Maria Elisabetha Motz

AMERICAN RECORDS

Rev. John Caspar Stoever's Records (also in Christ "Little Tulpehocken" Church Records):
George Schirman and wife of Tulpehocken had children:
  1. Simon, b. 22 Jan. 1743, bp. 23 Jan. 1743
    Sp.: Simon Schirman and wife

2. Anna Maria, b. 3 Oct. 1744, bp. 14 Oct. 1744
   Sp.: Philip Adam Schirmann and Adelheit Pfaffenberger
3. Joh. Simon, b. 19 Oct. 1746, bp. 26 Oct. 1746
   Sp.: Johannes Riegel and wife

Host Reformed KB, Tulpehocken Twp., Berks Co., PA:
Philip Sherman sponsored a child at Host in 1748.
George Sherman had a daughter Anna Barbara, bp. 4 May 1749.
A Mrs. Sherman sponsored a child of Valentin Heberling in 1750.

Georg Schirman and Lissa Catharina had:
   Catharina Elis., b. 1 Oct. 1756, bp. 17 Oct. 1756
   Sp.: Johannes Paffenberger and Cath. Elis.
   Elisab. Cathar., b.19 Mar. 1759, bp. 2 Apr. 1759
   Sp.: Philip Adam Schirman and wife.

Confirmed 1767:
Johannes Scharrmann, Adam's son.
Eva Elisabeth Scharrmann, Georg's daughter.
Susanna Scharrmann, Philip Adam's daughter.
Conf. 1768: Conrad Scharrmann, Georg's son.
Conf. 1772: Cath. Elis. Scharrmann

Married 15 Apr. 1755, John Bulman and Barbara Schirman.

Berks County Probate Records:
George Sherman of Heidelberg Twp., on 2 May 1787:   letters of administration were granted to Conrad Sherman, the second son; Anna Maria Sherman the widow, and Simon Sherman, the eldest son, renouncing.

Berks County Land Warrants, Pennsylvania Archives, Third Series:
Philip Adam Scharman, 25 acres, 15 Feb. 1755.
George Sherman, 115.1 acres, 18 Oct. 1770.

Altalaha Lutheran KB, Rehrersberg, Berks Co., PA:
Simon Schermann had children:
   1. Simon, b. 25 Mar. 1771
   2. Johannes, b. 6 Nov. 1772

Simon Shirman, Lancaster County, nat. 24 Sept. 1746.
Philip Adam Sherman, Heidelberg Twp., Berks County, nat. 10-11 Apr. 1761.
George Sherman, Tulpehoccon Twp., Berks County, nat. Fall 1765.

SCHIRMAN, GEORG JACOB
Lydia, 1749
S-H, I: 422

Niederhochstadt=
76879 Hochstadt, Pfalz

EUROPEAN RECORDS

Niederhochstadt Reformed KB:
Jacob Schirman and wife (unnamed) had a son:
    Georgius **Jacob**us, bp. 21 Dec. 1724
    Sp.: Jeorg Peter and Margaretha

Georg Jacob Schirmann and wife Maria Elisabetha had a son:
    Georg Jacob, b. 3 Feb. 1748; bp. 6 Feb. 1748
    Sp.: Georg Jacob Reintzel and Barbara

The door to the Reformed Church in Niederhochstadt

AMERICAN RECORDS

Berks County Land Warrants, Pennsylvania Archives, Third Series:
George Jacob Schirman, 2 different 25 acre tracts, both dated 19 June 1754.

Host Reformed KB, Berks Co., PA:
Georg Jacob Schirman and wife Eva Cunigunda had:
    Joh. Jacob, b. 2 Mar. 1755, bp. 30 Mar. 1755
    Sp.: Joh. Trautman and wife Eva Elisab.

Altalaha Lutheran KB, Berks Co., PA:
Georg Jacob Schermann (and wife) had a daughter:
    Elisabetha Juliana, b. 11 Sept. 1759, bp. 29 Sept. 1759
    Sp.: Jacob Kreutzer and Elisabetha Juliana Hoffmann

Jacob Shurman, Tulpehoccon Twp., Berks County, nat. 24 Sept. 1762.

SCHLINGENLOFF, JOHANN HENRICH   67112 Mutterstadt
Mortonhouse, 1729
S-H, I: 23, 25, 26
    Passengers on ship: Analis, Anna Christian, Henrich Schlengeluf

EUROPEAN RECORDS

Mutterstadt Reformed KB:
Johann Henrich Schlingenloff m. 14 June 1724 Anna Christina Gärtner.

She is possibly the Anna Christina Gärtner, bp. 28 Oct. 1697 at [74925]
Epfenbach, daughter of Hans Georg Gärtner, schoolmaster at [74937]
Spechbach, and his wife Apolonia. Their son, Conrad Gärtner, was the
Reformed schoolmaster at Mutterstadt.

AMERICAN RECORDS

Henry Slingloff was a member of the Church of the Brethren at
Germantown.

On 26 Aug. 1746, Bastian Höch and wife Johanna (nee Schilbert) deeded 1/2
acre and a house near Germantown to Theobald Endt and Henry Slingloff.

On 11 Aug. 1760, Theobald Endt and Henry Slingloff transferred this
property to Alexander Mack, Christopher Sower, Peter Leibert, and George
Schreiber to be used as a meeting place for the "members of the Religious
Society or Community of the people called Dutch (German) Baptists and
belonging to the Meeting of that People in or near Germantown."

Henry Slinglof nat. by Act. of 1735.

SCHMIDT, CASPAR   Ober Lustadt=
Royal Union, 1750   67363 Lustadt
S-H, I: 432

EUROPEAN RECORDS

Ober Lustadt Reformed KB:
Andreas Schmitt and Anna Margaretha had the following son:
    Caspar, b. 4 July 1730, bp. 7 July 1730

AMERICAN RECORDS

Six immigrants are listed together on the passenger list of the *Royal Union,*
and all are found in the Lustadt records: Henrich Hauenstein, Casper
Schmidt, Philip (X) Prike, Hans (X) Prike, Hans Michel Bauersachs, and
Andreas Hertzog.

SCHMIDT, CHRISTOPHER   67256 Weisenheim am Sand
York, 1725
    signed the ship's contract

EUROPEAN RECORDS

Weisenheim am Sand Reformed KB:
Christoph Schmidt, son of Wilhelm Schmidt, m. 9 May 1709 Elisabetha
Catharina, daughter of the late Johannes Wagner from Klein Odernheim [=
?55571 Odernheim am Glan]. They had children:
    1. Susanna, bp. 4 May 1710
    2. Leonhardt, bp. 30 Aug. 1711
    3. Magdalena, bp. 20 Aug. 1713
    4. Rohlandt, bp. 12 Jan. 1716
    5. Christoph, bp. 31 Oct. 1717
    6. Joh. David, bp. 10 Aug. 1719
    7. Susanna, bp. 21 June 1722

AMERICAN RECORDS

St. Paul's Lutheran KB, Red Hill, Montgomery Co., PA:
Leonhard and David Schmidt both appear sponsoring each other's children.

Christophorus Schmitt sp. a child of Philip Jacob Schellhammer [q.v.] in
1732.

Christopher Schmit and wife sp. children of Bartholomeus Gucker [q.v.] and Peter Walbert in 1732.

New Goshenhoppen Reformed KB, Montgomery Co., PA:
Member - David Schmidt.

Leonhard Schmid sp. a child of Joh. Adam Eucheling [q.v.] in 1732.
A Susanna Schmid sp. a child of Jacob Biseker, 1740.

Lorentz Schmid, son of David Schmid of Plumstet Twp., m. 15 Aug. 1769 Susanna Kolb, daughter of Geo. Michael Kolb, of Hanover Twp.

Jordan Lutheran KB, Lehigh Co., PA:
Roland Schmidt and Anna Maria had:
      1. Joh. Roland, b. 25 July 1749, bp. 14 Aug. 1749
         Sp.: Ulrich Burckholter and Barbara

SCHMIDT, JACOB   67256 Weisenheim am Sand
Adventure, 1727
S-H, I: 14
EUROPEAN RECORDS

Weisenheim am Sand Reformed KB:
Hans Wilhelm Schmidt and wife Anna Elisabetha had a son:
      1. Johann Jacob, bp. 14 May 1702

Lambsheim Reformed KB:
Joh. Jacob Schmidt, son of Wilhelm Schmidt, m. 8 Feb. 1724 Appolonia, daughter of the late Balthasar Storr. They had a son:
      1. Joh. Friederich, bp. 25 Feb. 1725

Jacob Schmit and wife had:
      2. Wilhelm, bp. 11 Apr. 1731
      3. Abraham, bp. 11 Apr. 1731
         Sp.: Wilhelm Schmit and Abraham Saler

AMERICAN RECORDS

New Goshenhoppen Reformed KB, Montgomery Co., PA:
Jacob Schmidt and wife Apolonia had a son:
      4. Johannes, bp. 11 Apr. 1737
         Sp.: Johannes Schuck and wife Anna Maria

St. Paul's Lutheran KB, Red Hill, Montgomery Co., PA:
Jacob Schmidt and Apolonia had:
> Anna Maria, b. Feb. 1742, bp. June 1742
> Sp.: Lorentz Lauffer [q.v.] and Elis. Margaretha

SCHMIDT, JOH. CASPAR   Lachen-Speyerdorf=
Thistle of Glasgow, 1730   67435 Neustadt an der Weinstrasse
S-H, I: 31, 32, 34

EUROPEAN RECORDS

Lachen Speyerdorf Reformed KB:
Johann Caspar Schmitt, single cartwright, son of the late Johann Görg
Schmitt formerly tenant farmer at Bruchhausen, Heydelberger Ambts
[Bruchhausen, Kr. Karlsruhe = 76275 Ettlingen], m. 20 Apr. 1727 Anna
Agatha, daughter of the late Johann Henrich Zinckgraff, formerly inhabitant
at Battenberg [67271 Battenberg, Pfalz]. They had:
> 1. Anna Barbara Catharina Agatha, b. 26 Dec. 1727,
> bp. 30 Dec. 1727
> Sp.: Anna Barbara Mergenthal, wife of Hans Görg Mergenthal
> of Bruchhausen.

[Schmitt is a very common name, and precise identification has not been
located in PA records; this immigrant is included here, based on the fact
that he drops out of the Lachen records, and appears on the same ship with
five others from Lachen-Speyerdorf.]

SCHMIDT, PHILIP   67251 Freinsheim
SCHMIDT, JOHAN PETER
Johnson, 1732   *Harle,* 1736, S-H, I: 156
S-H, I: 72, 76, 78   [J[a] Judith Schmitt age 20, A[n] Margreth 53]
[listed between Peter Gabel and
Jacob Neunzenhöltzer, both [q.v.] from Freinsheim]

EUROPEAN RECORDS

Freinsheim Lutheran KB:
[Gap in marriage record 1710-1715]
Philips Schmidt and wife Anna Margaretha had children:
> 1. Johann Peter, b. 18 Sept. 1712; conf. 1724, age 12
> Sp.: Johann Peter Brenner & Anna Maria Hüssgin

2. a daughter [Johanna Judith], b. 27 Jan. 1715; conf. 1727
3. Joh. Conrad, b. 9 Aug. 1719; died 1719
4. Anna Maria, b. 28 July 1721; died 1721

AMERICAN RECORDS

St. Michael's and Zion Lutheran KB, Philadelphia:
Peter Schmidt and wife Anna Margaretha had:
      1. Johanna Judith, b. 28 Sept.? 1745, bp. 30 Sept. 1745
      Sp.: Herman Bast and wife Johanna Judith

Herman Bast and wife Judith had:
      1. Catharina, b. 4 Sept. 1746, bp. 12 Sept. 1746
      Sp.: Lorentz Bast and wife Anna Margaretha, both Reformed
      2. Anna, b. 12 Jan. 1749, bp. 19 Jan. 1749
      Sp.: Michael Eve and wife Anna Catharina
      3. Elisabeth, b. 23 Mar. 1751, bp. 7 Apr. 1751
      Sp.: Lorentz Bast and wife Anna Margretha

Buried 30 Apr. 1765: Johanna Judith Bast, widow of Herman Bast. Born June 1715 in Freinsheim, Pfalz; to America in 1736. Married 1739 Herman Bast.

Philadelphia Will Book K: 218:
Herman Bast, Philadelphia. 22 Nov. 1754 - 27 Nov. 1754.
Exrs: wife Judith and brother Laurence Bast
Children: Maria Margaretta, Henry, John Henry, Anna and Laurence.
Wit.: Peter Miller, Jacob Grief.

SCHMITT, GEORG HEINRICH   Ober Lustadt=
Britannia, 1764   67363 Lustadt
S-H, I: 693

EUROPEAN RECORDS

Ober Lustadt Reformed KB:
Jörg Schmitt, Sr. and wife Maria Eva had a son:
      Jörg Heinrich, b. 31 July 1740, bp. 4 Aug. 1740
      Sp.: Jörg Henrich Hamelman and his mother Dorothea

In 1762 Jörg Henrich Schmitt, single, is listed as a sponsor at a baptism, then drops out of the record.
(see comment about the *Britannia* passengers following next immigrant.)

SCHMITT, JOH. ANDREAS Ober Lustadt=
Britannia, 1764 67363 Lustadt
S-H, I: 693

EUROPEAN RECORDS

Ober Lustadt Reformed KB:
Joh. Jacob Schmitt and wife Rosina had a son:
    Joh. Andreas, b. 12 July 1723
    Sp.: Joh. Andreas Schmitt and Anna Barbara

One Andreas Schmitt and Anna Barbara had children:
    1. Joh. Peter, b. 15 Sept. 1744, bp. 18 Sept. 1744
    2. Barbara, b. 15 Apr. 1757, bp. 17 Apr. 1757
    3. Dorothea, b. 21 May 1759, bp. 24 May 1759
or
One Andreas Schmitt and Elisabetha had children:
    1. Georg Adam, b. 21 Jan. 1751, bp. 24 Jan. 1751
    2. Jacob, b. 1 Nov. 1755, bp. 2 Nov. 1755

AMERICAN RECORDS

Seven passengers from Oberlustadt are listed together on the passenger list of the ship *Britannia* in 1764: Johann Bernhart Ott, **Johann Andreas Schmitt**, Christian Haushalter, **Georg Heinrich Schmitt**; further on the list are Johann Martin Ott, Carl Garaus (see Jahraus), Vallentin Stettler.

SCHMITT, JOHAN HEINRICH 67125 Dannstadt
Thistle of Glasgow, 1730
S-H, I: 31, 32, 33

EUROPEAN RECORDS

Dannstadt Reformed KB:
Joh. Henrich Schmitt m. 5 Feb. 1726 Anna Maria Muin. They had:
    Joh. Jacob, b. 8 Apr. 1729
    Sp.: Joh. Jacob Schröder and Anna nee Schmidt

Note on Anna Maria Schmidt's maiden name: elsewhere in the church record, it is given as Mouy, Moyse, possibly Huguenot in origin.

AMERICAN RECORDS

For additional identification of Schmitt as an immigrant, see *Pennsylvania Dutchman* Vol. 5, no. 13, Mar. 1, 1954, pg. 13.

Due to the very common name, exact identification of this immigrant in Pennsylvania records would require extensive research.

SCHMIDT, MELCHIOR   67454 Hassloch
Emigration record dated 1752
Not located in passenger lists.

EUROPEAN RECORDS

Hassloch Lutheran KB:
Conrad Schmid and wife Anna Margaretha had a son:
    Johann Melchior, b. 23 Aug. 1721; conf. 1735

Johann Melchior Schmid m. 12 Oct. 1744 Anna Maria ?Diener. They had:
    1. Maria Magdalena, b. 8 Nov. 1745, bp. 11 Nov. 1745
    2. Anna Elisabetha, b. 4 Jan. 1751, bp. 6 Jan. 1751

Emigration record:
Werner Hacker, *Auswanderungen aus Rheinpfalz und Saarland*:
#13443 Melchior Schmidt (Schmitt), *Beisass* in Hassloch with wife and two children, ages 7 years and one year. To PA, document dated 28 Mar. 1752.

SCHÖNICH (SCHÖNIG), CONRADT   67454 Hassloch
Pennsylvania Merchant, 1732
S-H, I: 66, 69, 70

EUROPEAN RECORDS

Hassloch Reformed KB:
[Georg] Lorentz Schönich, son of Joh. Jacob Schönich, *des Gerichts*, m. 2 Feb. 1708 Anna Maria, daughter of the late Jacob Rümli former *Gemeinsmann* and carpenter here. They had children:
    1. **Johann Conradt,** bp. 14 Nov. 1708.
        Conf. 1722 at Easter, age 13 years, 6 months.
    2. Johann Ulrich [q.v.], bp. 15 Oct. 1710
    3. Maria Magdalena, b. 20 Dec. 1713
    4. Anna Maria, b. 25 Nov. 1717

On 12 Nov. 1741, Maria Elisabetha, daughter of the late Isaac Schmid, gave birth to an illegitimate child. She named the father as Conrad Schönig, but the Pastor records in the church book that Conrad Schönig had gone some time ago to the New Land.

AMERICAN RECORDS

St. Michael's and Zion Lutheran KB, Philadelphia, PA:
Conrad Schönichs and Maria Elisabetha had:
1. Anna Maria, b. 9 Jan. 1745, bp. 26 May 1745
   Sp.: Johannes Schneider and wife.

SCHÖNIG, ULRICH age 27   67454 Hassloch
St. Andrew, 1741
S-H, I: 304
EUROPEAN RECORDS

Hassloch Reformed KB:
[Georg] Lorentz Schönich, son of Joh. Jacob Schönich, *des Gerichts*, m. 2 Feb. 1708 Anna Maria, daughter of the late Jacob Rümli former *Gemeinsmann* and carpenter here. They had children:
1. Johann Conradt [q.v.], bp. 14 Nov. 1708.
   Conf. 1722 at Easter, age 13 y. 6 mo.
2. **Johann Ulrich**, bp. 15 Oct. 1710
3. Maria Magdalena, b. 20 Dec. 1713
4. Anna Maria, b. 25 Nov. 1717

SCHOTTER, VALENTIN   67159 Friedelsheim
SCHOTTER, HENRY
St. Andrew, 1743
S-H, I: 349, 350, 352
(Surnames appear in lists as Shutter; did not sign.)

EUROPEAN RECORDS

Friedelsheim Reformed KB:
Valentin Schotter from Lachen [= 67435 Neustadt a.d. Weinstrasse] m. 17 May 1719 Anna Margaretha, daughter of Jacob Klemmer. They had children:
1. Joh. Hennrich, bp. 28 Jan. 1720

2. Maria Magdalena, bp. 16 Nov. 1721
3. Catharina, bp. 22 June 1724
    Sp.: Hennrich Klemmer (q.v.) and Catharina
4. Anna Rosina, bp. 28 Sep. 1727
5. Andreas, bp. 10 Apr. 1730
6. Joh. Jacob, bp. 18 Jan. 1733
7. Anna Barbara, bp. 16 Oct. 1735
    Sp.: Anna Barbara, daughter of Joh. Philip Heyger,
    master tailor at [67161] Gönnheim.

AMERICAN RECORDS

First Reformed KB, Lancaster:
Valentine Schotter and wife Anna Margaret had:
8. Matthew, bp. 12 May 1745
    Sp.: Matthew Hover and Dorothy

Henry Schotter m. 18 Aug. 1757 Anna Margaret Stauffer

York County Will Abstracts:
Henry Shotter of York (boro). Dated 20 Aug. 1797, probated 16 Sept. 1797.
Executors: Dorothea and Henry Shotter. Wife: Dorothea. Children:
Anna, Catharina, Elizabeth, Frederick, and Margaret.

SCHREYER, CHRISTIAN   67161 Gönnheim
Prelist, before 1727   67159 Friedelsheim

EUROPEAN RECORDS

Gönnheim Reformed KB and Friedelsheim Reformed KB:
Christian Schreier, son of the late Nicolaus Schreier m. 22 Apr. 1710 at
Gönnheim Elisabetha Kröff, daughter of Henrich Kröff of Alte Hosungen
in Ambts Wolfhagen, Hesse-Cassel (Altenhasungen = 34466 Wolfhagen).
They had children, baptized at Friedelsheim:
1. Hans Georg, bp. 15 Mar. 1716
2. Anna Catharina, bp. 12 June 1718
3. Johannes, bp. 23 Mar. 1721
4. Joh. Niclas, bp. 22 July 1725
    Sp.: Joh. Niclas Coblentz [q.v.]
5. Jacob, bp. not located

AMERICAN RECORDS

Trinity Lutheran KB, Lancaster, PA:
Christian Schreyer was sponsor for a child of Johannes Huber in 1735.

Christian Schreyer and wife Elisabetha were sponsors for children of Joh. Adam Müller in 1733 and 1738.

Mattheis Märcker m. 27 June 1738 Catharina Schreyer.

John Georg Schreyer (Conewago) had children:
> 1. John Georg, b. 24 Feb. 1739 (Rev. Stoever's records)
>   Sp.: John Georg Soldner and Anna Maria Immler
>   (He became a gunsmith.)
> 2. Catrina
>   Sp.: Ludwig Imler, Catrina Bart
>   (This child and the next 6 children are recorded
>   in St. Matthew's Church record, Hanover. The
>   dates are torn from the page.)
> 3. Jacob
> 4. Ludwig
> 5. Anna Maria
> 6. Mattheis   2 Feb.
> 7. Maria Elisabetha   Mar.
> 8. Cathrina   Dec.
>   Sp.: The parents and Conrad Käffhaber and the Pastor Bager

Conewago Reformed KB, Adams County, PA:
John Schreyer from Friedelsheim, Pfalz, and wife Maria Margaret, daughter of Gerhard Rener from Hundsbach [55621 Hundsbach b. Kirn, Nahe], Zweibrucken, had children:
> 1. Catharina, b. 17 Oct. 1746, bp. 6 May 1747
>   Sp.: John Nicholas Coblenz and wife
> 2. Anna Maria, b. 5 Sep. 1748, bp. 16 May (1749?)
>   Sp.: Maria Elizabeth Schreyer, grandmother,
>   and Catherine Koblentz
> 3. Joh. Jacob, bp. 17 Aug. 1765
>   Sp.: Ulrich Huber and Anna Maria

Nicholas Schreyer, brother of the above, and wife Catharina, daughter of Gerhard Rener, had children:
> 1. John Adam, b. __ July 1746, bp. 6 May 1747
>   Sp.: Adam Rener, single

2. Johan Christian, b. 16 Aug. 1748, bp. 3 Sep. 1749
   Sp.: the parents
   (This baptism recorded in St. Matthew's Lutheran KB, Hanover.)
3. Joh. Jacob, b. 2 Feb. 1751, bp. 25 Jan. 1752
   Sp.: Jacob Schreyer and Anna Margaret

Jacob Schreyer and Anna Margaret had children:
1. Susanna, b. 14 July 1748, bp. 4 Aug. 1749
   Sp.: Maria Elisabetha Danner
   (Recorded at St. Matthew's, Hanover)
2. Anna Margaret, b. 14 Oct. 1750, bp. 25 Jan. 1752
   Sp.: Georg Spengel and Anna Margaret
   (Recorded at Conewago Reformed KB)

Matthew Marger and Catharina had a child:
1. Henry, b. 1749, bp. 1750 (Conewago Reformed)
   Sp.: Henry Bischoff and wife

Christian Schreyer's will, dated 21 Nov. 1742, was filed at Lancaster on 18 Jan. 1744; from the names of the witnesses, it is obvious he was living at the Conewago settlement. He names the following children: Johannes, Jacob, and Nicklaus. He also mentions Matteis Marger (his son-in-law). The will is witnessed by: Andreas Schreiber, Augustus Scherer, and Johannes Georg Froschauer. It was proven by Jacob Weynand and Augustus Scherrer.

The English version of this will, recorded in Lancaster Co. Will Book X, Vol, 2, page 25, gives the name of the testator as Christian Shreyer. Names the children: John, Jacob, Nicholas: and records the witnesses as : Jacob Weyhand, Augustus Sharrer, Georg Hushom (!) and Andrery Shreyer (!).

Naturalized Maryland, October term, 1743: Jacob Shrier, John Shrier, Nicholas Shrier.

SCHUH, ULRICH age 48   67459 Iggelheim
SCHUH, JOH. JACOB age 20
Elizabeth, 1733
S-H, I: 113, 114, 115, 765, 766
   Other passengers on ship: Anna Elisabetha age 48, Eva Elisabetha age 17, Anna Elisabetha age 13.

EUROPEAN RECORDS

Iggelheim - Schifferstadt Reformed KB:
Hans Ulrich Schuh m. 6 Jan. 1709 at Igelheim Anna Elisabetha, daughter of the late Peter Kissling, former *Gemeinsmann* here. They had children:
1. Maria Christina, b. 8 Sept. 1709
2. Johann Jacob, b. 14 July 1713, bp. 16 July 1713 at Igelheim
   Sp.: Johann Jacob Beusch, shoemaker
3. Eva Elisabetha, b. 21 Jan. 1716, bp. 22 Jan. 1716 at Igelheim
   Sp.: Eva Elisabetha Schuh, single
4. Anna Elisabetha, b. 19 June 1720, bp. 20 June 1720
   Sp.: Johann Georg Kappelsman and Anna Elisabetha

SCHUI (JUY, SHUEY), DANIEL 67125 Dannstadt
Johnson, 1732 Oggersheim=
S-H, I: 71, 72, 73, 74, 75, 77 67071 Ludwigshafen am Rhein
 [Passengers on ship: Daniel Schwe, Maria, Lodewick, Margaretha]

EUROPEAN RECORDS

Oggersheim Reformed KB:
Daniel Juy, Sr., originally from Grigy, near Metz, France, m. 24 Jan. 1702
Judith Lavenant, originally from Thierache, Aisne, France. They had a son:
   Daniel, bp. 9 Apr. 1703

Daniel Juy was baptized 9 Apr. 1703 at Oggersheim [=67071 Ludwigshafen], the son of Daniel Juy, Sr. Daniel Juy Sr. m. 24 Jan. 1702 at Oggersheim Judith L'avenant. Daniel, Sr. and Judith had five children baptized at Oggersheim and two baptized at Dannstadt. Daniel Joui died 22 Oct. 1738 in Dannstadt, age 59 years. On 20 Feb. 1739 his widow Judith married the widower Johann Jacob Becker.

Died 30 Mar. 1746 at the Munchhof, Dannstadt: Judith Becker from the province Dirage, in Picardy, France (Thierache, Aisne), age approx. 64 years, daughter of the deceased Piere Lavenant, refugee from the mentioned province.

Dannstadt Reformed KB:
Daniel Juy m. 16 Oct. 1725 Maria Martha Schilling. They had children:
1. Ludwig Heinrich, b. 15 Oct. 1726
   Sp.: Ludwig Heinrich Frey and Elisabetha
2. Anna Margaretha, bp. 15 Feb. 1729
3. Johannes, b. 24 Nov. 1730, bp. 28 Nov. 1730
   Sp.: Jean Saar and Maria Magdalena nee Michet

The son Johannes, b. 1730, does not appear on the ship's list with the other family members. It is known that Daniel made a trip back to Dannstadt in 1748. On the ship *Edinburgh* 5 Sept. 1748 there is listed a Johannes Schue. Several other passengers on this ship were from this area.

AMERICAN RECORDS

Lancaster Will Book Y-2, p. 553:
Daniel Shuey settled in Bethel Twp., Lancaster Co., PA (now Lebanon Co.). He left a will dated 8 May 1770, probated at Lancaster 21 May 1777, naming his wife Mary Martha and the following children: dec'd son Ludwig Shuy, daughter Anna Margaret wife of Nicholas Pontius, Peter, Daniel, John, Martin, Catharina wife of Jacob Giger, Barbara wife of George Feeser and Elisabeth wife of Henry Moser.

Swatara Reformed Church, Jonestown, Lebanon Co., PA:
Daniel Schuy and wife Anna Maria (also Maria Martha) had:
1. Barbara, bp. 25 June 1741
   Sp.: George Meyer and Barbara
2. Catharina Elisabetha, bp. 8 June 1747
   Sp.: Peter Schell and wife Maria Catharina

Ludwig Heinrich Schuy and Maria Elisabeth had:
1. John Henry, bp. 9 Mar. 1748
   Sp.: Henry Sauder and Anna Marg. Schuy, single

Ludwig Schuy and wife Elisabeth had:
1. John Martin, bp. 15 June 1750
   Sp.: John Martin Schuy, single
2. John, bp. 7 Dec. 1752
   Sp.: John Schuy and wife Catharina

Martin Schuy and wife had:
   Elisabetha, b. 1 Aug. 1762
   Sp.: Ludwig Schuy and wife Elisabetha

Rev. John Casper Stoever's Records:
Johannes Schuy of Bethel, Lancaster Co. had a son:
   Johannes, b. 9 Jan. 1757, bp. 13 Mar. 1757
   Sp.: Johannes Lohmüller and Barbara Hautz.

St. Paul's (Klopp's) Reformed KB, Bethel Twp., Lebanon Co., PA:
Martin Schuy, Jr. and Catharina Elisabeth had:
(elsewhere in the record, his wife is given as Margaret Elisabeth)

John Martin, b. 1 Feb. 1775, bp. 19 Feb. 1775
Sp.: Martin Schuy and Elisabeth
John, b. 6 Feb. 1776, bp. 28 Feb. 1776
Sp.: John Schuy

Additional records for the extensive Shuey family may be found in the following church registers:
   1. Trinity Tulpehocken Reformed Church, Lebanon Co.
   2. Christ Lutheran Church, Tulpehocken, Berks Co.
   3. Klinger's Church, Lykens Valley, Dauphin Co.

SCHULTZ, JOHANNES age 35   67159 Friedelsheim
Loyal Judith, 1742   55270 Essenheim
S-H, I: 343, 324, 326
   (Note: the surname appears as Schültheis in the German records; always as Schultz in the Pennsylvania records.)

EUROPEAN RECORDS

Friedelsheim Reformed KB:
Gabriel Schültheis and wife Margaretha had children:
   1. Johann Martin, bp. 15 Oct. 1695 [q.v., Martin Schultz]
   2. Anna Catharina, bp. 7 July 1698 m. Jacob Weltzhoffer [q.v.]
   3. **Johannes,** bp. 10 June 1707
   4. Anna Maria, bp. 8 Nov. 1714
   5. Maria Magdalena, bp. 12 Dec. 1717

Anna Margaretha, wife of Gabriel Schultheis, died 20 July 1721. He m. (2) 21 Oct. 1722 Salome, widow of the late Hans Adam Böckel. Gabriel Schultheis died 15 Aug. 1730, age 60 years.

Essenheim Reformed KB:
Johann Christoph Horn from ?Eppenstein [?65817 Eppstein, Taunus] m. __? Jan. 1695 Anna Christina, daughter of Johannes Iber. They had a daughter:
   Anna Christina, b. 17 Nov. 1703, bp. 25 Nov. 1703
   Sp.: Christina, daughter of Hans Adam Brauneville

Johannes Schultheiss (Schultz) from Friedelsheim, m. 14 Mar. 1730 Anna Christina, daughter of Christophel Horn.

Buried 20 Dec. 1739 Christina, widow of the late Christopfel Horn, age 72 years, 11 months. (She was bp. 3 Nov. 1667, daughter of Hans Iber and Anna Ursula. Married 25 Feb. 1662: Johannes Ibert and Anna Ursula, daughter of Lorenz Schmal.)

Additional European Data:
Krebs and Rubincam, *Emigrants from the Palatinate to the American Colonies in the 18th Century,* Pennsylvania German Society 1953, page 29:
          "Schultz, Johannes. Of [55270] Essenheim. Married Christina. Issue: (1) Anna Mara, b. Jan. 1753; (2) H. Jacob; (3) Johannes. To America with wife 3 children in the beginning of May, 1742. Johannes Schultz arrived on the *Loyal Judith,* 3 Sept. 1742."

AMERICAN RECORDS

Creutz Creek Reformed KB, Hallam Twp., York County:
John Shultz and wife were sponsors in 1757; Jacob Schultz and wife were sponsors in 1759; Anna Maria Schultz was a sponsor in 1760 for a child of Valentine Heiger and Anna Catharina. It will be noted that these names correspond with the children of Johannes Schultz of Essenheim.

Christ Lutheran KB, York, burials:
Died 13 July 1758, Christina Schultz, born 11 Nov. 1705. Buried 15 July 1758 in the Reformed churchyard at Kreutz Creek.

Died 15 Sept. 1758, John Schultz, b. 10 June 1707, m. in 1728 to the late Christina nee Horn. They have two sons and a daughter, who survive, all married. His father was Gabriel Schultz, his mother Anna Margaret. Buried 17 Sept. 1758 in the Reformed cemetery at Kreutz Creek.

The house of Johannes and Christina Schultz is illustrated in Gibson's *History of York County, Pennsylvania* page 605 (1886). Originally in Hellam Township (later Spring Garden), the house contains a sandstone tablet in one wall, containing the inscription:

I7ANO3Z·HABICH· IOHANE ⌠CHVLTZ·VND CRI⌠TINA·⌠EINEEFR AVDIE/E⌠ HAV⌠BAVT

The year should probably be read as 1754, rather than 1734, since Schultz did not emigrate until 1742.

John Shultz, Hallam Twp., York Co. was naturalized 10 Apr. 1753, without oath.

SCHULTZ, MARTIN 67159 Friedelsheim
Pennsylvania Merchant, 1731
S-H, I: 43, 44, 45
   Cathrina Shultsone appears on list of women over 16

EUROPEAN RECORDS

Friedelsheim Reformed KB:
Gabriel Schültheis and wife Margaretha had a son:
   Johann Martin, bp. 15 Oct. 1695

Johann Martin's first marriage was not located in the church record, but his first wife Anna Barbara died there on 18 Dec. 1727, age 33 years, and 6 months. Their marriage was located in the **Billigheim Reformed KB:**
   Married 10 Apr. 1724 at Billigheim [76831 Billigheim-Ingenheim]:
Hans Martin Schultheis from Friedelsheim and Anna Barbara Hutmacherin.

Hans Martin Schultheis m. (2) 3 Sept. 1728 Anna Catharina, daughter of Hans Adam Krähmer of [67161] Gönnheim.

See the preceding immigrant, Johannes Schultz, for further detail on the family. They were step-brothers of Anna Elisabetha Beckel, wife of Ludwig Klemmer. (See Klemmer.)

AMERICAN RECORDS

Martin Schultz and Johannes Schultz were members of Rev. Lischy's Congregation on the Cadores, 17 Mar. 1745.

Rev. Jacob Lischy's personal records, York Co., PA:
Martin Schultz and wife Catharina had children:
     1. Christina, bp. 24 July 1745 at Creutz Creek
       Sp.: Johanes Schultz and Christina
     2. Johannes, bp. 6 Jan. 1754
       Sp.: Johannes Schultz, Jr.

Christ Lutheran KB, York, burials:
John Martin Schultz was born in Martinmas, 1694, son of Gabriel Schultz and Anna Margaret his wife, of Friedelsheim in the Palatinate. He married (1) in 1721 Barbara nee Bieber (or Büber) and lived in marriage with her for three years. They had two children, both died. He married (2) in 1728 Catharina, daughter of John Adam Kreamer of Gönheim. She is now his widow. They came to Pennsylvania in 1731 and had 4 sons (2 survive) and 7 daughters (6 survive, 3 are married). Also 7 living grandchildren. He died 5 Nov. 1761.

The surviving children of Martin Schultz are listed in a deed, recorded in
York: 1. Henry   m. Mary Magdalena
        2. Eve   m. George Reitzel
        3. Anna Maria   m. Peter Boger
        4. Catharina   m. Michael Weider
        5. Marilis   m. Andrew Comfort
        6. Christina   m. ----- Meyer
        7. Juliana   m. (1) Joh. Jacob Faubel
                             (2) Abraham Shineman
        8. Johannes

SCHUNCK, CASPAR   67112 Mutterstadt
Prelist

EUROPEAN RECORDS

Mutterstadt Reformed KB:
Caspar Schunck and wife Anna Barbara had children:
        1. Christian, bp. 16 Sept. 1714
        2. Elisabetha, bp. 29 June 1717

Mutterstadt Kontraktenrotokolle:
Record dated 1726: Caspar Schunck, citizen here, who had moved to
Pennsylvania, sold a tract of land to the esteemed Bernhard Reimer.
Recorded 6 June 1737.

AMERICAN RECORDS

New Goshenhoppen Reformed KB, Montgomery Co., PA:
Elisabeth Schunk sponsored a child of Abraham Transo [q.v.] in 1736.

Rev. John Caspar Stoever's personal records:
Joh. Christian Schunck, Joh. Caspar Schunck, and Frantz Schunck all served
as sponsors of three children of Wilhelm Heim [q.v.] of Coventry.

Chester County Will Abstracts:
Conrad Shymer of Vincent Twp. left a will dated 20 July 1780. He mentions
his grandchildren Isaac and Peter Shunk who are to have his place in
Pikeland, and grandson Conrad Shunk who is to have £100. Exrs: Isaac
Shunk and Shymer's wife Anna Margaret.

Simon Shunk, Chester Co. 23 Dec. 1785, Adm. to Peter and Isaac Shunk.

Montgomery County Will Abstracts:
Francis Shunk, Trappe. 19 May 1807 - 7 Juny 1807.
To Rebecca Vanderslice, farm and personalty. Exr.: Rebecca Vanderslice.
Wit.: Jacob Fry.

SCHÜPPING, JOHANN JACOB   67454 Hassloch
Ship data not located;
family disappears from records after 1741.

EUROPEAN RECORDS

Hassloch Reformed KB:
Johann Jacob Schüpping, son of the late Abraham Schüpping, former
Gemeinsmann here, m. (1) 28 Jan. 1722 Anna Catharina, single daughter of
Andreas Kauffmann, *Gemeinsmann und Huffschmidt* here. They had a son:
    1. Johan Jacob, b. 18 Feb. 1723, bp. 21 Feb. 1723; conf. 1736

Joh. Jacob Schopping, *Gemeinsmann und Huffschmidt,* widower, m. (2) 24
Feb. 1725 Eva Gertraut, widow of the late Philipp Lorentz Kauffman. [Her
first marriage record in 1714 gives her maiden name as Postel, daughter of
Johann Wendel Postel. Children of the second marriage:
    2. Maria Magdalena, b. 30 Nov. 1725, bp. 3 Dec. 1725; conf. 1739
    3. Maria Eva Catharina, b. 15 Feb. 1728, bp. 18 Feb. 1728;
        conf. 1741 [her confirmation is the last entry for the family in the
        Hassloch records.]
    4. Catharina Margaretha, b. 28 Jan. 1730
    5. Maria Christina, b. 18 Dec. 1732, bp. 17 Dec. 1732
    6. Catharina Margretha, b. 5 Feb. 1735, bp. 7 Feb. 1735
    7. Johann Nicolaus, b. 10 Jan. 1739, bp. 13 Jan. 1739

AMERICAN RECORDS

Great Swamp Reformed KB, Lower Milford Twp., Lehigh Co., PA:
Nicolaus Schubing (and wife, not named) had a son:
    1. Jacob, bp. 14 May 1767
        Sp.: _____ Holshauser and wife.

The family evidently soon moved to North Carolina, after this child's birth.
Johann Nicholaus Schupping served on a jury in Rowan County, NC in
1771.

SCHUSTER, DANIEL   Lachen-Speyerdorf=
Recovery, 1754   64735 Neustadt an der Weinstrasse
S-H, I: 660
EUROPEAN RECORDS

Lachen-Speyerdorf Reformed KB:
Peter Schuster, son of the midwife Agnes Schuster, m. 10 July 1720 at
Speyerdorf Maria Barbara, daughter of the late Stephan Schuster of
Speyerdorf. They had children:
1. Frantz, b. 21 May 1721, bp. 25 May. 1721
   Sp.: Frantz Scherer
2. Philipp, bp. 29 Oct. 1722
   Sp.: Philips, son of Stephan Schuster and
   Ursula ____(page torn).
3. Johann Peter, b. 10 Oct. 1724, bp. 15 Oct. 1724
   Sp.: Peter, son of Ernst Barthel of Speyerdorf
4. Johanna Catharina, bp. 26 Feb. 1727
   Sp.: Johanna Catharina, daughter of Johannes Möchtersheimer
5. Johann Jacob, b. 26 Oct. 1729, bp. 30 Oct. 1729; conf. 1743
   Sp.: Jacob Roth, der jung, and wife Anna Maria
6. Anna Barbara, b. 19 May 1731, bp. 27 May. 1731; conf. 1745
   Sp.: Anna Barbara, wife of Michel Kilian
7. Joh. **Daniel,** b. 26 Apr. 1733, bp. 3 May 1733; conf. 1747
   Sp.: Daniel Flammuth
8. Joh. Philips, b. 9 Nov. 1735, bp. 13 Nov. 1735
   Sp.: Philips Schuster

Another Peter Schuster with wife Catharina Margretha also appear in the
Lachen KB, having children during this same time period. They had a
daughter:
   Maria Elisabetha, b. 5 July 1733, bp. 13 July 1733; conf. 1748.

Emigration record:
Werner Hacker, *Auswanderungen aus Rheinpfalz und Saarland im 18.
Jahrhundert:* # 14225 Schuster, M. Elisabeth, Lachen. To America 30 years
ago. Record dated 1784.

AMERICAN RECORDS

First Reformed KB, Philadelphia:
Daniel Schuster and wife Maria Elisabeth had children:
1. Catharine, bp. 2 May 1762; died 19 Sept. 1762
   Sp.: Georg Krieger and Catharina
2. Maria Catharina, b. 27 July 1764, bp. 17 Aug. 1764

3. Maria Elisabeth, b. 27 July 1764, bp. 17 Aug. 1764
   Sp.: parents
4. Maria Eva, b. 21 Jan. 1767, bp. 5 Feb. 1767
   Sp.: Felix Fennel and Maria Eva
5. Joh. Daniel, b. 8 Nov. 1769, bp. 21 Dec. 1769
   Sp.: parents
6. Margaret, daughter of Daniel Schuster, died 7 June 1761.

Died Mar. 1770: Barbara Schuster, age 38 years.
Died 26 Apr. 1771: Daniel Schuster, age 37 years.
Died 3 May 1784: Maria Elisabeth Schuster, age 50 years.

SEBASTIAN, ADAM   67251 Freinsheim
Mortonhouse, 1729
S-H, I: 24
   [appears on list as Adam Bastian]

EUROPEAN RECORDS

Freinsheim Lutheran KB:
Joh. Michael Sebastian and wife Maria Catharina had a son:
      Johann Adam, bp. 29 Nov. 1709; conf. 1722, age 13.
      Sp.: Johan Adam Setzer, *Schultheis* at Kirchheim an der Ecke
      [73230 Kirchheim unter Teck].

[He arrived on the Mortonhouse with Andrew Bastian: see Andreas
Sebastian].

SEBASTIAN, JOH. ANDREAS   67251 Freinsheim
Mortonhouse, 1729
S-H, I: 24
[appears on list as Andrew Bastian]

EUROPEAN RECORDS

Freinsheim Lutheran KB:
Daniel Sebastian and wife Eva Catharina had children:
      1. Joh. Jacob, bp. 9 Aug. 1699 (Reformed KB)
      2. Anna Catharina, m. (1) Georg Daniel Seidemann [see Jacob
         Seidemann]; she m. (2) Jacob Barth [q.v.], emigrated 1736

3. possibly Joh. Michael [q.v.], conf. 1720
4. **Johann Andreas,** bp. 18 Aug. 1709
    Sp.: Herr Johann Andreas Seltzer and wife Maria Sophia
5. Johann Peter, bp. 1 July 1714
    Sp.: Joh. Peter Volandt and wife Anna Catharina
6. Johann Peter, bp. 22 Apr. 1716; died 22 July 1716

Daniel Sebastian was buried in Aug. 1725, in the Pastor's absence.

The old tower of the church in Freinsheim

AMERICAN RECORDS

Trappe Lutheran KB, Montgomery Co., PA:
Andreas Sebastian m. 27 Apr. 1730 Elisabeth Kraus.

Conf. 1751: Catharina Bastian, daughter of Andreas Bastian, age 19 years. Was neglected.
(The surname appears in Pennsylvania records as Bastian and Sebastian.)

New Hanover Lutheran KB, Montgomery Co., PA:
Buried 31 Oct. 1748, Anthon Bastian, son of Andreas Bastian.

Andreas Bastian and wife Maria Albertina had children:
    1. Michael, b. __ July 1744, bp. 16 Sept. 1744
       Sp.: Michael Bastian and wife
    2. Anthony, b. 3 Mar. 1747, bp. 26 Apr. 1747
    3. Anthony, b. 17 June 1749, bp. 30 July 1749
    4. Magdalena, b. __ Dec. 1752

Western Maryland Genealogy, Vol. 2, no. 3 (1986):
Frederick County Wills: Book A1, pg. 214-5:
Andrew Bostian was a wit. to the 1764 will of Jacob Syderman [q.v., Seidemann].

Western Maryland Genealogy, Vol. 7, no. 3 (1991):
Frederick County Wills, Liber GM#2, pg. 300-302:
Andrew Bostian, Frederick Co. Will dated 25 Nov. 1785, sick. Provides for wife Maria Alberdina. Children: Anthony, Jacob, Henry, Daniel, Cathrine Doll, John, George, Barbara Buryer, Christiana Smith, Michael, Salome Lock and Mary Bostian. Exr.: son Anthony. Wit.: Joseph Wood, Adam Creager, Peter Stephens. Proved 28 Jan. 1789 by Creager and Stephens.

SEBASTIAN, JOH. MICHAEL   67251 Freinsheim
Molly, 1727
S-H, I: 12, 13

EUROPEAN RECORDS

Freinsheim Lutheran KB:
Joh. Michael Sebastian was confirmed 1720. He may be a son of either Daniel Sebastian and Eva Catharina, or he may be a son of Joh. Michael Sebastian and Maria Catharina. Both couples appear in the Freinsheim Lutheran records, and both had sons who came to Pennsylvania in 1729.

AMERICAN RECORDS

New Goshenhoppen Reformed KB, Montgomery Co., PA:
Eva Maria, wife of Michael Sebastian, was sp. in 1736 for a child of Henrich
Schmid.

Trappe Lutheran KB, Montgomery Co., PA:
Eva Maria Sebastian sp. in 1735 a child of Heinrich Krebs. She sp. a child
of Balthasar Füller in 1751.

Conf. 1746: Jürg Michael Bastian, age 14, son of Michael.
Conf. at New Providence 6 May 1759: Regina Bastian, daughter of Michael
Bastian, age 12 years.

Jurg Michael Bastian and wife Maria Magdalena had children:
1. Christina, b. 4 Mar. 1756
2. Anna Maria, b. 27 Nov. 1757
3. Johann Michael, b. 13 Aug. 1759
   Sp.: Michael Bastian and wife
4. Philip Jacob, b. 1 May 1761
   Sp.: Michael Bastian and wife Eva Maria, grandparents

David Shultze's Journal, 1769:
Michael Bastian's wife was buried on the 12th (May).

Michael Sebastian, Philadelphia Co., nat. Sept. 1740.

SEIBEL, HENRICH   67454 Hassloch
Friendship, 1738
S-H, I: 225, 228, 230 [Appears as Henry Syble age 27 on A list.]

EUROPEAN RECORDS

Hassloch Lutheran KB:
Henrich Seÿbel, single, m. 12 Jan. 1734 Johanna Magdalena nee Boll(in).

Georg Henrich Seÿbel (Seibel) and Anna (Johanna) Magdalena had
children:
1. Ursula Elisabetha, bp. 4 Oct. 1734 at [67459] Böhl
   Sp.: Joh. Thomas Hermann and Ursula Elisabetha
2. Joh. Conrad, bp. 13 June 1736 at Hassloch
   Sp.: Joh. Conrad Merner & Maria Sara Possler(in).

The family of Henrich Seÿbel's wife:
Jacob Boll, shoemaker, and wife Maria Elisabetha had children:
   1. Anna Maria, b. 11 Aug. 1709; it is mentioned in the record of this
      baptism that the parents were married 9 June 1709 at Philipsberg
      [= 76661 Philippsburg].
   2. Maria Elisabetha, b. 24 Dec. 1711; she m. Joh. Ludwig
      Lindenschmidt [q.v.].
   3. Johanna Magdalena, b. 27 Aug. 1713, bp. 30 Aug. 1713
      Sp.: Johanna, daughter of Hilarius Weller, citizen and
      shoemaker at N(eu)Statt [67435 Neustadt a.d. Weinstrasse].
   4. Philippina Magdalena, b. 21 Nov. 1715, bp. 24 Nov.
   5. Emanuel, b. 2 May 1718, bp. 8 May 1718.

AMERICAN RECORDS

Tohickon Reformed KB, Bucks Co., PA:
(George) Henry Seybel and wife (Mary) Magdalena had:
   3. probably Eva Seibel, conf. Easter, 1758
   4. Christina, bp. 9 June 1754
      Sp.: Adam Dani and Christina.
   5. George Henry, b. 1 Dec. 1758, bp. 1 Jan. 1759
      Sp.: parents.

Henry Seibel's child died 6 June 1759, buried 7 June 1759.

Died 4 Sept. 1808, Henry Seipel (no age given).

Conrad Seybel m. 5 Feb. 1760 Hannah Cressmann. They had children:
   1. Jacob, b. 19 Dec. 1760, bp. 28 Dec. 1760
      Sp.: Henry Seybel and wife
   2. Elizabeth, bp. 4 Jan. 1762
      Sp.: George Henry Seipel.

SEIDEMANN, JACOB age 17   67251 Freinsheim
Harle, 1736
S-H, I: 155, 158, 160
   [with stepfather Johan Jacob Barth, q.v.]

EUROPEAN RECORDS

Lambsheim Reformed KB:
Georg Seidemann from [67256] Weissenheim am Sand and wife Susanna had a son:
> 1. Georg Daniel, b. 13 Oct. 1697 in Weissenheim am Sand.

Freinsheim Lutheran KB:
Georg Daniel Seidemann was conf. 1712.
Georg Daniel Seidemann m. 23 Dec. 1718 Anna Catharina, daughter of Daniel Sebastian. They had children:
> 1. **Johann Jacob,** b. 29 Apr. 1719; bp. 1 May 1719. Conf. 1732.
>   Sp.: Johann Jacob, single son of Johann Jacob Webel,
>   master miller at Gross Carlbach [67229 Grosskarlbach].
> 2. Susanna Catharina, b. 3 ?Apr. 1721
> 3. a son, b. 1722, no other data
> 4. Johannes, b. 1 Sept. 1724; bp. 3 Sept. 1724. Conf. Easter 1736.
>   Sp.: Johannes Retzer and wife Anna Maria
> 5. Johan Georg, b. 4 Nov. 1726; died 7 Feb. 1730

Died 25 July 1726 of a malignant fever, Georg Seidemann.
The widow Anna Catharina Seidemann m. (2) 27 Dec. 1726 Johann Jacob Barth [q.v.]

AMERICAN RECORDS

New Hanover Lutheran KB, Montgomery Co., PA:
Buried 17 Jan. 1748: an infant son of Jacob Seideman.

Western Maryland Genealogy, **Vol. 2, no. 3 (1986):**
Frederick County Wills: Book A1, pg. 214-5:
Jacob Syderman of Frederick Co. 1 Feb. 1764 - 14 May 1764.
Wife: Margaret. Two daughters Catharine and Margaret, remainder of estate when they come of age or marry, and the lands when my wife dies or remarries. Wit: Thomas Beatty, Caspar Creager, Andrew Bostian [q.v., Andreas Sebastian].

SELTZER, JACOB JR.   67251 Freinsheim
First arrival, prelist
Mortonhouse, 1729
S-H, I: 24
> [passengers on ship: Jacob Sellser, sworn formerly and Elisabetha Seller; also Jacob Seller, Jr. formerly in PA]

EUROPEAN RECORDS

Freinsheim Reformed KB:
Joh. Jacob Seltzer, son of Herr Joh. Jacob Seltzer, *Rathsverwandter* here, m. 13 Feb. 1726 Elisabetha, daughter of Rudolff Walter. They had one child bp. in Freinsheim:
> 1. Johannes, bp. 17 July 1727
>   Sp.: Joh. Martin Altstatt [q.v.] and wife Judith.

AMERICAN RECORDS

New Goshenhoppen Reformed Church, Montgomery Co., PA:
Jacob Seltzer and wife Elisabeth were sp. for a child of Wendel Weigandt [q.v.].

Jacob Seltzer nat. by Act 1729/30.

SEYLER, BALTHASAR   67251 Freinsheim
[name also appears as Sahler, Sailer, Seiler, Seeler]
Pennsylvania Merchant, 1731   *Harle,* 1736, S-H, I: 157
S-H, I: 43, 44, 45   [Catharina Elisabeth Seyler, 18]
   [other passengers on list: Barbel Selern]

EUROPEAN RECORDS

Freinsheim Lutheran KB:
Balthasar Seyler and wife Anna Barbara had children:
> 1. Johann Balthasar, b. 23 July 1705; conf. 1717; died 1720
>   Sp.: Hans Barthel Kopp and Anna Margretha Gifft
> 2. Anna Christina, b. 26 July 1708, bp. 8th Sunday p. Trin.
>   Sp.: Joh. Jacob ?Wierns and wife Anna Christina
> 3. Anna Elisabetha, bp. 7 May 1711; she m. 1729 Joh. Michael
>   Förster. Sp.: Meister Joh. Wolf Schranck and Anna Elisabetha
> 4. Johan Adam, b. 20 Apr. 1713, bp. in house
>   Sp.: Adam Gifft and Maria Elisabetha, his brother
>   Peter Seyler's wife
> 5. Johannes, b. 1 Oct. 1715, bp. 3 Oct. 1715 in house
>   [father mentioned as *Vorsteher* in this record]
>   Sp.: Johannes Retzer, master cooper, and wife Anna Maria
> 6. Catharina Elisabetha, b. 12 Feb. 1718, bp. 20 Feb. 1718
>   [She arrived on the *Harle,* 1736, with others from Freinsheim]

Sp.: Joh. Georg, son of Valentin Ranck, *Schultheis* at Ungstein
[=67098 Bad Dürkheim], and Catharina Elisabetha, daughter of
Lorentz Münch, Callstatt [= 67169 Kallstadt, Pfalz].
   7. Susanna Elisabetha, b. 19 Mar. 1721, bp. 23 Mar. 1721
      Sp.: Elisabetha, wife of Joh. Wolff Schranck at Callstatt

AMERICAN RECORDS

Trappe Lutheran KB, Montgomery Co., PA:
Balthaser Sählor sp. a child of Joh. Henrich Haas [q.v.] in 1741.
Balt. Sähler and wife sp. a child of Joh. Ludwig Missinger in 1746.
Balthasar Sähler and wife Anna Elisabetha sp. a child of Johannes Pfluger
in 1748.
Conf. 13 Apr. 1746: Johann Caspar Rahn, age 15, step-son of Balthaser
Sähler.

Philadelphia Wills and Administrations:
Baltzer Seyler   1750   est. # 78   Adm. F: 347.

Balthazar Sailor, Philadelphia Co., nat. Sept. 1740.

SEYLER, FELIX   67112 Mutterstadt
Phoenix, 1749
S-H, I: 407 [appears on list as Sailor; did not sign.]

EUROPEAN RECORDS

Mutterstadt Reformed KB:
Felix Seyler, son of the late Benedict Seyler from [74930] Ittling(en) in
Herrschafft Gemming(en), m. 3 June 1732 Anna Margaretha Bast, daughter
of the late Daniel Bast of [67158] Ellerstadt, Grafschafft Hartenburg.
   Written under the marriage record: "moved to Pennsylvania 1748."

Ittlingen Lutheran KB:
A Benedict Sailer and wife Maria Elisabetha had two children baptized 1699
and 1701.

A Benedict Sailer and wife Maria Appolonia had two children baptized 1706
and 1707, then drop out of the record.

There is no mention of a son Felix in either family.

See *Eighteenth Century Emigrants from German-Speaking Lands to North America,* Volume I: the Northern Kraichgau, by Annette K. Burgert, for other Sailer emigrants from Ittlingen.

AMERICAN RECORDS

Anita Eyster, "Notices by German Settlers in German Newspapers" in *Pennsylvania German Folklore Society,* Vol. III: p. 11:
Newspaper dated 1 Sept. 1751: Joh. Peter Seyler, not far from Falckner Swamp, near to Heinrich Deringer's, has been for more than 24 years in this land and his brother Felix Seyler came here two years ago and wrote a letter from the ship to Peter Seyler which went to the wrong place, so that he has only now received it and he would much like to know where his brother is. Felix came here from Ruchheim [67071] and when he sees this, he shall come to Peter or let him know where he lives. Or if anyone knows where he is or that he is not living, will they at the first opportunity send word to Heinrich Deringer's or to the printer here.

SEYLER, PETER   67251 Freinsheim
Johnson, 1732
S-H, I: 72, 73, 76, 78
   [other passengers on ship: Mateline (Magdalena) Seyler, children:
   Michael, Valentine, Matelina, Martha Seyler.]

EUROPEAN RECORDS

Freinsheim Lutheran KB:
Peter Seeler (Seyler) and wife Maria Elisabeth had children:
1. Maria Elisabetha, b. 19 May 1708, bp. 23 May 1708
   Sp.: Caspar Stichel from Herxheim [67273 Herxheim a Berg] and wife Maria Elisabetha
2. Johann Peter, b. 22 Nov. 1711, conf. 1726
   Sp.: Balthasar Seyler and Anna Barbara
3. Johannes, b. 11 Aug. 1715, died young
   Sp.: Johannes Mäurer, citizen at Gross Carlbach [67229 Grosskarlbach] and his wife Juliana
4. Maria Magdalena, b. 1 Jan. 1719, bp. 6 Jan. 1719
   Sp.: Friederich Reichart and wife Maria Magdalena from Herxheim [67273 Herxheim a Berg].
5. Johann Georg, b. 21 Sept. 1721, bp. 29 Sept. 1721
   Sp.: Johann Georg Bach and wife

Peter Seeler (Seyler) m. (2) 27 Dec. 1725 Maria Magdalena, youngest daughter of Wielhelm Krahmer from Obersieltzen [67271 Obersülzen]. They had children:

      6. Johann Michael, b. __ Nov. 1726, bp. 17 Nov. 1726
         Sp.: Herr Michael Sebastian and wife Clara
      7. Johann Valentin, b. 1 June 1728, bp. 6 June 1728
         Sp.: Herr Joh. Valentin Rauch, *Schultheis* at
         Ungstein [= 67098 Bad Dürkheim] and wife
      8. Anna Martha, b. 11 July 1730, bp. 16 July 1730
         Sp.: Anna Martha, wife of Gerhard Krähmer
         from Obersiel. [= 67271 Obersülzen], sister of the wife.

AMERICAN RECORDS

Trappe Lutheran KB, Montgomery Co., PA:
Conf. 13 Apr. 1746: Johann Michael Sähler, age 18, son of Peter Sähler; Valentine Michael Sähler, age 16, son of Peter Sähler; and Anna Martha Sähler, age 15, daughter of Peter Sähler.

Jurg Adam Protzman m. 22 Mar. 1750 Anna Martha Sahler.

Died 8 Dec. 1751, Peter Sähler.

Johann Michael Sahler, son of Peter Sahler, m. 11 Apr. 1751 in Providence Elisabeth Engel.

SPIES, ULRICH   Ober Lustadt=
St. Andrew, 1734   67363 Lustadt
S-H, I: 137, 141, 142
   [Passengers on ship: Uldrich Spies, Maria Dorothea Spies, Fredrick Treyster, Hans Martin Treyster, sick, Maria Barbara Spies, Hans Jacob Spies, Maria Elisabetha Spies]

EUROPEAN RECORDS

Ober Lustadt Reformed KB:
A Johan Leonhard Tröster and wife Maria Dorothea appear in the 1720s in the Ober Lustadt records. Joh. Leonhard Tröster d. 9 Aug. 1726, age 36 y.

Ulrich Spiess and Maria Dorothea had children:
      1. Anna Barbara, b. 30 Apr. 1729, bp. 1 May 1729
      2. Joh. Jacob, b. 1 Aug. 1731, bp. 18 Aug. 1731
      3. Anna Elisabetha, b. 28 Mar. 1733, bp. 29 Mar. 1733

AMERICAN RECORDS

Montgomery, *History of Berks County*, pg. 10 Bethel Twp. tax list:
Ulrich Spice, Frederick Trester and Martin Trester all appear in 1754.

Friederick Troester and wife of Tulpehocken had children:
    Maria Dorothea, b. 24 June 1746, bp. 6 July 1746
    Sp.: Ulrich Spiess and Maria Dorothea

Berks County Abstracts of Wills and Adm.:
Ulrich Spiess of Bethel Twp. on 12 Mar. 1761, adm. was granted to Jacob
Spiess, only son.

Host Reformed KB, Berks Co., PA:
J. Trösser had a daughter:
    Anna Elisabetha, bp. 4 Dec. 1748; Sp.: A. E. Spiess.

M. Trösser had a daughter:
    Anne Margareth, bp. 16 Dec. 1748; Sp.: Elis. Kantner.

STAUTER, HEINRICH   67361 Freispach
before 1752; not in S-H

EUROPEAN RECORDS

Gommersheim Lutheran KB:
Georg Jacob Stauter, son of Georg Stauter m. 10 Feb. 1722 at Freÿschpach,
Anna Barbara, daughter of the late Georg Weiss. They had:
    1. Maria Magdalena, bp. 4 Mar. 1727
    2. Anna Margreth, b. 5 Nov. 1729
    3. **Gallus Henrich,** b. 5 Jan. 1733
        Sp.: Gallus Henrich from [67366] Weingarten
        and Anna Maria, daughter of Joh. Adam Fahr

AMERICAN RECORDS

Trinity Lutheran KB, Lancaster:
Heinrich Stauter from Freyspach near Speyer, m. 16 Sept. 1760 Barbara
Hornung from [74193] Schwaigern.

Heinrich Stauder on communicants list, 2nd Sunday after Trinity 1752.

Heinrich Stauter and Barbara had children:
1. Eva Maria, b. 19 June 1761, bp. 21 June 1761
   Sp.: Martin Berntheusel and Eva Maria his wife
2. Johann Heinrich, b. 16 Jan. 1763, bp. 23 Jan. 1763
   Sp.: Benedict Garbel and wife Rosina
3. Heinrich Benedict, b. 21 June 1765, bp. 30 June 1765
   Sp.: Benedict Garbel and Rosina
4. Elisabeth Barbara, b. 15 Sept. 1769, bp. 8 Oct. 1769
   Sp.: Georg Beigel and wife Barbara

Married 20 Apr. 1782 by means of license, Jonas Metzger, widower, and Eva Stauder, single.

Trinity Lutheran KB, Lancaster, Burials:
16 Feb. 1780, buried in the afternoon, Gallus Henrich Stauder who died of a hemorrhage, aged 57 years, 1 month, 10 days.
(Note error in subtraction - he was in fact 47 years old at death.)

STEINEL, CHRISTOPH   67454 Hassloch
Alexander & Anne, 1730
S-H, I: 35, 36
   [appears on A list as Christian Princeland,
   on B list as Christof Steinlein?]

EUROPEAN RECORDS

Hassloch Lutheran KB:
Christophel Steinel of Hassloch m. 8 Jan. 1726 Anna Catharina Ziegler "is going in 1730 to the N[ew] Land."

AMERICAN RECORDS

Muddy Creek Reformed KB, Lancaster Co., PA:
Christopher Steinel and wife Anna Catharine sponsor three children:
   Anna Catharina Schlappach, b. 1743, daughter of Henry Schlappach;
   Maria Catharina Kern, b. 1743, daughter of Abraham Kern; and
   Joh. Christopher Kauffman, b. 1744, son of Justus Kauffman
   [Augustus [q.v.] Kauffman also from Hassloch].

STEMPEL, HANS JACOB, age 40   67157 Wachenheim a. d. Weinstrasse
STEMPEL, NICHOLAS, age 70   67125 Dannstadt
Mary, 1732
S-H, I: 93, 94, 95

EUROPEAN RECORDS

Wachenheim Reformed KB:
Joh. Jacob Stempel, son of Nickel Stempel, m. 15 Jan. 1715 Maria Elisabetha daughter of the late Henrich Schneider. They had:
1. Joh. Leonhard, b. 21 June 1716
2. Maria Appollonia, b. 7 Apr. 1719

New Communicants: 1703 Joh. Jacob Stempel.

Dannstadt Reformed KB:
Herr Joh. Nicolaus Stemple, Reformed schoolmaster, and wife Susanna had one child baptized here:
Johann Gottfrid, bp 1 Sept. 1723

AMERICAN RECORDS

St. Paul's (Klopps) Reformed KB, Bethel Twp., Lebanon Co., PA:
Gottfried Stembel and wife Anna Margaret had:
Anna Barbara, b. Feb. 1755
Sp.: John Heffler and Anna Barbara

Swatara Reformed KB, Lebanon Co., PA:
John Gottfried Stempfel and Margaret had:
Christine Margaret, b. 16 Aug. 1753
Sp.: Conrad Raumer and Christine Margaret Stempfel

Rev. John Casper Stoever's Records:
Married 22 May 1744, John Friederich Zeh and Maria Ottilia Stempel, Swatara.

Gottfried Stemple's wife was Margaret nee Speck and they later resided in Aurora, Monongalia Co., VA (now Preston Co., W. VA.)
Gottfried Stemple died there in 1798.

STETTLER, VALENTIN   Ober Lustadt=
Britannia, 1764   67363 Lustadt
S-H, I: 693

EUROPEAN RECORDS

Ober Lustadt Reformed KB:
Georg Stettler and wife Maria Chatarina had a son:
    Geo. Valentin, b. 3 Sept. 1740; bp. 4 Sept. 1740
    Sp.: Geo. Valentin Becker and wife Anna Margarethe

It is possible that the father also emigrated; a Georg (X) Stadler appears on the *Polly* in 1765 with others from Ober Lustadt. (S-H, I: 704).

AMERICAN RECORDS

Seven passengers from Oberlustadt are listed together on the passenger list of the ship *Britannia* in 1764: Johann Bernhart Ott, Johann Andreas Schmitt, Christian Haushalter, Georg Heinrich Schmitt; further on the list are Johann Martin Ott, Carl Garaus (see Jahraus), **Vallentin Stettler.**

STORCK, ANNA MARGARETHA   67126 Assenheim
_____, 1748

EUROPEAN RECORDS

Assenheim Lutheran KB:
Johann Christoph Storck and wife Anna Barbara had a daughter:
    Anna Margaretha, b. 29 Sept. 1719
    Sp.: Joh. Anthon Kohl and Anna Margaretha.
Notation in KB: (by Anna Margaretha Storck's name) *1748 nach PA gezogen.*

STRIGEL, CHRISTOPH   Ober Lustadt=
Polly, 1765   67363 Lustadt
S-H, I: 704

EUROPEAN RECORDS

Ober Lustadt Reformed KB:
Jörg Striegler and Maria Margaretha had children:
    1. Christina, b. 13 Dec. 1742
    2. Maria Ursula, b. 12 Sept. 1744

3. Jörg **Christoph**, b. 22 Oct. 1747; bp. 28 Oct. 1747
   Sp.: Christoph Lintz and Margaretha. Father deceased.

Died 17 Oct. 1747, age 37 years, Jörg Striegel.

AMERICAN RECORDS

Fourteen passengers on the ship *Polly* in 1765, listed in close proximity to one another on the list (S-H, I: 704), all appear in the Oberlustadt records: Andreas Heintz, Christian Wunder, Conrad Hauenstein, Georg Jacob Hauenstein, **Christoph Strigel**, Johann Leon[d] Devil (Deubel), Andres Ehresmann, Peter Zeiler, Georg Aadam Bresler, Johan Michael Dühmer, Jacob Wunder, Jacob Faut, Georg Simon Haushalter, Geo. Adam Teis.

STÜBLER, JOHANNES   Lachen-Speyerdorf=
STÜBLER, JOH. ADAM   67435 Neustadt a. d. Weinstrasse
Dragon, 1749
S-H, I: 423 [surname appears on list as Stiebler]

EUROPEAN RECORDS

Lachen-Speyerdorf Reformed KB:
Conf. 1743: J. Adam Stübler, son of Johannes Stübler, Lutheran.
Age 14 years, 6 months.

Hassloch Lutheran KB:
Johannes Stiebler (Stübler- also given as Johann Georg Stiebler) and wife Gertrud had children:
   1. Hans Adam, b. 26 Oct. 1727, bp. at Böhl [67459 Böhl]
   2. **Hanss Adam**, b. 6 Nov. 1728, bp. at Böhl
   3. Anna Margretha, b. 17 Dec. 1730 at Böhl

Emigration record:
Werner Hacker, *Auswanderungen aus Rheinpfalz und Saarland im 18. Jahrhundert:* # 14741 Stübler, Jacob(!), Lachen. Manumitted to PA. Record dated 18 Mar. 1749.

STURM, JOHANN JACOB   67105 Schifferstadt
Mortonhouse, 1728
S-H, I: 18, 19

EUROPEAN RECORDS

Schifferstadt-Iggelheim Reformed KB:
Christian Sturm, widower, m. 10 May 1695 Anna Barbara Gah from
Planckstatt [68723 Plankstadt]. They had children:
1. Maria Barbara, b. 31 Jan. 1696
2. Veronica, b. 29 June 1698
3. **Johann Jacob,** b. 13 Jan. 1701; conf. 1714
4. Maria Barbara, b. 31 Dec. 1702; she m. Joh. Jacob Brunner, q.v.
5. Johann Peter, b. 27 May 1705
6. Anna Elisabetha, b. 10 Jan. 1708
7. Johann Wendel, b. 28 Mar. 1709
8. Maria Catharina (Margareta or Elisabetha), b. 25 May 1711
9. Maria Catharina, b. 30 Sept. 1714
10. Maria Helena, b. 20 Mar. 1718, died 1722
11. Johannes, b. 26 Jan. 1723

Johann Jacob Sturm, son of Christian Sturm, m. Anna Benedictina Saur.
They had children:
1. Susanna, b. 21 Apr. 1726
2. Johann Wendel, b. 27 Nov. 1727

AMERICAN RECORDS

First Reformed KB, Lancaster Co., PA.:
Jacob and Annabina Diktina Storm had children:
3. Christina, bp. 29 June 1739
4. John Peter, b. 19 Nov. 1740; bp. 18 May 1741
   Sp.: John Peter Attich and wife Christina Attich.

Frederick Reformed KB, Frederick, MD.:
Jacob Storm and Maria Benedicta had children:
5. Maria Catharina, b. 6 Sept. 1748
   Sp.: Catharina Brunner
6. Charlotta, bp. 11 Aug. 1751
7. Anna Maria, b. 12 Feb. 1753

Frederick County Wills, A1: 105:
Jacob Storm, dated 27 Dec. 1756, probated early 1757. Children mentioned
in estate records: Vandel (Wendel), Jacob Jr., John, Peter, daughters
Susanna wife of [Martin] Cuntz, Anna Maria wife of Peter Brunner, Anna
Elisabeth wife of Adam Kyle, Maria Barbara wife of Jacob Turner, Christina,
Mary, Catharina, Charlotta and a second Anna Maria. Exrs: Stephen
Ransberger and John Bruner. Wit: Frederick Becker, Samuel Becker, and
Peter Tofeler.

THEISS, GEORG ADAM Ober Lustadt=
[Teis on ship list] 67363 Lustadt
Polly, 1765
S-H, I: 704

EUROPEAN RECORDS

Ober Lustadt Reformed KB:
Jörg Adam Theiss and wife Anna Margretha had children:
1. Jörg Simon, b 1 May 1763, bp 4 May 1763
   Sp.: Jörg Simon Deubel, single, and
   Maria Barb. Weppler, a widow; he d. 22 June 1763
2. Anna Margaretha, b. 7 Nov. 1764, bp. 8 Nov. 1764
   Sp.: Johannes Hamerschmidt and Anna Margretha.

He might be either:
Georg Adam, son of Joh. Georg Theis and Anna Christina (bp. 23 Aug. 1733), or Georg Adam, son of Andreas Theiss and Magdalena, (b. 9 Feb. 1739).

AMERICAN RECORDS

Fritz Braun and Friedrich Krebs. "Pennsylvania Dutch Pioneers from South Palatine Parishes", *The Pennsylvania Dutchman*, 8 (Spring, 1957):
TEIS, GEORG ADAM - arrived at Philadelphia with Georg Simon Haushalter [q.v.] on the ship *Polly,* 24 Aug. 1765, and his name is given in the ship's list immediately after Haushalter's. Perhaps he is identical with Jörg Adam Theiss, born at Ober or Niederlustadt, 9 Feb. 1739, son of Andreas Theiss and wife Magdalena.

THEISS, JOH. HENRICH Ober Lustadt=
Lydia, 1749 67363 Lustadt
S-H, I: 425

EUROPEAN RECORDS

Ober Lustadt Reformed KB:
Andreas Theiss and wife Maria Magdalena had a son:
Heinrich, b. 10 June 1731; bp. 10 June 1731
Sp.: Henrich Theiss

THOMAS, MICHAEL   67105 Schifferstadt
Thistle of Glasgow, 1730
S-H, I: 31, 33

EUROPEAN RECORDS

Iggelheim-Schifferstadt Reformed KB:
Michael Thomas, son of the late Christian Thomas, m. 10 Jan. 1713
Veronica, daughter of Peter Lang. They had children:
1. Christian, b. 1 Jan. 1714
2. Philip Heinrich, b. 12 Sept. 1715
3. Maria Catharina, b. 2 Feb. 1718
4. Hans Michel, b. 3 Oct. 1719
5. Gabriel, b. 9 June 1721
6. Johannes, b. 10 Mar. 1723
7. Joh. Valentin, b. 28 Sept. 1724
8. Anna Catharina, b. 29 May 1725
9. Johann Christoff, b. 20 June 1728
10. Johannes,twin b. 20 June 1728
11. Christoph, twin b. 2 Oct. 1729

Emigration record:
Werner Hacker, *Auswanderungen aus dem Früheren Hochstift Speyer nach
Südosteuropa und Übersee im XVIII Jahrhundert*, Heimatstelle Pfalz, 1969:
Michael Thomas, Klein-Schifferstadt, with wife and seven children, to PA.
Property valued at 555 florins, 1 July 1729.

AMERICAN RECORDS

Reformed Church Records, Frederick, MD.:
Gabriel Thomas and wife Anna Margaretha had children:
1. Catharina, b. 22 July 1747
   Sp.: Heinrich Sinn and wife
2. Barbara, bp. 7 May 1749
   Sp.: Christian Götzendanner and Anna Barbara
3. Gabriel, b. 8 Mar. 1753
   Sp.: Andreas Paullus and Anna Maria
4. Elisabeth, b. 22 Mar. 1755
   Sp.: Philip Henry Thomas and Catharina
5. Johannes, bp. 25 Sept. 1757
   Sp.: Valentin Thomas and Margaret

Michael Thomas and wife Barbara had children:
1. Jacob, b. 1748
   Sp.: Jacob Götzdanner

2. Michael, bp. 7 May 1749
   Sp.: Gabriel Thomas

Christian Thomas and wife Magdalena had children:
1. Anna Maria, bp. 11 Aug. 1751
   Sp.: Johannes Brunner and Anna Maria
2. Anna Barbara, b. 6 Jan. 1753
   Sp.: Michael Thomas and Catharina Barbara

Valentin Thomas and wife Margaretha had children:
1. Gabriel, bp. 24 Sept. 1752
   Sp.: Gabriel Thomas and Margaretha
2. Valentin, bp. 8 Apr.1757

Johann Thomas and wife Catharina had a daughter:
Anna Maria, b. 7 Mar. 1755
Sp.: Anna Maria Götzdanner

Philip Heinrich Thomas and wife Catharina had a son:
Johan Heinrich, bp. 25 Sept. 1757
Sp.: Gabriel Thomas and Margaret

Christoffel Thomas and wife Susanna Margaret had:
Susanna Margaret, bp. 29 Apr. 1759
Sp.: Catharina Thomas

TRANSU, ABRAHAM   67112 Mutterstadt
Thistle of Glasgow, 1730
S-H, I: 31, 33, 34

EUROPEAN RECORDS

Mutterstadt Reformed KB:
Abraham Dransol m. (1) 4 Feb. 1721 Elisabeth Muschler. They had children
(surname also appears as Trentsols):
1. Anna Katharina, bp. 15 Mar. 1722
   Sp.: Joh. Georg Schuler and Anna Catharina
2. Johann Philip, bp. 1 Nov. 1723
   Sp.: Joh. Philip Neumann and Maria Barbara Muschler,
   both single.
3. Anthon, bp. 22 Dec. 1726; d. in Mutterstadt

Abraham Dransu, widower, m. (2) 22 July 1727 Anna Margaretha Müller from Obersiltzheim (=67271 Obersülzen). They had a son:
  4. Isaac, b. 31 July 1729, bp. 5 Aug. 1729
      Sp.: Isaac DeFrene and Judith nee Weinacht

See also Fritz Braun, "Auswanderer aus der Umgebung von Ludwigshafen a. Rh. auf dem Schiff *Thistle of Glasgow* 1730," publication #8, *Schriften zur Wanderungsgeschichte der Pfälzer,* 1959.

AMERICAN RECORDS

New Goshenhoppen Reformed KB, Montgomery Co., PA:
Abraham Transou [also Trandsu, Transo] and wife had children:
  5. Joh. Abraham bp. 25 June 1731
      Sp.: Michael Schell
  6. Joh. Jacob bp. 28 July 1734
      Sp.: Jacob Keller and wife Anna Maria
  7. Elisabetha bp. 20 June 1736
      Sp.: Elisabeth Schunck

Philadelphia County Administration Book D, page 140:
Estate # 119, Letters of Adm. to Henry Calman and Jacob Weisler, widow Margaret Transon having renounced, adms. of Abraham Transon, late of the County of Phila., yeoman, 14 Nov. 1740.

Emmaus Moravian Church records:
Anna Catharina Knaus nee Transeau died 26 June 1799; b. 6 Mar. 1722, daughter of Abraham Transeau and wife Elisabeth *Münster.* She m. 1741 Sebastian Henry Knaus and had 11 children, 91 grandchildren, and 36 great grandchildren, of whom 73 grandchildren and 32 great grandchildren were living when she died.

Northampton County Wills:
Abraham Transue witnessed the will of Valentin Reimer in 1793.

Philip Transu, bp. 1 Nov. 1723, moved to Bethania, North Carolina, to the Moravian colony there. Additional records of this family can be found in *Records of the Moravians in North Carolina,* published by the North Carolina Historical Commission.

TREIBELBISS, JACOB   67454 Hassloch
Mary, 1732
S-H, I: 93-95
EUROPEAN RECORDS

Hassloch Reformed KB:
Jacob Treibelbiss, a carpenter from Switzerland, m. 2 Feb. 1706 Anna
Margareta, daughter of Henrich Bruchbacher. Their son:
>   Johan Jacob, bp. 10 Apr. 1709

Hassloch Beiträge:
Jacob Dreÿbelbiss from Veltheim, *Berner Gebieths,* Switzerland [possibly CH-
5106 Veltheim, AG] was granted citizenship rights in 1721.

AMERICAN RECORDS

Jacob Triebelbis (Dreibelbiss) resided in Berks County, in Richmond Twp.
He took out warrants on several tracts of land.

Christ Lutheran Church, Dryville, Rockland Twp., Berks County:
Jacob Treipelpies and his wife Barbara nee Burkhart had two children bp.
The names of the children are not given in the baptismal records; the
baptisms occurred in 1751 and 1756. There are several later records in this
church for members of this family.

Berks County Abstracts of Wills:
Jacob Treibelbis of Richmond Twp. 5 Feb. 1761 - 23 Feb. 1761.
Children: Abraham, Martin, Jacob, Mary Elisabeth, Mary Magdalene,
Catharine, Philebena. Sons are given tracts of land; each daughter is to
receive £150. Remainder equally divided. Exrs: son Abraham and friend
George Markly. Wit.: Balser Schwenck and Nicholas Bunn.

Jacob Triebelbis was nat. in Philadelphia 24 Sept. 1760.

TRÖSTER, HANS MARTIN   Ober Lustadt=
TRÖSTER, FREDERICH   67363 Lustadt
St. Andrew, 1734
S-H, I: 137, 139
> [Treyster on A list; Martin is listed with males over 16 and was sick;
> Fredrick Treyster is listed with Maria Dorothea Spies and three Spies
> children]

EUROPEAN RECORDS

Ober Lustadt Reformed KB:
A Johan Leonhard Tröster and wife Maria Dorothea appear in the 1720s in the Ober Lustadt records. Joh. Leonhard Tröster d. 9 Aug. 1726, age 36 y. (There are no early marriages recorded in the existing Ober Lustadt records; however, it appears that Tröster's widow married (2) Ulrich Spiess.)

Ulrich Spiess and Maria Dorothea had children:
1. Anna Barbara, b. 30 Apr. 1729, bp. 1 May 1729
2. Joh. Jacob, b. 1 Aug. 1731, bp. 18 Aug. 1731
3. Anna Elisabetha, b. 28 Mar. 1733, bp. 29 Mar. 1733

AMERICAN RECORDS

Rev. John Casper Stoever's Records:
Friedcrick Troester and wife of Tulpehocken had children:
  Maria Dorothea, b. 24 June 1746, bp. 6 July 1746
  Sp.: Ulrich Spiess and Maria Dorothea

Montgomery, *History of Berks Co.*, pg. 10, Bethel Twp. tax list:
Ulrich Spice, Frederick Trester and Martin Trester all appear in 1754.

Berks County Abstracts of Wills and Adm.:
Ulrich Spiess of Bethel Twp. on 12 Mar. 1761, adm. was granted to Jacob Spiess, only son.

Host Reformed KB, Berks Co., PA:
J[?F]. Trösser had a daughter:
  Anna Elisabetha, bp. 4 Dec. 1748; Sp.: A. E. Spiess.

M. Trösser had a daughter:
  Anne Margareth, bp. 16 Dec. 1748; Sp.: Elis. Kantner.

Christ "Little Tulpehocken" KB, Berks Co., PA:
Joh. Martin Tröster had children:
1. Joh. Martin, b. 20 Mar. 1743 [sic]; bp. 17 Mar. 1743
   Sp.: Ulrich Spies [q.v.] and his wife
2. Joh. Michael , b. 18 Nov. 1746, bp. 21 Dec. 1746
   Sp.: Joh. Michael Axer and his fiancee
3. Georg, bp. 11 Aug. 1751 at Blue Moutain Ref. KB, Berks Co.
   Georg Dollinger and wife
4. Anna Elisabetha, b. 18 June 1753, bp. 1 July 1753 by Pastor John Caspar Stoever; Sp.: Nicolaus Haeffner and wife.

Altalaha Lutheran KB, Rehrersburg, Berks Co., PA:
Martin Tröster had:
     5. Johan Wilhelm, b. 21 ___ 1758
       Sp.: Wilhelm Stein and Margaretha Gebhard
     6. Johannes, b. 3 Jan. 1760

Friederich Troester had:
     1. Maria Dorothea, b. 24 June 1746, bp. 6 July 1746
       Sp.: Ulrich Spiess and Maria Dorothea
     2. Johannes, bp. 24 Apr. 1753
       Sp.: Johannes Mayer and wife

Rev. John Casper Stoever's Records:
Frederich Troester (Swatara) had:
     John Heinrich, b. 2 Nov. 1747, bp. 22 Nov. 1747
       Sp.: John Heinrich Roetelstein and wife.
     John Jacob, b. 3 Feb. 1751, bp. 13 Mar. 1751
       Sp.: John Jacob Spiess and Elisab. Catarina Simon

Berks County Orphans Court Records:
Dated 6 Mar. 1763: Petition of Maria Dorothea Triester, daughter of Frederick Triester of Bethel, Yeoman, deceased. That she is between 14 and 20 years; asks court to appoint William Keiser her guardian; so appointed.

Petition of Margareta Triester, widow and Adm. of Frederick Triester, late of Bethel Twp., Yeoman, deceased. Has rendered an account of adm.; charges herself with £116, 13 sh. 1 pence; asks for allowance and distribution. Said deceased left children: George Frederick, aged 4; Maria Dorothea, aged 16; Jacob and John, both deceased under age. So directed.

TRÜB, JACOB   Lachen-Speyerdorf=
Sandwich, 1750   67435 Neustadt an der Weinstrasse
S-H, I: 449 [surname appears on list as Traub]

EUROPEAN RECORDS

Lachen-Speyerdorf Reformed KB:
Hans David Drüb (also appears as Trüb), son of the late Jacob Drüb, m. 24 Jan. 1708 Catharina Elisabetha, daughter of the late Jacob Hamman. Among their children were:
     Johann **Jacob** b. 24 Feb. 1719, bp. 1 Mar. 1719
       Sp.: Johan Jacob Meyss, son of Michel Meyss

Anna Barbara b. 20 May 1721, bp. 25 May 1721
Sp.: Anna Barbara, daughter of Görg Schmitt

Emigration record:
Friedrich Krebs, "Pennsylvania Dutch Pioneers" in *The Pennsylvania Dutchman* (1954-1956): from Lachen (Kreis Neustadt):
Jacob Trueb, son of David Trueb of Lachen and his wife Catharina Elisabetha Hammann, "residing in Pennsylvania" (document dated 29 Sept. 1772). Anna Barbara Trueb, sister of Jacob "likewise residing in PA" (Document dated 29 Sept. 1772).

UHLAND, MATHIAS   67125 Dannstadt
Allen, 1729
S-H, I: 27, 30
[Passengers on ship: Mathias Ulland, Johannes (under 15), Catharina].

EUROPEAN RECORDS

Dannstadt Reformed KB:
Mathias Uhlandt m. 4 Jan. 1714 Catharina (maiden name not given). They had children:
1. Johannes, bp. 4 Nov. 1716;
   Conf. Easter 1729, son of Mathes Uland
2. Maria Elisabetha, bp. 29 Aug. 1719
3. Johann Nicolaus, bp. 22 Oct. 1723
4. Joh. Adam, bp. 23 Jan. 1726

AMERICAN RECORDS

PA, Third Series, Lancaster County Land Warrants:
Matthias Uland, land warrant for 150A in Lancaster Co., PA dated 17 Feb. 1734.

Lancaster County Probate Records:
Mathias Uland d. intestate in Lancaster Co. in 1751.

Adam Uhland d. intestate in Lancaster Co. in 1752. His minor children are listed in Lancaster Orphans' Court Records, dated 5 Mar. 1754: Georg Michael Ulland, Joh. George Ulland, Catharina Ulland.

Swatara Reformed Church Records, Lebanon Co., PA:
Nicolaus Ullant and wife Juliana had the following child:
>   1. John Jacob, bp. 25 Dec. 1749
>   Sp.: Jacob Schober and wife Dorothy

Rev. John Casper Stoever's Records:
Johannes Ulandt m. 23 Apr. 1739 Elisabeth Lintner.

UHRIG, (URICH), JOHANNES, age 20   67259 Kleinniedesheim
Samuel, 1732
S-H, I: 59
> (appears as Ulerich on A List; signed Uhrig.
> Ages are incorrect on this ship list.)

EUROPEAN RECORDS

Gross- and Kleinniedesheim Lutheran KB:
Johannes Urich from Northeim [= 97647 Nordheim v. d. Rhön],
Bischoffsheim, m. 15 Feb. 1729 Maria Catharina Brüch. They had a
daughter:
>   1. Maria Magdalena, bp. 25 July 1730
>   Sp.: Bastian Heilman and Maria Magdalena

Emigration record:
Werner Hacker, *Auswanderungen aus Rheinpfalz und Saarland*:
#15325 Uhrig, Valentin and Johann, Kleinniedesheim, residing in
Pennvylania, 1748.

AMERICAN RECORDS

Rev. John Casper Stoever's Records:
Johannes Uhrich [Ulrich in Muddy Creek translation] m. 13 Sept. 1737
Margaretha BrennEisen, surviving widow of Valentin BrennEisen.

Lancaster County Will Abstracts:
Urich, John, Earl Twp. February 7, 1758. February 22, 1758.
Wife. (name omitted) Stepchildren: Conrad and Valentine Breneisen.
Exrs. Henry Swer and Valentine Opp.

UHRIG (URICH) VALENTIN   67259 Kleinniedesheim
Mary, 1742
S-H, I: 322
  signed Valentinus Ury

EUROPEAN RECORDS

Gross- and Kleinniedesheim Lutheran KB:
George Uhrich and wife Anna Catharina nee Gref had children:
  1. Johannes, b. __ Oct. 1710, to PA 1732 [q.v.]
  2. Valentin, to PA 1742
  3. Otillia, b. 1720 m. Johann Adam Schenk

Emigration record:
Werner Hacker, *Auswanderungen aus Rheinpfalz und Saarland*:
#15325 Uhrig, Valentin and Johann, Kleinniedesheim, residing in Pennsylvania, 1748.

AMERICAN RECORDS

Christ Lutheran KB, Stouchsburg, Berks Co., PA:
Valentin Urich and wife Maria Agat. nee Volzin had:
      Maria Elisabeth, b. 10 Oct. 1745, bp. 17 Nov. 1745 at home
      Sp.: Anna Elizabetha Lehmann

Conf. 1752: Joh. Matthias Urich, aged 18 years, son of Velte Uhrich.

Conf. 1759: Christian Uhrig, aged 17 years.

ULLRICH, PAUL   67112 Mutterstadt
Edinburgh, 1748
S-H, I: 372

EUROPEAN RECORDS

Mutterstadt Reformed KB:
Georg Ullrich and wife Anna Maria had a son:
      Paul, bp. 7 Jan. 1714
      Sp.: Paul Heypel (q.v., Heipel) and Anna

Paul Ulrich, son of the late Georg Ulrich, m. (1) 22 Feb. 1735 Anna Margaretha Spitznagel, Lutheran, daughter of the late Wilhelm Spitznagel from Effolderbach, Darmstadt region (Effolderbach = 63683 Ortenberg, Hess.).

Paul Ulrich, widower, m. (2) 4 Aug. 1739 at [67125] Dannstadt, Maria Catharina, daughter of the late Adam Christina of Dannstadt.

Paul Ullrich, widower, m. (3) 30 Oct. 1747 Susanna Buchholtz, widow.

No children of any of these marriages recorded in Reformed KB.

Hochstadt is noted for its fine wines.

ULRICH, GEORG JACOB
Queen of Denmark, 1751
S-H, I: 472

Oberhochstadt=
76879 Hochstadt, Pfalz

EUROPEAN RECORDS

Oberhochstadt Reformed KB:
Confirmed Easter, 1742: Georg Jacob Ulrich

Emigration record:
Werner Hacker, *Auswanderungen aus Rheinpfalz und Saarland*:
#15285 Jakob Ulrich, citizen at Oberhochstadt, manumitted in 1751.

AMERICAN RECORDS

Host Reformed KB, Tulpehocken, Berks Co., PA:
Georg Jacob Ulrich m. 16 Oct. 1753 Maria Elisabeth Wolff. [She was bp. 3 Oct. 1728 at Oberhochstadt, daughter of Jacob Wolff [q.v.]

Berks County Will Abstracts:
George Jacob Ulrich, Pinegrove. 2 Oct. 1786 - 30 Jan. 1787.
To son Valentine my whole estate with 250 A of land, paying £ 270 to each sister and to his mother Margreta Ulrich, £ 60. The daughters mentioned are Eva Barbara, Anna Maria, Catharina, Margreth Ulrich, Elisabeth Meyer, Eve Ulrich, Susanna Ulrich, and Christina. Also mentioned are Peter Bressler, John Bressler, and John Adam Brown who may have been sons-in-law. Exr: son Valentine. Wits.: Egidius Moyer and Christian Webber.

UNGEFEHR, HANS MARTIN   67245 Lambsheim
The Globe, 1723
[He signed charter agreement for this ship]

EUROPEAN RECORDS

Lambsheim Reformed KB:
Joh. Friedrich Ungefehr m. 8 Jan. 1678 at [67161] Gönnheim, Maria Magdalena, daughter of Hans Böhler of Genheim [67161 Gönnheim]. They had children:
    1. Friedrich, m. before 1720 Ursula ____.
    2. **Martin,** b. ca 1693, m. Juliana ____.
    3. Apollonia A. Ursula, single in 1720.
    4. Anna Juliana, single in 1720.
    5. Joh. Georg, b. 20 Sept. 1696; m. Apollonia ____.

The son, Martin Ungefehr, is mentioned in the Lambsheim records as a citizen 10 Nov. 1721. In 1722 his age is given as 29 years. He married before 1 June 1719 Juliana (maiden name not given). On 7 Apr. 1723, they sold their house. (*Kaufprotokoll der Gemeinde Lambsheim.*)

AMERICAN RECORDS

Augustus Lutheran KB, Trappe, Montgomery Co., PA:
Anna Juliana Ungefehrin was a bp. sponsor in 1733 for Anna Juliana Elisabeth, daughter of Johannes Morgenstern.

Rev. Jacob Lischy's personal records, York Co., PA:
Görg Ungefehr and wife Anna Margreth were sp. for a child of Joh. Niclaus Hoog in 1759. They were sp. in 1762 for a daughter of Joh. Adam Forney, and in 1763 they sp. a child of Johannes Sauer.

Görg Ungefehr and wife Margreth had a daughter:
        Anna Margretha, bp. 13 May 1764
        Sp.: Joh. Görg Carle and Anna Maria Saur(in).

Connected Survey Map, Digges Choice, York Co.:
George Unkefehr, tract # 25; George Ugafar, tract # 49.

UNRUH, GEORG age 30   Niederhochstadt=
Adventure, 1732   67879 Hochstadt, Pfalz
S-H, I: 84, 85, 86, 87
    Anna Barbara (Hannah Boble) Unruh, age 26 on ship's list

EUROPEAN RECORDS

Niederhochstadt Reformed KB:
The Niederhochstadt records start in 1709 and therefore not early enough to contain the baptisms of these emigrants. One Georg Unruh with a wife Anna Barbara appears in the Niederhochstadt records and had four children baptized there, from 1717 to 1734. However, this couple emigrated in 1732, and have no children mentioned in the ship's list; therefore, it appears that there were two men named Georg Unruh in Niederhochstadt. No Georg Unruh appears in the marriage records.

AMERICAN RECORDS

Philadelphia Wills, Book H: 493:
Will of Georg Unruh, dated 4 Jan. 1748; probated 8 Mar. 1747/48: My
brother Valentine Unruh and brother-in-law Jacob Wilhelm "shall be
Curators over all my goods." Wife Anna Barbara to have £ 50. Sister Anna
Catrina Wilhelm.   To Frederick Rutes (?) £ 10 (does not mention any
relationship). Brother Johannes Unruh to have £ 100 if he comes to live in
this country. If he does not come to live here, because he has no child, he
shall have an English crown. Valentine Unruh and Anna Catrina Wilhelm
to have what is left. Witnessed by Johannes Heberling and John Trautman,
who appeared 8 Mar. 1747/48 at Tulpehocken in Lancaster County.
("German will freely translated by Conrad Weiser.")

Christ Lutheran Church Records, Stouchsburg (Tulpehocken), Berks Co.:
Married 31 May 1748, Velte Herchelroth, widower, and Barbara Unruh,
widow of the late George Unruh.

George Unrook, Lancaster County, nat. by Act, 1739.

UNRUH, JOHANNES   Ober Lustadt=
Brothers, 1752   67363 Lustadt
S-H, I: 481
                         EUROPEAN RECORDS

Ober Lustadt Reformed KB:
Johannes Unruh and wife Maria Catharina had children:
  1. Johannes, b. 28 Oct. 1728
  2. Anna Catharina, b. 21 Oct. 1730
  3. Joh. Georg, b. 19 May 1732
  4. Maria Barbara, b. 22 Jan. 1734
  5. Joh. Andreas, b. 1 Mar. 1736

Johannes Unruh and wife Anna Apollonia had children:
  1. Nicolaus, b. 1 Sept. 1738
  2. Jörg Sebastian, b. 10 Nov. 1739
  3. A daughter, b. __ ___ 1742
  4. A daughter, b. __ ___ 1744

                         AMERICAN RECORDS

St. Michael's Evangelical Lutheran KB, Germantown, PA.;
Buried 11 Nov. 1776 Apollonia, wife of Johannes Unruh, age 75 years, 11
months, 28 days.

Germantown Reformed Church, Philadelphia Co., PA.:
George Sebastian Unruh m. 17 June 1764 Catharina Simon, Gresham Twp.
Georg Sebastian Unruh and wife Catharina had:
1. Apollonia, b. 3 Nov. 1762, bp. 12 Dec. 1762
   Sp.: John Unruh and wife Apollonia, grandparents
2. John, b. 11 Oct. 1765, bp. 20 Oct. 1765
   Sp.: John Unruh and wife Apollonia
3. Elizabeth, b. 7 Oct. 1768, bp. 24 Apr. 1769
4. Philip, b. 18 Oct. 1769, bp. 22 Apr. 1770
5. N.N., b. 13 Jan. 1773, bp. 12 Apr. 1773
   Sp.: George Kornman and Elisabetha Simon
6. Sebastian, b. 9 June 1775, bp. 8 Sept. 1776
7. William, b. 25 Apr. 1785, bp. 18 Sept. 1785
8. A child, b. 19 June 1788, bp. 29 Apr. 1789

Georg Nicholas Unruh and Catharina had:
1. Nicholas, b. 29 June 1770, bp. 25 Dec. 1770
2. Magdalena, b. 7 Aug. 1774, bp. 30 Apr. 1774

Died __ Aug. 1807 Geo. Nicholas Unruh, age 69 y. 11 m., 30 d.
Died 1813, Geo. Sebastian Unruh, age 74 y.
Died 16 July 1818 Catharine Unruh, wife of Sebastian Unruh, age 72 y. 10 mo. 2 days.

First Reformed KB, Lancaster, PA:
John Unruh m. 12 May 1761 Engel Lay.

UNRUH, VALENTIN   Niederhochstadt=
UNRUH, MARIA CATHARINA   76879 Hochstadt, Pfalz
St. Andrew, 1734
S-H, I: 137, 139, 141, 142
  [surname spelled Humief on A List; he signed Unruch]

EUROPEAN RECORDS

Niederhochstadt Reformed KB:
Hans Adam Unruh and wife Maria Catharina had a son:
        Johann Veltin bp. 17 Aug. 1710
        Sp.: Hans Veltin Wolff and Anna Christina

Joh. Valentin Unruh conf. 1723

AMERICAN RECORDS

Christ "Little Tulpehocken" Church, Berks Co., PA:
Valentin Unruh and wife had a child:
      Maria Catharina b. 28 Jan. 1743; bp. 20 Feb. 1743
      Sp.: Jacob Wilhelm and wife [q.v.]

Host Reformed KB, Tulpehocken, Berks Co., PA:
Anna Elisabeth Unruh, daughter of Valentine Unruh, conf. 1765. Valentin
Unruh and wife Maria Catharina sponsored several children at Host Church.

Berks County Deed Book 1, pg. 315: dated 15 Sept. 1749:
Valentine Unruh of the Manor of Plumton in Tulpehocon Twp., Lancaster
County, innholder (a brother and devisee of George Unruh late of said
manor, deceased) and Mary Catharine, his wife, to John Seller of the same
place, yeoman, 167 acres on Tulpehocon Creek in Lancaster County.

Berks County Abstracts of Wills:
Valentin Unruh, Tulpehocken, dated 13 June 1783; probated 25 Apr. 1788.
To daughter Maria Catharina Meyer's two sons, Daniel and Valentine, the
land I bought from John Womelsdorf, but they shall have no right while
their parents, Philip and Maria Catharina Meyer, live. They shall pay to their
brothers and sisters £800, of whom Barbara and Jacob are named. To Philip
Meyer's eldest daughter Maria Catharina, the land I cut off from Fitteler's
place, when she marries, and she is to pay £125 to her brothers and sisters.
To daughter Elizabeth Kintzer's children the land I dwell on, 120 acres, after
Jacob Kintzer and my daughter's deaths. Exrs: Philip Mayer and Philip
Kintzer. Wit.: Henry Seiler and Christian Seiler.

Berks County Tax Lists, Pennsylvania Archives, Third Series:
Tulpehocken 1767 Valentine Unruh taxed for 200 acres.

Valentin Unruw, Lancaster County, nat. Apr. 1744.

URICH, CHRISTOPH age 25   67454 Hassloch
Winter Galley, 1738
S-H, I: 199, 201, 203 [Stoffell Urick on A List]

EUROPEAN RECORDS

Hassloch Reformed KB:
Joh. Christoph Urich from [67360] Lingenfeld in Ambt Utsperg, m. 3 Nov. 1705 Anna Barbara, daughter of the late Henrich Guth. They had children:
1. Maria Barbara, b. 10 Jan. 1709
2. **Johann Christoph,** b. 7 Dec. 1711
3. Johannes, b. 28 Nov. 1715, conf. 1730
4. Maria Catharina, b. 13 Sept. 1719
5. Maria Clara b. 2 Mar. 1721
6. Joh. Philip, b. 30 Jan. 1725

AMERICAN RECORDS

Rev. John Casper Stoever's Records:
Christoph Uhrich (Tulpehocken) had children:
1. Maria Catarina, b. 29 Jan. 1739, bp. 24 Feb. 1739
   Sp.: Valentin Unruh [q.v.] and wife
2. Maria Appollonia, b. 21 Mar. 1740, bp. 30 Mar. 1740
   Sp.: Jacob Vollmer, Sr. and wife.

T. L. Montgomery, ed. *Frontier Forts of Pennsylvania*, Vol. I, Harrisburg, 1916; p. 71: Letter of Conrad Weiser dated Nov. 19, 1755 to Gov. Morris about "Indian invasion in Bethel and Tulpenhacon: A bold, stout Indian came up with one Christopher Ury, who turned about and shot the Indian right through his Breast."

Berks County Will and Adm. Abstracts:
Rosina Ury, widow of Christopher Ury, Tulpehocken, was granted Letters of Adm. 24 Mar. 1763.

UTREE, JACOB   67251 Freinsheim
The Globe, 1723
[He signed charter agreement for this ship]

EUROPEAN RECORDS

Freinsheim Reformed KB:
Joh. Jacob Utteri (name also appears as Utry, Utri) and wife Anna Maria had children:
1. Anna Catharina Elisabetha, bp. 9 July 1713
   Sp.: Michael Sebastian and wife Anna Catharina
2. Anna Maria, bp. 6 Oct. 1715
   Sp.: Joh. Jost Wigandt *aus Hessenlandt* and
   Anna Maria Henssel, daughter of Valentin Henssel

3. Joh. Jacob, bp. 8 Aug. 1717
    Sp.: Joh. Jacob Albert, single, and *Jfr.* Anna Christina Heyd
4. Joh. Jacob, bp. 24 Apr. 1719
    Sp.: Joh. Jacob Seltzer and wife
5. Maria Fronich, bp. 25 Oct. 1722
    Sp.: Maria Fronich Klauer, single

AMERICAN RECORDS

First Reformed KB, Philadelphia:
Joh. Bernhard Laufferschweiler and wife Maria, daughter of Jacob Utri, had
a daughter:
    Maria, b. 2 Dec. 1748, bp. 17 Dec. 1748
    Sp.: Maria Utrich and Thomas Mayer

Jacob Utri (also Utrich, Utterich) and wife Wilhelmina nee Bouton had
children:
1. Jacob, b. 7 July 1749, died 12 July 1749
    Sp.: Jacob Wyny and wife
2. Elisabeth, bp. 8 Nov. 1760
    Sp.: Georg Bouton and Elisabetha
3. Maria Veronica, bp. 16 Dec. 1762, died 4 Dec. 1785
    Sp.: Jacob Weinig from Manheim and Maria Veronica Utterich

Died 6 Aug. 1764- Wilhelmina Uttri, age 39 y. 2 m. 3 weeks.

Abstract of Philadelphia Will Book M: 425:
John Daniel Bouton, City of Philadelphia, Baker, "sick and weak in body".
Signed Apr. 13, 1759; prob. 24 Nov. 1762. Exrs: wife; son, George; and son-
in-law, Jacob Udree. Wit: Mathias Abell and Paul Isaac.
£ 0.5.0 to widow of my deceased son Frederick; to loving wife during her
natural life all my household goods, house, etc. and at her decease:
£ 100. to son George; £ 100. to daughter Wilhelmina; balance of estate to
three children:
Jacob (Bouton), George (Bouton), and Willhelmina Udree.

Philadelphia Wills and Administrations:
Jacob Uttery   1742   est. # 59   Adm. D: 264:
Letters of Adm. to Mary Uttery, widow of Jacob Uttery, cooper, late of
Philadelphia, dec'd, 19 Oct. 1742.

Jacob Uttrey, Philadelphia city, nat. 1740.

UTZ, DANIEL Ober Lustadt=
Brothers, 1752 67363 Lustadt
S-H, I: 481

EUROPEAN RECORDS

Ober Lustadt Reformed KB:
Joh. Georg Utz and wife Anna Maria had a son:
     Georg Daniel, b. 22 Oct. 1728, bp. 24 Oct. 1728

AMERICAN RECORDS

York County Will Abstracts:
Andrew Flickinger, Manheim, Twp. 1 Mar. 1784 - 9 May 1789.
Names several children, including a daughter Elizabeth married to Daniel
Utz. One of the exrs. is Daniel Utz.

Will of Daniel Utz, Manheim Twp. 1 June 1805 - 14 Dec. 1818.
Wife: Mary. Children: Andrew, Daniel, Mary wife of Henry Hoff, and
Elizabeth. Exrs: Daniel Dupe and Daniel Utz.

VETTER, JACOB 67251 Freinsheim
Mortonhouse, 1729
S-H, I: 24

EUROPEAN RECORDS

Freinsheim Reformed KB:
Conf. 1725: Jacob Vetter (his bp. not located in KB)
See 1731 emigrant Michael Vetter for a complete family record.

AMERICAN RECORDS

Oley Moravian Records, Berks Co., PA:
list of members, 1741: Jac. Vetter and Mich. Vetter.

Lancaster Moravian Records, Lancaster, PA:
Jacob Vetter, cabinet maker, b. 31 Dec. 1709 in "Frantzheim in der Pfalz"
[67251 Freinsheim]; died in Lancaster 13 June 1777, age 68. Came to
Pennsylvania in 1729. He resided first in Oley, then moved to Bethlehem,
then later to Lancaster. He m. (1) 1732 in Oley Maria Magdalena Bertolait.
She d. in Lancaster 28 Sept. 1755, age 46. They had nine children:

1. Johann Daniel, b. Oley 16 Feb. 1733
   (another record gives his b. date 27 Feb. 1734).
   He m. 14 Feb. 1759 Anna Fulmer.
2. Johann Gottlieb, b. Oley 28 Oct. 1735.
   He m. 28 Apr. 1761 Anna Margaret Roser.
3. Peter m. 2 Jan. 1764 Christina Riem
4. A son (no further information)
5. Stillborn son, Bethlehem, 8 Mar. 1745
6. Stillborn son, Bethlehem, 9 Mar. 1746
7. Nathaniel, b. 25 May 1747, bp. 5 June 1747, d. 13 Sept. 1773
8. Johann Jacob, b. 10 Feb. 1751
9. Maria Salome, b. 21 May 1753

Jacob Vetter m. (2) in Lancaster 17 Apr. 1756 Christina Metz. She was b.
in [55566] Meddersheim 26 Feb. 1732; died in Lancaster 23 May 1791. They
had six children:
   10. Catharina, b. 26 Oct. 1757, m. (1) William Bandon;
       m. (2) Michael Kapp
   11. Philip, b. 9 July 1759, d. 21 Nov. 1775
   12. Johannes, b. 10 Aug. 1761, d. 10 Apr. 1763
   13. Eva, b. 18 Sept. 1763, m. Philip Heinrich Daehne
   14. Elisabeth, b. 4 Aug. 1765, d. 4 June 1766
   15. Johannes, b. 25 Sept. 1767

Lancaster County Will Abstracts:
Jacob Fetter, Lancaster Borough. 13 Mar. 1777 - 7 July 1777.
Wife: Christiana Fetter. Children: Daniel, Godleip Peter, Jacob, John,
Salome, Catharine, and Eve. Exrs: Christiana Fetter and Henry Dehuff.

Jacob Vetter, Philadelphia, nat. Apr. 1743.

VETTER, MICHAEL   67251 Freinsheim
Pennsylvania Merchant, 1731
S-H, I: 43, 44, 45, 46 [surname appears as Feder]
[other passengers on ship: women: Katrina Feder, Helena Feder, Katrina
Feder. Children: Michael Feter, Katrina Feter.]

EUROPEAN RECORDS

Freinsheim Reformed KB:
Nickel Vätter (also Vetter) and wife Maria Elisabetha had children:
   1. Hans Georg, b. ca. 1695, conf. 1708, age 13

2. Hans Reichart [q.v.], bp. 7 Sept. 1698
3. Ottilia, bp. 25 July 1700
4. Joh. Philip, bp. 5 Mar. 1702, conf. 1717; d. 7 Apr. 1726
5. Joh. **Michael**, bp. 16 Mar. 1704, conf. 1719
6. Anna **Catharina**, bp. 3 Oct. 1706, conf. 1722. She is
likely the Katrina Feder (2) on the ship list.
7. Jacob [q.v.], b. 1709, conf. 1725
8. Maria **Magdalena**, bp. 4 Mar. 1711. She is likely the
Helena Feder on the ship list.
9. Margretha, bp. 25 Mar. 1714

Joh. **Michael** Vetter, son of Nickel Vetter, m. 2 July 1726 Maria **Catharina**,
daughter of the late Nicolaus Weber from Lamsporn [66894 Lambsborn] in
Zweybrücken. They had children:
1. Joh. **Michael**, bp. 7 Dec. 1727
2. Anna **Catharina**, b. 9 Aug. 1730, bp. 13 Aug. 1730

AMERICAN RECORDS

Michael Fetter purchased 100 acres of land in Philadelphia County on 26
Oct. 1736.

Oley Moravian Congregation, Berks Co.: list of members, 1741:
Jac. Vetter and Mich. Vetter

Trappe Lutheran KB, Montgomery Co., PA:
Michael Vetter from Alsace (Twp.) m. 30 Sept. 1747 in Colebrookdale Twp.
Maria Catharina Schmied, step-daughter of Simon Pelzen.

Michael Fetter, Alsace Twp., Berks Co., nat. 1761.

VETTER, REICHARDT 67251 Freinsheim
Mortonhouse, 1729 [name on list Rich[d] Fetter]
S-H, I: 24
[other passengers on ship: Anna Margarett Fetter]

EUROPEAN RECORDS

Freinsheim Reformed KB:
Nickel Vetter and wife Maria Elisabetha had a son:
Hans Reichart, bp. 7 Sept. 1698
[see immigrant Michael Vetter for a complete list of family]

Joh. Reichardt Vetter, son of Nicol Vetter, m. 7 Sept. 1723 Margaretha, daughter of Johann Philip Seyfriedt of [67259] Heuchelheim. They had children:

1. Lorentz, bp. 13 Dec. 1724
    Sp.: Lorentz Kopp and Margaretha
2. Elisabetha, bp. 26 Dec. 1726
    Sp.: Jacob Seltzer, Jr. and wife Elisabetha
3. Joh. Peter, bp. 22 Aug. 1728
    Sp.: Joh. Peter Bartscherer and Anna Catharina

AMERICAN RECORDS

St. Michael's and Zion Lutheran KB, Philadelphia:
Peter Vetter m. 20 Nov. 1750 Hanna Müller. They had:

1. Maria Elisabeth, b. 8 Apr. 1751, bp. 14 Apr. 1751
    Sp.: Michael Egolf, Elisabeth Vohmassin (Ref.)
    and Maria Stromann.

First Reformed KB, Philadelphia:
Lorentz Vetter m. 29 July 1750 Elizabeth Alowey, both from Whitemarsh, Philadelphia Co.

VISANANT, PHILIP PETER   67454 Hassloch
Snow *Lowther,* 1731   CH-1001 Lausanne, VD
S-H, I: 54-57
    with John Peter, Allena, John Adam

EUROPEAN RECORDS

Hassloch Reformed KB:
Philipp Peter Visinand from ?Cortier [?CH-1804 Corsier-sur-Vevey, VD], Switzerland, m. 9 July 1710 Anna Helena, daughter of Conrad Neff, *Gemeinsmann* and weaver here.

Philip Peter Fisenant and his wife Helena had children:

1. Anna Maria, b. 2 May 1711; bp. 6 May 1711
2. Johann Peter, b. 4 Feb. 1714; bp. 7 Feb. 1714
3. Joh. Nickolaus, b. 24 Feb. 1717; bp. 28 Feb. 1717
4. Johann Adam, b. 3 Sep. 1719; bp. 8 Sep. 1719
5. Heinrich, b. 27 Sep. 1722; bp. 4 Oct. 1722

Hassloch Beiträge:
1710: Philips Peter Eÿsenant from *Losano [=Lausanne, Sw.]* was granted citizenship rights in Hassloch.

Additional Data:
In an article "Schweizer Einwanderer in Edenkoben" published in *Pfalzische Familien and Wappenkunde,* Band 4, Heft 11 (1963) is the following entry:
Visinant (Wissinand), Francois "aus dem welschen Schweitzerland bey Lausanne geburtig." Hofmann im Kloster Heilsbruck. His wife was Anna, and they had a son Philip Peter, bp. 13 Apr. 1684.

In the Hassloch marriage records, 12 Apr. 1700, Frantz Fisinant m. Johanna widow of the deceased Martin ___. (Note: this entry very faded; both dates and names may be inaccurate.)

AMERICAN RECORDS

Muddy Creek Reformed KB, Lancaster Co., PA:
In 1743, Johan Peter, Adam, and Peter Wisenandt all signed the Reformed Church Doctrine.

Adam Wissenant and wife Anna Barbara had a son:
John Nicholas, bp. 31 July 1743 [also given as 30 Oct. 1743]
Sp.: John Nich. Fisser and Anna Sophia.

Peter Wiesenant and wife Maria Magdalena had:
John Nicholas, bp. 5 Feb. 1744
Sp.: Nicholas Fisser and wife Julianna

Muddy Creek Lutheran KB, Lancaster Co., PA:
Adam Wissenandt had a son:
Joh. Georg, b. 10 Apr. 1749, bp. 23 Apr. 1749
Sp.: Joh. Georg Brunner and wife.

Joh Peter Wissenand had children:
Joh. Peter, b. 22 June 1746, bp. 29 July 1746
Sp.: Joh. Nicolaus Zeller and wife Margaretha
Joh. Heinrich, b. 2 Oct. 1749, bp. 8 Oct. 1749
Sp.: the above.

Christian Lutz m. 17 Mar. 1746 Maria Magdalena Wissenandt, Muddy Creek.

Rev. John Caspar Stoever's Records:
John Peter Wissenandt and Maria Magdalena Suni [?Summi] were m. 7 Feb. 1737. [Also recorded in Muddy Creek Lutheran KB].

In the 1760s the Wisenants left Pennsylvania and moved to the Lincolnton, North Carolina area.

VOGT, JOHANNES   67454 Hassloch
Lydia, 1749
S-H, I: 421 with Joh. Jacob Rahn, [q.v.]

EUROPEAN RECORDS

Hassloch Lutheran KB:
Johann Sebastian Voigt from -----mühr, Anspach Jurisdiction, m. 18 Jan. 1713 Elisabetha Margretha Hoffmann from Weingenberg, Hessen-Darmstadt. Sebastian Vogt and Elisabetha had children:
1. Johannes, bp. 2 Sept. 1713; d. 14 Dec. 1713
2. Anna Maria, b. 7 June 1715; d. 6 Sept. 1716
3. **Johannes,** b. 14 Sept. 1717, bp. 19 Sept. 1717; conf. 1730
   Sp.: Johannes Riegel
4. Johann Henrich, b. 1 Mar. 1720, bp. 3 Mar. 1720

Died 3 Nov. 1722, Johann Sebastian Vogt, aged 37 years, 6 months.

AMERICAN RECORDS

New Hanover Lutheran KB, Montgomery Co., PA:
Johannes Vogt and Maria Magdalena had children:
1. Joh. Ludwig, b. 5 Nov. 1762, bp. 5 Dec. 1762 (Vogt)
2. Johannes Leonhard, b. 24 Feb. 1770, bp. 16 Apr. 1770 (Voigt)
3. Catharina, b. 26 Dec. 1772, bp. 2 May 1773 (Vioght)
4. Rosina, b. 29 Apr. 1775, bp. 20 Aug. 1775 (Voigt)

Northampton County Will Abstracts:
Shaerer, Valentine. Williams Twp., Yeoman. 23 Apr. 1793-10 Oct. 1797. Wife: Barbara. Children: Adam, Philip, Anna Barbara wife of John Transue. Mentions children of his step son John Vogt. Exr: son Adam. Wit: Jacob Arndt and George Knecht.

WAGNER, CARL   Niederhochstadt=
Janet, 1751   76879 Hochstadt, Pfalz
S-H, I: 474

EUROPEAN RECORDS

Niederhochstadt Reformed KB:
Caspar Wagener, son of the deceased David Wagener from Schmalkalde [98574 Schmalkalden] in Hesse, m. 8 Oct. 1709 Anna Maria, daughter of Hans Velte Laux. They had children:
1. Joh. Jacob, bp. 29 Nov. 1711
2. Joh. Georg, bp. 24 Sep. 1713;
   He m. 20 Nov. 1736 Anna Elisabeth Weiss
3. Valentin, bp. 17 Sept. 1715; probably d. young
4. Eva Barbara, bp. 30 Mar. 1717;
   She m. 17 Jan. 1741 Adam Jordan [q.v.]
5. Carl Heinrich, bp. 21 June 1719
6. Joh. Valentin, bp. 7 Jan. 1722
7. Johannes, bp. 21 June 1726

Carl Heinrich Wagner conf. 1734.

Carl Heinrich Wagner m. (1) 5 Jan. 1743 Anna Margretha, daughter of Johannes Laux. They had one child:
   Anna Elisabetha b. 11 Sept. 1743

Carl Heinrich Wagner m. (2) 29 June 1745 Maria Elisabetha Ringshausen. They had a child:
   Margretha b. 5 June 1746

AMERICAN RECORDS

One Joh. George Wagner appears in the Pennsylvania ship lists on the Lydia, 9 Oct. 1749, with the Bresslers.

Also a Caspar Wagner and Johannes Wagner arrived on the Queen of Denmark, 4 Oct. 1751, with several others from Niederhochstadt.

The surname is common, but these immigrants might be members of this family from Niederhochstadt.

See Adam Jordan for information on Eva Barbara Wagner Jordan.

WAGNER, CARL age 52   67157 Wachenheim an der Weinstrasse
WAGNER, ELIAS age 19
Plaisance, 1732
S-H, 79, 81, 82, 83

EUROPEAN RECORDS

Wachenheim Reformed KB:
Carl Wagner, son of the deceased Frederick Wagner, *zu ?Erfurt am Mayn,*
[?99085] m. 10 Mar. 1706 Maria Magdalena, daughter of the deceased
Johannes Brand. They had a child:
>Elias, bp. 29 June 1710
>Sp.: Elias Brand and Sybella.

AMERICAN RECORDS

Elias Wagoner, Philadelphia County, nat. as a Quaker, Apr. 1743

WAGNER, MATHIAS age 23   Niederhochstadt=
Adventure, 1732   76879 Hochstadt, Pfalz
S-H, I: 84, 86, 87

EUROPEAN RECORDS

Niederhochstadt Reformed KB:
Johannes Wagener was a bp. sp. in 1726 for a son of Casper Wagener [q.v.]
and his wife Anna Maria. Mathias Wagner was a brother of Johannes
Wagner, and according to documents in Pennsylvania, they were born in
Niederhochstadt, sons of _____? Wagner and Eva Magdalena. The
Niederhochstadt records do not start early enough to document their births.
They are mentioned in the Berks County Will (see below) of Wolfgang
Miller as his step-sons. The bequest in this will resulted in several deeds
about his property that went to these two step-sons. The step-son Johannes
Wagner, born in Niederhochstadt, remained in Germany and married
Catharina. They had a son Joseph who inherited his father's share of the
Wolfgang Miller estate. In 1771, Joseph Wagner, master stocking weaver,
was residing in Freudenthal, and with his mother Catharina, he released his
share of the Miller estate to Jacob Hoffman, master shoemaker residing in
Reading. This untranslated German deed is recorded at the court house in
Reading, Berks County Deeds, Vol. B-1, page 286 and following.

AMERICAN RECORDS

Berks County Wills:
Wolfgang Miller of Tulpehocken, dated 29 Nov. 1752; filed 29 Jan. 1753. One share of estate to grandchildren: Johannes, Christian, and Elisabeth Miller. One share of estate to wife Eva Madline. One share of estate to step-sons: Mathias and Johannes Wagner. "£15 current money of Pennsylvania shall be paid to my grandchild Johannes Miller, abovenamed, with a new suit of clothes when he goes the first time to the Lord's Table." Step Son Mathias Wagner and friend and neighbor Johannes Troutman, exrs. Witnessed by Hans Presler, George Presler, and Bernhard Mots. Also witnessed and translated by Conrad Weiser.

From this will, it would appear that Margretha, the first wife, died and Wolfgang Miller married (2) Eva Magdalena Wagner, a widow.

Rev. John Casper Stoever's Records:
Married 29 Apr. 1735, Joh. Mattheis Wagner and Elisabeth Stuep, Tulpehocken.

Mattheis Wagner (Northkill) had:
      Johannes, b. 22 Apr. 1756, bp. 30 May 1756
      Sp.: John Kaufman and wife Barbara
      Anna Catarina, b. 15 Sept. 1758, bp. 17 Sept. 1758
      Sp.: John Zerwe and wife Catarina

Michael Sauszer (Northkill) had:
      Catarina Elizabetha, b. 4 Oct. 1759, bp. 21 Oct. 1759
      Sp.: Mattheis Wagner and wife

Jacob Wagner and Maria Appollonia (Northkill)
      Susanna Catharina, b. 17 May 1761, bp. 24 May 1761
      Sp.: Mattheis Muench and wife

Berks County Orphans Court, dated 13 Aug. 1762.
(Mathias Waggoner died ca. May 1760)
On petition of Elizabeth Kramer, late Elizabeth Waggoner, Administratrix of Mathias Waggoner, deceased, the Court appointed Christian Gruber guardian for George Waggoner, Frederick Weiser for Mathias Waggoner and Philip Adam Scherman for Philip Waggoner children of Mathias Waggoner, deceased, above the age of 14 years, and said Frederick Weiser guardian of Maria Cathrine Waggoner, under 14 years.

    Petition of Jacob Waggoner, eldest son and heir at Law of Mathias Waggoner, deceased. That Mathias Waggoner died 2 years 3 months ago leaving a tract of 200 acres in Tulpehocken Township, that the widow is still living but married to George Kremer - that the said intestate left 8 children, all now living viz: Jacob, George, Mathias, Philip, Anna Kunyunt [?Cunigunda] (wife of Michael Sauser), Catharine Margaret (wife of Christopher Kern), Maria Madlena (wife of Michael Munch) and Catharine aged 4 years. Prays partition or valuation,etc. So ordered.

13 Nov. 1762:
Return of the Sheriff on the real estate of Mathias Wagner, deceased, whereby it appears the inquest had valued one-third part of 144 acres in Tulpehocken Township, said to be made over to said decedent by a certain Wolfgang Miller, deceased, in his last Will - it being suggested to the Court that the aforesaid third part was not of the estate of said Mathias Wagner, deceased, the Court ordered another valuation.

In Feb, 1763:
Return of Henry Christ, Esq., High Sheriff, on property of Mathias Wagner, deceased, - a tract of 200 acres in Tulpehocken Township. On oath of Jacob Fisher, Henry Ketner, and Adam Smith, and on affirmation of Peter Knop, Jacob Miller, Casper Stump, Jacob Conrad, George Brendle, John Steiner, Nicholas Hawk, John Albert, and Nicholas Kollar, that they viewed the tract of 200 acres in Tulpehocken, a tract of 150 acres over the Blue Mountains, surveyed to Mathias Waggoner in his life time and the tract of 144 acres in Tulpehocken Township, - one undivided 1/6 whereof was devised to the said intestate in July by Wolfgang Miller - they value the whole at £460, subject to dower of the widow, Elizabeth, and moneys due the propreitors. Jacob Wagner, eldest son and Heir at Law, accepts and gives Samuel Filbert and George Michael Minich, both of Bern, Yeoman, as sureties.

WAHL, WENDEL   Duttweiler=
Leslie, 1749   67435 Neustadt a. d. Weinstrasse
S-H, I: 419
                          EUROPEAN RECORDS

Duttweiler (Böbingen) Reformed KB:
Hans Wendel Wahl, son of the deceased Conrad Wahl, *Gerichtsverwandten* at Duttweiler, m. 7 Feb. 1708 Barbara Mühl, single, after 3 proclamations. They had:
    1. **Hans Wendel,** b. 21 Mar. 1709, bp. 24
    2. Joh. Casper, b. 19 Aug. 1712
    3. Hans Adam, b. 6 Mar. 1715

Wendel Wahl, son of the deceased Wendel Wahl, m. 4 Jan. 1740 Christina Hammel, daughter of the deceased Johannes Hammel from Lachen [=67435 Neustadt a. d. Weinstrasse]. They had children:

1. Maria Appollonia, b. 30 Dec. 1740; bp. 1 Jan. 1741
2. Anna Maria, b. 7 June 1743; b. 8 June 1743
3. Daniel, b. 3 May 1745, bp. 5 May 1745
4. Maria Kunigunda, b. 14 Aug. 1746, bp. 15 Aug. 1746
5. Hiob, b. 10 Oct. 1748, bp. 14 Oct. 1748

AMERICAN RECORDS

Berks County Will Abstracts:
Wendel Wall of Alsace Twp., yeoman. Verbal will given when the testator was "sick of the sickness whereof he died and in the house of his then habitation". Wife: Christina. Children: Peter, Jacob, Michael, and Mary. Exr.: wife Christina. Wit.: Johannes Kloos and Jacob Kisling. Will dated 15 Nov. 1764; proved 24 Nov. 1764. Letters Testamentary granted to Christina Wall, 3 Dec. 1764.

WALTER, ANTHONY age 32 Ruchheim=
Loyal Judith, 1743 67071 Ludwigshafen am Rhein
S-H, I: 335, 337, 338

EUROPEAN RECORDS

Ruchheim Reformed KB:
Ludwig Walther and wife Elisabetha had a son:
Anthoni, bp. 2 Mar. 1710

Anthoni Walter, son of Ludwig Walter, m. 8 Sept. 1730 Gertrauta, daughter of Andreas Schornick. They had children:

1. A daughter, bp. 30 Nov. 1731
2. Andreas, bp. 27 Nov. 1733
3. Peter, bp. 17 Mar. 1737

AMERICAN RECORDS

Zion (Bethel) Lutheran KB, Greenwich Twp., Berks Co., PA:
Anton(y) Walter and wife Elisabetha had;

1. Georg Peter, b. 22 Feb. 1765, bp. 5 Apr. 1765
   Sp.: Joh. Hearing and Eva Maria

2. Anton, bp. 3 May 1767
    Sp.: Georg Haering and wife
3. Johann Jacob, b. 24 Dec. 1768, bp. 22 Jan. 1769
    Sp.: Jacob Kimmel and wife

Anthy. Walter, Greenwich Twp., Berks Co., nat. Autumn, 1765.

WALTER, JOH. HENRICH age 33   67157 Wachenheim a. d. Weinstrasse
Glasgow, 1738
S-H, I: 204, 206, 208

EUROPEAN RECORDS

Wachenheim Reformed KB:
Niclas Walter and wife Anna Margretha had a son:
    Hans Henrich, bp. 23 May 1700
    Sp.: Henrich Wilhelm and wife Elisabetha

AMERICAN RECORDS

Henry Walter, Cocolico Twp., Lancaster Co., nat. 11 Apr. 1752

WALTER, RUDOLFF   67251 Freinsheim
Mortonhouse, 1729
S-H, I: 24, 25
    [other passengers on ship: Hannah Barbary Walder]

EUROPEAN RECORDS

Freinsheim Reformed KB:
Rudolff Walter and wife Anna Barbara had children:
    1. Elisabetha m. 1726 Joh. Jacob Seltzer [q.v.]
    2. Nickel, b. 16 July 1701, bp. 17 July 1701
        Sp.: Nickel Boseler and Anna Maria
    3. Anna Judith, b. 22 Sept. 1703, bp. 30 Sept. 1703
        She m. Martin Altstatt [q.v.]
        Sp.: Anna Judith, widow of Cunrat ?Witsch

   4. Joh. Christian, b. 18 Mar. 1707, bp. 23 Mar. 1707
      Sp.: Joh. Christian Caspar from [67273] Dackenheim
      and Anna Maria
   5. Anna Catharina, b. 17 Nov. 1709
      Sp.: Theobald Retzer, Lutheran, and wife Anna Catharina
   6. Anna Christina, b. 24 Sept. 1713, d. 9 Oct. 1713
      Sp.: Henrich Grossman and wife Anna Christina

AMERICAN RECORDS

Philadelphia Will Book H: 430
Anna Barbara Waltherin, Philadelphia (city) dated 10 Aug. 1747, probated
13 Nov. 1747. Widow.
Mentions eldest daughter Elisabeth and daughter Anna Judith.
Son John Nicholas Walther "absent and I do not know where he dwells or
if alive". If he returns within ten years, daughters are to pay him 50 pounds
out of estate.

WEBER, BLASIUS
Possibly prelist   67112 Mutterstadt
Before 1740
EUROPEAN RECORDS

Mutterstadt Reformed KB:
Andreas Weber m. 10 May 1718 Anna Sophia, daughter of the late Adam
Beyer from Oggersheim (=67071 Ludwigshafen). They had a son:
      Blasius bp. 22 June 1721
      Under this entry in the KB it is recorded that he was in the New
      Land in 1740.

AMERICAN RECORDS

Indianfield Lutheran KB, Franconia Twp., Montgomery Co., PA:
Blasius Weber and wife Maria Barbara had children:
   1. John, b. 22 July 1753, bp. 2 Sept. 1753
      Sp.: John Heitzman and Maria
   2. John George, b. 4 Sept. 1761, bp. 4 Oct. 1761
      Sp.: Adam Eckert and Rosina Kessler
   3. Anna Maria, b. 29 June 1763, bp. 28 Aug. 1763
      Sp.: Balthaser Spitnagel and Anna Maria

Conf. 1757, Anna Maria Weber, age 14, daughter of Blasius Weber.

Philadelphia Will Book Q, p. 66:
Blaze Weber of Montgomery Twp., County of Philadelphia. Dated 22 Sept. 1774, probated 8 Nov. 1774. Names wife Mary; sons: George, John; three daughters: Hannah Chrisman, Sarah Cope, and Mary. Son-in-law Jacob Cope and wife Mary executors.

Bless Weiber, Montgomery Twp., Philadelphia Co., nat. 10 or 11 Apr. 1761.

WEIDMAN, JOHANNES   67105 Schifferstadt
Allen, 1729
S-H, I: 27, 28, 30
   (Johannes Weightman on A List; Maria Phillis Whitman with women)

EUROPEAN RECORDS

Iggelheim-Schifferstadt Reformed KB:
Johannes Weitmann, single, m. 5 Apr. 1701 Anna Otilia, widow of Jacob Gizedaner. [See Getzendanner].

Johannes Waydman, widower, m. 24 Sept. 1716 Maria Felicitas, daughter of Ludwig Wirth Jr. of [67454] Hassloch. They had children:
      Johann Jacob, b. 10 July 1725
      Catharina Elisabetha, b. 27 Jan. 1727

Emigration record:
Werner Hacker, *Auswanderungen aus dem Früheren Hochstift Speyer nach Südosteuropa und Übersee im XVIII Jahrhundert,* Heimatstelle Pfalz, 1969:
Waydmann, Johann, Marientraut, with wife and three children, to America, 1 July 1729.

AMERICAN RECORDS

Philadelphia Orphans' Court Book 8: 51:
John Whiteman, warrant for land, dated 27 Jan. 1738, Frederick Twp., Philadelphia Co., PA. Land became property of his son Jacob Whiteman.

Jacob Weidmann (Whiteman) married Veronica _____ and had children:
      1. Andrew, eldest son
      2. George
      3. Jacob
      4. Catharina

WELTZHOFFER, JACOB   67159 Friedelsheim
Pennsylvania Merchant, 1731
S-H, I: 43, 44, 45, 46
(Katrina Velsover on list of women over 16, and Anna Velsover on list of children under 16.)

EUROPEAN RECORDS

Friedelsheim Reformed KB:
Jacob Weltzhoffer from Gronau [67127 Rödersheim-Gronau] married in 1723 (possibly 26 Dec.: date very faded) Anna Catharina, daughter of Gabriel Schultheis. They had children:
- 1. Johann Lorentz bp. 17 Sep. 1724
  Sp.: Lorentz Kissel and Anna Catharina
- 2. Anna Catharina bp. 14 Sep. 1727
  Sp.: Anna Catharina, widow of Lorentz Küsel
- 3. Johan Jacob bp. 1 Oct. 1730
  Sp.: Joh. Jacob Kratz and Eva Klingler from [67161] Gönnheim

AMERICAN RECORDS

Jacob Weltzhöffer appears on the list of members of the church on the Catores dated 17 Mar. 1745, with his brothers-in-law Martin and Johannes Schultz.

Jacob Welshover settled on land that was claimed by both Maryland and Pennsylvania, before 1736. A warrant for the arrest of these early settlers was issued by the Maryland government on 21 Oct. 1736. The name appears as Jacob Welchhutter on this warrant.

On May 23, 1737, Joseph Perry and Charles Higginbotham reported to the Maryland council that they have "apprehended several Dutchmen and others set forth in proclamation as disturbers of the peace." The list of names includes Jacob Welshover.

Jacob Weltzhoffer died in 1758. **York County Deed Book 2:** 449-451 names the following heirs:
      Katrina Welshofer, his widow; daughter Anna Katrina and her husband Valentine Heyer; daughter Maria Elizabeth and her husband John Comfort; daughter Eva and her husband Kilian Schmahl; son Jacob Welshofer.

For full citation of this deed see Valentine Heyer.

York Reformed KB, York, PA:
Jacob Weltzhoffer's son Jacob m. Anna Maria Basler and left a will dated 5 July 1798, probated 16 June 1815, naming the following children: Jacob, Henry, Mary, Catharine, Elisabeth, and Susanna.

An inventory of the estate of the immigrant Jacob Weltzhoffer was published in Wentz, *The Beginnings of the German Element in York County, Pennsylvania,* (Lancaster, 1916). Proceedings of the Pennsylvania German Society, Vol. XXIV, pages 205-207.

WICKS, CHRISTIAN   67112 Mutterstadt
Prelist, ca. 1725

EUROPEAN RECORDS

Mutterstadt Reformed KB:
Christian Wicks from Guckischberg, Canton Bern, Switzerland [CH-3158 Guggisberg, BE] m. 6 Jan. 1711 Rosina Barbara Röder. They had children:
1. Katharina, bp. 25 Mar. 1713
2. Christian, bp. 14 July 1715
3. Maria Elisabetha, bp. 11 May 1719
4. Anna Barbara, bp. 14 Mar. 1721

Mutterstadt Kontraktenprotokolle:
Record dated 15 Feb. 1725: Sebastian Reimer, citizen and judge here, and Anna Barbara his wife bought property from Christian Wix, as he had moved to Pennsylvania. In a later record, Johann Raparlie bought some of Christian Wix' property, and again it was noted in the record that he was in Pennsylvania. Recorded 7 June 1737.

AMERICAN RECORDS

Philadelphia Adm. Book F, p. 201:
Christian Wicks, Sr., of Exeter Twp. (Berks Co.) Schwartzwalt; will dated 2 July 1748. Mentions 4 eldest children by his first wife, 2 children by his second wife, and 3 children by his last wife, Maria Magdalena. The oldest child of second wife, named Anna Maria, to be brought up to her age with Michael Krauel, the other child of second wife to be brught up to its age with Christian Wicks, Jr. The land bought from son Christian to said son at valuation. Mentions Johannes Moyer of Tulpehocken. Adm. granted 21 Sept. 1748 to Maria Magdalena Wicks and Christian Wicks.

Newspaper *Weekly Advertiser,* 16 Oct. 1813:
Died on Friday the 8th inst. in Alsace Twp., Berks Co.: Mr. Christian Wix, aged 98 years, 3 months, 3 weeks, and 2 days. He was from the Palatinate of Germany.

Rev. Boos' personal records, Schwartzwald burials, Berks Co., PA:
Wife of Christian Wicks, b. 2 Dec. 1722; died 17 Mar. 1801.

WIEDERGRUNDEL, GEORG HENRICH   67259 Heuchelheim
Dragon, 1749
S-H, I: 423, 424
    [Indexed as 2 men in S-H: Geo. Henrich Witter and _____ Grundel]

EUROPEAN RECORDS

Heuchelheim Lutheran KB:
Georg Henrich Wiedergrundel, weaver, son of Joh. Peter Wiedergrundel of [67294] Gauersheim, m. 13 Jan. 1733 Anna Catharina Nuss, daughter of the deceased Joh. Georg Nuss. They had children:
     1. Joh. Philip, b. 22 Oct. 1733
     2. Joh. Jacob, b. 13 Dec. 1735
     3. Joh. Peter, b. 25 Oct. 1737
     4. Catharina Elisabetha, b. 20 May 1740
     5. Philip Henrich, b. 8 Jan. 1743
     6. Maria Magdalena, b. 25 May 1746
     7. Joh. Nicolaus, b. 9 July 1748
All died young.

AMERICAN RECORDS

Old Goshenhoppen Family Register, Lutheran Church:
Georg Henrich Wiedergrundel, b. 6 Mar. 1707, son of Joh. Peter and Maria Apollonia Wiedergrundel from [67294] Gaursheim. Till Mar. 11, he lived at Weilbrunn, Pfalz. Anno 1733, 13 Jan. he m. Anna Catharina, b. 29 Nov. 1709, daughter of Joh. Georg Nuss and Anna Catharina from Heuchelheim near Worms. Anno 1749 he came to America. All seven children died young. Georg Henrich Wiedergrundel, widower, m. 19 Sept. 1758 Catharina Hesin. They had:
     8. Anna Margaretha, b. 30 Sept. 1760

Berks County Will Abstracts:
George Henry Wiedergrundle, Rockland Twp. 2 Feb. 1786 - 10 May 1786.
"Of old age and sick and weak in bodily health". Wife: Maria Catharina.
Daughter: Anna Margaret wife of Peter Ritz, and her children (who are not
named). Mentions his dwelling abode and 20 acres of land adj. Henry
Hoffman and George Drey in Rockland Twp. Exr.: Paul Grosscup, Esq.
Wit.: Henry Hoffman and Henry Mertz.

WIGANDT, ELIAS   67251 Freinsheim
Polly, 1765
S-H, I: 704

EUROPEAN RECORDS

Freinsheim Reformed KB:
Jost Wigandt m. (1) 17 Feb. 1699 Anna Margaretha, daughter of Andreas
Scherrer.
Herr Jost Wigandt, widower, m. (2) 9 Feb. 1718 Catharina Philipina,
daughter of Herr Elias Isabart of Klein Carlenbach [67271 Kleinkarlbach].
Their son:
    Elias, bp. 6 Apr. 1721, conf. 1736

Elias Wigandt and wife Jacobea Scharlotta had children:
    1. Catharina, b. 23 Sept. 1748, bp. 26 Sept. 1748
        Sp.: Catharina Reck, widow
    2. Catharina Scharlotta, b. 14 Jan. 1751, bp. 17 Jan. 1751
        Sp.: Johannes Stock and Catharina
    3. Anna Maria, b. 18 Feb. 1753, bp. 21 Feb. 1753
        Sp.: Herr Joh. Jacob Reck and Anna Maria
    4. Sybilla Catharina, b. 14 Feb. 1755, bp. 16 Feb. 1755
        Sp.: Sybilla Catharina, daughter of Herr Jost Wigandt
    5. Maria Philippina, b. 4 Feb. 1757, bp. 6 Feb. 1757
        Sp.: Caspar Weilbrenner and Maria Philippina
    6. Catharina Philippina, b. 31 July 1759, bp. 1 Aug. 1759
        Sp.: Catharina Philippina, widow of Herr Jost Wigand
    7. Andreas, b. 26 May 1763, bp. 29 May 1763
        Sp.: Andreas Engle and Elisabetha

Herr Jost Wigand died 14 Feb. 1758, age 86 or 87 years.
Philippina, widow of the late Herr Jost Wyand, died 17 Oct. 1767, age 68
years.

AMERICAN RECORDS

See an article on "The Weand Family" in *Perkiomen Region, Past and Present,* Vol. I: 130-132 for detail on the family.

Falckner Swamp KB, Montgomery Co., PA:
Buried - Oct. 1807: Elias Wigand, age 85 years, 5 months.

New Goshenhoppen Reformed KB, Montgomery Co., PA:
David Wiant, son of Elias Wiant, b. 17 Aug. 1769
Sp.: David Levi and wife

Hocker, *German Settlers of Pennsylvania:*
newspaper Staatsbote, dated 20 Jan. 1779, pg. 158:
Elias Wieand, schoolteacher in Goshenhoppen

newspaper Philadelphische Correspondenz, dated 2 Nov. 1784, pg. 172:
Elias Wiand, Reformed schoolmaster in Goshenhoppen

WIGANDT, JOH. GEORG age 29   67251 Freinsheim
Loyal Judith, 1740
S-H, I: 282, 284, 285

EUROPEAN RECORDS

Freinsheim Reformed KB:
Jost Wigandt m. (1) 17 Feb. 1699 Anna Margaretha, daughter of Andreas Scherrer. They had a son:
        Joh. Georg, b. 11 June 1711, bp. 14 June 1711, conf. 1725

The father is mentioned as *Rathsverwandter* in this record.
Sp. at the baptism were Georg Hilbert, inhabitant at Gross Carlenbach [67229 Grosskarlbach] and Elisabetha, his wife, both Reformed.

AMERICAN RECORDS

Hocker, *German Settlers of Pennsylvania:* 82
Sower's newspaper, dated 23 Nov. 1759:
Georg Weyand, Upper Salford Twp., (Montgomery Co.)

Old Goshenhoppen Reformed KB, Montgomery Co., PA:
Jacob Weiant, son of Georg Weiant of Old Goshenhoppen, m. 4 Apr. 1775.
Salome Renn, daughter of the late Michael Renn of Old Goshenhoppen.

George Wyandt, Upper Salford Twp., Philadelphia Co., nat. Fall 1765.

WIGANDT, JOH. HENRICH   67251 Freinsheim
WIGANDT, JOH. JOST
WIGANDT, JOHANNES
Sally, 1770
S-H, I: 731, 732

EUROPEAN RECORDS

Freinsheim Reformed KB:
Jost Wigandt m. (1) 17 Feb. 1699 Anna Margaretha, daughter of Andreas
Scherrer. Their son:
     1. Joh. Peter bp. 8 Mar. 1700

Joh. Peter Wigand, son of Herr Jost Wigand, m. 6 May 1731 Magdalena
Eigenbrod, daughter of Joh. Daniel Eigenbrod. She was b. 2 Dec. 1708.

Joh. Daniel Eigenbrod, son of the schoolteacher here, m. 13 Jan. 1705 Anna
Maria, daughter of *Herr* D. Seltzer, *des Raths.*

Joh. Peter Wigand and wife Magdalena had eight children, including:
     Joh. Jost, b. 19 Oct. 1737, conf. 1755
     Sp.: Herr Joh. Jost Wigand and wife Catharina Philippina
     Johannes, b. 1 June 1746, conf. 1755
     Sp.: Johannes Pausch and wife Maria Juliana
     Johannes Wygand, son of the late Peter Wigand, m. __ Apr. 1768
     Catharina, daughter of Jacob Limbach from Weissenheim
     [? Weisenheim am Sand or Weisenheim am Berg].
     Joh. Henrich, b. 27 Jan. 1749, conf. 1766
     Sp.: Henrich Huck and wife

WIGANDT, JOHANN JOST   67251 Freinsheim
Brotherhood, 1750
S-H, I: 448

EUROPEAN RECORDS

Freinsheim Reformed KB:
Jacob Wygand m. 12 July 1701 Anna Catharina, daughter of ____ Magsamer.
Their son:

> Johann Jost, bp. 24 Oct. 1717, conf. 1733
> Sp.: Joh. Jost Haffner, single, and Elisabetha,
> daughter of Herr Jost Wigandt

Joh. Jost Wigand, son of the late Jacob Wigand, m. 14 Apr. 1744 Maria
Barbara, daughter of the late Joh. Adam Schaffner. They had:

> 1. Joh. Jacob, bp. 24 Jan. 1745
> 2. Anna Catharina, bp. 3 Sept. 1748

[An earlier Joh. Jost Wigandt, single, was a sponsor at a baptism in 1714.
The record mentions that he is from Obergrentzebach [=34621 Frielendorf]
in Hessen.]

Emigration Record:
Werner Hacker, *Auswanderungen aus Rheinpfalz und Saarland im 18.*
Jahrhundert:
#16209 Wigandt, Jost, citizen of Freinsheim, with brother-in-law Henr.
Schaffner, to PA. Record dated 9 Dec. 1749.

AMERICAN RECORDS

Roberts, *History of Lehigh County, PA,* Vol. 3: 1400-1405:
The family record published here gives two more children for Jost and
Barbara Wieand:

> 3. Jost Wieand b. 21 June 1754 m. Anna Margaretha Lang
> 4. Wendel Wieand b. 21 June 1757 m. Christina Herzog

New Goshenhoppen Reformed KB, Montgomery Co., PA:
Jost Weigandt and Barbara had:

> 5. Johannes bp. 5 Aug. 1759
> Sp.: Johannes Derr & Anna Maria
> 6. Anna Maria bp. 7 Oct. 1761
> Sp.: Anna Maria Wiand

Hocker, *German Settlers of Pennsylvania:* 66, 94:
Sower's newspaper, dated 12 Nov. 1757:
Jost Wiegand, New Goshenhoppen, one mile from Hansz Meyer's mill.

Sower's newspaper, dated 7 Oct. 1761:
Joost Wicand, New Goshenhoppen, born in Fresheim [67251 Freinsheim]
in the Palatinate, is preparing to go to Germany.

See an article on "The Weand Family" in *The Perkiomen Region, Past and
Present,* Vol.1: 130-132 for further information on the family.

WIGANDT, WENDEL   67251 Freinsheim
Mortonhouse, 1729
S-H, I: 24
EUROPEAN RECORDS

Freinsheim Reformed KB:
Jacob Wygand m. 12 July 1701 Anna Catharina Magsamer. Their son:
    Johann Wendel, bp. 14 July 1709
    Sp.: Wendel Albert, Reformed, and wife Anna Catharina

AMERICAN RECORDS

New Goshenhoppen Reformed KB, Montgomery co.:
Wendel Wiand (also Weigand) and wife Anna Margreth [nee Fischer,
daughter of Freinsheim emigrant Jacob Fischer, q.v.] had children:
    1. Sophia, bp. 20 June 1736
       Sp.: Johannes Fischer and wife Sophia
    2. Philipina, bp. 5 Feb. 1738
       Sp.: Daniel Schöner & Maria Catrina
       She m. 14 Nov. 1758 Andres Beyer
    3. Jacob, bp. 24 Sept. 1740
       Sp.: Jacob Seltzer and Elisabeth
    4. Anna Maria, bp. 4 Sept. 1742
       Sp.: Johannes Segler and wife
    5. Anna Maria, bp. 24 Mar. 1747
       Sp.: Johannes Sechler and wife

Buried 1787: Old Mr. Wendel Wiant b. 14 July 1709. Age 78 years.

Old Goshenhoppen Reformed KB, Montgomery Co., PA:
Wendel, son of Wendel Wiand of New Goshenhoppen, m. 9 Jan. 1770
Catharina, daughter of Erhart Weis of Old Goshenhoppen.

See Roberts, *History of Lehigh County, PA,* Vol. 3: 1400 and also "The Weand Family" in *The Perkiomen Region, Past and Present,* Vol. 1: 130-132 for further family data.

The Journals and Papers of David Shultze, Vol 2, pg 27:
Oct. 1768: On October 9 Wendell Wyant arrived happily in Philadelphia from Germany. His trip had lasted 46 weeks after he left Philadelphia. It took 8 weeks from Philadelphia to London and 8 weeks from England to Philadelphia.

Wendel Wiand, Philadelphia Co., nat. Apr. 1743.

WILDFANG, JOHANNES   Ober Lustadt=
St. Andrew, 1734   67363 Lustadt
S-H, I: 137, 139, 141, 142
   [Other passengers on ship: Elisabeth, George Michael,
   and Johannes Woolfang]

EUROPEAN RECORDS

Ober Lustadt Reformed KB:
Johannes Wildfang and wife Maria Elisabetha had a son:
      Joh. Sebastian, b. 16 Nov. 1732, bp. 18 Nov. 1732
      Sp.: Joh. Sebastian Herter and Maria Elisabetha

AMERICAN RECORDS

Host Reformed KB, Berks Co., PA.:
Sebastian Wildfang m. 20 May 1753 Anna Christina Breidschwerd.

Rev. John Casper Stoever's Records:
Sebastian Wildfang of Atolhoe had children:
      1. Peter, b. 18 Aug. 1753, bp. 26 Aug. 1753
      2. Elisabeth, b. 13 Dec. 1754, bp. 15 Dec. 1754

First Reformed KB, Philadlephia, PA.:
Sebastian Wildfang and wife Maria Christina had:
      3. Dewald, bp. 6 July 1760

St. Michael's and Zion Lutheran KB, Philadelphia:
Sebastian Wildfang and wife Maria Christina had:

4. Johannes, b. 7 Aug. 1762, bp. 15 Aug. 1762
   Sp.: Johann Peter Tartar and Maria Catharina.
5. Maria Barbara, b. 19 June 1765, bp. 30 June 1765
   Sp.: Bernhard Rub or Rieb? and Maria Barbara.

Swatara Reformed KB, Lebanon Co., PA:
George Michael Wildfang and wife Susanna Catharine had a child:
3. Susanna Catharina, bp. 28 Aug. 1753

Germantown Reformed KB, Philadelphia Co., PA:
Sebastian Wildfang was a contributor to the church in 1761.

Rev. John Casper Stoever's Records:
George Michael Wildfang m. 16 Mar. 1747 Sophia Catharina Veitheim, Tulpehocken.
George Michael Wildtfang of Tulpehocken had children:
1. Elisabetha Catharina, b. 6 Mar. 1748, bp. 3 Apr. 1748
   Sp.: George Schermann [q.v.] and wife
2. Maria Margaretha, b. 15 Oc.t 1751, bp. 27 Oc.t 1751
   Sp.: Leonhardt Fischer and Margaretha Speck

WILHELM, JACOB   Niederhochstadt=
St. Andrew, 1734   76879 Hochstadt
S-H, I: 137, 139, 141, 142
Passengers on ship: Jacob Wilhelm, Catharina Wilhelm, Jacob Wilhelm, Valentin Wilhelm.

EUROPEAN RECORDS

Niederhochstadt Reformed KB:
Jacob Wilhelm and Anna Catharina had children:
1. Johan Jacob, bp. 29 Mar. 1728
   Sp.: Jacob Ehsberger
2. Joh. Valentin, bp. 2 Dec. 1731
   Sp.: Joh. Valentin Bressler and Anna Maria

AMERICAN RECORDS

Christ "Little Tulpehocken" Lutheran KB, Heidelberg Twp., Berks Co.:
Jacob Wilhelm and wife had children:
3. Philip Jacob, b. 10 Jan. 1738; bp. 2 Feb. 1738
   Sp.: Jacob Schopff and wife

4. Johann Adam, b. 31 Oct. 1742; bp. 28 Nov. 1742
    Sp.: Bernhard Motz [q.v.] and wife

Host Reformed KB, Tulpehocken Twp., Berks Co., PA:
Jacob Wilhelm and wife Anna Barbara had children:
    1. Anna Barbara, b. 3 Nov. 1756; bp. 7 Nov. 1756
        Sp.: Johannes Schob and Anna Barbara
    2. Maria Apollonia, b. 3 Oct. 1757; bp. 16 Oct. 1757
        Sp.: Valentin Drees and Maria Apollonia Keller

Berks County Will Abstracts:
Jacob Wilhelm of Tulpehocken, will dated 8 Feb. 1783; probated 14 Jan.
1786. Provides for wife Anna Barbara. Son John Adam to have the place
with the Summerhill land and pay £600 to the other children (who are not
named). Letters of Administration to John Adam Wilhelm and Philip Jacob
Wilhelm. Witnessed by John Kantner and John Christ Seyler.

Lancaster County Land Warrants, Pennsylvania Archives, Third Series:
Jacob Wilhelm, 200 acres, 17 June 1737.

Jacob Wilhelm, Lancaster County, nat. Apr. 1744 (with Valentin Unruh).
Another Jacob Wilhelm and Anna Cath. Wilhelm both nat. 10 Apr. 1760.

WINCKELMAN, HENRICH   Lachen-Speyerdorf=
Prelist, 1709   67435 Neustadt an der Weinstrasse

EUROPEAN RECORDS

Lachen-Speyerdorf Reformed KB:
Henrich Winckelman, a joiner, and Anna, his wife, had children:
        Hans Henrich, bp. 21 Feb. 1683
        Sp.: Henrich Reiff, son of Jacob Reiff
        Joh. Rudolph, bp. 17 Feb. 1684
        Sp.: Rudolph Gründele(r), born at Mettmanstätten, Zürich [CH-
        8932 Mettmenstetten, ZH]; now in Edengoben [67480 Edenkoben].

Died 11 Jan. 1681- Henrich Winckler(!), the joiner here, his wife named
Elisabeth was buried.

Emigration records:
Annette K. Burgert, *A Century of Emigration from Affoltern am Albis, Canton Zürich, Switzerland:* pg. 22: Heini Winckelman and wife Lisabeth Büchin left [CH-8910] Affoltern am Albis, 3 Feb. 1680 with one daughter, to Lachen.

Annette K. Burgert, *Eighteenth Century Emigrants from German-Speaking Lands to North America,* Vol. II: The Western Palatinate: pg. 355:
Conf. 1700 at Rieschweiler: Henrich Winckelmann, son of Henrich Winckelmann of Mühlbach [=66509 Rieschweiler-Mühlbach], Pfalz.

Anna, wife of Henrich Winckelman, was buried in Rieschweiler in 1707. She was from [CH-8932] Mettmenstetten, ZH.

Krebs and Rubincam, *Emigrants from the Palatinate to the American Colonies in the 18th Century:* pg. 32:
Henrich Winckelmann, who has left with 4 other persons, from Höhmühlbach [= 66509 Rieschweiler-Mühlbach], Palatinate (1709).

Hans Ulrich Pfister, *Die Auswanderung aus dem Knonauer Amt,* 1648-1750: pg. 364:
Heinrich Winkelmann from [CH-8910] Affoltern am Albis, bp. 6 Feb. 1648, master joiner, went with his family for a couple of years to Lachen in 1680; then returned to Affoltern. In 1695 returned to the Pfalz and in 1697 was living in Höhmühlbach. He married (1) 7 Mar. 1671 in Affoltern Elisabeth Büchi from [CH-8353] Elgg, ZH. She died in Lachen 9 Jan. 1682. He married (2) 21 Feb. 1682 in Affoltern Anna Kleiner from [CH-8932] Mettmenstetten; she died in Höhmühlbach 8 Aug. 1707. Children:

    1. Anna, bp. 5 Dec. 1671, in 1689 in [67480] Edenkoben
    2. **Heinrich**, bp. 21 Feb. 1683 in Lachen
        conf. 1700 in [66509] Rieschweiler (see above).
    3. Rudolf, bp. in Lachen (see above).
    4. Adelheid, bp. 13 June 1685 in Affoltern,
        conf. 1702 in Rieschweiler as Magdalena
    5. Oswald, bp. 27 Feb. 1687, conf. 1704 in
        Rieschweiler as Jos.

WISSENANDT see VISANANT

WOHLFART, CONRAD   67454 Hassloch
Phoenix, 1749   74889 Sinsheim, Elsenz
S-H, I: 406

EUROPEAN RECORDS

Hassloch Reformed KB:
Joh. Friedrich Wohlfahrt, *Haffner Meister,* son of the late Georg Henrich Wohlfahrt formerly of Sintzheim [74889 Sinsheim], m. 8 Feb. 1719 Susanna, daughter of Johannes Müller. Their children:
1. Johan Conradt, b. 29 Nov. 1719, bp. 3 Dec. 1779
2. Johann **Conradt,** b. 8 Oct. 1720, bp. 9 Oct. 1720; conf. 1734
3. Anna Maria, b. 20 June 1723, bp. 24 June 1723
4. **Johann Friedrich,** b. 13 July 1724, bp. 16 July 1724; conf. 1740
5. Amelia Maria, b. 24 Feb. 1728, bp. 3 Mar. 1728; conf. 1741
6. Anna Margretha, _____ no dates, 1730

Susanna (Müller) Wohlfarth d. 17 Feb. 1733, age 39 years, 7 weeks, 4 days.

Joh. Friedrich Wolfahrt, widower, m. (2) 6 May 1733 Anna Christina, daughter of Isaac Schmiet.

Johann Friedrich Wolfarth and Maria Christina had:
7. Maria Elisabetha, b. 20 Apr. 1734, bp. 20 Apr. 1734
8. Hanss Philip, b. 10 Apr. 1735, bp. 12 Apr. 1735
9. Anna Maria, b. 29 July 1736, bp. 1 Aug. 1736
10. Hanss Philip, b. 20 May 1740, bp. 22 May 1740

Joh. Friedrich Wohlfarth d. 13 Oct. 1746, age 51 years, 2 months.

Conrad Wolfarth, son of the deceased Friedrich Wolfarth, m. 25 Jan. 1747 Maria Margretha, daughter of the deceased Philip Reyher.

Joh. Philip Rheyer, son of the late Hans Georg Rheyer of [67459] Böhl, m. 27 Aug. 1720 Anna Maria, daughter of Abraham Hess (? faded entry). Their daughter:
Maria Margretha, b. 19 Feb. 1725

[Maria Margretha (Reyher) Wohlfart was a cousin of Christophel Reyer, 1749 emigrant [q.v.], and a niece of Sebastian Rheyer, 1726 emigrant [q.v.].

Joh. Philip Reiher d. 25 July 1738, age 41 years, 8 months.

Emigration record:
Werner Hacker, *Auswanderungen aus Rheinpfalz und Saarland*:
#16539 Wohlfarth, Konrad, Hassloch, with wife to PA 23 Apr.1749

AMERICAN RECORDS

PA Series 6, Vol 6, Rev. Waldschmidt's Records:
Conrad Wohlfart and wife Maria Margaret had children:
    1. Elisabetha, b. 12 Mar. 1755 (Rev. Waldschmidt's records)
Millbach Reformed KB, Lebanon Co., PA:
    2. Eva, bp. 4 Sep. 1757   (The last 3 children bp. at
    3. Anna Maria, bp. 22 Apr. 1760   Millbach Reformed Church,
    4. Mary Susanna, bp. 27 Oct. 1765 Lebanon County)

Conrad Wolfhart took out a land warrant for 25 acres in Lancaster County, on 30 Mar. 1757.

WOHLFART, FREDERICK   67454 Hassloch
Phoenix, 1749
S-H, I: 406

EUROPEAN RECORDS

Hassloch Reformed KB:
Joh. Friedrich Wohlfarth was b. 13 July 1724, son of Friedrich and Susanna Wohlfarth. He was a brother of the Conrad listed above. Joh. Friedrich Wohlfarth was confirmed at Hassloch in 1740, age 15.

AMERICAN RECORDS

St. Michael's Lutheran KB, Germantown, Philadelphia Co., PA:
Frederick Wollfart, a young journey man, Reformed religion, m. 12 Nov. 1751 Maria Eva Brunner, a single person from the Philadelphia Lutheran congregation.

WOLFF, GEORG   Oberhochstadt=
Queen of Denmark, 1751   76879 Hochstadt, Pfalz
S-H, I: 472

EUROPEAN RECORDS

Oberhochstadt Reformed KB:
Georg Wolff and wife Maria Apollonia had children:
    1. Georg, b. 9 May 1736; bp. 13 May 1736
        Sp.: Georg Schard and Margaretha from Leymersheim
        [=76774 Leimersheim]

2. Barbara, b. 28 Aug. 1738; bp. 31 Aug. 1738
   Sp.: Jacob Rühling, Oberhochstadt, and Anna Barbara Wolff
   from Leymersheim [76774 Leimersheim]
3. Johannes, b. 9 Dec. 1740; bp. 11 Dec. 1740
   Sp.: Johannes Becker [q.v.] and Catharina (nee Meyer)
4. Daniel, b. 9 Mar. 1742; bp. 11 Mar. 1742
   Sp.: Daniel Meyer [q.v.] and Anna Catharina
5. Anna Catharina, b. 23 Jan. 1744; bp. 26 Jan. 1744
   Sp.: Johannes Becker and Anna Catharina from
   [67483] Kleinfischlingen
6. Jacob, b. 9 Aug. 1746; bp. 10 Aug. 1746
   Sp.: Jacob Wolff [q.v.] and Anna Margretha
7. Catharina, b. 26 Apr. 1749; bp. 27 Apr. 1749
   Sp.: Joh. Becker and Catharina (nee Meyer)
   from Fischlingen [=67483 Kleinfischlingen].

Niederhochstadt Reformed KB:
Maria Apolonia Meyer, wife of Georg Wolff, was bp. 23 Oct. 1710, daughter
of Michael Meyer and wife Anna. Sp.: Wilhelm Roth from Offenbach
[76877 Offenbach a. d. Queich] and Apolonia, his wife.

AMERICAN RECORDS

Host Church Cemetery Records, Tulpehocken, Berks County:
Daniel Wolf, b. in Oberhost [=Oberhochstadt] 9 Mar. 1742, son of George
Wolf and Apollonia nee Meier; d. 2 Apr. 1829.

Eva Catharina Wolf, b. 18 Apr. 1749 Oberhost [=Oberhochstadt], daughter
of Georg Wolf and Anna Maria; d. 8 Apr. 1839. [Note: This may be
Catharina, b. 26 Apr. 1749.]

One Geo. Wolf, Tulpohockon, Berks County, nat. 10/11 Apr. 1761.

WOLFF, JACOB   Oberhochstadt=
Queen of Denmark, 1751   76879 Hochstadt, Pfalz
S-H, I: 472, 473
   Also on ship's list: sons Daniel and George

EUROPEAN RECORDS

Oberhochstadt Reformed KB:
Jacob Wolff and wife Anna Margaretha had children:
   1. Johan Peter, bp. 6 Oct. 1726; conf. 1740

Sp.: Peter Mayer and Anna Catharina Mayer
2. Maria Elisabetha, bp. 3 Oct. 1728
   [See marriage below, at Host Church]
3. Johan Friderich, bp. 7 June 1730; conf. 1744
   Sp.: Joh. Friederich Lang and Anna Barbara
4. Johan Daniel, bp. 18 Feb. 1732; conf. 1747
   Sp.: Joh. Daniel Meyer and Anna Catharina [q.v.]
5. Johan Georg, bp. 10 Feb. 1734; conf. 1748
   Sp.: Georg Becker and Anna Maria
6. Anna Margaretha, b. 7 Jan. 1736
   Sp.: Joh. Jacob Frey and Anna Margaretha Becker
7. Eva Elisabetha, b. 15 Jan. 1738
8. Anna Margaretha, b. 28 Dec. 1739
   Sp.: Jacob Freyel and Anna Margaretha
9. Maria Barbara, b. 19 Apr. 1741
   Sp.: Maria Barbara Martel and Georg Michel Stoll
10. Maria Catharina, b. 4 Sept. 1744

AMERICAN RECORDS

Host Reformed KB, Tulpehocken, Berks Co., PA:
George Jacob Ulrich m. 16 Oct. 1753 Maria Elisabeth Wolff.

Berks County Will Abstracts:
George Jacob Ulerich of Pine Grove Twp., Berks County, left a will dated 2 Oct. 1786: named his wife Maria Elisabeth and children. Witnessed by Egidius Myer and Christian Webber.

Maria Elisabetha Ulrich, d. 4 Mar. 1805, Summer Hill records, Schuylkill Co.

For further data on this family, see 1750 emigrants Peter Wolff and Friederich Wolff.

WOLFF, GEORG MICHAEL age 44   Oberhochstadt=
WOLFF, CONRAD age 20   76879 Hochstadt, Pfalz
Friendship, 1739
S-H, I: 265, 268, 271

EUROPEAN RECORDS

Niederhochstadt Reformed KB:
Georg Michael Wolff from Oberhochstadt conf. 1712.

Oberhochstadt Reformed KB:
Georg Michael Wolff, widower, m. 6 June 1730 Juliana Maria Engelhart, b. in ?Kirsbach [?53539 Kirsbach]. They had a son:
> Joh. Bernhard, bp. 1 Jan. 1732
> Sp.: Joh. Bernhard Meyer and Anna Barbara Licht

Joh. Conrad Wolff conf. 1734 at Oberhochstadt.

AMERICAN RECORDS

Index Philadelphia Wills and Administrations:
George M. Wolfe, 1747, File #117, Adm. Book F, p. 124.

History of St. John's (Host) Church:
This published history states (p. 72) that Michael Wolff settled near Wolmelsdorf. He died in 1746 from a stroke of apoplexy. In the year 1755 Conrad, one of his sons, was killed by an Indian. Shortly thereafter, John Bernhard "unwilling to enter into legal contests with an unrighteous step-father, relinquished his patrimony and came penniless, to Lancaster."

Lancaster County Land Warrants, Pennsylvania Archives, Third Series:
Conrad Wolf, 100 acres, 21 Dec. 1752.

Lancaster County Will Abstracts:
Bernard Wolfe, 1756, Q-1-452. There were other Bernhard Wolffs in Lancaster County, since the name appears on later tax lists.

Lancaster County Administrations:
Georg M. Wolf 1748; Conrad Wolf 1757.

Note by compiler: Some of these Lancaster county records possibly pertain to another Wolff family. Another immigrant Georg Michael Wolf who died intestate before 1756 in Earl Twp., Lancaster County, also had sons named Conrad and Bernhard, but both were minors in 1756. That Georg Michael Wolf appears in the New Holland Lutheran Church records in 1734, and is therefore not the 1739 immigrant.

For details on the earlier Georg Michael Wolf, see: Burgert, Annette K., *Eighteenth Century Emigrants from German-Speaking Lands*, Vol. I: The Northern Kraichgau. Pennsylvania German Society, Vol. XVI (1983). Family #602.

WOLFF, NICHOLAS   Niederhochstadt=
Janet, 1751   76879 Hochstadt, Pfalz
S-H, I: 474

EUROPEAN RECORDS

Niederhochstadt Reformed KB:
Conrad Wolff and wife Anna Margaretha had a son:
    Nicolaus, bp. 28 July 1720; conf. 1735

Anna Margretha, wife of Conrad Wolff, d. 16 Jan. 1744, age 44 years.
Conrad Wolff, widower, m. (2) 5 May 1744 Anna Maria, widow of Valentin
Pressler.

Nickel Wolff, son of Conrad Wolff, m. 25 Jan. 1746 Maria Elisabetha
Bressler. Nickel Wolff and wife Elisabetha had children:
    1. Johannes, b. 29 Oct. 1746; bp. 1 Nov. 1746
        Sp.: Johannes Degen and Margaretha
    2. Valentin, b. 22 Apr. 1750; bp. 24 Apr. 1750
        Sp.: Valentin Fischer and Anna Margretha

AMERICAN RECORDS

Rev. John Caspar Stoever's Records:
Nicolaus Wolf of Bethel and wife had children:
    3. Carolus, b. 20 Oct. 1751; bp. 27 Oct. 1753
        Sp.: Carl Scheidt and wife
    4. Maria Margaretha, b. 22 Sept. 1753; bp. 27 Oct. 1753
        Sp.: Cunradt Rounner and Sister Margaretha

Berks County Tax Lists, Pennsylvania Archives, Third Series:
Nicholas Wolf, Bethel twp., 100 acres, 1767.

Berks County Abstracts of Wills and Administrations:
Nicholas Wolf, Bethel: on 8 Nov. 1784, administration was granted to
Elisabeth Wolf, the widow.

Nicholas Wolf, Bethel Twp., Lancaster County, nat. Fall 1765.

WOLFF, PETER   Oberhochstadt=
WOLFF, FRIEDERICH   76879 Hochstadt, Pfalz
Royal Union, 1750
S-H, I: 433

EUROPEAN RECORDS

Oberhochstadt Reformed KB:
Jacob Wolff and wife Anna Margaretha had 10 children. Two of the sons were:

> Johan Peter, bp. 6 Oct. 1726; conf. 1740
> Sp.: Peter Mayer and Anna Catharina Mayer
> Johan Friderich, bp. 7 June 1730; conf. 1744
> Sp.: Joh. Friederich Lang and Anna Barbara

For complete details on family, see 1751 emigrant Jacob Wolff from Oberhochstadt.

AMERICAN RECORDS

Host Reformed KB, Tulpehocken, Berks Co., PA:
Frederick Wolff and wife Eva Barbara (nee Meyer) had a son:

> Daniel, b. 27 Dec. 1756; bp. 16 Jan. 1757
> Sp.: Daniel Wolff and Anna Barbara

Berks County Tax Lists, Pennsylvania Archives, Third Series:
Hantz George Wolf, Tulpehocken, 100 acres 1767.
Frederick Wolf, Tulpehocken, 100 acres 1768.

WOLSCHLÄGER, JOHANNES   67256 Weisenheim am Sand
The Globe, 1723
[Signed the ship contract agreement]

EUROPEAN RECORDS

Lambsheim Reformed KB:
Johann Jacob Wollschläger and wife Margaretha of Weisenheim-am-Sand had children:

> 1. Joh. Heinrich, bp. 31 Aug. 1698
> 2. Anna Catharina, bp. 20 May 1700

3. **Johannes**, twin, bp. 1 Apr. 1703
4. Maria Barbara, twin, bp. 1 Apr. 1703

There are major gaps in the Weisenheim am Sand KB - one extends from 1689 to 1705. During this period, several years of baptisms for Weisenheim parents are recorded in the Lambsheim Reformed KB. These records date from 1696 to 1703.

AMERICAN RECORDS

Lancaster County Deed Abstracts:
C 508: Mentions a tract of land in Manheim Twp. containing 204 acres, part of patent 4 Aug. 1741 to John Woolslegle.

F 202: John Woolslegle and wife Anna granted 204 acres in Manheim Twp. to Jacob Downer.

L 275: John Woolslegle on 24 Nov. 1752 granted 204 acres, part of 408 acres patented to him to Jacob Downer and later devised 200 acres to Elisabeth Downer by will.

Lancaster County Will Abstracts:
John Woleslegle, Twp. omitted. 1 Nov. 1758 - 12 Dec. 1758.
Wife: Anna Woleslegle. Stepson: Jacob Donner. Brother: Frederick Woleslegle. Exrs: Anna Woleslegle and John Brubacher.

Nat. 1729/30 by Act of the Assembly: John Woolslegle, Lancaster Co.

WUNDER, CHRISTIAN   Ober Lustadt=
Polly, 1765   67363 Lustadt
S-H, I: 704

EUROPEAN RECORDS

Ober Lustadt Reformed KB:
Sebastian Wunder and wife Anna Maria had a son:
        Christian, b. 3 Jul. 1729, bp. 17 Jul. 1729

Christian Wunder and wife Catharina had children:
        1. Maria Eva, b. 16 Apr. 1757
        2. Anna Elisabetha, b. 6 Apr. 1759, d. 1763

3. Andreas, b. 18 Oct. 1761; bp. 21 Oct. 1761
   Sp.: Andreas Lehr and Catharina
   d. 4 Feb. 1763
4. Andreas, b. 27 Dec. 1763, bp. 28 Dec. 1763
   at Niederlustadt
   Sp.: Andreas Lehr and Catharina

AMERICAN RECORDS

Fourteen passengers on the ship *Polly* in 1765, listed in close proximity to one another on the list (S-H, I: 704), all appear in the Oberlustadt records: Andreas Heintz, **Christian Wunder**, Conrad Hauenstein, Georg Jacob Hauenstein, Christoph Strigel, Johann Leon[d] Devil (Deubel), Andres Ehresmann, Peter Zeiler, Georg Aadam Bresler, Johan Michael Dühmer, Jacob Wunder, Jacob Faut, Georg Simon Haushalter, Geo. Adam Teis.

Conewago Reformed Church Records, Adams Co., PA.:
Christian Wunder and wife Catharina had:
   Daniel, b. 7 Mar. 1772, bp. 28 June 1772
   Sp.: John [Georg] Peter Deisert [q.v.] and
   wife Wilhelmina

Emanuel Reformed KB, Hanover, York Co., PA:
Andreas Wunder and wife Catharina had children:
   1. Catharina, b. 22 Oct. 1788, bp. 12 Jan. 1789
   2. Johannes, b. 20 Aug. 1790, bp. 12 Oct. 1790
      Sp.: Christian Wunder and wife Cath.
   3. Jacob, b. 23 Oct. 1792, bp. 25 Dec. 1792

WUNDER, JACOB   Ober Lustadt=
Polly, 1765   67363 Lustadt
S-H, I: 704
EUROPEAN RECORDS

Ober Lustadt Reformed KB:
Sebastian Wunder and wife Anna Maria had a son:
   Joh. Jacob, b. 13 Jan. 1727; bp. 19 Jan. 1727
   Sp.: Joh. Jacob von Geruch *der alte* and Catharine

Jacob Wunder and wife Anna Maria had children:
   1. Jörg Adam, b. 6 Sept. 1751, bp. 8 Sept. 1751
   2. Jörg Adam, b. 7 Jan. 1753; bp. 10 Jan. 1753

3. Anna Maria, b. 22 Aug. 1755; bp. 24 Aug. 1755
    Sp.: Frantz Herder and Anna Maria
4. Valentin, b. 1 Apr.1 758; bp. 2 Apr.1758
5. Maria Barbara, b. 21 Oct. 1760; bp. 26 Oct. 1760
    Sp.: Valentin Hamerschmidt and Maria
    Barbara Bressler, both single
6. Christoph, b. 5 Jan. 1764; bp. 8 Jan. 1764 (Oberlust)
    Sp.: Christoph Hoffman and Catharina

AMERICAN RECORDS

Fourteen passengers on the ship *Polly* in 1765, listed in close proximity to one another on the list (S-H, I: 704), all appear in the Oberlustadt records: Andreas Heintz, Christian Wunder, Conrad Hauenstein, Georg Jacob Hauenstein, Christoph Strigel, Johann Leon^d Devil (Deubel), Andres Ehresmann, Peter Zeiler, Georg Aadam Bresler, Johan Michael Dühmer, **Jacob Wunder**, Jacob Faut, Georg Simon Haushalter, Geo. Adam Teis.

Germantown Reformed Church Records, Philadelphia co., PA.:
Died 16 July 1812 Jacob Wunder, age 85 y. 6 m. 1 w. 2 d.

Jacob Wunner and wife Maria had the following child:
1. Christina, bp. 9 Apr. 1769

Fritz Braun and Friedrich Krebs. "Pennsylvania Dutch Pioneers from South Palatine Parishes", *The Pennsylvania Dutchman*, 8 (Spring, 1957):
Hacker #6507 Anna Maria Horter, wife of Jacob Wunder:
Wunder, Johann Jakob - born at Oberlustadt, 13 Jan. 1727, son of Sebastian Wunder and wife Anna Maria; married Anna Maria Horter, born at Oberlustadt, 21 July 1729, daughter of Georg Horter and wife Anna Barbara.
[See also Joh. Valtin Horter].

WUNDER, NICHOLAS   Ober Lustadt=
St. Andrew, 1734   67363 Lustadt
S-H, I: 137, 141, 142
    Other passengers on list: Anna Maria Winder, Andreas,
    Anna Margaret, Marilis, Maria Catrina

EUROPEAN RECORDS

Ober Lustadt Reformed KB:

Georg Niclaus Wunder (Wender, Wenner) and wife Anna Maria had children:

1. Anna Maria, bp. 12 Apr. 1722
   Sp.: Hans Jörg Stadeler and Anna Maria
2. Andreas, b. 19 July 1725, bp. 22 July 1725
   Sp.: Andreas Schmid and Anna Appolonia
3. Anna Margaretha, b. 9 Feb. 1728; bp. 15 Feb. 1728
   Sp.: Joh. Andreas Lehr and Anna Margaretha
   Weppler, both single
4. Maria Elisabetha, bp. 17 Sept. 1730
   Sp.: Sebastian Sager and Agatha
   Wenner, both single
5. Maria Catharina, b. 14 Nov. 1733, bp. 15 Nov. 1733
   Sp.: Maria Catharina Weppler, single

ZAHNEISSEN, VALENTIN age 34   76831 Ilbesheim

Barclay, 1754

S-H, I: 595, 597, 599

[appears on A list as Saynhaysen; did not sign]

EUROPEAN RECORDS

Leinsweiler [76829] Reformed KB:

Valentin Zahneissen, son of the late Balthasar Zahneissen, former citizen and inhabitant at Mertzh(eim?) [= 67271 Mertesheim], m. 24 ?Sept. 1743 at Ilvesheim [Ilbesheim] Juliana, daughter of Joh. Adam Clements, *Gerichtsmann* at Ilvesh.(eim). Children:

1. Anna Othilia, bp. 7 June 1745
   Sp.: Peter Müller and Anna Othilia
2. Anna Maria, bp. 18 Dec. 1746
   Sp.: Joh. Bosch and Anna Maria
3. Joh. Adam, bp. 14 Sept.1748
   Sp.: Joh. Adam Clementz, son of
   Sebastian Clementz and Margaretha,
   daughter of the late Peter Hellmann.
4. Matthes, bp. 14 Jan. 1751
   Sp.: Matthes Wirtenberger and Catharina
5. Anna Maria, bp. 20 Apr. 1752

Emigration record:
Werner Hacker, *Auswanderungen aus Rheinpfalz und Saarland*:
#16578 Zahneissen, Valentin, with wife nee Clementzer, Ilbesheim, with two
children, manumitted to go to America, 1754.

ZEILER, PETER   Ober Lustadt=
Polly, 1765   67363 Lustadt
S-H, I: 704

EUROPEAN RECORDS

Ober Lustadt Reformed KB:
Peter Zeiler and wife Christina, Lutheran, had children:
1. Maria Margaretha, b. 11 Sept. 1761, bp. 13 Sept. 1761
   Sp.: Johannes Hausser and Maria Margaretha
2. Anna Margaret, b. 18 Oct. 1762, bp. 24 Oct. 1762
   at Niederlustadt [= 67363 Lustadt]
   Sp.: Johannes Hauser and Maria Margaretha, Lutheran
3. Daniel, b. 16 Nov. 1764, bp. 18 Nov. 1764
   at Niederlustadt
   Sp.: Daniel Deubel and Anna Elisabetha Schmitt

AMERICAN RECORDS

Fourteen passengers on the ship *Polly* in 1765, listed in close proximity to
one another on the list (S-H, I: 704), all appear in the Oberlustadt records:
Andreas Heintz, Christian Wunder, Conrad Hauenstein, Georg Jacob
Hauenstein, Christoph Strigel, Johann Leon[d] Devil (Deubel), Andres
Ehresmann, **Peter Zeiler**, Georg Aadam Bresler, Johan Michael Dühmer,
Jacob Wunder, Jacob Faut, Georg Simon Haushalter, Geo. Adam Teis.

Williams Township Congregation, Northampton Co., PA:
Daniel Zeiler and wife Anna Maria had:
   Abraham, b. 2 Nov. 1778, bp. 22 Nov. 1778
   Sp.: Peter Seler and wife Margreth

ZINN, HERMAN age 25   67157 Wachenheim an der Weinstrasse
Mary, 1732
S-H, 93, 94, 95
   [appears on ship list as Sin; did not sign]

EUROPEAN RECORDS

Wachenheim Reformed KB:
Herman Zinn, b. in [67149] Meckenheim, m. 7 Jan. 1728 Juliana Margaretha, daughter of the late Henrich Brickmann. Children:
1. Johannes Görg, twin b. Dec. 1729
2. Anna Elisabetha, twin b. Dec. 1729, died
3. Joh. Henrich, b. 2 Mar. 1732

AMERICAN RECORDS

Ephrata Cloister Cemetery:
Burials:

Georg Zinn	Sister Veronica Zinn
b. 2 Jan. 1730	b. 17 Nov. 1734
d. 12 Mar. 1802	d. 4 Jan. 1815
age 72 y. 2 mo. 10 d.	age 80 y. 1 mo. 17 d.

ZÜRCH, ANTHONY   Oberhochstadt=
Dragon, 1749   76879 Hochstadt, Pfalz
S-H, I: 423

EUROPEAN RECORDS

Oberhochstadt Reformed KB:
Confirmed Easter 1742: Anthony Zürch.

An early record in the Niederhochstadt KB indicates that Jacob Zürch was born in Switzerland.

Jacob Zürch and wife Maria Margaretha had children:
1. Philipp **Anton**, b. 28 Feb. 1729, bp. 6 Mar. 1729
   Sp.: Philipp Anton Doll at Edenkoben [?faded]
2. Anna Margaretha, b. 3 Dec. 1730, bp. 11 Dec. 1730
3. Stephan, b. 12 May 1736, bp. 13 May 1736
4. Maria Catharina, b. 22 Sept. 1739, bp. 27 Sept. 1739
   Sp.: Johann Jacob Frey from Oberhochstadt and
   Maria Catharina Bressler from Niederhochstadt, both single.

AMERICAN RECORDS

Tracey & Dern, *Pioneers of Old Monocacy, The Early Settlement of Frederick County, Maryland.* GPC, Baltimore, 1987, pg. 378:
Frederick County Muster Rolls, circa 1757: Capt. Peter Butler 34 days' service, Anthony Zerich.

pg. 282-283: Christian Thomas, son of Michael Thomas [q.v.] from Klein Schifferstadt, was first mentioned in Maryland records when he and his brother Hendrick Thomas were naturalized on 3 May 1740. Christian Thomas owned 210 acres with frontage along the Monocacy River. By his will dated 14 May 1777, Christian Thomas passed this land to his son Christian Thomas, Jr. The will also named a son Henry who had left Maryland about 1768, daughters Barbara Stoner and Mary Thomas, and a son-in-law Anthony Terrick (elsewhere Zerrick) to whose children Christian Thomas devised the home he had built in the town of Frederick.

Frederick Maryland Reformed KB, Frederick Co., MD:
Anthony Zürich and wife Magdalena had children baptized as adults:
1. Jacob, an adult, bp. 25 Mar. 1785
2. Catharina Richter, b. 20 Oct. 1762, bp. 14 Apr. 1786
3. Johannes, an adult, bp. 6 Apr. 1787.

Anthy. Serich, from Frederick in Maryland, nat. in Philadelphia, without oath, Fall, 1765.

Hochstadt today.

BIBLIOGRAPHY

Alguire, Joan. *York County, Pennsylvania Deeds,* Vol. I-III. Alguire Abstracts, South Holland, IL. 1982.

Anhaeusser, Heinz R. "Die Kaufhölzer" Eine Auswanderergruppe aus religiösen Gründe, von Lachen, nach den U.S.A." in *Pfälzisch-Rheinische Familienkunde,* Band 10, Heft 6, 1983.

Berkey, Andrew S., Ed. *The Journals and Papers of David Shultze.* 2 volumes. Pennsburg, 1952-1953.

Braun, Fritz. "Auswanderer aus der Mennonitengemeinde Friedelsheim im 19. Jahrhundert," in *Mitteilungen zur Wanderungsgeschichte der Pfälzer,* Folge 1 and 2, 1955.

_____. *Auswanderer aus der Umgebung von Ludwigshafen a. Rh. auf dem Schiff "Thistle of Glasgow" 1730,* publication #8, Schriften zur Wanderungsgeschichte der Pfälzer, 1959.

_____. "18th Century Palatine Emigrants from the Ludwigshafen Area," in *The Pennsyvlania Dutchman,* 1954; reprinted in Boyer, Carl. *Ship Passenger Lists, Pennsylvania and Delaware,* 1980.

Braun, Fritz, and Friedrich Krebs. "Pennsylvania Dutch Pioneers from South Palatine Parishes" in *The Pennsylvania Dutchman,* 8 (Spring, 1957).

Bunting, Elizabeth B. "The Bresslers/Presslers of Niederhochstadt" in *Mennonite Family History,* Vol. XI, No. 1, Elverson, Pa., 1992.

Burgert, Annette Kunselman. *Early Pennsylvania Pioneers from Mutterstadt in the Palatinate.* Worthington, Oh., 1983.

_____. *Eighteenth Century Pennsylvania Emigrants from Hassloch and Böhl in the Palatinate.* Worthington, Oh., 1983.

_____. *Colonial Pennsylvania Immigrants from Freinsheim in the Palatinate.* Myerstown, Pa., 1989.

_____. *Eighteenth and Nineteenth Century Emigrants from Lachen-Speyerdorf in the Palatinate.* Myerstown, Pa., 1989.

Burgert, Annette K. *Eighteenth Century Emigrants, Volume 1: The Northern Kraichgau.* Breinigsville, Pa., 1983; *Volume 2, The Western Palatinate.* Birdsboro, Pa., 1985.

_____. *Eighteenth Century Emigrants from the Northern Alsace to America.* Camden, Me., 1992.

_____. *The Hochstadt Origins of Some of the Early Settlers at Host Church, Berks County, Pa.* Worthington, Oh., 1983.

_____. *York County Pioneers from Friedelsheim and Gönnheim in the Palatinate.* Worthington, Oh., 1984.

Calendar of Maryland State Papers, No. 1, The Black Books. Baltimore, Md., 1967.

Chambers, Theodore F. *The Early Germans of New Jersey.* Dover, 1895.

Dotterer, Henry S. *The Perkiomen Region, Past and Present.* 3 volumes. Philadelphia, Pa., 1894-1901.

Durnbaugh, Donald, ed. *The Brethren Encyclopedia.* 3 vols. Philadelphia, Pa. and Oak Brook, Il., 1983.

Egle, William H. *History of Dauphin and Lebanon Counties, Pennsylvania.* Philadelphia, Pa., 1883.

Egypt Reformed Church Record, Lehigh Co., Pa., published in *Pennsylvania Archives,* Sixth Series, Vol. 6. Harrisburg, 1907.

Eyerman, John. *A Genealogical Index of Wills, Northampton County, Pennsylvania, 1752-1802.* Easton, Pa., 1897.

Eyster, Anita L. "Notices by German and Swiss Settlers in German Newspapers." Published in *The Pennsylvania German Folklore Society,* Vol 3, 1938.

Faust, Albert B. and Gaius M. Brumbaugh. *Lists of Swiss Emigrants in the Eighteenth Century to the American Colonies.* 2 volumes. National Genealogical Society, Washington, 1920-25.

Fendrick, Virginia S. *American Revolutionary Soldiers of Franklin County, Pennsylvania.* Chambersburg, Pa., 1944.

Fulton, Eleanore J. and Barbara K. Mylin. *An Index to the Will Books and Intestate Records of Lancaster County, Pennsylvania. 1729-1850.* Baltimore, 1981.

Giuseppi, Montague S., ed. *Naturalizations of Foreign Protestants in the American and West Indian Colonies.* Baltimore, 1979.

Hacker, Werner. *Auswanderungen aus Baden und dem Breisgau.* Stuttgart, 1980.

_____. *Auswanderungen aus dem früheren Hochstift Speyer nach Südosteuropa und Übersee im XVIII Jahrhundert.* Schriften zur Wanderungsgeschichte der Pfälzer, 28. Kaiserslautern, 1969.

_____. *Auswanderungen aus Rheinpfalz und Saarland im 18. Jahrhundert.* Stuttgart, 1987.

_____. *Kurpfälzische Auswanderer vom Unteren Neckar. Rechtsrheinische Gebiete der Kurpfalz.* Stuttgart, 1983.

Heads of Families at the First Census of the United States Taken in the Year 1790; Pennsylvania. Baltimore, 1970.

Hinke, William J. *A History of the Goshenhoppen Charge.* Pennsylvania Geman Society Proceedings, Vol. XXVII, 1920.

_____. *Life and Letters of the Rev. Joh. Philip Boehm, Founder of the Reformed Church in Pennsyvlania, 1673-1749.* Philadelphia, 1916.

_____. *Ministers of the German Reformed Congregations in Pennsylvania and other Colonies in the Eighteenth Century.* Lancaster, 1951.

_____. *Tohickon Union Church Records, Bucks County.* Proceedings of the Pennsylvania German Society, Vol. XXXI, 1925.

Hocker, Edward W. *Genealogical Data Relating to the German Settlers of Pennsylvania and Adjacent States from Advertisements in German Newspapers Published in Philadelphia and Germantown, 1743-1800.* Baltimore, 1981.

Humphrey, John. *Pennsylvania Births. Lancaster County, 1723-1777.* Includes baptisms from the Lititz Moravian Church. Washington, DC, 1997.

Jones, Henry Z, Jr. *More Palatine Families.* Universal City, Ca., 1991.

Jones, Henry Z, Jr. *The Palatine Families of New York: A study of the German Immigrants who Arrived in Colonial New York in 1710.* Universal City, Ca., 1985.

Jung, Hans and Irmgard König. *Die Einwohner von Maudach.* Frankfurt am Main, 1985.

Knittle, Walter A. *Early Eighteenth Century Palatine Emigration.* Philadelphia, 1937; reprinted Baltimore, 1965, 1970.

Krebs, Friedrich. "Pennsylvania Dutch Pioneers" in *The Pennsylvania Dutchman,* 1954. Reprinted in Carl Boyer, ed. *Ship Passenger Lists, Pennsyvlania and Delaware (1641-1825).* Newhall, Ca., 1980.

_____. "Annotations to Strassburger and Hinke's Pennsylvania German Pioneers." *Pennsylvania Genealogical Magazine, 21,* 1960: 235-48.

_____. "More 18th Century Emigrants from the Palatinate," in *The Pennsylvania Dutchman,* 1954; reprinted in Carl Boyer, ed. *Ship Passenger Lists, Pennsylvania and Delaware (1641-1825),* Newhall, Ca., 1980.

_____. "Palatine Emigrants from the District of Neustadt 1750" in *The Pennsylvania Dutchman.* May, 1953.

_____. "Eighteenth Century Emigrants to America from Palatine Parishes" translated by Anthony A. Roth in *Pennsylvania Genealogical Magazine,* Vol. XXVI, No. 1, 1969.

_____. "New Materials on the 18th Century Emigration from the Speyer State Archives," in Don Yoder, ed. *Rhineland Emigrants.* Baltimore, 1981.

_____ and Milton Rubincam. *Emigrants from the Palatinate to the American Colonies in the 18th Century.* Norristown, 1953.

Kuby, Alfred. "Schweizer Einwanderer in Edenkoben," published in *Pfalzische Familien und Wappenkunde,* Band 4, Heft 11, 1963.

Livengood, Candy C. *Genealogical Abstracts of The Laws of Pennsylvania and The Statutes at Large.* Westminster, Md., 1990.

Macco, H. F. *Swiss Emigrants and Huguenots to the Palatinate in Germany and to America 1650-1800.* Typescript and microfilm, Family History Library, Salt Lake City.

Mayhill, R. Thomas. *Deed Abstracts, Lancaster County, Pennsylvania, 1729-c1770 and Oaths of Allegiance*. Knightstown, In., 1979.

Montgomery, Morton L. *History of Berks County, Pennsylvania*. 2 vols. 1909.

Mutterstadt Kontraktenprotokolle (1714-1747), Landesarchiv Speyer, Briefprotokolle nr. 254. 736 pages.

Pendleton, Philip E. *Oley Valley Heritage: The Colonial Years, 1700-1775*. The Pennsylvania German Society, Vol. XXVIII, Birdsboro, Pa., 1994.

Pennsylvania Genealogical Magazine, Vol. XXVII, no. 1, article titled "Palatines and Servants". Philadelphia, 1971.

Pennsylvania German Church Records. From the Pennsylvania German Society Proceedings and Addresses. 3 vols. Baltimore, 1983.

Pfister, Hans Ulrich. *Die Auswanderung aus dem Knonauer Amt, 1648-1750*. Zürich, 1987.

Poller, Oskar and Peter Ruf. *Friesenheimer Bürgerbuch. Die Einwohner von Friesenheim, 1584-1814*. Frankfurt am main, 1989.

Rembe, Heinrich. *Lambsheim. Die Familien von 1547 bis 1800---für Maxdorf bis 1830---mit Angaben aus Weisenheim a. S., Eyersheim und Ormsheim*. Beiträge zur Bevölkerungsgeschichte der Pfalz, no. I. Kaiserslautern, 1971.

Roberts, Charles R. et al. *History of Lehigh County, Pennsylvania*. 3 volumes. Allentown, 1914.

Rogers, S. G. "Genealogical Gleanings from Orphans' Court Records of Lancaster County, Pennsylvania." *The Pennsylvania Genealogical Magazine,* Vol. XXIV, Nos. 1 & 2. Reprinted in *Pennsylvania Vital Records*. Baltimore, 1983.

Rupp, I. Daniel. *A Collection of Thirty-Thousand Names of German, Swiss, Dutch, French, Portuguese and other immigrants in Pennsylvania, 1727-1776*. Philadelphia, 1876.

Russell, Donna Valley, ed. "Frederick County, Maryland, Will Abstracts" in *Western Maryland Genealogy*. 1986-1991.

Schwarze, Rev. William N. and R. Rev. S. H. Gapp. *A History of the Beginnings of Moravian Work in America*. Bethlehem, Pa., 1955

Stahler, Fritz. "Franzosen, Schweizer, und Andere Auswärtige in den ref. Kirchenbüchern von Mutterstadt (1700-1800," in *Pfalzische Familien und Wappenkunde.* Ludwigshafen/Rh., Band 6, Heft, 5, 6, 7, 1968.

Stoever, Rev. John Caspar, records of, in Egle's *Notes and Queries,* 1892; reprinted Baltimore, Md., 1982.

Strassburger, Ralph B. and William John Hinke, ed. *Pennsylvania German Pioneers: A Publication of the Original Lists of Arrivals in the Port of Philadelphia from 1727 to 1808.* Volume I: *Introduction and Lists, 1727-1775.* Volume 2: *Facsimile of Signatures.* Volume 3: *Lists, 1785-1808, and Indices.* 1934; reprint ed., Baltimore, Md., 1966.

Tappert, Theodore G., and John W. Doberstein, eds. and trans. *The Journals of Henry Melchior Muhlenberg.* 3 vols. Philadelphia, Pa., 1942-48.

Tepper, Michael, ed. *Emigrants to Pennsylvania, 1614-1819: A Consolidation of Ship Passenger Lists from the PMHB.* Baltimore, Md., 1979.

_____. *Immigrants to the Middle Colonies: A Consolidation of Ship Passenger Lists and Associated Data from the New York Genealogical and Biographical Record.* Baltimore, Md., 1978.

_____. *New World Immigrants: A Consolidation of Ship Passenger Lists and Associated Data from Periodical Literature.* 2 vols. Baltimore, Md., 1980.

Tracey, Grace and John Dern. *Pioneers of Old Monocacy. The Early Settlement of Frederick County, Maryland. 1721-1743.* Baltimore, 1987.

Waldschmidt, Rev. John. His records published in *Pennsylvania Archives,* Sixth Series, Vol. 6. Harrisburg, 1907.

Weiser, Frederick S., ed. *Tulpehocken Church Records 1730-1800: Christ (Little Tulpehocken) Church and Altalaha Church, Rehrersburg.* Sources and Documents of the Pennsylvania Germans: VII. Breinigsville, PA: Pennsylvania German Society, 1982.

_____. *Daniel Schumacher's Baptismal Register.* Publications of The Pennsylvania German Society, Vol. 1, 1968.

_____. *Records of Pastoral Acts at Christ Lutheran Church, (Tulpehocken), Stouchsburg, Berks County, Pennsylvania.* 2 vols. Sources and Documents Series, Vol. XII and XIII. Pennsylvania German Society, 1991.

Weiser, Frederick S., ed. "Muddy Creek Moravian Records." in *Der Reggeboge,* Dec. 1976

_____. *Muddy Creek Lutheran Church Records and Muddy Creek Reformed Church Records.* Sources and Documents Series, Vol. V, Pennsylvania German Society, 1981.

_____. *Maryland Church Records* Series: Frederick Reformed, Monocacy Lutheran, and Frederick Lutheran Church Books. Manchester, Md., 1987.

_____. "Oley Moravian Church Records", published in *Der Reggeboge,* vol. 14, no. 1, Jan. 1980.

_____. *The Gift is Small, The Love is Great.* York, Pa., 1994.

_____. "The Earliest Records of Holy Trinity Evangelical Lutheran Church, Lancaster, Pennsylvania, 1730-1744", in The Pennsylvania Geman Society, Vol. 14, 1980.

Weiser, Frederick S. and Debra D. Smith. *Trinity Lutheran Church Records, Lancaster, Pennsylvania.* 3 vols. Apollo, Pa., 1988, 1995, 1998.

_____ and Vernon Nelson. "The Registers of Reeds Church." in *Anniversary Magazine of the Tulpehocken, 1723-1973.* Womelsdorf, PA; The Tulpehocken Settlement Society, 1973.

_____ and Glenn Schwalm. *Records of Pastoral Acts at Trinity Evangelical Lutheran Church, New Holland, Lancaster County, Pennsylvania. 1730-1799.* Pennsylvania German Society, Sources and Documents Series, Vol. II, 1977.

Wentz, A. R. *The Beginnings of the German Element in York County, Pennsylvania.* Proceedings of the Pennsylvania German Society, Vol. XXIV. Lancaster, 1916.

Williams, R. T. and M. C. *Index to Wills and Administrations, Philadelphia County, 1682-1782.* Danboro, Pa., 1971-72.

Wust, Klaus. "Direct German Immigration to Maryland in the Eighteenth Century (A Preliminary Survey).: *The Report: A Journal of German-American History 37.* (1978): 19-22.

_____. "The Emigration Season of 1738 -- Year of the Destroying Angel." *The Report: A Journal of German-American History 40* (1986): 21-56.

412

Wust, Klaus. "Feeding the Palatines: Shipboard Diet in the Eighteenth Century." *The Report: A Journal of German-American History 39* (1984): 32-42.

_____. "German Settlements and Immigrants in Virginia: A Bibliography." *The Report: A Journal of German-American History 33* (1968): 47-59.

_____. *The Virginia Germans.* Charlottesville, VA, 1969.

Wyand, Jeffery A. and Florence L. *Colonial Maryland Naturalizations.* Baltimore, 1975.

Yoder, Don, ed. *Rhineland Emigrants: Lists of German Settlers in Colonial America,* excerpted and reprinted from *Pennsylvania Folklife.* Baltimore, Md., 1981.

_____, trans and ed. *Pennsylvania German Immigrants, 1709-1783: Lists Consolidated from Yearbooks of the Pennsylvania German Folklore Society:* Baltimore, Md., 1980.

_____, ed. and transl., "Emigration Materials from Lambsheim in the Palatinate." in *Pennsylvania Folklife,* Winter 1973-74. Translation of Heinrich Rembe's work with additional notes on emigrants.

Land Records:
Pennsylvania Archives, Third Series:
Lancaster County Land Warrants, Vol. XXIV.
Berks County Land Warrants, Vol. XXVI.
Berks County tax Lists, Vol, XVIII.

Probate Records:
Adams County Will Abstracts
Berks County Orphan's Court records

Burgert, Annette K. and Marilyn N. Adams. *Abstracts of Dauphin County Wills.* Unpublished manuscript.

CD # 209: Family Tree Maker's Family Archives. *Genealogical Records: Pennsylvania Wills, 1682-1834.* Includes abstracts of the following Pennsylvania counties: Berks, Bucks, Chester, Cumberland, Delaware, Lancaster, Montgomery, Philadelphia, and York.

Lancaster County Miscellaneous Book.

Pfälzische Familien und Wappenkunde is the original title of a genealogical periodical that started publication in 1952 and continues to this day with the more recent title *Pfälzisch-Rheinische Familienkunde.* There have been numerous articles in this publication that pertain to the villages researched for this volume. Several of these articles contain information about the early Swiss settlers and their former villages of origin in Switzerland. A selected bibliography is presented here:

Burgert, Annette K. "Die frühen Siedler von Host Church, Berks County, Pennsylvanien und ihre Herkunft aus Hochstadt, Pfalz" Part 1, in *Pfälzisch-Rheinische Familienkunde,* Band 9, Heft 1 (1978). Part 2 in Band 9, Heft 2; Part 3 in Band 9, Heft 3.

Herzog, Heinrich. "Schweizer Namen im reformierten Kirchenbuch Freinsheim: in *Pfälzisch-Rheinische Familienkunde,* Band 9, Heft 4 (1979).

_____. "Freinsheimer im deutsch-reformierten Kirchenbuch Frankenthal 1618-1650" in *Pfälzisch-Rheinische Familienkunde,* Band 11, Heft 1 (1986).

_____. "Schweizer Einwanderer im Heiratsreg. des ref. KB Weisenheim a. Sand" in *Pfälzisch-Rheinische Familienkunde,* Band 12, Heft 10 (1993).

_____. "Hessische Einwanderer in Weisenheim a Sand 1654-1727" in *Pfälzisch-Rheinische Familienkunde,* Band 13, Heft 1 (1994).

Johnson, Arta F. "Schweizer in Klein Schifferstadt 1651-1775" in *Pfälzisch-Rheinische Familienkunde,* Band 12, Heft 7 (1992).

_____. "Schweizer in Haardt a. d. Weinstrasse 1678-1770" and "Schweizer in Dannstadt-Schauernheim 1673-1775" both in *Pfälzisch-Rheinische Familienkunde,* Band 12, Heft 8 (1992).

_____. "Schweizer in Iggelheim 1650-1775" in *Pfälzisch-Rheinische Familienkunde,* Band 12, Heft 9 (1992).

_____. "Schweizer in Gimmeldingen a.d. Weinstrasse 1678-1770" and "Schweizer in Mussbach a.d. Weinstrasse 1721-1775" both in *Pfälzisch-Rheinische Familienkunde,* Band 12, Heft 10 (1993)

_____. "Schweizer in Böhl 1700-1775" and "Schweizer in Duttweiler 1663-1770" both in *Pfälzisch-Rheinische Familienkunde,* Band 12, Heft 11 (1993).

Krebs, Friedrich. "Amerikaauswanderer des 18. Jahrhunderts" in *Pfälzische Familien und Wappenkunde,* Band 5, Heft 4.

Kuby, Alfred H. "Schweizer Einwanderer in Edenkoben," published in *Pfälzische Familien und Wappenkunde,* Band 4, Heft 10 & 11, 1963.

_____. "(Born) im 17. Jahrhundert - (died) im 18. Jahrhundert in Niederhochstadt" in *Pfälzisch-Rheinische Familienkunde,* Band 9, Heft 7 (1980).

Pressler, Gerd. "Niederhochstadter Familien im 30-Jährigen Krieg" in *Pfälzisch-Rheinische Familienkunde,* Band 9, Heft 11 (1981).

Rembe, Heinrich. "Einwanderung nach Lambsheim aus der Schweiz und anderen Nachbarländern, 1648-1750" in *Pfälzische Familien und Wappenkunde,* Band 2, Heft 3 & 4 (1955).

Stahler, Fritz. "Franzosen, Schweizer, und Andere Auswärtige in den ref. Kirchenbüchern von Mutterstadt, 1700-1800," in *Pfälzische Familien und Wappenkunde.* Ludwigshafen/Rh., Band 6, Heft, 5, 6, 7 1968.

GLOSSARY

Certain words have been left untranslated in the text, and appear in italics. These words usually refer to an occupation or an official status, and often have no equivalent English translation. Other words appear in the eighteenth century records that are now obsolete. An approximate meaning is offered for some of these phrases. The spellings are given as they appear in the eighteenth century records and may differ slightly from the currently accepted spelling.

Anwald = today, attorney or lawyer; checker of contracts, deeds, etc.
Gauerben Hubschultheiss = magistrate of the hereditary farm community
Gemeinsmann = citizen of a community with full rights
(des) Gerichts = member of the community court
Gerichtsmann = member of the court
Gerichtsschöffe = lay member of the court
Gerichtsschultheissen = court magistrate
Gerichtsverwandten = lay member of the court, juryman
gewesenen = former
Haffner Meister = master potter
Herr = a title of respect: schoolmaster, pastor, official.
Hoffmann = farmer
Huffschmidt = farrier
Jfr. = Jungfrau = single young woman
Licenter = tax official
Ludi Magister (Latin) = teacher
Meister = master (craftsman)
Messergerichtsverwandter = surveyor's court or council
Messerschultheiss = surveying or zoning official
Postleitzahlenbuch = postal code number book
(des) Raths = councilman
Rathsverwanden = mamber of the council
Schmid = smith
Schuldiener = school teacher
Schultheiss, -en = head of the village governing body
Schürmer = an inhabitant under the protection of the ruler
Unterschultheiss = deputy mayor
Vorsteher = lay leader of congregation

APPENDIX:

SWISS ORIGINS

Introductory remarks to Swiss Origins Appendix

Many of the families mentioned in the preceding pages are, in fact, originally of Swiss origin. Some of the Palatine church records used for this compilation mention these earlier Swiss origins, and often give the former commune, a fact that is essential for further research.

Various articles have been compiled presenting lists of these Swiss settlers in certain Palatine villages, and published in the genealogical periodical titled *Pfälzisch-Rheinische Familienkunde*. See the bibliography on pages 413-414 for a list of these articles and their compilers. Many of these lists and others that have not been published are consolidated in the following appendix.

A very special thank you to Dr. Arta F. Johnson of Columbus, Ohio for her work on these Swiss families, and for her permission to use the data here. In addition to her several articles published in the above named German periodical, Arta also compiled an extensive paper about the early Swiss settlers in Hassloch. Excerpts from that paper are also included in this appendix, with her kind permission, and will provide helpful clues to researchers working on those Swiss/Palatine families.

In this appendix, the Palatine villages appear simply by the village name; their zip code identification has been given elsewhere in the text. Villages in Switzerland are so identified. The two-letter abbreviation following the Swiss village name indicates the canton. The conventional Swiss postal abbreviations are used for all cantons found in the text:

AG	Aargau	GR	Graubünden
AR	Appenzell A. Rhoden	LU	Luzern
BE	Bern	SH	Schaffhausen
BL	Basel Land	TG	Thurgau
FR	Fribourg	VD	Vaud
GL	Glarus	ZH	Zürich

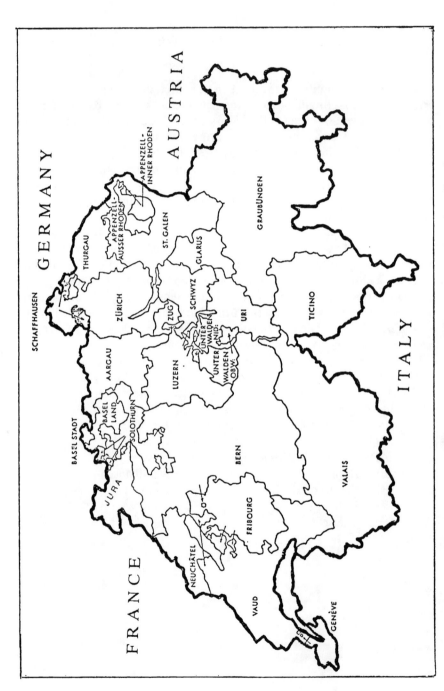

Map showing the cantons and boundaries of Switzerland

Person	Parent	Palatine Village	Year	Type of Record	Swiss Village
Abdorf, Benedict		Hassloch	1716	burial	Canton Zürich, Switzerland
Abeck, Elisabeth	Henrich AbEck	Gimmeldingen	1680	conf.	CH-8810 Horgen, ZH
Affholder, Anna	Benedict Affholder	Lachen	1665	m.	CH-3297 Leuzigen, BE
Affolder, Benedict	Benedict Affolder	Lachen	1668	m.	CH-3297 Leuzigen, BE
Albrecht, Hanss Jacob	Johannes Albrecht	Hassloch	1736	m.	From Switzerland
Allbrecht, Anna	widow of Jacob Mayer	Hassloch	1760	burial	CH-8174 Stadel bei Niederglatt, ZH
Altenberger, Johannes	Johannes Altenberger	Hassloch	1718	m.	CH-8173 Neerach, ZH
Alter, Martin	Hans Alter	Lachen	1668	conf.	CH-9000 St. Gallen
Ameter, Christian	Benedict Ameter	Duttweiler	1679	bp.	?CH-3705 Faulensee, BE
Angst, Henrich		Hassloch	1718	conf.	CH-8197 Rafz, ZH
Anneler, Johann Philipp	Christian Anneler	Hassloch	1716	bp.	From Switzerland
Aschmann, Hans Ullrich	Henrich Aschmann	Gimmeldingen	1694	conf.	?CH-8321 Madetswil, ZH
Bachman, Georg	Jacob Bachman	Lachen	1673	m.	?Embri, ZH
Baertschinger, Catharina		Lachen	1747	burial	CH-5600 Lenzburg, AG

421

Person	Parent	Palatine Village	Year	Type of Record	Swiss Village
Bähr, Johannes		Mutterstadt	1745	burial	CH-8805 Richterswil, ZH
Bähr, Veronica	Ulrich Bähr	Lachen	1714	m.	CH-8910 Affoltern am Albis, ZH
Bähr, Jacob m. Anna Maria Krey		Mutterstadt	1735	m.	CH-8805 Richterswil, ZH
Bardet, Jacob	Benedikt Bardet	Hassloch	1709	m.	CH-1831 Villard-sur-Chambry, VD
Baumann, Caspar	Jacob Baumann	Iggelheim	1716	m.	CH-5600 Lenzberg
Baumann, Jacob		Böhl	1717	m.	From Switzerland [see text]
Baumann, Hans Jacob		Lambsheim	1717	citizen	CH-4437 Waldenburg, BL
Baumberger, Hans	Felix Baumberger	Weisenheim a. S.	1663	m.	CH-8606 Nänikon, ZH
Baumgarten, Anna Barbara	Benedict Baumgarten	Lachen	1713	conf.	CH-3297 Leuzigen, BE
Baumgartner, Benedict	Benedict Baumgartner	Iggelheim	1719	burial	Weyler, BE [?CH-3251 or ?CH-3428 Wiler]
Bayn , Maria Ursula	Jacob Bayn (?Bein)	Hassloch	1709	m.	CH-8192 Aarüti, ZH
Beer, Veronica	Ulrich Beer	Lachen	1698	m.	CH-8910 Affoltern am Albis, ZH
Beer, Johannes	Ulrich Beer	Lachen	1696	m.	CH-8910 Affoltern am Albis, ZH

422

Person	Parent	Palatine Village	Year	Type of Record	Swiss Village
Beer, Elisabeth	Ulrich Beer	Lachen	1684	m.	CH-8910 Affoltern am Albis, ZH
Beer, Elisabeth	Uli Beer	Lachen	1682	conf.	CH-8910 Affoltern am Albis, ZH
Beer, Henrich		Hassloch	1717	conf.	CH-8910 Affoltern am Albis, ZH
Beer, Henrich	Henrich Beer	Gimmeldingen	1685	conf.	CH-8805 Richterswil, ZH
Beer, Henrich	Ulrich Beer	Lachen	1700	conf.	CH-8910 Affoltern am Albis, ZH
Beisch, Hans Jacob	Conrad Beisch	Iggelheim	1700	m.	?CH-8585 Eggethof, TG
Belle, Rudolff		Gimmeldingen	1690	burial	CH-3132 Riggisberg, BE
Belle, Rudolph	Rudolph Belle	Haardt a.d. W.	1686	conf.	CH-3132 Riggisberg, BE
Belli, Johannes	Hans Melchior Belli	Gimmeldingen	1683	conf.	CH-3132 Riggisberg, BE
Benninger, Ulrich		Böhl	1732	m.	From Switzerland
Bentz, Tobias		Mutterstadt	1726	m.	Altstetten, ZH = CH-8048 Zürich
Bentz, Anna Maria		Mutterstadt	1730	m.	CH-8450 Andelfingen, ZH
Bentz, Melchior		Mutterstadt	1727	m.	CH-8450 Alten, ZH
Bentz, Hans Adam	Ulrich Bentz	Hassloch	1707	m.	CH-3432 Lützelflüh, BE

423

Person	Parent	Palatine Village	Year	Type of Record	Swiss Village
Bentz?, Felix		Hassloch	1714	conf.	Riedt?, ZH
Berck, Magdalena	Hans Berck	Lachen	1663	conf..	CH-3549 Trimstein, BE
Berni, Johann Peter	Niclas Berni	Gimmeldingen	1689	m.	CH-3293 Douanne v. Twann, BE
Berrsche, Andreas		Hassloch	1707	citizen	CH-1531 Combremont, VD
Bertholf, Anthoni		Hassloch	1723	burial	from Switzerland
Bertsche, Felix	Hans Bertsche	Speyerdorf	1734	m.	CH-8154 Oberglatt, ZH
Biehler, Maria Margaretha	Peter Biehler	Hassloch	1713	m.	?Eshle, BE [?CH-3703 Aeschi, BE]
Bintz, Adam	Isaac Bintz	Speyerdorf	1736	m.	CH-8476/7 [Unter- or Ober-] Stammheim, ZH
Birer, David	David Birer	Gimmeldingen	1686	conf.	CH-4105 Biel, BL
Bittert, Hans Martin		Lambsheim	1674	burial	CH-4410 Liestal, BL
Bixel, Johannes		Hassloch	1717	conf.	CH-4900 Langenthal, BE
Bixel, Johannes		Hassloch	1722	m.	CH-4917 Busswil bei Melchnau, BE
Bleyenstein, Andreas		Mutterstadt	1737	burial	Canton Zürich

424

Person	Parent	Palatine Village	Year	Type of Record	Swiss Village
Bleyer, Barbara		Hassloch	1714	conf.	Bachenberg?, BE
Blum, Hanss Adam	Michael Blum	Lachen	1718	bp.	CH-3110 Münsingen, BE
Bollinger, A, Margaretha wife of Joh. Jacob Rothaug		Hassloch	1766	burial	Rued, BE [?CH-3711 Ried, BE]
Bollinger, A. Margaretha	Friedrich Bollinger	Hassloch	1725	m.	Ruth, BE [?CH-8630 Rüti, ZH or Ried, BE]
Bollinger, Felix		Hassloch	1719	conf.	CH-5200 Windisch, AG
Bollinger, Anna Barbara	widow of Jacob Bollinger	Hassloch	1734	burial	CH-8536 Gundetswil, ZH
Bordner, Johannes	Henrich Bordner	Gimmeldingen	1695	m.	?Mulhaussen, Schweitz
Bossa, Joseph		Hassloch	1683	citizen	CH-1630 Bulle, FR
Bossert, Barbara		Hassloch	1713	conf.	[?Porin or ?Norin]
Bossert?, Susanna		Hassloch	1713	conf.	Canton Zürich
Bosshardt, Johann Jacob	Joh. Jacob Bosshardt	Gimmeldingen	1766	m.	CH-8335 Hittnau, ZH
Bovon, David		Mutterstadt	1733	burial	CH-1837 Château d'Oex, VD
Bovon, Marie	Pierre Bovon	Mutterstadt	1736	burial	CH-1837 Château d'Oex, VD

Person	Parent	Palatine Village	Year	Type of Record	Swiss Village
Brendel, Henrich	Hans Brendel	Gimmeldingen	1683	conf.	?CH-4536 Attiswil, BE
Brendel, Henrich	Hans Brendel	Speyerdorf	1696	m.	CH-8135 Langnau am Albis, ZH
Brennel, Henrich	Hans Brennel	Lachen	1684	conf.	CH-8800 Thalwil, ZH
Brocher, Veronica she m. 1) Hans Nussbaum she m. 2) J.Michel Heberle	Georg Brocher	Iggelheim	1715	burial	Affholdren in d. Schweitz ?CH-3416 Affholtern im E., BE or ?CH-8910 Affoltern am Albis, ZH
Buche, Isac		Lachen	1681	burial	CH-8501 Hagenbuch, ZH
Bucher, Hans		Lachen	1680	m.	CH-3118 Uttigen, BE
Bug, Benedict		Hassloch	1728	citizen	?Kerbertz, BE
Bundt, Christian		Hassloch	1710	conf.	From Switzerland
Burgermeister, Johannes	Joh. Jacob Burgermeister	Hassloch	1780	m.	CH-8556 Wigoltingen, TG
Burgin, Andreas		Mutterstadt	1721	m.	CH-9428 Walzenhausen, AR
Burgin, Veronica	Urs Burgin	Kl. Schifferstadt		burial	Canton Basel, Switzerland
Burginon, Ludwig		Hassloch	1751	conf.	From Switzerland
Burginon, M. Elisabetha		Hassloch	1751	conf.	From Switzerland

426

Person	Parent	Palatine Village	Year	Type of Record	Swiss Village
Busehard, Veronica		Haardt a.d. W.	1702	bp.	CH-8211 Lohn, SH
Cavein, Jean Georg		Mutterstadt	1706	m.	? Villar, BE
Christen, Hans Jacob		Hassloch	1710	conf.	From Switzerland
Christen, Barbara		Hassloch	1715	burial	CH-4931 Leimiswil, BE
Cuntz, Felix	Caspar Cuntz	Hassloch	1730	m.	CH-8155 Niederhasli, ZH
Deege, Heinrich		Hassloch	1668	citizen	CH-4132 Muttenz, BL
Defréne, Philipp	Samuel Defréne	Mutterstadt	1736	burial	CH-1531 Dompierre, VD
Denni, Caspar		Mutterstadt	1702	m.	CH-3855 Brienz, BE
Diem, Johannes	Jacob Diem	Iggelheim	1718	conf.	CH-9103 Schwellbrunn, AR
Dobler, Hans Jacob		Hassloch	1725	conf.	From Switzerland
Doppler, Jacob	Salomon Doppler	Hassloch	1734	m.	From Switzerland
Dreyer, Hans Jacob		Mutterstadt	1716	burial	CH-4142 Münchenstein, BL
Drillinger, Elisabeth	Wendel Drillinger	Lachen	1681	m.	CH-8433 Weiach, ZH
Dups, Henrich	Henrich Dups	Lachen	1665	conf.	Loh, Knonauer Ampt, ZH

427

Person	Parent	Palatine Village	Year	Type of Record	Swiss Village
Ebrecht, Philip	Rudolph Ebrecht	Speyerdorf	1680	bp.	Uffeisten, ZH [?CH-8448 Uhweisen]
Egli, Jacob	Jacob Egli	Kl. Schifferstadt	1724	burial	CH-8627 Grüningen, ZH
Ehninger, Anna Barbara	wife of Georg Karn	Hassloch	1763	burial	CH-8500 Frauenfeld, TG
Eninger, Susanna	Jacob Eninger	Hassloch	1736	m.	From Switzerland
Epprecht, Hans		Lambsheim	1688	citizen	? Nierstadt, ZH
Erhard, Elisabetha	N. Erhard	Haardt a.d. W.	1698	conf.	CH-8561 Neuwilen, TG
Eyer, Melchior	Hans Eyer	Lachen	1681	conf.	CH-3132 Riggisberg, BE
Eysen, Hans		Weisenheim a. S.	1681	m.	?Nussbaum, Switzerland
Fehr, Anna		Dannstadt	1707	bp. Sp.	From Switzerland
Findeli, Peter	Ulrich Findeli	Lachen	1689	m.	CH-3550 Langnau im Emmental, BE
Fischer, Andreas		Hassloch	1718	conf.	From Switzerland
Fischer, Samuel	Samuel Fischer	Hassloch	1722	m.	CH-5600 Lenzburg, BE
Flachmüller, Frantz	Jacob Flachmüller	Weisenheim a. S.	1706	m.	Rickenbach, ZH [several Rickenbachs]
Floch?, Elisabetha		Böhl	1719	conf.	CH-8422 Pfungen, ZH

428

Person	Parent	Palatine Village	Year	Type of Record	Swiss Village
Forler, Henrich	Rudolph Forler	Gimmeldingen	1683	conf.	Canton Basel
Frandecker, Christina	Hans Jacob Frandecker	Duttweiler [Lachen KB]	1676	m.	Oberhofen, BE ?CH-3550 or ?CH-3653
Frankhauser, Johanna		Mutterstadt	1722	m.	Canton Bern, Switzerland
Freidiger, Barbara	Barthel Freidiger	Speyerdorf	1671	m.	CH-4704 Niederbipp, BE
Frey, Hans Henrich	Hans Henrich Frey	Speyerdorf	1711	m.	CH-8302 Kloten, ZH
Frey, Jacob		Hassloch	1669	citizen	CH-5728 Gontenschwil, AG
Frey, Nicolaus		Gimmeldingen	1739	burial	From Switzerland
Frischknecht, Thebes		Weisenheim a. S.	1676	m.	CH-9100 Herisau, AR
Frölich, Ulrich		Hassloch	1706	m.	CH-8155 Niederhasli, ZH
Fuchs, Barbara		Hassloch	1711	burial	From Switzerland
Fuchser, Anna Barbara married Peter Will	Moritz Fuchser	Mutterstadt	1747	burial	CH-3612 Steffisburg, BE
Funck, Anna wife of Philip Stiess	Hans Funck	Iggelheim	1714	burial	CH-8913 Ottenbach, ZH

429

Person	Parent	Palatine Village	Year	Type of Record	Swiss Village
Funk, Oswald		Mutterstadt	1708	burial	Canton Zürich
Furer, Magdalena	widow of Henrich Furer	Hassloch	1744	burial	?CH-3099 Hinterfultigen, BE
Gaffo?, Hans Ludwig	Felix ?Gaffo	Lachen	1672	conf.	?CH-8437 Zurzach, AG
Gärber, Anna Elisabetha		Mutterstadt	1726	m.	from Switzerland
Gavin (Cavein), Joh Georg		Mutterstadt	1706	m.	? Villar, VD (several Villars)
Geiger, Nicolaus		Lambsheim	1701	citizen	? CH-8305 Dietlikon, ZH
Genfe, Benedict		Lambsheim	1682	citizen	Biberen, BE = 3206 Rizenbach, BE
Giessen, Bernhard	Bernhardt Giessen	Lachen	1670	m.	Oltigen, BE = CH-3036 Detligen
Glatthardt, Bartel		Lambsheim	1678	citizen	CH-3812 Wilderswil, BE
Glor, Rudolph	Hans Ullrich Glor	Haardt a.d. W.	1700	m.	CH-5726 Unterkulm, AG
Glor (Klohr), Johannes	Hans Ullrich Glor	Haardt a.d. W.	1700	m.	CH-5726 Unterkulm, AG
Gommer, Peter	Hans Gommer	Lachen	1680	conf.	CH-2720 Tramelan, BE
Gotti, Anna Rashel	Christian Gotti	Hassloch	1707	m.	?Rochemont, BE
Götzendanner, Christian	Jacob Götzendanner	Kl. Schifferstadt	1723	m.	Switzerland

430

Person	Parent	Palatine Village	Year	Type of Record	Swiss Village
Graber, Susanna	Hans Graber	Hassloch	1712	m.	CH-3655 Sigriswil, BE
Greichi, Heinrich	Peter Greichi	Lachen	1710	conf.	?CH-3053 Münchenbuchsee, BE
Grof, Hans Ulrich	Henrich Grof	Niederlustadt	1707	conf.	Switzerland [Lachen KB]
Grumbach, Christian	Nicolai Grumbach	Lachen	1664	m.	CH-3454 Sumiswald, BE
Gründele, Rudolph		Edenkoben	1684	bp. Sp..	CH-8932 Mettmenstetten, ZH [Lachen KB]
Grundisch, A. Margaretha	Ulrich Grundisch	Haardt a.d. W.	1684	bp. Sp.	CH-3792 Saanen, BE
Grundisch, A. Margaretha	Ulrich Grundisch	Haardt a.d. W.	1684	m.	CH-3792 Saanen, BE
Gudt, Anna	Georg Nicolai Gudt	Lachen	1664	conf.	CH-8926 Uerzlikon, ZH
Guiene, Susanna Margreth	Piere Guiene	Hassloch	1720	bp. Sp.	From Switzerland
Gummer, Peter	Hans Gummer	Lachen	1687	m.	CH-2720 Tramelan, BE
Gut, Anna	Theobald Gut	Lachen	1665	m.	CH-8926 Uerzlikon, ZH
Guth, Rudolph		Hassloch	1716	conf.	?Woltzen, Switzerland
Guth, Hans		Hassloch	1730	burial	Canton Zürich
Guth, Johannes	Nicolai Guth	Lachen	1665	m.	CH-8926 Uerzlikon, ZH

431

Person	Parent	Palatine Village	Year	Type of Record	Swiss Village
Guth, Heinrich		Hassloch	1683	citizen	Unterlunnern= CH-8912 Obfelden, ZH
Gysi, Adam		Hassloch	1709	burial	From Switzerland
Gysi, Jacob		Hassloch	1710	conf.	CH-4434 Holstein, BL
Gyssi, Jacob		Hassloch	1710	m.	From Switzerland
Haberstock, Best		Lachen	1679	burial	By CH-5000 Aarau, AG
Haffner, Jacob	Andreas Haffner	Haardt a.d. W.	1749	m.	CH-8903 Birmensdorf, ZH
Haller, Rudolph		Hassloch	1710	conf.	CH-5734 Reinach, AG
Hämmerli, Samuel	Samuel Hämmerli	Mutterstadt	1760	burial	CH-5600 Lenzburg, AG
Hartmann, Veronica m Joh. Nicolaus Seel	Burckhard Hartmann	Haardt a.d. W.	1710	m..	CH-5617 Tennwil, AG
Hartmann, Samuel	Samuel Hartmann	Mutterstadt	1748	burial	? CH-5707 Seengen, AG
Hartmann, Veronica	Burckhard Hartmann	Haardt a.d. W.	1705	conf.	CH-5617 Tennwil, AG
Haser [Hauser], Anna	Melchior Hauser	Lachen	1663	conf.	CH-8911 Rifferswil, ZH
Hauser, Jacob		Lambsheim	1678	citizen	Reiersweyer ? = ? CH-8805 Richterswil, ZH Or ? CH-8911 Rifferswil, ZH

432

Person	Parent	Palatine Village	Year	Type of Record	Swiss Village
Hauser, Maria Catharina	Henrich Hauser	Lachen	1669	bp.	Oberhasen or Oberhofen, SH
Hauser, Anna	Melchior Hauser	Lachen	1665	m.	CH-8911 Rifferswil, ZH
Hausser, Anna Helena	Martin Hausser	Gimmeldingen	1750	m.	CH-8335 Hittnau, ZH
Hausser, Anna	Hans Georg Haussser	Hassloch	1748	burial	CH-9320 Steineloh, TG
Hausser, Anna		Hassloch	1718	conf.	From Switzerland
Hausswirth, Niclas		Lambsheim	1671	citizen	CH-4125 Riehen, BL
Hayni, Johannes	Benedict Hayni	Hassloch	1731	m.	From Switzerland
Hegy (Hoegi, etc), Felix		Lambsheim	1734	m. (2)	Uerzlikon, ZH = CH-8926 Kappel am Albis
Hellinger, Joh.'s wife		Speyerdorf	1738	burial	born in Switzerland
Henrich Maurer		Hassloch	1724	bp.	Canton Zürich, Switzerland
Hensler, Rudolff	Henrich Hensler	Gimmeldingen	1686	conf.	CH-8805 Richterswil, ZH
Herde, Veronica	Rudolph Herde	Haardt a.d. W.	1705	burial	from Switzerland
Heyler (?Jegler), Barbara	Sebastian Heyler ?Jegler	Mutterstadt	1704	m.	CH-4457 Diegten, BL
Hodel, Michael		Lachen	1724	burial	from Switzerland

433

Person	Parent	Palatine Village	Year	Type of Record	Swiss Village
Hofer, Anna Maria, widow	of Hans Ulrich Hofer	Lachen	1707	burial	CH-3251 Oberwil bei Büren, BE
Högi (Hegi), Joh. Jacob		Mutterstadt	1722	burial	from Switzerland
Högi (Hegi), Felix		Mutterstadt	1712	m.	Uerzlikon, ZH = CH-8926 Kappel am Albis
Hollinger, Jacob		Lambsheim	1682	citizen	CH-5600 Lenzburg, AG
Hubel, Hans Rudolph	Hans Hubel	Haardt a.d. W.	1686	m.	?CH-3451 Walkringen, BE
Huber, Henrich	Oswald Huber	Iggelheim	1717	burial	?CH-8932 Rossau, ZH or CH-8625 Gossau
Huber, Henrich	Johann Jacob Huber	Böhl	1730	m.	CH-8155 Oberhasli, ZH
Huber, Adam	Hans Jacob Huber	Lachen	1676	conf.	Klisch, ZH
Huber, Jacob		Hassloch	1669	citizen	CH-8902 Urdorf, ZH
Huber, Joh. Henrich		Hassloch	1770	burial	CH-8155 Oberhasli, ZH
Huber, Johannes		Hassloch	1724	conf.	From Switzerland
Hubert, Adam	Jacob Hubert	Lachen	1680	m.	Heisch, ZH [?Aesch]
Huggenberger, Johann Rudolff		Hainfeld (Gimmeldingen)	1756	m.	CH-5036 Oberentfelden, AG

Person	Parent	Palatine Village	Year	Type of Record	Swiss Village
Hubschmidt, Peter		Kl. Schifferstadt	1709	m.	From Switzerland
Hundner, Salome	Rudolph Hundner	Lachen	1668	m.	Nidermuchen, BE
Huntzicker, Rudolph	Rudolph Huntzicker	Lachen	1668	conf.	?Müchen, BE
Husser, Jacob	Hans Georg Husser	Gimmeldingen	1716	conf.	From Switzerland
Jacob, Veronica		Iggelheim	1744	m.	CH-8155 Oberhasli, ZH
Jacob, Johannes	Caspar Jacob	Iggelheim	1738	burial	Canton Bern, Switzerland
Jacque. David		Hassloch	1717	conf.	?Stomer, BE
Jegler (?Heyler), Barbara	Sebastian Jegler ? Heyler	Mutterstadt	1704	m.	CH-4457 Diegten, BL
Job, Hans	Hans Job	Hassloch	1703	m.	?CH-8903 Birmensdorf, ZH
Josy, Peter		Lambsheim			CH-3715 Adelboden, BE
Katterli, Veronica wife of Caspar Luetti	Johannes Katterli	Iggelheim	1715	burial	CH-4937 Ursenbach, BE
Keiser, Hans	Benedict Keiser	Lachen	1671	m.	CH-3297 Leuzigen
Keller, Christina	Ulrich Keller	Lachen	1664	m.	CH-3792 Saanen, BE

435

Person	Parent	Palatine Village	Year	Type of Record	Swiss Village
Keller, Hans Jacob		Mutterstadt	1714	m.	Canton Bern, Switzerland
Keller, Joh. Michael		Hassloch	1683	citizen	?CH-8505 Pfyn, TG [Pfruenn]
Keller, Joh. Jacob		Böhl	1729	bp. Sp.	From Switzerland
Keller, Joh. Jacob	Hans Georg Keller	Hassloch	1757	burial	CH-8215 Hallau, SH
Keller, Christian	Hans Georg Keller	Hassloch	1739	m.	CH-8215 Hallau, SH
Keller, Johannes	Hans Georg Keller	Hassloch	1740	m.	CH-8215 Hallau, SH
Kelter, Jacob	Johann Frantz Kelter	Mutterstadt	1736	burial	Seigneux, VD = CH-1599 Henniez
Kerle?, Joseph		Hassloch	1717	conf.	CH-3055 Brienz, BE
Kestle, Johannes		Lambsheim	1663	citizen	CH-9000 St. Gallen
Keyser, Barbara	Hans Keyser	Lachen	1665	m.	CH-3297 Leuzigen, BE
Keyser, Anna Barbara	Durres Keyser	Lachen	1688	m.	CH-3297 Leuzigen, BE
Keyser, Barbara	Ulrich Keyser	Lachen	1687	conf.	CH-3297 Leuzigen, BE
Keyser, Anna Barbara	Durres Keyser	Lachen	1681	conf.	CH-3297 Leuzigen, BE
Keyser, Hans	Ulrich Keyser	Lachen	1684	conf.	CH-3297 Leuzigen, BE

436

Person	Parent	Palatine Village	Year	Type of Record	Swiss Village
Keyser, Dureus	Benedict Keyser	Lachen	1665	m.	CH-3297 Leuzigen, BE
Kilheuer, Christophel		Lachen	1664	conf.	Not given, Switzerland
Kleis?, Hans Jacob	Hans Jacob Kleis?	Lachen	1685	conf.	CH-8932 Mettmenstetten, ZH
Klother, Tobias	Rudolph Klother	Duttweiler	1666	m.	?CH-8304 Wallisellen, ZH
Klutz, Barbara	Peter Klutz	Lachen	1704	conf.	Not given, Switzerland
König, Veronica	Sebastian König	Hassloch	1716	bp.	From Switzerland
König, Jacob	Lorentz König	Hassloch	1715	m.	Ausserrhoden, Appenzell
König, Barbara	Christmann König	Gimmeldingen	1679	m.	?Glitsch, Canton Bern
Krebs, Nickolaus	Peter Krebs	Hassloch	1713	m.	?Niederurach, BE
Krebs, Catharina	Nicolai Krebs	Duttweiler	1665	conf.	Switzerland [Lachen KB]
Krebs, Andreas		Hassloch	1708	m.	From Switzerland
Kreuter, Caspar	Peter Kreuter	Speyerdorf	1664	m.	Rockweyl, BE
Krieger, Bernhard		Hassloch	1710	conf.	CH-3368 Bleienbach, BE
Küburtz, Susanna Margr.	Moritz Küburtz	Hassloch	1705	bp.	Canton Bern, Sw.

437

Person	Parent	Palatine Village	Year	Type of Record	Swiss Village
Kuhn (Chun), Hans		Lambsheim	1672	citizen	From Switzerland
Kuhn, Philipp		Lambsheim	1671	citizen	? Grostall, ZH
Kühner, Johannes	Johannes Kühner	Haardt a.d. W.	1723	m.	From Switzerland
Kühner, Benedict		Gimmeldingen	1689	burial	?CH-3132 Riggisberg, BE
Kühner, Johannes	Johannes Kühner	Haardt a.d. W.	1708	conf.	From Switzerland
Kummer, Anna Barbara	Jost Kummer	Hassloch	1670	conf.	Bern, Switzerland [Lachen KB]
Kunkler, Barbara	Hans Kunkler	Hassloch	17715	m.	CH-3127 Thurnen, BE
Kunser, Hans Conrad	Henrich Kunser	Iggelheim	1719	m.	CH-8634 Hombrechtikon, ZH
Küster, Hans Conrad		Mutterstadt	1707	m.	Zürich, Switzerland
Lang, Adam	Henrich Lang	Lachen	1696	m.	Wirloss, BL = ?CH-8166 Würenlos, AG
Lappart, Barbara m. 1) Benedict ?Sattler m. 2) Caspar Lütti	Hans Lappart	Iggelheim	1727	burial	CH-4900 Langenthal, BE
Lehman, Barbara	Benedict Lehman	Lachen	1664	m.	CH-3297 Leuzigen, BE
Leuffer, Joseph		Weisenheim a. S.	1680	m.	From Switzerland

438

Person	Parent	Palatine Village	Year	Type of Record	Swiss Village
Liebensperger, Jacob	Cunrad Liebensperger	Duttweiler	1665	m.	CH-8546 Islikon, Gundetswil [Lachen KB]
Liesse, Hans Ulrich		Iggelheim	1701	m.	From Switzerland
Liessel, Anna Helena	Hans Peter Liessel	Gimmeldingen	1707	m.	CH-3099 Vorderfultigen, BE
Lischer (Löscher), Hans		Mutterstadt	1704	m.	CH-1510 Moudon, VD
Lischer, Susanna	Hans Lischer	Haardt a.d. W.	1697	conf.	From Switzerland
Lischer, Melchior	Hans Lischer	Lachen	1678	m.	Muchen, BE, ?CH-5037 Muhen, BE
Lischer, Susanna	Caspar Lischer	Lachen	1668	m.	Nidermauchen, BE
Löw, Joh. Jacob	Ulrich Löw	Mutterstadt	1744	burial	Rohrbach, BE (two of them)
Lütti, Catharina	Caspar Lütti	Iggelheim	1715	m.	CH-4937 Ursenbach, BE
Lütti, Johann Caspar	Caspar Lütti	Iggelheim	1726	m.	CH-4937 Ursenbach, BE
Lysi, Henrich	Jacob Lysi	Iggelheim	1720	burial	?Däuwyl, BE
Lysi, Hans		Hassloch	1713	conf.	?CH-8910 Zwillikon, ZH
Mag, Ulrich	Hans Henrich Mag	Lachen	1685	conf.	CH-8411 Dänikon, ZH
Margraue, Hans Nicolaus	Hans Margraue	Gimmeldingen	1681	conf.	CH-1095 Lutry, VD

439

Person	Parent	Palatine Village	Year	Type of Record	Swiss Village
Martin, Henrich	Johann Martin	Iggelheim	1716	conf.	CH-8155 Oberhasli, ZH
Martler, Margretha	Hans Wolff Martler	Duttweiler [Lachen KB]	1668	m.	CH-6000 Luzern
Massy, Samuel		Dannstadt	1703	burial	From Switzerland
Mattler, Henrich		Hassloch	1700	m.	CH-8426 Lufingen, ZH
Maurer, Anna	Benedict Maurer	Mutterstadt	1713	m.	CH-6248 Alberswil, LU
Maurer, Rudolf		Lambsheim	1703	citizen	Jais, BE = ? CH-1781 Jeuss, FR
Mayer, Jacob		Hassloch	1757	burial	Rohrwitz?, ZH
Mayer, Heinrich		Hassloch	1721	citizen	?CH-888102 Oberengstringen, ZH
Mayer, Heinrich		Hassloch	1707	citizen	Unter-Endingen, Unterwalden
Mayer, Anna, widow of Joh. Ludwig Kern		Hassloch	1759	burial	From Switzerland
Mayer, Veronica, widow of Joh. Georg Kauffmann		Meckenheim [Hassloch KB]	1774	burial	From Switzerland
Mayer, Anna wife of Henrich Bentz	Mathias Mayer	Mutterstadt	1735	burial	CH-8450 Alten, ZH

440

Person	Parent	Palatine Village	Year	Type of Record	Swiss Village
Meister, Anna Maria	Jacob Meister	Iggelheim	1731	burial	CH-3236 Gampelin, BE
Mertz, Joerg	Cyrillius Mertz	Weisenheim a. S.	1662	m.	St. Gallen, Switzerland
Meyer, Barbara	widow of Henrich Meyer	Hassloch	1736	burial	From Switzerland?
Meyer, Henrich		Hassloch	1718	conf.	Canton Zürich
Meyer, Veronica m. Jacob Weymann	Burckhardt Meyer	Hassloch	1701	m.	CH-8424 Embrach, ZH
Meyer, Joh. Jacob	Reformed Pastor, 1653-66	Lambsheim			CH-8400 Winterthur, ZH
Mohler, Mathes		Hassloch	1712	burial	From Switzerland
Mohler, Johann Georg	Mathes Mohler	Hassloch	1703	bp.	From Switzerland
Mohler, Anna Elisabetha	Mathes Mohler	Hassloch	1701	bp.	From Switzerland
Mohler, Henrich	Mathess Mohler	Hassloch	1734	m.	CH-4000 Basel
Mohler, Johann Henrich	Mathes Mohler	Hassloch	1711	bp.	From Switzerland
Monar, Abraham Benedict	Johann Monar	Weisenheim a. S.	1685	m.	Chabray?, BE [?CH-1581 Chabrey, VD]
Montay, Oubert		Hassloch	1700	bp. Sp.	From Switzerland

441

Person	Parent	Palatine Village	Year	Type of Record	Swiss Village
Moser, Anna Barbara	Joh. Jacob Moser	Hassloch	1665	conf.	Switzerland [Lachen KB]
Motte-, Susanna Margreth	Jaque (Jacob) Motte(t)	Hassloch	1720	bp.	From Switzerland
Müller, Samuel		Hassloch	1716	burial	From Switzerland
Müller, Stophel	Hans Müller	Lachen	1669	conf.	?Nidermauchen, BE
Müller, Susanna she m. Jacob Liesi	Johannes Müller	Iggelheim	1721	burial	?CH-Kallem, AG
Müller, Johannes		Hassloch	1707	citizen	CH-5600 Lenzburg, AG
Müller, Daniel	Conrad Müller	Schauernheim	1735	burial	From Switzerland
Müller, Joh. Samuel		Hassloch	1710	m.	CH-1831 Villard-sur-Chambry, VD
Müller, Joh. Daniel	Ottoni Müller	Hassloch	1718	m.	Villa---, Canton Bern, Sw.
Müller, Elisabeta she m. Johann Ernst Fick	Christian Müller	Iggelheim	1717	burial	CH-3700 Spiez, BE
Müller, Anna	widow of Samuel Müller	Hassloch	1719	burial	From Switzerland
Müller, Nickolaus		Hassloch	1719	m.	Canton Bern, Switzerland

442

Person	Parent	Palatine Village	Year	Type of Record	Swiss Village
Munier, Maria, m. Joh. Georg Diedenhoffer	Abraham Munier	Hassloch	1701	m.	CH-2720 Tramelan, BE
Munz, Peter		Lambsheim	1716	citizen	? Granaf, ZH
Nachbauer, Benedict		Lambsheim	1664	citizen	CH-4500 Solothurn
Nagel, Catharina	Elisabetha Nagel	Haardt a.d. W.	1718	bp.	From Switzerland
Neff, Cunrad	Hans Neff	Lachen	1687	m.	CH-9100 Herisau, AR
Nercker, Hans	Melchior Nercker	Weisenheim a. S.	1662	m.	Canton Zürich, Switzerland
Nercker, Balthasar		Weisenheim a. S.	1657	m.	From Switzerland
Neumann, Anna Maria married Phil. Härtel	Joh. Neumann	Mutterstadt	1743	burial	CH-3361 Höchstetten-Hellsau, BE
Neuschwanger, Daniel	Christian Neuschwanger	Haardt a.d. W.	1681	conf.	CH-3534 Signau, BE
Nicklar, Anna Barbara	Samuel Nicklar	Gimmeldingen	1679	conf.	CH-3293 Dotzigen, BE
Nieder, Susanna		Hassloch	1715	conf.	From Switzerland
Nuffer, Jacob		Hassloch	1719	m.	Canton Zürich
Nussbaum, Johann Georg	Hans Nussbaum	Hassloch	1705	bp.	CH-3073 Gümligen, BE

443

Person	Parent	Palatine Village	Year	Type of Record	Swiss Village
Oberli, Philippus	Johannes Oberli	Lachen	1664	m.	Not given, Switzerland
Oniger, Anna Barbara	Jacob Oniger	Hassloch	1732	m.	From Switzerland
Panchaud, Jonas Albert		Dannstadt	1726	m.	CH-8910 Affoltern am Albis, ZH
Peter, Joh. Peter	Joh. Jacob Peter	Lachen	1664	m.	?CH-8810 Horgen, ZH
Peter, Magdalena	Abraham Peter	Lachen	1688	conf.	CH-3271 Radelfingen b. Aarberg, BE
Pfeiffer, Peter		Weisenheim a. S.	1657	m.	From Switzerland
Pfisterer, Heinrich		Hassloch	1708	citizen	CH-8625 Gossau, ZH
Pfisterer, Caspar		Hassloch	1700	m.	CH-5026 Densbüren, AG
Pfrenger, Johann Jacob	Johann Jacob Pfrenger	Haardt a.d. W.	1692	m.	CH-3123 Belp, BE
Philipp, Hans Henrich	Caspar Philipp	Weisenheim a. S.	1670	m.	Canton Zürich, Switzerland
Pisterer, Cunrad	Hans Pisterer	Lachen	1698	m.	CH-8820 Wädenswil, ZH
Probst, Friederich	Mattheis Probst	Lachen	1704	m.	CH-3255 Erlach, BE
Probst, Mayrodt		Hassloch	1669	citizen	CH-8932 Dachelsen, ZH
Rapp, Magdalena		Hassloch	1717	conf.	?CH-3652 Hilterfingen, BE

444

Person	Parent	Palatine Village	Year	Type of Record	Swiss Village
Rauschenberger, Cunrad	Urban Rauschenberger	Lachen	1696	conf.	?CH-8418 Schlatt, ZH
Reichard, Veronica	Ulrich Reichard	Lachen	1664	m.	?Marwanger Ambt, BE
Rettemund, Niclaus		Speyerdorf	1712	bp. Sp.	CH-3251 Diessbach bei Büren, BE
Riess, Daniel	Niclaus Riess	Iggelheim	1714	burial	CH-3250 Lyss, BE
Ritz, Johannes	Michel Ritz	Hassloch	1745	burial	From Switzerland
Ritz, Michel		Lachen	1745	burial	?CH-9064 Hundwil, AR
Roht, Johannes	Ulrich Roht	Lachen	1668	m.	CH-4704 Niederbipp, BE
Roner, Maria Salome m. Niclaus Trommer	Joh. Roner	Iggelheim	1721	m.	CH-8439 Mellikon, AG
Rosche, Barbara	Peter Rosche	Lachen	1665	m.	CH-3652 Hilterfingen, BE
Roth, Dursus		Hassloch	1717	conf.	CH-5600 Lenzburg, AG
Rückli, Ludwig	Martin Rückli	Lachen	1688	conf.	CH-4705 Wangen an der Aare, BE
Rüdi, Henrich		Hassloch	1710	conf.	CH-4494 Ottingen, BL
Rudiman, Rudolph		Hassloch	1719	conf.	CH-8477 Oberstammheim, ZH

445

Person	Parent	Palatine Village	Year	Type of Record	Swiss Village
Ruhr?, Emanuel		Hassloch	1719	conf.	CH-5600 Lenzburg, AG
Sachser, Joh. Caspar	Ulrich Sachser	Mutterstadt	1735	burial	CH-9450 Altstätten im Rheinthal, SG
Sandmayer, Jacob	Jacob Sandmayer	Iggelheim	1720	burial	?CH-5704 Egliswil, AG
Sauter, Anna Barbara	Ulrich Sauter	Lachen	1704	m.	CH-8910 Affoltern am Albis, ZH
Sauter, Jacob	Henrich Sauter	Lachen	1665	m.	CH-8800 Thalwil, ZH
Sauter, Hans Heinrich	Heinrich Sauter	Lachen	1678	m.	CH-8800 Thalwil, ZH
Sauter, Jacob	Henrich Sauter	Lachen	1670	conf.	CH-8800 Thalwil, ZH
Schadt, Jacob	Hans Schadt	Lachen	1680	conf.	Dollikon, ZH = CH-8706 Meilen
Schenckel, Johannes		Hassloch	1744	burial	?Cleestadt, Switzerland
Schenk, Daniel		Hassloch	1723	conf.	From Switzerland
Scherer, Catharina		Hassloch	1710	conf.	From Switzerland
Schiveli, Anna Maria	David Schiveli	Hassloch	1724	m.	Biel, Switzerland
Schlabach, Maria Veronica widow of Henrich Schambach		Hochspeyer [Hassloch KB]	1776	burial	Canton Zürich, Switzerland

Person	Parent	Palatine Village	Year	Type of Record	Swiss Village
Schmidt, Johann Jacob	Johann Schmidt	Iggelheim	1715	m.	CH-3076 Worb, BE
Schmied, Caspar		Hassloch	1752	burial	CH-8225 Siblingen, SH
Schmitt, Anna Maria		Hassloch	1716	conf.	From Switzerland
Schmitt, Jacob	Felix Schmitt	Neustadt	1684	m.	CH-8114 Dänikon, ZH [Lachen KB]
Schmitt, Jacob	Hans Henrich Schmitt	Lachen	1672	m.	CH-8103 Unterengstringen, ZH
Schneberger, Anna	Ulrich Schneberger	Lachen	1684	bp.	?CH-3360 Herzogenbuchsee, BE
Schnebli, Elisabetha	Ullrich Schnebli	Haardt a.d. W.	1686	m.	CH-8910 Affoltern am Albis, ZH
Schneider, Hans	Peter Schneider	Haardt a.d. W.	1688	m.	CH-3425 Koppigen, BE
Schönthaler, Johannes	Nicolaus Schönthaler	Haardt a.d. W.	1681	m.	CH-3137 Gurzelen, BE
Schowalter, Bernhard	(Mennonite)	Lambsheim	1709	citizen	CH-4802 Strengelbach, AG
Schowalter, Rudolf		Lambsheim	1727	citizen	From Switzerland
Schuler, Jacob	Hans Ulrich Schuler	Mutterstadt	1735	burial	CH-8477 Oberstammheim, ZH
Schultheiss, Henrich		Hassloch	1717	conf.	CH-8712 Stäfa, ZH
Schurter, Hans	Cunrad Schurter	Lachen	1686	m.	Rohrweis, ZH = ?CH-8427 Rorbas

447

Person	Parent	Palatine Village	Year	Type of Record	Swiss Village
Schurter, Hans	Cunrad Schurter	Lachen	1672	conf.	?CH-8427 Rorbas, ZH
Schweitzer, Lisabeth	Henrich Schweitzer	Weisenheim a. S.	1672	m.	CH-8216 Oberhallau, SH
Schwendemann, Samuel	Samuel Schwendemann	Gimmeldingen	1684	m.	CH-3118 Uttigen, BE
Sieger, Christian	Christian Sieger	Haardt a.d. W.	1681	conf.	CH-1845 Noville, VD
Sigrist, Maria Magdalena wife of Henrich Schmidt	Joh. Jacob Sigrist	Iggelheim	1713	burial	?CH-4207 Bretzwil, BL
Spöri, Ursus		Hassloch	1701	m.	CH-3550 Langnau im Emmental, BE
Sprunglin, Barbara		Dannstadt	1726	m.	CH-8910 Affoltern am Albis, ZH
Staab, Henrich	Hans Jacob Staab	Gimmeldingen	1680	m.	CH-8810 Horgen, ZH
Stadler, Stefan		Lambsheim	1696	citizen	From Switzerland
Stahler, Elisabetha		Hassloch	1723	m.	From Switzerland
Stählin, Maria	Andreas Stählin	Iggelheim	1719	m.	CH-5024 Küttigen, AG
Stähly (Stehli), Johannes		Lambsheim	1730	citizen	CH-8376 Fischingen, TG
Stalter, Peter	Jacob Stalter	Lachen	1673	m.	CH-3456 Trachselwald, BE

448

Person	Parent	Palatine Village	Year	Type of Record	Swiss Village
Staub, Rudolph	Jacob Staub	Lachen	1664	m.	CH-8810 Horgen, ZH
Staub, Veronica	Henrich Staub	Lachen	1666	m.	CH-8810 Horgen, ZH
Staub, Henrich	Hans Jacob Staub	Lachen	1671	conf.	CH-8810 Horgen, ZH
Staub, Ulrich	Matheis Staub	Haardt a.d. W.	1681	m.	CH-4934 Madiswil, BE
Staub, Caspar	Jacob Staub	Lachen	1664	conf.	not given, Switzerland
Staufert, Hans Jacob	Hans Staufert	Haardt a.d. W.	1686	m.	CH-2553 Safnern, BE
Stauffer, Barbara m. Philipp Reinhard Kloss	Christian Stauffer	Iggelheim	1723	m.	?CH-3612 Steffisburg, BE
Steffen, Joh. Burckhardt	Peter Steffen	Hassloch	1715	bp.	From Switzerland
Steiger, Maria Elisabetha	Jacob Steiger	Dannstadt	1742	burial	CH-4704 Niederbipp, BE
Steiger, Conrad		Lambsheim	1674	citizen	From Switzerland
Stein, Joh. Jacob		Hassloch	1721	conf.	From Switzerland
Steiner, Susanna m. Johann Adam Heller		Haardt a.d. W.	1726	m.	Canton Bern, Sw.
Steinman, Johan Jacob	Hans Jacob Steinman	Hassloch	1722	bp.	?Dütingen, Sw.

449

Person	Parent	Palatine Village	Year	Type of Record	Swiss Village
Stern, Martin		Iggelheim	1679	m.	CH-3132 Riggisberg, BE
Stoll, Anna wife of Caspar Schmied		Hassloch	1752	burial	CH-8218 Osterfingen, ZH
Straub, Maria Catharina	Dorst Straub	Lachen	1680	bp.	Canton Bern
Stuck, Frantz		Hassloch	1754	burial	CH-3110 Münsingen, BE
Stück, Frantz	Johannes Stück	Hassloch	1727	m.	Canton Bern, Switzerland
Stück, Maria Margretha	Hans Stück	Hassloch	1722	bp.	CH-3110 Münsingen, BE
Stücker, Johannes		Hassloch	1734	burial	From Switzerland
Stump, Cunrad	Hans Stump	Lachen	1678	m.	Guntershausen ?CH-8357 or ?CH-8584
Suter, Anna Maria	Jacob Suter	Hassloch	1716	m.	CH-5034 Suhr, AG
Suter, Hans Jacob	Ulrich Suter	Hassloch	1718	bp.	From Switzerland
Tanne?, Elisabetha	Jacob Tanne?	Haardt a.d. W.	1682	m.	CH-3550 Langnau im Emmenthal, BE
Thüs, Hans Jacob		Iggelheim	1698	m.	Canton Bern, Switzerland
Trachsler, Catharina wife of Joh. Jacob Högi	Henrich Trachsler	Mutterstadt	1740	burial	CH-8903 Birmensdorf, ZH

450

Person	Parent	Palatine Village	Year	Type of Record	Swiss Village
Tragsell, Samuel	Hans Tragsell	Hassloch	1718	m.	From Switzerland
Traxel, Samuel		Hassloch	1713	conf.	From Switzerland
Treibelbiss, A. Barbara		Hassloch	1725	burial	From Switzerland
Trommer, Christoph	Niclaus Trommer	Iggelheim	1727	m.	CH-3714 Frutigen, BE
Trommer, Niclaus	N. Trommer	Iggelheim	1728	burial	CH-3714 Frutigen, BE
Trummer, Nickolaus		Hassloch	1715	conf.	CH-3714 Frutigen, BE
Visinand, Philipp Peter		Hassloch	1710	m.	?Cortier [?CH-1804 Corsier-sur-Vevey VD]
Voiblet, Margretha		Hassloch	1715	conf.	CH-2537 Vauffelin, BE
Volckert, Joh. Henrich		Hassloch	1769	burial	CH-8180 Bülach, ZH
Volckert, Henrich	Johannes Volckert	Hassloch	1736	m.	From Switzerland
Vollweyler, Caspar		Gimmeldingen	1716	m.	From Switzerland
Vollweyler, a son of	Henrich Vollweyler	Hassloch	1717	burial	From Switzerland
Vollweyler, Jacob	Felix Vollweyler	Gimmeldingen	1683	conf.	CH-8933 Maschwanden, ZH
Vollweyler, Johann Jacob		Haardt a.d. W.	1711	m.	From Switzerland

451

Person	Parent	Palatine Village	Year	Type of Record	Swiss Village
Wäber, Margaretha wife of Jac. Christ	Jacob Wäber	Iggelheim	1721	burial	CH-8232 Merishausen, SH
Walde, Anna	Hans Walde	Lachen	1687	m.	CH-8135 Langnau a. Albis, ZH
Wanner, Hans Cunrad	Hans Wanner	Lachen	1666	conf.	CH-8226 Schleitheim, SH
Weber, Peter		Hassloch	1717	conf.	CH-2578 Brüttelen, BE
Wedel, Margaretha	Jacob Wedel	Lachen	1670	conf.	?CH-8260 Wagenhausen, TG
Wedli, Hans	Heinrich Wedli	Lachen	1688	conf.	CH-8805 Richterswil, ZH
Weiersmüller, Melchior		Lambsheim	1722	citizen	CH-5034 Suhr, AG
Weinath, Anna Barbara	Hans Peter Weinath	Iggelheim	1716	m.	Madretsch, BE
Weiss, Peter	Hans Weiss	Lachen	1683	m.	CH-3611 Uebeschi, BE
Weiss, Anna Catharina wife of Niclaus Weynath	Joh. Jacob Weiss	Iggelheim	1714	burial	CH-8910 Affoltern am Albis, ZH
Weisslich, Henrich	Hans Weisslich	Haardt a.d. W.	1685	conf.	?Steiffen, ZH
Wendel, Abraham		Hassloch	1712	bp.	?Dabhein, Sw.
Werle, Henrich		Hassloch	1716	conf.	CH-5024 Küttigen, AG

452

Person	Parent	Palatine Village	Year	Type of Record	Swiss Village
Werndli, Anna Margretha	Abraham Werndli	Hassloch	1714	bp.	From Switzerland
Werthmüller, Nicolaus	Nick. Werthmüller	Hassloch	1702	m.	Canton Bern, Switzerland
Weymann, Jacob		Hassloch	1701	m.	CH-8704 Herrlisberg, ZH
Weynath, Peter		Hassloch	1712	m.	Madretsch, BE
Weynath, Abraham	Jacob Weynath	Hassloch	17712	burial	From Switzerland
Weynmann, Jakob		Hassloch	1701	citizen	CH-8704 Herrlisberg, ZH
Weyss, Anna		Hassloch	1718	conf.	CH-5638 Winterschwil, AG
Wicks, Christian m. Rosina Barbara Röder		Mutterstadt	1711	m.	CH-3158 Guggisberg, BE
Wider, Henrich		Hassloch	1713	conf.	CH-8117 Fällanden, ZH
Wilhelm, Johann Caspar	Ulrich Wilhelm	Hassloch	1711	m.	CH-5745 Safenwil, AG
Winckel, Ulrich	Ulrich Winckel	Lachen	1665	m.	CH-8408 Winterthur, Wülfingen
Wirth, Johannes		Weisenheim a. S.	1679	m.	?Hundswil, Sw. [? CH-9064 Hundwil, AR]
Wissler, Jacob		Lambsheim	1696	citizen	From Switzerland

453

Person	Parent	Palatine Village	Year	Type of Record	Swiss Village
Wolff, Anna Maria wife of Benedict Hoffmann	Joh. Henrich Wolff	Iggelheim	1725	burial	CH-5057 Reitnau, AG
Wollesberger, Jacob		Hassloch	1717	conf.	CH-8311 Winterberg, ZH
Würtz, Johann Ulrich, Pastor at Niedersaulheim	Joh, Würtz, Pastor at Schlatt, Canton ZH	Hassloch	1729	m.	CH-8418 Schlatt b. Winterthur, ZH
Zimmermann, Hans Jacob	Henrich Zimmermann	Gimmeldingen	1685	conf.	CH-8910 Affoltern am Albis, ZH
Zobel, Heinrich		Lambsheim	1687	citizen	Oberweningen, ZH= CH-8165 Schöfflisdorf
Zober, Caspar		Lambsheim	1674	citizen	From Switzerland
Zoller, Jacob		Hassloch	1723	conf.	From Switzerland

454

Notes on the Indexes

The first index, Index of Ships, contains the name of the ships and the year of arrival. The reader is referred to Volume III of Strassburger and Hinke, *Pennsylvania German Pioneers*, pp. 215-221, for a complete alphabetical listing of the known ship arrivals.

The second index, European Place Names, contains a listing of all European villages and place names mentioned in the text. In using this index, the researcher should consider the fact that quite often place names were misspelled in both the old German and American records. An attempt has been made in the text to provide identification and location by the inclusion of the European postal code. A few place names have defied positive identification. The places in Germany are indexed simply by the village name; further identification will be found in the text. Villages in Switzerland are so identified. The two-letter abbreviation following the Swiss village name indicates the canton. The conventional Swiss postal abbreviations are used for all cantons found in the text:

AG	Aargau	GR	Graubünden
AR	Appenzell A. Rhoden	LU	Luzern
BE	Bern	SH	Schaffhausen
BL	Basel Land	TG	Thurgau
FR	Fribourg	VD	Vaud
GL	Glarus	ZH	Zürich

The full name Index should be used with care (and with some imagination). The searcher should keep in mind the sound of the names and the fact that there was no consistent spelling used in this time period. (For example, Bressler and Pressler are the same surname, and both spellings are found in American and European records. Wissenandt, Fisinant and Visenant are all the same name.) We have included some suggestions to other possible spellings. The researcher should also keep in mind that given names were also inconsistent; a man named Johann Georg Müller might also appear in the records as Joh. Georg Müller, also as Hans Georg Miller, or Hans Jerg Müller. This same man might also appear in some records as simply George Miller, the second given name being usually the name by which they were known. This statement is also true of feminine names; a woman named Anna Barbara will often be found in other records as simply Barbara. The umlaut has been ignored in the alphabetical arrangement, out of consideration for American readers not familiar with European alphabetical arrangements.

European Place Name Index

466 European Place Name Index

NAME INDEX

Abdorf
Benedict, 421
Abeck
Elisabeth, 421
Henrich, 421
Abell
Mathias, 364
Abresch
Peter, 104, 186
Susanna, 104, 186
Aches
Leonhardt, 291
Acker
Antonius, 1
Casper, 1
Franz, 1
Hans Adam, 1
Maria Johanna, 1
Petrus, 1
Rudolff, 1
Acre
Casper, 1
Adam
Andreas, 71
Carl Ludwig, 27
Johanna Maria, 27
Affenstein
Anna Maria, 260
Affholder
Anna, 421
Benedict, 421
Affolder
Anna Catharina, 307
Benedict, 307, 421
Albert
Anna Catharina, 386
Joh. Jacob, 364
John, 374

Wendel, 386
Albertus
Wendel, 89
Albrecht
Hanss Jacob, 421
Johannes, 421
John, 2
Judith, 2
Aldebarger
John, 2
Maria Magdalena, 2
See Altenberger, 2
Aldenberger
See Altenberger, 1
Allbrecht
Anna, 421
Allbright
John, 206
Allstadt
Catharina, 2
Martin, 2
Alowey
Elizabeth, 368
Alstadt
Judith, 2
Martin, 2
Alstatt
Martin, 2
Nicholas, 2
Altenberger
Johannes, 1, 214, 421
John, 2
Maria Magdalena, 1, 214
Alter
Hans, 421
Martin, 421

Altmann
Johannes, 145
Maria Elisabeth, 145
Altstat
Martin, 2
Altstatt
Anna Judith (Walter), 376
Joh. Martin, 337
Johann Martin, 2
Johanna Judith (Walter), 2
John, 2
John Martin, 2
Judith, 2, 337
Martin, 2, 376
Nicolaus, 2
Am Endt
Anna Maria (Gemlich), 223
Hans Georg, 223
See Ament, 223
Amborn
Christoph, 186
Susanna (Klauer), 186
Amen
Catharine, 223
Amen
John, 223
Amend
Heinrich, 136
Henry, 223
Mary (Meck), 223
Ament
Johannes, 223
Maria Appolonia (Paulus), 223

Bach
Anna Catharina, 8-9,
111
Anna Catharina
(Cronoby), 111
Anna Elisabeth, 9
Anna Maria, 9
Catharina Margaretha, 9
Elizabeth, 10
Georg , 302
Georg Daniel, 8-9, 86
Georg Lorentz, 8
George Daniel, 10
Gg. Daniel, 9
Jacob, 9, 111
Joh. Georg, 8-9
Joh. Henrich, 8
Joh. Sebastian, 302
Johann Georg, 339
Johann Michael, 9
Johann Niclaus, 9
Johann Nicolaus, 8
Johannes Sebastian, 8
Maria Catharina, 8
Maria Clara, 8
Maria Magdalena, 9
Maria Margaretha, 9
Mary Magdalena, 10
Niclaus, 9
Phil. Jakob, 9
Philip , 111
Philip Jacob, 8-9
Philips Jacob, 10
Sebastian, 8-9
Susanna (Seidemann), 8
Bachman
Anna , 10
Anna Barbara (Sautor),
10
Anna Maria, 10
Christina, 11
Georg, 10, 421
Hans Henrich, 10
Heinrich, 10

Henrich, 10-11, 56
Jacob, 421
Joh. Henrich, 10
Louisa Sophia, 56
Michael, 2, 83
Sophia Louisa (Bock),
10
Bachmann
Anna Catharine, 11
Christina, 11
Heinrich, 10
Henry, 11
Back
Jacob, 68
Bader
Anna Margretha, 113
Eve (Laufer), 206
John Nicholas, 206
Baer
Maria, 82
Maria Agnes, 123
Baertschinger
Catharina, 421
Bager
Pastor, 321
Bahmer
Adam, 88
Elisabeth, 88
See Also Bohmer, 88
Bahn
Adam, 195
Eva, 194
Heinrich, 194
Bähr
Jacob, 422
Johannes, 422
Ulrich, 422
Veronica, 422
Bailey
Emanuel, 187
Baldnerin
Anna, 17
Bamberger
Agnesa, 12

Anna Elisabetha, 11
Anna Elisabetha
(Kremer), 11
Arnold, 11-12
Catharina, 12
David, 11
Elisabetha, 12
Hans, 11
Joh. Nicolaus, 11
Joh. Peter, 11
Johanna Catharina, 12
John, 12
Martin, 11-12
Mary Dorothea, 12
Rudolff, 11
Rudolph, 12
Bandon
Catharina (Vetter), 366
William, 366
Bär
Elizabeth, 123
Joh. Ulrich, 123
Maria Agatha, 123
Bardet
Benedikt, 422
Jacob, 422
Bart
Catharina, 70
Catrina, 321
Stephan, 70
Bartdorff
Jerg Adam, 35
Bartel
Ernst, 54
Joh. Adam, 54
Barth
Anna Catharina, 12-13
Anna Catharina
(Sebastian), 331, 336
Catharina, 12
Catharina (Sebastian,
12
Clemens, 12
Hans Peter, 13

Bauman (continued)
  Susanna (Müller), 17
Baumann
  Caspar, 422
  Catharina (Kühlwein),
    199
  Hans Jacob, 17, 422
  Jacob, 16, 422
  Johannes, 17
  Madlen (Lüdin), 17
  Matthäus, 199
  Susanna (Müller), 16
Baumänn
  Margretha, 163, 163
Baumberger
  Anna Margaretha
    (Lippert), 11
  Felix, 11, 422
  Hans, 11, 422
Baumgarten
  Anna Barbara, 422
  Benedict, 422
Baumgartner
  Benedict, 422
Bauniger
  Johannes, 97
Bauniger?
  Catharina Margaretha,
    292
  Johannes, 292
Baur
  Eva, 15
  Georg, 300
  Johann Henrich, 300
Baur Sax
  Georg Adam, 16
  Johan Nicolaus, 16
  Johann Valentin, 16
Baus
  Catharina, 185
Bayn
  Jacob, 422
  Maria Ursula, 422

Beaber
  Conrad, 112
  Lisa Margreth, 112
Bear
  John, 253
Beatty
  Thomas, 336
Beaver
  Conrad, 112
Bechdoll
  Anna Elisabetha, 36
Bechel
  Tobias, 19
Bechtel
  Anna Elisabeth, 33
  Anna Elisabetha, 18
  Anna Maria, 294
  Christian, 41
  Christoph, 110
  Elisabeth, 229
  John, 294
  Maria Elisabetha, 18,
    185
  Susanna, 110
  Tobias, 18, 33, 185,
    229
Bechtell
  Anna Elizabeth, 18-19
  Anna Margred, 18
  Anna Maria, 18
  Catharine (Bitting), 41
  George, 18, 41
  John George, 18
  John Nicholaus, 19
  John Nicklas, 18
  Nicholaus, 19
  Tobias, 18-19
Bechtloff
  Anna Christina
    (Münch), 18
  Anna Elisabetha (Koch),
    18
  Anna Maria, 18
  Hans Nickel, 18

  Hans Nicolaus, 18
  Sophia Catharina, 18
  Tobias, 18
Bechtluf
  Eliza, 17
  Tobias, 17
Beck
  George Felix, 108
  Henry, 204
  See Heck, 229
Beckel
  A. M. (Kindig), 20
  Anna Elisabeth, 33
  Anna Elisabetha, 19,
    327
  Anton, 34
  Catharina Elisabeth, 33
  Charles F., 20
  Christina , 229-230
  Christina (Kuster), 18,
    33
  Daniel, 33
  Elisabeth, 33-34
  Eva Elisabeth, 33
  Eva Elisabetha, 18
  Frederick, 20
  Friedrich, 19, 33
  Georg Frederick, 20
  Georg Valentin, 20
  George Valentine, 21,
    188
  Johann Gotthard, 33,
    229
  Johann Nicolaus, 33
  Johannes, 34
  Johannes Tobias, 34
  Lewis, 20
  Magdalena, 34
  Maria, 33
  Maria Elisabetha, 21
  Maria Margaretha, 18,
    229
  Phillip Jacob, 34
  Sybilla (Gossenberger),

DeFrene (continued)
Maria Catharina (Esch), 68
Maria Margaretha, 68
Peter, 68, 86, 224
Philipp, 427
Samuel, 427
DeFroen
Catharine, 68
Catherine, 68
Peter, 68
Degen
Anna Barbara, 278
Anna Catharina, 80
Georg Valentin, 201, 207
Henrich, 278
Johannes, 106, 396
Margaretha, 396
Degin
Anna Barbara, 278
Eva Magdalena, 241
Dehmer
Jacob Heinrich, 75
Joh. Michael, 75
Maria Agnes, 75
Dehuff
Henry, 366
Deickert
Anna Helena, 68
Joh. Michael, 68
See Dackert, 69
Deisert
Elisabeth, 70
Georg Peter, 69-70
Johann Georg, 70
Johannes, 70
John [Georg] Peter, 399
Juliana Margaret, 70
Maria Catharina, 70
Wilhelmina, 399
Wilhelmina (Hünd), 70
Deissert
Anna Margretha, 69

Johann Peter, 69
Johannes Georgius, 69
Peter, 69
See Deisert, 69
Deisserth
Anna Margretha, 69
Georg Peter, 69
Hans Peter, 69
Jeorg Henrich, 69
Joh. Daniel, 69
Maria Margretha, 69
Deissinger
Catharina (Mayer), 232
Delater
Anna Barbara, 71
Anna Elisabetha, 71
Catharina, 71
Christina, 71
David, 71
Elisabetha, 71
Jacob, 71
Joh. Henrich, 71
Maria Catharina, 71
DeLatere
Barbara, 71
David, 71
Johannes, 71
Delatre
Anna Barbara, 71
Anna Elisabetha (Geringer), 71
David, 71
Joh. David, 71
Dellarter
David, 71
Maria Catrina, 71
Demler
Georg, Pastor, 229
Dennhart
Joh. Nicolaus, 88
Nicolaus, 88
Denni
Caspar, 427

Deobald
Cath. Elisabetha, 92
Joh. Conrad, 262
Joh. Peter, 92
Johannes, 262, 298
Margretha, 92
Maria Catharina, 262, 298
Philip Lorentz, 92
Derein
Catharina, 153
Isaac, 153
Maria Catharina (Marquart), 153
Deringer
Heinrich, 339
Derr
Anna Maria, 385
Johannes, 385
Deschler
Catharina, 116
Detemer
Hans Michael, 72
Dethmer
Catharina, 72
Jacob, 72
Joh. Georg, 72
Maria Elisabeth, 72
Dettemer
Anna Margaret, 72
Elisabeth, 72
Jacob, 72
See Ditmer, 72
Dettenhelfer
Anna Maria, 79
Catharine, 79
Christopher, 79
Elisabeth, 79
George, 79
Juliana, 79
Michael, 79
Paul, 79
Sophia, 79

Eitel
Agnes, 171
Johan, 171
Eitzer
Elisabetha, 27
Jacob, 27
Eli
Barbara, 81, 81
Christian, 80-81
Daniel, 309
Hans David, 80
Joh. Jacob, 81
Maria Catarina, 81
Nicol , 81
Nicolaus, 81
Elie
Nichol, 80
Ely
Abraham, 80
Daniel, 80
David, 80
Elizabeth, 80
Geo. Theobaldt, 281
Jacob, 80
James, 80
John, 80
Nicholas, 81
Samuel, 80
Emerick
Jacob, 248
Emet
Anna Maria, 242
Emlich
Joh. Georg, 43
Emmenet
Johannes, 53
Emmerich
Christoph, 110
End
John Dewald, 17
Endt
Theobald, 312
Engel
Elisabeth, 340

Engelhard
Ludwig, 303
Engelhart
Juliana Maria, 395
Engle
Andreas, 382
Elisabetha, 382
Ulerich, 258
Englehart
George, 41
Eninger
Jacob, 428
Susanna, 428
Enssminger
Anna Catharina, 57
Epler
John, 116
Eppler
Elisabetha Dorothea, 15
Epprecht
Hans, 428
Erb
A.Marg. (Sauter), 300
Anna Margaretha
  (Sauter), 84
Anna Margretha
  (Sauter), 300
Catharina, 285
J. Jacob, 84
Jak., 300
Joh. Georg, 84
Joh. Jacob, 300
Johan Jacob, 84
Johann Jacob, 84
Erbach
Balthasar, 216
Mary Elisabeth, 216
Mary Eliza,, 216
Ergenbrod
Joh. Daniel, 257
Sophia Elisabetha, 257
Erhard
Anna Maria, 122
Elisabetha, 428

Hans Michael, 82
Hans Peter, 122
Maria Catharina, 82
Maria Elisabetha
  Catharina, 82
N., 428
Peter, 122
Philip Reinhardt, 82
Philip Reinhart, 82
Erhardt
Maria Christina, 82
Erisman
Andreas, 81
Anna Maria, 81
Barbara, 85
Georg Jacob, 85
Jacob, 85
Jörg, 81
Maria Eva, 81
Maria Ursula, 85
Erismann
Andreas, 81
Ernhard
Barbara (Andreas), 4
Ernst
Anna Katarina, 143
John Wendel, 143
Margretha, 143
Wendel, 143
Esch
Adam, 86
Anna, 68
Joh. Adam, 68
Maria Catharina, 68
Peter, 86
Samuel, 86
See von Esch, 86
Esh
Peter, 68, 86
Essel
Anna Maria, 232
Eucheling
Joh. Adam, 84, 314
Leonhard, 84

Gross (continued)
Anna Margaretha
(Reyher)
(continued)
(Reyher), 278
Johannes, 278
Josua, 54
Gross?
Christina Margaretha,
94
Joh. Christoffel, 94
Grosscast
Daniel, 114
John, 114
Grosscup
Paul, 382
Grosskost
Anna Elisabetha, 114
Anna Margaretha, 114
Anna Margaretha
(Heim), 114
Christoph, 114
Hans Philip, 114
Philip Daniel, 114
Wilhelm, 114
Grossman
Anna Christina, 377
Anna Margaretha, 186
Hans Jacob, 6-7, 186
Henrich, 6-7, 377
Jacob, 186
Margaretha, 6-7
Groves
John, 144
Susanna (Hallman), 144
Grow
Peter, 115
Gruber
Christian, 373
Grumbach
Anna Catharina,
115-116
Anna Maria, 115
Catharina, 116-117

Catharine, 117
Christian, 531
Christine, 117
Conrad, 115-117
Esther, 116
Eva Catharina, 115-116
Georg Heinrich, 115
George Henry, 116-117
Joh. Conrad, 115
Johann Adam, 115
Konrad, 115
Leonard, 116
Maria Marg., 117
Nicolai, 431
Grundel
See Wiedergrundel, 381
Gründele
Rudolph, 431
Gründeler
Rudolph, 389
Grundisch
A. Margaretha, 431
Ulrich, 431
Grüneisen
Johannes Jacob, 30
Maria Magdalena, 30
Grünewald
Catharina Barbara, 117
Johann Conradt, 117
Johann Jacob, 117
Johann Michel, 117
Johannes, 117
Maria Catharina, 117
Maria Magdalena, 117
Maria Margaret, 103
Maria Margaret
(Füsser), 117
Mathaes, 117
Philip , 222
Philip Lorentz, 103,
117
Grünewalt
Hann Filb, 117

Gryneisen
Johann Jacob, 30
Gucchus
John, 39
Guches
John, 38
Guchus
John, 38
Guck
Anna Maria, 235
Gucker
Barthold, 119
Bartholomeus, 118, 314
Catharina, 118-119,
199
Elisa Barbara, 119, 119
Elisabetha Barbara, 119
Eva , 119
Eva Lisabeth, 119
Johan Barthel, 118
Susanna, 118, 118-119,
167
Guckert
Anna Catharina
(Schmidt), 204, 206
Barthel, 204, 206
Catharina, 118
Joh. , 118
Joh. Barthel, 118
Guckes
John, 39
Mrs. John nee Bott, 39
Gudt
Anna, 431
Georg Nicolai, 431
Guiene
Piere, 431
Susanna Margreth, 431
Guisie
Elisabeth, 121
Jacob, 128
Joh. Jacob, 121
Philip Jacob, 121

Hamman (continued)
Maria Catharina
(Deobald)
(continued)
(Deobald), 298
Maria Catharina
(Theobald), 128
Peter, 128, 242,
298-299, 301
Philip, 128
See Also Sauerheber,
128
Susan, 129
Thomas, 129, 209
Hammann
Anna Barbara, 197
Anna Catharina, 128,
261
Anna Elisabetha, 128
Anna Margretha, 128
Catharina Elisabetha,
354
Georg Christoph, 129,
263
Georg Michael, 128
Görg, 197
Joh. Görg, 129
Joh. Jacob, 128
Johann Paul, 128
Johann Peter, 128
Peter, 298
Philip Lorentz, 128
Susanna (Raderli), 129
Thomas, 129
Hammel
Anna Catharina, 130
Anna Christina, 130
Anna Maria, 130
Anna Maria Barbara,
130
Christina, 375
Hans, 130
Hans Wilhelm, 130
Henrich, 243

Jacob, 130
Johann Henrich, 130
Johann Jacob, 130
Johannes, 130, 375
Maria Catharina, 130
Willhelm, 130
Hammen
Peter, 128
Philip, 128
Hammerich
Anna Margaretha, 127
Anna Margretha, 127
Hanss Georg, 128
Hieronimus, 127
Joh. Georg, 127-128
Johan Jacob, 128
Johann Henrich, 127
Johann Paul, 127
Johann Peter, 127
Johannes, 127
Maria Cretha, 127
Maria Elisabetha
(Biber), 127
Paul, 128
Philip Lorentz, 127
Hämmerli
Samuel, 432
Hamon
Thomas, 129
Hamrick
George, 128
Maria Elisabeth, 128
Hans
Anna Lucia, 277
Henrich, 127
Hieronimus, 127
Peter, 277
Härdi
Anna Margaretha, 2
Margareth Barbara, 2
Rudolph, 2
Hargate
Peter Sr., 153

Harlacher
See Horlacher, 167
Hart
Conrath, 133
Härtel
Phil., 443
Hartmann
Burckhard, 432
Samuel, 432
Veronica, 432
Hartranft
John F., 83
Häseler
M. Eva, 93
Matthaus, 93
Haser
Anna, 432
Hasin
Margred, 65
Hass
Eliesabetha, 236
Ludowich, 125
Hasslinger
Hans Adam, 197
Hast
Ludwig, 125
Hatzenböhler
Anna Catharina, 175
Hauck
Anna Christina, 69
Jacob, 117
Lorentz, 116
Peter, 117
Hauenstein
Anna Appolonia, 131,
168-169
Barbara, 130
Conrad, 48, 73, 76, 82,
130-131, 135, 146,
345, 399-400, 402
Georg , 85
Georg Jacob, 399-400,
402
Georg Jacob, 48, 73, 76,

Lauck?
Abraham, 248
Laucks
Anna Barbara
(Kuerschner), 207
John George, 174
Peter, 49, 207
Lauer
Anna Margreda, 221
Laufer
Barbara, 206
Catharina (Schmidt),
118
Catharine, 206
Christian, 118, 203
Elizabeth, 206
Eve, 206
Heinrich, 118
Laurence, 118, 206
Laurent, 205
Lorentz, 205
Philip, 206
Rachael, 206
Läufer
Anna Catharina
(Schmidt), 204, 206
Elisabetha (Fischer),
203, 205
Fronica (Caspar),
204-205
Heinrich, 204-206
Joh. Heinrich, 203, 205
Joh. Jacob, 204, 206
Johan Christian, 204,
206
Johann Laurent, 204,
206
Johannes, 204, 206
Joseph, 203, 205
Maria Ursula, 204, 206
Lauffer
Anna Maria, 205
Bardollomey, 204
Catharina, 206

Catharine, 205
Christian, 204-206
Elis. Margaretha, 315
Elisabeth, 205
Elisabeth Margareth,
206
Henry, 204
John , 205
John Adam, 204
Lorentz, 206, 315
Magdalena, 205
Maria Catharina, 206
Petter, 204
Susanna, 204-205
Susanna (Kemmerer),
205
Susanna Catharina, 204
Laufferschweiler
Joh. Bernhard, 364
Maria, 364
Laux
Anna Catharina, 207
Anna Margretha, 371
Anna Maria, 173, 173,
371
Anna Sybilla, 192
Barbara, 281
Catharina, 207
Eva Catharina, 207
Georg Theobald, 207
George , 207
Hans Peter, 241
Hans Velte, 371
Joh. Georg, 207, 371
Johan Jacob, 207
Johan Peter, 207
Johann Caspar, 207
Johannes, 371
Maria Gretha, 208
Maria Margareth, 208
Peter, 207-208
See Lauchs, 207
Lavenant
Judith, 323

Piere, 323
Lawfer
Laurence, 206
Lawrence, 207
Margaret, 206
Lay
Engel, 361
Laÿe
Anna Margaretha
(Fechter), 208
Johannes, 208
Martin, 208
Le Beau
Johannes, 208
Le Ru
Abraham, 213
Anna Maria, 213
Johan Jörg, 214
Le Ruh
Johann Georg, 214
Leaman
Ann Margaret, 210
Anne, 210
Christian, 210
Dority, 210
George, 210
Hans Adam, 210
Jacob, 210
John, 210-211
Ludwig, 210
Susannah, 210
Lear
John, 255
Lease
Leonhard, 93
Louise (Forney), 93
LeBeau
Abraham, 208
Anna (Croiiet), 208
Anna Margaretha, 208
Jean, 208
Maria Magdalena, 208
Lebo
Abraham, 209

Schirman (continued)
Joh. Jacob, 312
Joh. Simon, 310
Lissa Catharina, 310
Philip Adam, 310
See Schurmann, 309
Simon, 309
Schirmann
Georg Jacob, 311
Maria Catharina, 80
Maria Elisabetha, 311
Philip Adam, 310
Simon, 80
Schiveli
Anna Maria, 446
David, 446
Schlabach
Maria Veronica, 446
Schlappach
Anna Catharina, 342
Henry, 342
Schlengeluf
Analis, 312
Anna Christian, 312
Henrich, 312
Schley
Georg Thomas, 111
Maria (Giezendanner),
111
Thomas, 59
Schlingenloff
Anna Christina
(Gärtner), 312
Johann Henrich, 312
Schmahl
Christianus, 193
Eva (Welshofer), 379
family, 194
Kilian, 379
Killian, 157
Schmal
Anna Ursula, 326, 326
Lorenz, 326

Schmäyer
Daniel, 288
Schmeck
Johannes, 240
Margaretha, 240
Schmid
Andreas, 401
Anna Appolonia, 401
Anna Barbara, 307
Anna Elisabetha, 318
Anna Margaretha, 253,
318
Anna Margretha, 273
Anna Maria, 34, 61,
195
Anna Maria (Diener?),
318
Christina Margretha,
273
Conrad, 318
David, 314
Görg, 307
Henrich, 334
Isaac, 319
Joh. Henrich, 61
Johann Melchior, 318
Leonhard, 84, 314
Lorentz, 314
Maria Elisabetha, 319
Maria Magdalena, 318
Susanna, 314
Susanna (Kolb), 314
Schmidt
Adam, 239, 241
Anna, 113, 317
Anna Catharina, 204,
259
Anna Elisabetha, 75,
314
Anna Margaretha,
315-316
Anna Maria, 314-316
Apolonia, 314-315
Appolonia (Storr), 314

Balthasar, 113
Caspar, 313
Casper, 16, 53, 131,
154, 313
Catharina, 118
Catharina , 118
Catharina Elisabeth, 33
Catharina Margretha,
189
Catharina Ursula, 226
Christoph , 313
Christopher, 313
David, 313-314
Dorothea, 113
Elisabetha, 274
Elisabetha Catharina
(Wagner), 313
Esther Margaretha, 239
Georg , 259
Georg Valentin, 87, 189
Hans Nicolaus, 33
Hans Wilhelm, 314
Henrich, 448
Jacob, 34, 273, 314-315
Joh. Caspar, 315
Joh. Conrad, 316
Joh. David, 313
Joh. Friederich, 314
Joh. Heinrich, 118
Joh. Jacob, 314
Joh. Roland, 314
Joh. Wilhelm, 105
Johan Peter, 315
Johann , 447
Johann Jacob, 314, 447
Johann Peter, 315
Johanna Judith, 316
Johannes, 314
John Christian, 297
Leonhardt, 313
Magdalena, 238, 313
Margreth, 273
Maria Barbara, 34, 105
Maria Fronica, 166

Schumacher (continued)
  Johann Martin, 166
Schumann
  Anna Christina, 69
  Philipp, 69
Schunck
  Anna Barbara, 328
  Caspar, 328
  Christian, 328
  Elizabeth, 146, 350
  Elizabetha, 328
  Frantz, 146, 328
  Joh. Caspar, 328
  Joh. Christian, 328
  John Casper, 146
  John Christian, 145
Schunk
  Elisabeth, 328
  Elizabeth, 268
  Elizabeth (Reimer), 268
  Francis, 268
Schupping
  Johann Nicholaus, 329
Schüpping
  Abraham, 329
  Anna Catharina
    (Kauffmann), 329
  Johan Jacob, 329
  Johann Jacob, 329
Schurmann
  Anna Maria, 309
  Catharina (Heberling),
    309
  Catharina Elisabetha,
    309
  Eva Catharina, 309
  Georg, 309
  Joh. Carolus, 309
  Joh. Daniel, 309
  Maria Elisabetha, 309
  Philip Adam, 309
  Simon, 309
  Ulrich, 309

Schurter
  Cunrad, 447-448
  Hans, 447-448
Schuster
  Agnes, 330
  Anna Barbara, 171, 180,
    330
  Anna Elisabetha, 180
  Anna Helena, 171
  Anna Helena
    (Weyhenacht), 171, 180
  Anna Margreth, 233
  Anna Margretha, 301
  Anna Maria, 171, 180,
    180
  Anna Regina, 305
  Barbara, 331
  Catharina Elisabetha,
    180
  Catharina Margretha,
    330
  Catharine, 330
  Daniel, 330-331
  Frantz, 330
  Hans Michel, 301
  Joh. Daniel, 330-331
  Joh. Philips, 330
  Johann Jacob, 330
  Johann Matthes, 233
  Johann Peter, 330
  Johann Philip, 171, 180
  Johanna Catharina, 330
  Johannes, 180
  M. Elisabeth, 330
  Margaret, 331
  Maria Barbara, 330
  Maria Barbara
    (Schuster), 330
  Maria Catharina, 330
  Maria Elisabeth,
    330-331
  Maria Elisabetha, 330
  Maria Eva, 331
  Peter, 330

  Philip, 171, 180
  Philipp, 330
  Philips, 330
  Stephan, 171, 180, 305,
    330
Schuy
  Anna Marg., 324
  Anna Maria, 324
  Barbara, 324
  Catharina, 324
  Catharina Elisabeth,
    324
  Catharina Elisabetha,
    324
  Daniel, 324
  Elisabeth, 324-325
  Elisabetha, 324
  Johannes, 324
  John , 324-325
  John Henry, 324
  John Martin, 324-325
  Ludwig , 324
  Ludwig Heinrich, 324
  Margaret Elisabeth, 324
  Maria Elisabetha, 324
  Maria Martha, 324
  Martin, 324-325
  Martin Jr., 324
Schwab
  Anna Maria, 191, 216
  Johann , 216
  Johannes, 191, 216
Schwartz
  Conrad, 212
  Daniel, 263
  Elizabeth, 126
  Eva Marg. (Raderli),
    263
  Leonard, 126
  Maria Catharina, 173
Schwe
  Daniel, 323
  Lodewick, 323
  Margaretha, 323

Transeau
Abraham, 350
Anna Catharina (Knaus),
350
Elisabeth (Münster),
350
Transo
Abraham, 328
See Transou, 350
Transon
Abraham, 350
Margaret, 350
Transou
Abraham, 350
Elisabetha, 350
Joh. Abraham, 350
Joh. Jacob, 350
Transu
Abraham, 349
Philip, 350
Transue
Abraham, 350
Anna Barbara (Scherer),
305
Anna Barbara (Shaerer),
370
Elisabeth, 269
Johannes, 305
John, 305
Traub
See Trüb, 353
Trautman
Eva Elisab., 312
Joh. , 312
Johannes, 105
John, 360
Traxall
Nicholas, 286
Traxel
Samuel, 451
Treibelbis
Abraham, 351
Catharine, 351
Jacob, 351

Martin, 351
Mary Elisabeth, 351
Mary Magdalene, 351
Philebena, 351
Treibelbiss
A. Barbara, 451
Anna Margareta
(Bruchacher), 351
Jacob, 351
Johan Jacob, 351
Treipelpies
Barbara (Burkhart), 351
Jacob, 351
Trentsols
See Transu, 349
Trester
Frederick, 341, 352
Martin, 341, 352
Treyster
Fredrick, 340, 351
Hans martin, 340
Martin, 351
Triebelbis
Jacob, 351
Triester
Frederick, 353
George Frederick, 353
Jacob, 353
John, 353
Margareta, 353
Maria Dorothea, 353
Troester
Frederich, 353
Friederich, 353
Friederick, 341, 352
Johannes, 353
John Heinrich, 353
John Jacob, 353
Maria Dorothea, 341,
352-353
Trommer
Christoph, 451
N. , 451
Niclaus, 445, 451

Trösser
Anna Elisabetha, 341,
352
Anne Margareth, 341,
352
F., 352
J., 341, 352
M., 341, 352
Tröster
Anna Elisabetha, 352
Frederich, 351
Georg, 352
Hans Martin, 351
Joh. Leonhard, 340,
352
Joh. Martin, 352
Joh. Michael, 352
Johan Leonhard, 340,
352
Johan Wilhelm, 353
Johannes, 353
Maria Dorothea, 340,
352
Martin, 353
Troutman
Johannes, 248, 373
John, 190
Troxall
Michael, 286
Troxell
A., 271
Trüb
Anna Margretha, 200
David, 200
Hans David, 353
Jacob, 353
Trueb
Anna Barbara, 354
Catharina Elisabetha
(Hammann), 354
David, 354
Jacob, 354
Trumm
Margaret, 204